HANDBOOK

OF

SOUTH AMERICAN INDIANS

HANDBOOK

OF

SOUTH AMERICAN INDIANS

Julian H. Steward, *Editor*

Volume 4

THE CIRCUM-CARIBBEAN TRIBES

Prepared in Cooperation With the United States Department of State as a Project
of the Interdepartmental Committee on Scientific and Cultural Cooperation

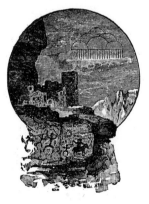

COOPER SQUARE PUBLISHERS, INC.
New York • 1963

SMITHSONIAN INSTITUTION
BUREAU OF AMERICAN ETHNOLOGY
BULLETIN 143

———————

Published by
COOPER SQUARE PUBLISHERS, INC.
59 Fourth Ave., New York 3, N. Y.
Library of Congress Catalog Card No. 63-17285
Printed in the United States of America

LETTER OF TRANSMITTAL

―――――

SMITHSONIAN INSTITUTION,
BUREAU OF AMERICAN ETHNOLOGY,
Washington, D. C., June 18, 1945.

SIR: I have the honor to transmit herewith a manuscript entitled "Handbook of South American Indians. Volume 4. The Circum-Caribbean Tribes," edited by Julian H. Steward, and to recommend that it be published as a bulletin of the Bureau of American Ethnology.

Very respectfully yours,

M. W. STIRLING, *Chief.*

DR. ALEXANDER WETMORE,
Secretary, Smithsonian Institution

CONTENTS

ILLUSTRATIONS

PLATES

XI

FIGURES

MAPS

PREFACE

By Julian H. Steward

It has always been supposed that the cultures of the Antilles and northern Venezuela should be classed with those of the Tropical Forests. Northern Colombia and Central America have been puzzling, however, for, though archeology reveals the presence in these areas of many elements of Mexican and Andean civilizations, the modern tribes are definitely Tropical Forest in character. The difficulty has been that the ethnology is known mainly from fairly recent studies of the few extremely deculturated tribes who remain and that the archeology has not been linked to the historic peoples except in a few instances.

Lothrop's summary (1937) of the ethnography found in early documents of the Conquest period of Panamá and his archeological work at the late pre-Conquest site of Coclé furnished cultural evidence of peoples who can scarcely be recognized as the precursors of the modern *Cuna*. More recently, Kirchhoff has undertaken a thorough perusal of all the available early chronicles bearing on the peoples around the Caribbean Sea, and he points out that, far from having a primitive culture such as that observed among their descendants of the past century, these tribes were actually highly developed. He finds also that the general pattern and content of these cultures were strikingly similar in most of the Circum-Caribbean area. It was mainly at his suggestion that the editor segregated the articles on the tribes of this area from those of volume 3 of the Handbook and grouped them in the present volume.

As the cultural relationships of tribes and groups of tribes cannot always be known until all the articles are assembled and viewed as a whole there are several instances, as seen in retrospect, in which tribes are placed in the wrong volume or in the wrong part of a volume. The Circum-Caribbean culture, or, as it is called in Colombia, the Sub-Andean culture, certainly includes the tribes of the South Colombia Highlands and of the Sierra de Santa Marta who are described in Volume 2 on the Andean civilizations. In fact, the *Chibcha* of Colombia are not properly classifiable as true Andean. Had it been possible to divide the volumes on a consistent cultural basis, the *Chocó, Cayapa,* and *Colorado* of western, lowland Colombia and Ecuador, the peoples west of Lake Maracaibo, and those of the lowlands of eastern Colombia should have been included with the Tropical Forest tribes who are described in Volume 3, and the hunting and gathering tribes of the Orinoco Basin and the *Ciboney* of the West Indies might have accompanied the Marginal peoples who are treated in the same volume.

The archeology is also somewhat divided between volumes. Special articles on the archeology of Central America, Venezuela, and the Antilles are presented in the present volume along with the ethnography. The archeology of Colombia, however, has been presented as a whole in Volume 2, although some of the prehistoric remains are undoubtedly attributable to the tribes encountered by the conquistadors.

One of the greatest difficulties in preparing the present volume was the direct result of the paucity of information on both the archeology and ethnography. As few of the aboriginal tribes survive today, ethnologists have largely ignored the area. Archeologists have done little but make surveys, except in the West Indies. It was consequently extremely difficult to find contributors who had a sufficient background of information to prepare articles without an enormous amount of original research, especially in the chronicles of the Conquest. Some groups of tribes were nearly omitted for want of someone who could do the necessary research. On the whole, the early sources have been used considerably less than was hoped, but the coverage of the area has been completed. The editor is especially grateful to Dr. Hernández de Alba for preparing last-minute summaries of the tribes of western Colombia and of the *Caquetío, Achagua,* and others in Venezuela. Hernández de Alba's articles are not exhaustive studies; they are merely preliminary essays hurriedly written to fill in gaps in the Handbook coverage in order to account for the more important tribes and to give the general features of their culture.

The Circum-Caribbean area is not only the least known of all South America, but it is perhaps the most important to problems of native American culture history. The editor and contributors feel with considerable satisfaction that the articles have succeeded in bringing a great deal of order to the previously confused anthropological picture of this area and that a basis is provided for future research on many fundamental problems that the Handbook helps point out.

ACKNOWLEDGMENTS

The editor wishes to express his gratitude to the Handbook staff and the Smithsonian editorial staff which have performed the enormous task of preparing the manuscripts, illustrations, and bibliography of this volume.

For permission to publish the illustrations used in this volume we are grateful to the Museo Nacional, San José, Costa Rica; the Peabody Museum of Archaeology and Ethnology of Harvard University; the Museo Nacional of Tegucigalpa, Honduras; the American Museum of Natural History, New York City; the Bureau of American Ethnology, Smithsonian

Institution, Washington, D. C.; and the American Geographical Society, New York City. We acknowledge also the kindness of the following individuals who furnished photographs for illustrations to the articles of this volume: Mrs. Doris Stone, Monseigneur Federico Lunardi, Dr. Frederick Johnson, Mr. Gerard Reichel-Dolmatoff, Dr. Alexander Wetmore, Llewelyn Williams, Batista Venturello, and the late John Verrill and Theodoor De Booy.

CONTRIBUTORS TO VOLUME 4

OF THE

HANDBOOK OF SOUTH AMERICAN INDIANS

ARMSTRONG, JOHN M., *Washington, D. C.*

GREGORIO HERNÁNDEZ DE ALBA,[1] *Bogotá, Colombia.*

ADOLFO DE HOSTOS, *Official Historian of Puerto Rico, San Juan, Puerto Rico.*

FREDERICK JOHNSON, *The Robert S. Peabody Foundation for Archaeology, Phillips Academy, Andover, Mass.*

ALFRED KIDDER II, *Peabody Museum of Archaeology and Ethnology, Harvard University, Cambridge, Mass.*

PAUL KIRCHHOFF, *Escuela Nacional de Antropología, Instituto Nacional de Antropología e Historia, México, D. F.*

SAMUEL K. LOTHROP, *Peabody Museum of Archaeology and Ethnology, Harvard University, Cambridge, Mass.*

ALFRED MÉTRAUX,[2] *Smithsonian Institution, Washington, D. C.*

JOHN MURRA, *Department of Anthropology, University of Chicago, Chicago, Ill.*

IRVING ROUSE, *Department of Anthropology, Peabody Museum of Natural History, Yale University, New Haven, Conn.*

JULIAN H. STEWARD,[3] *Institute of Social Anthropology, Smithsonian Institution, Washington, D. C.*

DORIS STONE, *San José, Costa Rica.*

DAVID B. STOUT,[4] *United States Naval Reserve.*

WM. DUNCAN STRONG, *Department of Anthropology, Columbia University, New York, N. Y.*

PEDRO GARCÍA VALDÉS, *Pinar del Río, Cuba.*

'1948

[1] Present address: Director, Instituto Etnológico de Popayán, Universidad del Cauca, Popayán, Colombia.

[2] Present address: Department of Social Affairs, United Nations.

[3] Present address: Department of Anthropology, Columbia University, New York, N. Y.

[4] Present address: Department of Sociology and Anthropology, Syracuse University, Syracuse, N. Y.

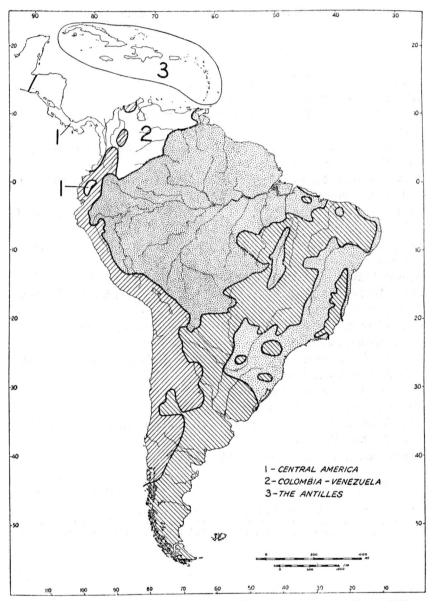

MAP 1.—Culture areas treated in Volume 4. (Stippled, the Tropical Forest Tribes, Volume 3; hachure down-slanted to left, the Andean Civilizations, Volume 2; and hachure down-slanted to right, the Marginal Tribes, Volume 1.)

THE CIRCUM-CARIBBEAN TRIBES: AN INTRODUCTION

By JULIAN H. STEWARD

The tribes described in the present volume are on the whole perhaps the least known ethnographically of any in the areas covered by the Handbook. Whether insular or on the mainland, they were readily accessible from the coast and were quickly overrun by the Spanish conquerors. The great majority of them have long been extinct culturally if not racially. Practically all that survive today were dislocated from their aboriginal habitats to new and often drastically different regions, and for 400 years they have been subject to influence not only from the Spaniards but from the descendants of Negro slaves who penetrated most of the Caribbean islands and coast.

In the Colombian Highland and North Coast Lowland the tribes have entirely vanished as cultural entities, and the only peoples now classed as Indians are a few refugee groups in the low rain forests of the Atrato River and the Pacific coast regions, the much acculturated, cattle-raising *Goajiro* on the Goajira Peninsula, some scattered primitive groups in the llanos and jungle on the western tributaries of the upper Orinoco River in eastern Colombia, and various culturally modified tribes around Lake Maracaibo. In Venezuela the descendants of the aborigines north of the Orinoco River are much mixed racially and have lost most of their native culture, the main exception being a considerable number of *Warrau* in the swamps of the Orinoco Delta. The Antillean tribes may be said to be extinct. In Central America the principal surviving Indians are the *Cuna* of Panamá, a few remnant groups in Costa Rica, the *Mosquito* and their neighbors of the lowlands of eastern Nicaragua, and strongly Hispanicized Indians of Honduras, especially the *Lenca.*

The chroniclers of the Conquest left relatively few and very fragmentary accounts of these tribes, though it is probable that more systematic utilization of their writings, both published and archival, will supply fuller pictures of aboriginal ethnology. Few of the surviving tribes have been visited by ethnologists. Professional studies have been made, though not all of them have been published, only of the *Lenca, Guaymí, Cuna, Chocó, Cayapa, Cágaba, Ica, Goajiro, Macoa (Chaké* or *"Motilones"), Yaruro,* and *Warrau.*

1

The Circum-Caribbean area has many archeological remains including mounds, burials, stone sculpture, ceramics, metallurgy, and other evidences of a rich culture. South of the *Maya* frontier in Honduras, however, these have received little more than superficial surveys. Coclé in Panamá and Tairona and San Agustín in Colombia (the last two described in vol. 2 of the Handbook) are exceptions. Only the Antilles have been worked with any thoroughness. Elsewhere the remains have not been dated sequentially in relationship to one another, and few have been identified with tribes occupying the regions at the Conquest. These materials, therefore, must be used with great caution in rounding out the ethnographic picture, for many of them may have great antiquity.

A comparison of data from the modern tribes with those from the earlier chroniclers and from archeology shows that all but the very backward and isolated tribes have suffered drastic changes. Gone are the intensive horticulture, the dense population, the large villages, the class-structured society, the mounds, temples, idols, and priests, the warfare, cannibalism and human trophies, the elaborate death rites, and even the technological and esthetic refinements evidenced in the early metallurgy, weaving, ceramics, and stone sculpture. The modern tribes who retain a predominantly aboriginal culture have come to resemble the Tropical Forest tribes (Handbook, vol. 3) rather than their own ancestors. They carry on small-scale slash-and-burn farming, and many of them now hunt and fish more than they till the soil. They live in small villages, weave simple cloth, and make only plain pots. Their society is unstratified, their religious cults are scarcely remembered, and the principal survival of former days is the shaman.

THE BASIC CIRCUM-CARIBBEAN CULTURE[1]

SOCIAL AND RELIGIOUS PATTERNS

The tribes carried on intensive farming, which outranked hunting, gathering, and fishing in its productiveness and which supported a dense population and large villages. The typical community was a large, compact, planned village of several hundred to several thousand persons. It consisted of pole-and-thatch houses arranged in streets and around plazas, and it was surrounded by a palisade. In the village were temples, special residences for chiefs, and storehouses.

[1] Dr. Paul Kirchhoff, who has been engaged in a thorough study of early accounts of the tribes around the Caribbean Sea, called attention to the fact that at the time of the Conquest there was great similarity between most of the tribes, attesting close historical connection. Unfortunately, his study could not be completed in time to utilize the results in the Handbook, but it is hoped that he may soon publish his detailed comparative survey of these peoples. The present summary is essentially a synthesis of the data in this volume and in the second volume of the Handbook, and it should be considered in connection with the comparable summary of the cultures of the Tropical Forest tribes given in volume 3 of the Handbook.

Society was characteristically stratified into three or four classes. The village chief stood at the social pinnacle, and in some areas he ruled over federations of villages or tribes. Characteristically, he lived in a large house, received tribute, had many wives and retainers (in Colombia he married his full sister, as among the *Inca*), wore special insignia and ornaments, was carried by his subjects in a litter, and at death his body was either mummified or desiccated and placed in a special house or temple, or it was buried, accompanied by wives and servants who were stupefied and interred alive (fig. 27), and often the chief's image was placed on the grave. There was rarely an organized priesthood, for in most of these tribes the shaman, and in some the chief, functioned as intermediary between the people and their gods. Similarly, the noble class tended to merge with that of the chiefs, except where extreme stratification occurred.

The basic social arrangement would have been one of chiefs and common people except for extreme development of warfare, which served the social hierarchy in several ways. Captive men were usually put to death for cannibalistic feasts and for human trophies, both of which enhanced their captor's prestige. Women were usually annexed to their captor's household, either as wives or servants, and their number was a measure of their master's social standing. Wealth was a major factor in the status of chiefs and nobles, and it was produced by these large households, together with some tribute from commoners and even from other tribes. It would seem, however, that male captives were seldom kept as permanent slaves except among the Antillean *Arawak*. Their ultimate fate and even that of the children they might breed in their captor's tribe was to be killed and eaten or sacrificed. Human sacrifice, therefore, made warfare also an important adjunct to religion in the Central American and Colombian tribes.

Social status was thus not entirely hereditary but depended partly upon individual achievement in warfare. Some Central American chiefs were elected. In many tribes shamans had great power. So far as status was hereditary in Colombia and Central America, titles and property tended to pass in the matrilineal line, from a man to his nephew, and in some cases matrilineal clans were interwoven with social classes. Sexual inversion of men, probably connected with shortage of women caused by polygyny, was common.

Religion centered around the temple cult. The temple was a special structure (it is uncertain how frequently it was set on a mound), which sheltered idols (pl. 89, *k*) to which offerings were made. Instead of a special organized priesthood, which was more common in Central America and may have come from the Meso-American tribes, the shaman seems usually to have been mediator with the deities; particularly he served as oracle and made sacrifices. In the Antilles, however, the *Arawakan* chief performed this function. The gods which were supplicated by the

Circum-Caribbean peoples are not clearly described, but those mentioned in myths and occasionally in ritual are usually celestial, the sun and moon being especially prominent and the stars frequently named. There is occasional evidence of a jaguar cult both in religious practices and in art motifs.

Considerable preoccupation with the dead is manifest in burial practices, and ancestors or ghosts are commonly named among supernatural spirits involved in religious beliefs. Urn burial (pl. 1, *bottom*) is Circum-Caribbean, and burial mounds occur everywhere but in the Antilles. Where archeological sequences are known these two methods seem to belong to fairly recent periods. Virtually all tribes disposed of a deceased chief with considerable ceremony, either desiccating the body (Antillean *Arawak*, where he became a god and temple idol; also, the Cauca-Atrato region of Colombia and Darién and Coclé in Panamá) or embalming it. When the chief was buried some of his retainers and wives were stupefied and interred with him, a practice found in all three areas.

MATERIAL CULTURE

Several facts indicate the importance of farming among these tribes as compared with that of the Tropical Forest. Fields seem to have been much larger and more permanent, resembling plantations rather than the frequently shifting, slash-and-burn plots. Hunting and fishing were secondary, and, although the cultures rim the Caribbean Sea, few settlements were actually on the coast; by contrast, the Tropical Forest villages were characteristically riparian and coastal. Circum-Caribbean men seem to have devoted proportionately much more effort to farming than to hunting and fishing, and in many tribes they performed tasks of cultivation that elsewhere fall to women. By inference, the much larger and more permanent Circum-Caribbean villages must have required a more assured food supply.

Domesticated plants varied somewhat, and the greatest number of species was found in northern Colombia, where, in addition to maize, sweet manioc or yuca, beans, sweetpotatoes, and peppers, which were the usual staples, the tribes grew many fruits and cacao. Bitter manioc had a very limited distribution, its spread in this area evidently having been post-Colombian.

Hunting and fishing were practiced, and fish nets, fishhooks, fish drugs, harpoons (pl. 56, *right*), spears, stone axes, and bows and arrows (unfeathered among several tribes) were general in the area. As in parts of the Amazon Basin, the bow and arrow had evidently spread at the expense of the spear and spear thrower; these weapons have a strong negative correlation. Arrow poison was Circum-Caribbean with a few gaps, and the poison was generally of animal-derived, putrified ingredients in contrast to the vegetable poisons used elsewhere in South America.

The more important technological traits were: loom-weaving (pl. 40) of domesticated cotton, but ornamentation of cloth often by painting rather than by woven-in patterns; twilled and woven basketry (pl. 54, *e*, *f*); developed ceramics, especially with plastic, applied, and incised decoration, and in zoomorphic, anthropomorphic, and tripod forms; dugout canoes and water travel (most developed on the South American, Panamanian, and Antillean coasts; somewhat less so in the Sub-Andean areas and the remainder of Central America, where overland travel by roads was more characteristic); and stone axes, slings, and the weapons mentioned above. Metallurgy was best developed in Colombia and Panamá (pl. 20; figs. 37–40), where gold and copper were smelted and alloyed, but gold was probably worked in a few other parts of Central America, and in the Antilles gold was taken from placer mines. Gold objects, however, reached all tribes by trade.

Some technologies which characterize the Marginal tribes in various parts of South America survive with a restricted distribution among Circum-Caribbean tribes. The use of wild basts and a netting technique for making hammocks and carrying-bags is found among the *Lenca* and *Talamanca,* in northern Venezuela, in the region west of Lake Maracaibo, and probably among the Antillean *Arawak.* Coiled basketry is reported nowhere except among the *Chocó* (fig. 63). Bark cloth (pl. 53, *d*, *e*) extends from the western Amazon through the *Toro* and *Chanco* of the Cauca River and the tribes of the North Colombian Lowland to the *Talamanca* Division and Caribbean Lowland tribes in Central America, and stone bark-beaters are found archeologically (pl. 14, *d*, *e*) somewhat beyond this distribution in Nicaragua and northeastern Honduras, but they are comparatively late in the *Maya* sequence. There was also extensive use of decorated calabash containers (pl. 54, *c*), a Tropical Forest trait which tends to have a somewhat negative correlation with elaborated ceramics.

Garments were made of woven cotton, the most common being the woman's apron and the man's breechclout, but various mantles or cloaks were also worn. The skull was artificially deformed, usually frontally or fronto-occipitally, and the nose and ears, but not the lips, were pierced for ornaments. Ornaments were made of gold, even where gold was not worked, and of stone (precious and semiprecious stones in Central America), shell, and other materials.

In food preparation, the most common utensils used were stone metates, mortars, pottery jars and griddles, and babracots.

Among items of household furniture, carved wooden and stone stools (pls. 26, 49, *a*, *b*; 88, *l*; figs. 43, 44) were characteristic, the latter taking elaborate animal forms in the archeological sites of coastal Ecuador and Central America. The platform bed occurred throughout the area, but, as in the Montaña east of the Andes, it seemingly was being replaced by the hammock in lowland areas; in most tribes both were found.

Among esthetic and recreational elements were chicha and chicha troughs (pl. 62), tobacco, coca, some form of game with a rubber ball which was probably played on special courts, hollow-log drums, skin drums (pl. 54, *a*), rattles, shell trumpets, panpipes, and flutes (pl. 68, *top, left*).

ORIGINS OF THE CIRCUM-CARIBBEAN CULTURE

To understand the origins of the Circum-Caribbean culture it is necessary first to classify its general structure and content with reference to other South American cultures. Considered in general terms, South American cultures may be classed roughly in four types: (1) the hunting and gathering, or Marginal; (2) the Tropical Forest; (3) the Circum-Caribbean and Sub-Andean; and (4) the Andean.

The Marginal tribes had a sociopolitical structure, which lacked classes and was based essentially on kinship ties, and a material culture, which lacked certain key technologies found among the other three groups. They carried on no farming and, if ceramics, basketry, and weaving were present, their pots were crude, their baskets twined or coiled, and their fabrics twined or netted. The other three groups had farming, ceramics, twilled basketry, and loom weaving, and they differed from one another in the variety and esthetic patterning of their products rather than in the essential processes.

In addition, the Circum-Caribbean and Andean peoples resembled each other and differed from those of the Tropical Forest in their sociopolitical and religious patterns. Highly productive farming in the Andes and around the Caribbean Sea made possible a dense population and large villages which formed the basis of a class-structured society with chiefs, nobles, commoners, and slaves. In parts of Guiana and among the coastal and river *Tupí*, where resources of the sea and rivers supplemented farming, and in certain tribes of the Mojos-Chiquitos area of eastern Bolivia, a tendency to a similar class-structured society is evident. Characteristically, however, the Tropical Forest peoples, like the Marginal tribes, had small villages and an unstratified society, each community consisting of an extended lineage or being organized on other kinship lines. The Andean and Circum-Caribbean tribes also had a developed temple-priest-idol cult, whereas Tropical Forest religion, more like that of the Marginal peoples, centered around shamanistic practices, with only a few group ceremonies conducted by the shaman.

The Circum-Caribbean tribes differed from the civilized peoples of the Andes and México in the elaboration of the basic sociopolitical and religious patterns. Among the latter, social classes were more complicated, more fixed by heredity, and more strongly endogamous. In the Circum-

Caribbean area status was somewhat mobile and, though hereditary rank was not absent, status often could be attained through warfare. The civilized peoples had achieved political states, with rulers of dominions and even empires, and their warfare was directed toward conquest and tribute. The Circum-Caribbean tribes had only incipient states, and warfare furthered personal ambition rather than political ends. Its purpose was cannibalism, display of human trophies, capture of female slaves, and, in some cases, taking of sacrificial victims. In religion, México and the Andes had succeeded in separating shamanism from temple worship, and they had a special class of priests dedicated to community worship in temples. The Circum-Caribbean peoples also had temples, but their shamans performed not only as priests but also as medicine men.

In their material arts the civilized peoples of México and Perú excelled mainly in the elaboration of the processes which they shared with the Circum-Caribbean tribes. The greater variety of crops and better methods of cultivation made their farming more productive. Their pottery was better made and esthetically far superior, especially in painted decoration; their weaving involved many special techniques; and their handling of stones, whether in construction or in sculpture, outranked that of the Circum-Caribbean peoples. The Andes also had metallurgy, which became part of the Circum-Caribbean culture, and domesticated animals, which did not. The Circum-Caribbean cultures are distinguished from the civilized peoples not only by their lack of the latter's elaborations but also by their possession of certain material items probably derived from the Tropical Forest.

Other embellishments that distinguish the civilized peoples from those of the Circum-Caribbean are certain intellectual accomplishments, such as quipus and scales in Perú and writing and astronomy in México. Some Andean elaborations reached all the Circum-Caribbean peoples, and others reached those of Colombia and Venezuela, who are called sub-Andean to distinguish them from the peoples of Central America and the Antilles. Certain Mexican elaborations similarly reached Central America.

The classification of South American cultures into four general types has developmental implications. Hypotheses concerning the origin and spread of the traits and complexes, however, must take into account the ecological adaptations of human societies through exploitative techniques to a variety of natural environments.

That the Andean and Mexican civilizations differ from the Circum-Caribbean culture more in elaboration than in essential form or content means that they grew out of something generally similar to it and that each acquired its own emphasis. It must be postulated, therefore, that a Formative Period culture once extended from México to the Andes, and perhaps farther. This culture appears to have been an essentially Highland one, though in certain localities it probably incorporated elements, particularly material ones, that were more especially adapted to the tropical rain forests.

To judge from the Circum-Caribbean culture, the Formative Period culture had the following general characteristics: There were fairly large and permanent communities that rested upon adequate subsistence, principally farming.   Society was characteristically class-structured , and there may have been incipient states, though the Circum-Caribbean level of organization would suggest that warfare was directed more toward trophy taking (mainly head and bone trophies) and cannibalism, both being means of gaining social prestige, than toward conquest and tribute, features that go with a class system that is fixed by heredity.   That chieftainship was well developed is implied in the complex early burial types found archeologically in many regions; elaborate burial for the chief is a feature of the Circum-Caribbean culture.   In religion there was a temple-priest complex, but the shaman probably performed the priestly functions. The gods may have been represented by idols.   A very wide inter-American distribution suggests that the principal deities were celestial ones, that place and animal spirits were important, that human sacrifice may have been practiced, and that offertories and shrines were used.

A fairly adequate subsistence based particularly on maize farming in the Formative Period is implied not only by the known antiquity and wide distribution of maize but by the evident size and stability of many early archeological sites.   Agriculture was becoming man's task, and hunting and fishing were diminishing in relative importance.   The latter, however, were practiced locally, and, to judge by their wide distribution in the hemisphere, devices available for hunting included traps, nets, snares, deadfalls, pitfalls, spears, and spear throwers, and for fishing included drugs, hooks, and nets.   Hunting and fishing, however, affected the general patterning of these cultures only insofar as local abundance of certain species augmented or took the place of farming as the basis for a dense population and stable communities.

There is archeological evidence that construction of mounds, elaborate graves, and possibly of temples and roads were carried on in the Formative Period.   Such features in turn presuppose fairly organized, stable populations.

Inter-American distributions, both archeological and ethnological, show that the essential technologies of the Formative Period included ceramics, especially with plastic and incised treatment, loom weaving, domesticated cotton, netting, stone metates, stone grinding and polishing, and coiled basketry.

On the basis also of archeological and ethnological distributions other material items available to the Formative Period culture, though not necessarily part of it in all localities, were: breechclouts, aprons or wrap-around skirts, cloaks and mantles, sandals, ear and nose ornaments, necklaces, head deformation, body paint, tattoo, featherwork, mirrors, stone axes, wooden and stone-head clubs, panpipes, single-head skin drums, flutes, and rattles.

As the New World civilizations developed from the Formative Period culture, each acquired specialized features and styles; México became readily distinguishable from the Andes, and subareas of each became distinguishable from one another. It is at present difficult to ascertain to what extend localities differed in the occurrence of the essential Formative Period features and in the stylistic handling of them. Archeology has so emphasized style as a criterion of prehistoric cultural differences that localities may well appear much more unlike than they really were.

The Circum-Caribbean culture corresponds to the postulated Formative Period culture in the presence of the essential ecological adaptations, the socioreligious patterns, and the technologies and traits of material culture. It also has special traits and specialized handling of traits that are peculiar to the Mexican and Andean civilizations. In addition, it has several material items that are more particularly associated with a tropical rain forest environment. The following chart shows the interareal linkage of Circum-Caribbean traits with México, the Andes, and the Tropical Forest; also, differences.

LINKAGES OF ELEMENTS IN THE CIRCUM-CARIBBEAN AREA [1]

Culture	Andean	South American Tropical Forest	Mexican
Subsistence	Tropical fruits (plus maize, potatoes, quinoa, etc.)	Manioc Coca* Domesticated duck Meat smoked on the babracot	Domesticated turkey
Houses and furniture	Platform bed Stone stool	Pole-and-thatch construction Pile house Communal house Palisaded village Hammock Wooden stool	Wooden stool
Clothing and ornaments		Penis cover Labrets†	Leather sandal*
Technologies	Metallurgy	Bark cloth* Decorated calabashes	Bark cloth*
Weapons	Sling Mace-head club*	Vegetable arrow poison† Pellet gun or blowgun	Animal arrow poison* Sling
Social traits	Chief's litter†	Captives for cannibalism	Ritual cannibalism

[1] Elements marked with an asterisk are limited to South and Central America; those marked with a dagger to South America and the Antilles. (See also Kidder II, 1940; Nordenskiöld, 1930; Kroeber, 1939; Lothrop, 1940.)

LINKAGES OF ELEMENTS IN THE CIRCUM-CARIBBEAN AREA [1]—Continued

Culture	Andean	South American Tropical Forest	Mexican
Religious traits	Idols Stone-cist grave* Deep-shaft grave* Mummification or desiccation of body Burial of retainers with chief	Mound burial*	Idols Stone-cist grave Ritual incense* Flayed-skin deities
Warfare	Flayed-skin trophies	Human sacrifice for cannibalism*	Flayed-skin trophies
Esthetic and recreational traits	Alter-ego monolith* Chontales monolith* Jaguar stool Manabí-type stone slab* Pottery ocarina*	Ball game with court Coca Chicha Wooden chicha trough Hollow-log drum	Ball game with court Chicha (pulque) Hollow-log drum

[1] Elements marked with an asterisk are limited to South and Central America; those marked with a dagger to South America and the Antilles. (See also Kidder II, 1940; Nordenskiöld, 1930; Kroeber, 1939; Lothrop, 1940.)

This list shows that the preponderant linkage of Central America is with South America and inferentially that at least after the Formative Period the cultural flow in Central America was predominantly from south to north. The occurrence of *Chibchan* languages through Panamá and Costa Rica north to the *Ulua-Sumo-Mosquito* group seems clear evidence of tribal migrations from South America, and the failure of a number of Central and South American ethnographic traits, such as coca, manioc, palisaded villages, hammocks, bark cloth, blowguns, developed metallurgy, mummification, burial of a chief with his retainers, and many art styles, to extend to or at least to take hold in México points to the origin of the particular elaborations of the Central American-Circum-Caribbean culture in South America. Some of the Central American-Andean elements, however, such as alter-ego statutes, Manabí-type carved stone slabs, deep-shaft graves, and others seem to have considerable antiquity in Ecuador (Handbook, vol. 2, p. 781), suggesting that the flow has been from south to north since the Formative Period traits began to assume specialized regional characteristics.

México influence in Central America is not wanting, but most of it seems to have come fairly recently with the migrations of the *Nahuatlan* tribes from México, and its elements, such as tongue piercing, jade working, an organized priesthood, steam bath, ritual incense, Chacmool statues, Nicoya Polychrome pottery, and the game of voladores, have a limited distribution in Central America and did not reach South America.

The many traits assumed to have come from the Tropical Forest involve perishable materials, and, though some of them might have been preserved in sites on the arid coast of Perú, archeology elsewhere can throw no light on their antiquity or origin. It is likely that those that require forest materials, are adapted to a hot climate, and have an ethnographic distribution predominantly in the rain forest areas came from such regions. For some items, however, such an origin must be accepted with caution. The blowgun, for example, now has a Tropical Forest distribution, but it also has been found archeologically in the Early Periods of Perú.

The general inference of these considerations is that the Circum-Caribbean developed out of an early culture with characteristics that are thought of as Andean. Its class-structured society may represent a response to intensive farming and a fairly dense population coupled with pressures of warfare rather than a specific complex derived from some single center of origin. Many of its special elaborations, however, both in element content and in stylistic handling, are derived from the Andean and Méxican civilizations, especially the former. It even appears that its specific resemblances to the Andes may have been greater at some early prehistoric period than at the Conquest. Meanwhile, its distribution in tropical and semitropical regions made it receptive to many material items which the Tropical Forest added at some undatable period.

DISTRIBUTION OF THE CIRCUM-CARIBBEAN CULTURE

The Circum-Caribbean culture is found in areas that are largely highland but that have neither the great altitude nor the continuous mountain masses of the Andes or the Plateau of México. To a great extent, the environment is tropical or subtropical.

The portions of Colombia where the Andean Cordillera breaks down into a series of smaller mountain blocks with comparatively low valleys between them are more or less coincidental with the distribution of Sub-Andean cultures. The tribes of the Southern Colombian Highland (Handbook, vol. 2, p. 911) really belong to this class. To the north of them tribes of the upper Cauca River were essentially Sub-Andean, though lacking a few characteristic features. The peoples of the Cordillera Central between the Cauca and Magdalena Rivers and of the Cordillera Occidental west of the Cauca also belong in this group. Farther west, the *Chocó* of the Pacific Coast lowlands are definitely Tropical Forest in culture. The North Colombia lowlands on the Atlantic coast are Sub-Andean, and a very similar culture continues through Panamá, Costa Rica, Nicaragua, and Honduras to the *Maya* frontier in northwestern Honduras. The greater part of Central America is mountainous, but there are no great continuous mountain masses. It is possible that some less-developed peoples had survived in certain parts of Central America, ıor example, the *Sumo, Jicaque,* and *Paya* of the East Coast Lowlands of Nicaragua, but the Conquest Period culture is not sufficiently well known to clarify this point.

Where the Cordillera Oriental branches off from the Cordillera Central in southern Colombia, the Sub-Andean culture continues north through the *Pijao* and *Panche* to the *Chibcha (Muisca)*, whose culture is Andean primarily in having achieved political states (Handbook, vol. 2, p. 887), and its distribution continues to the north of the *Chibcha* toward Lake Maracaibo. Approaching Venezuela the mountain chain forks again southwest of Lake Maracaibo, and, as Kirchhoff points out in "The Northeastern Extension of Andean Culture" (this volume, p. 349), one branch runs west of Lake Maracaibo to the Sierra de Perijá and onward toward the Sierra de Santa Marta, and the other runs northeast skirting Lake Maracaibo on its southeast side and becoming the Cordillera de los Andes in Venezuela. The tribes of the Cordillera Oriental north of the *Muisca (Chibcha)* are little known except for a few data on the *Lache,* who adjoined the *Muisca* on the north, and on the *Chitarera,* somewhat farther north. These peoples were definitely Sub-Andean or Circum-Caribbean in their general culture elements and patterns. East of the Andes, the *Betoi, Achagua,* and other tribes of eastern Colombia are Tropical Forest.

The group of tribes extending northward to the Sierra de Santa Marta and the Goajira Peninsula, west of Maracaibo, seem to have lacked most of the essential features and should probably be considered Tropical Forest peoples. The *Timotean* peoples of the Venezuela Andes, however, were definitely Sub-Andean, and, despite breaks in its continuity, marked even by hunting and gathering tribes of northern Venezuela, the Circum-Caribbean culture is somewhat resumed among the *Carib* tribes who were spread along the north coast of Venezuela to the Delta of the Orinoco. A break is again encountered in the Lesser Antilles, which had been invaded by the *Carib,* probably in the last century before the Conquest, but the Circum-Caribbean culture is found again among the *Arawak* of the Greater Antilles, and it extended as far as Cuba and Haiti, where the primitive hunting and gathering *Ciboney* still survived.

A general hypothesis is offered to explain this distribution. In the first place, it is probable that the fundamentals of this culture were spread from a single source. The occurrence of such specific items as gold-embellished litters among the Antillean *Arawak* as well as in the Andes and of definitely Colombian art motifs in Central America cannot be explained by independent invention. They imply intertribal contact so strong that it must have facilitated the diffusion of many other traits. At the same time, the social and political patterns required a basis of intensive farming that supported large permanent villages. If diffusion of the Circum-Caribbean culture from a single source is postulated, therefore, it must have involved the essential technologies and subsistence as well as the sociopolitical and religious features.

Theories of the origins of American civilizations have always tended to push the ultimate origin to the area that is least known scientifically. The basis of Mexican culture was sought first in México and then in the Andes, and when developmental stages were not found in Perú, ultimate origins were again pushed to the least-known areas, the jungles east of the Andes. That many individual Highland traits were ultimately derived from the jungle is quite probable. That the essential sociopolitical patterns and esthetic elaborations of the basic technologies came from an area that still can support only slash-and-burn farming and small communities organized on a simple kinship or unstratified basis is highly improbable.

The alternative hypothesis is that the patterns characteristic of the Circum-Caribbean cultures were Highland-derived and that at one time they formed a substratum which extended from the Andes to the Mexican Highlands. This substratum probably included the elements listed for the Formative Period culture. Out of it grew the Mexican culture, which emphasized the temple cult and war achievements, and the Peruvian civilization, which elaborated sociopolitical structure and material arts. A corollary hypothesis is that at a fairly early period, perhaps when the culture was less environmentally specialized than later or when it had greater vigor and adaptability, it thrust widely into regions where it later ceased to exist sometime before the Conquest. It failed particularly in savanna and tropical rain forest areas. This hypothesis not only helps explain such breaks in the distribution of high cultures as that between the Central Andes and the *Chibcha* of Colombia or that between South America and México, but it accounts for gaps in the occurrence of the Circum-Caribbean culture, such as those west of Lake Maracaibo, in northern Venezuela, and between the north coast of Venezuela and the Antillean *Arawak*, and it also explains certain archeological remains. In the llanos of eastern subtropical Bolivia are mounds and causeways that antedate the historic people. In the same area the social classes and the temple-priest complex found among the Mojos-Chiquitos tribes and even as far east as the *Xaray* on the upper Paraguay River (Handbook, vol. 3) may represent survivals of an early Sub-Andean complex. Stirling (personal communication) reports large mounds on the lower Marañón River of eastern Perú where only primitive tribes were found in the historic period. In Colombia, east of the Cordillera Oriental, are ancient stone structures, and great causeways are found in the llanos of eastern Colombia nearly to the Orinoco River. Ethnologically, the occurrence of mummification among the *Piaroa*, east of the upper Orinoco, and idols among the *Sáliva* suggests earlier Highland influence. Stone-faced terraces and stairways of large monolithic stones in the Sierra de Santa Marta, neither built by the historic *Cágaba*, are evidence of a thrust northward, west of Lake Maracaibo. If the stone structures of the *Tai-*

rona area along the coast north of the Sierra de Santa Marta can be attributed to the *Tairona* themselves, they may represent a local survival in strength of the earlier culture. In the southern Colombia Highlands, the elaborate stone sculpture and architecture of San Agustín is apparently fairly old, and surpasses anything attributable to the peoples found at the Conquest. The general style and the alter-ego motif of this sculpture is found widely on stone statues in Central America north to Nicaragua.

These threads of evidence are at present very tenuous and await archeological verification in the rain-forest areas. It is purely speculative to maintain that all these thrusts were contemporary. On the other hand, there would seem to be some causal connection between the thrusts of a Highland culture into the lowlands or forests at many different places and their consistent failure. If cultures of an Andean or Sub-Andean type were carried by actual movements of peoples into sparsely populated lowlands or tropical forests, they would at first find little opposition. The culture, however, seems to depend upon dense populations clustered in large stable villages. This is difficult to maintain in tropical rain forests, where slash-and-burn farming is carried on, and it is perhaps significant that the *Maya*, who were unique in maintaining a high civilization outside a Highland area, had settlements dispersed around religious centers. As the lowland became more densely settled owing to better farming, intensified warfare would not only be a factor requiring more highly nucleated settlements but it would add to the precariousness of their tenure.

Present data, therefore, could be interpreted to mean that the Circum-Caribbean culture originated from an early Sub-Andean stratum that may have been carried in part by migrations of peoples into thinly populated areas. Population pressure and the necessity of adapting to non-Highland environments eliminated some of the more typical Andean traits, but the basic patterns and many specific elements survived in simpler but unmistakable form.

In historical terms, this hypothesis may be extended to account for the origin of the Tropical Forest culture. In Volume 3 it has been suggested that the Tropical Forest complex has the technologies which characterize the Circum-Caribbean peoples and that these technologies appear to have spread down the Guiana coast and by water up the Amazon. The Circum-Caribbean cultures near the mouth of the Orinoco would supply a source for these traits; indeed, archeology of the lower Amazon yields pottery that in many respects is surprisingly like the Circum-Caribbean.

This thesis suggests that subsequent to the early expansion of the Highland cultures there may have been some deculturation which was checked at a Circum-Caribbean level. The Circum-Caribbean culture retained the general form of the Highland culture, and even added material items from the Tropical Forest, but it was not able to maintain the sociopolitical, religious, and material elaborations of the civilized peoples. The Conquest initiated another period of drastic deculturation which eliminated all but the bare technological processes, and, though the cultures may still be regarded as essentially aboriginal, the modern peoples resemble those of the Tropical Forests rather than their own ancestors. Loss of lands, wars of the Conquest, and European diseases contributed to a reduction of the population, and influence from both Spaniards and Negroes modified the cultures. In a more fundamental sense, however, it would seem that the class-structured society, the temple-idol complex, and the wars for slaves and for victims for sacrificial rites and human trophies formed strongly interrelated patterns which were destroyed by European religion and by laws which prohibited many of the key practices. With the loss of these patterns, the artistic refinements that were expressions of them also perished. What was left was simple technologies—farming in unfavorable areas, weaving plain cloth, manufacture of unadorned ceramics, canoe making, and the like—and unstratified social groups with weak chiefs, with warfare reduced to mere defensive fighting, and with religion reduced to shamanistic practices without temples or idols. In short, the culture stepped down to the Tropical Forest level.

THE SUB-ANDEAN TRIBES OF WESTERN COLOMBIA

The peoples described in Hernández de Alba's articles in this volume on the "Tribes of the North Colombia Lowlands," "Tribes East of the Cauca River," "Tribes of the Cauca-Atrato Region," and "Tribes of the Upper Cauca River" conform to the general Circum-Caribbean pattern, but were Sub-Andean in the possession of certain specific Andean items, such as liana bridges, salt working, copper smelting and alloying with gold, construction of roads and hilltop forts, war banners, marriage of a chief to his sister, and other features not found elsewhere around the Caribbean Sea. Archeology reveals traits not reported for the Conquest Period tribes. Some of these traits, such as the carved stone statues of San Agustín and Tierradentro, evidently belong exclusively to a very early period. Other archeological traits, such as shaft-and-chamber burials, stone-cist burials, and negative-painted and monochrome-incised ceramics, have specific stylistic resemblances to Early Period remains of the North Highlands of Perú, but in generalized form they may well have survived to the Conquest among some Colombian tribes.

Although the great ethnographic diversity in Western Colombia undoubtedly reflects to some degree the fragmentary information of our sources, archeology suggests a comparable local difference, and there seems little doubt that Colombia's extreme local geographic diversity has been an important factor in splitting the area into cultural provinces.

SOCIAL AND RELIGIOUS PATTERNS

All tribes of Western Colombia, except the *Chocó*, a Tropical Forest people, were sedentary, intensive farmers who lived in large planned and probably palisaded villages. The village, and in some instances the tribe or dominion, was controlled by a chief of exalted status and great power. Under the chief were nobles, commoners, and slaves. Among the *Carrapa*, *Picara*, and *Paucura*, the chief married his sister, a system which the *Inca* used to preserve the purity of the emperor's divine descent. The chiefs seem usually to have been succeeded by their sons, but a matrilineal tendency is evident in the frequent marriage of a chief to his sister's daughter. The *Fincenú* even had female chiefs. Evidences of the chief's high position are his very large number of wives and retainers, his special insignia and ornaments, the gold-adorned litter in which he was carried, the special obeisance and etiquette accorded him, and the burial of a number of his wives and retainers with him. Development of states through federation or imperialism, though less advanced than among the *Chibcha*, is recognizable among the *Quimbaya*, *Tolú*, *Cenú*, and *Mompox* of the North Colombia Lowlands, the *Lile* of the upper Cauca River, and the *Ancerma*, *Catío*, and other tribes of the Cauca-Atrato region. In several cases, the chief received tribute from federated or subjugated tribes.

Subchiefs and nobles evidently comprised a distinct and somewhat endogamous class, and below them were the commoners and finally the slaves. Warfare was essential to this class system, for cannibalism and the display of human trophies were means of gaining prestige, and captives constituted a slave group. The extent to which the upper strata were really warrior classes is not clear, but the existence of regular armies and the frequent reports of female warriors, who acquired military fame no less than the men, show the great importance of warfare. Human trophies consisted of flayed skins and even arms and legs stuffed with ashes (*Lile*, *Gorrón*, *Ancerma*, and some tribes east of the Cauca) and skulls that were either painted (*Ancerma*) or had their features restored with modeled wax. These trophies were displayed on poles. Cannibalism is reported among all tribes except possibly those of the North Colombia Lowlands. East of the Cauca River, prisoners were fattened before they were killed and eaten, and in the Cauca-Atrato region, the *Caramanta* ate not only captives they had taken but slaves bought from other tribes for the sole purpose of eating them. East of the Cauca River and in the Cauca-Atrato region, captives were also used as sacrificial victims in religious rites.

Temples and idols probably occurred everywhere except on the upper Cauca River. In the North Colombia Lowlands, the "great temple" of the *Fincenú* accommodated 1,000 people, and in the Cauca-Atrato region, the *Ancerma* temple was on a large hill ascended by bamboo stairs. In both cases, the temple was entered only by priests and chiefs. Idols of painted or gold-sheathed wood were kept in these sanctuaries, but among some tribes, such as the *Caramanta, Pozo,* and *Arma,* who built no temples, people kept idols in their own dwellings (as among the Antillean *Arawak*) and made offerings to them on special altars.

There seems to have been no special priesthood. On the upper Cauca and among the *Evégico,* shamans communicated with the deities, who were not represented by idols. "Priests" are mentioned among the *Ancerma,* but it is possible that they were shamans, as seems to have been the case among the North Colombia Lowland tribes. In any case they served as oracles and made offerings to the idols.

The nature of the deities and the purposes of the temple or idol worship seems to have varied considerably. The *Fincenú* apparently had animal idols, including the jaguar. The *Carrapa* lacked idols but made offerings to the Sun. The *Ancerma* principal deity, Xixarama, was the parent of the sun and moon. The *Nutibara* god, Guaca, was represented as a jaguar, and the *Catío* had celestial deities.

Human sacrifice is recorded for the *Pozo, Arma, Quimbaya. Picara, Paucura,* and *Caramanta,* but its nature and purpose are seldom revealed. The *Arma* and *Quimbaya* performed the rite on a special platform. The *Caramanta* cut out the victim's heart to control the weather, and the *Pozo* made sacrifices before going to war.

The shaman served as doctor as well as priest. In the North Colombia Lowlands, he seems to have treated patients in the temple with the help of the gods, using tobacco for purification. The *Ancerma* shaman massaged and sucked his patient and blew the sickness into the air.

MATERIAL CULTURE

Western Colombia had the essential Circum-Caribbean traits of material culture: pole-and-thatched houses, often on piles (Cauca-Atrato); planned, compact, palisaded villages; wooden stools (upper Cauca); stone metates; hammocks (North Colombia Lowlands, *Quimbaya*); platform beds (*Ancerma*); dugout canoes; gold mining and goldworking; calabash containers; pottery, often with negative-painted designs; woven cotton textiles; breechclouts, aprons, and cloaks or mantles; featherwork; ear and nose ornaments, especially of gold; skull deformation (*Pozo, Quimbaya*); matting; probably basketry but techniques not known; the chief's litter; spear and spear thrower (east of Cauca, Cauca-Atrato, Province of Aburrá); the bow and poisoned arrow (more northern: Province of Aburrá, east of Cauca(?), North Colombia Lowlands); darts; slings (North Colombia Lowlands, east of Cauca, Province of Aburrá); clubs, harpoons; flutes; drums; shell trumpets; coca; and chicha.

Specifically Andean traits found here but rarely encountered elsewhere around the Caribbean Sea are: manufacture and trade of salt; copper smelting and alloying with gold (upper Cauca and east of Cauca) and many specialized metallurgical processes; road construction (*Arma, Catío, Abibe, Nutabe, Urezo, Aburrá*); liana or vine suspension bridges; aqueducts (*Aburrá*); rain gutters and storage vessels (*Catío*); gold pincers (*Quimbaya*); war banners (east of the Cauca); maces (Province of Aburrá); balsa canoes (*Cenú*); markets; wrapped funeral bundles (*Gorrón*); and a system of weights and measures.

The Tropical Forests may be the origin of the following Western Colombian traits that had a limited distribution in the Circum-Caribbean area: cultivation of the pixiuva palm; bark cloth (*Chanco, Arma*); labrets (*Pozo, Arma*); ligatures around the arms and legs; and the use of deadfall traps, boiling water, and pitfalls with sharp stakes in house defense (*Antiochia*).

Special features of more restricted distribution were: wells (North Colombia Lowlands); artificial fish ponds (*Gorrón*); the rearing and fattening of young pecarries (*Urabá, Yamici*); mute dogs (?) (*Aburrá;* cf. Antillean *Arawak*); pottery ocarinas (east of the Cauca); and gold armor(?) (*Arma*).

The only information about crisis rites concerns burial, the more complicated forms of which were reserved for chiefs. The *Cenú* and *Yapel* of the North Colombia Lowlands and the *Nore, Gauca,* and probably the *Catío* and *Guazuzú* of the Cauca-Atrato region buried a chief in a mound-enclosed vault but gave commoners ordinary earth burial. The *Ancerma* and *Caramanta* of the Cauca-Atrato region and the tribes east of the Cauca and of the upper Cauca buried chiefs in a deep pit. The *Ancerma* first desiccated the body, but the *Quimbaya* cremated it and buried the ashes. It is not certain whether these pits correspond to the shaft-and-chamber burials found archeologically in the Quimbaya, upper Cauca, Tierradentro, and Nariño zones. Many of the latter may belong to a very early period.

THE NORTHEASTERN SUB-ANDEAN TRIBES

The Highland tribes in the Cordillera Oriental north of the *Chibcha* and in the Andes which stretch toward the coast on both sides of Lake Maracaibo not only seem to represent a marked break-down of Sub-Andean culture but fail to supply many essential links with the north coast of Venezuela to the east and with the Antillean *Arawak*. One has the feeling that the data are too fragmentary to give a coherent picture. It is possible, of course, that tribal movements, for example, of the *Cariban Motilones* and their neighbors, may have broken the continuity. Even the *Timote* of the Venezuelan Andes, who have the strongest Sub-Andean complex, do not wholly fill the bill, for they seemingly lacked such an essential trait as metallurgy. Archeology has not yet corrected the difficulty, for metallurgy has not been found in Venezuela. Archeology does, however, provide evidence of Andean influence in the stone terraces and rock-lined tombs of the Andes south of Lake Maracaibo and in the mounds and causeways in the llanos of Colombia west of the Orinoco River. It also suggests that the culture of the northeast coast of Venezuela was formerly more like that of the Orinoco and West Indies.

THE CORDILLERA ORIENTAL AND VENEZUELAN ANDES

The *Lache* and *Chitarera,* immediately north of the *Chibcha,* and the *Timote* of the Venezuelan Andes seem to have had the most complete Sub-Andean culture. Some of the tribes between them, such as the *Zorca,* were perhaps more typically Tropical Forest.

These tribes cultivated the essential food plants, including a considerable number of fruits. The *Timoteans* had permanent, often terraced fields, and used water-storage tanks and irrigation ditches. Large, planned, permanent, and perhaps palisaded villages were also characteristic of the *Timoteans, Corbago,* and *Lache;* one *Lache* town had 800 stone houses. *Chitarera* and *Zorca* villages, however, were small. The large communities would seem to have afforded a basis for developed chieftainship and a class structure on the Circum-Caribbean pattern. The only evidence of this is a reference to noblemen and the statement that some *Timotean* chiefs ruled whole valleys. There is no reference to special burial for chiefs, or to litters. Evidence of a temple cult comes from the *Lache,* who built a "House of the Sun," like the *Chibcha* temple, and from the *Timoteans,* who had a temple in the center of every town. These latter temples held idols made of pottery, wood, stone, or cotton thread, and they were entered only by the priests, who made offerings of manufactured objects, foods, beads, and deer parts to the gods. More specifically Andean was the *Timotean* belief in gods of mountain peaks and lakes, and their rituals performed on mountaintops and in caves. But human sacrifice was missing.

Virtually nothing is known of the war complex, though warfare seems to have been of some importance. There is evidence of somewhat regimented military operations in the Cordillera Oriental and of taking prisoners among the *Timoteans.* Cannibalism is not mentioned, and the straw-stuffed human heads, arms, and legs found among the *Corbago,* though suggesting the war trophies of Western Colombia, may have been the tribe's own dead.

These Sub-Andean tribes lacked metallurgy but had some of the other essential Circum-Caribbean material traits: loom-woven textiles of cultivated cotton; ceramics; cotton tunics and mantles (*Timote* women pinned theirs at the left shoulder with a wooden or gold pin): necklaces and breastplates, especially of bone; liana suspension bridges; clubs; spears; apparently either the bow and unpoisoned arrow (the *Chinato* poisoned theirs) or else the spear thrower, but not both; shields; shell trumpets; drums; rattles; chicha; coca; tobacco taken in jellylike form; and metates. Hammocks are not mentioned.

TRIBES WEST OF LAKE MARACAIBO

In the area west of Lake Maracaibo there seems to have been great local cultural variation. Traces of Sub-Andean culture are not wanting, but most information comes from the modern *Chaké, Cágaba,* and *Goajiro.* These tribes are definitely not Sub-Andean and conform more nearly to the Tropical Forest patterns, but the *Chaké* and *Cágaba* may have changed during the historic period. Some use of stone construction in the *Tairona* area suggests a limited survival of Sub-Andean culture.

The modern *Chaké* cultivate a considerable number of plants, but their fields are not permanent. As a corollary, their villages are small and their society unstratified. Their religion evidently lacks any trace of the temple cult; a harvest festival with chicha drinking and castigation of one another with bow staves is reported. In the Sierra de Santa Marta, archeology suggests the earlier presence of more advanced agriculture, but the modern people make only rough stone terraces and practice elementary irrigation. Modern *Cágaba* villages are small and lack social strata and chiefs. They are governed by priests, who wear spirit masks and conduct seasonal ceremonies in the village temple, which also serves as the men's house, but there are no idols. Supernatural beings include various spirits and human ancestors. The *Goajiro* have been so completely modified by their early adoption of cattle that little trace of aboriginal culture remains. They are intensive nomadic herders, with farming secondary. Wealth, represented by cattle, gives social status, but the basic social structure is matrilineal sibs. So far as is known, the *Goajiro* had no trace of a temple cult, and their religion is limited to beliefs in a culture hero, bush spirits, and a god or gods of thunder, lightning, and drought. They have shamans who function solely as medicine men, performing with the aid of a spirit-helper. The *Goajiro* had some warfare, and possibly slaves were taken, but cannibalism, human sacrifice, and human trophies are not recorded from any of these tribes.

Burial customs give no hint of the elaborate Circum-Caribbean methods used in disposing of deceased chiefs. The *Chaké* expose the body and later bundle up the bones and place them in a cave, perhaps a reflection of Andean procedures. The *Cágaba* and *Goajiro* practice primary earth burial, and the *Goajiro* rebury in an urn.

Weaving is done on the true loom by the *Chaké, Cágaba,* and *Goajiro,* the first two with agave fibers and domesticated cotton, the *Goajiro* with wild cotton. The *Cágaba, Chaké, Arhuaco,* and *Goajiro* also make netted carrying bags. The *Chaké* make a variety of twilled and woven baskets, but the *Cágaba* make only a few mats and boxes, the *Goajiro* no baskets. Crude pottery is made throughout the area. Metallurgy is not reported. Other elements present are: bows and arrows (unfeathered among the *Chaké*; poisoned with animal-derived ingredients, *Goajiro*); fish drugs (*Chaké*); fish nets (*Cágaba*); babracot (*Chaké*); and metate (*Chaké*, *Cágaba*). The pre-Columbian presence of dogs is doubtful. The *Chaké* are un-Andean in shunning salt. The platform bed is absent, but the *Cágaba* and *Goajiro* use the hammock, and the *Cágaba* have wooden stools. The long cotton tunics of the *Chaké,* the cotton blankets worn by *Goajiro* women and by the *Coanoa,* and the *Cágaba* gowns are Andean traits, and so are *Coanoa* nose and ear ornaments made sometimes of trade gold. *Goajiro* men wear breechclouts. The *Chaké* and *Cágaba* use carrying baskets; canoes are not ascribed any of these tribes. The *Cágaba* make complicated log bridges. Coca, chicha, tobacco, drums, hollow-log drums (*Goajiro*), flutes, trumpets, and rattles are found.

TRIBES OF NORTHWESTERN VENEZUELA

The tribes of the northwestern portion of Venezuela between Lake Maracaibo and Cabo Codera (p. 469) seem to have formed a somewhat tenuous link in the Circum-Caribbean culture between the *Timoteans* and the tribes north of the Orinoco River. In religion and political organization the *Arawakan Jirajara* and *Caquetío* have certain specific resemblances to the *Arawakan Taino* of the Antilles.

The political unit was the village, which had its own chief, but the *Jirajara* had a tribal war chief and the *Caquetío* had a tribal chief of general power and prestige. The *Caquetío* chief was accredited with supernatural power to control natural phenomena and plant growth, he was carried in a hammock, and he received special treatment at death. Under the chief were nobles, warriors, and rich men, each forming a special class. At death, leading men were burned and their ashes drunk, but the head chief's body was desiccated, placed in his house in his hammock with a wooden image below him, and later cremated and his ashes drunk.

These tribes were extremely warlike, but the functional role of warfare in sociopolitical life is not known.

There was some kind of community temple (adoratorio) where offerings were made by shamans to the sun and moon and where shamans practiced divination with tobacco ash and communed with spirits while taking tobacco and a narcotic herb. Each house was also a place of worship in that it had its own idols. Human sacrifice was practiced: young girls were beheaded and their blood offered to the sun in order to obtain rain. Shamans not only served as priests but they also cured illness by sucking out the disease-causing object.

Agriculture was best developed among the *Caquetío* and *Jirajara*. Near Barquisimeto, irrigation was carried on. Salt was manufactured and traded. Items of material culture reported include: pile dwellings; clubs; bows and arrows (poisoned among the *Jirajara*); fish drugs; hammocks; women's front apron, skirt (*Jirajara*), or a string passed between the legs; men's calabash penis cover or string to tie up the penis; body paint; chief's feather, gold, and pearl ornaments; dugout canoes; carrying bags; ceramics; woven cotton bags, garments, and hammocks (the weaving technique unknown); trumpets; tobacco; masato, which may have been fermented, i.e., chicha; and a maguey drink, perhaps similar to pulque.

TRIBES OF NORTHERN VENEZUELA

Connections between the Andes and the Antilles, though somewhat broken in the Cordillera Oriental and the Cordillera de Mérida, are partly resumed among some of the *Cariban* tribes of the area between the Orinoco River and the north coast of Venezuela (p. 481). The linkage, however, is mainly in material and social features; the temple cult is lacking. As archeology suggests that resemblances of this area and the Antilles were somewhat greater at an earlier period, the historic inhabitants may not have transmitted the Circum-Caribbean culture to the Antilles; possibly they merely acquired it by contact with those who did transmit them.

SOCIAL AND RELIGIOUS PATTERNS

Intense farming is indicated not only by a considerable list of plants, including bitter manioc and rows of fruit trees, but by irrigation (*Cumanagoto*) and in some tribes the performance of the main labor by men. Villages were very large (as many as 200 houses among the *Aruacay*), carefully laid out, and surrounded by one to three palisades. (*Piritú* villages may have been smaller, for they were abandoned at a death.) Social classes were well developed, with a powerful chief and frequently various subchiefs; and there were some federations. The chief was carried in a gold-adorned litter, and on the Unare River he had a harem of 200 wives (attended by eunuchs, according to the chroniclers!). His decrees were promulgated from an artificial mound, and he had power of life and death over his subjects. Often these chiefs had magical power and were also shamans. The *Caracas* had graded military classes with distinctive insignia. Traces of Sub-Andean death practices are found here, though it is not clear whether they were restricted to chiefs: desiccation of nobles and hanging the body in the house (*Chiribichi*); roasting and burial, with subsequent reburial or cremation (*Piritú*); burial in a clay and log tomb with an image on top (*Aruacay*). The *Cumaná* dried the body and drank the bone powder and fat. Little is known of commoners or slaves, except that the latter, who probably were war captives, were objects of trade. There was considerable warfare, carried on with fairly well organized armies which included female warriors. The principal weapons were bows, arrows with animal-derived poison, spears, shields, clubs, and, on Trinidad, spear throwers; these were kept in arsenals. The *Cumanagoto, Marcapana,* and *Palenque* were cannibalistic, and the *Piritú* drank powdered enemy hearts in chicha. The only record of human trophies is *Piritú* flutes of human bone. Human sacrifice is not reported.

Religion lacked the temple cult. The sun and moon were supreme beings. Ceremonies had some.connection with deer and fish, and offerings of first fruits and of various valuable objects were made to the earth and ocean. The *Palenque* had hunting and fishing magic. The shaman, who had great power and social prestige and frequently was also the chief, came nearest to performing priestly functions when he served as oracle, communicating with spirits in caves so as to learn the future. He cured sickness by sucking out or causing the patient to vomit the disease-causing evil spirit. Witchcraft and divination with "yopa," a narcotic snuff, are reported. The *Piritú* used flagellation in battle magic and the ant ordeal in girls' puberty rites.

MATERIAL CULTURE

Material culture includes the following elements: textiles of woven wild cotton; pottery; basketry; salt making; dugout canoes; hammocks; excellently carved wooden stools; the calabash penis cover, penis thread, or breechclout for men; the apron, breechclout, or drawers for women; head deformation; profuse ornaments of many materials including trade gold and pearls (the *Guaiqueri* had pearl fishing) ; tattooing; domesticated turkey, Muscovy duck, and bees; fish harpoons, nets, traps, and hooks; bird snares and bird lime; the babracot; chicha; tobacco; hollow-log drums(?) ; flutes; shell trumpets; and rattles (used by shamans).

THE ANTILLES

Three waves of cultural influence had swept the Antilles: first, the primitive hunting and gathering *Ciboney* coming probably from Florida; second, the *Arawak,* who were typically Circum-Caribbean and came from South America; third, the *Carib,* who were Tropical Forest rather than Circum-Caribbean, and also came from South America. At the Conquest the *Ciboney* occupied part of Cuba and Haiti. The *Arawak* held the remainder of the Greater Antilles, but they had been driven from most of the Lesser Antilles by the *Carib,* probably in a very recent prehistoric period.

THE ARAWAK

SOCIAL AND RELIGIOUS PATTERNS

The *Arawak* lacked some of the more important Circum-Caribbean cultivated plants but nonetheless depended more upon farming than on fishing, and they tended to live away from the seacoast. Their villages, which consisted of as many as 3,000 persons, were carefully planned, and each enclosed a ball court. Commoners occupied communal houses, but the chief, who had great prominence, lived in a special house of his own. In the hierarchy of chiefs, the head chief ruled a province, which was divided into as many as 30 districts, each under a subchief, and a district consisted of 70 to 80 villages, each with a headman. A chief had power of life and death, and he controlled civil, military, and religious affairs, there being no separate priesthood. He bore titles, was treated with special etiquette, and, to complete the parallel with Colombia, he was carried in a gold-decorated litter and upon his death he was either disemboweled, dessicated, and kept as an idol (zemi), or he was buried, accompanied by several of his wives. Ranking below the chief were the nobles who formed a council, the commoners, and the slaves. The society had matrilineal inheritance but lacked clans.

It is probable that the slave class came from war captives, but the *Arawak* evidently departed from the Circum-Caribbean pattern in lacking cannibalism and human sacrifice. There was some warfare, however, and on St. Croix Island, female warriors are reported.

Arawakan religion had the functional equivalent of the priest-temple-idol complex, but the elements and organization were somewhat distinctive. Evidently combining the guardian spirit concept with fetish worship, there was a large number of idols called zemis. These were made of different materials, and they represented plant, animal, and human spirits, often those seen in dreams. A common type found archeologically is a three-cornered stone. Each zemi served a special purpose, and every person had one or more in his house. The zemis were offered food, and people fasted and took emetics and snuff while invoking their help. Because the chief's zemis were the most powerful in a community, he conducted group celebrations in their honor.

A more specific Circum-Caribbean trait is the public séance which shamans held in caves to communicate with zemis and other spirits. In addition to zemis there was belief in nature spirits and in human ghosts, which were feared. Celestial deities are mentioned, and the sun and moon were connected with the myth of human emergence from a cave. Shamans conformed to the ritual pattern in taking snuff and emetic before singing, shaking a rattle, and sucking the cause of disease from a patient.

The dead were usually buried in the ground or placed in a cave, but the head was always kept in a basket in the house. Children sometimes received urn burial.

MATERIAL CULTURE

The *Arawak* material and technological culture seems to have included most if not all the Circum-Caribbean elements. With the aid of irrigation, they grew potatoes, peanuts, beans, and arrowroot, but they evidently either lacked hard-kernel maize or ate their maize before it matured. This may explain why they used the mortar but not the metate. They also had bitter manioc and squeezed the poison out of it with the tipití, but these traits may have been acquired in the historic period. The pepper pot was a characteristic dish. The *Arawak* hunted with clubs, dogs, bird decoys, drives, and corrals, and they used calabash masks for taking ducks. The absence of the bow, except among the *Ciguayo* (who used featherless arrows that were sometimes poisoned), and the presence of the spear thrower suggest that the spread of the former at the expense of the latter elsewhere may have been comparatively recent. In warfare, clubs and stones (on Trinidad, the sling) were also weapons. Fishing devices included the usual items: nets, weirs, hooks, harpoons, and baskets. The domesticated parrot is of local interest, and the somewhat puzzling mute dog may be related to a similar animal ("perro mudo") of the *Aburrá* of Colombia.

Other typical Circum-Caribbean traits found among the Island *Arawak* are the woman's apron, frontal head deformation, ear and nose piercing, the platform bed for chiefs and hammocks for commoners, carved stools of both stone and wood, dugout canoes, carrying baskets, twilled basketry, pottery with plastic forms and with one-, two-, and three-color positive and negative designs, and wooden bowls. Metallurgy was restricted to gold, which was taken from placer mines and worked by hammering, but objects of gold-copper alloy were obtained by trade. The presence of true weaving is uncertain; hammocks, bags, and aprons may have been netted of cotton. The rubber-ball game, cigars, hollow-log drums, gourd rattles, shell trumpets, chicha, and coca (?) are all Circum-Caribbean, but the use of emetics and of snuff taken through a Y-tube is exceptional.

THE CARIB

The *Island Carib* were very similar to the *Arawak* in material culture, but their social and religious patterns were more like those of the Tropical Forests, and their ferocity and cruelty in warfare were very reminiscent of the *Tupí*. They made continual raids and took female captives as wives, but tortured, killed, and ate male captives and made trophies of their bones. Socially they were extreme individualists and attached little importance to rank or to chieftainship. Prestige was acquired by achievement, and a boy's powers were tested in his puberty rites. Although captive wives were kept in a slave status and occasionally a slave was buried with his or her master, the children of captive women were freemen. Lacking social classes, kinship relations were of great importance, and the village tended to consist of an extended matrilineal family.

A reflection of *Arawakan* religion is seen in offerings made to guardian spirits, which were not, however, represented by idols. The importance attached to the dead people is shown not only in the great fear of ghosts but also in the shaman's practice of keeping his ancestors' bones as a source of power and the belief that his ancestor's spirit assisted him in obtaining a spirit helper. Shamans cured by means of sucking. They also held public séances. Ritual elements included fasting, scarifying—both were present in boys' and girls' puberty rites—and feasts with much use of chicha. Among mythological supernatural beings were an unnamed power in Heaven, various astral beings, especially the sun and moon, and a culture hero from heaven.

The *Carib* usually practiced earth burial, but sometimes they cremated a chief and drank his ashes with chicha.

In material traits the *Carib* differed from the *Arawak* in making great use of bitter manioc, which they prepared with the manioc grater and the tipití, in their failure to use salt, in the certainty that they wove cotton, and in their expert navigation in large, planked, dugout canoes. Their weapons included bows and poisoned arrows, javelins, and clubs. The *Carib* lacked the ball game and had other athletic contests instead, but they used cigars, single-head skin drums, gourd rattles, conch-shell trumpets, and one-string gourd instruments.

CENTRAL AMERICA

DISTRIBUTION AND ANTIQUITY OF THE CIRCUM-CARIBBEAN CULTURE

In instances when early documents and the archeology of the protohistoric period give a reliable picture of the aboriginal peoples, the cultures are so strikingly different from those of the modern tribes that it is difficult to recognize that the latter are descendants of the former. In the absence of Conquest period data, this drastic deculturation makes it extremely difficult to ascertain the native distribution of the Circum-Caribbean culture.

The *Cuna* who live between the Panamá Canal and Colombia must once have had a Circum-Caribbean culture, for, though their modern sociopolitical organization is of a Tropical Forest type, archeological remains of the late prehistoric period and documents of the early post-Conquest period supply many of the missing traits. The tribes southwest of the Canal, who probably belonged to the *Guaymí* group, had a culture very similar to the aboriginal *Cuna*. The chroniclers describe these people as cultivating many large cleared areas where today there is jungle and as having a stratified society.

The *Talamanca* Division is also undoubtedly classifiable as Circum-Caribbean, though they have a few traits, such as netted bags, bark cloth, clans, boys' puberty ceremonies, and communal houses, that are usually associated with less-developed cultures. It is possible that in some instances these features occurred in isolated, culturally retarded tribes, but on the whole they appear to have persisted in true Circum-Caribbean contexts. Archeology of the general *Talamanca* area, however, reveals unexpectedly developed features: house and burial mounds, courtyards, and monoliths in the Pacific region and grouped burial and habitation mounds in the Highland. Associated with these are carved stone statues, many of them with the alter-ego motif or other features linked with South America. There is also archeological evidence of metallurgy in gold and of three-legged or four-legged stone zoomorphic metates or stools. These archeological materials have not been interrelated sequentially, and none but a few ceramic types have been identified with modern tribes. Though animal-form metates were used by the historic tribes, there is no certainty that they were not taken from old sites. At least one mound group appears to have been occupied at the Conquest. Perhaps it is assignable to the Meso-American tribes, for it does not fit the ethnographic picture of the Talamancan peoples. Many of the other mounds and stone carvings could well antedate the historic tribes.

Among the tribes of the Caribbean Lowlands of Nicaragua and Honduras, ethnological data show the Circum-Caribbean complex in greatest strength among the *Mosquito* of the Eastern Coastal Plain and among the *Sumo*. This impression may merely reflect insufficient information about other tribes, though the *Jicaque* and *Paya* appear to have been on a distinctly lower level. Archeology discloses definite *Maya* influence in the Ulua-Yojoa region, but this influence is not manifest in the culture of the *Jicaque* who occupied this region at the Conquest. On the northeast coast of Honduras and the Eastern Coastal Plain of Nicaragua the archeology has a non-Mexican character, and the monoliths and stone statues are of South American types. In *Jicaque* and *Paya* territory there are a great many indications of a high culture, such as mound groups, paved roads, canals, monoliths, stone statues, and offertories, but their age and relationship to the Conquest Period tribes are uncertain. If certain stone-faced mounds can be assigned to the Sula-*Jicaque* and the *Paya*, the post-Conquest deculturation of these tribes must have been very great. On the Eastern Coastal Plain the mounds, monoliths, goldwork, and stone animal-form metates seem congruent with the cultural level of the *Mosquito*, but here too the archeological materials are undated and many of them may represent a much earlier period. The same holds for the Highland area with its burial and habitation mounds, its alter-ego, chacmool, and various small stone statues, its stone-cist and mound burials, its carved stone slabs, and its stone metates and stools. The region of the Caribbean Lowland tribes has the modeled and tripod ceramic complex of Stone's Central American "Basic Culture" (p. 169), which apparently persisted from a fairly early period to the Conquest, but the only correlation with historic tribes is that Luna polychrome and incised Zapatero monochrome, both associated with urn burial, were made by the *Ulva*, and that the Bold Geometric polychrome and North Coast Appliqué styles probably pertain to the *Lenca, Jicaque,* and *Paya.* These wares, though distinctly non-*Mayan,* extended to the *Maya* frontier in the Ulua-Yojoa district, where they blended with *Mayan* styles.

In the Northern Highlands the modern *Lenca* have lost most traces of a Circum-Caribbean culture, but if the site of Tenampua in Central Honduras really belonged to them, they had a very high culture at the Conquest. This hilltop site is fortified with stone walls and has a ball court and numerous terraces and mounds, some of them stone-paved. This and other hilltop sites may be connected with the supposed *Lenca* pilgrimages in the last century to their aboriginal village sites and with their modern custom of visiting hilltop shrines to commune with the spirits. But the ceramics of these sites have not yet been identified with the Bold Geometric and Bold Animalistic polychrome and North Coast Appliqué pottery styles that were probably made by the Conquest period *Lenca.* If the structural complex represented at Tenampua is actually Conquest Period *Lenca,* the Circum-Caribbean culture must have existed in some strength in Highland Honduras, and it may have considerable antiquity, for the ceramic traditions of the *Lenca* are fairly old in the area.

SOCIAL AND RELIGIOUS PATTERNS

Panamá.—Aboriginal villages of the *Cuna* are not described, but communities southwest of the Canal had as many as 1,500 people, were palisaded with living fences, and each had a large, many-roomed, and well-provisioned house for the chief. Modern *Cuna* villages are seemingly much less impressive. The Conquest Period *Cuna* had four social classes, though today they have merely extended matrilineal households. Southwest of the Canal the aboriginal classes were: (1) The head chief, who controlled several villages; (2) the nobles, who captured their retainers in war or inherited them; (3) commoners, who might marry nobles; and (4) slaves, who were war prisoners. Ceremony attending the chief is not fully described, except that he was carried in a litter and had many wives and slaves. A chief or noble was either buried with wives and retainers who had been stupefied, or his body was desiccated and seated in a room or placed in a hammock. Similar burial is indicated in the Coclé area, and Sitio Conte had archeological evidence of burial of a headman with many wives and quantities of gold and other valuable objects. Secondary urn burial is reported archeologically on the Atlantic Coast and deep-grave burial on the Pacific.

Warfare was well developed and there were standing armies. Captives were taken, and the early *Cuna* killed male enemies so that the sun might drink their blood; a man accredited with 20 such victims received a title. Southwest of the Canal acquisition of territory as well as prestige were war objectives.

There are no records of a temple cult, except what human sacrifice and the shaman's fetishes (see below) suggest. There was formerly sun worship. The modern *Cuna* are Christians. They have a considerable ceremony for girls a year after their puberty confinement. The priest or shaman burns cacao in a brazier, smokes cigars, and chants with the aid of a mnemonic board. These elements enter other shamanistic activities, and the shaman also uses wooden fetishes, perhaps survivals of or derived from an idol cult. With their aid he prognosticates, finds lost objects, and cures disease, sending his fetish's soul to bring back that of the patient.

The mnemonic boards bear a kind of conventionalized system of pictures and symbols, but they are not true writing in any sense inasmuch as the symbols are peculiar to the individual and cannot be interpreted by other shamans.

The Talamanca Division.—Farming in the *Talamanca* Division was more important at the time of the Conquest than today, and it supported palisaded villages which consisted of a large house or a group of houses, possibly some of them communal, to judge from modern dwellings. Early documents report feudal states among the *Guaymí*, the *Talamanca* Division, and the *Guetar*. The *Bribri* even conquered the *Terraba* in the early 19th century, and they exercised political control over the *Cabecar*. *Bribri* chieftaincy rests in a single family and must be a survival of an older class system, though the main *Bribri, Cabecar,* and *Terraba* headmen were said to be elective war chiefs. Chiefs wore gold ornaments and special insignia. The *Guetar* had nobles, commoners, and slaves, the last being captive women and children; captive men were sacrificed.

Social stratification among the Circum-Caribbean tribes seems generally to have been at the expense of clan systems, and this was certainly true of the Mexican and Andean civilizations. The *Bribri*, however, had exogamous matrilineal clans and moieties, and the modern *Guaymí* evidently have exogamous clans. Evidence of avuncular marriage and matrilineal descent appears among some of the West Colombian Sub-Andean tribes. Though usually superseded by classes, a clan system is not incompatible with them, as shown by the Northwest Coast culture of British Columbia and Alaska, which combined a strong class system with matrilineal clans and moieties. Perhaps in Central America we have traces of an old *Chibchan* clan organization.

Warfare was an important feature of social life, for its purpose was to obtain women and children as slaves and men as sacrificial victims. *Bribri, Cabecar,* and *Terraba* warriors formed a special class and received special burial.

Kinds of burial accorded chiefs and nobles are not reported, but some of the usual practices were present: embalmed bodies placed in mortuary buildings (*Guetar*), inhumation, and various kinds of secondary burial

Whether archeological deep-shaft graves in Veraguas and stone-cist graves in Chiriquí were connected with the historic tribes is not known; the latter are thought to be late prehistoric.

The temple cult is not mentioned, and concepts of supernatural beings are not known, but the *Bribri* and *Guetar* are accredited with a formal priesthood. The *Guetar* sacrificed human beings at every moon and at burial feasts.

An unusual *Guaymí* feature, reminiscent of more primitive tribes, is a secret ceremony in which boys are instructed, their faces painted, and their teeth chipped (Negro influence?), after which they may marry.

The Caribbean Lowlands.—The modern Caribbean Lowland tribes have a considerable list of cultivated plants (p. 220), but their farming is slash-and-burn. Their early villages consisted of 100 to 500 people living in one or more communal houses. Sociopolitical features are little known. The chief, though elected by the elders, had supreme power. A hereditary, matrilineal tendency is evident among the *Mosquito,* but no clans are mentioned. A *Mosquito* chief was sewed up in a mat, and slaves, servants, and sometimes a shaman were buried with him. That mummification was practiced is uncertain. The *Sumo* may have made gold and clay masks of deceased chiefs.

Warfare was well developed among the *Mosquito, Sumo,* and perhaps the *Paya.* The first two tribes accorded military rank and insignia to all men, and they subjected boys to tests as part of their puberty training. The *Mosquito* fought wars to take captives and the *Sumo* to kill their enemies, make trophies of their teeth and fingernails, and reputedly to eat them.

There is no record of a temple cult, and only the shaman is reported in recent times. His main function is to cure sickness, which he does by means of trances, dancing, singing, using painted sticks and carved figures, and driving the disease-causing spirit out of the patient. He also placates evil spirits. Among supernatural beings are the sun, moon, various astral gods, and a remote sky deity called "Our Father."

At death, the corpse is left in the hut, which is abandoned. A *Mosquito* wife exhumes and carries her husband's bones, and there is an anniversary mourning ceremony.

An unusual ritual element is the steam bath for pubescent girls and mothers of newborn infants, a North American trait, and circumcision among the *Sumo.*

The North Highlands.—Little information on the Conquest Period ethnology of this area has been assembled, and the modern *Lenca* reveal scant traces of the Circum-Caribbean socioreligious culture. They now seem more Honduran than Indian. Their villages and houses are of the modern Honduran type, but if hilltop forts and mound groups such as Tenampua (above), belonged to the *Lenca,* a very developed

Circum-Caribbean community type with characteristic social and political features must have been present. Some towns still have hereditary chiefs, and the modern two-class system may be a modified vestige of native social stratification.

Warfare in recent times usually has involved boundary disputes, but at one time a warrior ate the heart of his slain enemy to obtain his valor.

There is no evidence as yet that associates any complicated methods of burial with the *Lenca*.

A few native religious elements are recognizable today: pilgrimages to sacred hills to commune with spirits; great veneration of the sun; agricultural ceremonies with drinking of chicha and offerings of burned copal; shamanistic curing through offerings of white chickens and copal to crosses on sacred hills; divination by shamans, who throw colored beans from a calabash; ritual chicha drinking; copal burning as an offering; and fumigation of persons. Some of the archeological hilltop sites may be old *Lenca* religious centers, evidencing a very rich native religious complex.

MATERIAL CULTURE

The material culture of the modern tribes of Central America has lost the intensity and esthetic refinements of the Conquest Period, but the essential technologies are present.

The principal crops are maize, sweet manioc, sweetpotatoes, peppers, kidney beans, lima beans, gourds, calabashes, and several fruits. Bitter manioc was not pre-Columbian. It reached the *Cuna* and the Caribbean Lowlands in the 17th century; the latter probably obtained it from the *Carib*. Whether irrigation was practiced must be ascertained archeologically. Two *Talamanca* subsistence traits that are found also in northern Colombia are the cultivation of the pejibaye palm (*Guilielma utilis*) and the raising of wild peccaries. The Muscovy duck may have been kept by the Caribbean Lowland people and by the *Lenca*. Domesticated turkeys are kept by the *Lenca*, but their pre-Columbian distribution is not known. Apiculture in the Caribbean Lowlands is an exceptional feature. The aboriginal presence of the dog is uncertain.

Central American hunting techniques include bows and arrows, blowguns, spears, slings, traps, snares, game drives with nets (*Cuna*), and pitfalls. The spear thrower was used in the Darién region and occurred archeologically at Coclé, but it seems to have been superseded since by the bow and arrow. *Cuna* arrows are unpoisoned, but poisoned arrows were used southwest of the Canal and occasionally by the *Talamanca* Division. The Caribbean Lowland tribes used animal-derived poison, and their arrows were unfeathered. The blowgun was probably used everywhere to shoot clay pellets, but the *Cuna* adopted the blowgun with a poisoned dart in the historic period. Various chipped blades found archeologically may have been knives. There were also axes and celts. The principal fishing devices were arrows, hooks, nets, traps, spears, drugs (Caribbean Lowlands, *Lenca*), and harpoons (Carribbean Lowlands). The production and trade of salt was of some importance.

The metate and mortar for grinding food and the babracòt for smoking meat were used in food preparation. Pottery griddles occur in the Caribbean Lowlands. Three-legged and four-legged stone metates (or seats) occur throughout Central America, but whether they were made by the historic tribes is a problem for archeology.

Basketry was made by all tribes, but weaves are not described, except that the *Cuna* used twilling, wickerwork, and coiling, and the *Talamanca* a hexagonal weave. Bark cloth is reported for all areas except the North Highlands (*Lenca*), but archeological stone bark-beaters show that it was probably general. Loom weaving of domesticated cotton formerly occurred in all tribes, except perhaps the *Talamanca* Division, which now uses wild cotton. A wild bast and a netting technique were used for hammocks (*Talamanca* Division) and carrying bags (*Talamanca* Division, Caribbean Lowlands, *Lenca*). Ceramics, though now plain, were once predominantly of the plastic, incised traditions. There were, however, a few polychromes (e. g., at Coclé and the Bold Geometric ware of the *Lenca, Jicaque,* and *Paya* and the Luna polychrome of the *Ulva*). Negative-painted ware from Chiriquí and from Honduras may be ascribable to some of the *Talamanca* Division peoples. The negative-painted and the plastic-incised wares are probably part of the old Circum-Caribbean culture. Some authors attribute the polychromes to Meso-American influence.

In Panamá, metallurgy in gold and gold-copper alloys was highly developed as far as Veraguas, but it faded out in Costa Rica. Some gold is found archeologically in the Caribbean Lowlands, but it may represent trade objects. Approaching the *Maya* frontier, copper bells occur archeologically, perhaps originating from the secondary and comparatively late center of metallurgy in México. In the central part of Central America there is an apparent and unexplained gap in the distribution of metallurgy and negative-painted pottery.

Central American clothing includes: the penis cover (*Cuna*); men's breechclout (*Talamanca* Division, Caribbean Lowlands); the woman's wrap-around skirt; various mantles of bark cloth with painted designs (*Talamanca* Division) or of textiles with woven-in designs (Caribbean Lowlands); some skin garments (*Lenca*); sandals (*Lenca*); skin sandals (*Paya*); skin, moccasinlike footgear (*Mosquito*); ear, nose, and other ornaments of gold, precious stones, and feathers; head deformation (Caribbean Lowlands); scarification (*Talamanca* Division); tattoo as insignia of rank (*Cuna*); and chipped teeth (Caribbean Lowlands—Negro influence?). Mirrors were found at Coclé.

Household furniture consists of platform beds, hammocks (all but the *Lenca*), wooden stools, stone stools (?), and gourd and calabash containers. Dugout canoes in the Darién region were described as huge and pearl-inlaid; southwest of the Canal they had cotton sails. Dugouts also occurred in the Caribbean Lowlands. For carrying objects on land, the Panamanian tribes used carrying baskets and the balance pole, but the other tribes used netted bags. Paved roads, a conspicuous feature in the Honduran Highlands, may have been made by the historic tribes.

The aboriginal musical instruments were shell trumpets, panpipes, calabash rattles, flutes, musical bows (Caribbean Lowlands), skin drums, goblet-shaped drums (Caribbean Lowland), hollow-log signal drums (*Cuna*), whistles, and pottery ocarinas. Chicha and tobacco are general. Tobacco or coca was chewed in the *Cuna* and the *Talamanca* Division. Pottery pipes were used by the *Talamanca* Division, and cigars by the *Cuna*.

A ball game was played in a special court by the *Cuna* and, if Tenampua is a *Lenca* site, by the *Lenca* also.

THE MESO-AMERICAN TRIBES

The more important Meso-American tribes are a number of *Nahuatlan*- and *Chorotegan*-speaking peoples distributed principally along the Pacific coast of Nicaragua and Costa Rica. They are thought to have migrated to this region from México comparatively recently, some within two to four centuries before the Conquest and others even later. They are accredited with introducing certain polychrome ceramic wares to Central America, and some of their traits, such as the game of voladores, the custom of tongue piercing, and certain religious practices, are definitely Mexican, not Circum-Caribbean. On the whole, however, they seem to have adopted the Circum-Caribbean culture and to have contributed very little to it.

SOCIAL AND RELIGIOUS PATTERNS

Meso-American communities consisted of houses arranged in streets around a plaza where temples and chiefs' "palaces" were built, often on low mounds. Society was stratified into three hereditary classes: (1) Chiefs, priests, and nobles; (2) commoners; and (3) war prisoners, who performed menial labor but were ultimately sacrificed and eaten. Acquisition of wealth, however, improved social status. Politically, a council had great power, and among the *Chorotega* it selected the chief. *Nicarao* chieftaincy was probably hereditary, though the council also had considerable power.

Warfare was highly developed, and there were trained armies. War was waged to settle boundary disputes and to obtain slaves for sacrifices and for cannibalism. The taste for human flesh was so great that slaves were bred in order that they might be slaughtered.

The temple cult was served by a special priesthood, which performed ceremonies to the various gods on holy days, at the cacao harvest, and on such occasions as birth and death.

MATERIAL CULTURE

Many crops were cultivated, the most important being maize, cacao, and tobacco.

Weaving techniques are not mentioned; the fibers of cotton, agave, and palm were used. Ceramics were well developed and included polychromes of Mexican origin. The presence of metallurgy is uncertain. Dugout canoes and rafts were made. Clothing and ornaments included the men's breechclout and sleeveless tunic of woven cotton (*Nicarao*), women's skirts (*Nicarao*), the woman's decorated breechclout (*Orontiña*), gold beads, identifying tattoo marks, head deformation, and men's tongue and ear piercing.

Chicha was made, and coca was chewed with lime. The Mexican game of voladores was played, but the ball game is not reported.

THE TROPICAL FOREST PEOPLES

THE PATÁNGORO AND THEIR NEIGHBORS

In general, these tribes lacked the intensive farming, especially of fruits, and the salt making of northern Colombia. Their technology is little known. They made pottery but lacked metallurgy and apparently used no canoes. Villages were palisaded and were of fair size, consisting of 80 to 90 houses each, with a ceremonial building in the center. Highland traits present are the platform bed, head deformation, and liana bridges. Men went naked and women wore aprons. Unlike most Sub-Andean tribes, the *Patángoro* were organized in exogamous matrilineal clans rather than social classes. Warfare was strongly developed; weapons included the bow and poisoned arrow, lances, boiling water, deadfall doors, and sharpened stakes placed in pits. Captives were taken not for ritual purposes but for cannibalism, which was so strongly developed that human flesh constituted an essential food. All captives were killed at once, either being cooked or else cremated, ground, and mixed with chicha, an Amazonian trait. There is no evidence of a temple-priest complex, though the *Amaní* shaman concealed himself behind a wall to answer questions, which is reminiscent of the oracular functions of the Sub-Andean priest. Deities were celestial, including one which sent thunder and lightning. These tribes practiced earth burial and believed in an afterworld that was so pleasant that people sometimes committed suicide. Shamans apparently had both human and animal tutelary spirits, and they cured disease by sucking.

THE GUAYUPÉ AND SAE

These tribes, occupying the llanos and forests on the eastern slope of the Andes south of the *Chibcha*, had a general Tropical Forest culture with perhaps a few Sub-Andean traits. They were farmers and lived in palisaded villages of multifamily houses arranged around a plaza that had a ceremonial building. They had no class system, but old men apparently had superior status and formed a council. Chiefs were elected, and their prestige is indicated only in their use of stools and feather blankets and their claim to half the bride price paid at each marriage. A deceased chief was cremated, and his ashes were ceremonially drunk in chicha by his successor.

There was much warfare, but slave taking, cannibalism (except *Sae* funerary cannibalism), and human trophies are not reported. At their initiation boys were whipped and pricked with lances to make them good warriors.

The special religious house was perhaps comparable to that of the Tropical Forests rather than to the Andean temple. The sun and moon, who were man and wife, were the gods, and the jaguar and other animals were evil beings. No ceremonialism is mentioned except shamanistic curing, which was accomplished by sucking out the disease-causing object.

Subsistence was based on farming, bitter manioc probably being one of the crops. The technology is not well known, but cotton was grown and must have been woven, though feather instead of cotton blankets are mentioned as articles of clothing. Except for these blankets and some gold, shell, and feather ornaments, people went naked. These tribes used hammocks, wooden stools, dugout canoes, spears, lances, clubs, bows and arrows, slings, and shields. They took coca and tobacco to obtain visions.

THE BETOI AND THEIR NEIGHBORS

The *Betoi* and their neighbors may be classed as Tropical Forest in culture, although in some respects they were little more developed than the hunting and gathering tribes to their east in the llanos of eastern Colombia. They were farmers but carried on much hunting and fishing. Their villages were small and were frequently moved. Each consisted of one or more communal houses sheltering an extended family. In some cases the village apparently was limited to a single extended family, and local exogamy was therefore practiced. The village head man was the oldest person or one of the older persons of the community. An anomalous feature found among the *Airico* was hired laborers, paid with shell disk money.

Religion was limited to belief in a sun god (*Betoi*) and other mythological beings, but there were no priests or idols. The shaman performed as medicine man and used snuff of "yopa" powder. There were no temples or group religious ceremonies, but each village had a festival house in which men assembled to drink chicha.

These tribes carried on warfare, using clubs, bows and arrows (poisoned among the *Lucalia*), axes, and lances, but the purpose and nature their fights are not known.

Female infanticide is reported. The dead always received direct earth burial.

Manufactures were limited to ceramics, bark cloth, mats (*Anabali*), calabashes, and dugout canoes. *Betoi* chiefs wore bark-cloth garments; *Jirara* and *Airico* women wore genital covers made of leaves. Bodily adornment consisted only of paint and feather crowns. Musical instruments mentioned are flutes, fifes, and wooden signal drums.

THE OTOMAC AND GUAMO

These tribes contrast sharply with their primitive hunting and gathering neighbors, and their presence in the area is unexplained. It is of interest that archeology in the llanos of Venezuela shows an early extension of an Andean culture nearly to the Orinoco River. Kirchhoff (p. 439), however, likens these people to Central American tribes.

The villages were reputedly large, but chiefs seem to have controlled groups of houses, not whole villages. Though life was regimented with respect to warfare, there is no evidence of a class system. Warfare was mainly against *Carib* raiders, and women participated in battles, helping the men.

There was no temple cult. The moon, probably a supernatural being, had a special connection with women. The *Otomac* believed they were descended from stones. The shaman performed as medicine man and cured by sucking out stones. Curing was also accomplished by smearing blood on the patient; a child's tongue was pierced and his own blood smeared on his body. Circumcision was practiced at puberty. No Andean burial forms are reported; a body was given earth burial and later reburied in a cave.

Subsistence was based on fairly intensive farming which was done by men on flood plains, but food plants were limited to one kind of maize, sweet manioc, pineapples, and several roots. People slept on the ground under palm-leaf mosquito nets. Industries included the manufacture of finely woven cotton, ceramics, calabash containers, palm-fiber baskets and bags, and dugout canoes. Clubs, bows, and unpoisoned arrows were among the weapons. Feathers and other ornaments were worn in profusion, but there was no gold, and the only garment mentioned is men's wide cotton belts. In their festivities people drank chicha, took coca, played the trumpet, and bled themselves. They also played the rubber-ball game.

THE ACHAGUA AND SÁLIVA

The *Achagua, Sáliva,* and probably some of the adjoining tribes, such as the *Puinave,* were well advanced above the *Guahibo* and their other hunting and gathering neighbors, but they had few Andean or Sub-Andean features. Their probable possession of patrilinear, totemic, exogamous sibs and an ancestor cult links them mainly with the *Tucanoan* tribes of the Northwest Amazon (Handbook, vol. 3).

These tribes were farmers, and they had fairly large, palisaded villages, many of which evidently consisted of a single communal dwelling and a separate men's clubhouse. The villages were probably impermanent, however, for they were moved at the death of an occupant. There is strong evidence that the *Achagua* had patrilinear, exogamous, totemic sibs, each perhaps localized. The village had a chief but accorded him few privileges except that of access to vestal virgins of some kind. A *Sáliva* chief had to endure a pepper and ant ordeal before taking office. There were no social classes. The main grouping outside the family was sexual: men foregathered and held drinking bouts in their clubhouse, from which women were barred.

Trophy taking, cannibalism, and capture of slaves and sacrificial victims are not reported, and there was no warrior class. The *Achagua* and *Sáliva* fought mainly defensively against predatory tribes, such as the *Carib, Caberre,* and others, which sought to enslave them.

Presence of the temple cult is suggested only by the *Sáliva* sculptured "demons," which were consulted as oracles. The *Sáliva* held ceremonies in honor of the Creator, and they also worshiped the sun and moon. *Achagua* masked men represented deities in a ceremony from which women were excluded. (Cf. the *Tucanoan* ancestor cult, Handbook, vol. 3, p. 889). The *Achagua* also had a first fish ceremony. Among their gods were a supreme being and special gods of cultivated fields, riches, fire, fate, and madness, and one that holds the earth. Witchcraft and divination were strongly developed in this area.

The *Sáliva* shaman sucked, blew on, and anointed his patient in order to cure him and purified people and objects with smoke from a cigar containing copal.

The *Achagua* practiced female infanticide. At a *Sáliva* funeral special paraphernalia and trumpets were used and later thrown into the river. The body was buried and subsequently disinterred, cremated, and the ashes drunk with chicha. The *Achagua* buried in a sealed grave.

The main items of *Achagua* material culture were: Bitter manioc and the tipití; bows and poisoned arrows (the *Caberre* were the principal producers of poison); fish nets; fish drug (barbasco); basketry shields; well-developed basketry; netted hammocks and women's skirts, probably both of hemp or other wild bast, but no true weaving; men's breechclouts; ceramics in some variety of forms; calabash vessels; wooden stools; dugout canoes and pole rafts; body paint; shell bead necklaces (used also as money) ; necklaces and ear and nose ornaments of pearls; silver pins (post-Columbian?), but no goldwork; tattoo, but not as an insignia of status; hollow-log drums; trumpets; and "yopa" snuff used for divination.

THE PACIFIC COAST TRIBES

The low, densely forested and now unhealthy regions of the Pacific coast stretching from Ecuador to the junction of Panamá with South America was occupied by peoples with backward cultures. On the Colombia coast were the *Chocó*. On the Ecuadorian coast Andean influence from the Highlands and from the Peruvian coast had implanted advanced cultures (see Handbook, vol. 2, p. 780), which surrounded a primitive enclave, the *Cayapa* and *Colorado*, who adjoined each other on the western slope of the Cordillera.

THE CHOCÓ

The *Chocó* were slash-and-burn horticulturists, but they grew only food plants and lacked domesticated cotton and tobacco. They relied considerably on fishing, using nets, spears, arrows, and a drug, but no hooks, and on hunting with the blowgun and dart and the bow and unfeathered arrow. They made bark cloth, twilled and woven basketry, calabash containers, pottery, dugout canoes, one-piece wooden stools, men's loincloths, women's wrap-around skirts, ear and nose ornaments, and round pole-and-thatched houses, often on piles. They had coiled basketry, one of the few modern survivals of this technique which North and South American peripheral distributions and archeological evidence show to have been very old and once probably very widespread. They lacked metallurgy. Textile weaving was introduced only recently. Like the Andean tribes, they slept on the platform bed, but they had the hammock as a cradle.

Chocó society was not stratified; instead there were exogamous, patrilineal lineages that were probably clans. Chieftainship was weakly developed, there is no evidence of a war complex with trophies and cannibalism, and shamanism takes the place of the temple cult. Some Highland influence has crept into the local context, however, for the shaman's fetish staff, which is believed to contain his spirit helper, and the infant's doll, which is alleged to embody its guardian spirit, may well reflect the idol complex of neighboring tribes. Shamanistic curing through exorcising malignant spirits is a somewhat distinctive practice, and the wooden models of boats with spirit images used in training shamans are unique. Supernatural beings, besides guardian spirits and spirits' helpers, include the culture hero, good and evil spirits, and ghosts. A girl's puberty observance involved her isolation, as usual, but the use of the scratching stick is another old, widespread element that usually has survived only in peripheral areas. The main musical instruments are the panpipes, flutes, skin drums, and hollow wooden drums. The ceramic art is anthropomorphic and zoomorphic.

THE CAYAPA AND COLORADO

The *Cayapa* and *Colorado* differ from the *Chocó* in specific elements rather than in the general organization of their culture. According to tradition, they descended from the Highland and thus may once have had a more developed culture. Information about them is comparatively recent, but there is little to suggest Andean patterns. Their culture, like that of the *Chocó*, is Tropical Forest in many specific elements. A trans-Andean spread of some of these appears very possible in view of the fact that the *Colorado* actually traveled across the Andes to the *Canelo* on the eastern slopes to obtain fish poison.

The *Cayapa* and *Colorado* cultivate not only food plants but cotton and coca (*Cayapa*), and they keep guinea pigs. The *Colorado* take fish with nets, traps, hooks, and drugs. Houses of both tribes are frame and thatch, those of the *Cayapa* being on piles. The *Cayapa* sleep in hammocks, the *Colorado* on platform beds. The bow and arrow and the dugout canoe were used by the *Colorado* but not by the *Cayapa*. Both have blowguns, but the former shoot darts from them, the latter clay pellets. Cotton weaving, twilled basketry, metates, and crude pottery are probably common to both tribes, but metallurgy is not reported for either. Calabashes somewhat replaced pottery among the *Cayapa*. Dress of earlier periods showed Highland influence, even the poncho being reported. Fronto-occipital head deformation was recently found among the *Colorado*.

Villages are small, those of the *Colorado* consisting of one house, those of the *Cayapa* of three or four pile dwellings, each sheltering several families. Perhaps the social unit inhabiting the *Cayapa* house is a patrilineal lineage, for there is some tendency to patrilocality. Chieftainship is not well developed, nor are there social classes, a temple cult, or a war complex. At the time of the Conquest, however, the *Colorado* were described as warlike and "idolatrous," but as lacking chiefs.

There are few data on puberty observances, except the *Colorado* nose-piercing and cayapi-drinking rite for boys. The games which the *Colorado* played as part of mourning wakes are a Highland trait. Both tribes bury their dead.

Musical instruments of probable aboriginal origin are panpipes, flutes, drums, and rattles.

Religion involves good and bad spirits; the latter cause lightning, thunder, and other evils. Among the *Colorado* and probably the *Cayapa*, shamans deal with these spirits. To cure disease the *Cayapa* shaman exorcises an evil spirit, and he also sucks. Two ritual elements link the

Colorado with the Montaña: the belief that disease is caused by the intrusion into the body of sharp spines, which the shaman "sucks" out, and the use of cayapi (*Banisteriopsis caapi*).

THE HUNTING AND GATHERING TRIBES

The principal distribution of the hunting and gathering, or Marginal, tribes is in the Gran Chaco, Patagonia, and Tierra del Fuego (Handbook, vol. 1) and around the perimeter of the Amazon Basin (Handbook, vol. 2). The second group includes the *Shirianá, Waica, Guaharibo, Auaké, Calianá,* and *Maracaná* of the Amazon-Orinoco watershed. Other primitive hunting and gathering tribes, who are described in the present volume, occupied the llanos or plains of the Orinoco Basin and a portion of the Antilles. The *Guaiquerí* and *Guamontey* were scattered along the lower Orinoco River; the *Guahibo, Chiricoa, Yaruro,* and others lived west of the upper Orinoco in western Venezuela and eastern Colombia; several groups lived in the plains around Barquisimeto near the Sub-Andean *Timoteans* in the Venezuelan Andes; and the *Ciboney* were a Marginal peoples of the Antilles.

These tribes unquestionably represent retarded groups, peoples who remained in dry plains, where farming was not suitable, or in isolated places, where the Circum-Caribbean and Tropical Forest cultures did not reach them. They have in common the absence of the technological and socioreligious features of the more advanced peoples rather than the presence of any characteristic complexes.

TRIBES OF THE ORINOCO BASIN

All these tribes were hunters, fishers, and gatherers. The *Yaruro* formerly cultivated a little maize but have now given it up. There were no permanent villages; the *Guaiquerí* and *Guamontey* lived in movable grass-covered houses; the *Guahibo* simply sleep under trees or portable mats or in hollow trees, and the *Yaruro* in temporary palm-covered shelters. The *Guahibo* sociopolitical unit is the band of about 30 persons, who hunt and make war under the leadership of a headman. They are described as nomads, leading a gypsylike life. The *Yaruro* social unit is the extended matrilocal family, but there are also exogamous moieties. In warfare it is possible that the pre-Conquest *Guahibo* took slaves to use in trade, but there was no cannibalism. Religion is virtually unknown. *Yaruro* mythology holds that the moon goddess, who is the sun's wife, is the creator, and there is a story of a culture hero. *Yaruro* shamans seem to get their power from the moon, which helps them cure sickness. In their performances they smoke cigars, drink chicha, and take a narcotic root.

Hunting devices include bows and arrows (which the *Guahibo* sometimes poisoned). The *Yaruro* use disguises, harpoon arrows, fish arrows, and fishhooks. The *Guaiqueri, Guamontey,* and the tribes around Barquisimeto used to cook in skin-lined earth ovens, and the *Guahibo* and *Yaruro* over a fire. The last two tribes use wooden mortars. The *Yaruro* have pots but rarely boil food in them. None of these tribes uses salt.

Few of the Circum-Caribbean and Tropical Forest technologies are present. The *Guahibo* and *Yaruro* make woven baskets, but there is no loom weaving. The only recorded textile manufacture is hammocks, and these are netted of palm fibers. Pottery is made by the *Guahibo* and *Yaruro,* that of the former being "beautifully" decorated. The *Guahibo* make decorated calabash containers.

The *Guahibo* use carrying baskets and dugout canoes, the *Yaruro* the carrying net and rafts.

Clothing is limited to the *Guahibo* men's penis cover and the *Yaruro* men's breechclout and women's girdles. The *Guahibo* have body paint but no ornaments; the *Yaruro,* labrets, arm and leg bands, and necklaces.

The *Guahibo, Yaruro,* and the tribes of Barquisimeto have the hammock; the *Guaiqueri* and *Guamontey* used to sleep on skins on the ground.

The *Guahibo* use rattles, flutes, and panpipes, and they take parica snuff for magical purposes and when going to war.

THE CIBONEY OF THE ANTILLES

The little-known and now extinct *Ciboney* occupied the Guaicayarima Peninsula of Haiti and at one time the greater part of Cuba. They are thought to have come to the Antilles from Florida. They represented a marginal survival of very primitive hunters and gatherers, and they are known mainly through archeology.

These people depended primarily upon sea foods, lived in caves or temporary shelters, and practiced primary and secondary earth burial and cremation. They used clubs, various shell artifacts, chipped-flint daggers, clubs, stones (thrown with slings?), breechclouts, and shell ornaments. There is no record of their basketry and weaving, but they lacked farming, houses, pottery, metallurgy, metates, zemis, and other traits characteristic of the *Arawak* and did only a little work in ground or polished stone, which was manifest especially in stone mortars, axes, and balls. The bow is reported but may be post-Conquest.

PART 1. CENTRAL AMERICAN CULTURES

CENTRAL AMERICAN CULTURES: AN INTRODUCTION[1]

By FREDERICK JOHNSON

Central America may be defined culturally as the region extending from the Atrato and San Juan River Valleys in Colombia nearly to the western boundary of Honduras (map 1). It has a fundamental unity in what may be a basic cultural tradition or cultural substructure. This basic culture has a distinctly South American cast, and the region marks the northern limit of culture complexes which were probably derived from South America. The region has, however, been exposed to influences from the northern, that is, the Meso-American cultures. The continuing stream of cultural diffusion from both the north and south has produced a strong overlay of foreign elements which gives many local cultures a superficial similarity to those of neighboring regions. These tend to obscure the basic cultures.

GEOGRAPHY

The culture area of Central America is not coterminous with a geographical province.[2] Central America includes several portions of a larger geographic region which extends north to the "Great Scarp" of Oaxaca, México, and south to the northern terminus of the Andes, the eastern slopes of the Atrato River Valley. This region is part of the Antillean Mountain System and is distinct from the great Cordilleras of North and South America. The Antillean System comprises a series of east-west trending crustal folds, which have given rise to the present river valleys and ridges of northern Honduras and central Nicaragua. A major vulcanism of Pleistocene and Recent date has modified the topography, particularly of the western termini of these earlier mountains, and a series of volcanoes welded into a number of gigantic pedestals are distributed in a great arc between Tehuantepec and Costa Rica. A smaller, sigmoid-shaped arc of volcanoes, of lower altitude, begins with the Cordillera de Tala-

---

[1] This introduction incorporates data furnished by Stone, Kirchhoff, Strong, Stout, and Lothrop.

[2] The archeological and ethnological subdivisions do not always coincide with geographical divisions, although they are designated by geographical names. Cultural and geographical terminology has been correlated so far as possible, but discrepancies remain.

43

manca in Costa Rica and continues eastward, following the Cordillera de
San Blas and the Serranía del Darién in Panamá. The vulcanism closed
a portal connecting the Caribbean Sea and the Pacific, now the area included in the Nicaraguan Lowland. Other changes in level and the deposition of volcanic materials formed the Isthmus of Rivas, cutting off from
the sea the basins of Lake Managua and Lake Nicaragua. The consequent
rise of the levels of the lakes turned the drainage into the San Juan River
Valley, leading to the Caribbean Sea. (Cf. esp. Ricketson, 1940; Schuchert,
1935.)

Along the Caribbean coast, Lowlands of varying width have been
formed. These are flood plains, alluvial fans or areas of little or no slope,
which have been built up by the deposition of materials eroded from the
Uplands. The Lowlands bordering the Pacific—the Pacific Borderlands
—are less extensive, being composed largely of deposits of volcanic material and recent alluvium.

The orogeny of the region has been one of the principal factors in the
development of a number of areas which can be classified according to
their topography and other general features. The mountain masses divide
areas affected by the warm moist winds of the Caribbean from those dependent upon the winter winds and summer monsoons characteristic of
the Pacific Ocean in these latitudes. This general condition is partially
obscured by a complication of factors which have not yet been thoroughly
studied. The climate of different areas and even of restricted localities is
influenced by the topography, particularly the orientation of the mountains
with respect to prevailing winds. Even this characteristic is subject to
exceptions, the nature of which varies in the different areas.

The Caribbean coast and the Uplands of Central America which drain
into the Caribbean Sea differ greatly from other areas because of the highly
specialized environment. This area is covered with a dense tropical forest.
The moist winds from the Caribbean bring a rainfall of 100 to 200 inches
a year. Some areas have even more precipitation. The so-called dry
season is really a period of less rain. Depending upon circumstances,
especially upon the orientation of the slopes toward the prevailing winds,
the rainfall varies slightly in different areas but has a negligible effect on
the significant features of the environment.

PANAMA

Darién.—Darién is the area between the Atrato River Valley and the
gap in the backbone of the Isthmus of Panamá, the site of the Panamá
Canal. The two ranges that comprise the central structure of Darién lie
close to the Caribbean coast and the western shore of the Golfo de Urabá.
The southeasterly extremity turns inland to form the western side of the
lower reaches of the Atrato River. The southern end of the Serranía del

Darién becomes lost in a plain. West of this, paralleling the Pacific coast of Colombia, lie the hills which are the northern extremity of the Cordillera de Chocó.

The southern and western slopes of the two ranges are drained by the westerly flowing Río Chepo, also called Río Bayano, and the Río Chucunaque-Tuira, which empty into the Golfo de San Miguel. The watersheds of these two relatively large systems comprise the major part of the area of the region. The valleys are of low relief; they have been described as plains. The Atrato River Valley, draining into the Golfo de Urabá, is wide and also of low relief. Toward the south, above the headwaters of the Atrato, the character of the relief continues, but the gradient dips to the south and the San Juan River runs southward to enter the Pacific at Punta Charambira in Colombia.

Darién is covered, for the most part, by several types of tropical forest. Onshore winds bring moisture from the warm Caribbean resulting in a rainfall varying between 100 and 200 inches a year. The northern slopes of the mountains and most of the interior valleys are covered with a dense tropical forest. Dry and wet seasons follow in regular succession over the entire area, but they are much more marked in the drier area bordering the Pacific coast, where offshore winds blow part of the year. In the latter area the distribution of the tropical forest is irregular, but the vegetation is lush, owing to large quantities of water caught in the poor drainage.

Western Panamá.—West of Darién an expanse of savanna borders the Pacific and extends as far as the mountains of Chiriquí, Panamá. The environment of this area is similar to all lands occupying the Pacific side of Central America. The climate is largely determined by accidents of location with respect to winter winds and summer monsoons, which bring out clearly marked dry and wet seasons. With the exception of local areas where the topography and other features affect the rainfall, these savannas and the Pacific coast in general support areas of semideciduous or scrub forest, between which grasslands flourish. The climate, though hot, is favorable, and the inhabitants could live above bare subsistence levels.

Between the Lowlands of the coast and the higher parts of the Uplands lies an area of hills and low ridges which topographically are part of the mountain systems. The environment of this little-known zone is very complex, but it appears to be analogous to that of the savannas. The cool nights, the occasional rains during the dry season, and possibly the specialized fauna and flora make it hospitable to human occupancy; at least some sections have, in the past, supported a relatively large population.

The Isthmian Tropical Forest.—This area extends westward from the Panama Canal, a very arbitrary boundary, to the Nicaraguan Lowland. It includes the Caribbean watershed which, in Panamá, is clearly bounded by the divide separating it from the Pacific slopes. The inland boundary in Costa Rica is very irregular and hard to fix. It follows the limits of the Caribbean drainage, excepting some areas on the upper reaches of some of the larger rivers.

The area is divisible into a Coastal Lowland zone and an Upland zone. The Coastal Lowland is largely a poorly drained alluvial plain, much of it swampland, especially along the shore, behind the barrier beaches and along the meandering and irregularly flooding rivers. Except for occasional intrepid travelers, the Panamanian Lowland has not been explored since the Spaniards lost interest in the area. A section of the Lowland, west of the Laguna de Chiriquí, sometimes called the Talamanca Plain, has been reclaimed. Strong onshore winds cause heavy surf to beat against the barrier beaches and to form sand bars blocking the river mouths. Navigation by canoe is hazardous if not impossible on the sea, but water travel is possible in the Laguna de Chiriquí and in the lower reaches of the rivers.

With the exception of sections of Costa Rica, very little is known of the Upland zone. This area is marked by steep slopes and deep valleys in which swift rivers flow through rocky channels. In general, the climate of the Uplands is healthier than that of the Lowlands.

Discussion and interpretation of the significance of the population pattern of the Isthmian Tropical Forest began in the 16th century, but the characteristics and necessities of life are still poorly understood. At the time of the Spanish conquest, when the aborigines did not have steel tools, it seems almost certain that very large areas of it had been cleared, and it appears to have been inhabited by a relatively large population. As a rule the headquarters of the several divisions of the population were located in the Uplands. Furthermore, there are vague suggestions of seasonal migrations of at least a portion of the population between the coastal Lowlands and the Uplands. After the Conquest, the characteristics of the occupancy of this area changed. The population became smaller and more sedentary, and much of the cleared land reverted to impenetrable jungle. For several reasons, not the least of which was the forbidding environment, the Spaniards concentrated their attention only upon the ports of entry and the lines of communication to the Pacific watershed, where, from their point of view, life was easier. From the time of its abandonment until a very few years ago, the Tropical Forest had been neglected by Europeans and remained an area in which refugee tribes could exist unmolested by their erstwhile conquerors.

THE SOUTHERN HIGHLANDS

The mountains between the Province of Chiriquí and the Nicaraguan Lowlands may be divided into a number of subareas.

Southern Costa Rica.—This subarea includes the Cordillera de Talamanca and its eastward extension into the Province of Chiriquí, the Cordillera Brunquena, and the various basins and lowlands which lie within the mountain system and which border the Pacific coast. The most important basin is a structural depression drained by the Río Diquis. The northern portion of this basin, called the Valle General, is drained by the Rio General and the Río Cabagua, tributaries of the Río Diquis. The Terraba Plain occupies the southern and eastern portion of this depression bordering the Cordillera Brunquena, through which the Río Diquis has cut a narrow canyon. To the south lies the Peninsula of Osa, a hilly region running in a southeasterly direction to form the Golfo Dulce. The peninsula is nearly cut off from the mainland by a low swampy area.

The north shore of the Golfo Dulce is hilly and the slopes rise abruptly from the coast. To the east, however, lies an area of Lowland savanna and swampland, which extends eastward along the Pacific coast of Panamá. The short valley of the Río Coto and its tributaries opens onto these Lowlands and meanders across them to its mouth on the Golfo Dulce. The Lowland is interrupted by the hills surrounding the Pico Burica and the low ridge running south to Punta Burica.

Central Costa Rica.—This is an area of relatively high altitude. Northeast of Cartago and San José, four great volcanic cones, varying in altitude from 9,120 to 11,220 feet (2,779 to 3,409 m.), stand in a row, their bases merged into a massive volcanic pedestal. Between these and the mountains to the south lies the intermontane basin known as the Meseta Central. This basin, lying at an altitude between 2,000 and 4,000 feet (about 650 to 1,300 m.), is complex in structure and its surface is distinctly hilly. The southeastern part of the Meseta is drained by the Río Raventazon, which empties into the Caribbean north of Puerto Limón. The northwestern part of the Meseta Central is drained by the Río Grande, which enters the Golfo de Nicoya a little southeast of Puntarenas. The Cordillera Volcánica, extending in a northeasterly direction from the Meseta Central, gradually decreases in altitude until, in Nicaragua, it forms only a hilly belt between Lake Nicaragua and the Pacific.

The Nicoya Area.—This area lies to the south of the Cordillera Volcánica, from which it is separated by the relatively wide and low valley of the Río Tempisque, which empties into the head of the Golfo de Nicoya. The Peninsula de Nicoya is a range of hills to the south of this valley, running in a southeasterly direction to form the Golfo de Nicoya. The western margin of the area, fronting the Pacific, is composed of a low range of hills.

The climate of all the southern or Costa Rica Highland area is exceedingly complex. Over most of the region the influences of the Pacific Ocean cause a dry and a wet season, but the differences between these seasons are not always extreme. Certain regions, particularly along the northern and eastern boundaries, are affected by trade winds from the Caribbean. Climate also varies with altitude and with the orientation of slopes in relation to prevailing winds and the sun. One slope of a valley may receive abundant rains, while a nearby slope is infertile because little or no rain falls upon it. The General Valley, the Terraba Plain, and the Meseta Central are well-watered, fertile areas. The Lowland areas bordering the coast are very wet, having meandering rivers and most of them being poorly drained. Some of them are covered with mangrove swamps. The semideciduous and scrub forests of the Uplands give way to areas of lush vegetation in the wetter sections of the Lowlands.[3]

THE NICARAGUAN HIGHLANDS

This region lies north of the Nicaraguan Lowland. It is closely related, geologically, to the Guatemalan Highlands, though not so high, and is composed of a volcanic plateau with the highest elevations in the south. The steep escarpment of the plateau faces toward the Lempa River Valley of El Salvador and continues southward bordering the Golfo de Fonseca and the northeastern side of the Nicaraguan Lowland. The east-west pattern of the folded and faulted structure of the mountains is obscured by volcanic deposits in the south, but the older structure is revealed in the north. The easterly pointing spurs dip beneath the sea along the north coast of Honduras. The Bay Islands are, presumably, peaks of these submerged ranges. The Highlands are characterized by steep-sided mountains rising above high intermontane basins and plateaus.

The climate and vegetation patterns of the Northern Highlands are complex chiefly because extreme ranges of altitude are combined with a wide variation in the orientation of the slopes in relation to the prevailing winds and the sun. "In valleys and basins or on mountain slopes which are protected from the rain-bearing winds, the oak-pine forests, characteristic of the tierra templada and the tierra fría, may descend as low as 2,000 feet (about 650 m.). No parts of the country are high enough to be above tree line; but there are extensive savannas in relatively high places, such as those east of Tegucigalpa" (James, 1942, p. 689). In the eastern sections of the Nicaraguan Highlands, where the warm, moist winds from the Caribbean are forced to rise over the eastern slopes, the rainfall is very heavy and the forests are exceptionally thick. On the lower slopes of the mountains there is a drier belt, but the rainfall is sufficient to support a tropical rain forest. At high altitudes in Nicaragua the rainfall is more moderate and the temperature lower, permitting the growth of the oak and pine forests. These highlands mark the southernmost distribution of North American species of pines.

THE NICARAGUAN LOWLAND

This is a structural depression which runs in a northeasterly direction from the Caribbean Sea. The Tropical Forest extends up it nearly to San Carlos, where Lake Nicaragua empties into the Río San Juan. The forest

---

[3] For a brief description of the environment, cf. James, 1942.

also covers sections of the valleys of tributaries of the San Juan, particularly those which drain the southern watershed of the Lowland. The northern side of the Lowland has a drier climate, perhaps because the orientation of the adjoining slopes produces local "rain shadows."

THE EASTERN COASTAL PLAIN

This area in Nicaragua is the largest lowland plain in Central America. It is an alluvial plain, poorly drained by the meandering rivers which cross it. Huge portions of it are swampland unfit for human habitation. The people build their villages on natural levees bordering the rivers or upon the low rises near the coastal lagoons. The coast has a complicated series of sand bars and barrier beaches, behind which there are extensive lagoons. The latter fostered the development of a partially maritime existence among the coast dwellers. The Upland slopes, facing the Caribbean, support the heaviest tropical forest in Central America. This did not, however, prevent the people from inhabiting the river valleys in great numbers.

THE NORTHERN COASTAL PLAIN

This is a fringe of Lowland in Honduras which skirts the spurs of the mountains and extends for varying distances up the river valleys. It receives great quantities of moisture from the Caribbean and supports a tropical forest. It is probable, however, that less rain falls here than elsewhere on the Caribbean coast. These Lowlands are composed of alluvial deposits washed off the slopes or deposited at the mouths of the rivers. Though of limited extent, they are usually poorly drained and dotted with swamps. The adjacent Uplands also support a tropical forest, which extends inland to a very irregular line where the "Caribbean" and "Northern Highland" environments meet. For reasons not yet well known, the tropical forest occurs also in some of the northerly and higher sections of the Honduran Plateau.

TRIBAL DIVISIONS AND HISTORY [4]

THE CUNA-CHOCÓ DIVISION [5]

At the time of the Conquest the Darién region was inhabited by tribes speaking dialects belonging to two languages which the Spaniards named *Coiba* and *Cueva*. The meaning of these names in terms of existing dialects or tribes is not clear; perhaps *Coiba* was a larger linguistic category. *Cueva* may now be extinct, having been spoken by a tribe which is no longer extant. On the other hand, elements of *Cueva* may be present in the dialect spoken by the modern San Blas *Cuna*.

The Chocó Group.—The designation *Chocó*, as a tribal name, does not occur in the early literature, though Oviedo y Valdés (1851–55, vol. 4,

---

[4] The locations of the Central American tribes are shown on map 2.
[5] The data on the *Cuna* and *Chocó* are briefed from a manuscript submitted by D. B. Stout.

p. 121) mentions a chief named Coquo, and the name Chocó was applied to a province in 1575 (Wassén, 1935, p. 42).

Beginning with Balboa in 1511, the Conquistadors made a series of explorations through various parts of the *Chocó* area. In most cases they were driven back by the *Chocó*, who were to be feared because of their poisonous weapons and perhaps also for their cannibalism. Successful entry of the country was not accomplished by Europeans until 1654, when missionaries established themselves there. They remained until 1687, and their work was carried on for a time by neophytes. Latterly, the *Chocó* have been a peaceful people; in fact, during the 19th century they were described as more docile and less jealous of their independence than the neighboring *Cuna*.

The *Chocó* have remained aloof from the influences of the Europeans. They have never been employed away from their homeland in large numbers, nor have they engaged in trade of commercial proportions. Negroes were introduced into the area very early and they have mixed with some of the *Chocó*. These Negroes have replaced the Indians along the lower courses of the rivers.

The *Chocó* of modern times are composed of three groups: (1) The *Northern* or true *Chocó*, (2) the *Southern Chocó*, and (3) the *Catío*. The *Northern Chocó* appear to be the most populous of the three. They dwell on the lower courses of the rivers flowing into the Golfo de San Miguel and along the rivers of the Pacific coast of Colombia. There is a concentration of this group on the Río Baudó and on the Río Saija. The *Southern Chocó* are concentrated about the Río San Juan, particularly on the Río Docordó and on the Río Micay. The *Catío* dwell in the eastern parts of the Atrato River valley.

The Cuna Group.—The *Cuna* are divided into two sections. The mainland *Cuna* inhabit the headwaters of the rivers on the Pacific slope of eastern Panamá, several small settlements in the lower Atrato Valley, and the eastern shore of the Golfo de Urabá. The San Blas *Cuna* inhabit the small islands along the Caribbean coast between the Golfo de San Blas and Cabo Tiburón. Throughout the historic period the area occupied by the *Cuna* has been steadily shrinking. The land vacated in the south and about the Golfo de Urabá has been taken up by Negroes and *Chocó*.

European and Negro contact began to affect the *Cuna* culture in 1540, and many Indians were enslaved. To escape this some of the *Cuna* retreated up the river valleys. Meanwhile bands of escaped Negro slaves settled on the borders of *Cuna* territory, where their descendents may still be found.

Contact with Europeans was continued during the 17th and 18th centuries, when English and French pirates were based on the *Cuna* islands. Of significance also is the Scotch Darién Colony and the French Colony which existed between 1690 and 1757 at Concepción. After the treaty

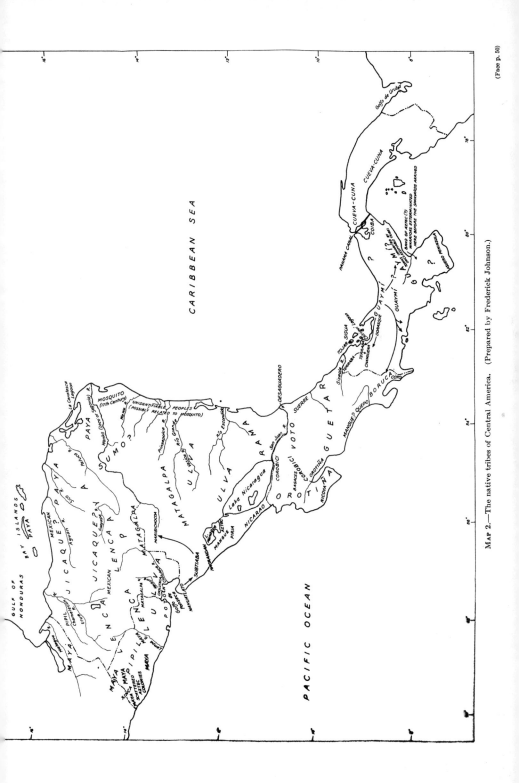

Map 2.—The native tribes of Central America. (Prepared by Frederick Johnson.)

of 1790 the *Cuna* lived at peace with the Spaniards. Subsequent to 1821 the government of New Granada accepted in principle their independence.

About the middle of the 19th century an extensive trade in tortoise shell, ipecac, vegetable ivory, and rubber developed. At the present time trade flourishes though it is largely restricted to coconuts. Formerly, *Cuna* men shipped aboard the English and American ships, which came at irregular intervals. Now, however, a regular trade is maintained by companies established at Colón, and the *Cuna* men have gradually given up the sea to work on the mainland.

No missions were established among the mainland *Cuna* between the 17th and 19th centuries. In 1907 Catholic and Protestant missionaries were finally established among the San Blas *Cuna*. They opened schools, which were later augmented by government-supported schools. Some of the pupils have continued their schooling in Panamá City and Colón. This educational activity was interrupted in 1925 when one faction of the San Blas *Cuna*, encouraged and guided by an American, staged a revolution and attempted to form an independent government. Since then the reservation boundaries and laws, first established in 1915, have been clarified. The Panamanian Government has reservation offices at two islands, but the San Blas *Cuna* have title to the island and a strip of the coast. They possess the power to withhold from outsiders permission to buy, settle, or establish businesses on their island.

THE TALAMANCA DIVISION [6]

The Guaymí Group.—The term *Guaymí* was first loosely applied to the people living in the vicinity of the Laguna de Chiriquí. By 1578 the people inhabiting the Miranda Valley on the Río Cricamola were identified as the *Guaymí* tribe, and soon after it was noted that they also inhabited the area to the east as far as the Río Calovebora. The Indians on the southern, or Pacific, slopes of the Cordillera were not identified as *Guaymí* until 1631, when this term was applied to Indians living in Guabala and San Felix. A more definite record of *Guaymí* living in the environs of the village of Chiriquí was made in 1638.

During the 16th century small groups of *Guaymí* broke off from the main tribe and moved westward to various locations along the Caribbean slopes of the mountains. These groups were allied for varying lengths of time with other tribes, e. g., the *Terraba*. During the first part of the 17th century the Spaniards moved as many groups of *Guaymí* as they could conquer to southwestern Panamá. Later, other tribes were moved from the Tropical Forest area to the Pacific coast, and the *Guaymí* moved

[6] The information about the *Guaymí* was obtained by Frederick Johnson during 1932 and 1933. The two expeditions to Panamá and much of the subsequent research were carried on under the auspices of the Peabody Museum, Harvard University. The information presented here is briefed from an unfinished manuscript and is published by courtesy of the Museum.

eastward into the central part of the coastal Lowlands of Chiriquí. Since this time the *Guaymí* have been, in fact still are, withdrawing into regions as remote as possible from European settlements.

Recent studies have tended to emphasize the opinion of former students that the *Guaymí* inhabited the savanna area at the time of the Conquest. There is no proof of this, because the tribes inhabiting the savannas cannot to be classified in such detail. Several different languages were spoken in the savannas, but there is no proof that any one of these was *Guaymí*. The distribution of *Guaymí* on the savannas, based on vocabularies obtained since the beginning of the 19th century, may well represent only the location of descendants of *Guaymí* who were moved to the many mission towns during the 16th and 17th centuries. It is probable that some of the people indigenous to the savannas spoke languages related to *Guaymí*, just as they possessed a number of culture traits common to the whole region.

The present-day *Guaymí* are composed of the *Guaymí* proper and a mixture of numerous groups who have fled from European domination. The people occupy most of the northern and sections of the southern slopes of the Cordillera, particularly of the Serranía de Tabasara. In general the *Guaymí* do not frequent the coastal regions in large numbers or, if they do, they do not occupy them for long periods of time.

The modern boundaries of the *Guaymí* are indefinite, for this group is surrounded by peoples of mixed blood who are under more direct control of the Panamanian Government. In general the *Guaymí* are found between the Panamá–Costa Rica boundary and the longitude of Santa Fé, Province of Veraguas. Mixed but unclassifiable groups, some of whom acknowledge their aboriginal descent, are found scattered about Chiriquí and Veraguas, particularly on the Asuero Peninsula.

Pinart's (1885, p. 438) identification of subtribes of the *Guaymí* is substantially correct. It is likely that these subtribes are the remnants of aboriginal sociopolitical divisions.

The *Mové* have their headquarters in the Miranda Valley and on the Río Cricamola. They also live on the Caribbean slopes of the mountains between the Laguna de Chiriquí and the Río Belén. Scattered members of this group may be found in the Highlands of Chiriquí and on the Pacific slopes of the Serranía de Tabasara.

The *Murire* live in the eastern sections of the Serranía de Tabasara and are said to inhabit sections of the Caribbean coast and Upland as far east as the Río Coclé del Norte. Strongly Hispanicized remnants live in the eastern sections of the Pacific watershed. In the west, the *Murire* and *Mové* either occupy neighboring localities or else representatives of one group live among the others.

The *Muoi* have practically disappeared as a unit if present information can be trusted. At one time they lived about Chorcha and along the Río

Fonseca in the Province of Chiriquí, a location to which they may have migrated after 1600.

The Talamanca group.—*The Dorasque.*—In contrast to some linguistic classifications this tribe, politically and socially, was apparently closely allied to the *Changuena* at the time of the Conquest. This relationship may be followed through the incomplete records into the latter part of the 19th century. In the 16th century the *Dorasque* were living between the *Changuena* and the *Guaymí.* Boundaries mentioned are the Río Guarano and the Río Cricamola. Following the conquest the *Dorasque* joined the *Changuena* in order to combat the Spaniards and to protect themselves from the raids of the *Mosquito* and the English buccaneers. The attacks of the latter are said to have resulted in a retreat into *Terraba* territory and an amalgamation or at least a federation with them. Finally, the combined *Terraba* and *Dorasque-Changuena* retreated to the former home of the *Changuena.* After this the movements of the *Dorasque* are obscure until the very last records of them. The *Dorasque,* allied with some *Changuena,* were to be found south of Cerro Horqueta, on the Río Chiriquí and in the environs of Caldera, Potrero de Vargas, Dolega, and possibly Guabala. Dolega was an ancient mission of the *Dorasque.* It is doubtful if any true *Dorasque* are alive today.

The Changuena.—This tribe was said by the early Spaniards to be located in the mountainous region southwest of Almirante Bay, along the Río Robalo, and about the headwaters of the Ríos Changuena, Bun, and Puan. Andrade (1709) says that they numbered about 5,000. A few *Changuena* were reported living in their native region by Gabb (1875, p. 486). In 1900, a few families, said to be *"Chelibas"* and closely related to the Changuena, were living to the north of the Volcán de Chiriquí on the headwaters of the Changuinola River. Other *Changuena* moved to the Pacific coast with the *Terraba* and *Dorasque.* They are said to have settled in regions northeast of Burica and the Golfo Dulce. They are now extinct or inextricably mixed with the *Bribri, Terraba,* and *Guaymí.*

The Terraba.—The *Terraba* lived in the Lowlands and lower Uplands between the Ríos Sixaola and Changuinola. They also occupied some of the islands at the mouth of the Laguna de Chiriquí. The *Tojar,* either a subtribe or a name synonymous with the *Terraba,* lived on the island of Tojar as late as 1763. The *Terraba,* particularly a subgroup called the *Quequexque,* were said to occupy lands adjacent to *Guaymí* territory. Some of the *Terraba* were removed to a mission in southeastern Costa Rica, now the village of Terraba. Other groups migrated in company with the *Dorasque* and *Changuena.*

The Boruca.—Doris Stone (1943) correctly notes that the modern *Boruca* are probably composed of a mixture of tribes indigenous to the

Terraba Plain and neighboring regions. Probably, also, the tribe includes increments from tribes moved into the region in the 16th and 17th centuries. The early information is equivocal. The *Boruca* may be the descendants of the *Coto,* who were enemies of the *Quepo.* On the other hand, the *Boruca,* first identified as a tribe living in the environs of Pico Burica, may have counted the *Quepo* and *Coto* as subtribes. This latter alignment is used here because the earliest information which has come to hand implies some such political organization. The language of the *Boruca* has been classified with that of the *Dorasque* and *Changuena.* That of the *Quepo* has been linked, at least by implication, with the *Guetar* language. The data prevent the construction of any satisfactory conclusion. (Peralta, 1901, p. 130; Lehmann, 1920, vol. 1, p. 201; Stone, 1943.)

The Bribri.—The origin of the name *Bribri* is obscure. It first appears in the literature of the 19th century, and it may have been derived from *Viceita* or some equivalent form. In 1709 it was suggested that the 7,000 *Viceitas* could be removed to Boruca, but nothing concerning the outcome of this proposal has come to light. Nothing is known of their early home. Gabb (1875, p. 486) places the *Bribri* on the east side of the Río Coen, where they occupied all the Lari, Uren, and Zhorquín River Valleys. The same author says that the term *Biceita* was not known as a tribal name in 1875. Peralta (1890, p. 70) says that the Río Sixaola flows, from its sources to the sea, through the territories of *Cabecares* and *Viceitas.*

The Cabecar.—It is impossible to identify this tribe in the earlier documents. It is probable that, like the *Bribri,* they were closely related to the *Guetar,* although some authors claim that their language was distinctive (Pinart, 1900; Lehmann, 1920). The first definite record of their location was made by Gabb (1875, p. 486), who says that the *Cabecar* lived between the frontiers of civilization and the western banks of the Río Coen.

The Central Costa Rica group.—*The Guetar.*—The *Guetar* were named for a chief, Huetar, who lived to the north and east of Punta de Herradura. In addition to Huetar himself, the records mention four other chiefs who controlled political divisions of varying sizes and importance. These chiefs were named Garabito, Guarco, Pacaca, and Asseri. The actual political system and its divisions are obscure and puzzling. It is possible, though believed by some to be doubtful, that there was a strong intertribal organization even before the Conquest. The territory ruled over by the chiefs mentioned above extended from the eastern shore of the southern section of the Golfo de Nicoya across Costa Rica to the Caribbean. On the Caribbean coast the *Guetar* inhabited the area extending from the vicinity of Port Limón northward to the region about the mouth of the Pacuare River.

The Northern Costa Rica group.—*The Voto.*—"These Indians occupied the valleys of the San Carlos, Pocosal and Saraqui Rivers. To the south they extended to the Cordillera Central, and probably across these mountains into the Province of Alajuela" (Lothrop, 1926 b, p. 16). The *Voto* were a separate tribe, but they were tributary to the *Guetar* chieftain Garabito. Doris Stone (correspondence), following Gabb (1875), says that the *Voto* "continue today as the *Rama* in Nicaragua." Remnant groups may have been absorbed by the *Rama.* At the present writing, however, the only way to distinguish the two tribes is through detailed linguistic analysis, and until this has been accomplished Gabb's statement must remain tentative.

The Suerre.—The *Suerre* lived on the Atlantic coast of Costa Rica behind the Laguna de Tortuguero and around the mouths of the Ríos Raventazón and Pacuare. Four chieftains were said to be members of this tribe, but nothing is known concerning them. They were named Suerre, Chiuppa, Camachire, and Cocori.

The *Guetar, Voto,* and *Suerre* tribes were conquered very early, and members of other tribes, particularly from southern Costa Rica, were moved into their villages. The languages of the three tribes were closely related to those spoken in southern and eastern Costa Rica. The known characteristics of their culture indicate the same close relationship with the tribes to the south. These three tribes had, however, little if any formal relationship with their neighbors. The existing records have been summarized by Lothrop (1926 b), the principal source of the preceding notes.

The Corobici.—The *Corobici* take their name from a chieftain encountered by Gil González Davila. In early Spanish times the *Corobici* lived along the southern shores of Lake Nicaragua between the Río Frío and the Cordillera Volcánica. Some claim they inhabited the Solentiname Islands in Lake Nicaragua; others say that the people on these islands were a branch of the *Rama.* Probably the *Corobici* occupied a tongue of territory extending westward across the Cordillera de Tilleran and through the valley of the Río Tenorio to the northern shore of the Golfo de Nicoya. As the Spaniards conquered the country the *Corobici* retreated to the plains about San Carlos. Later, as *Guatuso,* they occupied the inaccessible region about the headwaters of the Río Frío and perhaps also the valleys of the Ríos Zapote, Guacalito, and Cucaracha to the west (Rivet, 1924, p. 681). Apparently separate enclaves, which may have been either indigenous or fugitive groups, were to be found in the region between Bagaces and Esparata. About the middle of the 18th century these groups raided and plundered the countryside, but they were driven back to the north across the Cordillera. Between that time and about 1860 the *Guatuso* lived in comparative seclusion in the upper sections of the Río Frío Valley. Recent exploration and conquest of the valley has resulted in the decimation of the *Guatuso*. Some were captured and sold as slaves in Nicaragua. (Lothrop, 1926, b; Conzemius, 1930; Fernández, 1889, pp. 622–640.) At the present time remnants of the *Guatuso* live in upper sections of the Río Frío.

Some students do not agree with the location and implied relationships given above. Lines (1938 a) states that the *Guatuso* were originally *Guetar* and that, because they were neighbors of the *"Chontal"* and *"Chorotega,"* their "race" has become very mixed. Conzemius (1930, p. 105) implies that the *Corobici* are different from the *Guatuso,* and he believes that the latter are descendants of the people who live in Aranjuez and El Garabita. These two towns and the descendants from the original inhabitants are now believed to be *Guetar*. A note by Conzemius to the effect that some *Guatuso* on the Río Frío are actually *Rama* Indians may well be due either to recent undocumented wanderings of the latter or to variations in the interpretation of linguistic data. The early data cannot be interpreted in this way.

Doris Stone (correspondence) quotes the statement by Oviedo y Valdés to the effect that the *Corobici* inhabited the Chara and Pocosi Islands in the Golfo de Nicoya, and she is led to suspect that the Nicoya Peninsula was once *Corobici* territory. This suspicion is not based upon records made during the Conquest or later, for it is recorded that this territory was occupied by the *Orotiña* during and subsequent to the 16th century. In this case, Oviedo's statement refers only to the islands. The delimitation of the habitat of the prehistoric *Corobici* depends upon the discovery, on the peninsula and elsewhere, of cultural material which may be identified as the product of *Corobici* industry.

The Rama.—The records indicate that the *Rama* probably lived on the Caribbean coast of Nicaragua between Bluefields and the Río San Juan. Some authors believe that their southern border lay at the Río Punta Gorda. The location of the northern boundary is by no means certain. At the present time the principal settlement of *Rama* is on Rama Key in the Laguna de Bluefields. A few scattered settlements are found between this island and Punta Gorda. Conzemius (1930, p. 94) says that the language is spoken by about 270 persons.

The former western boundary of the *Rama* is indeed vague. They appear to have inhabited the San Juan River Valley and probably sections of the hinterland to the north. The *Melchora* (Squier, 1852, p. 79; 1853 a, p. 94 f), a group of unknown origin, were probably *Rama* living in the middle reaches of the Río San Juan. Vague suggestions of the existence of political units justifies the assumption that the *Rama* were confined to the area east of Lake Nicaragua. There is the possibility that *Rama* families, or small enclaves of this tribe, have lived among the *Guatuso* since the middle of the 18th century, if not before. (For arguments identifying *Rama* groups in northwestern Costa Rica, cf. Conzemius, 1930.)

THE CARIBBEAN DIVISION: EAST COAST[7]

The information from the accounts of the first conquerors and the few colonists of this region is exceedingly small in quantity, and it is equivocal. Some references employ the term *"Chontal,"* but it is impossible to know whether these refer to enclaves of "foreign" origin or whether this term was applied by early writers to the ancestors of the present population. The Lowlands and the lower Uplands of the hinterland were inhabited by peoples now called the *Mosquito* and *Sumo*. Unfortunately, the records made previous to the end of the 17th century supply information for but a small section of the Mosquito coast. Early information about the inland peoples is practically nonexistent.

The Mosquito coast was discovered by Columbus on his fourth voyage. Between that time and the middle of the 17th century the country was only occasionally visited by Europeans. The coast became a refuge for the English buccaneers who, after the middle of the 17th century, established themselves at Cabo Gracias a Dios. The ensuing alliance between the English and Indians resulted in the expansion of the territory of the local tribe at the expense of its aboriginal neighbors. Effective raids, particularly against Spanish settlements, were made along the coast as far south as the Laguna de Chiriquí. As a consequence of this alliance the aboriginal culture was profoundly modified.

By 1688 the buccaneers were masters of the Mosquito coast and they made the *Mosquito* chief governor general of it under the jurisdiction of the English Government at Jamaica. Before long the English established a protectorate over the coast and even sent troops there in 1744. Spain protested this action, and following the treaty of 1786 England evacuated the territory. Spain was, however, unable to establish effective control in the region.

In 1821 the English protectorate was renewed. The *Mosquito* Chief was crowned King in 1825, and it was claimed that his territory extended from Cabo Gracias a Dios to the Laguna de Chiriquí. Later the southern boundary was relocated at the Río San Juan. The *Mosquito* King ruled until 1860 when, through the intervention of the United States, the English ceded part of their territory to Honduras and the remainder to Nicaragua. A section lying between the Río Hueso and the Río Rama, extending inland to longitude 84° 15′ N., was set aside as a reservation governed by the natives under Nicaraguan sovereignty. The population of this reservation was composed for the most part of English-speaking "Creoles," the mixed descendants of Jamaican Negroes and *Mosquito* and some *Rama* Indians. The majority of the aboriginal groups lived outside the reserve. After a long series of difficulties the Nicaraguan Government, in 1894,

---

[7] The following information is a rearrangement of data submitted by Kirchhoff. Data from manuscripts by Doris Stone and Frederick Johnson have been added.

took possession of the reservation incorporating it into the republic as the Department of Zelaya, now the Department of Bluefields.

The Mosquito group.—The account of the fourth voyage of Columbus and the few 17th century descriptions of the Mosquito coast are difficult to evaluate in terms of the more adequate later descriptions. It is probable that *Mosquito* were living between Cabo Gracias a Dios and the Río Wawa. Either the inhabitants of much of the coast to the south were unknown or else early descriptions of them have been lost. The first satisfactory record was made by Exquemelin in 1672. He found them divided into two subtribes, one located at Cabo Gracias a Dios and the other at "Mostique" (Sandy Bay?). Contemporary writers (e. g., Raveneau de Lussan, 1689; "M. W." in 1699 [1752]) mention the wreck of a slave ship, in 1641, which freed about 200 Negroes. These took refuge among the *Mosquito* at Cabo Gracias a Dios, and, as has been emphasized by many writers down to the present day, they were largely responsible for the primary introduction of African traits into the culture of the Mosquito coast.

Some 150 years after Exquemelin's observations (1672) the *Mosquito* occupied all important river basins between Cabo Gracias a Dios and the Río San Juan. They had also disrupted the distribution of the fugitive populations who had attempted to settle in the Lowland regions between the San Juan and the Laguna de Chiriquí. By the beginning of the 19th century bands or subtribes of *Mosquito* were identifiable. Today 5 of these, with a population of about 15,000, are known. These appear as distinct political units, but their languages may differ only slightly. Attempts to point out differences in their ethnology (cf. esp. Conzemius, 1932) are significant, but further detailed study in the field is necessary before they may be fully accepted.

Inevitably, most of the *Mosquito* have mixed with Negroes. Latterly, mixtures between the Indian-Negro-European populations and the *Mosquito* have been frequent. The strongest mixture of Negro blood has been observed among the *Baldam* and *Cabo*. The *Baldam* were first known about Sandy Bay, but a part of the group has migrated to the Laguna de las Perlas. The *Cabo* live along the coast between Sandy Bay and the Río Grande. The *Mam* moved to the Río Patuca, absorbing some of the indigenous *Paya* and driving the remainder to the west. The *Wanki* remained in the valley of the Río Wanks and, according to Conzemius, they are moving up the river. By 1932 they had reached the town of Bocay. The *Tawira* live a short distance from the Coast, between Sandy Bay and the Río Grande. The *Mam* and *Wanki* call the *Mosquito* living south of Cabo Gracias a Dios "Tawira" (heavy-haired). The *Cabo* and *Baldam* call themselves "*True Mosquito.*"

The Sumo group.—*Sumo* is a generic name given by the *Mosquito* to a number of tribes speaking a language closely related to *Mosquito*. They now number between 3,000 and 4,000 people, and they occupy the lower Uplands and upper sections of the river valleys west of the Caribbean coast in Honduras and Nicaragua. Almost nothing in the 16th-century documents can be construed as a description of the *Sumo*, and, as a matter of fact, little was known of them until the very last of the 17th century. Beginning with the 18th century, the increasing amount of information, principally from travelers' accounts, defines 10 subtribes of which 6 are now either extinct or combined with other groups.

Some *Twahka* live in five villages located in Honduras along the middle reaches of the Río Patuca. These are slowly being absorbed by the *Mosquito*. Other members of the *Twahka* have migrated to Nicaragua, where they live in the lower reaches of the Ríos Waspuk, Lakus (Lecus?), Wawa, Cuculaya, Hamaco, and even Prinzapolca and Río Grande. The closest linguistic relatives of the *Twahka* are the *Panamaka*, who prefer to call themselves "*Twahka*" (= *True Sumo*).

The *Panamaca* live along the tributaries of the Wanks River. Relatively pure groups have been found on the Ríos Bocay, Pis Pis, and Kwabul (?). Two groups of *Panamaca* have moved to the upper reaches of the Río Prinsapolca and the Río Grande.

The *Bawahka* were expelled from the Ríos Wawa and Cuculaya by the *Twahka*. They live today on the Río Banbana.

The *Ulva*, the southernmost *Sumo*, live today along the upper reaches of the Río Grande and the Río Escondido. It is likely that other unrecorded enclaves are still extant. Early knowledge of this tribe in eastern Nicaragua is scanty. They were probably neighbors of the *Rama*, occupying a stripe of territory between Lake Nicaragua and the coast. They also occupied sections of southern Jinotega and were distributed to the west along the northern slopes of the Nicaraguan Lowland, extending through Honduras into eastern El Salvador (Ponce, 1873, vol. 1; Squier, 1860 a). They occupied the western parts of their territory in company with *Chorotega, Nahuatlan,* and possibly even *Lenca, Matagalpa,* and other groups.

Owing to continuous wars with the *Mosquito*, the *Kukra* have only recently been exterminated as a subtribe, but individuals still live in their native haunts, i. e., about the Laguna de Bluefields and on the Corn Islands. The *Yosco* [8] lived on the Río Tuma in territory which was invaded by the *Panamanca* and *Ulva*. Tradition has it that the *Yosco* were killed off because they were sodomites. The *Prinsu* lived on the lower Río Prinsapolca, a region now inhabited by the *Tawira*. The *Tunla*, speaking a dialect resembling *Bawahka*, were a mixture of *Prinsu* and *Tawira*. The *Boa* formerly lived on the upper Río Kewaska (?), and the *Silam* and the *Ku* inhabited the valley of the Río Waspuk.

---

[8] It is believed by some that the *Yosco* language differed from other *Sumo* dialects (cf. Mason, J. A., 1940; Johnson, 1940).

THE CARIBBEAN DIVISION: NORTH COAST

North Coast group.—*The Paya.*—Stone (1941, etc.) advances the idea that the term *"Taia"* recorded by Columbus is an early spelling of the modern term *Paya.* The territory of the *Paya*, she believes, lay between the Aguán River Valley and the Wanks River and extended southward to the Olancho and Jamastran Valleys. The date of the establishment of these boundaries corresponds with the settlement of the country following the Conquest. It is possible that there was a southward drift of the *Paya*, who took refuge in the interior from the Spanish attacks on the coast. Possibly the interior boundaries were modified by this movement. More conservative interpretations locate the early *Paya* along the coast between the Patrum and Wanks Rivers.

Conzemius (1927–28) lists the towns of El Carbón and El Dulce Nombre (Culmí), saying that 250 to 300 *Paya* Indians may be found in each. Also, 30 *Paya* live in El Payal, on the Paulaya River, and 40 Indians live in Puskira, located on the Plantain River 15 km. (about 10 miles) from the coast. Stone (1941) accepts Squier's statement that the *Seco* on the Tinto River were a band of *Paya.* If these are the *Seco* mentioned by Young (1842) they should be located on the Río Sico (Seco), a tributary of the Río Negro (also called Tinto) in northeastern Honduras. The descendants of the *Seco* of the Río Sico are to be found in the neighborhood of El Carbón (Conzemius, 1927–28). Stone (1941) also says that the *Towka* were probably *Paya.* Conzemius believes that these people were *Sumo*, as their name suggests. The identification of the original inhabitants of Catacamas is difficult. Stone believes that they were *Paya*, and Conzemius says that they may have been *Sumo.*

In 1921 there were a few more than 600 *Paya* (Conzemius, 1927–28). At the end of the 18th century Ramón de Anguiano estimated that there were 10,000 to 12,000 *Paya.* This estimate seems to be greatly exaggerated. Sapper (1899) estimated 825. Kirchhoff believes that Fray Espino was referring to *Paya* when he said, in 1674, that he settled 6,000 in 7 villages. It is probable that Espino was referring to *Jicaque.*

The Jicaque.—Stone (cf. esp. 1941) has, through recent interpretations of the documents, thrown new light upon the *"Jicaque* Area." She has emphasized the possibility that the term *Jicaque* is of *Nahuatlan* origin and that it was used as one of the "terminos provinciales," as were such terms as *Chontal, Pupuluca*, and, to a more limited extent perhaps, *Lenca* and *Paya.* In her opinion *Jicaque* was applied to peoples speaking languages and having cultural traditions which differ from the present-day *Jicaque.* This opinion depends largely upon the interpretation of Vázquez (1714–16), from whom later writers drew much of their material.

In later times the term *Jicaque* was used by anthropologists to designate the language spoken by the inhabitants of Yoro, southern Atlantida, and Cortés. Because of difficulties with tribal terminology it is still impossible to trace the history of the people now called *Jicaque* back into proto-historic times. However, Von Hagen (1943) has attempted to identify earlier groups. He locates more recently extinct groups and completely Hispanicized remnants in the Sierra de Omoa, the Ulua-Chamelicón Valley, and in the Departments of Yoro and Atlantida. He also accepts 18th- and 19th-century identifications of the *Jicaque de Palmar* and the *Jicaque de Yoro*. The *Jicaque* tribe, which he names *Torrupan*, left the town of Yoro in 1865 and moved to their present location on the Montaña de la Flor.

THE NORTHERN HIGHLAND DIVISION

The Matagalpa group and tribe.—Information concerning the *Matagalpa* is limited. They spoke a language related to *Ulva* and *Sumo*. At the present time knowledge of them is confined almost exclusively to their language. The early information indicates that the language was spoken in northwestern Nicaragua and southwestern Honduras. An enclave speaking a language related to *Matagalpa,* usually called *Cacaopera,* was identified soon after the Conquest in northeastern El Salvador. Remnants, strongly Hispanicized, have been reported near Cacaopera in eastern El Salvador. Other groups have been located along the Nicaraguan-Honduran frontier, around the Pantasma Valley, near Esteli in Nicaragua (Stone, correspondence), and at Lislique. Another group has been located near the town of Matagalpa.

The Lenca group.[9]—The term *Lenca* first appears in the chronicle of Padre Francisco Vázquez (1714–16), who uses the reports of a Franciscan friar, Padre Espino, to recount the conquest of the Honduran Province of Teguzgalpa (Tegucigalpa). Vázquez designates certain Indians as members of the *Lenca* nation, e.g., *Paraka,* but at the same time includes the *Jicague* as speaking the *Lenca* tongue. He makes the following significant statement, however: ". . . the *Lenca* Indians of confused language, and treacherous character and inconstant" (Vázquez, 1714–16, lib. 5, trat. 1, cap. 7, p. 447). Squier (1858) was the first to apply this term to the Indians in southwestern Honduras, particularly those around Quajiquiro, in the present Department of La Paz, and in Intibucá. The language of these people differs from the idiom of the *Paraka* and other people who are still found in parts of eastern Honduras. We must, therefore, accept *Lenca* as a general term to cover a number of different peoples and dialects, both those of definite interrelationship and those which may have only remote if any connection with one another.

Words ending in "-ique," "-quin," "-guara," and "-gua" are *Lenca* (Squier, 1908; Lehmann, 1920). The former distribution of the *Lenca* can be traced fairly accurately by the place names on the present-day maps of Honduras and El Salvador. At the present time we designate as *Lenca*

[9] This section was written by Doris Stone.

the Indians inhabiting the mountainous regions of the Departments of La Paz, Intibucá, southern and southeastern Gracias in Honduras, and the northeastern portion of the Republic of El Salvador.[10]

Tribal divisions, population, and distribution.—The *Lenca* seek high country and isolated peaks and hillocks, cultivating their cornfields in the small sloping cavities of the hillsides and in the Upland narrow valleys. Each community is formed by a separate tribe, often with a slight difference in dialect (Squier, 1858; also personal observation of the writer). To-day, unfortunately, the language has almost entirely disappeared, surviving only among the elders in the more remote towns, e. g., Quajiquiro. The villages in the *Lenca* area receive their names from the tribes inhabiting them.

La Paz, according to the Honduran Government statistics, has 18,589 pure-blooded Indians: 8,861 males and 9,728 females. The chief pure-Indian towns in La Paz are: Gualazara, Muyén, Guascupuscua, Chinacla, Ato Viejo, Santa Elena, Mata Palo, Pitahayas, Barrancarai, Aguanquete-rique, Quajiquiro, Sabana Larga, Tepanguare, Lepaguare, Ranteca, Chichicaste, Guaspopolo, Guidinmani, Chiderique, Orovila, Sigamaní, Choacapa, Inchulile, Guanga, Guascotoro, Pule, Upa, Apacilina, Gruiraca-ray, Suyate, Kukinca, and Yarula.

Opatoro, Cacaoterique, Puringla, and Cabañas (formerly Similatón) have also a large Indian population, although some Hondurans live in the townships.

Intibucá has 32,707 Indians: 15,669 males and 17,083 females. The pure-Indian towns are: Semane, Chogola, Malguare, La Silimaní, Guas-cotoro, Monquecagua, Quiaterique, Misiure, Oloas, Siquire, Yace, Chupu-cai, Segua, Cangual, Jagua, Cacauchagua, Cacahuatal, Masaya, Cotala, Yamaranguila, Jiquinlata, Coloraringua, El Talquekzal, Kiragüira, Guatateca, Cosongra, Cirisma, and Dolores, the former Yolula. Intibucá, the town, has Honduran inhabitants, and their number seems to be increasing. In addition to this, a portion of the community, called La Esperanza, is completely Honduran, which quite naturally influences the life of the indigenous side. A street is the dividing line between the two towns. Many of the Indians from Intibucá have moved to Yamaranguila to be more to themselves.

Gracias has a total of 5,659 Indians. Gracias, however, was at one time very heavily populated by Spaniards. The Departmento is a meeting ground for the *Chorti* from Copán and Ocotepeque, with the remnants of what were possibly the ancient *Pipil,* who are still found around Ocotepeque. Only the southeastern part of the Department is occupied by *Lenca,* the exact number of whom is not known. In this section some

---

[10] Ponce (1873), among others, describes a tribe named *Poton* who inhabited southeastern El Salvador. The identity of this group is not clear. That they were a discrete unit seems certain. Their language has been identified as *Maya, Ulva, Nahuatlan,* and *Lenca* by different authors, but as yet no satisfactory decision can be made.—FREDERICK JOHNSON.

of the towns can be classed as *Lenca,* e. g., Cerquin, Congolón, Tixila, Gualcixe, and Guanajulque.

In El Salvador most of the towns on the northeastern frontier have some *Lenca* inhabitants.

THE MESO-AMERICAN DIVISION [11]

There have been at least four migrations from the north into Central America of peoples known as Meso-Americans (Kirchhoff, 1943). To these may be added the possibility of a less extensive but significant tendency of the *Lenca* to push southward. The consequences of the migrations were that when one group replaced another in a restricted area repercussions were felt over the length and breadth of the land. Although the first of these movements began during the middle of the Christian Era, they were continuing at the time of the Spanish Conquest. The tribes herein discussed were thus in a state of flux, and so, to a lesser degree perhaps, were their indigenous neighbors.

The mapping of the tribes in this division is particularly difficult. Discussions of their location are many and few agree (cf. Lehmann, 1920; Johnson, 1940; Stone, 1940 b, 1941). As these Meso-American immigrants carved living space for themselves out of lands formerly owned by indigenous peoples, their territory inevitably changed with the fortunes of their conflict with indigenous tribes. The scene of this struggle, when first viewed by the Spaniards, was inevitably a complicated one: Peoples speaking several languages and possessing different cultural traditions were trying to exist as local entities, though occupying neighboring towns scattered over the countryside without regard for linear boundaries. The "aboriginal" population had been fragmented through the conquests by waves of people with different cultural heritages.

The present location of a few of the remnants of these peoples is shown on map 2. Most of these tribes are extinct, at least as units identifiable with those recorded in the 16th and 17th centuries. Remnants have taken refuge in regions on the fringes of the modern population, which is relatively heavy in this area. These remnants are strongly Hispanicized and, to some extent, mixed with other Indian populations, which were moved into the region during early Colonial resettlement programs or which were attracted to it because of economic motives, the region recently having been almost completely Europeanized.

The Chorotega group.—The tribes of this group, named with terms which probably designated dialects, were the descendants of the first definitely identifiable migration from the north. Their language is related to that spoken by the *Otomi, Popoloca, Mazateca,* and *Chiapanec* of México. *Choluteca* was spoken along the northern shores of the Golfo de Fonseca. *Mangue* was spoken in the area between Lake Managua

---

[11] This section combines data contributed by Doris Stone and Frederick Johnson.

and the Pacific. Stone (correspondence) has identified an enclave speaking *Mangue* near Quepos in Costa Rica, but its "tribal" identity is not revealed. *Nagrandan* and *Dirian* are two enclaves speaking some form of *Mangue;* they are named after chiefs. The *Orotiña* occupied the Nicoya area, extending westward to Lake Nicaragua. They also were discovered on the north shore of the Golfo de Nicoya west of Puntarenas.

The Maribio group.—The second migration ended when a tribe, whose language was first called *Maribio* and later named *Subtiaba,* settled in the area about León in Guatemala. After the Conquest the *Subtiaba* were reduced to a few survivors living to the east of their 16th-century home. Squier obtained a vocabulary from *Subtiaba* remnants living about the town of Subtiaba. The *Maribichicoa* were a group which split off from the *Subtiaba* during a famine which occurred before the Conquest.

The Nahuatlan group.—The third and fourth migrations to this area were composed of peoples speaking several forms of *Nahuatlan.* These people brought with them some of the historical and other traditions of their parent nation and the penchant for incorporating their contemporary history into their extensive folklore. The earliest of these migrations brought the *Nicarao* who, by the end of the 11th century, had settled on the Isthmus of Rivas. Of the other enclaves, the time of arrival can be determined only in the case of those groups which arrived just before the Spanish Conquest. The *Nahuatlato* lived on Punta Conseguina until 1586, when they were moved to the towns of El Viejo and Chinandega. The *Desaguadero,* apparently a commercial colony, lived on the delta of the Río San Juan. The identity of the *Bagace* is not certain, but apparently some people spoke *Nahuatlan* near that town. The *Sigua,* with members of the *Terraba* and other tribes, occupied the Island of Tojar and part of the delta of the Changuena River. Other small groups speaking *Aztec* or *Pipil* but lacking specific names have been identified in various parts of Honduras and Nicaragua. Their approximate location is indicated on the map.

CLASSIFICATION OF TRIBES IN CENTRAL AMERICA

Division	Group	Tribe	Subtribes and Synonyms
Cuna-Chocó ...	Chocó	Northern or True Chocó	Cholo, Empera, Emberak, Citará, Paparo, Andagueda.
		Southern Chocó	Nonamá, Noaname.
		Catío	
	Cuna	Mainland Cuna........	Cunacuna.
		San Blas Cuna	Chucuna, Tule, Mandinga, Bayano, Chepo, Chucunaque, Paya, Caiman.

Division	Group	Tribe	Subtribes and Synonyms
Talamanaca ...	Guaymí	Northern Guaymí ...	Murire, Muoi, Move, Valiente, Culantro, Nuite, Norteño, Bukuete, Artieda, Chaliva. (For additions, cf. Lehmann, 1920, and others.)
		Southern Guaymí....	Protohistoric and early historic enclaves located in the savanna area. (Cf. Lothrop, 1937.)
	Talamanca ...	Dorasque [1]	Dorace, Dorado, Irabalo, Chiriluo, Suasimi, Chumulu, Dolega, Thorasque.
		Changuena	Changuina, Chaliba [2] Shelaba. [2]
		Terraba	Tojar, Techi, Tirub, Tirribi, Techbi, Tichbi, Depso, Norteño, Quequexque, Terrebe, Brururau.
		Boruca	Burica, Brunka, Quepo, Burucaca, Turucaca, Coto.
		Bribri	Blancos, Valientes, Biseita, Veceita, Biceyta, Abicetava, Talamanca, Urinama, Tariaca, Pocosi, Lari, Uren.
		Cabecar	Cavecara, Coen, Chirripo, Tucurriqui, Estrella.
	Central Costa Rica	Guetar	Guarco, Garabito, Pacaca, Asseri, Huetar, Brusela (?).
	Northern Costa Rica	Voto	Barba.
		Suerre	Chiuppa, Camachire, Cocori.
		Corobici	Guatuso, Los Tices (?).
		Rama	Melchora.

[1] Some authors classify the *Dorasque* with the *Guaymí* on the basis of scanty linguistic evidence. Equally acceptable data indicate that this tribe originally had political if not closer relationships with their other neighbors. The arrangement here does not deny the validity of classifications based on other types of data.

[2] These terms are also used as synonyms for the *Sigua*, a colony speaking *Nahuatlan*.

Division	Group	Tribe	Subtribes and Synonyms
		Mosquito (early name for tribe)	Meskito, Missko, Moscos, Miskito, Moustiques, Moustiquais, Muskitoe, Mustic, Sambo.
	Mosquito	Mam .... Wanki	Cueta.
		Baldam .... Kabo Tawira	Baymuna.
	Sumo		Sumu, Smu, Simu, Zumu, Soomoo, Soumou, Soomu, Smoo, Smou, Simou.
		Twahka	Taga, Tagua, Taguaca, Tahua, Teguaca, Teuko, Tao, Touco, Thuaco, Tuaco, Toca, Towka, Toaka, Tauzzka, Tauachka, Tukaca, Towcka, Tauca, Towa, Tuaca, Twaxka, Twa'ka, Tocka, Tawasca, Tuaca, Tucoa, Laku, Coco, Wasabane, Pispi.
Caribbean Lowland: East.		Panamaca	Panamaga, Ponamaka, Pnamaka.
		Bawahka	
		Ulva [3]	Ulwa, Ulua, Culoua, Ulawa, Ulba, Uluwa, Vulva, Vulwa, Vulua, Wulua, Woolwa, Gaula.
		Kukra (extinct)	Kukara, Kokora, Cookra, Cukra, Kokra, Cucura, Cookera, Cockerack, Cackera.
		Yosko (extinct)	Yusku, Yusko.
		Prinsu (extinct)	Prinzu, Prinzo, Prinzoo, Prinsoo.
		Tunla (mixed group)	Tungla, Tungola, Tongula, Toongla, Tonga, Tumbla, Tumba.
		Boa (extinct)	Poa, Pua.

[3] It is possible that the *Ulva* should be classified as a group as well as a tribe.

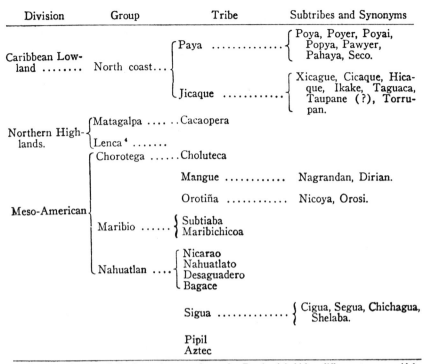

Division	Group	Tribe	Subtribes and Synonyms
Caribbean Lowland	North coast...	Paya	Poya, Poyer, Poyai, Popya, Pawyer, Pahaya, Seco.
		Jicaque	Xicague, Cicaque, Hicaque, Ikake, Taguaca, Taupane (?), Torrupan.
Northern Highlands.	Matagalpa	Cacaopera	
	Lenca [4]		
Meso-American	Chorotega	Choluteca	
		Mangue	Nagrandan, Dirian.
		Orotiña	Nicoya, Orosi.
	Maribio	Subtiaba Maribichicoa	
	Nahuatlan	Nicarao Nahuatlato Desaguadero Bagace	
		Sigua	Cigua, Segua, Chichagua, Shelaba.
		Pipil Aztec	

[4] The organization of the *Lenca* is not understood. Peoples inhabiting different towns could be classified as tribes and named after the towns. However, until the relationship of these towns is known it seems better not to list them here.

BIBLIOGRAPHY

Alba, C., 1928; Andagoya, 1865; Anderson, 1914; Andrade, 1709; Angulo, 1862; Avila, [1524]; Bancroft, 1874–76, 1883–90; Bard, 1885; Berckenhagen, 1894; Berendt, 1876; Blessing, 1899; Bonilla, J., 1702; Brinton, 1895; Captain General of Guatemala, 1742; Cardenas Palomino, 1684; Carrión, 1648; Ceballos, 1610; Col. Doc. Inéd. Amer., 1864–84; Col. Doc. Inéd. de Colombia, 1891–94; Conzemius, 1921, 1927–28, 1928, 1929, 1930, 1932; Coronado, 1564; Costa Rica–Panamá Arbitration Documents, 1913; Criado de Castilla, 1575; Dampier, 1699; Davidson, 1935; Diego y Gutiérrez [1534]; Edwards, 1823; Espinosa, 1514, 1516, 1519; Exquemelin, 1678 (1893); Fernández, 1881–1907, 1889; Fernández Ferraz, 1892; Fernández Guardia and Fernández Ferraz, 1892; Flores, 1611; Gabb, 1874, 1875; Gagini, 1917; Garret y Arlovi, 1711; González y Gutiérrez, [1540]; Habel, 1878; Hackett, 1916; Harrower, 1925; Haya Fernández, 1719; Heath, 1913, 1927; Irias, 1853; James, 1942; Johnson, 1940; Juan and Ulloa, 1748; Kirchhoff, 1943; Lade, 1744; de Laet, 1640; Landecho and San Millan, 1559; Lara, 1912; Lehmann, 1915, 1920; Lines, 1938 a; Lothrop, 1926 b, 1937, 1942; Lutz, 1922; MacNiel, 1886; Maldonado, 1662; Margil, 1703; Mason, J. A., 1940; Matamoros, 1675; "M. W.," 1752; Oviedo y Valdés, 1851–55; Pavon, 1578; Pector, 1888–89; Peralta, 1883, 1890, 1892, 1901; Pim and Seeman, 1869; Pinart, 1885, 1887 a, 1887 b, 1900; Pinedo, 1709; Pittier de Fábrega, 1895, 1898, 1903, 1938 a, 1938 b, 1941; Ponce, 1873; Prince, 1913 a, 1913 b; Quiroga, 1535; Raveneau de Lussan, 1689; Rebullida, 1698; Requejo Salcedo, 1908 (1842); Ribera, 1571; Ricketson, 1940; de Rivera, 1569;

Rivet, 1911, 1924; Royal Cedula, 1521, 1740; Ruiz de Campos, 1631; Sáenz, 1675, 1676; Salinas y de la Cerda, 1651; Sandoval, 1638, San Francisco y Rios, 1703; San José, 1697; San José and Rebullida, 1699; Sapper, 1899; Schuchert, 1935; Seeman, 1853; Semano, 1536; Skinner, 1920; Sójo, 1605; Squier, 1852, 1853 a, 1856, 1858, 1859, 1860 a, 1860 b, 1908; Stewart, 1942; Stone, 1940 a, 1940 b, 1941, 1942, 1943; Strong, 1935; Strong, Kidder and Paul, 1938; Termer, 1914; Thomas and Swanton, 1911; Urcullu, 1763; Vázquez, 1714–16; Villacorta Calderón, 1942; Von Hagen, 1943; Wassén, 1935; Young, 1842.

The Archeology of Central America
THE ARCHEOLOGY OF CENTRAL AMERICA:
AN INTRODUCTION

By Wm. Duncan Strong

The geographic position of Central America, linking as it does the two great western continents (map 1), gives the area a great importance to the student of native peoples and cultural movements in pre-Columbian America. History and ethnology furnish much data on these later processes, but only archeology can reveal the earlier population and cultural interchanges that occurred during the as yet uncounted millennia from the first human occupation until the time of the Conquest. It is unfortunate, therefore, for present purposes that scientific archeology in the area has until now merely scratched the surface of what is obviously a rich and promising field.

Archeological materials from the various countries in Central America are abundant, but unfortunately the bulk of these are the result of treasure-hunting or chance discovery and lack scientific documentation. Nowhere in the isthmian region has archeological research uncovered cultural materials of demonstrable antiquity. When we consider the very limited amount of truly scientific exploration and stratigraphic excavation yet accomplished in the region this is hardly surprising. The occurrence of associated human and bison tracks in consolidated lava deposits in Nicaragua, however, strongly suggests that early cultural materials will be found here when more work is accomplished. At the other end of the time scale too little is yet known regarding the actual association of aboriginal cultural materials and documented historic or protohistoric sites. Lothrop has presented some evidence of this sort linking the historic and prehistoric in Panamá, Costa Rica, and Nicaragua, and similar beginnings have been made in Honduras. However, the historic approach must be emphasized far more than it has before the findings of archeology can assume their full significance in association with the relatively rich record of history and ethnology.

There follow brief articles on the present status of archeology in the various provinces of Panamá by Lothrop, who has been closely associated with recent work in this area. In regard to Costa Rica and Nicaragua very little has been published since the monumental summary, "Pottery of Costa Rica and Nicaragua," by Lothrop (1926 b), which appeared two decades ago. As a result, these two countries are here treated together by Strong in what is little more than a digest of Lothrop's two volumes with certain new findings added. Honduras has been the scene of certain stratigraphic excavations in recent years and is, therefore, summarized by Strong in a separate article. Finally, a general article on Central American archeology by Stone presents materials and an individual interpretation resulting from recent surveys in most of these countries.

It would be of great value to include a section concerning the archeology of the northern border of Central America as viewed from South America, notably including El Salvador and Guatemala, but this has not proved possible. There has been a great deal of recent exploration and excavation in these countries, particularly by the Carnegie Institution, but little of this material has yet appeared in print. The interpenetration of northern and southern cultural influences in Central America during the millennia of native occupation prior to the Conquest was naturally complex and variable in direction. From an archeological standpoint the territory included in the present Republic of Honduras seems today as logical a northern boundary for direct South American culture thrusts as any that might be chosen. However, the scientific findings and publications of tomorrow may well revise this judgment on numerous time levels.

THE ARCHEOLOGY OF HONDURAS

By Wm. Duncan Strong

INTRODUCTION

The archeology of Honduras (see map 3) is perhaps even less generally known than that of Costa Rica and Nicaragua, since it has never been made the subject of a general monograph such as that of Lothrop (1926 b, vols. 1, 2). On the other hand, northwestern Honduras has in recent years been the scene of several careful stratigraphic excavations. Hence, the all-important factor of relative time and cultural succession is not quite so obscure here as it is in southern Central America. This factor, coupled with the extremely spotty nature of present archeological knowledge concerning Honduras, necessitates a less generalized treatment than was possible in Costa Rica and Nicaragua and permits a somewhat more careful analysis of the nature of certain northern and southern prehistoric cultural thrusts as they intermingled along this very important borderland between predominantly South American and northern cultures and peoples.

For purposes of convenience we shall consider three rather arbitrary regions in Honduras. These are partially geographic and partially cultural in nature, their choice being determined quite as much by the haphazard distribution of available archeological data as by ecological factors. These tentative regions are (1) the northeast coast including the Bay Islands, (2) the Ulua-Yojoa region, and (3) central and southwestern Honduras. Of these, the northeast coast is geographically an extension of the Eastern Coastal Plain in Nicaragua (map 3), and the second region, centering around the Ulua River and Lake Yojoa, comprises most of northwestern Honduras. The third "region," central and southwestern Honduras, while geographically self-explanatory, is obviously neither a natural nor a cultural unit. From present inadequate surveys its southwestern portion would seem to have been predominantly *Maya* and *Pipil*, whereas central Honduras, on the basis of even less satisfactory surveys, seems to have been dominated by the *Lenca*. Of the earlier cultures in central and southwestern Honduras we as yet know nothing. The only detailed archeological reports on this region concern the famous *Maya* city of Copán. Since *Maya* civilization is so obviously of more northerly provenience it is discussed here primarily in regard to the manner in

71

which it impinges on the other Honduran cultures, historic and prehistoric. In the Ulua-Yojoa region we have considerable and significant evidence in this regard, but so far, little such evidence is available for southwestern or central Honduras. Since treatment of such major manifestations of *Maya* culture, as are represented at Copán and adjacent *Maya* sites, logically do not fall within the scope of a South American handbook, the reader will be referred to other sources in this regard.

Each of the three "regions" of Honduras will first be considered separately in the following discussion and the major sources will be indicated. Then such ethnic correlations as seem justified will be mentioned. Subsequently, the close relationships that exist between all three regions will be outlined and wider comparisons made. Owing to the fact that ceramic styles are better known than other cultural materials and therefore seem historically more significant, they may seem to be unduly stressed. This state of affairs, however, merely indicates the early pioneer stage so far attained concerning the archeology of Honduras.

THE NORTHEAST COAST REGION

EVIRONMENT

The northeast coast of Honduras is a swamp, savanna, and mountain area drained by the Aguán, Sico, and Paulaya (which unite to form the Black) and Patuca Rivers. (See map 3.) To assign southern limits to this area on archeological grounds is as yet impossible. For present purposes, however, we shall arbitrarily consider these as being formed by the Cordillera de Pijol in the west, and the northern rim of the valleys of the Guayape and Guampú Rivers (which together form the Patuca) in the east. On the Caribbean this northeast coast region in the same arbitrary manner can be considered as terminating on the west near the mouth of the Ulua River, and to the east at Cape Gracias a Dios on the modern Nicaraguan border. Present archeological knowledge of all this area is largely based upon reports resulting from hurried survey trips rather than on extensive excavations. The major sources on the northeast coast are Spinden (1925), Strong (1935), and Stone (1941).

SITES AND REMAINS

Mound groups.—The larger sites on the northeast coast of Honduras are marked by notable mound assemblages. These may be either irregular or formally laid out around rectangular courts. They consist of earth, rough stone, or both. In some cases earth mounds have outer walls composed of boulders or stone rubble. One large habitation area in the Bay Islands, the "Eighty Acre" site, consists of a large number of low refuse or house mounds, whereas the Plan Grande site on the island of Bonacca

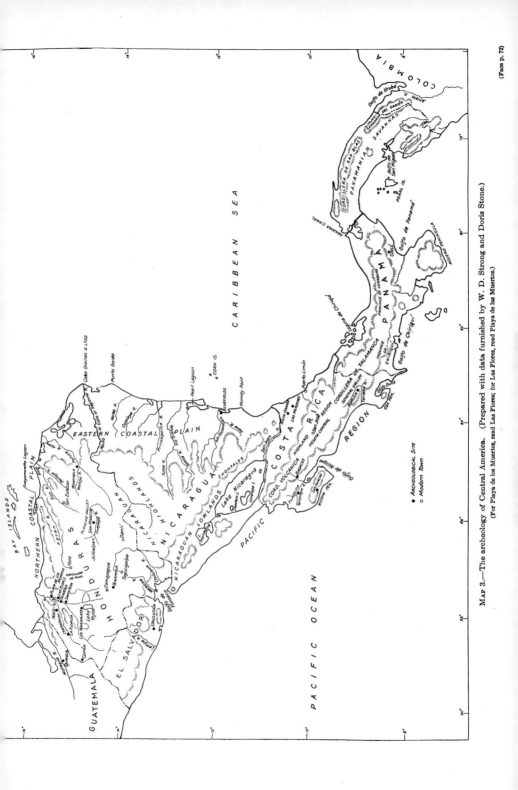

Map 3.—The archeology of Central America. (Prepared with data furnished by W. D. Strong and Doris Stone.)

(For Playa de los Muertos, read Las Flores; for Las Flores, read Playa de las Muertos.)

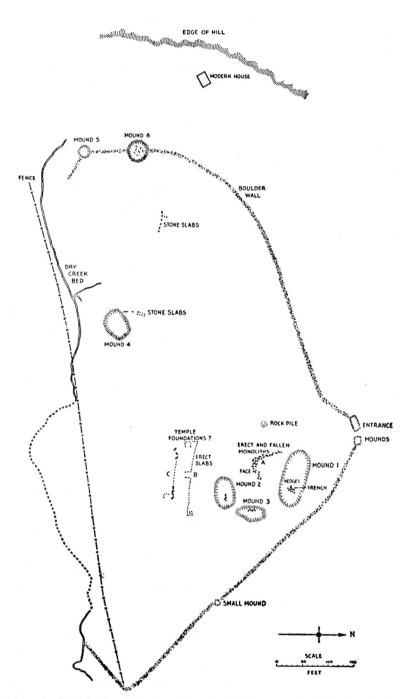

FIGURE 1.—Sketch map of the Plan Grande site, Bonacca, Bay Islands, Honduras.
(After Strong, 1935, fig. 35.)

is a vast enclosure bounded by a boulder wall around irregular earth mounds (fig. 1). Inside the wall at Plan Grande are also large rectangular foundations made of low erect stone slabs, and there is also a large irregular alignment of erect and fallen monolithic slabs of great size (Strong, 1935, p. 131). The "Eighty Acre" site was apparently a town, whereas Plan Grande suggests a ceremonial center.

On the adjacent mainland, in the vicinity of Trujillo, Stone (1941, p. 47) mentions an interesting mound complex apparently closely related to certain Bay Island cultural manifestations. These sites are marked by shell heaps, long, flat, habitation mounds, and circular ceremonial mounds. Unfortunately, data on the careful excavations of Junius Bird at one of these sites have not yet been published. To the north, in the Aguán Valley, Stone (1942, p. 380) describes two types of mounds, one of unworked stone, the other of earth with stone facings. Both types occur in irregular groupings and the earth mounds are the larger. This last mound type Stone assigns to the historic Sula-*Jicaque*. To the south, on the Tonjagua River near San Esteban, she describes a large, stone temple-mound ascended by a 7-foot stairway of large stones, surrounded by smaller mounds. This site she assigns to the historic *Paya*. Spinden (1925) reports numerous circular or oval village sites with moats and, at Bonito farm, mentions an oval, boulder enclosure containing a large temple-mound ascended by rough, stone-slab steps. Strong (1935, p. 160) has described a number of similar sites from the pine-forest area between the Olancho Valley and the north coast. These sites are marked by large earth mounds arranged to form rectangular enclosures. Long stone causeways or paved roads often lead from such sites to the nearest stream, and impressive but uncarved monoliths occur at several of them. On the headwaters of the Bonito River is a rather unique ruin with well-made stone walls consisting of three large rooms. The center room contains five large stone altars (Strong, 1935, p. 161; cf. Stone, 1941, p. 52). There are many earth and boulder mounds in the vicinity. The most easterly site so far described from the northeast coast region is at the junction of the Guampú and the Patuca Rivers (Strong, 1934 a; 1935, p. 161). This ruin, at Wanquíbila, consists of a complex arrangement of great earth mounds, some 100 yards (100 m.) long and 30 feet (about 10 m.) high, around a series of plazas. The earth mounds have burned-clay cores. The easterly occurrence of such great earth mounds arranged around plazas is important since similar sites occur in eastern Costa Rica (Costa Rica and Nicaragua, p. 131). The great intervening area between northeastern Honduras and Costa Rica is too little known to tell whether this distribution is continuous.

Canals.—The reported occurrence of artificial canals around Guaymoreto Lagoon has been mentioned. A similar canal is reported as separating Helena Island from Roatán in the Bay Islands (Strong, 1935.

FIGURE 2.—Incised design on erect stone at ceremonial site on Claura River northeastern Honduras. (After Spinden, 1925, fig. 4.)

p. 74). In neither case are present data adequate to determine the exact nature or function of such presumably artificial waterways.

Roads.—Stone-paved roads on the Bay Islands (Strong, 1935, p. 140) and similar roads connecting mounds and streams at northern mainland sites have also been mentioned.

Stone monuments.—Stone monuments are scarce on the northeast coast with the exception of clusters of large, erect monolithic slabs such as those which occur at Plan Grande (fig. 1). These menhir-like monuments (occasionally phallic) seem most characteristic of the area as a whole, although at times attempts at decoration occur. Spinden (1925, p. 539) discovered a plinth of this type on the northern mainland decorated with an elaborate incised design (fig. 2). The design is of particular interest since it depicts the widely distributed, overlapping-fanged monster, the head of which is surmounted by another creature (or headdress) suggesting the "alter ego" motif. A small steatite figure from an offertory spring on Bonacca Island is likewise surmounted by the figure of an animal (fig. 5, *right*). This use of the "alter ego" motif is similar to that employed in Nicaragua.

Petroglyphs.—Petroglyphs similar to those in eastern Nicaragua occur at several sites on the northeast coast of Honduras.

Offertories and burials.—Hilltop offertories on the Bay Islands consist of masses of broken pottery and contain numerous other specimens (Strong, 1935, pp. 142-143). Probably burials also occur in such sites, but the evidence in this regard is not clear. A Bay Island Polychrome pot (pl. 5, *c*) containing what appears to be a priest's outfit of some 487 carved green stone, shell, and copper ornaments (Strong, 1935, p. 53) occurred in one such site on Roatán Island. On offertory in a mineral spring on Bonacca Island (Strong, 1935, p. 123) and another in a hot spring in the Black River Valley (Stone, 1941, p. 28) seem quite similar. Spinden (1925) has described offertories on the northeast mainland where great stone tables, carved stone bowls, and metates occur (pl. 1, *top*).

On the northeast coast both flexed and extended burials have been reported in shell heaps. Urn and skull burials with some traces of cremation occur in the Bay Islands (pl. 1, *bottom*) and probably on the mainland as well. Burials likewise occur in caves, house mounds, and probably in connection with hilltop and other offertories. Further exploration and careful excavation are needed to define clearly the relative importance and exact nature of all these aboriginal manifestations.

CERAMICS

Introductory note.—In regard to ceramic styles on the northeast coast, certain of those on the Bay Islands have been described by Strong (1935) and on the mainland by Stone (1941). Monochrome pottery seems to be the most abundant ware in the region, and the majority of these ceramics can be considered as belonging to what is here designated as the North Coast Appliqué style. Recent comparison of the ceramic groups that I formerly designated as Bay Island Plain and Elaborate Monochrome (Strong, 1935), and Stone (1941) as Bay Island ware or "Paya" pottery, with those Highland Costa Rican types included by Lothrop (1926 b, vol. 2) within his Highland Appliqué Wares (p. 135) convinces me that these are all basically the same. For this reason the term North Coast Appliqué style for the Honduras variant seems fitting, since it points out the basic similarity to Highland Appliqué but allows for slight local differentiations. The designations "style" and "type" are employed in the present section, since this permits the use of the term "ware" for wider categories, such as monochrome versus bichrome, etc., which is not the case in discussing Costa Rica and Nicaragua (p. 126), where Lothrop's terminology is followed.

North Coast Appliqué style.—North Coast Appliqué style ceramics can, at present, be divided into three types: (*a*) Bay Island Monochrome type, so designated since the type was first defined here (Strong, 1935); (*b*) Ulua Marble Vaselike type (an awkward term but descriptive); and (*c*) Simple Painted type. Other types will doubtless be distinguished, but for the present these will suffice. North Coast Appliqué style ceramics, as a group, are predominantly monochrome, the surface ranging from rough unslipped to slipped and polished, the color from brown to red, and decoration being achieved by means of both appliqué and incision.

Bay Island Monochrome type.—The Bay Island Monochrome type (pls. 2, 3, *a–d*, and fig. 3) contains numerous forms, including rounded

FIGURE 3.—North Coast Appliqué style vessel forms, Bay Islands, Honduras. (After Strong, 1935, fig. 38.)

vessels with necks of varying height, cylindrical vessels with annular and tripod bases, and shoe-shaped, boat-shaped, and effigy vessels. Some vessels lack handles, but a wide variety of handles and modeled lugs occurs. Tripod legs are common, often elaborated in the form of human or animal heads, but legs seem generally shorter than is the case with Costa Rican Tripod Ware. Many small, ornate but crudely made vessels were apparently constructed primarily for ceremonial deposition (Strong, 1935, pls. 7, 8).

Ulua Marble Vaselike type.—The second type of vessel (pl. 5, *d*, *e*), is generally cylindrical, with an annular or flat base. The pots are decorated by incision and some appliqué, including ornate animalistic lugs. Rim and base are often decorated with incised step or scroll designs, and

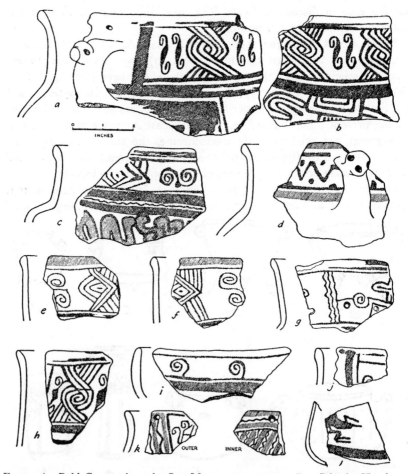

FIGURE 4.—Bold Geometric style, San Marcos type pottery, Bay Islands, Honduras. (White: red, brown, or orange; hatching: dark brown or dull black). (After Strong, 1935, fig. 11.)

the complex central design centers around a grotesquely conventionalized face surrounded by interlocking scrolls. The resemblance between these pottery vessels and the well-known, and exquisite, marble vases of the Ulua Valley is very striking (pl. 5, compare *d, e, f*). It is generally believed that pottery vessels of this type were made in imitation of the marble vases, but recently Stone (1941, p. 29) has suggested that the pottery vessels are the original prototype. Since this type of North Coast Appliqué style ceramics occurs in other associations in the Ulua-Yojoa region the problem will be discussed later.

Simple Painted type.—While the bulk of North Coast Appliqué pottery is monochrome, at least one limited type has simple painting in addition to basic decoration by appliqué and incision (pl. 3, *e, f*). This type seems so close to the Simple Painted Wares of Highland Costa Rica that it has here been similarly designated, the Simple Painted type. The type is less adequately defined even than the above. In all probability it contains pieces that blend with certain polychrome styles. Form, texture, and basic decoration, however, all indicate that the Simple Painted type or types pertain to the larger, North Coast Appliqué style rather than to any of the polychrome styles. In general, North Coast Appliqué style pottery seems to occur in somewhat variant forms throughout the entire northeast coast region as here defined. The exact boundaries of this distribution, and the finer type distinctions, remain to be determined.

Bay Island Polychrome style.—The most distinctive northeast coast polychrome style is that here designated as Bay Island Polychrome (formerly called Bay Island Polychrome I by Strong, 1935). The type is as yet poorly defined but appears to center on the Bay Islands and on the adjacent mainland, around and back from Guaymoreto Lagoon. (See map 3, p. 72). It is a thin polychrome ware characterized by an orange slip with complex designs in red and black (for color, see Strong, 1935, pl. 1). A cream-white slip is sometimes employed with black and red designs. The slip and paint appear to be rather easily eroded. Forms (fig. 5) are much the same as in North Coast Appliqué, but a pear-shaped vessel with flat, annular, or tripod base seems to predominate (pl. 5, *c*). Adequate examples are not available for complete design analysis, but these appear to be complex and florid. The main distinguishable design is a plumed deity or monster, perhaps the plumed serpent, with a foreshortened body (pl. 5, *c*). The main body design seems to be repeated in even more conventionalized form on the rim band and, probably, by the modeled lugs. It is a highly conventionalized art and suggests indirect Mexican or *Chorotegan* influence. Not only vessel forms but also modeled lugs are often identical with examples in the North Coast Appliqué style. For this reason, and also because no utilitarian vessels in Bay Island Polychrome style have been noted; it seems probable that the style represents a ceremonial aspect added to the more widespread monochrome Appliqué ceramic tradition. We shall discuss the probable significance of this in a later section.

Other styles and types.—The other polychrome styles so far distinguished on the northeast coast seem more representative of the Ulua-Yojoa region. One of these is the Ulua Bold Geometric style (formerly called Bay Island Polychrome II, Strong, 1935), which occurs on the Bay Islands and on the mainland. The examples of Bold Geometric style so far noted in the Bay Islands and on the adjacent mainland (fig. 4 and pl. 3, *g, h,*) seem to be of the later or San Marcos type on the Ulua River, which is characterized by the predominance of textile and geometric designs. Another polychrome style represented in casual finds from the Bay Islands (Strong, 1935, pl. 18, *a, c, e*) and the north coast suggests the Ulua-Mayoid style, and most of these seem to belong to the later or Las Flores type (pl. 6, *j–n*). Finally, a few sherds of Plumbate

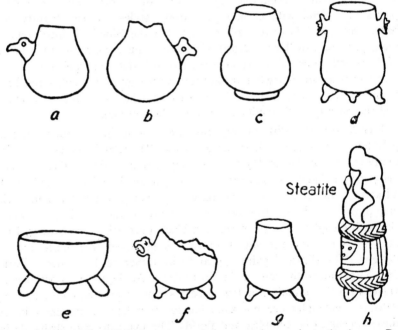

Figure 5.—Bay Island Polychrome vessel forms and carved steatite image, Bay Islands, Honduras. (After Strong, 1935, fig. 37.)

ware, in association with Bay Island Polychrome and Appliqué, were found on Barburata Island (Strong, 1935, p. 117). These ceramic styles and types will be discussed in connection with the Ulua-Yojoa region. A considerable variety of other pottery objects occur on the northeast coast; these include grotesque appliqué figurines, figurines on stools, crude realistic human faces, modeled whistles, and cylindrical and flat pottery stamps. The majority of these are figured by Strong (1935).

Ceramic stratigraphy.—So far no clear stratification of ceramic types has been reported from the northeast coast. Strong (1935, p. 145) pointed out that Bay Island Polychrome I and the more elaborate North Coast Appliqué were related and believed that both overlay the plainer monochrome pottery deposits in at least one Bay Island offertory site. This evidence is entirely observational and is not closely enough controlled to accept without further verification. His incorrect assumption that, stylistically, the Bold Geometric (Bay Island Polychrome II) style represented a degeneration from Bay Island Polychrome I and is therefore presumably later has already been corrected (Strong, Kidder, and Paul, 1938, pp. 119–120). We turn now to a brief consideration of other classes of artifacts in the northeast coast region.

NONCERAMIC ARTIFACTS

The nonceramic culture of the Bay Islands, so far as known, has been described in some detail elsewhere (Strong, 1935). For the remainder of the northeast coast region such data are scattered but, in general, indicate a rather close relationship to the Bay Islands.

Metals.—Metalwork seems to be rare in this region but does occur. Copper bells, including some cast to represent a feline face (pl. 4, *bottom*), were included in a votive cache within a Bay Island Polychrome vase (pl. 5, *c*) on Roatán Island, and a few other objects of copper including copper celts have been found (Strong, 1935). Gold or other metal objects have not been reported.

Ground stone.—Ground-stone objects, so far reported, include many carvings of a green stone (Strong, 1935; Stone, 1941). Though a few of these are of true jadeite the majority are of softer materials such as talc. These include a variety of human heads often elaborately plumed and feline faces (pl. 4, *top*). A large number of these, in association with a votive celt (Strong, 1935, pl. 12), were found in the previously mentioned hilltop offertory on Roatán Island. According to Stone (1941, p. 47, fig. 39), such carvings, including ax-gods (or votive celts) and very large cylindrical beads, are particularly common in sites around Guaymoreto Lagoon on the mainland adjacent to the Bay Islands. As previously noted, both Bay Island Polychrome and Bold Geometric style ceramics occur in this area. Stone (1941, p. 52) points out various resemblances such as the common occurrence of votive celts of greenstone in this small section of Honduras and in the Nicoya Peninsula in Costa Rica. Bay Island Polychrome ceramics are also somewhat reminiscent of the Nicoya Polychrome Ware, and the possibility that the Bay Islands and the adjacent Honduras mainland were, in some manner, more or less directly influenced by the Mexicanized or *Chorotegan* cultures of western Nicaragua and Costa Rica should be carefully considered in future studies. This is of particular interest since, generally, the pre-

FIGURE 6.—Bay Island Polychrome pottery, Bay Islands, Honduras. (White: orange-red; black: black; hatching: purplish red; cross-hatching: darker red.) (After Strong, 1935, fig. 21.)

historic cultures of the northeast coast of Honduras seem more closely related to the Highland than to the Pacific regions to the south.

To return to a consideration of ground-stone work on the northeast coast, simple marble bowls occur (Strong, 1935, p. 127), but the more elaborate type of Ulua marble vase has not been reported despite the fact that a very similar ceramic type occurs (p. 78 and pl. 5, *d, e*). The most characteristic stone bowl in this region is cylindrical, with or without legs, and with sculptured lugs and decorative bands in relief. These vessels often occur in votive caches (pl. 1, *top*). Such bowls are beautifully made and are often decorated with textile motifs. There is doubtless some cultural connection between this type and the Ulua Marble vases of similar form, as well as with similar stone vase types in Costa Rica. As in Highland Costa Rica, large stone tables occur (pl. 1, *top*), as do three-legged forms suggesting giant metates. A characteristic metate form on the northeast coast has three squared legs and a flat, ungrooved working surface surmounted by a bird, mammal, or conventionalized reptilian head. Legless mealing stones are common. Mullers are usually cylindrical, and a few giant specimens with anthropomorphic carving in relief have been found. As in Highland Costa Rica, stone pot-rests with legs and incised decoration have been reported from the Bay Islands (Strong, 1935, p. 108). Other polished stone artifacts include celts ranging from large to small size (the latter often of greenstone), T-shaped axes (which are sometimes perforated), a variety of mace heads (including star and mammiform types from the Bay Islands which are identical with specimens from Nicoya), grooved bark-beaters of both the cylindrical-handled and ovoid types, and a wide variety of carved and plain pendants and beads (all types illustrated, Strong, 1935).

Chipped stone.—Chipped-stone artifacts are not so common or striking as the above but do occur. (See W. and D. Popenoe, 1931, fig. 1.) They have been reported so far mainly from the Bay Islands. The finest specimens are beautifully chipped knives, of honey-colored stone, from the Bay Islands (Strong, 1935, pl. 16). They suggest sacrificial use. Ovoid obsidian points from the same islands may have been used either as knives or for projectile points (Strong, 1935, fig. 15). Small notched arrow points occur at Lancetilla on the mainland (W. and D. Popenoe, 1931, fig. 1). Prismatic flakes of obsidian seem to be a widely distributed and ancient type of knife in prehistoric Honduras. Crudely chipped T-shaped axes are rather abundant also.

Miscellaneous.—Other classes of artifacts known from the northeast coast include both shell- and bonework. Perforated conch shells, presumably used as trumpets, occur commonly at coastal sites. In association with the votive cache on Roatán Island, a six-pointed star and other pendants, labrets, danglers (of *Oliva porphyria*) and beads of shell were found (Strong, 1935, pl. 15). Perforated animal teeth, some with decorative carving, and various fragmentary bone implements constitute the only known artifacts of this material. From the above list it is obvious that, while perishable materials are rare in northeast coast sites, the list of nonceramic artifacts is still considerable. As indicated in the next section, this does not seem to be true of most sites in Ulua-Yojoa region.

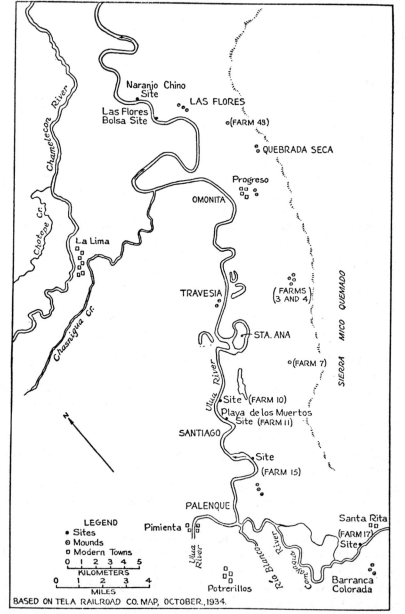

FIGURE 7.—Sketch map of the lower Ulua and Chamelecón Rivers, Honduras. (After Strong, Kidder, and Paul, 1938, fig. 5.)

THE ULUA-YOJOA REGION

SUMMARY OF RESEARCH

As discussed here this region can be regarded as representing a sampling of northwestern Honduras. Intensive archeological work, however, has so far been accomplished at only a few sites on the lower Ulna, Chamelecón, and Comayagua Rivers and around the northern end of Lake Yojoa. Surveys around the southern and western borders of this northwestern district (Yde, 1938) indicate that the majority of larger sites there are predominantly *Mayoid*. Such sites are not considered here. However, it must be remembered that, to date, the northwestern region of Honduras as a whole has been barely sampled by scientific archeologists, although it has long been and continues to be a collector's paradise. For this reason the following outline must be regarded as exploratory rather than definitive in outlining apparent culture sequences in an obviously rich and complex area. The region was first called to scientific attention by the work of Gordon (1898). The early Playa de los Muertos culture was isolated and defined by Popenoe (1934), and her work was followed up by the stratigraphic excavations of the Smithsonian Institution–Harvard University Expedition of 1936. (See Strong, Kidder, and Paul, 1938.) Stone (1941) has excavated at Travesia and has surveyed much of the area. Yde (1938) has also surveyed the region, and his report includes a good bibliographic and site index up to 1937. Culture-sequence data are to be derived primarily from Popenoe (1934) and Strong, Kidder, and Paul (1938).

SITES AND REMAINS

Mound groups and associated features.—The prehistoric structures of the Ulua-Yojoa area are similar to those of the northeast coast but in many cases are larger and more elaborate. In the Ulua Valley are a number of mound sites most of which are more or less formally arranged around plazas (Gordon, 1898, fig. 3). The mounds are usually of earth, often with burned-clay cores and sometimes capped or surrounded by rough stones. Some stone stairs, causeways, and encircling walls occur. Cut stonework and carving seems to be rather rare except at sites of probably *Mayoid* affiliations (Yde, 1938). No definitive work in mound sites has been accomplished except at Travesia (Stone, 1941), where stuccoed terraces, steps, altars, and courts have been uncovered. One of these terraces, believed to be a temple, was marked by the occurrence of crudely carved anthropomorphic designs on rock slabs (Stone, 1941, p. 61). Outlying "cache" mounds near the site contained masses of pottery of mixed styles and types. A somewhat similar site on the Chamelecón at Naco also has stucco-covered small pyramids and long earth mounds arranged around courts (Strong, Kidder, and Paul, 1938).

A ball court and stuccoed-house floors of various colors are also of interest at Naco, which is an historic *Nahuatl* site. Earlier sites on the Ulua and its immediate tributaries are refuse heaps, or burial grounds exposed by the cutting of the river and locally called Playas de los Muertos,

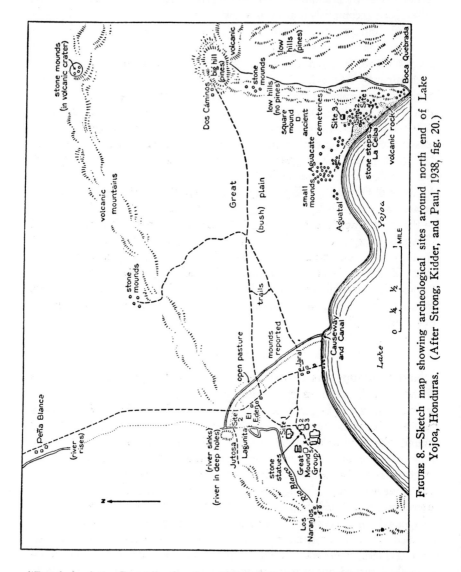

FIGURE 8.—Sketch map showing archeological sites around north end of Lake Yojoa, Honduras. (After Strong, Kidder, and Paul, 1938, fig. 20.)

"Beaches of the Dead." Gordon (1898), Popenoe (1934), and Strong, Kidder, and Paul (1938) all worked in these deeply sedimented sites. Adjacent to Lake Yojoa one large, formally arranged mound group is located at Los Naranjos (Yde, 1938; Strong, Kidder, and Paul, 1938), and many groups of low burial and habitation mounds occur in groups around the lake. The burial mounds, prior to the extensive looting of recent years, were rich in beautiful polychrome pottery. A canal, or earth causeway, 5 kilometers long, leading from the Río Blanco to the Lake, is an unusual and interesting feature here (fig. 8, and Strong, Kidder, and Paul, 1938).

Stone monuments.—Large stone sculpture is not abundant in the Ulua-Yojoa region. Gordon figures a crude anthropomorphic statue from near the Ulua (fig. 12, *c*), and several sculptures have been described from near Los Naranjos on Lake Yojoa (Yde, 1938; Strong, Kidder, and Paul, 1938, pl. 16). The most striking of these include a conventionalized serpent head of *Mayoid* type, a crudely realistic human torso with folded arms, a large apelike head which may belong to the body, and a cylindrical statue suggesting a giant roller pestle with a crude human figure in low relief and a columnar base. The last three statues are not *Mayoid* in style and suggest Nicaraguan or Costa Rican affiliations.

Burial places.—Along the Ulua, Chamelicón, and Comayagua Rivers the occurrence of both ancient and more recent prehistoric burial grounds, originally covered by sedimentation and later exposed by river erosion, has been mentioned. The earliest of these cemeteries so far excavated (Popenoe, 1934) pertains to the Playa de los Muertos culture and contained both flexed and unflexed burials. Later burial grounds of the polychrome pottery period excavated at Las Flores, the upper stratum at the Playa de los Muertos site, and Santa Rita, on the Ulua and lower Comayagua Rivers, contained badly preserved extended and some bundle burials. The burial mounds of the polychrome pottery period at Lake Yojoa are composed of black humous soil, and no skeletal parts were recovered except a few fragments of dental enamel. Earlier records of burials uncovered in this general region (Strong, 1935, p. 151) are interesting but lack scientific detail or later confirmation. Much more specific information on ancient methods of disposing of the dead, as well as concerning the physical types represented at various periods, can be obtained in the Ulua-Yojoa area, but the present published record is too inadequate for any generalizations to be drawn.

CERAMICS

Introductory note.—In regard to the complex ceramics of the Ulua-Yojoa region, the present discussion will be largely limited to those pottery styles and types which have been more or less stratigraphically placed. It is unfortunate that the final report on the 1936 Smithsonian Institution–Harvard University expedition incorporating the materials secured by Gordon (1898), Popenoe, et al., is not available. However, the major stratigraphic groupings have been outlined in a preliminary report (Strong, Kidder, and Paul, 1938), and an attempt will here be made to define and illustrate, briefly, but perhaps more specifically, the ceramic styles and types so far defined in the region under discussion.

Naco style.—On the Contact, or early historic, level the ceramic complex revealed at Naco is very distinctive. Both historic documentation and direct association with European materials indicate that aboriginal material from this site pertains to a late *Nahuatl* occupation. For present purposes we can designate this entire ceramic complex as the Naco style, since the present sample is inadequate for final subdivision into types. The most striking Naco ware has a white slip with painted geometric and curvilinear decorations on both surfaces in black and red (pl. 6, *a–g*). Plumed figures are apparently represented in some cases. Tripod bowls with a unique, four-pointed foot are characteristic. A small proportion of unpainted and a few painted sherds have either heavily incised or raised geometric designs on the inner surface (Strong, Kidder, and Paul, 1938, pl. 4). Textile-marked sherds also occur. These will probably form the basis for quite distinctive types. As is true at all other sites in Honduras, plain, utilitarian ware is far more abundant than decorated ware at Naco.

Ulua-Comayagua polychrome sequences.—Concerning the sequence and association of the rich polychrome pottery styles of the Ulua-Comayagua Valleys we have the pioneer work of Gordon (1898), the careful stratigraphic excavations of the Smithsonian Institution–Harvard University expedition of 1936 (Strong, Kidder, and Paul, 1938), and the later work of Stone (1941) at Travesia. The preliminary establishment of styles and types in a sequential series rests mainly on two sites, Las Flores on the Ulua River and Santa Rita on the lower Comayagua River. The details of stratification and methods employed are given elsewhere (Strong, Kidder, and Paul, 1938), but it may be stated that a 5.4-meter (about 18 feet) refuse deposit at Las Flores yielded prehistoric but relatively late polychrome ceramic types, whereas a similar deposit at Santa Rita revealed materials similar to Las Flores in the upper level but also had several continuous lower levels marked by somewhat earlier but closely related ceramic types. A still lower, discontinuous cultural level at Santa Rita yielded a quite different and earlier ceramic style, Ulua Bichrome, which will be discussed later. Considering the Las Flores-Santa Rita excavations as one overlapping unit, we can say that two major ceramic strains or decorative styles persist throughout the entire period represented by the 33- to 39-foot (10 to 12 m.) refuse accumulation. One of these major styles has been designated as Ulua Mayoid (pl. 8) and, as the name indicates, is obviously of *Mayan* and northern inspiration. The other major style has been designated as Ulua-Bold Geometric (pl. 7) and probably finds it closest analogues to the south and east in northern and central Honduras. Each of these styles can be more or less arbitrarily split into at least two types: the

Ulua-Mayoid into the Las Flores type (upper and later) and the Santa Rita type (lower and earlier); the Ulua-Bold Geometric into the San Marcos type (upper and later) and the Comayagua type (lower and earlier).

In the following description only the most salient characteristics of each style and selected type can be mentioned. It must be remembered that, since both styles occur intermingled throughout the same deposits, they were in all probability made by one, apparently culturally and ethnically composite, population. Under such circumstances a blending of ceramic traditions in numerous individual pieces is expectable and occurs. However, objective classification of these rich materials into the styles and types, representing the poles around which likenesses appear to cluster, reveals a remarkable stylistic dichotomy which undoubtedly has ethnological significance.

Ulua-Mayoid style.—The Ulua-Mayoid style as a single unit is rich and complex. Exclusive of the plain, utilitarian types, which are abundant but cannot be discussed here, the Ulua-Mayoid style is characterized by polychrome painting, rich design, modeling, use of molds, and engraving or incising. The most characteristic decorated form is a straight-walled, cylindrical vase with elaborate, polychrome designs.

Las Flores type.—The Las Flores, or later, type of the Ulua-Mayoid style (pl. 6, *j–n*) is characterized by red, black, white, or purple designs on a buff, orange, or red slip. These designs are complex, conventional, and at times rather crude. The over-all occurrence and flamboyancy of design in this type create a somewhat florid impression. The designs often seem to represent monstrous masks (pl. 6, *j*) or reptilian forms, and rim bands with skeuomorphic glyphs occur. The Las Flores type of straight-walled vase is relatively thick and usually has hollow cylindrical or rectangular tripod feet and two projecting monkey-head lugs (Strong, Kidder, and Paul, 1938, pl. 5, *f, g.*) Designs are sometimes outlined with incisions as well as painting, and both incised and well-carved designs occur (pl. 6, *m,* and Strong, Kidder, and Paul, 1938, pl. 5, *b, d, k, n*). In addition to the cylindrical vases there is a considerable variety of forms including small bowls and low jars. These latter forms often include single pieces decorated with various degrees of blending between the Mayoid and the Bold Geometric decorative traditions.

Santa Rita type.—The earlier or Santa Rita type, of the Ulua-Mayoid style is similar to the above but is finer in composition and decoration (pl. 8). Designs in red, black, white, purple, and (rarely) blue occur on white, black, and orange backgrounds. Though certain of these are very complex (pl. 8, *e*) the majority are more realistic (pl. 8, *a, b, d*) than in the Las Flores type. Seated or standing priestly and "dancing" figures (pl. 8, *a, b*) are of common occurrence. Some are definitely of the "processional" *Maya* type. The Santa Rita type vertical-walled vase is usually of thinner and of harder ware than the Las Flores type. It commonly has a flat bottom with no lugs (pl. 8, *a, b, d*). Flat plates on high tripod legs (pl. 8, *e, f*), elaborate modeled forms (pl. 8, *c*), and a considerable range of smaller jar and vase forms also occur in the Santa Rita type.

Mayoid carved pottery.—Mayoid sculptured and incised pottery (pl. 6, *m*) occurs in the lowest levels at Las Flores and in the upper levels at Santa Rita, and at both sites this carved subtype is in direct association with the Ulua Marble Vaselike ceramic type previously described (p. 78) as occurring in the northeast coast region. (Compare pl. 5, *d, e,* with Strong, Kidder, and Paul, 1938, pl. 6, *d-f.*) This association of Mayoid carved wares with Ulua Marble Vaselike vessels and sherds is significant and offers some objective basis to Stone's belief (p. 101) that *Maya* workmanship, as well as local artistic inspiration, was involved in the creation of the Ulua Marble Vase style. At present our ceramic classification is too broad to place exactly the Ulua Marble Vaselike ceramic type other than to say that it seems to form a link or cross tie between the upper (Las Flores) and lower (Santa Rita) levels (and ceramic types) of both the Ulua-Mayoid and Ulua-Bold Geometric styles in the Ulua district. (Cf. Strong, Kidder, and Paul, 1938, p. 51.)

Ulua-Bold Geometric style.—The Ulua-Bold Geometric style, as a whole, is quite distinctive from the Ulua-Mayoid style. The two styles, however, occur associated in the same sites, and various writers have erroneously attempted to arrange them in an evolutionary sequence. (See Strong, Kidder, and Paul, 1938, pp. 119–120.) Just as the vertical-walled vase best typifies the Ulua-Mayoid style, so a large-mouthed swollen-bodied olla with two vertical handles having monkey-head lugs (pl. 7, *a, b, d, e*) is the most characteristic Ulua-Bold Geometric style form. In regard to colors, a clear yellow to orange-red slip decorated with interlocking textile, geometric, and conventionalized animal designs in red and black is most common. Handled bottles (pl. 3, *g*), tripod (pl. 7, *c, f*) and open bowls, as well as other forms also occur.

San Marcos type.—The later, or San Marcos type, of the Ulua Bold Geometric style is named after a site in the Olancho District where the type was early segregated as an isolated unit (pl. 7, *a,* and Strong, 1934 b, fig. 54). At Las Flores and Santa Rita, the San Marcos type of Ulua-Bold Geometric occurs in the upper levels, intermingled, and sometimes blended, with Las Flores type ceramics of Ulua-Mayoid tradition. The typical San Marcos type monkey-handled vessel (pl. 7, *a, b*) is large and is often characterized by a broad band of interlocking textile design below the rim (pls. 6, *i;* 7, *a*). Body designs are usually geometric in red and black. Samples of San Marcos type pottery from Olancho and the northeast coast seem somewhat brighter in color than those from the Ulua-Yojoa region. (Cf. pls. 7, *a,* with 7, *b, c.*)

Comayagua type.—The earlier, or Comayagua, type of Ulua-Bold Geometric occurs in the lower levels at Santa Rita. It is very similar in form to the San Marcos type, but the characteristic monkey-handled and other vessels are somewhat smaller, thinner, and harder in composition. Geometric and textile designs occur on bowls, low vases, and large-handled vessels, but the most characteristic design on the Comayagua type consists of distinctive conventionalized birds, bats, and other animals (pl. 7, *d, e*). These unusual elongated designs often occur on both the body and the neck band of the vessel (pl. 7, *d*). Colors in the Comayagua type consist of bright yellow to orange backgrounds with striking black and red designs. In the lower levels at Santa Rita the Comayagua type of Ulua-Bold Geometric occurs in close association, and occasionally blends, with Santa Rita type ceramics of the Ulua-Mayoid style or tradition. Such, briefly, is the somewhat complex but sociologically significant association of polychrome ceramic wares as at present known in the Ulua region.

Ulua-Yojoa polychrome comparison.—The picture sketched in above regarding the association of polychrome ceramic styles on the Ulua is apparently repeated in equally interesting but somewhat condensed form for the Lake Yojoa district. Lake Yojoa sites are shallower but may be as old as or older than those on the Ulua. The beautiful ceramic collections so far collected from Lake Yojoa are in even greater need of thorough classification than are those from the Ulua. However, sufficient associational data are now available (Strong, Kidder, and Paul, 1938) to indicate that Lake Yojoa polychrome wares, like those of the Ulua, are grouped around at least two major stylistic poles and that these styles are associated together in time and place and occasionally blend on individual pieces. For all that, the two major styles are strikingly distinctive in cultural and artistic inspiration. These major styles are here termed the Yojoa-Mayoid (pl. 9, *c-f*) and the Yojoa Bold Animalistic (pl. 10, *a–d*). They occur together in rather shallow refuse deposits (Strong, Kidder, and Paul, 1938, p. 76, et seq.) and also in individual burial offerings in low mounds (pl. 9, *e–h*). So far they have not been split into earlier and later types. Yojoa-Mayoid style pottery is very similar, and often identical, with the Ulua-Mayoid, although the ware itself seems technically inferior. It is obviously of *Maya* inspiration. However, the decision whether the Ulua- and Yojoa-Mayoid styles should be grouped together must await adequate classification. The second style, Yojoa-Bold Animalistic, is characterized by the use of elaborate, conventionalized zoomorphic and geometric designs. The Yojoa-Bold Animalistic is seemingly quite distinctive from the Ulua-Bold Geometric style but would seem to have been derived from a related artistic tradition. This common stylistic basis is particularly striking in comparing conventionalized Yojoa bird and zoomorphic designs with those on Comayagua type vessels from the Ulua (pls. *7, d, e*; *10, a-d*). The Yojoa-Bold Animalistic style blends more closely with the Mayoid style than on the Ulua, but the origin of the animalistic style itself would seem to be non-Mayoid. Bold Animalistic designs often occur on, or in, open bowls, but monkey-handled ollas as well as tripod vessels with conventionalized designs similar to Ulua-Bold Geometric vessels also occur in the mixed Lake Yojoa polychrome deposits (pl. *10, e, f*). The intermingling, in time and place, that occurs between the two major styles, Mayoid and Bold Animalistic, is strikingly illustrated (pl. *9, e–h,* and Strong, 1937, figs. *75, 77*) in the contents of one Lake Yojoa grave that contains one fine Mayoid processional vessel (pl. *9, f*), one Bold Animalistic vessel with geometric neck designs (pl. *9, g*), and a third style (pl. *9, h*), closely related to the last, designated as Naranjos I by Stone (1941, fig. *75*).

Thus, segregation of styles according to burial contents at Lake Yojoa confirms the stylistic associations also specifically established in the refuse deposits. Space is lacking to amplify this necessarily complex discussion, but it seems clearly indicated that during the period characterized by ornate polychrome pottery in both the Ulua and Yojoa regions two quite distinctive ceramic decorative styles were contemporaneously in vogue among the same populations. Both styles persisted together, intermingling in part but still distinctive, over a considerable period of time. One of these traditions was definitely northern and Mayoid. In regard to the other we can only say at present that it was not Mayoid, may well have been local, and perhaps had southern affiliations.

A still further parallel in ceramic and stylistic associations between the Yojoa polychrome deposits and those of the Ulua is the common occurrence in both of Ulua Marble Vaselike vessels in association with Mayoid carved or sculptured vessels (pl. *10, g, h*). Much careful distributional and stratigraphic as well as grave segregation work remains to be accomplished before we can delimit these complex and frequently hybridized styles in space and time and objectively subdivide them into an adequate number of types. Stone's work (1941) at Travesia indicates that Yojoa Bold Animalistic type vessels occur at Ulua sites, apparently in direct association with Mayoid and Bold Geometric style pottery. However, the excavation data presented, demonstrating the association between various structures at Travesia and between these and the wide range of ceramic styles and types encountered, leave much to be desired. Very early ceramic types (Stone, 1941, p. 57, fig. *85, b, e, j*), quite possibly included in the fill of later mounds, are discussed as if they were actually contemporary with polychrome wares demonstrably later at other sites. As subsequent discussion (p. 117) points out, this seems highly improbable.

Various pottery objects.—A wide variety of modeled human and animal figures, modeled whistles, molds, handled incensarios, candelarios, and both flat and roller stamps, all made from pottery, occur in refuse deposits and graves characterized by the Ulua and Yojoa polychrome pottery styles (Gordon, 1898; Strong, Kidder, and Paul, 1938, fig. 7; Stone, 1941). The majority of these are of monochrome pottery, but there is no doubt as to their association with the polychrome horizons. Earlier forms than these do occur (pls. 11, *n, r;* 12, *j, k*), and, while some of these are fairly distinctive, even they have not yet been analyzed carefully enough to be safely classified unless their exact provenience is known. As for the riot of modeled and molded figurines and similar objects associated with the polychrome wares, not even a preliminary classification has yet been attempted. For this reason attention is called to their occurrence and the promising problems they present. A condensed discussion here of such complex and as yet unclassified materials, however, would have little value.

Early horizons.—Turning now to the ceramic complexes or styles which can be objectively demonstrated as preceding the polychrome wares of the Ulua-Yojoa region in time, we have three which belong to what Thompson (1943) has termed the Formative Period in Middle American prehistory. None of these ceramic styles is fully known and none has as yet been carefully classified. However, their major characteristics and relative age are quite clear, and these may be briefly outlined.

Ulua Bichrome.—The first of these has been tentatively designated as Ulua Bichrome (Strong, Kidder, and Paul, 1938, pp. 61–62, fig. 6 and pl. 9). The provenience of this material is clear; it lay below and was separated by a sterile sand layer from the lowest polychrome levels (Strong, Kidder, and Paul, 1938, fig. 6). Two Ulua Mayoid sherds of the finest Santa Rita type which occurred above the sterile sand layer capping the Ulua Bichrome deposits have been illustrated elsewhere (Strong, Kidder, and Paul, 1938, pl. 9, *t*). However, owing to the depth of this excavation and its flooding by the rising river, the available sample of Ulua Bichrome pottery is small. All sherds from this deep horizon are monochrome or bichrome, and polychrome sherds are totally lacking. Aside from the coarse utilitarian ware, which has not yet been analyzed, the Ulua Bichrome ceramic materials are highly distinctive. One type, having an orange slip decorated with faded red or black linear designs (pl. 11, *g*), is apparently Usulután Ware. The decoration on this type closely resembles negative painting because of the brighter slip and dull, faded designs. Some of the pieces may prove to be negative-painted when carefully studied. One coarse sherd from a flat tripod vessel has crisscross red lines on a dull white slip. The majority of the thin, orange and red, slipped sherds seem to come from small flat-bottomed vessels having small, solid, tripod or tetrapod feet. The occurrence of rocker-

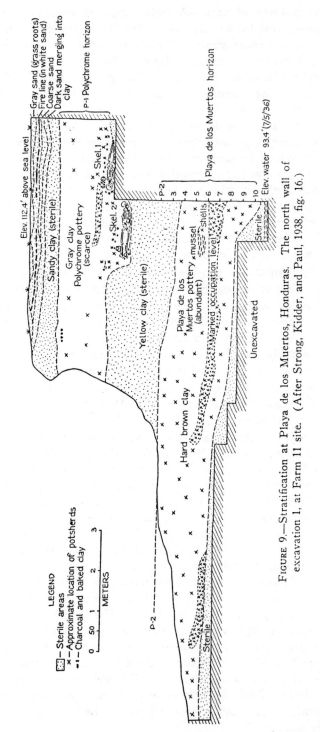

FIGURE 9.—Stratification at Playa de los Muertos, Honduras. The north wall of excavation 1, at Farm 11 site. (After Strong, Kidder, and Paul, 1938, fig. 16.)

stamp decoration is of interest (pl. 11, *b*).   Everted lips with broad incisions on the upper surface (pl. 11, *d, n*), swollen, comma-shaped lips, and a few simple painted designs are among the specific characteristics which link the present small sampling of Ulua Bichrome with the Playa de los Muertos ceramic style.   Aside from pottery, the only other clay artifact type from the Ulua Bichrome horizon was a vertical stamp with geometric design (pl. 11, *i*).

Playa de los Muertos style.—As previously stated, the Playa de los Muertos horizon in Honduras was first isolated in a series of deep burials

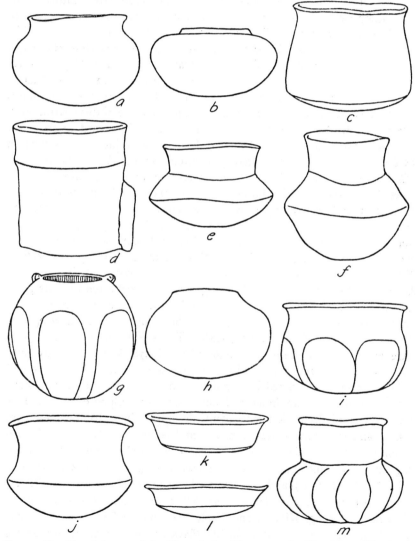

FIGURE 10.—Vessel forms of the Playa de los Muertos style, Ulua River, Honduras. (After Popenoe, 1934, and Strong, Kidder, and Paul, 1938, fig. 17.)

by Dorothy H. Popenoe (1934). Gordon's mixed collections secured near the same site include a considerable number of complete Playa de los Muertos pottery vessels (Gordon, 1898, pl. 7, *n–u,* and possibly *a–c, d, e, h, i*), indicating that his deepest excavation had reached this burial horizon. These include the majority of unbroken vessels he figures. However, a detailed analysis of Gordon's materials has not yet been attempted. In 1936 the Smithsonian Institution–Harvard University expedition's excavation at Farm 11 (Playa de los Muertos, fig. 7) revealed a strikingly clear, discontinuous stratification, with Ulua Polychrome Period refuse and burials above, and Playa de los Muertos culture refuse and occupation levels below, the two cultural horizons being separated by 2 meters of sterile yellow clay (fig. 9). Stone (1941, pp. 56–57) obscures a very clear situation when she confuses this clean-cut major stratification between two distinct cultural horizons with Popenoe's remarks concerning possible slight differences in the Playa de los Muertos burials alone. The ceramics from the Playa de los Muertos living levels and burials are rather complex, and only a bare outline of their major characteristics can be given here. As was the case in regard to the Ulua Bichrome horizon at Santa Rita, the deep Playa de los Muertos horizon at Farm 11 did not yield a single polychrome sherd. Vessel forms (figs. 10, 11) in the Playa de los Muertos style include straight-walled, but irregular, vases with flat bottoms; lower, open bowls of composite silhouette; round-bottomed pots with constricted orifices and necks ranging from direct lips to tall, flaring spouts (Strong, 1937, fig. 76, *upper left*) ; similar pots with single spouts (including human and animal effigy vessels), and open bowls with thick lips, comma-shaped in cross section. The great bulk of the ware is of monochrome type, and five subtypes have been distinguished: (1) Unslipped, rough, bricky-red to sooty gray, (2) slipped and polished orange-red to brown, (3) dark gray to black, highly polished ware, (4) slate-gray to buff, highly polished ware, and (5) ware with a chalky, white wash. The second, or painted, type is rare but forms a definite ingredient of the Playa de los Muertos style. Irregular areas are painted with red, red and black, and red and buff colors, sometimes outlined by incisions, while a few sherds have blotchy white designs on both inner and outer surfaces. Opposed to this rare and haphazard decoration with paint, decoration by polishing, broad incising, and modeling is very common and is competently executed. Incision with broad lines occurs on necks, bodies, and everted lips. Modeling on vessels includes human and animal effigies of some complexity (fig. 11, *b;* pl. 5, *a*) and the human hand in relief. Paneling, the use of flanges, and some filleting also occur. Further details are given elsewhere (Strong, Kidder, and Paul, 1938, pp. 73–75), but a complete and distinctive study of all available Playa de los Muertos materials has not yet been made. It is obviously an important and early style, char-

FIGURE 11.—Vessel forms of the Playa de los Muertos style, Ulua River, Honduras. (After Popenoe, 1934, and Strong, Kidder, and Paul, 1938, fig. 18.)

acterized by competent polished and incised decoration, as well as a little rather amateurish and, apparently, experimental work in simple painting.

Aside from pottery, the clay figurines known actually to have come from deposits of the Playa de los Muertos cultures are particularly interesting (pl. 12, *j, k;* fig. 11, *i*). All these are hand-modeled, but both a solid, naturalistic, and unslipped form (pl. 12, *k*) and a hollow, conventionalized, slipped and polished form (pl. 12, *j*) were recovered from the refuse deposits. Popenoe's burials yielded both an elaborate naturalistic (fig. 11, *f*) and a cruder conventionalized form (fig. 11, *i*). Gordon (1898, pl. 10, *d, f, g*) figures three of the solid, seated, and naturalistic forms, as well as others which may belong to the Playa de los Muertos horizon. It is obvious that a variety of figurine types is represented in the Playa de los Muertos cultural horizon, as is even more true of the later, more complex Ulua-Yojoa polychrome horizons. Since the figurine forms are so complex in both horizons and those of neither group have been either carefully studied or classified, it is extremely hazardous to speak of a "Playa de los Muertos type" of figurine heads of unstated provenience as Stone does (1941, fig. 45). Likewise, the theory that this ancient culture, or integral units of it, survived "until quite late" times in the Ulua Valley (Stone, 1941, p. 57) must be based on more closely controlled evidence than has yet appeared to support it.

The Playa de los Muertos culture awaits adequate definition and description based upon further study and skilled excavation, but there can be no doubt that it is one of the very early and formative ceramic cultures of Middle America.

Yojoa "Monochrome" style.—The third early culture revealed in Honduras was discovered at Los Naranjos near Lake Yojoa (Strong, Kidder, and Paul, 1938, pp. 111–125, figs. 31, 32). Two excavations carried through the upper layers containing Yojoa polychrome cultural materials penetrated through a meter of sterile yellow clay and gravel into a deeper and hitherto unknown cultural horizon. This horizon has been barely tested, since time was then lacking to explore it thoroughly. The pottery sample from this early level has been tentatively designated as the Yojoa "Monochrome" style, since the bulk of the material is of this type. However, a very few two-color sherds are present, and this tentative name for the style should probably be changed when this cultural horizon has been more thoroughly explored. The Yojoa "Monochrome" ware is seemingly very crude and simple (pl. 11, *n–t*) and is crumbly in texture, and some of the sherds appear to be waterworn. Rim sherds show a majority of low, slightly flaring lips. Some of these are swollen, and both vertical and slightly flaring rims are present. The majority of basal sherds are from small, flat-bottomed vessels. No spouts, handles, lugs, or feet are present in the available collection (about 700 sherds). Only 12 sherds show traces of slip or paint. The others range in color from dull buff, through dull red, to a grayish black. Despite the obvious erosion on many sherds, the majority do not appear to have been slipped or painted. The painted sherds include eight that have faded red or pinkish slip (pl. 11, *q*), two with a dull white slip or wash, and two that have definite areas painted a dull red and black on the inner surface. Three figurine fragments (pl. 11, *n–r*) are of solid, unslipped clay and are apparently hand-modeled. These bear some resemblance to the cruder Playa de los Muertos type of figurine. If the present sample is at all adequate, this, the oldest known Lake Yojoa pottery style, appears to be the most primitive ceramic type yet encountered in Honduras, and possibly in all Central America. Technically, since a few sherds are painted, we should designate this ware as Yojoa Bichrome. However, the great majority of sherds are unpainted, and all of them are definitely inferior in texture and finish to either the Playa de los Muertos style or the Santa Rita Bichrome style. For this reason it has been tentatively designated as Yojoa "Monochrome" subject to change when an adequate sample is at hand for classification.

No very obvious relationship, other than the prevalence of monochrome, small, flat-bottomed vessels, exists between Yojoa "Monochrome" ceramics and the Ulua Bichrome style and even less between the former and the Playa de los Muertos style. This is very puzzling, since local people have dug up typical, spouted, incised and painted, Playa de los Muertos vessels (pl. 5, *a, b*) at this same site. The occurrence of these two obviously early styles, as well as the rich Yojoa polychrome styles in the upper levels, at Los Naranjos makes this site one of very great promise in regard to the possibility of determining the nature and sequence of a number of prehistoric cultures in Honduras. This promise is enhanced by the fact that, unlike the deeply sedimented archeological horizons on the northern river banks, these similar early horizons at Lake Yojoa seem to be relatively quite shallow.

NONCERAMIC ARTIFACTS

Concerning nonceramic artifacts from the Ulua-Yojoa region the outstanding fact is the paucity of the record. This can be partially accounted for on the grounds that the majority of pieces reaching our museums have been collector's items, such selection being in vogue even among scientific archeologists until rather recent times. However, the results of recent excavations where every artifact has been preserved are not strikingly different. In this regard the work of the Smithsonian Institution–Harvard University expedition in 1936 revealed very little nonceramic material from sites on the Ulua and Comayagua but relatively more from sites near Lake Yojoa. The reasons for such local differences are not clear. There follows a synoptic discussion of such materials mentioned in the literature. This could undoubtedly be amplified were it possible to include a study of all museum collections from this region.

Metal.—Metalworking seems to have been uncommon in the Ulua-Yojoa region, and the few pieces on record seem to be mainly the result of trade in late periods. At Las Flores, one barbless, copper fishhook was the only metal object encountered in the entire season's work on the Ulua and at Lake Yojoa (Strong, Kidder, and Paul, 1938, p. 41). A report that gold objects had been found in burial mounds at Lake Yojoa (Stone, 1934 a) seems to have no foundation in fact. Blackiston (1910) reported a great cache of copper bells (similar to those from the Bay Islands, pl. 9) from a cave near the Chamelicón River. According to Spinden these probably formed part of a *Toltec* trader's outfit. Steinmayer (1932) gives an analysis of one copper celt from the Ulua. Spinden states also (1925, p. 54) that one of two Ulua marble vases uncovered near Santa Ana contained a Costa Rican gold amulet of the type traded in to Chichen Itzá in a late period. From the sporadic nature of the record there seems to be little doubt that trade in metallic objects in the Ulua-Yojoa region was late and relatively unimportant. As regards metalworking the evidence is equally meager. Las Casas (see Strong, 1935, pl. 11) speaks of the native traders encountered by Columbus in the Bay Islands as having "small copper hatchets to cut wood and bells and some medals, [as well as] crucibles to melt the copper." Gordon (1898, fig. 34) illustrates "crucible-like objects of clay," but there is no evidence that they were thus employed. The occurrence of one copper fishhook with a burial at Las Flores indicates that copper was used in the later polychrome period. However, until contradictory evidence is at hand, metalworking, or even extensive trade in metals, does not seem to have been characteristic of the Ulua-Yojoa region.

Ground stone.—*Marble vases.*—In ground stone the carved marble vases of the Ulua are justly outstanding (pl. 5, *f*). The art style represented on such vases has been analyzed by Gordon (1898) and Stone (1938) and need not be discussed in detail here. The finding of several of these vases has been reported by archeologists (Spinden, 1925; Steinmayer, 1932; Stone, 1938, p. 39), but in each case the data concerning the exact provenience and association of such discoveries are tantalizingly vague. Spinden's statement that a Costa Rican gold amulet of late type occurred in one of these vessels has previously been mentioned. Every effort was made by the Smithsonian Institution–Harvard University expedition in 1936 to secure even a fragment of such a vase in situ so that the type could be positively correlated with the ceramic sequence, but none were encountered.

Lacking adequate data on the marble vases themselves, one is forced to fall back upon known occurrences of the Ulua Marble Vaselike ceramic type (pp. 78–79), which is indubitably closely related to the Ulua marble vase in style (pl. 5, *d-f*). The possible range in time represented by this interesting ceramic type is indicated in figure 15 (p. 113). This ceramic type on the Ulua occurs overlapping the Las Flores and the Santa Rita polychrome periods, but its earliest and latest extensions in time are uncertain. Throughout its known occurrence on the Ulua it seems to be closely associated with Mayoid sculptured and carved pottery. As previously stated, this does suggest that the fullblown Ulua Marble vase style was the result of a fusion of two art styles, the one Mayoid, and the other the one that was responsible for the Bold Geometric tradition in Ulua ceramics.

Since the great majority of Ulua Marble Vaselike vessels are so standardized, they suggest cheaper copies of rare objects rather than originals, or prototypes, as Stone (1941, p. 29) has recently suggested. Spinden (1925, p. 540) derives the two-handled, cylindrical, and decorated stone bowls, characteristic of northeastern Honduras (pl. 1, *top*), from the *Maya* pottery vase of this type, whereas Stone (1938, p. 10) believes that the pottery form may well have been derived from the more southerly stone vessels. The pottery sequence at Las Flores and Santa Rita tends to support Stone's view, since two-handled, tripod vases of Mayoid type are late here and associated with the Ulua Marble Vaselike type, whereas the early Mayoid cylindrical vases at Santa Rita are flat-bottomed and without lugs, as is also true in early periods in the great *Maya* cities. Unfortunately, the northeastern Honduras and Costa Rican type of double-banded stone bowl has not yet received any careful study, but it seems probable that it is a southerly form of which the delicate, annular-based Ulua marble vase is merely a highly specialized and very important type. The fact that it was so often copied in pottery, which is distributed beyond the range of the marble vases themselves, bears this out.

Until further evidence comes to hand the Ulua Marble vase seems best explained as representing a localized, and relatively late, artistic climax in the Ulua region. It would seem to have been derived from an older, southern, stone bowl-working tradition, locally combined on the Ulua with a delicacy of execution which may well have been borrowed from associated artists of *Mayan* extraction. That its form and design remained relatively static over a considerable period, as demonstrated by the known time range of its pottery imitations, suggests that this vase form and its elaborated feline and scroll motifs had the very highest ceremonial importance in all northern Honduras.

Metates, manos, pestles.—The flat, undecorated, three-legged metate seems to have been the characteristic form in the Ulua-Yojoa region. At Lake Yojoa, sites of the polychrome pottery period had three-legged metates, the majority of which had a broad grinding groove. Flat, ovoid lapstones were common there. Manos are usually cylindrical or rectangular. A conical stone pestle was found at Las Flores. Three shallow bed-rock mortars at Los Naranjos on Lake Yojoa seem unique. In the older "Monochrome" horizon at Lake Yojoa rectagular manos with battered ends and fragments of sandstone grinders occurred.

Miscellaneous objects of ground stone.—The recorded range of other polished artifact types in the region is not large. From Ulua sites of the polychrome pottery period it includes rectangular bark beaters, large and small celts (including those of greenstone), and a square, flat, polished knife (Santa Rita). From Lake Yojoa sites of the same period came double-ended hammerstones; large and small celts (including those of jadeite and other greenstone); cylindrical and ovoid bark-beaters; an ovoid wedge, or chisel, of greenstone; small round stone balls; and jadeite and brown stone beads. Jadeite and greenstone carved faces and plaques have been collected on the Ulua and at Lake Yojoa, apparently from the polychrome horizon, but there are no good records for such discoveries. (See W. and D. Popenoe, 1931, fig. 6.) In the Old Playa de los Muertos refuse deposits polishing stones and jadeite beads were recovered, and Popenoe (1934) found celts, a rough stone knife, and jadeite amulets, pendants, and beads with burials of this culture. These have not yet been described in any detail. This lack of detailed information on work in jadeite and allied materials, from either the polychrome or the Playa de los Muertos deposits, is extremely unfortunate since it prevents any comparison of earlier and later forms.

Chipped stone.—Work in chipped, or flaked, stone in the Ulua-Yojoa region is even more scantily represented than are ground-stone forms. The prismatic flake knife of obsidian occurs in historic Naco and practically all other earlier sites. A cache of these knives with needle-sharp points occurred with a burial at Las Flores, as did T-shaped obsidian drills and very crudely retouched stone flakes. In the Lake Yojoa polychrome deposits were obsidian and quartzite side scrapers, prismatic obsidian knives, and one planoconvex, obsidian dart point with a tapering stem. The Playa de los Muertos horizon yielded prismatic obsidian knives and retouched obsidian flakes, while the "Monochrome" horizon at Lake Yojoa contained obsidian flakes and one flint side-scraper.

Miscellaneous.—Work in other materials was even less abundant; perforated conch shells occur at Ulua sites, a perforated bone at Las Flores, ground-down animal ribs at Santa Rita, and necklaces of shell beads with Playa de los Muertos burials (Popenoe, 1934).

Even though the above summary includes only a small proportion of the nonceramic materials so far recovered, but not recorded, from the Ulua-Yojoa region, the list is still strikingly limited. On the Bay Islands, and adjacent mainland, offertory caches seem to have yielded the largest range of artifact types, but if such occur in the Ulua-Yojoa region they have not yet been reported. It is undoubtedly significant that rich refuse deposits such as those at Las Flores, Santa Rita, Playa de los Muertos, and the Yojoa burial and habitation mounds yield abundant ceramic but very few other artifact types. Conditions of preservation in this humid jungle country are notably bad, and stone materials are rather scarce; hence, the most probable explanation is that outside of pottery and a few stone artifacts, the material culture of these advanced peoples was largely based on the use of wood, fiber, bone, and shell, of which all but the smallest traces have disappeared. The textile-marked pottery at Naco, like the abundant spindle whorls occurring there and, more rarely, in polychrome period sites, all bears out the record of history that this was an advanced center for the textile arts. Further evidence of this sort must be carefully sought for if the full record of a series of very important Middle American cultures is to become clear.

CENTRAL AND SOUTHWESTERN HONDURAS

SUMMARY OF RESEARCH

Concerning the archeology of this large and important region it is impossible at the present time to write any systematic account. With the exception of the great *Maya* city of Copán, with which we are only indirectly concerned in this summary, there has not been one piece of systematic excavation work in the entire area. The few archeological surveys so far attempted have covered only a small portion of the area. For this reason a brief synopsis of certain observations and a consideration of certain major problems in the region must suffice. For present purposes we will subdivide the region into the following subareas: (*a*) Copán and the upper Chamelicón River Valley; (*b*) the Comayagua Valley; (*c*) the Tegucigalpa area; (*d*) the Olancho Valley; and (*e*) the Pacific or Fonesca Bay area.

Copán and the upper Chamelicón River Valley.—A number of sites on the upper and lower Chamelicón River have been described by Yde (1938), Strong, Kidder, and Paul (1938), and others. Those on the lower river, around and above Naco, appear to be *Mayan,* and the majority of stone carvings from sites on the upper Chamelicón, such as La Florida and El Puente, are undoubtedly *Mayan* (Yde, 1938). The same is true in regard to Paraíso, on an affluent of the Motagua River, as well as a considerable number of sites on the upper Copán River. (See map, fig. 24, *a;* Yde, 1938, p. 49.) Aside from one distinctive stone carving from La Florida (fig. 12, *b*) no non-*Mayan* remains have so far been encountered in the very limited archeological surveys so far attempted in this rich area.

Non-Mayan stone sculpture.—Whether the *Mayan* occupation of the site of Copán itself was preceded by that of another and earlier culture seems to be a disputed question. The vast majority of the stone carving and construction work at this great site is undoubtedly *Mayan,* but certain stone carvings and ceramic types encountered in the older horizons of the city may pertain to an earlier occupation. Since these and similar evidence of cultural interpenetration have a direct bearing on the problem of culture sequence in Honduras, they must be briefly considered, although any detailed discussion of Copán or other *Mayan* sites is beyond the scope of the present summary.

Among the numerous stone statues in southwestern Honduras that are definitely *Mayan* in inspiration there are several which seem to have other cultural affiliations (fig. 12). Two of these, thought by Lothrop to be non-Mayoid, were found built into the foundations of stelae (5 and 4) at Copán and presumably antedate the *Mayan* occupation at that site (fig. 12, *d*; Lothrop, 1921, fig. 70, *d, e*). Lothrop believes that these two statues, one of which has since disappeared, are stylistically related to both Nicaraguan and Guatemalan Highland statues of non-*Mayan* origin. The same is thought to be true regarding an "alter ego" statue at La Florida (fig. 12, *b*) and the crude anthropomorph from the Ulua (fig. 12, *c*) figured by Gordon. A feline figure or a tall pedestal from Octopeque Province in southwestern Honduras (fig. 12, *a*) is also similar to "peg-based" statues from Nicaragua, Costa Rica, and the Guatemalan Highlands. Richardson (1940, p. 410) doubts the suggested relationship between the substelae statues at Copán with the Nicaragua-La Florida type of sculptures for the following reasons: (1) There is no "alter ego" motif in the Copán statues; (2) they are not on a pedestal, column, or pillar; (3) they have necklaces, clothing, and feather ornaments, which are more characteristic of *Mayan* than Nicaraguan sculpture; (4) the neck appendage on one Copán statue differs from such appendages found in Nicaragua; (5) they are merely delineated on a boulder and not entirely sculptured out; and (6) the figure from stela 4 is of local Copán stone. He believes, however, that the two statues in question are far removed from the traditional *Mayan* style at Copán and may well be related to the "crude group" at Kaminaljuyú; and he suggests that they might belong to an early non-*Mayan* horizon represented by the early occurrence of Usulután ware at Copán. This opens interesting possibilities, since at Kaminaljuyú, in the Guatemalan Highland, rather similar "crude" statues, are said to be associated with what has been termed "Archaic" pottery (Richardson, 1940, p. 399).

Ceramic correlations with Formative Maya.—Unfortunately, the published data concerning the sequence of ceramic styles at Copán and southern *Maya* sites are as yet far from adequate. Vaillant's earlier correlation (1927) of ceramic styles and dated stelae is not adequately illustrated and should be brought up to date. Various interesting suggestions made by Longyear (1940, 1942) are based on first-hand study of both older and recent ceramic collections from Copán and other *Mayan* sites, but his published articles are very brief and generalized. However, the following suggested pottery correlations between Petén and *Southern Maya* seem plausible and have a direct bearing on the sequence and probable dating of

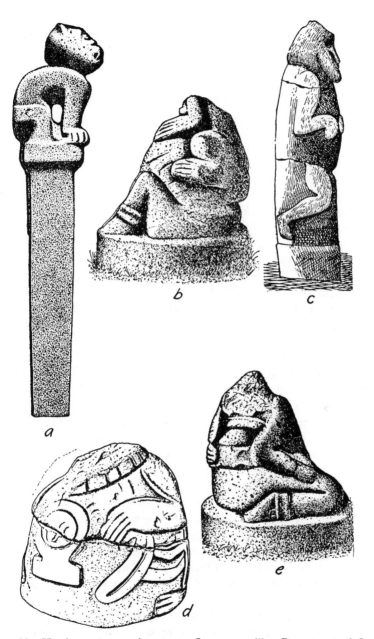

FIGURE 12.—Honduras stone sculptures. *a,* Jaguar on pillar, Department of Ocotepeque (height 4 ft. 2 in. (1.28 m.)).   *b,* Human figure, La Florida, Department
of Copán (height 2 ft. 8 in. (0.80 m.)).   *c,* Stone statue, Ulua River. *d,* Human
figure, Copán site, from foundations of stela 4 (height, approximately 4 ft.
(1.22 m.)).   *e,* Other side of *b.*   (After Richardson, 1940, figs. 35–37; *c,* after
Gordon, 1898, fig. 4.)

prehistoric cultures in Honduras. These will become more applicable to the Honduras area when the full sequence of cultures in Highland Guatemala has appeared in print. However, the Petén data are more accessible at the moment.

According to Longyear (1942, p. 391), the most primitive-appearing ceramics in the southern *Maya* area are the Yojoa "Monochrome" deposits. (See p. 98.) This, as yet little known, ceramic type does not exactly correspond with any of the Petén-*Maya* prepolychrome styles. The presence of crude, hand-molded figurines and the discovery of other traits may eventually link it with the Mamom phase in the north and the Playa de los Muertos in the south, or it may prove to be earlier than either. The Playa de los Muertos style, with its broad, incised designs, single-color painting, and solid figurines, apparently links up with the Mamom phase to the north (Smith, 1940, p. 249). There are some general resemblances between Playa de los Muertos monochrome vessels and the incised, fluted or plain, bottle-necked vessels associated with cremations found in caverns about 4 miles from Copán (Gordon, 1896, 1898). This last type of pottery has not been reported from the main Copán ruins. It is apparently early, but it is too little known at present to be safely classified.

The Ulua Bichrome style (including Usulután ware) is stylistically linked with deep deposits at Cerro Zapote in El Salvador (Lothrop, 1927 a) which also contain Usulután ware. Longyear (1942) suggests that the batik process employed on ceramics of the second or Chicanel phase in the Petén at Uaxactún may also be temporally and stylistically related to the Cerro Zapote and Ulua Bichrome ceramic styles.

Thus, these two prepolychrome phases in western Honduras, the Playa de los Muertos and the Ulua Bichrome, are apparently related to two similar *Maya* (or proto-*Maya*) phases in the Petén, the Mamom, and Chicanel. As Longyear states (1942, p. 393), "Any dating for these early levels is necessarily tentative, but since 9.0.0.0.0. or A. D. 435 in the Goodman-Martinez-Thompson correlation, is given for the upper limit of the Chicanel [Thompson, 1939, p. 240] we can take this date at present as signifying the close of the prepolychrome horizon in the south also." More recently Thompson (1943) has given A. D. 300 as the closing date for the Formative or Mamom-Chicanel phases in the Petén. In any event, actual dates as applied to this borderland area are to be considered as approximations at best.

Ceramic correlations with Classic Maya.—In regard to the later polychrome styles in western Honduras, apparent correlations with Petén-*Maya* sequence exist, but there are bad gaps in the present record. Tzakol-phase ceramic characteristics are said to be rare, but they do occur at Copán (Longyear, 1942, p. 393), whereas both Santa Rita and Las Flores type Ulua-Mayoid style characteristics are apparently lacking in such horizons at Copán. The Tepeu phase in the Petén finds representative forms both at Copán and apparently in the Ulua-Mayoid Santa Rita type pottery. A characteristic Tepeu form is a flat-based, thin-walled, cylindrical vase decorated with human figures and glyph bands, and without thickened lips, tripod feet, or lugs. As previously indicated (p. 89), this type of vase is characteristic of the earlier Santa Rita type ceramics in the Ulua-Mayoid series. As Longyear (1942, p. 393) suggests, the temporal positions of the (earlier) thin-walled and (later) thick-walled vases actually overlap in western Honduras, but the former occurs only in the early Santa Rita ceramic type of the Ulua-Mayoid style. According to Longyear (1942, pp. 393-394), the Tepeu phase, in the Petén, lasts from 9.10.0.0.0 (A. D. 633) until 10.8.0.0.0 (A. D. 987), and this span of time may well include the Tepeu forms at Copán and the Santa Rita ceramic type on the Ulua River. Another occurrence, recently reported from Copán (Longyear, 1940, pp. 269-270), is the discovery of Teotihuacan (II–IV) types of pottery in association with "fairly early Copán horizons." These are apparently trade wares from Kaminaljuyú in the Guatemala Highlands. In time, this intrusion apparently more or less coincides with the Tzakol-Tepeu phases, tentatively dated above. Thompson (1943, p. 122) dates these Mexican influences in Kaminaljuyú as circa A. D. 350–650. Heretofore, Mexican influence in Honduras and El Salvador was believed to have begun with the *Toltec,* who, traditionally, migrated southward from the 10th to the 12th centuries, following the breakup of the *Toltec* Empire. The fact that Teotihuacan-Mexican influences were present in Copán at least several centuries prior to these traditional dates must be borne in mind when the complex problems involving various Mexican versus *Mayan* influences in contemporary and later Honduras cultures are considered. As Longyear (1942, p. 395) also points out, a known terminal point in the Mexican occupation of Honduras is marked by the Naco style pottery at that site (p. 88), which is dated as just subsequent to A. D. 1500 by its demonstrated association with Spanish Colonial pottery.

Summary of ceramic correlations.—To summarize this important but necessarily complex and incomplete treatment of the known relationship between Honduras and northern, i.e., *Mayan* and Mexican, ceramic styles, the following outline seems tenable: The two prepolychrome horizons, Playa de los Muertos and Ulua Bichrome (Usulután) in western Honduras, correspond in certain general characteristics to two similar early horizons, Mamom and Chicanel, in the Petén. The earliest date for these horizons is speculative, but the latest appears to be from about A. D. 300 to 435. Between these and the later polychrome horizons in western Honduras there is at present a complete break, which is not the case in the Petén. This is due to the fact that the Tzakol phase in the Petén (A. D. 435 to 633) is almost entirely unaccounted for in western Honduras, either at Copán or on the Ulua. The next, or Tepeu phase, in the Petén (A. D. 633 to 987) is apparently represented at Copán (Longyear,

1942, p. 393), and possibly on the Ulua, by the Santa Rita type of the Ulua-Mayoid style. However, the fact that Ulua-Mayoid style pottery generally seems to be rare or lacking at Copán and that Copán style ceramics are generally lacking on the Ulua—but that both styles occur together in El Salvador (Longyear, 1940, p. 270)—presents a puzzling problem which more adequate data regarding Copán and stratigraphic excavations in El Salvador seem most likely to solve. Nevertheless, despite the present inadequacy of the record at Copán, and in the remainder of northwestern Honduras, wide cultural correlations of considerable depth are already clearly apparent. These important matters will be discussed further in the conclusion of this section, but here we must return to a brief survey of prehistoric central and southwestern Honduras.

Comayagua Valley.—In the Comayagua Valley, or more technically, the Humuya River Basin, only the site of Tenampua on a hill crest southeast of the town of Comayagua has been at all carefully explored. Despite the surveys of Squier (1853 b, 1869), Lothrop (1927 b), Popenoe (1928, 1936), and Yde (1938), there is still considerable disagreement as to the exact plan of the site. Popenoe, who gives the most complete map (fig. 13), shows 99 structures, whereas Squier counted over 400 mounds (Yde, 1938, p. 22). Tenampua was apparently a hilltop fortress and, possibly, a religious shrine. Despite a limited water supply, Popenoe notes three artificial reservoirs or water holes; the abundance of worn-out metates suggests occupation during considerable periods of time. The site is strongly fortified by stone walls, as well as by nature (fig. 13), and the surface of the mountain top is covered with numerous terraces and rough mounds. The latter fall into three main groups, which are formalized in arrangement. Yde (1938, p. 22) on the basis of Popenoe's map (fig. 13) believes that the site was erected during at least two periods of construction. The mounds are of earth paved with stones, or of rough rocks paved with slabs. Crude stone stairways ascend the terraces and certain mounds. Two long mounds with slanting inner walls faced with stone slabs 3¼ feet (1 m.) in height form a ball court. According to Yde (1938, pp. 19–21), this has a stucco floor. Certain rocks at the site are inscribed with simple geometric patterns. Strange to say, the ceramic complex from this important site has never been described. Squier (1869) figures a remarkable painted vessel from here, with handles and legs suggesting twisted cords. It contained chalcedony beads and a pottery whistle. A few sherds of polychrome ware collected by Squier are now in the American Museum of Natural History. They do not conform to any Honduran ceramic type with which the author is familar. Popenoe figures another tripod vessel (fig. 14) whose polychrome bird design somewhat suggests the Yojoa Bold Animalistic style previously described (p. 91). Other elaborately painted, tripod bowls, as well as incised pottery, are mentioned by Squier (1869). He also noted much broken pottery and burned human

PLATE 1.—**Ceremonial cache and urn and skull burials, Honduras.** *Top*: Ceremonial deposits of stone bowls, metates, and tables near Plantain River, northeastern Honduras. (After Spinden, 1925, fig. 1.) *Bottom*: Urn and skull burials, Bay Islands, Honduras. (After Strong, 1935, pl. 2.)

PLATE 2.—North Coast Appliqué style vessels, northeastern Honduras. (After Stone, 1941, figs. 13–15.)

PLATE 3.—**Northeast Coast Honduras pottery types.** *a–d*, North Coast Appliqué
style; *e–f*, North Coast Appliqué style, Simple Painted type; *g–h*, Bold Geometric style, probably San Marcos type. (After Stone, 1941, figs. 16 and 11.)

PLATE 4.—**Stone and metalwork, Bay Islands, Honduras.** *Top:* Small green stone anthropomorphic carvings. (Scale: Upper left specimen 1¼ in. (3 cm.) wide.) *Bottom:* Modeled copper bells. (Scale: Lower left specimen 1⅛ in. (2.7 cm.) high.) (After Strong, 1935, pls. 11 and 10.)

PLATE 5.—**Honduras ceramic and marble vessels.** *a, b,* Playa de los Muertos style, Bichrome type vessels from Lake Yojoa. *c,* Bay Island Polychrome style vase. (In orange, dark red, and black.) *d, e,* Ulua Marble Vaselike type vessels, Bay Islands. *f,* Ulua Marble vase (University of Pennsylvania Museum. Note similarity with *e*). (After Strong, Kidder, and Paul, 1938, pl. 15; Strong, 1935, pls. 1 and 24; and Stone, 1938, fig. 6.)

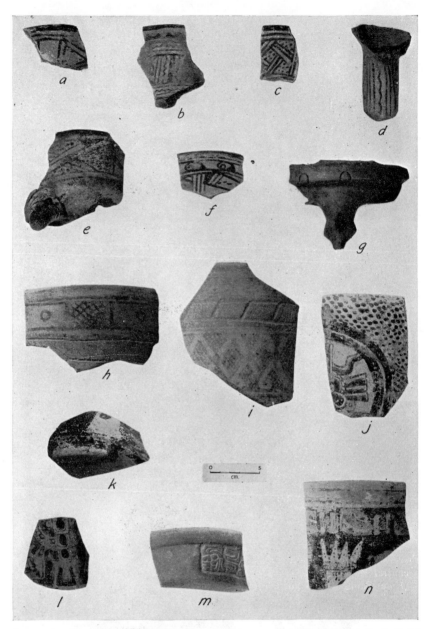

PLATE 6.—**Honduras pottery styles and types.** *a–g*, Naco style; *h*, *i*, Bold Geometric style, San Marcos type; *j–n*, Ulua Mayoid style, Las Flores type; *m*, Mayoid carved subtype. (After Strong, Kidder, and Paul, 1938, pls. 3 and 5.)

PLATE 7.—**Bold Geometric style pottery.** *a*, San Marcos type (San Marcos, central Honduras); *b*, *c*, probably San Marcos type; *d*, *e*, *f*, Santa Rita type. (From Santa Rita, Ulua River, Honduras.)

PLATE 8.—**Ulua Polychrome vessels, Mayoid style, Santa Rita type, Santa Rita, Honduras.**) (After Strong, Kidder, and Paul, 1938, pl. 8.)

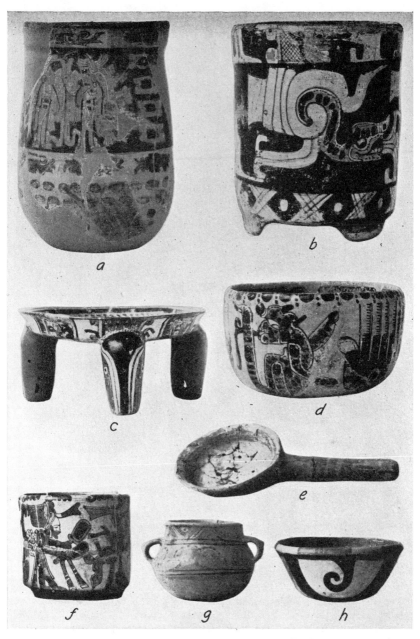

PLATE 9.—**Yojoa Polychrome vessels, Lake Yojoa, Honduras.** *a–d*, Mayoid style; *e–h*, group of vessels from a single grave at La Ceiba, Lake Yojoa, Polychrome Period; *e*, uncertain style; *f*, Mayoid style; *g*, Bold Animalistic style; *h*, Bold Animalistic style, Naranjos I type. (*e–h* on different scale than others.) (After Strong, Kidder, and Paul, 1938, pl. 12; and Strong, 1937, fig. 75.)

PLATE 10.—**Yojoa Polychrome and other vessels, Lake Yojoa, Honduras.** *a–d*, Bold Animalistic style; *e–f*, Bold Geometric style; *g*, Crude Ulua Marble Vaselike type; *h*, Mayoid carved subtype. (After Strong, Kidder, and Paul, 1938, pls. 13 and 14.)

PLATE 11.—**Early ceramic types, Honduras.** *a–m*, Ulua Bichrome from deepest level, Santa Rita; *n–t*, Yojoa Monochrome, Los Naranjos. (After Strong, Kidder, and Paul, 1938, pls. 9 and 15.)

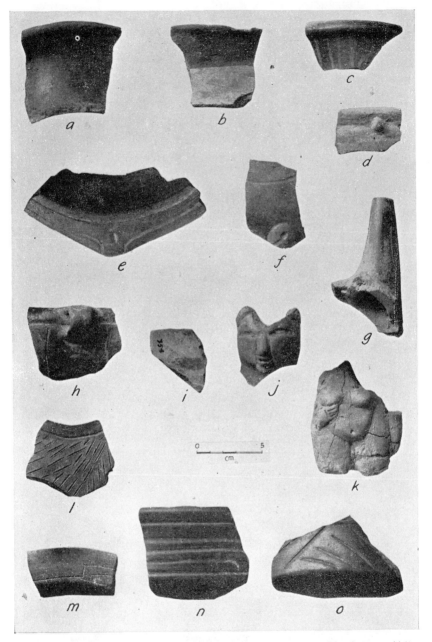

PLATE 12.—**Playa de los Muertos style sherds and figurines, Honduras.** (After Strong, Kidder, and Paul, 1938, pls. 10 and 11.)

and animal bones at the site. A comprehensive and objective description of Tenampua ceramics is very badly needed. Plain stone metates, with and without legs, and broken ovoid mullers are abundant at the site.

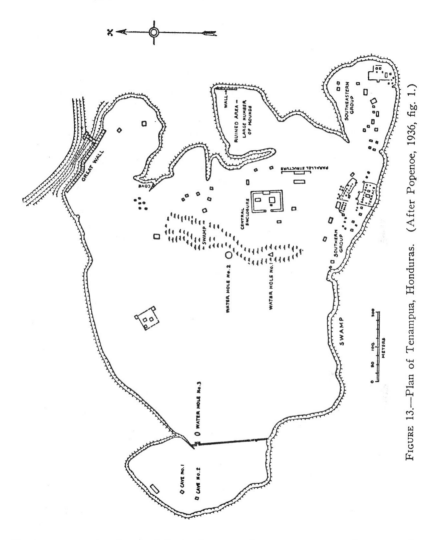

FIGURE 13.—Plan of Tenampua, Honduras. (After Popenoe, 1936, fig. 1.)

Popenoe uncovered an elaborately carved stone metate of openwork Nicoyan or Costa Rican type. Small stone balls and obsidian lance points complete the reported artifact inventory from this important site. Popenoe (1936, pp. 560, 571) suggests that Tenampua may be identified with the *Lenca* fortress of Guaxeregin destroyed by Montejo, but Yde (1938, p. 21) denies this possibility on geographic grounds. No post-Contact materials have been reported from the site. Both Popenoe and Yde agree that the main structures and artifact types at Tenampua do not appear to be *Mayan* or Mexican in character but rather show strong Nicaraguan and Costa Rican influences. However, the true significance of this superficially well-known site will not become clear until it has been the scene of more inten-

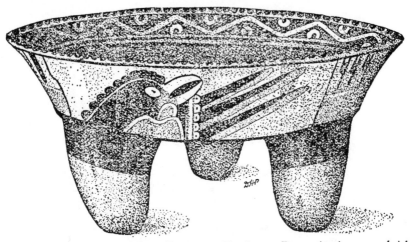

FIGURE 14.—Pottery vessel from Tenampua, Honduras. Decoration in cream, brick red, and dark brown. (After Popenoe, 1936, fig. 2.)

sive excavations, accompanied by adequate ceramic and other artifact type analyses.

Concerning the various mound groups and similar sites, as well as a few artifacts all briefly mentioned as occurring in or near the town of Comayagua, at Yarumela, at the north and south ends of the Comayagua Valley, and around the town of Siguatepeque, the reader is referred to Yde (1938, pp. 11–27). Long ago Squier (1859) pointed out that the local Indians, presumably *Lenca*, still made annual pilgrimages to their immediately pre-Conquest village sites in the vicinity of the historic town of Comayagua, and mentions at least five such ruins within a league (about 3.5 km.) of the town. None of the important Contact sites have yet been identified nor described. Pottery from such sites would presumably be *Lenca*. Here is a promising lead to the historic approach in Honduras archeology which remains to be developed. Until more exploration and scientific excavation have been accomplished in this part of central Honduras the nature of prehistoric southern and northern cultural interpenetrations, now becoming obvious slightly to the north, will remain obscure so far as concerns one of the most immediate sources of southern elements.

Tegucigalpa area.—In the valley of the upper Choluteca River, in that part called Río Grande, is located the city of Tegucigalpa, the modern capital of the Republic of Honduras. Unlike the Comayagua Valley, that of Tegucigalpa is surrounded by high mountains on all sides, and apparently it was thinly occupied in pre-Columbian times. It is at present a center for mining activities, but apparently the native peoples of the region, like those of northwestern Honduras, were little interested in gold and silver. In any event, no ruins or mound sites have yet been reported[1] from this pleasant and fertile valley, and the few artifacts described in print as coming from here offer little tangible information (Yde, 1938, pp. 8–10). Passing toward the Olancho Valley, Wells (1857, p. 244) describes and figures some sort of natural or artificial structure made of blocks of stone on a hilltop 1 league north beyond the crossing of the Guampú River on the Talanga road. Neither the drawing nor the description conveys a clear picture of what was actually encountered. Recent investigations in this vicinity have not verified Wells's account. No vestiges of such a structure now exist, nor does it appear likely that there was a building (personal communication from Doris Z. Stone.).

Olancho Valley.—The Olancho Valley, another gold-producing region, was early the scene of conflicts between the followers of Cortez in the north and Pedrarias in the south. Unfortunately, we know little of the archeology of this important central area except that there are a number of large mound groups in the valley (Strong, 1934 b, p. 47; 1935, pp. 159–160). There are several mound sites on the Olancho and Guayape Rivers, in the vicinity of Juticalpa. One of these, called Dos Quebradas, consists of a great number of earth and stone mounds covering an enormous area. The majority of these are small, suggesting house mounds, but some are large, ranging from 30 to 40 feet (10 to 13 m.) in height. One of them is covered with large granite slabs, many of which formerly stood erect. The largest, about 12 feet (4 m.) high, had recently (before 1933) been knocked down by lightning. Broken pottery is abundant at the site. The most striking pottery is of Bold Geometric style. Both monkey-handled ollas and large tripod vessels of composite silhouette occur. The latter have hollow feet, modeled to represent alligator or other reptile heads, which contain rattles. Colors consist of a dull yellow or a brighter orange slip with red and black designs, which are either geometric, textilelike, or, occasionally, symbolic and vaguely suggesting aberrant Mayoid, Mexican, or *Chorotegan* motifs. In addition, North Coast Appliqué pottery of the less elaborate forms occurs at the site. A pottery earplug, a small celt of greenstone, and the obsidian flake knives were also found.

At San Marcos, on the Guayape River, are large earth mounds with the same ceramic types. The Bold Geometric Ware available from San Marcos forms one stylistic unit that has here been designated as the San Marcos type of Ulua Bold Geometric (p. 90 and pl. 7, *a*). North Coast Appliqué pottery of simple form also occurs at San Marcos and is the

---

[1] Stone has conducted recent investigations in this region, locating numerous ruins. A report of this work will eventually be published by Peabody Museum, Harvard University.

only style present at other earth-mound groups noted in Olancho. Other types of artifacts are rare on the surface of these sites. Excavation at San Marcos, or elsewhere in the Olancho region, was very superficial, but it is obviously a promising and important area.

The apparent absence in Olancho Valley sites of Mayoid forms, and the predominance of the Bold Geometric style, throw a faint but promising gleam of light on the probable source of this Bold Geometric element in the Ulua-Yojoa mixed deposits. Careful excavations in this promising central region should give vitally needed information concerning the cultural relationships that existed in prehistoric times between northwestern Nicaragua, the northeast coast regions of Honduras, and the *Maya* borderlands along the Ulua River, Lake Yojoa, and the El Salvador–Guatemala frontiers.

Pacific or Fonseca Bay area.—It seems anticlimactic to close our discussion of central and southwestern Honduras with only a brief quoted paragraph on the Pacific or Fonseca Bay area, which should, by reason of its geographic position, be the key to the prehistoric interrelationship between Honduras, El Salvador, and Nicaragua. However, as the work of Rivas is unavailable at the time of writing, we can quote only the following: "A young German photographer, Fritz Wellerman, living in Tegucigalpa, has collected a number of small stone figures from Zacate Grande Island in Fonseca Bay, and Prof. Pedro Rivas of Tegucigalpa observed large idols, pottery, and mounds on the same island; in his 'Monografia . . . . de la Isla Tigre y Puerto de Amapala' [Rivas, 1934, p. 26] he describes a 4 km. long and 2 km. wide zone where these artifacts occur" (Yde, 1938, pp. 18–19). Thus we conclude our incomplete survey of the very incompletely known, but highly important, archeological region of central and southwestern Honduras.

ETHNIC CORRELATIONS IN HONDURAS

THE POTTERY TIME CHART

As was the case in Costa Rica and Nicaragua, ceramic wares or styles prove to be the most effective links between the historic and the prehistoric periods in Honduras. Other traits of material culture may later prove to have equal or even greater value, but at present inadequate excavation prevents detailed structural comparisons, and the remaining inventory of comparable artifact types does not approach pottery decoration as a sensitive index of cultural change and ethnic affiliation. For this reason a diagrammatic chart has been prepared of known Honduras ceramic styles and types, with a tentative estimate of their probable duration (fig. 15).

This chart includes the northeast coast and Ulua-Yojoa regions. It does not include the Copán (*Mayan*) sequence, since full data are not now available, nor does it cover central and southwestern Honduras, since no adequate scientific data are available from these regions. Sequence of styles and types in figure 15 rests primarily on demonstrable, stratigraphic sequences in the Ulua-Yojoa region (Strong, Kidder, and Paul,

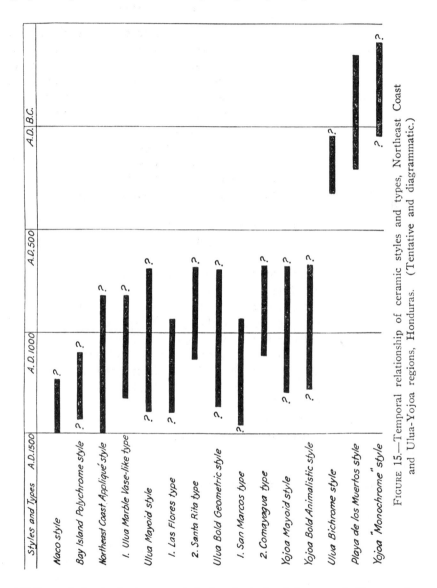

FIGURE 15.—Temporal relationship of ceramic styles and types, Northeast Coast and Ulua-Yojoa regions, Honduras. (Tentative and diagrammatic.)

1938), and the basis for actual dating is derived from probable correlations between undated Honduras and dated *Mayan* styles previously discussed in regard to Copán and the Petén (p. 106). In the present sections we are primarily concerned with those ceramic styles and types which directly, or indirectly, lead up to historic tribes or ethnic groups. The earlier, discontinuous, ceramic horizons dated prior to A. D. 500 will be mentioned again in the final section.

A CONSIDERATION OF CERAMIC STYLES

Naco style.—The Naco style (fig. 15) is definitely historic and of Mexican origin. It occurs at a documented site in direct association with European porcelain sherds. The style seems to be late prehistoric in México and evidently pertains to the latest Mexican or *Nahuatl* intrusion into Honduras. Whether this occupation should be called *Aztec, Pipil,* or *Nahuatl* remains to be determined. Similar Mexican groups are known to have been located near Trujillo, in Olancho, near Comayagua, and in Chapagua and Papayeca on the northeast coast (Stone, 1941, pp. 15–16). None of these sites, nor the ceramics associated with them, have yet been located or described. The problem of Mexican intrusions into southern Central America is extremely complex. Thompson (1943, p. 122) points out that there may have been three rather than two main periods of Mexican migration. In any event, Naco style ceramics and the associated cultural complex at Naco clearly mark a terminal point in the last intrusion since it has a post-1500 date.

Bay Island Polychrome style.—Considering the ceramic styles in order, one can say little concerning the Bay Island Polychrome style (fig. 15) except that it is apparently late. The extremely conventionalized and florid decoration accords more closely with the later Las Flores type of the Ulua Mayoid than it does with the earlier Santa Rita type. However, Bay Island Polychrome is a distinctive style despite the fact that its vessel forms blend with those of the North Coast Appliqué style. It is also rather unusual in being associated with Plumbate ware. In México, Thompson (1943, p. 128) states that three centuries intervened between the disappearance of the Plumbate export trade and the Conquest. Whether this was so in Honduras we do not know. No Contact material has been found with Bay Island Polychrome, although it is associated with metalwork which appears to be late in this part of Honduras. This fact, and the apparent relationship between Bay Island Polychrome and North Coast Appliqué, suggest that the basic ethnic affiliations of the former will eventually prove to be similar if not identical with those of the latter. The particular cultural intrusion, however, that led to the development of this localized polychrome style remains to be determined.

North Coast Appliqué style.—North Coast Appliqué style ceramics have been extended into the historic period on somewhat shaky grounds (fig. 15). Stone (1941, p. 20) has attempted to demonstrate that the Northeast Coast Appliqué style pottery occurs in historic *Paya* sites. Near the old town of San Esteban Toyazua, established as a *Paya* mission in 1807, 284 years after the Conquest, Stone found abundant pottery of this style. No Contact materials, however, are reported, and the case for historic identification still rests on the fact that North Coast Appliqué ceramics occur in most parts of the recorded territory of the *Paya*. It is highly probable that the *Paya* did make pottery of this style, but this cannot be regarded as indisputably demonstrated as yet. However, in the case of the neighboring *Jicaque*, at Cangelica and Subirana, Stone (1942, p. 380, fig. 43) did find ceramics, including some of a generalized North Coast Appliqué style, in reputedly *Jicaque* sites associated with glass beads. It is on this slender but tangible bit of evidence that I have here extended the North Coast Appliqué style into the historic period (fig. 15). The style, as represented in these protohistoric finds, had apparently degenerated from its earlier prehistoric elaboration in the *Paya* country (Stone, 1941) and on the Bay Islands (Strong, 1935), but enough incision, appliqué work, and modeling on monochrome ware remain to link safely these various manifestations.

We have previously mentioned the close relationship that exists between Highland Appliqué in Costa Rica and Nicaragua, and the North Coast Appliqué style in Honduras. In both north and south the appliqué style occurs in territories occupied almost exclusively by *Chibchan,* or probably *Chibchan*-speaking peoples, and there is a high probability that the style pertained to the *Guetar* in the south and the *Paya, Jicaque,* and related peoples in the north. As to the age of this ceramic style in the north, as in the south, we have as yet no direct evidences. It has been assigned a terminal date here (fig. 15) owing to the fact that the North Coast Appliqué style contains the Ulua Marble Vaselike ceramic type which, on the Ulua River, stratigraphically overlaps the two Ulua-Mayoid style types, Las Flores and Santa Rita (fig. 15). How much earlier this or other types of the North Coast Appliqué style may have been made in Honduras remains to be determined. This is an important problem, since it involves the probable time of a major *Chibchan,* or a related southern Central American thrust from the south into the north.

Ulua-Mayoid style.—In regard to the Ulua-Mayoid style (fig. 15; pls. 6, *j–n;* 7) there is a distinct possibility that the latest Las Flores type persisted into early historic times, but we have as yet no tangible proof of this. The ethnic linkage of the style with the *Maya* rests on its clear relationship to known *Mayan* styles in the north rather than on any direct historic evidence, although *Mayan*-speaking peoples are known to have occupied this northwestern region in historic times. (See linguistic map, p. 50.) The sequence and characteristics of the two types included in this style, Las Flores and Santa Rita, and their apparent tenuous connections at Copán, have already been discussed. Perhaps the outstanding thing about this definitely *Mayan* style on the Ulua, and again in the Lake Yojoa district, is the fact that it does not occur by itself, as is the case in most *Maya* sites to the north, but is often found in direct association with other styles, Bold Geometric and Bold Animalistic (fig. 15 and pls. 7, 9), which do not seem to be at all *Mayan* in inspiration. This, coupled with the fact that neither type of the Ulua-Mayoid style occurs at Copán during its earlier "great period" of the dated stelae, leads one to conclude that the Ulua River and Lake Yojoa populations that made the Ulua and Yojoa Mayoid pottery, as well as that of Bold Geometric and Bold Animalistic styles, were mixed, part *Maya* and part alien. This leads to a consideration of the latter styles as well as the probable ethnic composition of this alien, or non-Mayoid, element at such mixed Ulua-Yojoa sites.

Non-Mayan styles of the Ulua-Yojoa region.—The non-*Mayan* ceramic elements in these interesting composite sites on the Ulua River, and at Lake Yojoa, are as follows: The Bold Geometric style (including the earlier Comayagua and the later San Marcos types), the Bold Animalistic style, and the Ulua Marble Vaselike type of the North Coast Appliqué style. The Bold Geometric style does not occur, so far as known, in predominantly *Mayan* territory, but it does occur, either isolated or associated with North Coast Appliqué style ceramics, in the Olancho district of central Honduras (see p. 111), on the Bay Islands, and on the adjacent mainland. The Olancho region is in the heart of historic *Lenca* country, the Bay Islands were probably *Paya* territory, and the adjacent mainland is *Paya* and *Jicaque* country. (See linguistic map, p. 50.) In protohistoric sites in the Yoro district, presumably *Jicaque,* typical Bold Geometric style handles with raised, monkey-head lugs (Stone, 1941, figs. 42, *l;* 43, *k'*) occur in association with North Coast Appliqué style ceramics. The Ulua Marble Vaselike pottery type to pertain to the *Lenca, Jicaque, Paya,* and related peoples east of the occurs on the Bay Islands and the adjacent mainland, in historic *Paya* territory. Thus, this general northeastern ceramic complex including Bold Geometric and North Coast Appliqué styles and types would appear Ulua. The exact affiliations of the Yojoa Bold Animalistic style are not so clear, since the style occurs in El Salvador under as yet unknown circumstances, but in Honduras it centers in *Lenca* territory and is apparently related to the Bold Geometric style, which again occurs isolated in *Lenca* territory. Thus, the non-Mayoid ceramic element in the mixed Ulua-Yojoa polychrome sites would, therefore, appear to be predominantly *Lenca* and *Jicaque,* with possibly some *Paya* ingredients (Ulua Marble Vaselike type ceramics). This is the general southern or easterly ceramic complex which met, occasionally blended with, but also for a considerable period existed side by side with, the *Mayan* ceramic tradition along its southern borders in the Ulua-Yojoa region.

The sociological basis for this state of affairs can only be surmised. It seems logical, however, to postulate that *Mayan* and *Lencan,* as well as *Jicaque* groups, had intermarried and formed numerous composite communities along the Ulua and at Lake Yojoa. In such communities the two schools of pottery-makers had in each case largely maintained their group artistic traditions over a considerable period despite parallel changes in both traditions through time and some blending in the less typical ceramic forms. The record in the ground fully justifies such an interpretation, but much more extensive work in structures, as well as in refuse heaps and burial deposits, is needed before full light can be thrown on this extremely interesting case of peaceful cultural inter-action between peoples of apparently quite differently derived cultural traditions. It is tempting to visualize a period after the "fall" of the "Old *Maya* Empire" at Copán when the scattering *Maya,* abandoning their great stoneworking tradition and stela cult, pushed in small groups to the north and east, accepting extended hospitality from the various alien peoples of their southern borderland. That something of this sort occurred seems quite possible, but since neither the exact nature of the "fall of Copán" nor the full details of this interesting cultural amalgamation to the north are as yet clear, such speculations are premature. In any event, it is obvious that cultural interrelationships along this border area were not only complex but also extremely interesting from both the historical and the sociological viewpoint.

Discussion.—In regard to the attempt to establish definite historic correlations between sites, ceramic complexes, and historic tribes, the efforts of Stone (1941, 1942) are highly praiseworthy. However, the extremely complex cultural interactions in aboriginal northwestern Honduras, as well as the many obscurities of early post-Conquest history, make this a very difficult and meticulous task. Thus, the postulated correlations between the historic *Paya* and the North Coast Appliqué ceramic style (Stone, 1941), while highly probable in a general sense, is still not historically established. Furthermore, it is misleading to attempt to limit the identification of such a widespread ceramic style to only one of the many linguistic groups, or subgroups, such as the *Paya,* which appear to have been associated with it. Similarly, in regard to the *Jicaque,* where the historic correlation (like that at Naco) is based on an actual association with Contact materials, the limited ceramic sample seems to contain at least two definite styles, the North Coast Appliqué and the Bold Geometric.

In the case of the *Lenca* linguistic groups the situation promises to be even more complex. While no absolute historic *Lenca* ceramic correlations have yet been established, there is a high probability that the Bold Geometric ceramic style, the Bold Animalistic style, possibly the North Coast Appliqué style (in the north), and certain of the ceramic styles encountered at Tenampua are all *Lenca.* Such linguistic designations, particularly in regions of high culture, apply to a wide variety of cultural groups which have specialized in certain areas and also developed over a long period of time.

From the archeological standpoint each historic datum point which can be established with reasonable certainty, such as that at Naco for the late *Nahuatl* and at Cangelica and Subirana for the obscure *Jicaque,* is a very definite gain. Such correlations must, however, be carefully interpreted in terms of the larger cultural wholes and realities of which they are a part. Above all, they must be considered in terms of scientifically demonstrated temporal relationship. An example of such disregard is the obviously erroneous statement that certain Ulua Bichrome incised and rocker-stamped sherds should be classified as historic "Sula-*Jicaque*" (Stone, 1942, p. 379, fig. 31), despite the fact that while simple incision occurs in practically all horizons, rocker-stamping (pl. 11, *b*, and Strong, Kidder, and Paul, 1938, pl. 9, *e*) and Usulután ware are strictly limited to this one early horizon in Honduras and do not occur at all in the "Sula-*Jicaque*" sample. Similarly, the point already raised regarding the assertion that the Playa de los Muertos ceramic type persisted until "quite late during the Indian occupation of the Sula-Ulua" (Stone, 1941, p. 57) is based on uncontrolled evidence which, if accepted, would refute the findings of two carefully controlled stratigraphic excavations (Popenoe, 1934; Strong, Kidder, and Paul, 1938). However, in dealing with these earliest known Ulua Bichrome and Playa de los Muertos horizons in Honduras (see fig. 15), or with the possibly earlier Yojoa "Monochrome" horizon, we have reached a point where the nonconformity of the temporal sequence in Honduras (between circa A. D. 600 and 300, see fig. 15) indicates that further attempts at any direct historic correlations are as yet unjustified.

GENERAL CONSIDERATIONS

The earlier statement that the western boundary region of modern Honduras seemed to mark a meeting point between northern and southern prehistoric cultures seems justified in the light of present-day archeological knowledge. Such knowledge is at present inadequate in both space and time coverage, but what objective data we have reveal a fascinating interplay of cultural forces in this area. Along the Ulua River at Lake Yojoa, and in all probability south through El Salvador, *Maya* cultures of the later polychrome pottery periods are seen to meet and intermingle with those from the south. These southern cultural elements were apparently carried by such native groups as the *Lenca, Jicaque,* and *Paya,* although the *Paya* seem more closely identified with an appliqué monochrome pottery tradition which is apparently derived from, or basic to, the Highland region in Costa Rica.

The sources of the polychrome pottery styles associated with this southern or Honduras cultural element, i.e., Bay Island, Polychrome, Bold

Geometric, and Bold Animalistic, are as yet uncertain. They occur by themselves and isolated from *Mayan* or Mexican styles in northern and central Honduras, but they may originally have been derived from *Chorotegan* or Mexican culture centers in western Nicaragua and Costa Rica. Until we have objective excavation data from the great archeological blank now formed by south-central Honduras, El Salvador, and practically all Nicaragua, the answers to such questions can only be guessed at. A similar unanswered question involves the exact relationship that existed between the various *Mayan* ceramic styles on the Ulua, at Lake Yojoa, at Copán, and in El Salvador, as well as their respective relationship to the earlier or Formative Period. The answer to these questions may be found in El Salvador, but further excavation and publication are vitally needed in the other regions as well. Concerning the various Mexican intrusions into Honduras and southern Central America our only objective data at present are a few such terminal points as Naco. Until more is known about the relative time and nature of such Mexican invasions we cannot hope to understand the role played by the Meso-American cultures in Central America either in the western Nicaraguan and Costa Rican culture centers, nor in its wider peripheral manifestations.

With the possible exception of Copán, there is at present in Honduras a complete break in continuity between the polychrome pottery horizons and what may be termed the Formative cultures of northern Middle America. In Honduras these include the Ulua Bichrome, the Playa de los Muertos, and, probably, the Yojoa "Monochrome" horizons. The last, contrary to an earlier estimate (compare fig. 15 with Relative Chronological Chart, Strong, 1943, p. 42), may be the oldest of the three, but it is too little known at present to even suggest wider correlations. There are, however, already clear indications of relationship between the Ulua Bichrome and the Playa de los Muertos horizons on the one hand and the Mamom-Chicanel (*Maya* or proto-*Maya*) phase in the Petén area on the other. When more information is available concerning the comparable early periods in the intervening Guatemala Highland area, the nature and direction of these relationships should be clearer. However, to the south of Honduras no evidences of any comparable early culture horizon are yet known until one reaches the Coast of northern and central Perú. Here the Early Ancón-Supe, or Chavinoid, cultures seem quite similar in cultural content and probable age to the Playa de los Muertos horizon in Honduras. (See Strong, 1943, pp. 31–33 and Relative Chronological Chart.) How significant such spatially distant cultural correlations may prove to be it is too early to say. It seems obvious, however, that careful and deep excavations in strategic sites in the intervening regions of southern Central America and northern South America should go far toward solving this and other important problems which no amount of speculation or specimen-collecting can hope to touch.

BIBLIOGRAPHY

Blakiston, 1910; Gordon, 1896, 1898; Kidder (see Strong, Kidder, and Paul, 1938); Longyear, 1940, 1942; Lothrop, 1921, 1926 b, 1927 a, 1927 b; Paul (see Strong, Kidder, and Paul, 1938); Popenoe, D., 1928, 1934, 1936; Popenoe, W. and D., 1931; Richardson, 1940; Rivas, 1934; Smith, 1940; Spinden, 1925; Squier, 1853 b, 1859, 1869; Steinmayer, 1932; Stone, 1934 a, 1938, 1941, 1942; Strong, 1934 a, 1934 b, 1935, 1937, 1943; Strong, Kidder, and Paul, 1938; Thompson, 1939, 1943; Vaillant. 1927; Wells, 1857; Yde, 1938.

THE ARCHEOLOGY OF COSTA RICA AND NICARAGUA

By Wm. Duncan Strong

INTRODUCTION

As is true of most of Central America, only the most obvious or generalized archeological provinces have as yet been distinguished in Costa Rica and Nicaragua. (See map 3.) To date, demonstrated culture sequences are unknown; hence, it is impossible further to subdivide these larger areas into those which existed during successive periods prior to the Conquest. For present purposes we shall, therefore, take Lothrop's two main archeological areas (1926 b, vol. 1, fig. 1, p. xxv), the Pacific region and the Highland region, and add to these another region that is even less known, the Eastern Coastal Plain. In general, the Pacific region, as considered here, includes what Johnson (p. 44) has designated as the Pacific Borderlands. It includes also the Nicoya Peninsula, which, from a strictly geographic standpoint, can also be included with the Southern Highland area. Too little detailed information is available to tell whether the Boruca area belongs archeologically with the Highland or the Pacific region. For present purposes it is included with the latter. In regard to the Pacific region it is known to be archeologically rich, but, with one exception, it has as yet received little systematic excavation. The Highland region in Costa Rica is fairly well known, since it includes the thickly inhabited "Meseta central." However, as Lothrop pointed out in 1926, we have to thank Hartman for the only published scientific excavation work in either the Pacific or the Highland region. Unfortunately, in 1946, this strange state of affairs is still true. As regards the Eastern Coast Plain, which from the archeological standpoint apparently includes the Nicaraguan Lowland, this vast jungle area is still largely unexplored scientifically; hence, very little can be said about it.

The names and locations, as well as a brief sketch of the history of Costa Rican, Nicaraguan, and other Central American tribes, have already been presented (pp. 49–64). The distribution of native culture types in Costa Rica, Nicaragua, Honduras, etc., at the time of the Conquest is discussed at considerable length in a subsequent section (pp. 185–193). Here we shall confine our treatment to a description of the archeological remains

121

themselves, making use of tribal names only in the few cases where the association between ethnological and archeological materials or horizons has been demonstrated on a sound historical basis. Such exact correlations are highly to be desired but are lamentably rare in Central America. On the other hand, numerous correlations between historic tribes and archeological remains have been suggested, and certain of these will be mentioned subsequently, taking care to distinguish the few proved ethnoarcheological associations from those that seem probable or merely possible. Since the admirable archeological summary of Costa Rica and Nicaragua by Lothrop (1926 b, vols. 1, 2) has not yet been superseded, this work forms the basis of much of the present outline and should be consulted for further details, particularly concerning ceramics, lists of sites, and general bibliography. The present account adds certain more recent findings and interpretations.

THE PACIFIC REGION

Surface structures.—The prehistoric structures of Costa Rica and Nicaragua are not particularly striking. In the Pacific region flat-topped mounds of earth and stone occur, often surmounted or surrounded by stone statues. There are no records or evidences of temples on such mounds. According to historic accounts, mounds stood in the temple courtyards. The irregular arrangement of mounds and statues in the Pacific region is indicated by an example from Zapatero Island, Nicaragua (fig. 16). Mounds of stone that are presumably domiciliary reach a size of 200 feet (60 m.) in length, 60 feet (18 m.) in width, and 10 feet (3 m.) in height. Small, low mounds of earth and stone are more common. Many of these are apparently raised house sites. Small circular mounds 20 to 40 feet (6 to 12 m.) in diameter were also used for burial and, in some cases, a short stone column with or without carving surmounted the mound. On Ometepe Island in Lake Nicaragua burial mounds are surrounded by a ring formed of stone slabs set on end. Refuse heaps, often of large size and considerable depth such as that at Filadelfia, are reported. A number of these appear to be rich in potsherds and should offer excellent stratigraphic possibilities. (See Lothrop, 1926 b, vol. 2, List of sites, p. 421 et seq.). Shell mounds occur at several places on the coast of Nicaragua and Costa Rica. Stone "dump heaps" or "quarries" marked by incomplete stone statues, seats, and metates are reported in the Terraba Plain, and an extensive flint quarry or workshop at Tablón, Nicaragua.

Stone statues.—The stone statues of the Pacific region are well known and occur both with mounds and in isolation. They range roughly from 4 to 12 feet (1.2 to 3.6 m.) in height and represent human beings, animals, or both (pl. 13 and fig. 17). Examples from the Nicaraguan lake region are among the most striking. Stone statues of the Pacific

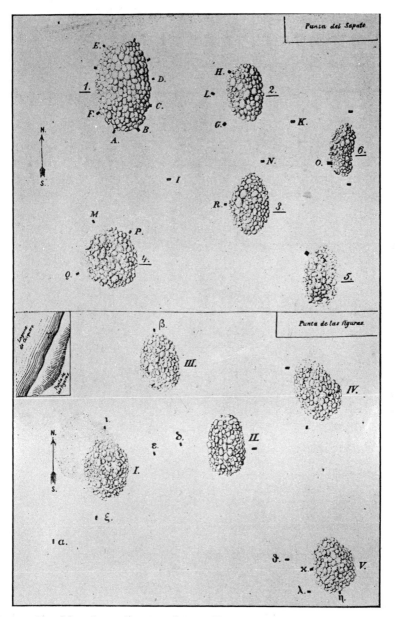

Figure 16.—Mounds on Zapatero Island, Nicaragua. (After Bovallius, 1886.)

FIGURE 17.—Stone sculptures from Costa Rica and Nicaragua. *a,* Human figure, Copelito, Nicaragua (height approximately 5 ft. (1.50 m.)). *b,* Human figure with "alter ego" motif, Nacasola, Costa Rica (height approximately 8 ft. (2.40 m.)). *c,* Human figure, El Silencio, Nicaragua (height approximately 5 ft. (1.50 m.)). *d,* Human figure from Copelito (height approximately 4 ft. 6 in. (1.37 m.)). *e,* Human figure, La Libertad, Nicaragua (height approximately 5 ft. 4 in. (1.63 m.)). (After Richardson, 1940, figs. 39, 38; *b,* after Cabrera, 1924.)

region usually have a columnar base, often with a simple capital on which the figure rests. One common type, suggesting the "alter ego" or guardian-spirit motif, is a human figure seated or standing, carrying on the shoulders or over the head an alligator or other animal. Sometimes the head of the human figure is enclosed in the jaws of this animal. Characteristically, in the lake region this animal head is huge. Other types of human figures have gorgets on the breast or held in the hand, have tenons on top of the head, or have the lower part of the face covered by a mask suggesting the bill of a duck or other bird. Recently a unique type of columnar human statue with elaborate low relief carving has been reported from the western slopes of the Cordillera east of Lakes Managua and Nicaragua (Richardson, 1940). In a subsequent article (Stone, this volume, pp. 173–174) cruder human and animal statues (often with peg bases) and small groups of large stone balls from the Terraba Plain are described. In addition to the large statues and realistically carved human figures, a wide variety of elaborately carved jade and other stone celt-shaped pendants occurs. Large numbers of these have been recovered from graves on the Nicoya Peninsula (fig. 21). (See Hartman, 1901, 1907.)

Regarding the stylistic and temporal affiliations, particularly of the larger statues, there has been much discussion but as yet little agreement (compare Lothrop, 1926 b, vol. 1, p. 93, with Richardson, 1940, pp. 412–416.) The styles are highly distinctive and seem of local or perhaps of more southerly origin, but whether certain types are ancient and underlie *Maya* horizons to the north, as Lothrop believes they do, or are late and possibly associated with post-Conquest materials, as Richardson believes possible, must await systematic excavation and correlation in the area. Certainly the majority of larger statues in the Pacific region seem very distinct from *Mayan, Nahuatl,* or other northern forms and suggest South American rather than northern relationships. The stylistic relationship of the numerous petroglyphs carved on boulders with designs ranging from simple and realistic to complex and highly conventionalized figures also remains to be determined by more comprehensive study.

Burial.—Burial methods in the Pacific region of Costa Rica and Nicaragua include the use of urns, cremation, and inhumation. Three types of urns were used: boot-shaped, circular, and boat-shaped. Both articulated and disarticulated bodies occur in urns as well as the ashes of cremated bodies. Urn burials are reported from many coastal sites (see Lothrop, 1926 b, vol. 1, p. 97). Inhumation, often in mounds, was practiced in all parts of the Nicaragua region and was almost universal in Nicoya. Preservation of osseous material is very bad, but where determination is possible secondary or bundle burials seem most common. An example of unmarked grave arrangements at the well-known site of Las Guacas on the Nicoya Peninsula is characteristic (fig. 18). At

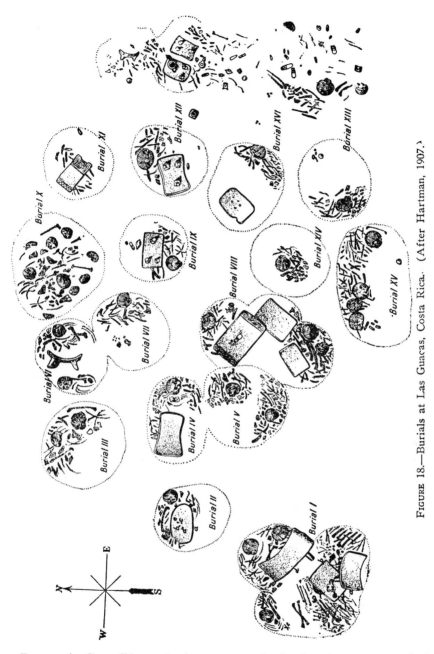

FIGURE 18.—Burials at Las Guacas, Costa Rica. (After Hartman, 1907.)

Bagaces in Costa Rica and other more northerly sites graves are marked by four stone columns at the corners. This corresponds to a grave type found in the Chiriquí[1] region.

---

[1] Chiriquí is used here as the designation of an archeological area and does not refer to the Chiriquí tribe, which may or may not have left the archeological remains in the region.

Ceramics.—According to Lothrop (1926 b, vol. 1, p. 105), the ceramics of Nicaragua and Costa Rica, despite borrowing and blending on the borders, form a unit when compared to pottery from the *Maya* and *Lenca* areas to the north or the Chiriquí region to the south. Certainly the finer, particularly the polychrome, vessels from this region are distinctive, but recent work in Honduras and in southwestern Costa Rica indicates that the monochrome wares of Chiriquí, Costa Rica, Nicaragua, and northwestern Honduras have many characteristics in common. Lothrop's detailed study (1926 b, vols. 1, 2) is largely based on museum collections, and recent field work indicates that here selection of finer, showier pieces has led to undue emphasis on polychrome and elaborate pieces as opposed to the much more abundant monochrome and simpler vessel types. This is pointed out by Stone (this volume), but it must be remembered that Stone is particularly referring to southwestern Costa Rica, whereas the most abundant polychrome pottery seems to come from Nicoya and western Nicaragua. Lothrop's analysis of Costa Rican and Nicaraguan pottery is still the most complete available; hence, with the above warnings pointed out, it will be very briefly outlined here. For full description, analysis, and illustration, the reader is referred to Lothrop's beautifully illustrated volumes.

The two main ceramic divisions in the Pacific region comprise the Polychrome and Monochrome Wares. The most important Polychrome group has been designated Nicoya Polychrome. (For a synoptic presentation of ceramic groups, see fig. 19.) Nicoya Polychrome Ware has been found from the Nicoya Peninsula to Fonseca Bay but is especially typical of southwestern Nicaragua and northwestern Costa Rica. As is true of other groups, briefly mentioned here, it includes numerous styles and types which await more detailed classification. Common Nicoya Polychrome vessels are egg or pear-shaped jars, set on annular bases or tripod legs, and tripod bowls supported by animal-head legs. Animal effigy jars are also common. The finest vessels are elaborate and brightly painted.

Painted designs are of various colors outlined in black. It is the perhaps unwarranted impression of the present writer that the use of a white or light background color is particularly striking on many pieces. Designs appear to be geometric and when analyzed usually prove to be conventionalized animals. Modeled vessels represent the turkey, macaw, jaguar, monkey, armadillo, and human head. Painted animals include man, jaguar, plumed serpent, 2-headed dragon, monkey, crab scorpion, and alligator.

Under-slip Incised Ware is a second Polychrome group. The design here has been incised prior to application of the slip through which it is visible. In addition, this ware is decorated with painted designs in Nicoya Polychrome style. Motifs include the earth monster, feathered serpent and its derivatives, as well as simple geometric forms. In 1926 the known

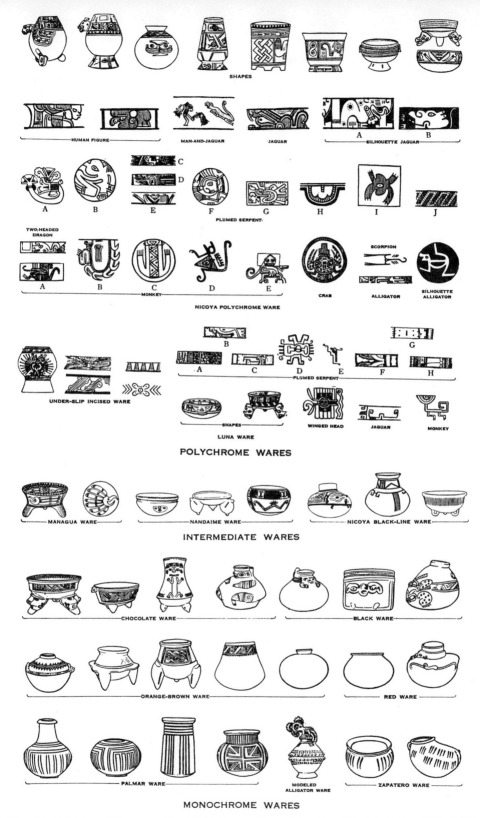

FIGURE 19.—Costa Rican and Nicaraguan pottery of the Pacific area. Forms and decorative motifs. (After Lothrop, 1926 b, pl. 193.)

distribution of this ware extended from the Nicoya Peninsula to Lake Nicaragua, and similar types were reported from near Veracruz in México.

The third main Polychrome group is Luna Ware, reported from northern Guanacaste (Costa Rica) to north-central Nicaragua but appearing to center on the islands of Lake Nicaragua. A creamy-white slip on which patterns are painted in thin-line technique is its most striking characteristic. Bowls supported by annular bases or tripod legs are almost the only forms represented. Designs are almost entirely derived from those on Nicoya Polychrome Ware. Life motifs are more limited and until analyzed appear to be purely geometric.

Intermediate between the Polychrome and Monochrome groups are three wares which are decorated chiefly by incising. The first, Managua ware, is limited in distribution almost entirely to the district between the two great Nicaraguan lakes. Its characteristic shape is a flaring rimmed bowl supported by solid tripod legs. Painted designs are either plumed serpent or apparently allied bird designs. The incised designs, often found on bowl floors, suggest *Aztec* "pepper grater" bowls. Nandaime Ware has a distinct red slip but is allied with the Polychrome Wares by its modeled and painted decorations. One Nandaime type has bulbous tripod legs and incised designs on the vessel floor. It is reported from central Guanacaste north along the Pacific probably to Fonseca Bay. Nicoya Black-line Ware seems to be found mainly in central Guanacaste. It may have a red or white slip, or no slip at all. Modeled forms are those of the Monochrome Ware series, and painted designs are either distinctive or are taken from the Polychrome group.

The Monochrome Wares are distinctive in regard to shape, color, and methods of decoration. Of the seven in this group the first four—Chocolate, Black, Orange-Brown, and Red Wares—are named from the color of their slips. Their decorations are modeled and incised. White paint is often rubbed into the incised design. Incised designs are usually geometric though some life forms occur. Motifs are built up through combinations of geometric units. Effigy vessels are very common, and modeled heads and other features are applied to the outer walls in the same fashion as in the Polychrome Wares. Life forms include the human figure, alligator (and alligator "god"), great horned owl, monkey, turtle, jaguar, armadillo, and snake (rare).

The other three Monochrome Wares are designated Palmar, Modeled Alligator, and Zapatero. Palmar Ware is a local ceramic group distinguished by simple patterns made with a broad incised line. This design is emphasized by touches of red paint. Modeled Alligator Ware is made of coarse unslipped clay. There is usually a cover on which is a modeled alligator. The sides of the cover and the base are adorned with lumps representing alligator scutes. Zapatero Ware includes large burial urns and smaller related forms. It, too, is composed of coarse clay, but the outer surface is usually polished and often decorated with broad red lines and small modeled figures of distinctive types.

Most if not all of the Pacific region ceramic wares are represented by a variety of other pottery artifacts, of which figurines and whistles are most abundant. These in many cases are synonymous. Nicoya Polychrome figurines are particularly interesting, since they represent a seated spread-legged type with "coffee-bean eyes." Lothrop takes issue with Spinden on the grounds that this apparently late type could hardly be directly related to those of the Archaic or Middle Cultures of the Valley of México. Nicoya Polychrome figurines are mold-made. Those of other wares are apparently both of mold-made and hand-modeled types. Figurines seated on elaborate stools are an interesting form. Zapatero Ware figurine forms, notably a howling dog and an old person with a container on her back (Lothrop, 1926 b, vol. 2, p. 273), are obviously related to Ulua River specimens in Honduras (compare Strong, Kidder, and Paul, 1938, fig. 7, c, g, h, r). Pottery drums, clay rattles, miniature vessels, painted and incised spindle whorls and cylindrical stamps all occur. Clay labrets are abundant. Similar forms of jade are found on the Nicoya Peninsula, but the Chiriquí gold type appears to be lacking. Two possible snuff tubes are on record, but tobacco pipes seem to be lacking. Since we lack temporal or other significant classifications for these interesting ceramic forms they need only be mentioned here. For further details the reader is referred to Lothrop (1926 b, vol. 2, pp. 258–282) and Hartman (1907).

In regard to the apparent great predominance of Monochrome Wares in the southern portion of the Pacific region, the reader is referred to a subsequent article (this volume, p. 187; also Stone, 1943, p. 80). As indicated previously, the center of distribution of most of the Polychrome Wares would seem to be the coastal and lake areas of Nicoya and western Nicaragua. Obviously, the decorative styles and techniques of many of these wares or types merge, but only many careful distributional and stratigraphic studies can hope to work out their exact spatial and temporal relationship one to another. Such studies still remain to be accomplished in the field.

Metallurgy and jade work.—Work in metal does not seem to be abundant in the Pacific region. Goldwork is rare and when found appears to be of the simpler Chiriquí forms. Jade, on the other hand, if we use the term in its broadest sense, seems to have been used extensively, as indicated by the findings of Hartman and others on the Nicoya Peninsula. Lehmann (1910) among others, has suggested that in certain areas of Middle America predominant interest in jade or greenstone seems to preclude an interest in the working of gold.

Stonework.—In regard to stonework, despite the account of flint quarries where the Indians of Subtiaba are said to have made arrowheads as late as 1890 (Lothrop, 1926 b, vol. 2, p. 435), very few chipped artifacts are recorded. Hartman (1907, pl. 32, No. 7) figures one large, stemmed point. The most elaborate of the ground-stone artifact types is the cere-monial metate from the Nicoya region (pl. 13, *f*, *g*). This is char-acterized by three legs in contrast to the 4-legged form of the Highland and Chiriquí regions. Hartman notes that the Nicoyan metates have either triangular or circular legs. Both types are elaborately decorated, the former with a projecting animal head and geometric patterns; the latter is usually larger and has animal decorative patterns. Manos, or grinding stones, are larger than the width of the metate. A stirrup-shaped grinding stone, with an ornamental handle, is an interesting form (fig. 20, *left*). The full function of these very elaborate metates is unknown.

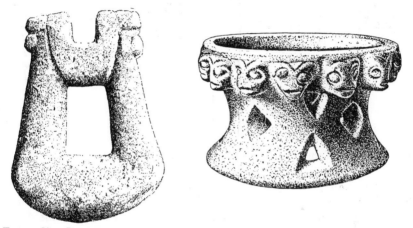

FIGURE 20.—Costa Rican stonework. *Left*: Stirrup pestle. *Right*: Stone stand, Las Mercedes (diameter of stand, 6 in. (15.2 cm.)). (After Lothrop, 1926 b, figs. 16 and 259.)

Quite possibly they were used as seats. Simple legless forms were prob-ably used for ordinary household purposes on the Pacific, as seems to have been the case in the Highlands. The elaborate, legged metate type, representing a decorative peak for the Americas in this regard, occurs south in the Chiriquí region and north into central and eastern Honduras.

Maces or club heads of stone are very typical in Nicoya graves (pl. 14, *a*, *b*). Hartman classifies these as having human, mammal, and bird heads; as representing two-legged monsters or alligators; or as round or star-shaped. The latter forms, including mammiform heads, have a wide distribution both to the north and south.

Bark beaters of stone are of two types (pl. 14, *d*, *e*). One of these is a flat disk, grooved around the edges for attaching a handle, and ridged on the two flat surfaces. The other is cylindrical, with the enlarged end ridged and the smaller end serving as a handle. The disk type, as Lothrop points out, is widely distributed, occurring in various parts of México, Guatemala, Costa Rica, and Colombia. Both types occur in Honduras (Strong, 1935, pl. 16, *k-m*). In México and in Honduras certain primitive tribes now use a hardwood club similar to the cylindrical stone form. Polished celts of amygdaloid and oval shape occur, and chipped double-bladed as well as T-shaped chipped axes are common (pl. 14, *h*). Monolithic, ground-stone, double-bladed axes (pl. 14, *f, g*) occur in the Nicaraguan lake region but seem more abundant on the east coast of that country.

As previously mentioned, jade amulets, particularly celt-shaped pendants, are very characteristic of the Nicoya region. (See fig. 21; also

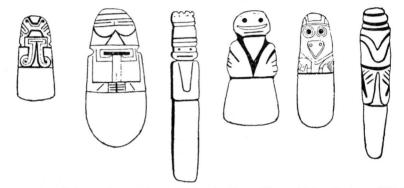

Figure 21.—Jade pendants, Nicoya Peninsula, Costa Rica. (After Lothrop, 1921.)

Hartman, 1907.) Many of the smaller amulets have been sawed off from larger celts. Objects of true jadeite or nephrite are actually rare compared to those made of similar but softer minerals. Circular stone disks, possibly gorgets, are common grave finds (pl. 14, *c*). Identical objects of slate have been found in mounds in northeastern Honduras. Some stone atlatl pegs, similar to those from northwestern South America, are found in Nicoya (fig. 22). The elaboration and range of all these

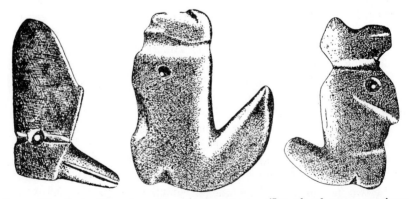

Figure 22.—Costa Rica stone spear-thrower pegs. (Length of center specimen, 2⅛ in. (5.4 cm.)). (After Hartman, 1907.)

various carved stone artifact types in the Pacific region are well shown by Hartman (1907). There is an obvious relationship between the designs on the smaller carved artifacts, on the larger stone statues, and on various pottery vessels, but, lacking true time perspective based on stratigraphy, the historic sequences remain to be worked out.

THE HIGHLAND REGION

For present purposes the term Highland region is used geographically in a somewhat larger and looser sense than the same term is employed by Lothrop. This was also true in regard to the Pacific region. (See sketch map, Lothrop, 1926 b, vol. 1, fig. 1, p. xxv). Lothrop distinguishes several subareas in the Highland region (1926 b, vol. 2, p. 285) and points out that the large area west of San José is still largely unknown. Logically, this would be the region archeologically transitional between the central and eastern Highlands and Nicoya. For the known Highland region he sees such a close relationship with prehistoric Chiriquí archeological materials as to suggest Chiriquí origins for the Highland culture later modified by northern influences. Since the *Guetar* peoples are historically the only known inhabitants of what Lothrop defines as the Highland region, he states that "the archeological remains must necessarily be attributed to them" (1926 b, vol. 2, p. 285). Such an inclusive statement is obviously open to criticism, since this could be true only if the *Guetar* had always been there or if no evidences of ancestral or earlier alien groups had ever been encountered. That no such temporal or ethnic distinctions have yet been made, in an area through which early migrations of necessity must have passed, clearly indicates how small our archeological knowledge of the region actually is. This being the case, we shall not attempt here to define either major or minor archeological area boundaries but shall limit the discussion to those major characteristics which at present seem to characterize the Highland region as a whole and tend to distinguish it from the Pacific region.

Surface structures.—As in the Pacific region, the most characteristic prehistoric structures of the Highlands are mounds. In the central valleys these are rubbish heaps of irregular shape, but on the Atlantic slope they are grouped so as to enclose courts or series of courts. An example of such aligned structures at Las Mercedes in Costa Rica is given here (fig. 26). The upper figure (fig. 26) shows smaller burial mounds (surface and cross section) located near the main group of structures. The latter (fig. 26, *lower*) center around a circular mound 100 feet (30 m.) in diameter and 20 feet (6.5 m.) in height. This mound consisted of a circular wall of river boulders filled in with earth. Hartman found evidence that large stone statues found nearby had once stood on the upper rim of the central mound. In western Nicaragua statues usually occur around the base of mounds. European articles were also found in typical graves at this site, suggesting that at least part of it was late. In addition to Hartman, Alanson Skinner excavated at Las Mercedes (Lothrop, 1926 b, vol. 2, pp. 451–467) and a large part of the Minor Keith collection was also secured here. (See Mason, 1946.) At several Highland sites occur circles of stones filled with debris ranging up to a diameter of 70 feet (21 m.). These are believed to be habitation mounds, although burials also occur in them (Lothrop, 1926 b, vol. 2, pl. ccii).

Statues.—Large stone statues of Lake Nicaragua type are reported from the eastern shore of that lake, extending southward into the Highland region across the Río San Juan as far as the vicinity of Puerto Limón. The "alter ego" motif, when it occurs in Costa Rica, is usually indicated by a small, complete animal or the head of the human figure (pl. 15, *b*), although large animal heads in this position do occur. (Compare fig. 17, *b*, example from Guanacaste.) The stone statutes from the Chontales region east of Lake Nicaragua, previously mentioned, seem likewise to be characterized by small complete animal figures surmounting the human head. Chacmool type statues, characterized by a recumbent figure with a bowl inset in the stomach, occur rarely in western Nicaragua and across to the Atlantic coast of Costa Rica. México is believed to be the center of distribution of the Chacmool type (Richardson, 1940, p. 403).

Smaller, realistic human figures of stone appear to be the most abundant type of stone statuary (pl. 15, *a-c*). Available literature suggests that such figures are as characteristic of the Highland region as small, celt-shaped, human amulets are of certain parts of the Pacific region, but this may be illusory. If true it is of interest, since celt-shaped human amulets are rather common in northeast Honduras, whereas human figures of stone are not. This is curious, since in general the northern coastal cultures of Honduras seem to bear a closer resemblance to the Highland than to the Pacific cultures of Costa Rica and Nicaragua.

Lothrop distinguishes three types of small human stone figures in the Highlands (pl. 15). The first consists of standing figures usually grasping an object in each hand. Often a human head is held, sometimes with a head in one hand and an ax in the other. This general style is repeated in the goldwork (pl. 17, *a*). A second consists of a human head, usually about half life size, cut squarely across the neck. These may be larger replicas of the decapitated heads held by standing figures. Similar heads occur in pottery. The third is a seated human figure with the arms resting on the knees and placed across the body. Often such figures are blowing a whistle or eating. These are usually only a few inches high, but specimens 2 feet (60 cm.) in height have been found. They resemble the Mexican seated stone figures known as "Indios tristes." Stone statuary of all sizes in Costa Rica and equally objects made of gold, deserve far more comprehensive study than they have yet received.

Mason's study of the stonework in the Minor Keith Collection improves our knowledge of stone sculpture in Costa Rica.

Burial.—Rectangular stone cists were commonly used for disposal of the dead in the Highland region. Hartman distinguishes four main types. Characteristic of the Cartago Valley is a cist built entirely of flat stone slabs. In the vicinity of San José cists are usually oval in form, built of river boulders, and have no roof. On the Atlantic slope large cists occur in which river boulders are used for walls and floors, but flat stone slabs form the roof. The fourth type, found on the western side of the Cartago Valley, consists of cists made of small, square-cut stone slabs used like bricks. Rectangular graves and globular stone cists are also reported by Hartman from the same mound at Santiago. These cist burials usually occur in mounds, or in stone circles apparently marking hut rings. Sometimes as many as three tiers of cists occur, with burials

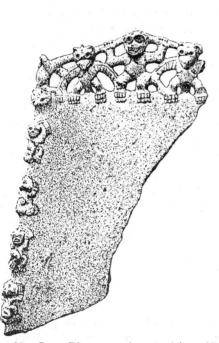

FIGURE 23.—Costa Rican carved stone slabs. (Specimen at left, 19 in. (48.4 cm.) wide.) (After Lothrop, 1926 b, fig. 179.)

touching. This crowding apparently leads occasionally to odd-shaped cists. Where burials are very crowded and cists small, as in the Cartago Valley, it is presumed that secondary burials occur. Elsewhere, as on the Atlantic slope, extended burials are said to be more common. As was true in the Pacific region, preservation of bones is very bad, and the proportion of direct inhumations to cist burials cannot be determined.

The majority of the objects described in sequel come from graves and cists or from their vicinity. This is also true of many of the small stone figures previously mentioned. Particularly characteristic of the Highland region are large, thin, elaborately carved stone slabs (fig. 23). Decorations on the sides of these are in low relief and often there are animals, such as monkeys or birds, carved in the round on the tops. Skinner found one of these in situ, standing erect in the middle of a cemetery at Anita Grande, and it is quite possible that these ornate slabs served as grave markers. Lothrop points out their stylistic similarity to decorated slabs from Manabí in Ecuador. The suggested resemblance to carved stonework from Chavín de Huantar in Perú does not seem to the present writer to be so close as in the case of the Manabí examples.

Ceramics.—In regard to ceramics from the Highland region, Lothrop states (1926 b, vol. 2, p. 293) that in almost every ware examined one finds strong traces of the virile art of Chiriquí to the south. Certain Highland ware designations, such as Red-line, Lost Color, Maroon, Tripod, and Handled, have previously been used to designate Chiriquí pottery groups. The Highland wares so designated pertain to the same class of pottery as in Chiriquí, modified but slightly by a different locale. Lothrop regrets the lack of data from the intervening provinces of Talamanca and Boruca in comparing the respective fictile and other arts of Highland Costa Rica and Chiriquí. However, this gap is here partly filled by Stone's paper (this volume, p. 170 f.), which in part deals with these areas. Stone corroborates the close relationship between Costa Rican and Chiriquí ceramics indicated by Lothrop.

In the territory lying east of Nicoya and extending to the Atlantic slope, northern and southern extensions not being indicated, which Lothrop (1926 b. vol. 2, pp. 295–389) terms the Highland region, four main ceramic groups are distinguished. These include (1) Polychrome Wares, (2) Simple Painted Wares, (3) Monochrome Wares, and (4) Appliqué Wares. (See fig. 24.) The Highland Polychrome Ware represents a relatively small group, not comparable in amount or importance with Nicoya and other Polychrome Wares from the Pacific region. Lothrop further points out that the majority of Highland Polychrome designs and shapes are borrowed from the Pacific region, although considerable local modification exists. Elsewhere in the present volume (p. 172) Stone states that many of the painted pottery pieces from Boruca and Talamanca have forms characteristic of the Monochrome Wares.

POLYCHROME WARE

SIMPLE PAINTED WARES

MONOCHROME WARES

APPLIQUÉ WARES

FIGURE 24.—Costa Rican and Nicaraguan pottery of the Highland area. Forms and decorative motifs. (After Lothrop, 1926 b, pl. 194.

These observations again emphasize the fact that the elaborate Polychrome Wares seem to center not only in the Pacific region, but particularly in Nicoya and western Nicaragua.

The Simple Painted Wares include Red-line, Yellow-line, White-line, Black-line, and Lost Color Wares. The first four are characterized by designs painted in the respective color upon a red or, rarely, a cream slip. Geometric patterns are common, some of these being derived from the Chiriquí alligator motif. A tripod bowl supported by animal heads is the most distinctive form, but each ware contains various forms apparently taken over from the Appliqué Wares. Lost Color, or Negative Painted, Ware is decorated with light designs against a darker background. The usual wax process appears to have been employed on this type of vessel. Designs are geometric, curvilinear, and zoomorphic. Lost Color Ware is not abundant in the Highland region and appears to be little more than a specialized extension of a common Chiriquí technique. As is true of all Highland Wares, its relative age is undetermined, but its forms are generally those of the above.

There are five subdivisions of Highland Monochrome Wares according to Lothrop. These are: Maroon Incised (related to Lost Color Ware and marked by incised patterns on vessels with a maroon slip), Chocolate (apparently derived from its Pacific region prototype), Red-lip (lip red with unslipped band below on which painted, modeled, or incised decoration occurs; related to Nicoya Black-line group), and Red, characterized by a red slip, its forms falling into two divisions, one connected with the Pacific region, the other differing from Stone Cist Ware only in clay and slip.

The four Appliqué Wares are apparently the most typical and abundant of the Highland region. These are the Curridabat, Tripod, Stone Cist, and Handled Wares. As a rule, the Appliqué Ware vessels are of coarse, gritty paste, usually burnished rather than slipped. Decoration consists primarily of the application of buttons or ribbons of clay to the outside of the vessel, but this does not exclude painting, incising, and modeling. All four types of decoration sometimes occur on the same vessel and, in certain subtypes, appliqué decoration is absent. The dividing line between these wares is often obscure, and they blend into one another in no apparent succession. The dividing line between Stone Cist and Handled Wares is particularly obscure.

There are two groups of Curridabat Ware; one is distinguished by one or more small ridges encircling the neck or shoulder; the other consists of smaller vessels with painted instead of raised designs. Decoration is appliqué (most common; apparently representing alligator scutes), modeled, incised, and painted. All the forms are simple. In regard to subtypes, occasional provenience, and wider distributions the reader is referred to Lothrop (1926 b, vol. 2, pp. 332–355).

Tripod Ware consists of vessels which are set on tall tripod legs and either represent animals or have modeled animals upon them. The vessels are often elaborately decorated and tend toward the grotesque. Modeling is very common, but a few painted forms occur. At Curridabat, in Costa Rica, the type site for ware of that name, Hartman (1907) found broken Tripod Ware vessels at depths of 2 to 4 feet (0.6 to 1.2 m.) underground, and at 4 to 7 feet (1.2 to 2.1 m.) he encountered numerous upright Curridabat jars. He observes that these two wares formed 90 percent of the pottery at this site. Tripod Ware has a wide distribution marked by local variations. It is particularly characteristic of northeastern Honduras.

Stone Cist Ware is composed of globular jars, often set on short tripod legs and decorated with appliqué animal forms, ribbons (often punctured), or buttons. Modeled forms include the alligator, man, tree, frog, and snake. The paste is sandy; the color normally brick red; burnishing is more common than slipping; and specimens are very friable. This general type is also widely distributed. It is very characteristic of northeastern Honduras.

Handled Ware is similar in composition to the above but is less elaborately, one might say grotesquely, decorated. Handles are large and include single, paired vertical, and paired horizontal forms. This ware is closely related to its Chiriquí name-giver. As Lothrop indicates, the basis of classification of this ware, like many of the others, is not entirely satisfactory and awaits revision based on more extensive, as well as intensive stratigraphic, excavations.

Like the Pacific, the Highland region has various ceramic forms which do not fit into present pottery classifications. It also has a number of pottery objects other than vessels. Hollow cylindrical pot stands, sometimes with Atlantean supports, are common. Often the upper ring is surmounted by small faces (fig. 20, *right*). These objects of either pottery or stone were presumably used to support round-bottomed vessels which are the usual type. Incense burners of Red Ware with modeled handles are similar to Honduran and Mexican forms. The handles often represent an alligator or serpent. Large pottery heads of several types, similar to those in stone, also occur. Nearly all on record came from the Las Mercedes district. Figurines are much less common than in the Pacific region. Human figures are most common; standing figures in costume and pensive figures seated on stools occur. A common type with painted geometric designs belongs to the class of Chiriquí Alligator Ware. These are usually seated, sometimes on stools, and usually have spread legs. Canoe- or boat-shaped vessels containing human paddlers are a distinctive type. In addition, dogs, jaguars, birds, and composite or double animals are represented. Whistles, usually human or animalistic in form, pertain to various ceramic wares. Rattles occur in the form of tripod legs, incense-burner handles, or even sealed pots. Gourd-form rattles are represented. Pottery drums are less common than in the Pacific region but do occur. Some of these are of Highland Polychrome Ware. Cylindrical pottery stamps are also found in the Highlands.

Metallurgy.—Though excellent examples of jade or allied stone carving have been found in the Highland region graves, goldwork is apparently more common. Most of this exquisitely worked material has been dug up by treasure hunters, and much of it has been melted down. However, large collections are to be found in Costa Rican and other museums. Unfortunately, no comprehensive studies of Costa Rican goldwork are available and little can be said about it here. Many forms in goldwork are the same as those in Highland ceramics or in stonework. The techniques employed seem generally to be the same as those used in the Chiriquí area. Human figures holding trophy heads or other objects, mammals, birds, alligators, frogs, and bells are all represented. (See pl. 17, *a*.) The entire problem of metalwork in Costa Rica and the rest of Central America calls for much more study than it has yet received. On general grounds, however, we can state that the Highland region links up with the Chiriquí area in yielding considerable amounts of stylistically similar goldwork. The Pacific region, however, with the possible exception of the Boruca region, seems largely to lack metalwork, or to yield merely a few simple and presumably borrowed forms.

Stonework.—Considering work in stone, again we have no data on chipping techniques, but various ground-stone objects are excellently made. The Highland metate differs from the Nicoya form in being oblong instead of rectangular and having three legs instead of four. It also has a ridge around the edge of the grinding plate necessitating a short handstone or mano. Often the Highland metate is formed like an animal, particularly the jaguar, having the head at one end and the tail curled and attached to a leg to form a handle (fig. 25). It is so closely related in form and style to the metate of the Chiriquí area that there are no clear rules to distinguish between the two. As in Nicoya, very elaborate forms occur (pl. 15, *d*), complex in execution and rich in forgotten mythological sym-

FIGURE 25.—Metate from Cartago, Costa Rica. (After Lothrop, 1926 b, fig. 181.)

bolism. The animal-form metate occurs as far south as Ecuador and is rather common in northeastern Honduras.

In the Highlands, as in the Pacific region, it is impossible to distinguish positively between certain elaborate mortuary metates and probable seats or stools. However, one Highland form definitely suggests a seat. This type consists of a round plate encircled by a ridge and supported on a tall, openwork pedestal. Decoration consists of pierced slits, triangles, diamonds, or Atlantean figures. Similar forms occur in pottery and wood which cannot be successfully used as a grinding surface; hence the use of such objects for seats seems probable. This pedestal-type seat, or stand, is distributed throughout the Highland and Chiriquí regions. A similar form without the plate is identical with the pot stands made of pottery and apparently performed the same function. Stone bowls, some of which resemble pottery forms and are elaborately carved, also occur in the Highland region. The polished ax of the Highland region is usually diamond-shaped in cross section, and this type is common also in the Chiriquí region. Another type is chipped and not polished. A double-bitted, chipped ax form occurs, but the monolithic ax is not reported.

THE EASTERN COASTAL PLAIN

This, the third region mentioned in the present brief archeological survey of Costa Rica and Nicaragua, contains topographic variations (see Introduction, p. 121) but may be considered as generally coterminous with part of the Atlantic Plain and all the Nicaraguan Lowland. It comprises a huge triangular area extending from the Talamanca Plain in Costa Rica north along the Caribbean into Honduras and, widening rapidly to the northwest, to the eastern base of the Cordillera in northern Costa Rica and central Nicaragua. This vast jungle-covered area, extending from rolling foothills eastward to the swampy Mosquito coast, is not very well known from the geographic and is almost unknown from the archeological standpoint. Despite the fact that the region includes over half of the combined area of Costa Rica and Nicaragua and forms an essential archeological link between Honduras and the Highland region on the south and the Pacific region on the west, very little can be said at present concerning its archeology. For this reason only a brief summary of previously published materials (Strong, 1935, pp. 166–167) is given here.

Le Baron gives a plan of a small ceremonial site on the Prinzapolca River consisting of three rude monoliths set up to form a triangle, which is paved with rocks. One monolith had a crude face incised at the top and others had simple circular or geometric petroglyphs. No artifacts were found. On the Rama River, which enters the Caribbean near Monkey Point, Spinden (1925) notes the occurrence of small mounds containing abundant pottery. Painted and modeled ware, including tripod bowls, figurines, whistles, etc., were found here. Cookra Hill, near the south end of Pearl Lagoon, formerly had ancient graves from which gold amulets, a marble mace head of Nicoyan type, abundant pottery, and other artifacts have been removed.   Near Bluefields occur large and interesting

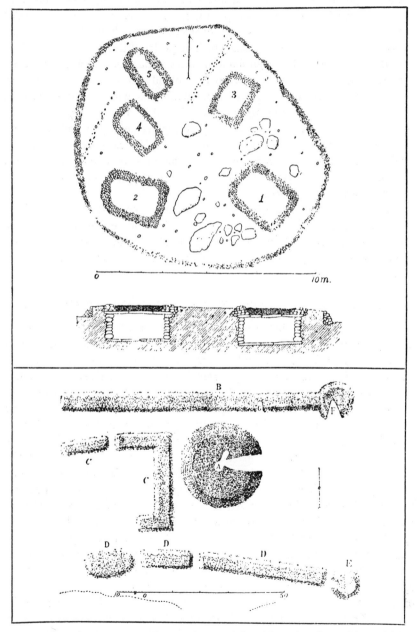

FIGURE 26.—Burial mound and general map of Las Mercedes, Costa Rica.   (After Hartman, 1901.)

shell heaps. Pottery from these is usually unslipped but is elaborately modeled. One type, with tripod feet decorated with faces and containing rattles, suggests a local variant of Costa Rican pottery (Tripod Ware). A small stone figure of a man and two interesting types of monolithic axes, figured by Lothrop (see pl. 14, *f*, *g*), come from here. Spinden calls attention to stone bowls with projecting heads, tripod supports, and a band of interlaced decoration, which come from this area. (See Honduras, pl. 1, *top*.) The well-made metates with animal heads from eastern Nicaragua form a link between (Highland) Costa Rica and northern Honduras. Spinden also states that small pots with plastic decoration and gold figurines are said to have been found in the Pis Pis mining district. He observed many elaborate petroglyphs near falls and rapids on these eastern rivers. At the junction of the Yasica and Tuma Rivers, within the wet belt and in the vicinity of mounds, he found two carvings of the Lake Nicaragua type. One of these depicted a man with an alligator clinging to his back.

From the surveys made by Spinden it thus appears that eastern Nicaragua forms a cultural link between the Highland region of Costa Rica to the south, and the Bay Islands and the Honduran coast to the north. Too little is yet on record, however, to attempt a more detailed comparison of types.

ETHNIC CORRELATIONS IN COSTA RICA AND NICARAGUA

Exact correlations between archeological manifestations and documented historic sites or ruins formerly occupied by specific tribes are as yet unknown in Costa Rica and Nicaragua. Whether available documentation and adequate archeological remains at historic sites exist cannot be determined until more serious attempts in that direction have been made. However, western Nicaragua, particularly the lake region, as well as various parts of Costa Rica seems very promising in this regard. This is indicated by the fact that rather close territorial correlations have already been demonstrated, particularly by Lothrop, between certain ceramic wares and the historic territories of certain distinct linguistic and ethnic groups. Such generalized correlations should not be pushed too far, but when objectively arrived at they do have rather strong inferential value. Needless to say, these will be greatly strengthened when (1) specific historic sites have been carefully worked and (2) when demonstrable sequence or time order can be established. A simpliste "one to one" correlation between the ethnic group known to have occupied a specific region at the time of the Conquest and all, or a great majority, of the archeological remains in that region must always be subject to suspicion. This is particularly true in the more favorable parts of an isthmian area where both linguistic distributions and history indicate that numerous migrations have occurred. However, until painstaking excavation brings

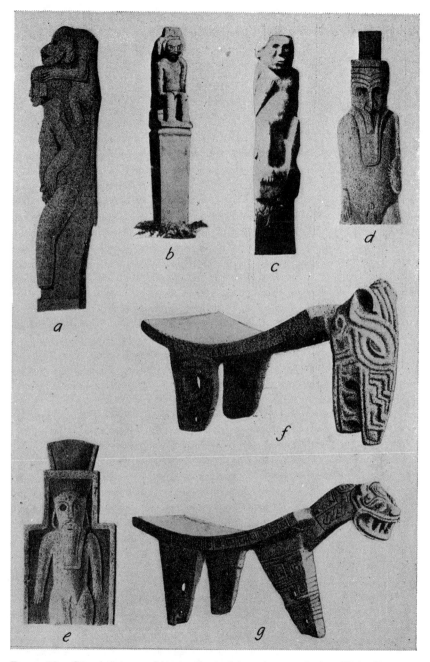

PLATE 13.—**Stone statue and seats, Central America.** *a, b, d, e,* From Zapatero Island, Nicaragua. (After Bovallius, 1886, and Squier, 1852.) *c,* Comitán, México. (After Seler, 1901.) *f, g,* From Nicoya Peninsula, Costa Rica. (After Holmes, 1908.)

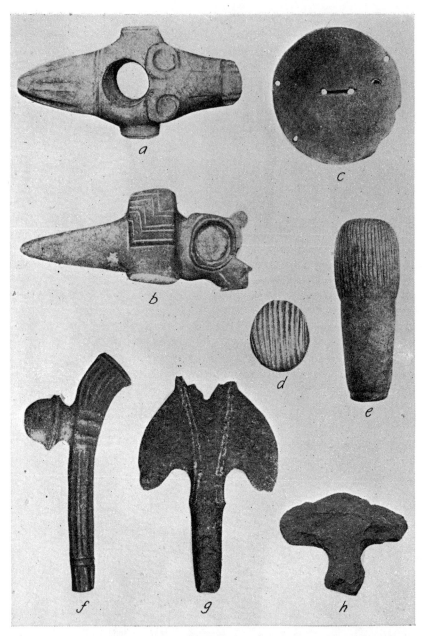

PLATE 14.—Stone artifacts from Costa Rica and Nicaragua. *a, b,* Club heads, Nicoya Peninsula, Costa Rica; *c,* disk, Costa Rica; *d, e,* bark beaters, Filadelfia, Costa Rica; *f–h,* axes. (Length of *f,* 12.5 in. (31.5 cm.); length of *g,* 8 in. (20.2 cm.); height of *h,* 7 in. (17.8 cm.).) (After Lothrop, 1926 b, pls. 10–12.)

PLATE 15.—**Stone carvings, Costa Rica.** *a, c,* Figures from Las Mercedes.
(Respective heights, 14 and 10.5 in. (35.5 and 26.5 cm.).) *b,* Statue. *d,*
Ceremonial metate, San Isidro de Guadaloupe. (Length of top 24.5 in.
(62.5 cm.).) (After Lothrop, 1926 b, pls. 205, 138, and 140.)

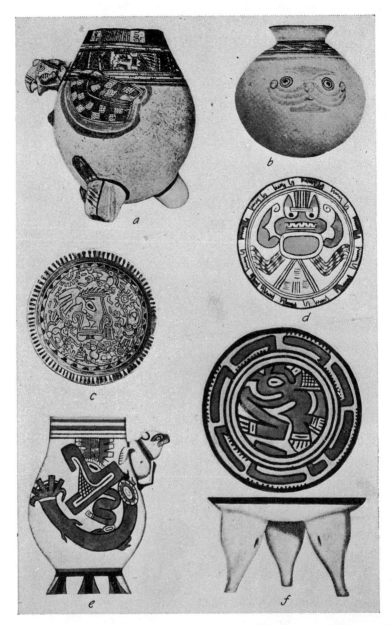

PLATE 16.—**Nicoya Polychrome, Costa Rica and Nicaragua.** *a*, Macaw effigy
jar, Bolson, Costa Rica. (Height, 11.5 in. (29.2 cm.).) *b*, From Filadelfia,
Costa Rica. (Height, 9 in. (23 cm.).) *c*, From Ometepe Island, Nicaragua.
(Diameter, 9 in. (23 cm.).) *d*, Bowl interior, crab motif in light red, dark
red, orange, and black on white. (Diameter, 5.5 in. (14 cm.).) *e*, Plumed
serpent motif jar, Nicoya Peninsula, Costa Rica, in red and black on yellow.
(Height, 10.5 in. (26.7 cm.).) *f*, Plumed serpent decoration from tripod
interior, Nicoya Peninsula, Costa Rica, in red and black on orange. (Diameter, 5.5 in. (14 cm.).) (After Lothrop, 1926 b, pls. 14, 23, 30, 71, 46 and 47.)

PLATE 17.—**Central American goldwork and pottery.** *a*, Gold figurines, Costa Rica; *b*, Nandaime ware, Nicaragua; *c*, Nicoya Black-Line ware, Costa Rica; *d*, Under-Slip Incised ware, Nicoya Peninsula, Costa Rica. (Height, 9 in. (23 cm.).) *e*, Plumbate ware, Ulua Valley, Honduras. (Height 7 in. (18 cm.).) (After Lothrop, 1926 b, pls. 78, 97, 99, 84, and 20.)

PLATE 18.—**Central American pottery types.** *a, b,* Black-Line ware, Las Mercedes and Anita Grande, Costa Rica. (Diameters, approximately 9 and 6 in. (23 and 15 cm.).) *c,* Curridabat ware, Costa Rica. (Diameter, approximately 4 in. (10 cm.).) *d,* Luna ware, Nicaragua. (Width, 4.5 in. (11.4 cm.).) *e,* Lost-Color pattern, Las Mercedes. *f,* Yellow-Line ware, Las Mercedes. *g,* Red-Line ware, Las Mercedes. (Diameter, 6.5 in. (16.5 cm.).) *h,* Tripod ware, Las Mercedes. (Height, approximately 6 in. (15.2 cm.).) *i,* Highland Polychrome ware, Costa Rica. (Height, 4.5 in. (11.4 cm.).) (After Lothrop, 1926 b, pls. 159, 171, fig. 93, pls. 161, 157, fig. 192, pls. 175, 143.)

true time perspective, the establishment of such gross correlations is at least a promising first step.

The most striking of these correlations is that existing between the distribution of Nicoya Polychrome Wares and peoples of *Chorotegan* (the *Chiapanecan* of Thomas and Swanton, 1911) and *Nahuatl* speech. Territorially this double distribution includes the Peninsula of Nicoya, the Isthmus of Rivas, the west coast of Nicaragua, the islands of Lake Nicaragua, and parts of southern Salvador. As Lothrop (1926 b, vols. 1, 2) demonstrates in considerable detail, Nicoya Polychrome pottery is not only the most elaborate painted ware in Costa Rica and Nicaragua but also is characterized by design and technical elements of older *Mayan* and later *Mexican* origin. The presence of what he considers to be older *Mayan* motifs in Nicoya Polychrome leads him to the belief that the *Chorotegan* groups, longer in residence, were responsible for the bulk of this ceramic ware, whereas the later *Nicarao* and other *Nahautl* (Mexican) peoples adopted it and introduced later northern motifs into Nicoya Polychrome but did not develop a distinguishable subtype of their own. Since linguistic considerations indicate northern origins for both *Chorotegan* and *Nahuatl* peoples, while history and legend give the *Chorotegan* temporal priority in this region, Lothrop's correlation agrees with the available evidence.

On similar distributional and territorial grounds, Chocolate Ware, Black Ware, Orange-Brown Ware, perhaps Red Ware, and Alligator Ware may also be largely assigned to the *Chorotegan* peoples. Another ware, Managua, is limited in shape and design and has been found almost entirely within the boundaries of one *Chorotegan* tribe, the *Mangue*. Nandaime Ware has been found from Guanacaste in Costa Rica to Nandaime in Nicaragua and probably extends north to Fonseca Bay. Because this distribution includes the *Subtiaba* as well as the *Chorotegans*, Lothrop believes Nandaime Ware was made by people of both linguistic groups. Similar dual authorship is suggested by Lehmann (1910) and Lothrop in regard to Nicoya Blackline Ware, since it commonly occurs at sites in *Coribici* (*Chibchan*) territory and also in *Orotiña* (*Chorotegan*) territory as well. East of the Nicaraguan lakes the territory of the *Ulvan* tribes and the known distribution of Luna and Zapatero Wares more or less coincide. Luna Ware, through its association with large boot-shaped burial urns in which were found post-Caucasian objects, is apparently protohistoric. According to Lothrop, this coincidence between *Ulvan* occupation and the above wares is strong for Luna Ware, but he states that Zapatero Ware cannot be so definitely delimited.

All the foregoing ceramic and tribal correlations refer to the Pacific region. In regard to the Highland region we have previously (p. 131) quoted and criticized Lothrop's somewhat wholesale assignment of all the known archeological materials to the historic *Guetar* (*Chibchan*). Stone

(1943, p. 75) points out some of the difficulties encountered in assigning prehistoric remains to specific historic tribes in Costa Rica. However, the known historic occupation of the entire southern and eastern Highland region by tribes pertaining to the *Chibchan* linguistic stock does establish at least a priority in their favor. The marked concentration of large statues of so-called *"Chorotegan* type" within the area mainly occupied by *Chorotegan* peoples, particularly in the Nicaraguan lake region, offers some justification for this nominal linkage. As previously stressed, however, the styles of these large monuments are so variable and their present distribution and relative age are so uncertain that this problem must be left open. Certainly the concentration of jade (greenstone) work on amulets, etc., in Nicoya and adjacent areas historically occupied by the *Orotiña* and other *Chorotegan,* as well as Mexican, peoples suggests a partial correlation. Similarly, the fact that goldwork is equally characteristic in the Highland region and in Chiriquí, where only *Chibchan* tribes are known to have lived in historic times, tends to link goldworking with peoples of this linguistic stock, the major affiliations of which are with northern South America. All the above correlations have some degree of probability and indicate very important leads. However, the final assignment of technical trends, ceramic wares, monumental styles, and all other archeological complexes in Costa Rica and Nicaragua to historic tribes, prehistoric groups, and relative temporal position in both the Pacific and Highland regions must await far more careful and extensive excavation work than either of these areas has yet received. As for the Eastern Coastal Plain, it still remains an almost complete archeological terra incognita.

BIBLIOGRAPHY

Hartman, 1901, 1907; Johnson, 1940; Kidder (see Strong, Kidder, and Paul, 1938); Le Baron, 1912; Lehmann, 1910; Lines, 1938 b; Lothrop, 1926 b; Mason, 1945; Paul (see Strong, Kidder, and Paul, 1938); Richardson, 1940; Spinden, 1925; Stone, 1943; Strong, 1935; Strong, Kidder, and Paul, 1938; Swanton (see Thomas and Swanton, 1911); Thomas and Swanton, 1911.

THE ARCHEOLOGY OF PANAMA

By Samuel K. Lothrop

INTRODUCTION

For many years the primitive inhabitants of Panamá were known only through archeological remains discovered in the Province of Chiriquí, and it was generally supposed that a more or less uniform culture extended throughout the Isthmian region. Since 1930, however, evidence has come to light which radically changes this picture, and at present we can distinguish four or more cultures in Panamá. In spite of the small area they occupied, each culture was radically distinct from the others, although features were sometimes borrowed, as might be expected among neighbors. From continental South America to the west the principal culture areas are named Darién, Coclé, Veraguas, and Chiriquí (map 4). Several regions in Panamá are archeologically still unknown, and it is definitely possible that other cultures may be discovered.

The cultural diversity disclosed by Panamanian archeology is in accord with early historical accounts. These indicate that a fairly uniform speech, physical type, material culture, and social organization once extended throughout Darién from South America to a point beyond the Canal. The town of Chame, which still exists, is given as the limit of Darién culture in the 16th century. From Chame to the west both speech and physical type varied greatly. It is constantly stated in Spanish documents that neighboring aboriginal settlements could communicate with each other only through interpreters. Unfortunately, no ancient vocabularies have come down to us, and so we cannot know the extent of linguistic variation. Today the few surviving Indians speak *Guaymí, a Chibchan* dialect.

Regarding physical type, various 16th-century observers point out that there was great variation in skin color and in stature. At least two accounts exist of the natives of Escoria, who were both taller and more heavily bearded than the Spaniards. We can say nothing about the beards, but excavations in Coclé have revealed the presence of individuals who must have stood over 6 feet (1.9 m.) in life.

A suggestion of cultural diversity with wide implications arises from the description of a native ball court (juego de pelota). This definitely was not of the Mexican or Central American type, for it was compared

143

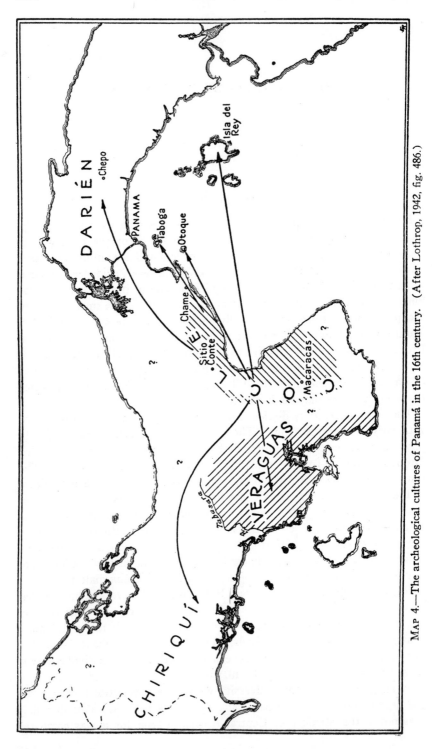

Map 4.—The archeological cultures of Panamá in the 16th century.   (After Lothrop, 1942, fig. 486.)

to the *Arawak* ball courts seen by the Spaniards in the West Indies, which differ radically from those of the mainland.

Any discussion of Panamá must consider the question of antiquity, because Panamá is the most obvious route to South America and because man must have passed through the isthmian region, even if he did not permanently settle there, in the remote past. It has been suggested that a crudely chipped celt found by Linné on the Atlantic coast may be of great antiquity. This seems improbable, because chipped celts or chipped and partly polished celts were manufactured both in Panamá and Costa Rica until the time of the Spanish Conquest. It is fair to state, therefore, that no proved trace of man in the far past has yet been found in Panamá or, in fact, nearer to Panamá than Nicaragua.

The cultures to be described may be regarded as historic; that is to say, they were flourishing when the Spaniards came. Evidence obtained from excavations in Coclé suggests that Coclé culture was blooming at least two centuries before the Conquest. The complexity of the oldest known remains, dating only from the early 14th century, is such that a fairly long past must be postulated. This is especially true of the intricate symbolism shown in pottery designs. The prototypes, however, remain to be found.

DARIEN

The term Darién applies geographically to the portion of Panamá lying between the Canal and continental South America. Archeological research in this area commenced in 1522 when Gonzalo Fernández de Oviedo y Valdés, later the royal historian, opened "certain sepulchers which were inside a hut," with the hope of finding gold. Present knowledge of archeological remains, however, is based largely on the work of S. Linné (1929), who conducted excavations on both coasts of the Isthmus.

The Darién first seen by the Spanish explorers was very different from the Darién that exists today. Owing to advanced agricultural practices, much of the now-prevalent jungle evidently had been cut down. Descriptions exist of huge and beautiful houses, giant canoes inlaid with mother-of-pearl—in short, a scale of material culture much more advanced than the surviving archeological remains indicate. A suggestion of ancient cultural complexity, however, comes from the mythology and ritual of the present *Cuna* Indians, ably studied by Nordenskiöld (1938), Ruben Néle, and Pérez Kantule. (See also, this volume, p. 257.)

Burial custom.—History and archeology alike indicate considerable variety in the burial customs of Darién. Oviedo y Valdés, (1851–55), the best historical authority, states that burial was a rite reserved for the nobility as well as for such wives, retainers, and captives as were selected to accompany their lords to another world. The living destined for the grave either took poison voluntarily, were buried alive while stupified by intoxication, or were killed in some unspecified manner. Bodies of the common people were abandoned to the beasts and birds.

In Darién it was customary among certain ruling families to bury the wives and servants in the ground but to desiccate and preserve the body of the chief. To this end the body was dried out by means of surrounding fires. It then was disposed of in one of two ways. Some families maintained a special house or room where their ancestors were seated in order along the walls. In other instances the bodies were wrapped in mantles and placed in hammocks. Linné (1929) points out that the *Cueva* today place the dead in hammocks slung in pits, which subsequently are filled with earth, and he has published a map showing the distribution of various types of mummification.

Linné's excavations revealed the presence of secondary urn burials on the Atlantic coast of Darién and of inhumations in deep graves on the Pacific.

Ceramics.—The pottery in general is coarse. Decoration consists of modeling, filleting, and incising (pl. 19, *c–e*). Tall annular bases are typical. Sufficient material is not available for close comparisons, but the pottery may be described as definitely Isthmian in character with stylistic links both to the south and north.

On the Pearl Islands, Linné discovered typical Darién pottery associated with round house sites and also polychrome pottery of Coclé style associated with rectangular house sites. He demonstrated by microscopic studies that both were manufactured locally and suggested that the polychrome ware was produced by Indians transferred from the mainland after the Conquest. Stratigraphic studies in Coclé endorse this opinion.

Stone objects.—Objects of stone are not common in Darién. The elaborate metates typical of western Panamá have not been found east of the Canal, but small mortars occur (pl. 20, *b*). Celts usually are small and are polished (pl. 20, *a*).

COCLE

The aboriginal culture which takes its name from the Province of Coclé occupies the Pacific watershed of Panamá to the southwest of the Canal. It is found chiefly in Coclé Province and the adjacent Asuero Peninsula, including the Provinces of Herrera and Los Santos. This well-watered region in large part today consists of open plains and is dedicated to cattle raising, but to the south and west the land is hilly and increasingly more rugged. To the north lies the little-known Cordillera and the continental divide. Archeological remains in the area here outlined are better understood from a technical point of view than are those from other parts of Panamá because detailed records of excavation have been published and because much material with accurately recorded provenience exists.

The Spaniards first reached Coclé and the Asuero Peninsula in 1515 and continually raided it for several years thereafter because the natives possessed gold in greater quantity than hitherto had been encountered in the New World. The discovery of even greater wealth in México and western South America, however, soon attracted the stream of adventurers to those regions, leaving this part of Panamá in an isolated desuetude from which it is only today emerging. The few surviving Indians now live in the high mountains.

No remains exist today above ground of the old Indian settlements except occasional lines of stone columns, the function of which is still unknown. Refuse beds, however, have been disclosed in the banks of rivers to indicate the sites of primitive villages. Many of these contain burials accompanied by funeral furniture in great quantity.

Burial customs.—Burial in the ground, as in Darién (q.v.), was a right confined to chiefs, the nobility, and their wives and retainers. In 1519 the Spaniards discovered and described the body of the Cacique Parita prepared for burial in sumptuous array, including gold ornaments which weighed 355 pounds.

The most famous burial ground, today known as Sitio Conte, is situated on the Río Grande de Coclé. Here scores of graves have been opened and carefully plotted and their contents recorded. These graves are of several types, one of which evidently represents the burial of chiefs. In these, the main occupant was seated on a stone slab, on which his body seemed to have been desiccated by fire, surrounded by the extended bodies of his retainers (fig. 27). Above and around the bodies, funeral offerings and jewelry were piled in great abundance. Over 200 pottery vessels were found in several graves.

Excavation of these graves presented a difficult technical problem. In many cases the funeral offerings were several layers deep and had been trampled into a compacted mass before the grave was closed. At times graves were reopened and the contents pushed aside to make room for more bodies. Frequently, in digging a grave, an older burial was encountered. This might be robbed for the benefit of the new burial or it might be cut through and the contents scattered, and so the deeper burial actually is the more recent.

The contents of the grave are so complex that we can merely list the more frequently found types of objects. Tools and implements include metates, sharpening and grinding stones, polishing stones, crudely chipped stone blades, bone points, stingray points, bone spear throwers, stone shaft straighteners, drills, mirrors, and chisels of gold or stone. Two types of celts are characteristic of the locality. One is pear-shaped with a polished blade and roughly chipped poll (fig. 28). The other is wedge-shaped and polished all over (pl. 20, c). Stone artifacts with the exception of jewelry are crudely made.

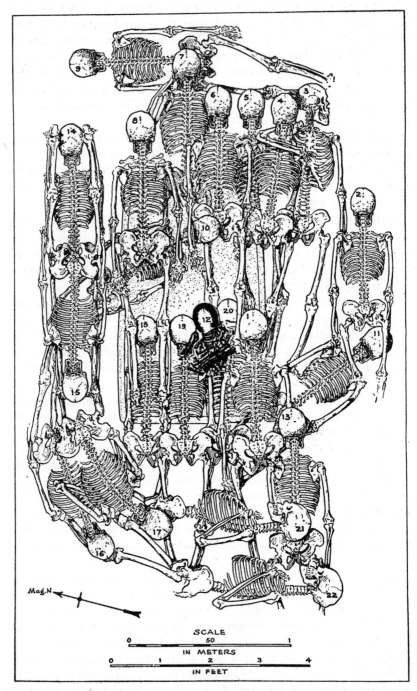

FIGURE 27.—Coclé grave plan. Skeleton 12, the owner of the grave, has fallen from a seated position. (After Lothrop, 1937, fig. 31.)

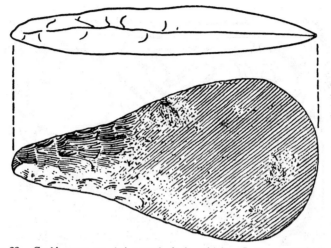

FIGURE 28.—Coclé stone ax (⅓ actual size). (After Lothrop, 1937, fig. 53.)

Ceramics.—Pottery, found in abundance, is complex in character, for not only are there many distinct wares, but the designs are intricate and vary with period (figs. 29–36). Several ceramic shapes are typical only of Coclé. Among these are slightly curved plates about 12 inches (30 cm.) in diameter, deeper and smaller bowls with flaring walls, and carafes with globular or angular bodies and tall, flaring necks. Occasionally vessels are decorated with filleting or incising and suggest the pottery of Chiriquí or Darién, but the vast majority of vessels are purely local in character. Most of the pottery was coated with varnish, perhaps copal, which disappears when re-exposed to the air and light.

The outstanding pottery ware of Coclé is the polychrome (figs. 30–35). Colors include black, brown, dark red, light red, purple (which sometimes verges on blue or gray), and green. The designs typically depict various monstrous beasts which combine aspects of several animals. Attempts at naturalism either in painting or modeling are rare. Also typical are beautifully executed scroll patterns, of which there are a bewildering number.

Ornaments.—Jewelry and ornaments are scarcely less complex than the pottery. We may mention headbands and hats of gold. Shirts were adorned with golden disks with beaten designs (pl. 20, *d*), running up to 12 inches (30 cm.) in diameter, or with sets of smaller golden disks. In

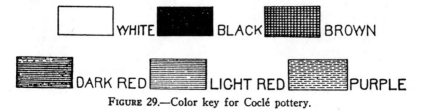

FIGURE 29.—Color key for Coclé pottery.

FIGURE 30.—Early Polychrome, Coclé. Tray showing crocodile-headed bird motifs (approximately ¼ actual size). (After Lothrop, 1942, fig. 7.)

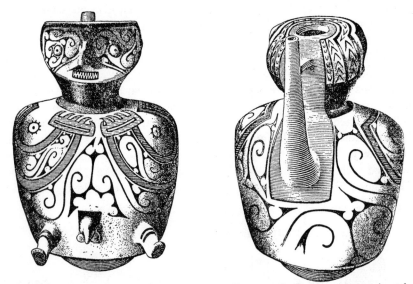

FIGURE 31.—An Early Polychrome spouted effigy vessel, Coclé. (Approximately ⅓ actual size). (After Lothrop, 1942, fig. 123.)

FIGURE 32.—Early Polychrome, Coclé. Plate interiors. *a*, Herringbone Pattern (⅛ actual size); *b*, crocodile-headed bird pattern (³⁄₁₆ actual size); *c*, conventionalized bird and turtle motifs (³⁄₂₀ actual size); *d*, "S" scrolls (⅟₁₆ actual size). (After Lothrop, 1942, figs. 15, 83, 50, 33.)

FIGURE 33.—Early polychrome, Coclé. (Approximate sizes: ¼, ¼, ⅓, ⅙, and ⅓). (After Lothrop, 1942, figs. 108, 11, 116, and 98.)

FIGURE 34.—Late Polychrome, Coclé.   Fish and claw motifs from a pedestal plat·
        (¼ actual size).   (After Lothrop, 1942, fig. 144.)

FIGURE 35.—Late Polychrome, Coclé. (Approximate sizes: carafes, ⅙; bowls, ⅖). (After Lothrop, 1942, figs. 10, 176, and 174.)

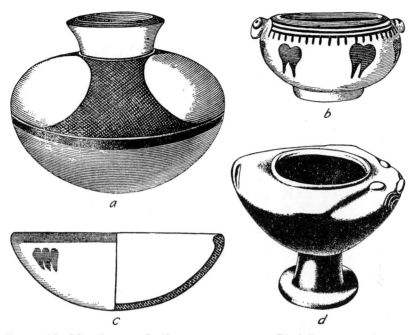

FIGURE 36.—Miscellaneous Coclé pottery types. *a*, Black-line geometric ware
(approximately ⅛ actual size); *b*, *c*, red-line bowls (approximately ⅖ actual
size); *d*, Late smoked ware (approximately ⅕ actual size). (After Lothrop,
1942, figs. 237, 251, and 332.)

the nose, rings of gold, serpentine, or opal were inserted (fig. 37, *b*, *c*).
Ears were decorated either with long rods of gold or stone or with large
spoollike ornaments of gold (fig. 38; pl. 20, *e*). Necklaces were of hollow
golden beads (one necklace is 3 m. (10 feet) in circumference) **or of**
boars' tusks, sharks' teeth, dogs' teeth, serpentine, agate, shell, or bone.
For fingers there were gold rings, and for wrists bracelets of gold, agate,
or bone. Sometimes the forearms were encased in cuffs of gold, and there
were golden greaves for the legs. There are many forms of pendants,
shaped like men, birds, crocodiles, monkeys, etc., which may be of gold,
agate, serpentine, whale-tooth ivory, or bone (pl. 20, *a*, *b*; figs. 37, *a*; 39).
This is but an incomplete list with no attempt to describe the infinite
variety of forms.

Peculiar to Coclé are composite pendants made of gold **and some other**
material. Among these combinations are ivory, pottery or resin figures
with overlays of sheet gold, and also various animals with heads of cast
gold and bodies of emerald (fig. 40), agate, or quartz. Many objects of
sheet gold are found which once were overlays on now rotted wooden
forms.

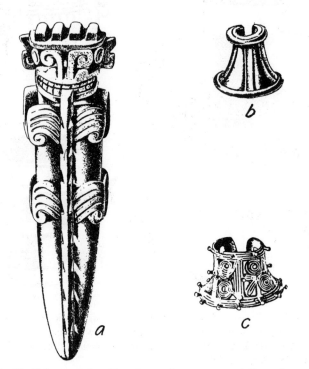

FIGURE 37.—Coclé ivory and goldwork. *a*, Ivory representation of crocodile god; *b*, *c*, gold nose clips (actual size). (After Lothrop, 1937, figs. 162 and 121.)

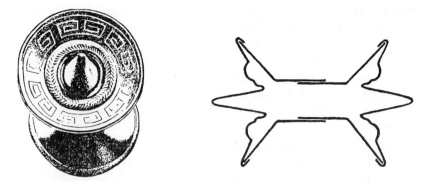

FIGURE 38.—Coclé ear ornament. At right is cross section of method of joining (actual size). (After Lothrop, 1937, figs. 128 and 127.)

PLATE 19.—**Artifacts from Darién, Panamá.** *a*, Stone celt, Puturgandi (much reduced). *b*, Stone mortar, Pearl Islands (much reduced). *c*, Pottery vessel from La Gloria (approximately ⅖ actual size). *d*, Vessel from Puerto Piñas, Río Juan Domingo (approximately 1/12 actual size). *e*, Vessel from Garachine, Santa Barbara (much reduced). (After Linné, 1929, figs. 2, 40, 45, 12, 29.)

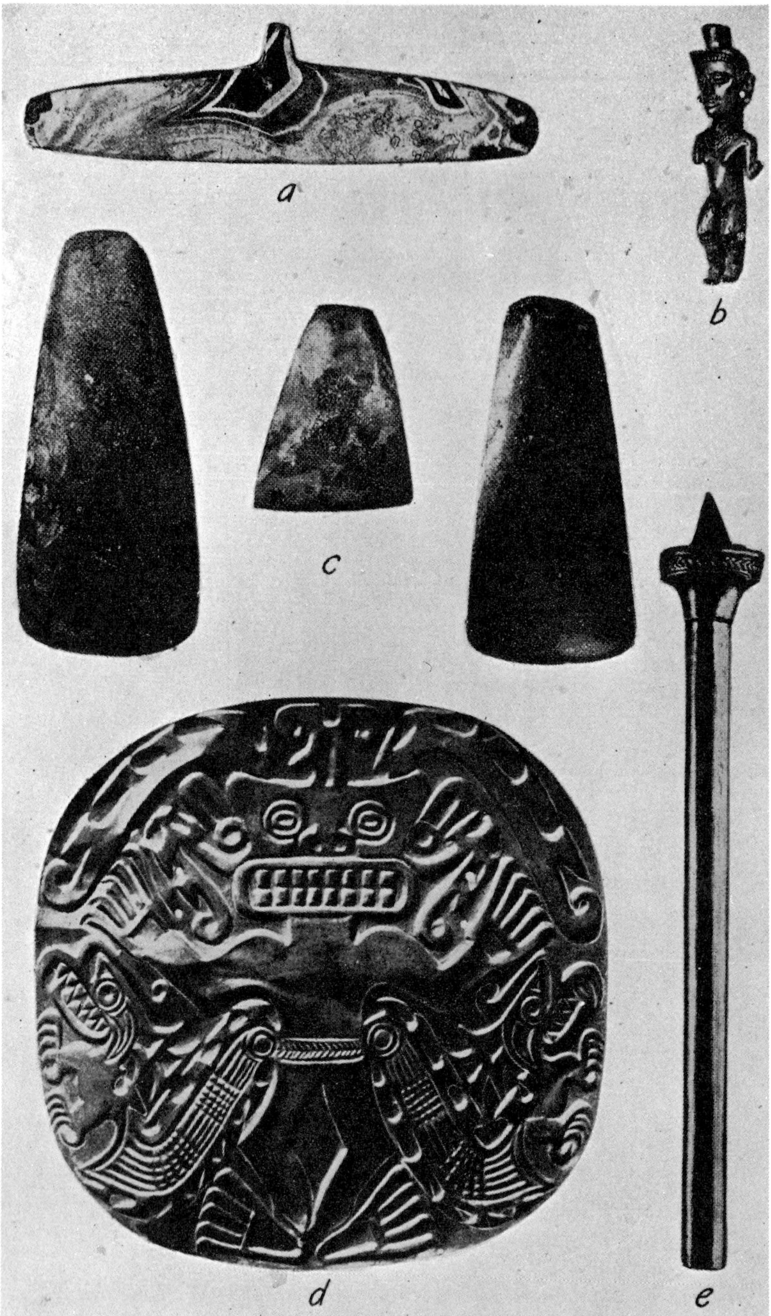

PLATE 20.—**Artifacts from Coclé, Panamá.** *a*, Agate pendant (approximately 2/5 actual size). *b*, Gold pendant (approximately 2/5 size.) *c*, Stone celts (approximately 2/3 actual size). *d*, Gold disk representing the crocodile god (approximately 3/8 actual size.) *e*, Gold-covered ear ornament (approximately 3/5 actual size.) (After Lothrop, 1937, pl. 3, figs. 56, 90, 124.)

FIGURE 39.—Coclé gold pendants. *a*, Curly-tailed monkey; *b*, crocodile; *c*, woman. (All actual size.)   (After Lothrop, 1937, figs. 170, 155, 148.)

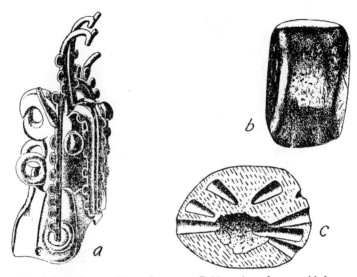

FIGURE 40.—Gold and emerald pendants. *a,* Gold setting; *b,* emerald from setting; *c,* emerald in cross section, showing systems of drilling. (All actual size.) (After Lothrop, 1937, figs. 181 and 180.)

Metallurgy.—From a metallurgical point of view the artifacts of Coclé are most closely related to those of the western Isthmus (Chiriquí and Veraguas) and Colombia. The chief metallurgical processes are casting, hammering, welding, soldering, and gilding. Many objects were hollow-cast over a clay core by the cire-perdue method, which makes possible the creation of elaborate filigree work. Gilding was chiefly by the mise-en-couleur process. Alloys are combinations of gold and copper with silver present as an impurity (tumbaga). Relatively pure copper objects are found, but most of the pieces which now appear to be copper actually contain some gold and originally were gilded. Ornaments made by cold-hammering are relatively more numerous than in any region except the former *Inca* Empire.

Trade.—The Coclé area was unusually active in trade, and the *Coclesano* maintained commercial relations with distant lands. For instance, agate, which came to Coclé apparently from northern Colombia, was manufactured in products of Coclé style and then shipped toward Central America. Coclé pendants of agate have been found not only in Veraguas and Chiriquí but as far away as Oaxaca in México. Coclé received objects of gold from the *Sinú* and *Quimbaya* regions in Colombia, emeralds from Colombia or more probably Ecuador. Gold pendants from Coclé, on the other hand, have turned up in Yucatán.

This trade activity in part explains the basis of Coclé art. Beyond that, however, are stylistic traditions from farther away, from the Amazon Basin and Perú. These must have blended with a cultural current from the north, responsible chiefly for the introduction of polychrome pottery. Cultural links cannot be explained in greater detail without further elucidating the problem of cultural origins.

Antiquity.—Coclé culture evidently is not of great age. The remains now known probably all date within two centuries of the Conquest. This statement is based partly on trade contacts with other areas and partly on internal evidence, such as the rate of accumulation of refuse, stratification, and the chronological interrelationship of graves as demonstrated by the identification of individual pottery styles.

Collections.—Large collections from Coclé may be seen in the Peabody Museum, Harvard University; the Museo Nacional de Panamá; and the University Museum (Philadelphia). Smaller collections exist in the American Museum of Natural History; the Museum of the American Indian, Heye Foundation; and the Peabody Museum, Yale University.

VERAGUAS

The Province of Veraguas, which fronts on both oceans, has a width of little more than 50 miles facing the Pacific. Flanking this area are the vigorous cultures of Coclé and Chiriquí. In the intervening territory one might expect a blending of the two, but this is not the case. On the contrary, in southern Veraguas there flourished a radically distinct culture, extending an unknown distance into the interior. No village sites or refuse beds have been discovered as yet, but many graves have been opened and rifled, largely for the benefit of the tourist trade.

Burial customs.—Veraguas graves usually are located high up on the mountain ridges. Their presence is indicated by a slight depression in the ground, at the edge of which a few small boulders were sometimes placed. Excavation reveals a tubular grave shaft, a meter or more in diameter, extending to a depth of 3 to 7 m. (10 to 23 feet). The shaft usually is not verticle but slopes slightly. At the bottom there is a chamber, made either by enlarging the grave shaft or by digging a short horizontal tunnel. On the floor of the grave is a bed of river boulders on which the body evidently lay in an extended position. No skeletal remains are found, but the position of the body is sometimes outlined by objects placed around it, rarely present in large numbers. The grave shaft is filled with the earth excavated from it or sometimes with stones.

The type of grave here described has no counterpart in Central America or the Isthmian region, but it corresponds closely to the deep-shaft graves found in Colombia.

Stone objects.—Artifacts of stone generally are unlike those of Coclé or Chiriquí. Celts, for instance, are shaped like an elongated bell in outline and are diamond-shaped in cross section. Small chipped blades with a tang form an equilateral triangle in cross section. Metates are rectangular or oval and have three or four legs. The 3-legged metates sometimes have a carved panel suspended below the grinding surface, a curious form found also in the vicinity of San José de Costa Rica. Four-legged metates may be jaguar effigies with protruding head and tail, similar to a type found in Chiriquí and Costa Rica, but the Veraguas specimens are very much larger and relatively thinner than those found in other regions.

Ceramics.—The pottery very rarely is painted, with the exception of vessels which obviously were imported from Coclé or from the Asuero Peninsula. It is improbable that the inhabitants of Veraguas did not know how to fire colors, as their close neighbors were adepts. Evidently they preferred, or had inherited, the tradition of adorning pottery vessels by incising and filleting.

Several pottery shapes apparently were developed locally. Among these are globular jars with huge, flaring strap handles. A curious and common variant is a vessel with a flat base and top constructed to resemble the upper half of the vessels just described. Another characteristic type is shaped like a small barrel placed horizontally with a tall tubular neck protuding from its side. There are a number of effigy bowls with double walls (gutter rims), a feature also found at Santarém in the Amazon Valley and, very rarely, in Peruvian pottery of *Inca* style. Tripod legs are not uncommon, but, unlike those found in other areas, they usually consist of looped ribbons of clay.

The relationship between Veraguas pottery and that of adjacent areas may be summarized as follows: Trade took place to the south and east for at least two centuries before the Spanish Conquest. At first Veraguas purchased from Coclé, but later Veraguas exported pottery as well as acquired it. On the other hand, there is little evidence that Veraguas traded pottery with Chiriquí, but the potters of the later region sometimes copied Veraguas types in the local clay. Veraguas did, however, export objects of metal to Chiriquí in large quantity.

Metallurgy.—Veraguas metalwork with authenticated provenience has reached museums in such quantity that it may be discussed with some assurance. It consists largely of cast pendants representing birds, frogs, fishes, jaguars, and men. A stylistic peculiarity of the region is that the protruding eyes often are tiny bells. In Coclé cast objects usually were hollow or had a clay core. In Veraguas, however, hollow-casting was not practiced and the artifacts invariably have an open back. Metallurgical analysis indicates that almost all objects are of tumbaga, a gold-copper alloy. Frequently the gold content is so reduced that the metal has oxydized and appears to be copper. When cleaned, however, a gilded surface appears, originally obtained by the mise-en-couleur process. Analysis reveals also that the native gold of Veraguas differs from that of Coclé because it contains a higher content of silver as an impurity.

Collections.—Comprehensive collections of Veraguas archeological material exist only in the Museo Nacional de Panamá and the Peabody Museum (Harvard University). There is a small but authenticated metal collection in the University Museum (Philadelphia).

CHIRIQUI

The Province of Chiriquí has given its name to an ancient culture that flourished in western Panamá and the southern half of Costa Rica. Boundaries cannot be defined with precision, but in general the present political division between the Provinces of Veraguas and Chiriquí corresponds to the southeastern archeological frontier. To the north this culture extends through the central Cordillera of Costa Rica as far as El General. Archeological remains from Chiriquí exist in great abundance owing to the fact that gold was discovered in the ancient graves nearly a century ago. During the period of greatest exploitation in the 1860's, it is reported that gold ornaments to the value of £10,000 annually were melted down by the Bank of England.

No technical archeologist has made detailed studies of the remains of Chiriquí in situ. Hence our knowledge of this culture is based on popular articles published many years ago and on the detailed and well-illustrated studies of museum collections published by Holmes (1888) and MacCurdy (1911). A paper by Osgood (1935) reclassifies the ceramic remains on a more modern basis and, so far as is possible, correlates them with various types of graves.

No evidence of Chiriquí culture exists above ground, except a few pictographs, vaguely South American in style (fig. 41), and stone columns which mark the sites of graves.

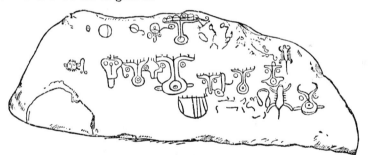

FIGURE 41.—Pictograph, Chiriquí country. The piedra pintal at Caldera. (After Holmes, 1888.)

Burial customs.—The popular literature of the 19th century, reviewed by MacCurdy, indicates that two principal types of tombs are found in Chiriquí: rounded or rectangular in outline, both with rough stone walls (fig. 42). There was no distinct floor, and the tombs were covered either by a layer of river boulders or by flat slabs. Several variant forms may be defined which, at present, are not of archeological significance. Skeletal remains usually have disintegrated, but the size of the graves suggests that they normally contained a single body, interred a meter or two below the ground level. In type, size, and depth the Chiriquí graves may be vaguely compared to the so-called *Guetar* burials in northern and northeastern Costa Rica, but they are totally unlike the deep graves of Veraguas or the multiple burials of Coclé.

Artifacts are not found in quantity with individual Chiriquí burials, and so the great number that have come to light is the result of opening many thousands of graves. Perishable materials, such as wood or bone, have

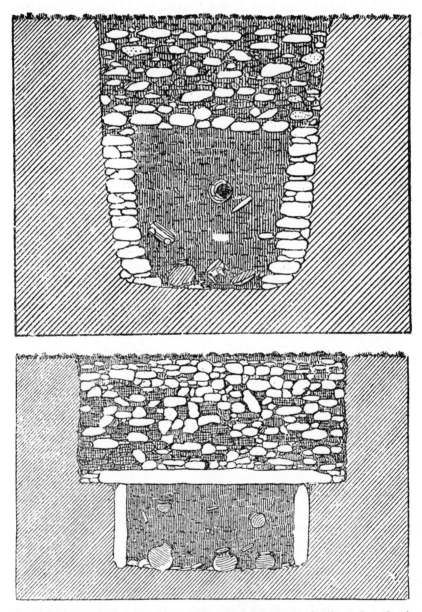

FIGURE 42.—Chiriquí grave types. *Top:* Oval. *Bottom:* Quadrangular, showing surface pack of river stones and positions of grave artifacts. (After Holmes, 1888, figs. 1 and 2.)

totally disappeared, and the surviving objects are of stone, pottery, or metal.

Stone objects.—Stone tools consist of a few simple forms. There are small chipped blades, triangular in cross section—a form also typical of Veraguas. Celts may be pear-shaped in outline, with polished blades and roughened polls—a type also found in Coclé. In addition, there are celts with a flaring blade, polished all over. Stone chisels have narrow blades and thick, roughened handles.

Metates, or grinding stones, usually are effigies representing a jaguar. The grinding surface is either rectangular or oval, and often it is surrounded by a small raised flange. In addition, there are circular grinding stones (sometimes called stools) supported by Atlantean figures or latticed columns. These forms, illustrated in figs. 43 and 44, are equally

FIGURE 43.—Chiriquí stone metates. *a*, Jaguar metate with rectangular top; *b*, jaguar metate with guilloche ornamentation. (Size: ½ and ¼ actual, respectively.) (After MacCurdy, 1911, figs. 26, 28.)

FIGURE 44.—Chiriquí stone metates or stools. (After MacCurdy, 1911, pl. 4.)

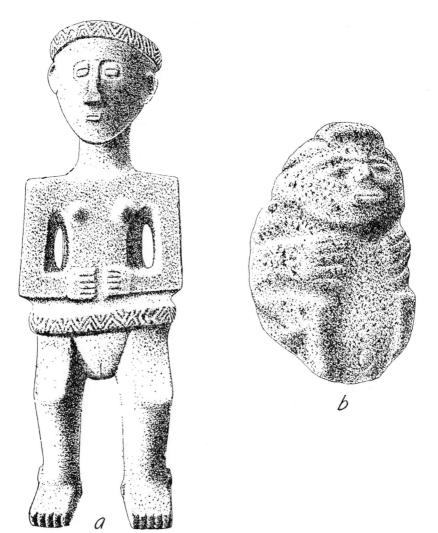

FIGURE 45.—Chiriquí stone statues. a, The "Panama Venus" (⅛ actual size);
b, crude human image from Bugarita (¼ actual size). (After MacCurdy, 1911,
figs. 40a and 38.)

typical of the *Guetar* area to the north in Costa Rica but, with some exceptions in Veraguas, do not occur to the east and south of Chiriquí. Small stone statues, usually crudely carved, also recall the *Guetar* area (fig. 45).

Stone jewelry in Chiriquí consists largely of objects obtained by trade. These include jade pendants from the Nicoya Peninsula in northwestern Costa Rica as well as agate beads and animal effigies, typical of Coclé and northern Colombia.

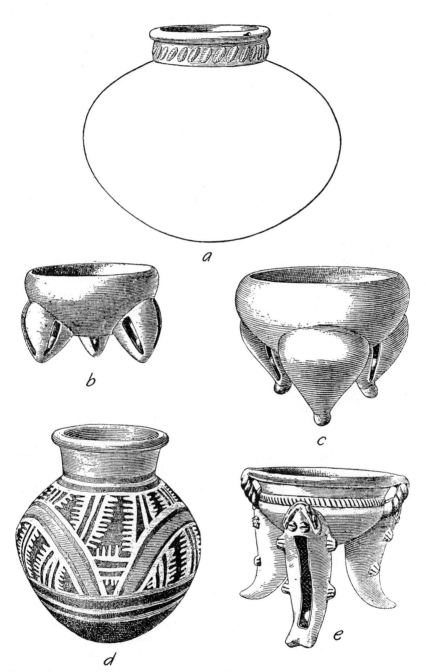

FIGURE 46.—Chiriquí pottery types. a-c, Armadillo ware (a, ½, and b, c, ⅖ actual
size); d, lost-color or negative painted ware (⅜ actual size); e, tripod ware
(¼ actual size). (After MacCurdy, 1911, fig. 85, pls. 6, 31, and 23.)

Ceramics.—Pottery vessels from the graves of Chiriquí exist by the thousands. In general, they are small and globular with relatively thick walls. Jars have no basal support, but bowls often have tripod legs. These may be conical and pointed or bulbous and mammiform, both shapes being typical of Central America. There are also tall, elongated tripods, a type with affinities both in Central and South America.

Holmes distinguishes 11 and MacCurdy 14 distinct pottery wares. The so-called Polychrome ware of both these classifications consists in fact of trade pieces from Coclé and the Asuero Peninsula, representing a culture not known at the time these authors wrote. The other wares may be divided into two groups, one being purely local in style, the other closely related to the *Guetar* pottery of northern Costa Rica.

Typical of the local groups is Armadillo ware, a thin buff ware distinguished by delicately rounded outlines (fig. 46, *a–c*). Decoration is confined to modeled relief on the neck, shoulders, or tripod legs. There also is an important pottery type decorated by negative painting (fig. 46, *d*). Except for the technique of adornment, this group shows little resemblance to the well-developed negative painting of northeastern South America, but slight links may be noted with the negative painting of the *Guetar* area. The so-called Alligator ware of Holmes and MacCurdy is really a local polychrome, painted in black and red on a white slip. The name comes from the fact that most the designs represent crocodiles or stylized elements derived from the crocodile (fig. 47).

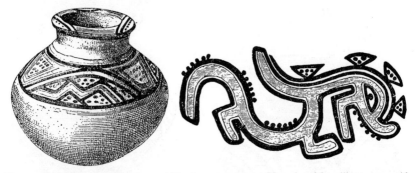

FIGURE 47.—Chiriquí pottery. Alligator ware. *a*, Vessel with alligator motifs (approximately ⅓ actual size); *b*, alligator design. (After MacCurdy, 1911, figs. 235 and 208.)

Among the Chiriquí pottery types with *Guetar* affiliations are Red-line ware, White-line ware, Handled ware, Tripod ware (fig. 46, *e*), Maroon ware, and Chocolate ware. The resemblance between the two areas is so close that it is often difficult to tell the provenience of individual vessels unaccompanied by field data. Evidently the two cultures share in part a common base, but not enough evidence is available to discuss the question of origins.

Typical of the Chiriquí area are small pottery figurines with polychrome decoration. These often are hollow animal effigies with a whistle incorporated in them.

Metal objects.—Chiriquí metal objects almost invariably are cast, apparently of gold. This is about all that can be said at present, in spite of the numerous specimens in museums and private collections. The reason for this caution is that recent excavations have shown that a large part of the so-called Chiriquí gold is the product of trade with Veraguas. Until the local Chiriquí styles can be determined and their metallic content analysed, therefore, intelligent discussion is not possible.

Antiquity.—We have mentioned trade between Chiriquí and other regions, which include the Nicoya Peninsula and *Guetar* area in Costa Rica, as well as Veraguas, the Asuero Peninsula, and Coclé in Panamá. Correlation with chronological studies made at the Sitio Conte in Coclé indicates that the culture of Chiriquí was contemporaneous at least in part, and flourished for two centuries or more before the Spanish Conquest.

Collections.—Major collections from Chiriquí are housed in the following museums: American Museum of Natural History, Brooklyn Museum, Museum of the American Indian (Heye Foundation), Museo Nacional de Panamá, Peabody Museum (Harvard University), Peabody Museum (Yale University), University Museum (Philadelphia), United States National Museum.

BIBLIOGRAPHY

Bancroft, 1882, 1883–90; Holmes, 1887, 1888; Linné, 1929; Lothrop, 1919, 1937, 1942; MacCurdy, 1911; Mason, J. A., 1942; Nordenskiöld, 1938; Osgood, 1935; Oviedo y Valdés, 1851–55; Verrill, 1927.

THE BASIC CULTURES OF CENTRAL AMERICA

By DORIS STONE

INTRODUCTION[1]

Central America, the land link of the two American continents, presents some of the most complicated problems in New World archeology. In western Central America, nearest México, archeologists have, for the most part, concerned themselves with the outstanding features of this region, the great *Mayan* and Mexican ruins. The other problems of the Central American area as a whole, and particularly eastern Central America, nearest the South American Continent, have scarcely been touched by archeological investigation. These problems are concerned with what appear to be the basic local cultures which are evident throughout Central America. Evidences of these essentially Central American cultures are found in relatively unmixed state with regard to outside influences, and they are also found blended with *Mayan* and Mexican complexes. The present discussion is an attempt to describe and place in their proper geographical and cultural setting these basic cultures of Central America. Cultures and archeological sites dominantly *Mayan* or Mexican are outside of the scope of this treatment and of the Handbook; however, they are referred to in those instances where their presence has a cultural and historical bearing upon the fuller exposition of the other Central American problems.

THE BASIC CENTRAL AMERICAN CULTURES AND THE Q-COMPLEX

The concept of a basic Central American culture, or cultures, is formulated upon the general horticultural-ceramic level of New World development. Its implications are in no way connected with the presumed early peopling of Central America or with a hypothetical cultural level equivalent to the early American hunting and gathering horizons found in other parts of the New World. It is based, specifically, upon a ceramic-stonework complex, which is manifested in varying intensity, from southern México to Costa Rica. Lothrop has called attention to a series of stone sculptures of non-*Maya* affiliations which may be considered as a component of a basic Central American complex (Lothrop, 1921, pp. 311–319; 1926 a, pp. 163–171; 1926 b, vol. 2, pp. 400–404; 1940, p. 420).

[1] Refer to map 3 for sites discussed in this paper.

In 1928 Lothrop and Vaillant (Vaillant, 1930, p. 81) grouped these traits of stone carving together with a number of ceramic elements, and temporarily designated the agglomeration as the "Q-complex." The Q-complex traits as ultimately listed by Vaillant (1934, p. 90) are these:

1. Spouted vessels.
2. Effigy vessels, either modeled or with filleted features and extremities.
3. Shoe-form vessels.
4. Vessels decorated by filleting, modeling, incision, or polishing to the virtual exclusion of painting.
5. Tetrapod supports.
6. Elongated tripod legs.
7. High annular bases (occasionally pot stands).
8. Usulután ware.
9. Slipped hand-made figurines.
10. Crude stone monuments.
11. Negative painting.
12. Shallow spouted trays.

With two exceptions[2] the Q-traits are all elements which can justifiably be considered as part of an old Central American culture stratum. In the following discussion it will be seen that they recur throughout Central America. The Q-complex, however, must not be considered as representing a particular tribe or culture, for the same 12 traits are not found associated from site to site. In this sense it is not a complex. Rather, these features represent a number of ideas common to the Central American region and, for the most part, having an early inception in the culture history of the region. In line with this last, it should be noted that a number of Q-elements were discovered at Playa de los Muertos in the Sula-Ulua Plain of northwestern Honduras (Vaillant, 1934, pp. 87–97; Popenoe, 1934, pp. 61–85). This Playa de los Muertos culture was found underlying typical *Mayan* ceramics (Strong, Kidder, and Paul, 1938).

COSTA RICA

CERAMICS

A salient archeological fact concerning Costa Rica is that a fundamental monochrome ceramic style extends throughout the whole area. Lothrop called attention to this when he observed the similarity between *Guetar* (Meseta Central) and *Chiriquí* ceramics (Lothrop, 1926 b, vol. 2, p. 293). At the time he wrote little was known of the intervening section of Talamanca and Boruca, which last includes the General Plateau and the Terraba Plain. It is our contention that the similarity referred to by Lothrop is not the result of *Chiriquí* influence or contact but of a fundamental

---

[2] Negative painting is absent in western Costa Rica and in Nicaragua and is picked up again in the Pipil area of Salvador (Lothrop, 1926 b, vols. 1 and 2; 1933, footnote 2, p. 51). Its presence in eastern Costa Rica is the result of South American or Mexican influence or trade. (See also Kidder II, 1940.) Shallow spouted trays are rare in non-*Mayan*, non-Mexican regions, and are not considered here as an essential Central American trait.

sameness of the pottery of this entire area which has persisted in spite of individual or localized changes. It is necessary to examine this basic monochrome pottery complex, and later to consider other elements associated with this ceramic division.

The characteristics of this important monochrome style, and the regions wherein it occurs most frequently, can be outlined in the following manner:

SPOUTED VESSELS: Found throughout the monochrome ware (pl. 22, *j,* from the Nicoya Peninsula).

EFFIGY VESSELS: Found throughout Costa Rica, but especially in the Highland and *Guetar* section and the General Plateau (pl. 22, *c* and *f,* from the Nicoya Peninsula, and pl. 23, *a,* from Buenos Aires, Valle General, *Boruca* region).

SHOE VESSELS: Although they seem to extend all over Costa Rica, they are less common than the other types. (See Lothrop, 1926 b, vol. 2, pp. 254, 256, and pl. 123, *d, f*; also pl. 22, *f.*)

VESSELS DECORATED BY FILLETING, MODELING, INCISION, APPLIQUÉ, AND PUNCTATE PATTERNS: These are usual and extend all over Costa Rica (pl. 21, *b, c,* from the *Guetar, e* from *Boruca,* and pl. 22, *a* and *e,* from the *Boruca* and the *Suerre* areas, respectively).

ELONGATED TRIPOD LEGS: Very usual all over, particularly in the *Boruca* area (pl. 21, *e*).

ANNULAR BASES AND POT STANDS: Found throughout (pl. 24, *i-k,* from the *Guetar* and *Suerre* regions).

VESSEL SUPPORTS IN THE FORM OF ANIMAL AND HUMAN HEADS: Very frequent among the *Guetar;* less so in the *Boruca* section where, when they occur, they are generally a modified form of animal and very rarely a human head (pl. 21, *b,* from the *Guetar,* and pl. 21, *d,* from the *Boruca* region; also pl. 24, *b,* from the *Guetar*).

SUBGLOBULAR VESSELS USUALLY WITHOUT, BUT SOMETIMES WITH THREE LEGS OR WITH RING BASES (e.g., see Lothrop, 1926 b, vol. 2; pp. 346–350; also pl. 22, *a* and *e.*): Common throughout.

Six of the ceramic traits listed above are Q-elements, while the seventh, vessel supports in the form of animal or human heads, has a wide distribution in Central America and might well be included as a Q-characteristic. The eighth, subglobular vessels, may perhaps more rightly be considered along with the shoe vessels, as they often appear closely connected and one may be an outgrowth of the other (Lothrop, 1926 b, vol. 2, fig. 236, p. 349; and cf. pl. 22, *a, c, e,* and *f*). Of the other five ceramic traits listed by Vaillant as part of the Q-complex, only one, the tetrapod vessel, can be considered with the monochrome pottery. In the Costa Rican area tetrapodal supports are rare and when present are more usual on animal figurines (see Lothrop, 1926 b, vol. 2, fig. 270, p. 374) or on clay counterparts of the four-legged metate. (See pl. 25, *b* and *c,* from the *Guetar.*)

With the exception of some polychrome wares encountered in the Costa Rican Highlands, which Lothrop considers as an off-shoot of Nicoya Polychrome ware (Lothrop, 1926 b, vol. 2, p. 295), there is only one other example of polychrome pottery which is essentially non-*Chorotegan* in origin. This is the obvious adaptation of the monochrome basic type to reappear in a polychrome form. (See pls. 21, *b,* and 24, *i,* both from the *Guetar* area.) Excellent examples of this are shown by Lothrop (1926 b, vol. 2, pl. 142, fig. *b*; fig. 194, *b,* p. 308; and pl. 142, fig. *a*). In fact, the whole class of pottery known as "Red-line ware" is a painted adaptation of the fundamental monochrome style.

The figurine and figurine whistle are found both as monochrome and polychrome specimens in Costa Rica (see pl. 24, *n-r; p* and *q* are from *Coto* and *Boruca* regions; the rest are from the Meseta Central or *Guetar* area) and should be included in a consideration of basic Central American ceramics. Probably in no region of the New World is there greater diversity of the subject portrayed by the figurine whistle as within Central America. Figurine whistles in zoomorphic shapes have a wide distribution although more limited in spread than those with the human figure. A human, generally female, figure with opened legs and a tendency to a broad flattened head (see, e.g., pl. 24, *l-q;* Lothrop, 1926 b, vol. 2, pl. 125) is the most prevalent type. This shape occurs with slight differences, or localizations of style, throughout the Central American area.

STONE SEATS AND METATES

The first objects in stone to be considered are forms whose exact use has not been determined but which as a matter of convenience have been classed under the broad terms of "seats" and "metates." These objects are of two types, one with three and one with four legs. Both groups are common on the mainland, whereas the four-legged variety is very rare on the Nicoyan Peninsula.[3]

The tetrapod metates or seats are frequently in the form of a jaguar with the tail curved and attached to a hind leg, thus serving as a handle. These are very common in the *Boruca* and the *Guetar* regions (pl. 26, *h,* from the *Guetar* area; also Lines, 1939, fig. 9, p. 12), although they are found throughout the Costa Rican mainland. Four-legged metates without the jaguar head and tail are found in greater numbers in the *Guetar* area around the San Juan Plain and in the Meseta Central. These, as is true of all the Costa Rican stonework, range in size from the very large to the minute. A characteristic of this class of metate is a raised border or edge around the bowl or seat. (See fig. 26, *h;* also Lothrop, 1926 b, vol. 2, pl. 141.)

The three-legged group has the wider distribution, extending throughout Central America. In Costa Rica there are two divisions, those from the mainland and those from Nicoya Peninsula. Typical of Nicoya are slablike legs cut in openwork and a seat with protruding edges (Lines,

---

[3] The everyday grinding stone throughout mainland Costa Rica was a heavy stone slab without legs or decoration (Hartman, 1901).

1939, figs. 26, 27, pp. 20–21 and pl. 26, *f, g,* and *j*). The mainland specimens are at times very elaborate with complicated carvings on narrow legs (Lines, 1935, fig. 1, p. 9, and fig. 3, p. 13) and often like the tetrapod metates, with a slightly raised border around the seat or grinding plate. The similarity of the tripod mainland type metate to those from *Chiriquí* has been noted by Lothrop and also by Mason (Lothrop, 1926 b, vol. 2, p. 290; 1937, pp. 95–96; Mason, J. A., 1945, pp. 52–53).

STONE FIGURES

Crude stone monuments in the sense of large monoliths rudely carved in human form are strangely lacking on the Costa Rican mainland but appear on the Nicoya Peninsula (Richardson, 1940, fig. 39, *b,* p. 413). Smaller figures of a type related to monolithic images, such as have been found in the neighboring territories of Panamá and Nicaragua (for Panamá, see Verrill, 1927, figs. 17, 18; for Nicaragua, see Richardson, 1940, fig. 39, *a, c*), do occur in the *Boruca* area (pl. 27, *b*), while various types of stone figures, both large and small, are found all over Costa Rica (pls. 27–29; also Hartman, 1901, pl. 3, figs. 1, 3; pl. 11, figs. 2, 3; pl. 12, figs, 2, 3; pl. 15, fig. 1). Anthropomorphic and zoomorphic monoliths have a massive, blocklike appearance, even when well executed. The salient characteristic, however, is a tenon or peg which is unsculptured and was apparently designed to be stuck into the earth as a supporting base to stand the figure erect (Lines, 1935, fig. 9, p. 25; fig. 11, *c,* from El Palmar; Stone, 1943; for Nicaragua, see Lothrop, 1926 b, vol. 2, p. 433, San Pedro del Lobago). Sometimes with figures of four legs the tenon is absent.

Another feature characteristic of many of these animal images is a human face suspended from the tongue. (See pl. 29, *g.*) There are also human figures with a snake or a snake's head hanging from the mouth (pl. 27, *h.*) This is characteristic of many figures from the *Guetar* area, although it is also present in the *Boruca* region.

A different group of stone figures, which likewise have what might be classed as a tenon or peg-base, consists of the jadeite pendants or ax-gods which occur from the Valle General through the *Guetar* area and in quantities on the Nicoya Peninsula. The base of these jadeite pieces may be only a retention of the original "ax-god" form, but their distribution is similar to that of the tenon-based monoliths. It is possible that these pendants are a relatively late development. Certain of the pendant figures also have a snake coming from or connected with the mouth. Some pendant figures in the Río Jiménez section of the *Guetar* territory do not have pronounced ax-god bases.[4]

---

[4] The presence of these jadeite pendants in the Valle General has been noted by the writer at the site of Pejevalle; Hartman (1901) shows examples from the *Guetar* area; and Hartman (1907) illustrates many from the Nicoya Peninsula. (For discussion of the "ax-god" type of figure, see Stone, 1941.)

STONE DUMPS

Stone dump heaps, or perhaps better named "quarries," have been reported in the Terraba Basin in southeastern Costa Rica (Stone, 1943) and at Las Mercedes on the San Juan Plain (Hartman, 1901). None have yet been noted on the Nicoya Peninsula.

STONE BALLS

Smooth stone balls, ranging from 1 to 7 feet (0.35 to 2.4 m.) in diameter, have been found in the Terraba Plain (pl. 30; Stone, 1943). In the Valle General the largest ball yet encountered has a diameter of 4 feet (1.4 m.). This is one that came from a site in the hills by the Pacuare, a branch of the General River. There are four stone balls at the site, two at the north and two at the south of an area 1 km. long. There are many graves within this kilometer. In the Meseta Central, part of the *Guetar* area, balls 2 feet (0.7 m.) in diameter have been reported (Stone, 1943). As yet no large balls have been found on the Nicoya Peninsula. Smaller balls were found by Hartman (1901, pl. 4, figs. 6, 7) on the north coast, but those of small size are not considered here. Hartman (1901, p. 42) also calls attention to some large balls from Siquirres. He does not give the diameter of these, however.

PETROGLYPHS

Small rocks and boulders left in the natural form but with incised designs are found throughout Costa Rica (pl. 31, *bottom*). Generally the patterns are curvilinear, but sometimes simple animal figures or even attempts at human figures appear. They are all simple line drawings, almost childlike in conception. We can trace these petroglyphs from the eastern frontier of Costa Rica near Piedra de Candela, westward through the General or *Boruca* region to the Nicaraguan frontier.[5]

BURIALS

Burials of different kinds are found in Costa Rica, with no one type occuring independently of the others. Cremation is most typical, the ashes being placed within an urn. A large number of graves, both urn burials and deep graves, are marked by a stone shaft or column. In northern

---

[5] The following is a list of sites from where such stones have been reported: Piedra de Candela, Piedra Pintada near Java Creek, Río Volcán (Lothrop, 1926 b, vol. 2, p. 445), Rivas, Palmares, Quisará (pl. 31, *bottom*), Quebrada Grande (Lothrop, 1926 b, vol. 2, p. 443), Santa María de Dota (ibid., p. 445), Cuericí near La Muerte (ibid., p. 444), La División (ibid., p. 443); in the Meseta Central at Alajuelita, Santa Domingo de Roble, Juan Viñas, Orosi (Hartman, 1901, p. 186, fig. 479), Agua Caliente (ibid., p. 189, fig. 482), the San Juan Plain (Hartman, 1901, pl. 15, figs. 2, 3); and on or near the Nicoya Peninsula at Liberia (Lothrop, 1926 b, vol. 2, p. 427), Hacienda de Mogica (ibid., p. 428), Pasondito (ibid.), Lofieros (ibid.), Hacienda de Guachipilín and Hacienda de Guayacanal and Río Colorado (ibid., p. 425).

Costa Rica stone-cist graves are found in quantity, although they occur in other parts of the republic. The Nicoya Peninsula has a greater variety of burial forms, from shell-mound burials[6] to urn burials, mound burials, and inhumations (Lothrop, 1926 b, vol. 1, p. 97).

NICARAGUA

CERAMICS

In the Nicaraguan area certain ceramic types, which fundamentally belong in the monochrome group as noted in Costa Rica, appear only slightly modified. Spouted vessels, effigy vessels (pl. 23, *b,* from Ometepe Island), and vessels whose decoration is characterized by filleting, appliqué, modeling, incising, and punctate designs are found throughout the Pacific area (pl. 22, *d,* from Muymuy, a site near the boundary of the two departments Matagalpa and Chontales; Lothrop, 1926 b, vol. 2, pp. 387–388). These "basic Central American" elements persist, despite what may be Mexican influences, and are noted particularly in the Black ware, Red ware, Zapatero ware, and certain types of orange-brown ware (ibid., pl. 193). The same traits, but even less touched by other cultures, with the exception of spouted vessels which have not yet been reported, occur on the Caribbean side, in country which is historically associated with the *Rama* (Spinden, 1925). In fact, the monochrome ware typical of Costa Rica is so much a part of the archeology of the Nicaraguan east coast that Strong (1935, p. 167) has suggested that this section formed a cultural link between the northern coast of Honduras and Costa Rica.

Shoe-form vessels are found in quantity in the area around Lake Nicaragua, particularly on Zapatero Island (Lothrop, 1926 b, vol. 2, pp. 254–257).

Elongated tripod legs occur in the Pacific area, but the examples known to the writer are for the most part polychrome and contain, as does most of the polychrome ceramics of southern Nicaragua, too many Mexican elements to permit any clear discussion of relationship. On the other hand, tripod legs ornamented with faces, similar to tripod legs from Costa Rica, are found on the Caribbean coast where Mexican influence was less strong (Spinden, 1925), while effigy heads as vessel supports are prevalent (pl. 24, *e*) from Muymuy.

Annular bases are also common, but, as is true of most of the ceramics from the Pacific region, the specimens available are generally polychrome and Mexicanoid (Lothrop, 1926 b, vol. 1, fig. 61, p. 162). Likewise, sub-globular vessels with and without three legs, or with a ring base, are very prevalent in the Pacific area (Lothrop, 1926 b, vol. 2, p. 235).

As in Costa Rica, known examples of tetrapod vessels are rare.

Figurines and figurine whistles continue from Costa Rica north and westward (Lothrop, 1926 b, vol. 2, fig. 149, p. 260; pl. 125, *h-j;* fig. 150, *c,*

[6] At Culebra Bay there are a number of shell mounds with burials.

p. 261). The form of the human figurine with stylized flattened head and a tendency to opened legs persists, despite specializations or localized distinction.[7] The figurine whistle appears in a variety of subjects, certain ones having a distribution which is easily traceable. One of the most popular forms is a bird whistle. The human figurines from Zapatero Island (Lothrop, 1926 b, vol. 2, fig. 165, p. 273; fig. 167, a; fig. 167, b; although not from Zapatero Island, is in the same style) are particularly important as they are more crudely executed than the Nicoya polychrome type and are generally monochrome. (Compare these with pl. 24, n, from Costa Rica.) Spinden (1925) reports, but does not illustrate, figurines and whistles from the Caribbean region in territory associated with the Rama. He notes that they were found in connection with ceramic types considered here as part of the basic Central American complex.

METATES

The stone complex continues into Nicaragua, where certain elements appear to have been more strongly developed than in Costa Rica. Although much has been written on Costa Rican metates, very little is known about those in the Nicaraguan area, despite the tendency of archeologists to connect the Atlantic coast of both countries (Kidder II, 1940, p. 454). The grinding stone generally cited is the three-legged Nicoya variety (Squier, 1852, vol. 1, p. 272, pictures one from León). Spinden (1925) reports Costa Rican style metates from the Caribbean region.

STONE FIGURES

The outstanding stone trait in Nicaragua, however, is found in the peg statues. These take the form of large stone figures representing human beings and are of two types, the Chontales group (Richardson, 1940, pp. 412–414) and what may be called the alter-ego group (Richardson, 1940, pp. 405–408; Kidder II, 1940, pp. 452–453), or representations of human beings with animals on their backs, and at times with a human head within their jaws. The Chontales style is found on the eastern border of Lake Nicaragua in the vicinity of Subtiaba around León (Squier, 1852, vol. 1) and, in particular, on many of the islands of Lake Nicaragua, especially Zapatero Island (Squier, 1852, vol. 2). Both types appear on the Caribbean coast (Spinden, 1925; Strong, 1935, p. 167).

STONE DUMPS

"Workshops" have been reported from Corlobalo (Lothrop, 1926 b, vol. 2, p. 424), Cerro Tablón (ibid., p. 435), and San Pedro del Lobago (ibid., p. 433), in Nicaragua.

---

[7] Compare figurines referred to above with those in the same volume on pl. 128, or Luna ware figurines.

STONE BALLS

Smooth stone balls have not yet been reported from Nicaragua.

PETROGLYPHS

Petroglyphs cut on rocks or boulders, or rock walls, have been noted throughout the Pacific region of Nicaragua. (For exact locations, see Squier, 1852, vol. 2, pp. 21–26, fig. 19, pp. 65–66; Lothrop, 1926 b, vol. 1, pl. 8, figs. 12, 13; vol. 2, pp. 421, 423, 426, 428, 429, 431–435.) They continue on the north coast at Prinzapolca, at the confluence of the Yasica and Tuma Rivers (Spinden, 1925), and near Doris farm at El Gallo on the Río Grande de Matagalpa.

BURIALS

The majority of the reports concerning aboriginal interments in Nicaragua mention urn burials in the Pacific section (Lothrop, 1926 b, vol. 2, pp. 421–437), while the Caribbean side remains archeologically unknown. Stone-walled graves have been reported by Bransford (1881, p. 60), however, on Ometepe Island in Lake Nicaragua, which may have been associated with the *Corobici.*

Graves marked by stone shafts, although rare, are found in the western section (Strong, 1935, p. 163), while mound burials appear throughout this section but with less frequency on the eastern coast.

HONDURAS

CERAMICS

The general monochrome ceramic complex as it appears in eastern Central America continues into Honduras, where its focus was the *Paya* territory, which includes, of course, the Bay Islands (Strong, 1935; Stone, 1941). Throughout the *Paya* region the pottery characteristics noted in Costa Rica persist, apparently untouched by the obvious Mexicanization which can be seen in many of the Nicaraguan wares. In the Sula-Ulua Plain, at a site called Melchior, and in the immediate vicinity, there may have been a *Paya* colony, for the same traits are found as those within the *Paya* region.

These monochrome wares extend southward into the Comayagua Valley, where they occur but with less frequency. The ceramics of the Sula-Jicaque region as known consist of a related monochrome, incised ware (Stone, 1942). In the Sula-Ulua Valley a bichrome type has been given the name Ulua bichrome (Strong, Kidder, and Paul, 1938, p. 123; pl. 9, except fig. *t*).

In this same section there is also an ancient non-Mexican culture somewhat distinct from the monochrome complex already discussed in relation to Costa Rica and Nicaragua and belonging to more or less the same time period as the Ulua bichrome style. This is the Playa de los Muertos culture and pottery complex.[8] The Playa de los Muertos ware is technically superior to the monochrome wares of the Caribbean area of Costa Rica and Nicaragua but manifests certain of the same basic forms and styles, namely, spouted forms, effigy form, shoe-form vessels, and fluted, incised, and modeled ware (Gordon, 1896, pl. 7; Popenoe, 1934). There is a peculiar type of effigy vessel associated with Playa de los Muertos. This is a fat, rounded figure with a single large loop handle (Popenoe, 1934, fig. 12, p. 75; Strong, Kidder, and Paul, 1938, fig. 18, b, and pl. 15, fig. a).

Generally considered to be as old as Playa de los Muertos pottery, Usulután ware, a bichrome group so far found in greatest quantity in eastern El Salvador (Lothrop, 1927 a, pp. 175–177; 1933, pp. 47–53), is found in Honduras also. Usulután ware, the decoration of which resembles but is not negative painting (Lothrop, 1933, particularly footnote 2, p. 51), is found in Honduras from the Sula-Ulua Valley southward, including Olancho, Comayagua, and Tegucigalpa, all *Lenca* or part *Lenca* country. Usulután ware evidences so many of the traits found in the Playa de los Muertos pattern that it has been suggested that this ware may have formed a part of Playa de los Muertos bichrome ceramics (Strong, Kidder, and Paul, 1938, pp. 74–75).

Certain elements of the Central American complex of the *Paya*, and at the same time certain traits found in quantity in western Central America and the Pacific area of Nicaragua, and less frequently in Costa Rica, are almost entirely absent in *Paya* territory. The elongated tripod leg, for example, is an important feature of *Paya* ceramics (Stone, 1941, fig. 36) but is rarely found in the Sula-Ulua Plain. Spouted vessels, on the other hand, are not common in *Paya* territory but appear frequently in the Sula-Ulua region, where they are chiefly associated with the Playa de los Muertos culture (pl. 22, h, from Yoro, Sula-*Jicaque* territory, and pl. 22, i, from Lake Yojoa). Both monochrome (pl. 22, i) and polychrome (pl. 23, c) effigy ware is also common. Spouted and effigy vessels extend into ware of definite *Maya* type and continue through the Comayagua Plateau southward to the Salvadorean border.

Interestingly enough, shoe vessels are found in the *Paya* region, in the Playa de los Muertos deposits, and in the Comayagua–Lake Yojoa region, where they are found in remote and almost hidden locations, such as caves or old graves high in the hillsides. (See pl. 22, g, from Siguatepeque; and Yde, 1938, pp. 26–27, e.g., mentions a shoe-form vessel with a turkey head and wings which comes from a cave by Siguatepeque. This is now in the Tulane University Museum in New Orleans.)

---

[8] As a class, Playa de los Muertos pottery has generally been referred to as monochrome, but Strong, Kidder, and Paul (1938, pl. 10) discern a Playa de los Muertos bichrome.

Tetrapod vessels are very rare in *Paya* country (Stone, 1941, fig. 33, *e, f*) but are found to some extent in the Sula-Ulua Plain, in the upper Chamelecón Valley (Yde, 1938, fig. 25, p. 50), and in the Comayagua-Yojoa region (ibid., pp. 70–71) and are very common in the *Lenca* area of southwestern Honduras (pl. 25, *f,* from Marcala).

Effigy-head vessel supports, both painted and occasionally unpainted, are characteristic of southern Honduras, appearing in the Departments of El Paraíso near Danlí, in Choluteca at La Ola, a historical *Ulva* site (Ponce, 1873, vol. 1, p. 339) at Santa Inez Creek near El Zamorano in the Yeguare Valley, in the Comayagua area (pl. 24, *c, d,* and *g*), and in the *Lenca* region of southwestern Honduras always as animal, never as human, heads (pl. 24, *f,* from Intibucá, and pl. 25, *f*).

The flatheaded, partially opened-leg figurine of the monochrome group appears, as would be expected, in *Paya* territory. Examples similar to the Zapatero Island figurines noted in Nicaragua (Lothrop, 1926 b, vol. 2, fig. 165, *b, c,* p. 273) have been found in the Guaymoreto Lagoon section of the Honduran north coast (Stone, 1934 b, pp. 130–131). The specimen shown on plate 24, *m,* from Sula-*Jicaque* country in the Department of Yoro, Honduras, is better executed but is also reminiscent of certain Nicaraguan figures (Lothrop, 1926 b, vol. 2, fig. 158, *c,* p. 267). This type is fairly numerous in both the Sula-*Jicaque* region and in the mixed culture zone of the Sula-Ulua Plain. In the *Lenca* area of Gracias, Honduras, and El Salvador, the figurine head is of more importance than the body, which either does not appear (pl. 24, *l,* from Intibucá) or has dwindled in size even beyond that of the Sula-*Jicaque* figure referred to above.

The figurine whistle of the monochrome class noted in Costa Rica and Nicaragua occurs also in the *Paya* area (Spinden, 1925; Strong, 1935, pl. 27, figs. *a–c*) and in the Sula-Ulua-Comayagua region and has been reported from Olancho.

Within the Playa de los Muertos ceramic pattern is a distinctive type of figurine which, although often suggesting the extended-leg figure (Gordon, 1896, pl. 10, figs. *d, g*), has a natural-shaped head. Besides this, the whole object is executed with a skill and a lack of formalization as a rule unknown in Central American art. This type is limited to a relatively small area in Honduras, extending from the Sula-Ulua Valley through the Comayagua region. Figurine whistles or figurine subjects other than the human beings do not appear to have been associated with Playa de los Muertos culture. However, jadeite ax-gods are associated.

STONE SEATS AND METATES

Three-legged seats and metates of definite Costa Rican style, some even with a slightly raised edge, are typical of the *Paya* area (Stone, 1941, fig. 34) and occur, as in the former region, in a variety of sizes, from the miniature to the overlarge. They appear in the Sula-Ulua Valley at Melchoir (pl. 26, *c–e*) by Palenque Hill (Stone, 1941, fig. 99, p. 96), in the Jamastran Valley near the Nicaraguan frontier, and occasionally in the Comayagua area. No tetrapod specimens have as yet come to the attention of the writer.

STONE FIGURES

Animal figures with peg bases have been found in southwestern Honduras (Richardson, 1940, fig. 36, *a*) but not as yet in the other sections. However, the same technique of carving, the same stylization, with exception of the base, is evident on the animal representations in stone from the *Paya* area, and in the Ulua Valley near Santa Barbara. (Compare Stone, 1941, figs. 28, 34, *c* and *f*, and pl. 29, *e*, from Santa Barbara, with pl. 29, *d*, from El Palmar in *Boruca* country.) Human figures with peg bases occur in the Sula-Ulua Valley (Gordon, 1896, fig. 4, p. 12), at Los Naranjos at Lake Yojoa. (See Strong, Kidder, and Paul, 1938, pl. 16, fig 1; fig. 3 might have been a peg-base statue before it was broken. The interesting feature of this image is the position of the hands (Stone, 1934 a, pp. 125–126; Lothrop, 1921, fig. 69, *b*, and p. 314); compare with pl. 27, *b*, from El Palmar, Costa Rica.) Images with peg bases, although of a different stylization, are found also in the Copán section (Richardson, 1940, fig. 35, *c*, p. 404).

From southern Honduras, including the islands in the Bay of Fonseca, the territory of the historic *Mangue* (that is, from Nacaome and Perspire) and of the *Ulva,* from La Ola in Choluteca, comes still another type of peg figure (pl. 28, *a–c, f–g,* and *j*). This extends in a degenerate form north to Tegucigalpa (pl. 28, *k*) and has already been noted in the *Boruca* area of Costa Rica (pl. 28, *i*, from La Ola, Terrabá Plain, *Boruca* region). This is similar to the statue illustrated by Gordon from the Sula-Ulua Valley. The type often has a sharp spiny ridge or ridges down the back (pl. 28, *a'*), a feature of a group of Costa Rican stone images which have been termed "sukia" figures (pl. 29, *c*, from Guapiles, *Guetar* territory; Lines, 1938 a). Statues related to those from southern Honduras have been found at San José de Colinas in the Department of Santa Barbara (Yde, 1938, fig. 19, p. 40) and near Naco in the Chamelecón Valley (pl. 28, *h*). Occasionally a second human head instead of a peg is used (turn pl. 28, *j*, upside down). In Gracias, and near San Lorenzo by the Bay of Fonseca, "sukia" figures identical with those of the *Guetar* region of Costa Rica have been found (pl. 29, *a*, from San Lorenzo, and pl. 29, *b*, from Gracias). This style of statue does not have a peg base.

Jadeite ax-gods also are common in *Paya* territory (Stone, 1941, fig. 39) and are found to a lesser extent in the Sula-Ulua and Comayagua areas and in the vicinity of the city of Tegucigalpa (personal observation of the writer).

STONE DUMPS

The only examples of stonework shops or deposits have been reported from *Paya* country (Spinden, 1925, e.g., fig. 1).

STONE BALLS

In Honduras, stone balls larger than the ordinary ball used in the bola have been found in Tenampua in Comayagua (Popenoe, 1936, pp. 569–570), at Travesia in the Sula-Ulua Plain (Stone, 1941, p. 94), and at San José de Colinas in the Santa Barbara region (Yde, 1938, fig. 19, p. 40).

PETROGLYPHS

Petroglyphs of the type encountered in Costa Rica are scattered over Honduras. They are found in *Paya* country, for example on the Plantain River (Spinden, 1925, fig. 2). They are found also in Olancho outside of Guaymaca, at Tenampua in Comayagua (Popenoe, 1936, pl. 4, fig. 2), at Los Gallianos near Yarumela likewise in Comayagua, at Aramecina in the Goascorán valley (Squier, 1908, p. 299), in the immediate vicinity of the city of Tegucigalpa toward the southeast, at Nueva Armenia by the upper reaches of the Nacaome River, and at Cerquin in Gracias (pl. 31, *a*). Much of this region was occupied by the *Lenca*.

BURIALS

Burials are of various types. Stone-cist graves are rare but occur in the *Paya* area. Here also are what may be urn burials both in caves and outside (Stone, 1941, fig. 6, p. 23). Some of these are cremated remains. Urn and skull burials occur on the Bay Islands (Strong, 1935). In the Sula-Ulua Plain, at Melchoir, stone shafts marking graves occur (pl. 32). There are similar shafts on the Bay Islands (Strong, 1935, p. 135), although it is not known whether burials are located beneath them. A report of cave burial likewise comes from the Bay Islands (Strong, 1935, p. 32). In the Sula-Ulua Plain, in the Sula-*Jicaque* territory, up the Sulaco River, and in part of the Comayagua area burials seem to have been in mounds; but in the region of Lake Yojoa, in addition to mound burials, bodies were placed in the crevices of large rocks on the islands in the lake. In the Comayagua region also, and in all the *Lenca* country of southwestern Honduras, caves were used for burials. There is as yet no report on the burial types from southeastern Honduras.

EL SALVADOR

CERAMICS

The monochrome-stone complex is stronger in eastern, or the ancient province of Chaparrastique, than in western El Salvador. However, the spread of basic elements is noticeable throughout. Only one trait, an elongated tripod leg, seems to have disappeared or never reached the Salvadorean area, while the others persist, particularly in the east.

As in Nicaragua, the ceramics of El Salvador which may be seen in the collections are usually polychrome. These show, however, a combination or a persistence of monochrome traits. An important inclusion among the painted ceramics is Usulután ware, most common in eastern, although found in both eastern and western, El Salvador.

Spouted, effigy, and shoe-form vessels and vessels with annular bases are very frequent in the east. (See Spinden, 1915, fig. 61, pp. 458, 482; Lothrop, 1927 a, fig. 24, *f*. The vessel shown in fig. 24, *f*, is similar to one from the *Guetar* section, which is now in the Museo Nacional in Costa Rica. See also fig. 18, *e–g*, and material collected by John Longyear III, Peabody Museum, Harvard University.)

Modeled, incised, and punctate patterns are also prevalent.

As in the *Lenca* territory, tetrapod vessels are common, extending throughout eastern and western El Salvador (pl. 25, *a*).

Effigy supports on vessels, both polychrome and monochrome, are found in El Salvador (material collected by John Longyear III, Peabody Museum, Harvard University). Many supports portray human heads and are as a whole similar to those in Costa Rica. The animal-head legs are as a rule conventionalized, as in the *Lenca* area of Honduras, and have small snoutlike bases, sloping foreheads, and two holes or indentations for eyes. Sometimes they are so formalized that the eyes are omitted. The indented or sloping forehead is a characteristic of *Lenca*-area pot legs. Loop handles with raised heads are typical of the *Lenca* region and are common in eastern El Salvador. Also numerous are monkey-head lugs, likewise characteristic of the *Lenca* area (pl. 24, *a*).

Figurines in eastern El Salvador are found in a variety of styles, which include Playa de los Muertos, bird and animal representations related to the Sula-Ulua region as well as to Nicaragua and Costa Rica, and a version of the conventionalized flatheaded type so prevalent in eastern Central America. (See Lothrop, 1927 a, fig. 23, p. 209; Stone, 1941, fig. 1, p. 13. Compare Lothrop, 1926 b, vol. 2, fig. 157, *a*, from Nicaragua, with Stone and Turnbull, 1941, pl. 8, fig. *g*, from the Sula-Ulua Plain, and with Stone, 1941, fig. 1, *l–k*, from eastern El Salvador.) In fact, Lothrop (1927 a, p. 211) attributes the flatheaded figurine to *Chorotegan* influence. We have seen that, with the exception of a possible enclave of *Maribio* (Lehmann, 1920, 2:647–649) in the north, basically Central American nations inhabited this area. It is not surprising, then, to find this figurine type extending into the eastern Salvadorean region.

Cuscatlan, or western El Salvador, is more closely bound with Guatemala than the section east of the Lempa River. Here, at Cerro Zapote, San Jacinto, El Salvador, Lothrop and Larde y Larin found stratified remains, in the lowest level of which were figurines reminiscent of red-ware figurines from Costa Rica (Lothrop, 1927 a, p. 175) and tetrapod vessels (ibid., p. 176).

STONE METATES

The stone complex continues also into El Salvador. Curiously enough, the usual metate, particularly in the east, is a four-legged variety, some-times with an extended animal head (Lothrop, 1927 b, fig. 8, p. 31). Around Quelepa, rectangular stones without legs but with a deeply hol-lowed grinding basin have been found. (Information from John Longyear III, Peabody Museum, Harvard University.) Such grinding stones are common in Costa Rica in the *Talamanca* and *Boruca* sections.

STONE FIGURES

Spinden (1915, p. 459, fig. 63, p. 460) has noted that animals portrayed in stone, although rare, are heavy and massive and that the human figures are sculptured with the arms and legs in relief against the body. We have followed this method of carving and representation north and west from southeastern Costa Rica. Lothrop (1927 b, fig. 7, p. 30) publishes a stone figure of a man which he notes is a common type in the coastal region. This is identical to figures from the *Lenca* area in the Department of Gracias in Honduras and is reminiscent of the "sukia" figures of Costa Rica. (Cf. with pl. 29.)

Quantities of small jadeite ax-gods with peg bases occur in eastern El Salvador. (Information from John Longyear III, Peabody Museum, Harvard University; also see Lothrop, 1927 b, p. 33.)

PETROGLYPHS

Petroglyphs are found in northeastern El Salvador, and caves with pictographs are reported (Spinden, 1915, p. 450).

STONE DUMPS

Stone dump heaps or quarries have not been reported from this area.

STONE BALLS

Stone balls have not been reported.

BURIALS

Little has been reported on burial customs in El Salvador. The writer has heard of burial caves in the northeastern section but has never seen them. In the western half of the republic, *Maya* and Mexican methods of burial are prevalent.

GUATEMALA

CERAMICS

As might be expected, there are certain centers where non-*Maya,* non-Mexican traits are predominant in Guatemala and where there occurs a monochrome ware with a definite relationship to that which has been traced throughout Central America. This monochrome ware at times underlies polychrome *Maya* horizons and at times is associated with them. The centers known at present for this basic style are Uaxactún and Holmul in the Petén (Vaillant, 1930, pp. 79–80), Chamá in the Alta Verapaz (Butler, 1940, pp. 250–267), Zacualpa (Wauchope, 1941, pp. 211–231, particularly pp. 229–231) and Salcajá in the Highlands, Chukumuk and neighboring sites around Lake Atitlán (Lothrop, 1933), and the Fincas Arevalo and Miraflores near Guatemala City (Lothrop, 1926 a). Usulután ware is generally associated with this monochrome style, and Lothrop (1933, p. 48) has listed the following locations where it has been noted: Chukumuk, Xikomuk, the Fincas Arevalo and Miraflores, Semetabaj, Zacualpa, Salcajá, and the Departments of Sacatepequez and Alta Verapaz. This list includes practically every known site at which the monochrome complex occurs.

Following more exactly the locations of the various monochrome ceramic types, we find spouted vessels at Holmul (Vaillant, 1930, fig. 6, pp. 79–80), at Chamá in period III (Butler, 1940, p. 262), at Chukumuk associated with Usulután ware (Lothrop, 1933, p. 47), and at Salcajá (Vaillant, 1930, p. 81).

Effigy vessels, tetrapod supports, and vessels decorated by filleting, modeling, incising, and punctating (appliqué patterns are not so common) occur at most of the sites named above.

Subglobular pots are common, particularly in the Lake Atitlán region (Lothrop, 1933, figs. 13, *e;* 20, *b*).

Shoe-form vessels are rare but have been reported from Chipal, a site similar to Chamá in the Alta Verapaz (Butler, 1940, p. 262), Saculeu (Wauchope, 1941, p. 224), and Zacualpa (ibid., p. 229). According to most reports the shoe-form vessels are late.

Ring bases and pot stands are fairly common.

Effigy-head vessel supports, although having a general distribution, appear more frequently in Zacualpa than in the other sites (Wauchope, 1941).

Figurines and figurine whistles in the Guatemala area are rare and are marked for the most part by outside influences. Flatheaded figurines are unknown to the writer. Lothrop illustrates certain other types from Chuitinamit, one of which is a figurine whistle in human form. The position of the legs is reminiscent of certain Salvadorean and Sula-Ulua figures and may perhaps be an adaptation of the monochrome style seen throughout Central America. (See Lothrop, 1933, fig. 61, *h,* p. 96.)

METATES AND STONE SEATS

Metates of southern Central American type are rare. One stone seat and a portion of another were found at Chuitinamit (Lothrop, 1933, p. 86, fig. 53). These are actually seats and not grinding stones, differing slightly from those seen in eastern Central America, although Strong mentions what may be miniature stone seats in the Bay Islands of Honduras (Strong, 1935, p. 131).

PETROGLYPHS

Petroglyphs on rocks and boulders have been reported from the lake district (Lothrop, 1933). The pattern, however, is not the typical scroll and crude curvilinear design noted in the other regions of Central America. There is a possibility, of course, that the more complicated cultures of the *Maya* and the *Pipil* may have influenced the style of these rock carvings.

STONE FIGURES

The most marked development of the stone complex in Guatemala seems to have been the peg statues. They have, generally speaking, the same distribution as the other objects associated with the Central American basic cultures, occurring principally in the Lake Atitlán region (Lothrop, 1933, fig. 10, *b*, p. 27; fig. 63, *b*, *c*, p. 99; fig. 64, p. 100), and outside of Guatemala City at Finca Arevalo (Lothrop, 1926 a). In the Peabody Museum, Harvard University, is a peg or tenon statue from the Guatemalan Highlands (pl. 27, *i*). There is very little difference between this statue and the *Boruca* peg figures.

OTHER FEATURES

Stone dump heaps and balls are not reported in Guatemala, and there is only one mention of stone-cist graves. This is at Zaculeu (Saculeu), and their relationship to the stone-cist graves of the other regions of Central America is not definable at present (Hartman, 1901, p. 192). As in the Sula-Ulua Valley of Honduras, there seems to have been no special form of interment. It is interesting, however, that at least one body has been found placed under boulders as on the islands in Lake Yojoa, Honduras (Lothrop, 1933).

SUMMARY AND DISCUSSION

An attempt has been made here to present what is considered to be the basic cultural matrix of Central America as disclosed by the archeological evidence. In doing this it has been necessary also to show how those cultural features of the region, which are here considered basic Central

American, are related and intermingled with traits essentially *Mayan* or Mexican. Throughout Costa Rica we can follow this basic monochrome ceramic-stone complex into southeastern Nicaragua up through Zapatero Island in Lake Nicaragua and, as far as our scant knowledge of the region permits, through the Caribbean section into and through the *Paya* territory in Honduras to the Sula-Ulua Valley. This complex is technically and artistically simpler than the more complicated traits of the *Maya* and Mexican cultures. This eastern Central American region, outlined above, seems to have remained, for the greater part, un-Mexicanized and undisturbed by invasions from the north and west. Here the basic culture apparently has persisted with little interruption.

On the Caribbean side the basic complex can be followed up the Segovia and Jamastran Valleys and across the divide south to the Pacific and north and west through the Choluteca Valley into eastern El Salvador and southern Gracias. Here many of its traits persist almost untouched by the neighboring and relatively recently arrived Mexican peoples. Farther north in Honduras, in the Departments of Tegucigalpa, Comayagua, La Paz, Intibucá, and the northeastern portion of Copán, and in parts of the Chamelecón Valley into the Sula-Ulua Valley, and even in Guatemala, are vestiges of the spread of this same complex, which is most obvious in the stonework and in ceramic traits such as lugs, handles, and an appliqué technique especially noticeable on effigy vases.

On the Pacific side of Central America the aboriginal populations were disturbed and in part conquered by peoples from the north, coming from territory now belonging to México. Some of these tribes, for example, the *Chorotega-Mangue,* apparently arrived in Central America so far in the past as to seem almost indigenous in this area and were themselves followed and intruded upon by the later migrations of the *Subtiaba,* the *Nahua* or *Nicarao,* and the *Aztec.*

Mixed with this spread of Mexican influences were certain definitely *Maya* elements which, outside of what is generally accepted as *Maya* territory, may have been the results of trade or of an earlier extension of the *Maya* to the eastward. *Maya* traits are found from Guatemala through El Salvador and western Honduras (Lothrop, 1939), beyond the region of Lake Yojoa through the Comayagua Plateau and the Sulaco Valley, and in sketchy locations in the present Departments of Tegucigalpa, Choluteca, and El Paraíso in Honduras, the Cuá River, a branch of the Segovia River, in Nicaragua (Lehmann, 1910, p. 748), the area around Managua, Nicaragua (information from Francis Richardson, Carnegie Institution of Washington), and the Nicoya Peninsula in Costa Rica. This *Maya* influence is particularly evident in the painted ceramics, especially in the pictorial designs and in the cylindrical vase form. In Honduras in the Sula-Ulua and Comayagua Valleys, the headwaters of the Sulaco River, at Esquías, and in Costa Rica on the Nicoya Peninsula have been found carved marble vases of a type which the writer considers to be of *Maya* workmanship but of a *Paya-Maya* inspiration (Stone, 1941).

From this it is evident that there were two cultural centers in Central America. The first is most clearly seen on the Caribbean coast, extending from the *Paya* area of Honduras through the Costa Rican mainland and into South America, and south through the *Ulva-Matagalpa* of southeastern El Salvador and southern Honduras and Nicaragua to the *Corobici* of the Nicoya Peninsula. The second is that of Highland peoples such as the *Lenca* tribes of Honduras and El Salvador. The first is characterized by the monochrome ceramic-stone complex, referred to above, while the second shows evidence of subsequent influence from the *Maya* and the Mexican peoples.

The monochrome ceramic-stone complex of the first or Caribbean culture center is, perhaps, seen to best advantage in Costa Rica. The pottery is characterized by subglobular forms and annular bases. Vessels have short necks and zoomorphic handles. A flatheaded human figurine[9] of pottery should also be included in the Caribbean group, although a variety of subjects served as models for the figurine or figurine whistle within this area. The appliqué patterns, so much a part of what has been termed Red Line ware and Stone Cist ware, have a universal distribution throughout Costa Rica. In southeastern Costa Rica these types are less common; even there, however, the principal ceramic type is a subglobular bowl with raised and often appliquéd figures as ornamentation. Lothrop relates this type, along with elongated tripod vessels, which are an important feature of *Boruca* region ceramics, to the *Chiriqui* (Lothrop, 1926 b, vol. 2, p. 412; Stone, 1941, 1943). The monochrome appliqué ware of the *Boruca* and *Guetar* country has its counterpart in a similar style found in the *Paya* region of northeastern Honduras; and appliqué pottery also continues in a modified form among the Sula-*Jicaque* and, less frequently, in *Lenca* territory and Guatemala (Lothrop, 1933, pp. 31–34, figs. 12, *e*, *g;* 13, *f;* 15, *a*, and pp. 47–53; Stone, 1942, p. 382, fig. 43). In these latter regions and on the Pacific side appliqué pottery is blended with polychrome pottery but persists in keeping certain of its monochrome or appliqué characteristics.[10]

At present it seems reasonably clear that this monochrome ceramic complex reached its highest development in the Central American Caribbean region, and no other culture has been found to underlie it as far as the Ulua Valley.

The roots of the second culture center were chiefly in the western and southern portions of Central America and in part coincide with the

---

[9] This flatheaded figurine style is concentrated in eastern Central America and northern South America (Lothrop, 1926 b, vol. 2, figs. 148, 166; Arango C., 1929, fig. 4).

[10] The distribution of appliqué ware includes, outside of the Central American area, Highland Colombia, Ecuador, and Perú in South America (Lothrop, 1926 b, vol. 2, p. 409). It occurs also in less complicated forms in the Antilles (Rouse, 1939, pp. 110–113; pls. 1–5) and in simple forms in Venezuela (Lothrop, 1926 b, vol. 2, p. 410).

spread of the monochrome complex. As a result both complexes were closely bound together. Many of the elements that appear as characteristic of both centers seem to have been transmitted through the Sula-*Jicaque*, who not only were closely allied both culturally and geographically with the *Paya* but also stretched far into *Lenca* territory (Stone, 1941, 1942). Characteristic of both Sula-*Jicaque* and *Lenca* ceramics are lugs with raised animal heads. These can be divided into two classes. One has a head so formalized, or perhaps so degenerated, as to appear only a raised nubbin on the lugs (pl. 21, *a*, from Marcala), often with two holes for eyes, and occasionally with merely two small indentations in a triangular-shaped button (Strong, Kidder, and Paul, 1938, pl. 14, fig. *d;* also pl. 25, *e*, from Siquatepeque). The other class has protruding well-formed heads generally of monkeys (pl. 24, *a;* also Yde, 1938, fig. 46, p. 72). Both types depend largely on the use of paint to perfect the facial details, but the second style is never found without paint, whereas the first often appears as monochrome ware. Another important feature of the ceramics from these areas is the effigy head of an animal on or as the vessel support. This, especially in Sula-*Jicaque* pottery, is often merely suggested by an indentation at the knee of the pot leg. The use of the whole head and also the use of indentation is, however, a characteristic *Lenca* style.

The patterns of Chukumuk brown ware in Guatemala are reminiscent of Sula-*Jicaque* ceramics. (Cf. Lothrop, 1933, fig. 12, with Stone, 1942, fig. 43.) Lothrop has already pointed out that the subglobular vessel with tripod legs, such as occurs at Chukumuk, Guatemala, has been found also at the Fincas Arevalo and Miraflores, at Zacualpa, and at Salcajá; and all are comparatively early. He suggests that this is South American influence[11] into northern Central America (Lothrop, 1933, p. 33). In fact, continual attention is called to the Costa Rican-Nicaraguan influence noted at many of the Guatemalan sites (Lothrop, 1933, pp. 44–45, 47–48).

The Playa de los Muertos types, with which should be associated Usulután ware, emphasize further the blending of cultures. Many figurines in the *Boruca* area of Costa Rica, for example, are portrayed in positions similar to certain Playa de los Muertos figures. (Cf. Popenoe, 1934, fig. 12, p. 75, with pl. 24, *p*.) Playa de los Muertos as a ceramic style extends through the Sula-Ulua Plain, through the Comayagua Valley into eastern El Salvador, and in part, minus figurines, into Guatemala.[12]

In the *Lenca* territory certain traits stand out and are traceable through the Central American area. Tetrapod vessels are characteristic of *Lenca*

---

[11] The present author prefers to attribute this influence to the two Central American centers, the Caribbean and the Highland, and not with South America.

[12] Vessels similar to Playa de los Muertos are common in Colombia (Arango C., 1929, vol. 1, fig. 11; vol. 2, fig. 1) and particularly in Perú (Strong, 1925, pl. 48). The same pottery types have an analogy in Uaxactún, Guatemala (Strong, Kidder, and Paul, 1938, p. 122), and in the Chukumuk ware from the Guatemalan lake district (ibid., pp. 122–123).

PLATE 21.—**Tripod styles from Costa Rica and Honduras.** *a,* From Marcala, Honduras, *Lenca* Territory; *b, c,* from *Guetar* area, Costa Rica; *d, e,* from the *Boruca* region, Costa Rica. (*b, c,* Courtesy National Museum, San José, Costa Rica; others, courtesy Doris Stone.)

PLATE 22.—**Some basic Central American ceramic types.** *a*, San Isidro, General Valley, *Boruca* region; *b*, Comayagua Valley, Honduras; *c*, *f*, *j*, Nicoya Peninsula, Costa Rica; *d*, Muymuy, Matagalpa area, Nicaragua; *e*, *Guetar* area, Costa Rica; *g*, Siguatepeque, Honduras; *h*, Yoro, Sula-*Jicaque* country, Honduras; *i*, Lake Yojoa, Honduras. (*c*, *e*, *f*, *j*, Courtesy National Museum, San José, Costa Rica; others, courtesy Doris Stone.)

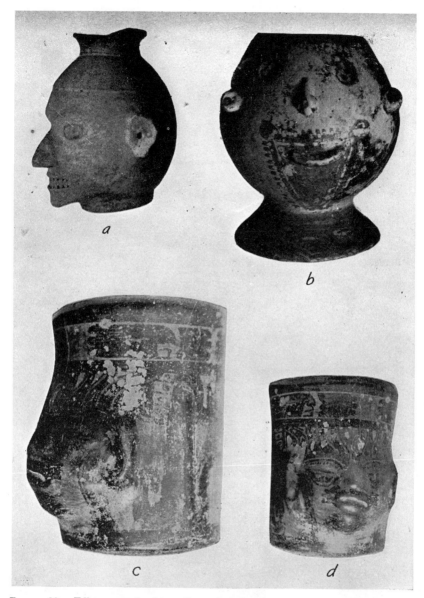

PLATE 23.—**Effigy vessels from Central America.** *a*, Buenos Aires, General Valley, *Boruca* region, Costa Rica; *b*, Ometepe Island, Nicaragua; *c*, *d*, two views of a vessel from Las Vegas, Comayagua Valley, Honduras. (*a*, *b*, Courtesy Doris Stone; *c*, *d*, courtesy Federico Lunardi.)

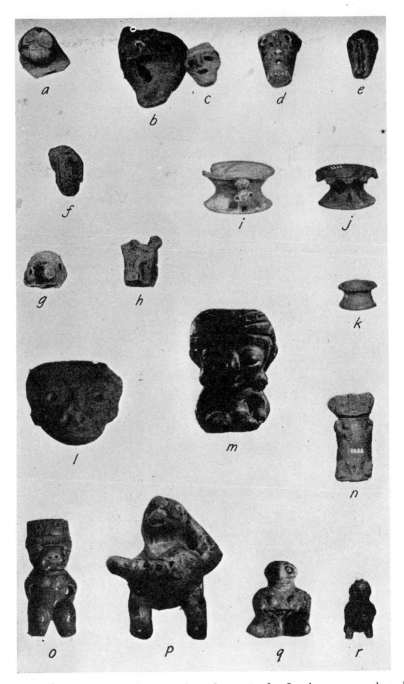

PLATE 24.—**Central American pot legs, lugs, stands, figurines.** *a, c, d, g, h,* Comayagua Valley, Honduras; *b, i–k, n, o, r, Guetar* area, Costa Rica; *e,* Muy- muy, *Metagalpa* area, Nicaragua; *f, l,* Intibuca, *Lenca* territory, Honduras; *m,* Yoro, Sula-*Jicaque* territory, Honduras; *p, Coto* region, Costa Rica; *q, Boruca* region, Costa Rica. (*i–k, n, r,* Courtesy National Museum, San José, Costa Rica; others, courtesy Doris Stone.)

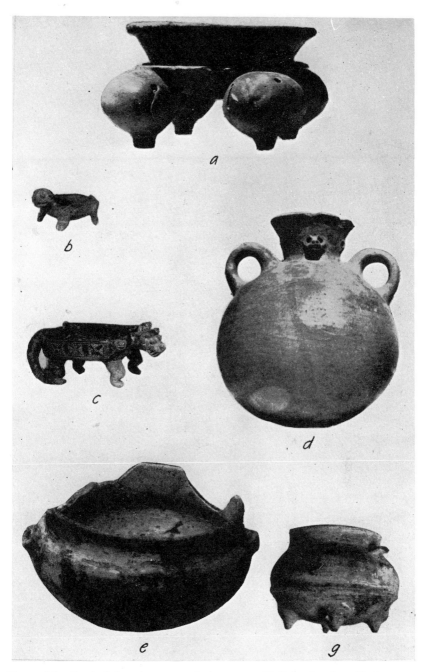

PLATE 25.—**Central American ceramic types.** *a*, El Salvador; *b, c, Guetar* area, Costa Rica; *d*, Lake Yojoa, Honduras; *e*, Siguatepeque, Honduras; *f*, Marcala, *Lenca* territory, Honduras. (*b, c*, Courtesy National Museum, San José, Costa Rica; others, courtesy Doris Stone.)

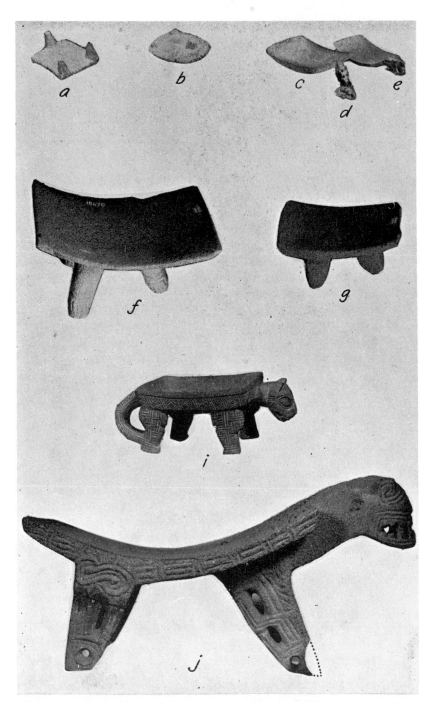

PLATE 26.—**Stone seats or metates from Central America.** *f, g, i,* Nicoya Peninsula, Costa Rica; *c–e,* Melchoir, Sula-Ulua Valley, Honduras; *h, Guetar* area, Costa Rica. (*f–i,* Courtesy National Museum, San José, Costa Rica; others, courtesy Doris Stone.)

PLATE 27.—Stone peg figures from Costa Rica and Guatemala. *a–g*, Terraba Plain, *Boruca* area, Costa Rica; *h*, *Guetar* region, Costa Rica; *i*, Guatemala Highlands. (*i*, Courtesy Peabody Museum, Harvard University; others, courtesy Doris Stone.)

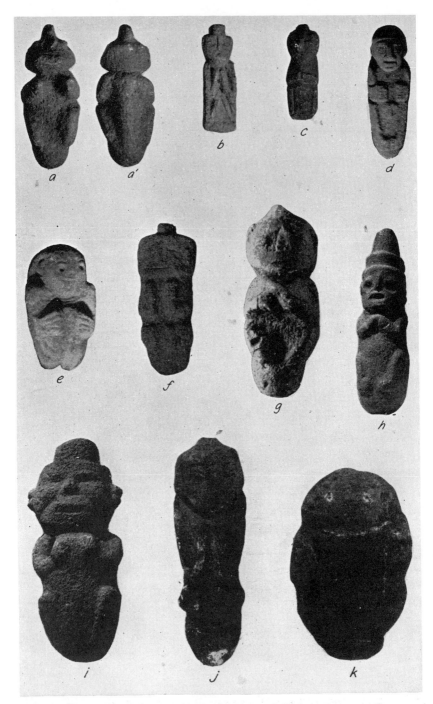

PLATE 28.—**Stone peg figures from Costa Rica and Guatemala.** *a–c*, Gueguensi Island, *Ulva* territory, Honduras; *d, e, i*, Terraba Plain, *Boruca* region, Costa Rica; *f*, Sacate Grande Island, Honduras; *g*, Nacaome, Honduras; *h*, Naco, Honduras; *j*, San Lorenzo, Honduras; *k*, Humuya Creek, Tegucigalpa, Honduras. (Courtesy Doris Stone.)

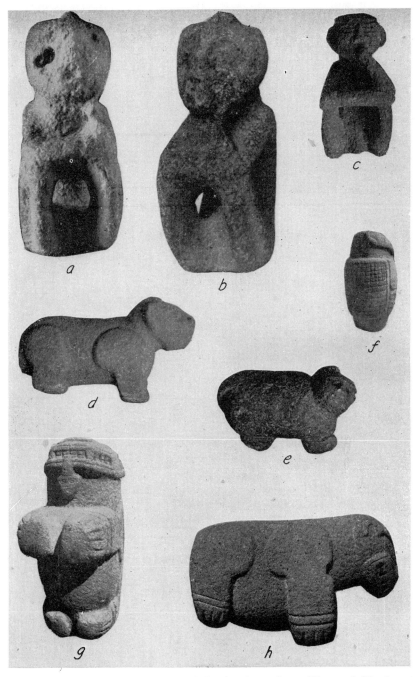

PLATE 29.—**Stone sukia and animal figures from Costa Rica and Honduras.**
a, San Lorenzo, Honduras; b, Department of Gracias, Honduras, *Lenca* territory; c, *Guetar* area, Costa Rica; d, f, g, Terraba Plain, *Boruca* area, Costa
Rica; e, Santa Barbara, Honduras. (b, Courtesy National Museum, Tegucigalpa, Honduras; others, courtesy Doris Stone.)

PLATE 30.—**Stone balls in the Terraba Plain.** The *Boruca* region, Costa Rica. (Courtesy Doris Stone)

PLATE 31.—**Petroglyphs, Honduras and Costa Rica.** *Top:* Cerquin, Gracias, *Lenca* area, Honduras. *Bottom:* Quisara, General Valley, *Boruca* area, Costa Rica. (Courtesy Doris Stone.)

PLATE 32.—**Stone grave markers from Honduras.** The Sula-Ulua Plain.
(Courtesy Doris Stone.)

pottery (pl. 25, *f*) and continue in numbers into what may have been originally *Xinca* country, such as Atitlán, as well as in other sections of Guatemala, where they occur frequently in Usulután ware (Lothrop, 1933, p. 49). It has been suggested that tetrapod vessels, annular bases, and pot stands are South American in origin (Thompson, 1936, 140–141, p. 16). The concentration of tetrapod vessels in the *Lenca* area and their gradual diminution toward eastern Central America argue against this thesis, however, and place the tetrapod vessel within the Highland culture center. The annular base and pot stand occur too frequently in Central America to permit the ready acceptance of a South American origin, although they belong both with the Caribbean and with the Highland groups.

Painted fine-line decoration and a formalized painted or even slightly raised eye or face on the vessel side (fig. 25, *d*, from Lake Yojoa, and pl. 25, *e;* also see Stone, 1941) are other *Lenca* area traits which are found in *Ulva-Matagalpa* territory and continue eastward through Nicaragua, e.g., Nandaime Ware (Lothrop, 1926 *b,* vol. 1; pp. 217–22). Fine-line monkey vessels, with extended monkey-head handles and with raised animal heads as legs, also follow more or less the same distribution and seem to have their center in the *Lenca* area of Honduras and northeastern El Salvador. At the same time they show influences from the *Paya* region of the Honduras north coast (Stone, 1941).

The earliest ceramic types from Cerro Zapote, in western El Salvador, a region that at one time may have been *Xinca* or even *Lenca,* evidence a close relationship to the ceramics of eastern El Salvador, namely the Departments of Usulután and San Miguel (Lothrop, 1933, p. 59), which are principally *Lenca,* although in part *Ulva,* territory. The *Xinca* as well as the *Lenca* were a Central American group who apparently developed their culture within the region of Central America and served as a channel for diffusion between the cultures of Central America and those of the *Maya* and their Mexican neighbors.

The carrying of culture traits by the *Lenca* is apparent not only in the north of Central America but also in the southern area. Remains from the territory of the *Corobici,* which originally seems to have included southwestern Costa Rica and the region of Lake Nicaragua, evidences this same blending of traits associated with both the Caribbean and Highland centers. The *Lenca* seemingly formed a link connecting the *Xinca* and the Pacific side of Central America.

In regard to stonework the distribution of metates in Central America presents an interesting but confusing problem. It is difficult to determine just what objects should be called metates and what should be classed as seats. Aside from this, stones which were obviously used for grinding purposes are common all over the Costa Rican mainland. These are nothing more than large rocks with hollow portions which served as a bowl and without even a sign of legs or of adornment. In southern or eastern Costa Rica, exclusive of the Nicoyan Peninsula, the prevalent type of metate or seat, other than the grinding stones mentioned above, was the four-legged variety. This type extended as we have seen all over the mainland, but in the North Coast area, e.g., Mercedes, and in the Highland region, the four-legged type is found along with the three-legged. In Nicoya, although four-legged metates occur, the usual grinding stone has three legs. The three-legged class continues throughout Nicaragua and the *Paya* area of Honduras into the Comayagua Valley, and over into Guatemala, where, interestingly enough, in the area which is definitely *Maya,* the metate with legs is generally replaced by metates without legs.[13] This last type is not the unworked crude grinding stone found in Costa Rica but is the grinding portion of the legged metate without the supports (Stromsvick, 1935). The four-legged metate appears again in quantity in eastern El Salvador, where the three-legged variety is practically nonexistent.

It is reasonable to suggest from this survey that the 3-legged metate was preferred by the Caribbean group. The 4-legged grinding stone was apparently confined to the Pacific side. Whether this tetrapod variety belongs fundamentally with the Highland centers or whether it originally developed in the Caribbean centers cannot be determined until further archelogical work is done, particularly in *Ulva* country, such as Choluteca in Honduras and the adjoining region in Nicaragua.

Concerning the peg statues, these stone figures are characteristically Central American and apparently non-*Mayan.* They have been linked with the *Chorotega* (Lothrop, 1926 b, vol. 1; p. 93) and tentatively with the *Pipil* (Thompson, 1941, pp. 52–56). Some investigators have suggested a South American origin (Richardson, 1940, pp. 414–416; Kidder II, 1940, pp. 452–453). Figures on pedestals, pegs, or columns, however, extend throughout the Central American area, and their presence in the Costa Rican Highlands and *Boruca* region, where the culture appears to have been more unified and less affected by foreign influences, suggests equally the possibility of a Central American origin. The various types of peg figures, e.g., those of the Chontales group (Richardson, 1940, pp. 412–416), of the Ulua-Yojoa area (Gordon, 1896, p. 12, fig. 4; Strong, Kidder, and Paul, 1938, pl. 16, fig. 1), of southwestern Honduras and the Guatemalan Highlands (Richardson, 1940, p. 406), and of the smaller statues of the *Boruca* area in Costa Rica and the *Ulva* area in southern Honduras and eastern Salvador, though differing in details of technique and dress are nonetheless tenon or peg statues. Some of these from *Boruca* territory, as we have seen, are identical with those of the Ulua region.

---

[13] Tetrapod metates have been found in *Maya* country in the Chultunes of Labna, but this appears to be the exception rather than the rule (Gordon, 1896, p. 19).

The peg apparently is intended as an unseen support in the earth. The differences in the pegs, from a blunt roundness to an elongated shaft, we consider localized stylizations which developed from a common fundamental idea. The entire statue was usually an architectural feature to be used in association with mounds or buildings.

It is also highly probable that many of the large peg statues were relatively late, executed by Mexican people or at least directly influenced by them. (For discussion of the time element in connection with these statues, see Richardson, 1940, pp. 412–415; Kidder II, 1940, pp. 452–454.) In the Nicaraguan lake area in particular, where Mexican traits were predominant, it is reasonable to accept the view that many of these figures were Mexicanized, e.g., the birdman class pointed out by Lothrop (1926 b, vol. 1, pl. 7, figs. *a-c*, and Thompson, 1941, pp. 48–49).

Stones or boulders with incised designs, often with scrolls similar to the curved monkey tails on many of the polychrome vessels in the Sula-Ulua and Comayagua Valleys in Honduras and in the Pacific region of Nicaragua, occur throughout Costa Rica, Nicaragua, and the *Paya* region of Honduras and are found also in the *Lenca* area of Honduras and northeastern El Salvador. In Guatemala the petroglyphs that exist in the lake district are more elaborate and may be the result of influence of higher developed cultures or may have no relationship to the petroglyphs found in connection with basic Central American ceramics and stonework. In the cave of Labna, however, Central American types are intermingled with a few *Maya* motives (Gordon, 1896). In the Antilles and in northern South America the Central American type is common (Lothrop, 1926 b, 1:94). There is as yet no clue to the significance of these petroglyphs, but their spread covers the greater part of the Central American area as well as the regions to the south and the north outlined above. At present petroglyphs in Central America cannot be assigned to any particular culture center.

Raised burial mounds are found in the *Maya* and Mexican occupied regions, or where *Maya* or Mexican influence predominated, but are not so common in the other zones. In Costa Rica urn burial is most prevalent, but on the north coast stone-cist graves are also numerous. In Nicaragua, Honduras, and eastern El Salvador, non-*Mayan*, non-Mexican burials are generally in urns or in caves.[14] Although what might be called a form of urn burial (Lothrop, 1933, p. 22) and cave burial (e.g., at Lanquín in the Alta Verapaz) has been found in Guatemala, there is too much chance of other cultures such as *Maya* and *Pipil* being represented, and the subject must wait further investigation.

---

[14] Geologically, few caves exist in Costa Rica.

SPECULATIONS

Certain ceramic forms and other cultural traits which we feel may well have been originally developed in Central America by people of that region have been considered as elements of a basic Central American culture. Two centers of influence may be localized within the so-called basic culture pattern, the Caribbean and Highland groups or centers. The Caribbean center seems to have had the wider extension in Central America. This greater distribution of the Caribbean type may indicate that it was a more potent influence than the Highland culture type. On the other hand, influences of the Highland culture center may have been obscured by the impact and intermingling of strong *Maya* and Mexican characteristics, thereby creating the impression that the Caribbean type was a "purer" and more vigorous strain in Central America.

It is significant that many of the fundamental ceramic traits of these two centers of Central American culture occur in northern South America, Ecuador, and Perú. The same is true of the petroglyphs discussed as a part of the basic Central American complex. Carvings of a similar style are common in both northern South America and the Antilles. Stone stools likewise extend into northern South America, but the metate as found in Central America reaches its highest development in the Caribbean center and disappears as one progresses southward. In South America the alter-ego motive occurs in Perú and in the San Agustín Valley in Colombia (Sarmiento, 1941, pp. 14, 18). Among the San Agustín monuments are several with a serpentlike form tending from the mouth and held to the chest of a human figure (ibid., p. 16). In addition there is also a raised, slablike headdress which is reminiscent of the *Ulva* and of certain figures of the *Boruca* and the *Guetar* regions. Many of these massive monuments rest on a very small peg or pedestal base.

The relative time position of a great many of these South American parallels to the basic Central American traits is not known. Where it is known, however, it is usually early. The early position of these traits in South America checks, roughly, with the relatively early time position of the datable, pre-*Maya*, Playa de los Muertos culture of Honduras. The Playa de los Muertos complex shows a greater similarity to an early Peruvian horizon than any other ceramic unit in Central America.

It is not reasonable to suppose that ancient Peruvians or other northern South Americans would have traversed the area of eastern Central America northward to the Sula-Ulua and there to have left as a distinct culture so many of their traits when elsewhere in Central America there are only scattered items. It seems more reasonable that the Playa de los Muertos group is a part of, and a specialization out of, an early, widespread inter-American cultural horizon. The general cultural uniformity in eastern Central America suggests that this early widespread horizon, of which the Central American basic cultures were a part, continued through to the historic level under relatively static conditions as regards culture change. Such a hypothesis, however, should not overlook the fact that undoubtedly more recent South American traits came into Central America as the result of trade, or, perhaps, migratory groups. We have not concerned ourselves with these elements in the above discussion, in order to give a more definite idea of the characteristics which are possibly of Central American origin.

BIBLIOGRAPHY

Arango C., 1929; Boyle, 1868; Bransford, 1881; Briceño-Iragorry, 1928; Brinton, 1885, 1887, 1895, 1901; Butler, 1940; Col. Doc. Inéd. Amer. y Oceanía, 1864–84; Cortes, 1908; Fernández, 1881–1907; Franco Inojosa and González, 1936; Gabb, 1886; Gómara, 1749; Gordon, 1896; Hartman, 1901, 1907; Johnson, 1940; Juarros, 1936; Kidder II, 1940; Larde y Larin, 1940; Lehmann, 1910, 1920; Lines, 1935, 1938 a, 1939; Lothrop, 1921, 1926 a, 1926 b, 1927 a, 1927 b, 1933, 1937, 1939, 1940; Martyr, 1511; Mason, J. A., 1940, 1945; Oviedo y Valdés, 1851–55; Peralta, 1883, 1901; Pittier de Fábrega, 1904; Ponce, 1873; Popenoe, 1934, 1936; Popenoe, W., and Orton, 1921; Radin, 1919; Richardson, 1940; Rouse, 1939; Roys, 1932; Sapir, 1937; Sapper, 1897 a, 1907; Sarmiento, 1941; Schuchert, 1935; Schuller, 1928; Spinden, 1915, 1925; Squier, 1852, 1860 a, 1908; Steward, 1929; Stoll, 1938; Stone, 1934 a, 1934 b, 1940 a, 1940 b, 1941, 1942, 1943; Stone and Turnbull, 1941; Stromsvick, 1935; Strong, 1925, 1935, 1940; Strong, Kidder, and Paul, 1938; Thomas and Swanton, 1911; Thompson, 1936, 1941·; Torquemada, 1723; Vaillant, 1930, 1934, 1940; Vásquez, 1714–16; Verrill, 1927; Wauchope, 1941; Yde, 1938.

THE POST-CONQUEST ETHNOLOGY OF CENTRAL AMERICA: AN INTRODUCTION

By Frederick Johnson

Previous to the arrival of the Spaniards the culture of the Indians of Central America had been modified by the infiltration both of isolated culture traits and of complete complexes. It is probable that some of these modifications were forced upon the region by conquests, that is, by armies or at least by powerful bands of people. This influence was not overwhelming, however, for, regardless of its extent, the innovations were American in character and could be assimilated without disrupting the major trends of local developments. The Spanish Conquest was different, being carried on by means of an unprecedented military organization and involving a radically new economic system. Furthermore, its expressed intent was to mold the aboriginal culture into a form that could be dominated and controlled by Europeans.

Under Spanish influence a mixed culture developed, consisting of indigenous traits which the Indians could not or would not give up, together with a number of traits of foreign origin. Some of the latter were sought by the aborigines, for example, metal tools and other articles, which replaced the aboriginal ones as fast as the supply permitted. Many domesticated crops, especially bananas, sugarcane, rice, coffee, and oranges, and animals, particularly pigs and chickens, were quickly adopted. Some features, including social and religious concepts, were forced upon the Indians. The process of mixing and adjustment was not the same everywhere, however; each tribe reacted in its own peculiar manner, and the various Spanish leaders utilized different approaches. Moreover, some Indian groups submitted to Spanish domination more readily than others. The immediate result was a confusion, which is reflected, perhaps, by the contradictory information in the early documents. Once a relationship tolerable to both the Spaniards and Indians had been established, the progress of acculturation proceeded with less difficulty. However, in spite of 400 years of European aggression, some tribes still maintain many of the features of their aboriginal cultural tradition. As the contact between the Indians, Mestizos, and Whites of Central America

195

becomes more intense, these features will be further modified; in fact, acculturational changes are now taking place with an impressive rapidity.

The most striking influence on the Indian culture is that from the Spaniards, but Negro elements, to which too little attention has been paid, are also present. In the early mid-16th century, African slaves escaped from the Spaniards and organized communities as discrete enclaves, which promptly established intimate contacts with the Indians. The possible effects of the Negroes upon aboriginal culture should not be minimized. Another source of cultural influence came from the *Carib* Indians who, in the 18th century, were transported in considerable numbers to the Bay Islands and subsequently migrated to the mainland. They are probably responsible for some Central American culture traits which have been labeled "West Indian." It is necessary, however, to distinguish between West Indian traits that were brought by the *Carib* and those that may have reached Central America before 1700.

The role which geographic factors played in the development of Central American culture was vital, but unfortunately it has not been studied. Each cultural division has a few traits of restricted distribution which are obviously conditioned by the environment. It was probably in part for environmental reasons that the route of invasion taken by Meso-American tribes paralleled the Pacific coast and crossed sections of the Highlands. The few colonies which the Meso-Americans sent into the Tropical Forests were mere outposts, some of which succumbed to the environment, while others, probably under environmental influence, adopted the indigenous culture. The colonies which retained their Meso-American features were evidently not established long enough before the Conquest for local environmental and cultural influences to have changed them.

Environment was, however, only one of many factors responsible for the distribution of aboriginal culture. Exclusive of the Northern Highland and Meso-American Divisions, each culture in Central America is distributed over the Tropical Forests, the Pacific Borderlands, and the Highlands. Social and political organization are much the same everywhere. It is these cultures, especially among the tribes of Darién, the *Talamanca* Division, and the tribes of the northern and eastern coastal regions of Honduras and Nicaragua, which have a majority of traits of South American origin and which seem least affected by the differences in environment. They differ from one another only in detail.

The Spanish Conquest completely disrupted the trend of aboriginal events. During the past 400 years some tribes have become extinct and new tribes have developed out of the remnants of former organizations. Their territory has changed greatly. (Cf. map 5, for the period 1700–1900.) It seems possible that geographic factors have become more important than at any previous time. When the Spaniards landed they had to plunge into the Tropical Forest, an environment which they did not understand very well. They attempted to subdue the region but they were not wholly successful. Through military action and political intrigue they were able to conquer some tribes and to obliterate others, but there always remained aboriginal nuclei on the flank of their lines of communication through the Forests to the Highlands and the Pacific Borderlands. In these latter areas the Spaniards found themselves more at home, and, in spite of temporary setbacks, the expeditions sent west of Panamá City and south of ports of entry on the Caribbean were successful.

After conquering the Highlands and the Pacific Borderlands, the Spanish conquistadors transferred their interest from the Tropical Forest to the riches of México and Perú, making certain only that areas around the ports of entry and lines of communication were safe from any threat from the aborigines. The remainder of the Tropical Forest was virtually ignored, partially because it was useless to them. The remnant Indian groups were thereafter able to preserve their isolation in the Tropical Forest. Some tribes had not moved from their native haunts, but many others had been shifted about because of the military campaigns and the colonizing policies of the Spaniards. Despite the vagaries of history, which resulted in contacts of varying intensity with Europeans, these tribes still exist as cultural and, to a limited extent, as political entities in the Tropical Forest. The very small refugee enclaves and the partially Hispanicized *Lenca* now inhabit the more remote regions of the Highlands, but the bulk of the population which retains an Indian culture is found in the Tropical Forest and along its inland fringes.

It is obvious that the preceding hypothetical and speculative observations oversimplify a complex development in a region where all features are highly variable. Nevertheless, such a statement serves to combine possible interpretations of previous sections with the description of specific culture traits included in the present section. Before this statement can be greatly improved we need more accurate and more comprehensive geographic studies and also more detailed studies of the native and mixed populations of Central America. This latter includes further research into their territory.

In the following descriptions an attempt has been made to indicate the possibilities of such a study. Where feasible, the descriptions of 16th-century culture are separated from modern observations. If this were done in more detail and for all areas, the course of acculturation over the past 400 years would be more clearly brought out. Even as it is, what is often called the degeneration of culture is quite apparent.

Native industries have been choked out by the influx of European goods, which were often better suited than native objects for certain purposes. The native ceramic industry, once a significant outlet for artistic expression, produces only utilitarian wares, and these are now made in insufficient quantity to meet the demand. Only rarely are ceremonial vessels made, and even more rarely are wares decorated. Similarly, the weaving industry now produces only distinctly utilitarian fabrics, in contrast to the textiles, particularly those made on the Pacific coast, which the Spaniards admired. Metallurgy is no longer practiced, even by the descendants of tribes which had been most expert. Other industries have similarly declined, and only items of definite utility value are now made. In some cases, even the latter are no longer identical with the aboriginal ones, for they include innovations introduced by Europeans.

The changes in size and distribution of the population have affected the manner of living. Village or community life has taken on certain aspects of European tradition. Communal houses have been broken up. Single-family houses are now more common, and there is a tendency toward the reduction in number of house types. The "el" roofed house with or without walls may now be the most common type. These developments have had far-reaching effects upon the social customs of practically all tribes. The zeal of the missionaries has destroyed much of the ancient religion, but the more conservative groups retain many aboriginal features. It would be interesting to discover how many Christian and African concepts have been incorporated into these Indian religions and to determine the number and character of the Indian beliefs which have been adopted by the Church.

The present survey and tentative comparisons of early and modern culture traits bring to light several hypotheses which merit much future study. The aboriginal cultures of the Pacific Borderlands have been practically obliterated, and those of the Highlands have been superseded by a culture which is largely of Spanish origin. Of extreme interest, however, is the strongly Hispanicized culture of such tribes as the *Lenca*. In these a great many aboriginal features are still recognizable. In the Tropical Forests the Indians have become restricted to isolated regions, but their culture appears to retain much that is aboriginal. The culture traits first recorded after the Conquest reveal a number of local cultural divisions, but data collected during the past 50 years suggest greater homogeneity. The striking fact of the Tropical Forest people is that since the Conquest their culture has been simplified or decultured, rather than Hispanicized. During the past 400 years the more sophisticated aboriginal traits have disappeared; art, some industries, special costumes, the class system which supported a leisure class of nobles, and such are gone. The surviving culture is largely that concerned with subsistence and utilitarian pursuits, but even these have been modified by Spanish influence.

THE MESO-AMERICAN DIVISION[1]

By Frederick Johnson

INTRODUCTION

A satisfactory description of this Division is prevented by the contradictory and fragmentary nature of the data. The Central American culture traits which appear to have originated to the north and west of the eastern boundary of Guatemala[2] cannot, for various reasons, be ascribed with certainty to the tribes which have been identified. Ferdinand Columbus and other early explorers of the coasts of Honduras and Nicaragua describe clothing, ornaments, body decoration, weapons, and such which are Meso-American in character, but it is questionable whether the *Paya, Jicaque, Sumo,* and *Mosquito* possessed them. Actually these traits may have occurred only among the enclaves of immigrants who came from the lands to the north and west. Or they may have diffused into these regions and been adopted by the ancestors of the present tribes, who subsequently lost them. Records of Meso-American traits in the scattered localities in Central America which were not, as far as we know, inhabited by tribes of Meso-American origin are difficult to evaluate. These traits may have come through diffusion or they may have been actually carried in by small groups of travelers or traders.

The data on identifiable tribes can be treated with more confidence. Three groups of tribes living in Central America at the Conquest have, through their characteristically Mexican dialects, traditions, and culture elements, been identified as immigrants from México (maps 2 and 5). On the basis of traditional history, tribes of the *Nahuatlan* Group have been identified either with the *Toltec-Chichimec,* speaking the *Nahuatl* language, or with the *Aztec,* speaking *Nahuatl* (Mason, J. A., 1940; Johnson, 1940). It is probable that the *Toltec-Chichimec* tribes left Mexico during the 12th-century revolutions and migrations. The *Aztec,* on the other hand, appeared in Central America in the 15th and 16th centuries, having been sent out from México on trading and colonizing expeditions. The history of the *Maribio* and *Chorotega* Groups is controversial if not obscure. The languages and some culture traits are closely related to those of México. It has been postulated that these two groups of tribes

---

[1] For a definition of Meso-America, cf. Kirchhoff, 1943.

[2] Kirchhoff (1943) includes the *Lenca* in his Meso-American area. In the Handbook the *Lenca* are included in Central America, because they have many features which are common to the Central American region. The existence and significance of traits suggesting relationships to the north and west have not been emphasized.

199

represent earlier migrations to the region. Many of the traits of recent "Mexican" origin may, however, have developed in South America and spread northward, so that the Meso-Americans borrowed certain traits before they disseminated them.

After examining the historical data and making first-hand field observations himself, Lothrop (1940, p. 427), commenting on the culture of the *Nahuatlan* Group, exclusive of the *Nicarao,* says that, "they had abandoned anything recognizable as Mexican except their religion and speech and, in western Nicaragua and northwestern Costa Rica, some rare polychrome pottery patterns. Instead they adopted the manner of living practiced by their neighbors, Chorotegan and Talamancan tribes, probably as a result of intermarriage. In other words, the southward drift of the *Nahua* [*Nahuatlan*] from the 12th to 16th centuries did not, so far as we know, influence South American culture and by its nature could not be expected to do so." To a lesser extent this statement applies also to the *Chorotegan* and *Maribio* Groups.

An account of the culture of the Meso-American Groups is hampered by the lack of knowledge of the different tribes. With few exceptions, available data pertain to the *Chorotega* and the *Nicarao.* Oviedo y Valdés (1851–55), by far the best source, segregated some of his descriptions into these two divisions but all too frequently used the term "Nicaraguan." This term may have originated from *Nicarao,* but certain cultural items appear to have been *Chorotegan* or, perhaps, ascribable to other tribes. There is virtually no information on *Maribio* culture and on most of the *Nahuatlan* settlements.

CULTURE

SUBSISTENCE ACTIVITIES

Agriculture was highly developed among all these tribes. The slash-and-burn type common to the region must have been universally employed. The most important of the many crops were maize, cacao, and tobacco. Hunting and fishing supplied important additions to the diet.

VILLAGES AND HOUSES

Houses of the common people were thatch-roofed. Possibly the tree houses found on islands and along rivers were also those of the common people. The early writers devoted considerable attention to the "palaces" of the kings and nobles. These were composed of several varieties of rectangular houses each with a special use and all arranged about a rectangular plaza. Some had porticos. Temples were structurally similar to houses. Both temples and palaces were often built upon low earth mounds. Towns consisted of temples and palaces scattered about the countryside, each surrounded by houses apparently laid out along streets. Little or nothing is said about the location of the houses of the common people.

DRESS AND ORNAMENTS

Nicarao men wore sleeveless tunics of woven cotton cloth and breech-clouts made of a long strip of cloth wound about the body and passed between the legs.   Sandals were made of deer hide and tied on with straps. Women wore skirts reaching to the knees.   Women of high rank wore ankle-length skirts and "neck-cloths" which covered their breasts.   The costume of *Orotiña* men was very similar to that of the *Nicarao,* but the former tied a thread to the prepuce.   *Orotiña* women were said to wear an elaborately decorated breechclout, the ends of which passed over a narrow belt and hung down to form small aprons front and back.

According to Oviedo y Valdés, the *Nicarao* and the *Chorotega* took great care of their hair.   They decorated it in many ways and wore combs in it.   A man shaved his head in various fashions to indicate his social position and his success in battle.   Men were said to pierce their tongues and ears, and some were said to scarify (?) the penis.   Women also pierced their ears and wore quantities of necklaces, some of gold beads and medallions.

Body painting and tattooing were common.   The followers of the caciques bore identifying marks.   Elaborate body painting was used on ceremonial occasions.   Cranial deformation was common.

TRANSPORTATION

Dugout canoes were used, and a type of raft is described.   Paddles were made by fastening large pearl-oyster shells or pieces of board to the ends of a shaft.

MANUFACTURES

Weaving.—Textiles were made by all tribes.   Thread was spun from cotton, agave, and palm fibers.   The Spaniards greatly prized these textiles, particularly those made by the *Orotiña,* who dyed their threads with purple obtained from a shellfish (*Purpura patula*).   Mats and hammocks were woven of threads made from the coarser fibers.

Ceramics.—One of the greatest industries was pottery making, which the explorers and travelers praised highly.   Oviedo mentions particularly the black ware made on Chira Island in the Golfo de Nicoya.

Metallurgy.—Goldworking is mentioned, but it may not have been a major industry among the peoples of "foreign origin," i.e., the Meso-Americans.   The industry is more completely described for tribes of the *Talamanca* Division.   Early records and subsequent archeological work indicate that a center of the industry may have been in western Panamá and southwestern Costa Rica.   At any rate there was an extensive trade in objects made in this region and also in the raw materials.

Social organization and marriage.—The social organization of the people in Nicaragua was characterized by three hereditary classes. A person could improve his status, however, by acquiring wealth. The priests, who were usually nobles, were in a class more or less by themselves. "Slaves were usually prisoners of war, and their lot was a hard one, for, after a period of toil, they were often sacrificed to the gods and eaten" (Lothrop, 1926 b, p. 47).

According to Oviedo y Valdés (1851–55, bk. 42, ch. 1), marriage among the *Nicarao* might be arranged in several ways. The first is reminiscent of the *Aztec* custom. The fathers of the couple which wished to marry agreed to the union and the man's father gave a large banquet. The marriage ceremony was performed by the cacique, who joined the fingers of the left hands of the couple by slipping a little sheath over them. The couple then sat in silence beside a small ceremonial fire until it was "consumed," when the marriage was considered sealed. Feasting and the presentation of gifts were then in order. Theoretically, a woman should remain a virgin until married, and the bridegroom was permitted to reject a woman who was not a virgin.

In a second form of marriage a prostitute might acquire a husband. Oviedo implies this to have been characteristic of the *Nicarao,* but Lothrop (1926 b, p. 59) believes that it may have been a *Chorotega* custom, which perhaps was adopted by the *Nicarao.* If an unmarried woman became a prostitute and, despite supporting her progeny, acquired wealth, she might build and furnish a house on land obtained from her father and her consorts. She then chose one of her consorts for a husband, and after a marriage feast the couple lived together as man and wife. This feast was sometimes prolonged by the eating of the corpses of the rejected suitors, who, having helped provide the house, had committed suicide.

Nobles were permitted to have one wife and several female slaves. Bigamy is not defined, but it was punished by expropriation of property and exile. An adultress was beaten and returned to her father, who claimed her property. The woman was disgraced; the man was beaten by the husband but not otherwise penalized.

There were a number of general rules, which were possibly *Nicarao* customs, though some may have been *Chorotega* practices. Marriage was permitted with anyone except a member of one's immediately family. Intrafamily marriage was encouraged on the grounds that it strengthened family ties. A man convicted of rape had to ransom himself from the girl's family or become its slave. When a slave had relations with his owner's daughter, both lovers were buried alive. The position of women seems to have been good. They exercised considerable authority in the house, having the power to punish their husbands and to make them provide food and perform many household tasks. One of the principal duties of the women was to barter and sell the goods, usually in the markets.

Chorotega customs have not been described specifically. The common people were apparently monogamous, but the upper classes might be polygynous. *Orotiña* caciques had the right of jus primae notis.

Prostitution was a recognized institution among the *Chorotega* and *Nicarao*. Also, there were recognized periods of sex license, particularly during certain ceremonies.

Political organization.—There were two types of government among these tribes, but the information does not permit a description of the type found in each tribe. A democratic form, perhaps characteristic of the *Chorotega,* has been described, particularly by Oviedo y Valdés (1851–55, bk. 42, ch. 1). A council of old men was selected by popular vote. It chose for its supreme head a "captain general," who acted as chief, particularly in war. If he were killed in battle another chief was chosen. Apparently the council had considerable power, for it could kill the chief it had elected and choose another. This system was so strong that the Spaniards had to abolish it. They dissolved the councils and established repartimientos governed by appointed caciques, thus creating a sort of feudalism which they could control.

A feudal form of government is also described by Oviedo y Valdés (1851–55, bk. 42, ch. 12). Lothrop (1926 b, p. 48) summarizes this: At the head of the state was the cacique (called teyte by the *Nicarao*), who probably came by his office through a hereditary-elective system. In addition, there was a council (monexicos) composed of various elders (guegues), who were elected for a term of four moons. The cacique theoretically could not act unless supported by the council, which could not meet unless he summoned it. The council appointed various officials, presumably from their own number, and these were paid for their services in maize, cacao, or mantles.

The laws of the *Chorotega* and *Nicarao,* reported mainly by Oviedo y Valdés (1851–55, bk. 42, ch. 3), concerned adjustments made personally between an offended person and the criminal. This legal system, as Lothrop (1926 b, p. 63) says, was on a different basis from that of the *Aztec,* among whom "there existed a complicated system of tribunals, each with its particular composition and jurisdiction, and the right of appeal to a higher court was acknowledged."

ECONOMIC ORGANIZATION

Chorotega and *Nicarao* commerce centered in the markets. Each town had a market in which all commodities, even slaves, were traded. A special official enforced all its regulations. Cacao was employed as money in the markets as well as outside them, and maize and cotton were also bases of exchange. Men were forbidden to enter the market of their native towns, for these were run by the women and boys. Strangers, however, could enter them to trade.

WARFARE

These tribes were continually at war, and the art of warfare was highly developed, particularly among the *Chorotega* and *Nicarao*. The young men were carefully trained and organized in companies which stood regular watch and were constantly ready for battle. The principal cause of war, said Oviedo y Valdés (1851–55, bk. 42, ch. 3), was boundary disputes, but the desire to obtain slaves for sacrifice probably also was a motive. War was declared through a messenger, who followed standard procedure (Lothrop, 1926 b, p. 50). Usually the cacique did not accompany the army, a war leader being appointed by the council or by the cacique with the approval of the council.

CANNIBALISM

"Cannibalism was widespread. Although of ceremonial origin, it appears that the taste for human flesh had become highly developed, and that slaves were bred in captivity for consumption just as any other domestic animal might be; also there is evidence that raids were conducted in hope of plunder and high living in the form of human flesh" (Lothrop, 1926 b, p. 35).

ESTHETIC AND RECREATIONAL ACTIVITIES

Two *Chorotega* and *Nicarao* games are described. One, voladores, is still known in México. The other was a sort of seesaw, two men swinging from the end of a beam which revolved upon a horizontal pole, supported on two crotched uprights. (Cf. illustrations in Oviedo y Valdés, 1851–55; also Lothrop, 1926 b, p. 53.)

Many beverages, some highly intoxicating, were used. Coca mixed with lime was chewed, particularly by the *Nicarao*.

RELIGION AND MYTHOLOGY

Religious practices were marked by several types of human sacrifice and various observances to celebrate different cults. The *Nicarao* and the *Chorotega* had a number of gods, each with distinctive attributes. Priests formed a special caste and officiated at the ceremonies held at the temples. Ceremonies to the various gods celebrated the cacao harvest, the holy days in the calendar, and such occasions as birth and death. Various types of witchcraft and divination were practiced.

The mythology of these tribes centered about the gods. There was a creation myth, various beliefs concerning the soul and death, and explanations of several natural events. (Cf. Lothrop, 1926 b, for an excellent discussion of religion.)

BIBLIOGRAPHY

Johnson, 1940; Kirchhoff, 1943; Lothrop, 1926 b, 1940, Mason, J. A., 1940; Oviedo y Valdés, 1851–55.

THE NORTHERN HIGHLAND TRIBES: THE LENCA

By Doris Stone

INTRODUCTION

The question of the classification of the *Lenca* language is very important. It is known largely through inadequate data published by Squier (1858) and Membreño (1897). According to different authors, it is related to South or North American languages or is affiliated with unidentified languages, such as the *Xinca*. Some students have postulated that it is unrelated to any known linguistic family. (For a more detailed discussion, see Mason, J. A., 1940; Johnson, 1940; Stone, 1941; and article on languages in Handbook, Vol. 5.)

The *Lenca* area (maps 2 and 5) is marked by a significant variation in dialect, physical type, and political, social, and economic organization. Each township has characteristics which set it off from its neighbors. This heterogeneity obscures the position of the *Lenca* in relation to the rest of Central America.

The *Lenca* are being slowly acculturated and absorbed by people of Mestizo descent. There is, however, some conservatism which seeks to preserve the aboriginal culture, thus increasing the difficulty of adjustment to changing conditions. An example of the desire of groups to maintain their former cultural habits is found among the *Guajiquiro*. Formerly famed as warriors, they now seek employment in the army or the police force.

CULTURE

SUBSISTENCE ACTIVITIES

Farming.—The life of the modern *Lenca* village centers around the milpa. The male members of a family generally spend 5 or 6 days a week in a straw hut built near the field. They return bringing food to the village at the end of a week. The principal crops, many of them of European origin, are maize, wheat (which is threshed with flails), plantains, "chatos" and fig-bananas, cacao, a little coffee, varieties of gourds, sugarcane, vegetable pear, squash, beans (black beans are preferred in this section, but various types are planted), a little tobacco, yuca, and chili peppers. In certain places, such as Marcala and Santa Elena, oranges are an important crop. Around the town of Intibucá peaches are grown in quantities. In parts of El Salvador peanuts are cultivated. (For land tenure and working, see pp. 212–213; and for agricultural ceremonialism, p. 215.)

Wild foods.—The chief noncultivated food of the *Lenca* is the palm. The hearts of the royal and suyate palms and the early sprouts of the pacaya palm (*Chamaedorea* sp.) are favorites. Blackberries, wild guayabos, granadillas, and other fruits are eaten in the season.

Hunting.—All Highland Indians hunt, either singly or in pairs; occasionally larger groups hunt deer. Sometimes dogs are used for pursuing deer and jaguars. Generally, however, a man depends only on his bow and arrow. Songbirds are caught in cane traps.

Fishing.—The *Lenca* are not ardent fishermen. Expeditions to poison fish are organized by the town leader, but women are not permitted to participate. A river is dammed with stones, and a cane net or funnel is placed in an opening of this dam, its mouth facing upstream. The poisonous barbasco vine is broken into lengths and thrown into the water. The stunned and dead fish come to the surface and are carried by the current into the trap. The leader, or his representative, divides the catch according to the amount of work performed by each individual.

Domestic animals.—Dogs, chickens, and a few pigs, ducks, and turkeys are the usual possessions. Very rarely the Indian owns a horse and a cow, and sometimes the town owns a few head of cattle. In Intibucá particularly, goats and some sheep are raised.

Food preparation.—Generally food is boiled in pots placed on a hearth built of three stones. Very rarely a clay oven is found outside the house, either incorporated in the house wall or built separately. New metates have three short feet, but the highly prized old metates brought from ancient sites have four and even five legs. Some metates are simply boulders having a slightly concave surface. The manos vary in length.

The most important foods are maize, salt, chili, and beans. Salt is believed to come from the sun, which the *Lenca* still hold sacred. Chilis are supposed to give strength and to act as a purgative and a stimulant. Whenever a *Lenca* departs on a journey he carries chilis mixed with tortillas or tamales.

Food is eaten from calabashes or from the vessel in which it was cooked. It may be wrapped in a tortilla or in a flat maize cake. Essential to every meal are tortillas and rounded tamales (also called totapostes), which are made of maize or of maize and chili, wrapped in shucks, and roasted in the ashes of the hearth. Steamed whole ears of roasted maize and beans are staples. These are supplemented by yuca, bananas, plantains, squash, and the other produce of the farm and forest. Boiled or raw eggs are eaten, and on rare occasions fowl is wrapped in banana leaves and boiled or roasted in the ashes.   Meat and fish are generally cut into strips, dried and smoked.

Food storage.—Selected ears of ripe maize in the husk are carefully piled to the ceiling in a corner of a room.   These last from one season to another.   In sections of the Department of Intibucá, maize kernels are kept in a perpendicular, hollowed log, which is covered with a thick cloth.

VILLAGES AND HOUSES

The villages are laid out as any modern Honduran town.   A "cabildo," which is usually distinguishable by the wooden fence and gate around the porch, often serves both as the "commandancia" and the house of the local authority.   All *Lenca* towns have churches.

The typical *Lenca* village house is made of adobe and has a roof thatched with straw or grass or, rarely, covered with tiles.   Infrequently, walls are made of wooden slabs.   The most modern houses in the larger towns are built of adobe and have tile roofs.   The average dwelling has one room, with a front porch that is open on the sides but covered by an extension of the roof supported by three vertical wooden posts (fig. 48).

FIGURE 48.—*Lenca* house.

Often, especially when the roof is tile, two additional wooden posts are placed at corners of the house in the adobe and at the inner edge of the extension over the porch. In certain settlements, for example, Santa Elena, there is a porch at the rear, which is sometimes used as a kitchen. The houses are generally very low (a mounted man can reach the edge of the roof). The foundation of the adobe house is a low stone wall plastered with mud. The wall consists of cane or wooden poles set vertically upon this foundation. These vertical poles are laced with horizontal poles or cane and plastered with mud, which generally contains some gravel. Some of the wooden or cane supports protrude on the outside. In making the roof, dried grass or straw is tied to a framework of cane or poles. Dirt floors are usual, except that the porch floor may be covered with cobblestones.

Household furniture.—In the colder regions the hearth is in the center of the room; elsewhere it is in a corner or by a side wall. Beds or shelves are made of wooden frames interlaced with vines and hung from the ceiling by vines. They serve many purposes. The wealthy Indians make frame beds of woven vines supported on sticks and covered with skins. In most houses the family sleeps on the floor around the fire.

Calabashes are hung on forked sticks, which are stuck in the walls or tied to the shelves. On the floor are the metate, a small pile of firewood, the maize granary, and very occasionally a stool. Frequently, a wooden cross is attached on the outside of the house to the wall or roof to keep off the evil spirits.

DRESS AND ORNAMENTS

Clothing.—*Lenca* dress is highly variable. About 1925, in the villages of Chinacla and Guajiquiro, Department of La Paz, the women had one type of costume for daily use and another for ceremonial occasions. The latter was given to a bride-to-be by her future husband who purchased it in Guatemala, generally in Esquipulas. It consisted of a white huipil, a blue skirt with white or red lines forming large squares, and a red or multicolored belt. It was worn with a quantity of coin and bead necklaces (M. Bonilla, ms.).

This costume is no longer worn. The modern dress everywhere is generally an Indian version of the 19th-century Spanish Colonial style. In the Departments of La Paz and Intibucá many villages still retain their distinctive local style. Trade with El Salvador has stimulated continual changes, however, so that there exists much local freedom in the details of dress. In Guajiquiro, for example, the women wear wide, gay colored skirts with contrasting vertical rows of colored cloth, which are repeated on the blouse. They grease their hair and wear a multitude of silver rings and bead necklaces, often with coins. The men wear dark jackets and pants and, whenever they can afford it, felt hats. On feast days some add plaits of junco, a palm-leaf fiber, as hatbands, and varicolored ribbons and feathers (M. Bonilla, ms.).

FIGURE 49.—*Lenca* woman's dress, Santa Elena.

The dress of Opatoro women is always very bright, with a preference for red and yellow. The blouse has a series of vertical bands of contrasting colors coming in two lines and reaching from the upper part of the breast to the waist, where they almost meet. This gives the effect of a bodice, the intervening space between the two lines being filled with horizontal bands also of contrasting colors. A yokelike collar, about 3 or 4 inches (7.5 to 10 cm.) wide, of the same color as the blouse encircles the garment, leaving a space between the beginning of the breast and the neck. The dress continues upward and ends in a narrow band a little above the start of the throat, giving to the whole the appearance of an old-fashioned guimpe. The artificial guimpe has vertical bands of contrasting colors. The sleeves are three-quarters length with two horizontal, colored bands below the elbow and a sort of drooping flounce for a cuff. The skirt is wide, with colored bands at the top of a bottom flounce.

The Opatoro women wear their hair in long braids, into which are plaited many gay-colored ribbons, and stick a number of combs set with cheap glass stones in their hair. These combs are bought in El Salvador by the men. The men use pants and shirts of drill, both of the same color and generally with a narrow blue stripe. They carry a machete at their belt. The Santa Elena women wear the kind of dress shown in figure 49. The skirt is rolled at the waist and is worn higher in the front than in the back. The blouse has a small peplum, almost like a bustle in the rear. The Yarula dress is fairly similar to that of Santa Elena, differing only in a small detail at the neck which ends in a narrow protrusion like a dickey. The skirt has two rows of inverted V's on the bottom. All *Lenca* women are very fond of silver rings, usually made of melted coins, quantities of necklaces of beads and coins, and charms, both the typical church scapulas and those they make themselves of gay-colored thread. These charms supposedly have power to ward off evil. On their heads they wear bright silk shawls, in the manner of the non-Indian women. On special occasions they put a man's hat decorated with a band of ribbon on top of this shawl.

Sandals differ slightly throughout the region. The most common style has a strap between the fourth and the big toe. However, horizontal straps across the toes are frequently seen. A type which comes from Marcala and Santa Elena (pl. 33, *top*) has an outer rim as well as buckles all around the foot. This type is not usual in the more isolated communities.

TRANSPORTATION

Trails.—True *Lenca* country is very wild and grand, with steep rugged mountains, the highest in Honduras. The trails follow the mountain crests with their numerous outcroppings of limestone bedrock and less frequently of volcanic tuffs. The protruding limestone rock, tall pines, and scarce underbrush make travel in the wet season very difficult, for the large rock layers tend to be slippery, and the land washes away quickly. The trails throughout the *Lenca* country are cut into the outcroppings in such a manner as to permit the passage of men and animals. It is impossible to know if these were in use before the Spanish Conquest, but they are found on the modern *Lenca* trails, even on those not intended for beasts of burden.

Carrying devices.—In the *Lenca* area both sexes carry objects in a net bag (pl. 33, *bottom*), which is supported by a tumpline or swung over one shoulder. The size of the bag varies according to need. Babies are carried on the back in a shawl. Commonly, a woman carries a net bag loaded with wood and, on top of it, a child in a shawl. Sometimes large hide sacks are carried by the men.

The *Lenca* travel on foot. In the more isolated sections the laboring men, who make long journeys laden like beasts of burden, practice the old custom of tying stones to their toes in order to enlarge their feet. It is believed that large feet improve their grip on the rough and steep trails. Rarely the *Lenca* ride horseback using saddles made of a single piece of leather and wooden stirrups copied from the 16th-century Spanish types. The few horses which belong to the Indians are not broken to the bit but are ridden with a rope halter.

MANUFACTURES

Basketry.—Baskets are made of pine needles and of caña brava, a wild cane. Certain villages, e.g., Chinacla, are famous for their baskets. There is no shape or size peculiar to the *Lenca.* Many baskets are copied from gourds; others are smaller and have either separate covers or covers attached to the handles. Sometimes the baskets are colored, the cane being dyed before weaving. Cochineal, achiote, and indigo are the principal tints employed. These are found either wild in the forest or, especially cochineal, are brought from El Salvador. Some of the *Lenca* make hats of leaves, generally of the suyate palm, cut into strips, braided and sewed together.

Weaving and cordage.—The *Lenca* are said to have woven cloth in the past century, but today the industry has disappeared. Cordage for net bags and such is made from the fiber of the suyate palm, pinuela, and maguey. The fibers are spun with wooden whorls operated by two persons who stand 10 to 30 yards apart. Netting needles are made of bamboo, wood, or palm. Rope is made from the same material as the thread, the suyate palm-leaf fiber being in most demand for ropes used in house construction. Rope is also made of twisted hide.

Skin preparation.—The *Lenca* have always used the skins of wild animals. In the past century, jaguar, watusso, and deer skins served as the dress of many men. Today skins are frequently worn as an apron or are used for blankets or bedding. In certain isolated villages they are slung over the shoulders as a cloak or shirt. Skins of wild animals as well as of cows are scraped, then stretched and dried in the sun. No curing agent is used.

Pottery.—The women make coiled pottery. The favorite shape is a rounded jug or bulge-bowl with two handles. Modern painted pottery is not of aboriginal origin. A few vessels are colored, either solidly or half one color, half natural. The paint is of foreign manufacture and comes from El Salvador or Tegucigalpa. Pots are fired in kilns built into the earth and rising only slightly above the surface. The vessels are covered with large slablike broken pieces of baked clay and are fueled with wood.

Gourds.—Gourds of certain types are not only eaten but are utilized as water jugs, as models for baskets, and even as masks for dances. For a water jug the gourd is cleaned through a perforation in the top, and most of the seeds and pulp are extracted. Pebbles or earth with pebbles are then put inside it, and, after drying in the sun, it is shaken so that the stones and earth rub the sides clean.

Fire making.—Fire is made by striking together two white or hard stones so that the sparks fall on dry cotton, which is carried in a short hollowed stick or on dried leaves and pine needles.

Candles are made from the wild waxplant (*Myrica cerifera*), a common forest weed. The berries are crushed and boiled, and the residue is placed in wooden molds with a fiber wick.

Starch.—A yuca starch is used by the Indians for medical purposes, such as plasters, and is sold to non-Indian towns for stiffening clothes. The root is peeled, ground very fine on the metate, and sun-dried on a hollowed plank or log until it is gummy.

Weapons.—The long bow is of palm wood. The arrows are relatively short. "Killing" arrows have an iron point, $3\frac{1}{2}$ to $4\frac{1}{2}$ inches (about 9 to 11 cm.) long. "Stunning" arrows have rounded cork-shaped wooden butts reinforced with iron bands and very small protruding iron knobs at the ends. The primary arrow release is used. Quivers are narrow hide cylinders.

SOCIAL, POLITICAL, AND ECONOMIC ORGANIZATION

Formerly, each *Lenca* community maintained its integrity in its relationship to other towns and was strictly endogamous. The cacique and the council (casicasgo) controlled the village land. This council was composed of the cacique, the curandero (called in many places inteligente), the priest or soothsayer (called hechicero, "witch"), and the town elders. It officiated in all disputes involving the town. When an intertown problem arose the council of each town met and clarified its position, after which the two councils met together to settle the matter. If no agreement could be reached, the towns went to war. In 1888 disputes concerning the location of the town boundaries of Santa Elena (the ancient Jocoara), Opatoro, Polorós, and Arambala arose. The councils of the towns could not reach an agreement and war ensued. The Honduran Government intervened, and now these and nearly all other towns have their own legal title to land.

The town, though modified by European influences, is practically the only vestige of the ancient tribal organization. In certain towns the cacique still inherits his office; in others he is elected. The village, not the individual, owns the land, but its distribution varies with each settlement. In some villages the local authorities, such as the alcalde and the jefe politico, give the allotments; in others, the village elders with the alcalde; in a few, the cacique; and in still others, as in Guajiquiro, the land is communal, that is, it is worked by the town without dividing it into separate portions.

In the cases of communal farming the cacique distributes the produce of the town. What is not consumed locally is saved for trade, which the

PLATE 33.—**Lenca manufactures.** *Top:* Santa Elena and Marcala type sandals.
Bottom: Net carrying bag. (Courtesy Doris Stone.)

PLATE 34.—**Lenca Indians.** *Top:* Typical Intibucá fences. *Bottom:* Wearing a gourd mask at dance of festival of the patron saint of the town. (Courtesy Doris Stone.)

cacique controls. The amount of land given to a person is counted in tareas—approximately the amount of land one man can work in a day. Four to eight tareas per man is the usual allotment. When the soil grows poor the Indian complains to the authorities and proves that he needs another piece. The land is cultivated by the individual with the help of his sons. In some places, as around Opatoro, laborers are assigned to work with him.

The structure of the aboriginal class system has been modified almost beyond recognition. There appears still to be an upper and a lower class. The first includes the cacique, his immediate family, and the council members and their families. The lower class is composed of the laborers, who seem to take no part in the running of the village affairs.

Personal property excludes land, but consists of one's house and its contents and livestock. In general, a widow retains her husband's property and deeds it over to the son when he is 18 years old, though she may retain the house. If there are no sons, the property goes to the deceased's oldest brother. If there is no brother, the council assigns the property to the nearest male relative.

A woman who commits adultery may be killed by her husband, but the man involved is not punished. Criminals are forced by the council to work 2 or 3 days without food.

CANNIBALISM

Cannibalism was rarely practiced by the *Lenca*. On rare occasions the heart of an enemy was eaten in order that the enemy's valor might be acquired. Such practices are now forbidden by the Honduran authorities.

LIFE CYCLE

Childbirth.—*Lenca* childbirth involves little ceremony. A woman delivers her child into a bed of leaves on the floor of the house, using a stooping position during delivery. She may give birth alone, cutting the cord with a bamboo or steel knife and burning it, or her husband may cut the cord. In cases of prolonged labor, her husband or another woman may burn certain leaves under her. This simple ceremony is called zahumería.

Very infrequently today the old custom of providing the newborn with a "nagual" is practiced. The maternal grandmother presents the baby with an animal, such as a snake, frog, or toad, and with chicha, maize, beans, and other foodstuffs. The "nagual" is, or was, an important quasi-religious object which the child always kept, even taking it to bed.

Pregnant women are believed to possess extraordinarily strong eyes, that is, their own combined with those of the fetus. They are not allowed to witness the birth of either human beings or animals, for these eyes are reputed to kill the newborn.

Marriage.—Girls marry when they are between 12 and 14 years of age, boys between 14 and 18. Marriages are usually prearranged by the parents of the couple, although there is no set rule. When the boy does the courting, he throws pebbles at his prospective sweetheart when she is washing clothes by a stream or bathing and leaves a load of wood in front of her house. If the girl and her family approve the match, they bring the wood into the house. At the age of puberty the boy lives with his family-in-law-to-be for several months or longer, while the girl lives with the boy's family. If the parents approve of the boy and girl, the latter returns to her parents' house and lives with the boy. Should this period of trial marrage turn out satisfactorily, it may be terminated and the marriage made permanent by a feast and merrymaking. Otherwise both parties are free to separate and choose other mates. Usually the newly married couple stays with the girl's family for 1 or 2 years before establishing a home for themselves. The *Lenca* are polygynous, and a family head may have three or four wives. When a man is through with a woman he may arrange for her to live with her children in a separate house, but he is responsible for her food.

Death.—When a man dies his widow walks around the house moaning and singing for 1 day. A feast is held, and quantities of chicha are drunk for 9 days. Formerly, the deceased was placed on one of the hanging beds or shelves throughout the merrymaking, but the law now requires burial on the day of death. Feasting, drinking, and sometimes music may, however, go on for the full 9 days.

ESTHETIC AND RECREATIONAL ACTIVITIES

Masks and dances.—Calabash masks are painted, but wooden masks are not. The latter are very simply carved, and human teeth are added to them. Occasionally they are named, e.g., in Intibucá one mask is called "Capitán Mayor." All masks are used in ceremonial dances, which are performed by the councilmen, generally at the festival of the patron saint of the town (pl. 34, *bottom*). Sons learn the dance steps from their fathers. The hechicero is in charge of the ritual which accompanies the dancing. Marcelina Bonilla (ms.) describes a dance at Santa Elena in which the men wore feathered caps over their painted calabash masks and cotton clothes (manta)—a shirt and pants with a cow's tail sewed to them. The dancers circled, the steps being interspersed with much knee bending. In another dance of the same village a large lancelike stick is thrown into the air and caught with much dexterity, mimicking, and contortion. In some dances, such as those in Intibucá, flags are carried, as well as tall bastions of the church with small silver crosses on the ends.

Musical instruments.—*Lenca* drums are of wood with hide heads, which are tuned with quills. Bamboo flutes have three or four stops. Rattles are made of gourds attached to a stick.

Alcoholic beverages.—Chicha, an intoxicating drink made from maize, is supposedly purifying and ritualistic. The kernels are boiled with water and brown sugar in a clay pot, which is then covered with a cloth and left to ferment. The excrement of goats or sheep wrapped in a rag may be added after fermentation has begun in order to strengthen its flavor. This custom, however, is slowly disappearing. In parts of El Salvador chicha may be flavored with peanuts, and in Honduras with pineapple peelings.

RELIGION

Many *Lenca,* although nominally Catholic, still retain certain aboriginal beliefs. Sacred mountains and hills, considered as holy places in pre-Conquest times, now have wooden crosses on their summits. The *Lenca* still have a profound respect, or even adoration, for the sun.

Their life, which depends on agriculture, is marked by periodical offerings to the seasons or to the crops. Planting and harvesting ceremonies are celebrated throughout the *Lenca* area. When it is time to clear the land, chicha is drunk, copal is burned to the four directions, and straw or corn-shuck crosses are put in the centers of the fields. At sowing time chicha is drunk, copal is burned, and bonfires are built outside the fields. Drunkenness is explained by the belief that chicha purified the soul and expels bad thoughts. The soul is thus purified for the sacred business of planting. Throughout the *Lenca* country men abstain from sexual intercourse at this time. They stay at the milpas, and women live in the towns. When maize is in the silk, copal is burned and chicha is drunk. At this time also the women are forbidden to visit the milpa, for it is feared that they might contaminate the crops.

When the fields are harvested and it is time to divide the produce, masked men dance around the piles of grain to the music of drums, rattles, and whistles. Offers of food are made to the sun. The hechicero is in change of this ceremony. At this time he promises the cacique to defend the council.

Many of these Highland Indians make a yearly pilgrimage on April 24, the day of San Gaspar, the patron of Taubelve, to Taubelve in the relatively low hills south of Lake Yojoa. There is not much doubt that this visit has its roots in pre-Conquest days. Taubelve is supposed to mean in *Lenca* "House of the Tiger" (Squier, 1858). Here many years ago a cache of what may have been pre-Colombian copper bells was discovered in a cave. The *Lenca* go to mass at the nearby church of La Misión and then visit the cave, where they hold their own secret communion with the spirits within. They remain 2 to 4 days at Taubelve, sleeping in the roads and fields or wherever they can and drinking great quantities of chicha.

In all *Lenca* communities the most sacred day of the year is that of the patron saint of the village. Often the saint is carried on a visit to the patron of a friendly neighboring town. Such excursions are always the occasion for heavy chicha drinking by both sexes, for dancing by the men under the leadership of the hechicero, and usually for feasting.

SHAMANISM AND MEDICINE

The shaman (inteligente or curandero) occupies an important place in the life of the village. He is charged with the curing of the sick through both ritual means and the application of practical remedies. When he has a patient to be cured he offers white chickens and copal at the crosses on the sacred hilltops, after which he returns to the ailing person and gives him certain curative drinks.

Formerly some soothsayers were women. They prophesied the future by throwing different-colored beans from calabashes as one would throw dice.

Certain general cures are usually given by the inteligente, but others may be prepared by anyone. For indigestion every portion of the body is massaged, pulled, and stretched. For fevers the patient is wrapped in as much cloth as possible to produce sweating, or a cure called ruda is administered. Certain leaves are heated and rubbed on the sick person. Excrement, burned to a powder, is sometimes taken internally. Of the many plants and herbs used as medicine by the *Lenca*, the most popular ones are listed below:

Hoja del aire (*Bryophyllum pinnatum*). The leaves are boiled and taken for colic.
Malba and pavana. The leaves of these low bushes are covered with oil and placed on afflicted parts in order to reduce inflammation.
Tuna, or nopal. The leaves of this member of the cactus family are rubbed with oil or grease, heated, and then used as a plaster for cases of colic.
Siguapate. The leaves of this bush ara placed on the forehead to cure headache.
Pasote and ipacina. A tea made of the leaves of this plant combined with manzanilla and a variety of mint is used as a vermifuge.
Grama, maize milk, and cañafistola (*Cassia* sp.). Teas made of these are used to cure kidney trouble.
Sauco (usually *Salix chilensis*). An infusion of the leaves and flowers of this willow is set in the sun for 2 days and used to cure coughs.

MYTHOLOGY

Herrera y Tordesillas (1730, vol. 3) recorded a legend of a goddess named Comicahual. The tale is still told around Puringla and Guajiquiro, but the name of the deity has been modified to Comitzahual.

In certain communities, such as Opatoro, the belief is held that people can change themselves into animals and back again into people. The inhabitants claim that this has actually happened to a woman from this village. They say she turned herself into a pig, and the whole town, infuriated, kicked her and beat her, as a pig, until she was black and blue. The pig ran into the forest and changed back to the woman, who was found the next day in her house, bruised from head to foot.

LORE AND LEARNING

Ordinary products are measured by baskets, which carry the equivalent of 4 pounds. This is the standard medium in the interior of Honduras, and the *Lenca* do not use any other measure. Time is measured by the amount necessary to accomplish a certain task (tarea) and is stated in terms of tareas and fractions thereof. Space is measured by the distance that can be covered in a day's walk, but the Spanish measure, vara (32 inches), is also used in certain places for smaller distances.

The year is divided into 54 moons and has 336 days. It is divided into the seasons of sowing, harvesting, preparing the soil, the time of the appearance of the young corn, the blossoming, etc. Each of these periods has its own meaning and is often celebrated by ceremonies held in the fields.

BIBLIOGRAPHY

Bancroft, 1890, vol. 3; M. Bonilla, ms.; Herrera y Tordesillas, 1730; Johnson, 1940; Juarros 1808–18 (1936); Lehmann, 1920; Lothrop, 1939; Mason, J. A., 1940; Membreño, 1897; Milla y Vidaurre, 1879–1919; Palacio (*in* Squier, 1860 a); Pedraza (*in* Col. Doc. Inéd., 1898–1900); Ponce, 1873; Relación Breve y Verdadero (see Alonso de San Juan, 1873); Relaciones de Yucatan, 1898–1900; Squier, 1858, 1859, 1860 a, 1869, 1870; Stoll, 1938; Stone, 1940 b, 1941; Torquemada, 1615 (1723); Vásquez, 1714–16.

THE CARIBBEAN LOWLAND TRIBES:
THE MOSQUITO, SUMO, PAYA, AND JICAQUE

By Paul Kirchhoff

INTRODUCTION

The modern *Paya* and *Jicaque* enclaves in the Caribbean Lowlands may not all be the descendants of the people so named by the first explorers (maps 2 and 5). It is possible that the culture of the people first discovered on the coast was similar to that from which the present-day *Mosquito* and *Sumo* culture has evolved, although the north coast probably had culture traits that differed significantly from those of the *Mosquito* and *Sumo*. It is impossible to describe the post-Conquest changes of the culture of the *Paya* and *Jicaque*. It seems reasonably certain, however, that during the past 400 years the east coast people and the people now known as the *Paya* and *Jicaque* have converged culturally. We can, then, describe these peoples as a unit, although hypothetically their cultures have developed out of the ruins of a more complex aboriginal background.

Less important but significant features of the culture may be ascribed to the contact with the *Black Carib* Indians, who were brought to the Bay Islands in 1796 and whose descendants have settled on the mainland. The importance of the early Negro influence has already been noted.

CULTURE

SUBSISTENCE ACTIVITIES

Farming.—A type of slash-and-burn agriculture is employed by all tribes. Every season the men clear new farmlands and burn the slash. Planting and cultivating is done with a digging stick. This is woman's work, except among the *Jicaque* (Von Hagen, 1943), and the women also harvest the crops. Some fields have combinations of crops, such as maize, beans, and peanuts; others are reserved for single crops, especially the tubers.

A list of agricultural products may be found below. Sweet manioc, an important *Mosquito* crop, is grown by all tribes. Bitter manioc, probably introduced by the *Carib,* is important to some *Paya* and *Jicaque.*

219

Maize is believed to be unimportant except in the higher lands, e.g., among the *Ulva*. The *Jicaque* grow it as a commercial crop but do not use it extensively as food. Pineapples are important to the *Paya*. Chili peppers and opuntia, the latter used for raising cochineal, a dye-producing insect, appear to be recent introductions. Plants introduced by the Europeans vary in importance, but plantain is now one of the most basic foods of the region. Quantities of wild foods of all kinds form an important part of the diet.

Hunting.—The bow and arrow was once important to many tribes but has been partially or wholly replaced by the gun. The bow has not been reported from the Corn Islands. Spears or javelins were formerly used for hunting. Slings, traps, and snares were used prinicipally for birds. For the blowgun, see page 224.

LIST OF FOODS GROWN BY THE PEOPLE IN THE CARIBBEAN LOWLANDS:

AMERICAN ORIGIN:
Sweet manioc.
Bitter manioc.
Maize.
Pejivalle (pejibaye) palm.
Sweetpotato.
Eddoe (tania).
Gourd.
Pumpkin.
Squash.
Chayote.
Tomato.
Bean (red and black).
Pineapple.
Tobacco.
Cotton.
Achiote (*Bixa orellana*).
Cacao.
Pataste.
Papaya.
Avocado.
Guava.
Chirimoya.
Zapote.
Coconut.
Usi.
Ficus.
Yam.
Opuntia.
Peanuts.

FOREIGN ORIGIN:
Rice.
Sugarcane.
Coffee.
Mango.
Breadfruit.
Tamarind.
Citrus fruits.
Plantain.
Banana.

Hunting is exclusively a male occupation. Communal hunts lasting several days and hunting by torchlight have been reported. Dogs are used frequently to chase the game. Hunters may imitate the calls of animals, sometimes using bone whistles.

Fishing.—Women fish with hooks, which were originally made of bone. Men fish in groups of varying sizes. Fish are shot with the bow and arrow, speared with single- or multipronged spears, taken with traps of various types, or frightened so that they jump into canoes. Torches are used at night to attract the fish. Fish are poisoned by parties of men. Women and men whose wives are pregnant or menstruating cannot join such expeditions (*Jicaque*). Rotenone-bearing plants are crushed in the water above a weir from which the stupefied fish are removed.

Harpoons with floats attached are used for large fish and for manatees, the latter being taken in the lagoons and at sea. Harpoons with long retrieving lines but without floats are used for sea turtles. The *Sumo* lasso young crocodiles.

Domesticated animals.—No early source mentions dogs, but they are now common. Pigs, sheep, goats, cattle, horses, and cats have been introduced. The people tame a great variety of wild birds and several species of mammals. The latter are even suckled by the women. Species of native bees are kept in hives near the houses.

Food preparation.—Food may be boiled, sometimes in coconut milk. Meat and fish are broiled or roasted in hot ashes, and fish may be fried in coconut oil. The *Paya* fry green pineapple. Salt is used as a condiment but rarely as a preservative. Sauces of red peppers, lime, and salt are made by the *Mosquito*. The *Paya* use chili as a sauce or as a substitute for other food. Tamales are made of manioc. Maize dough, sometimes soured (*Mosquito*), is wrapped in leaves and baked. This and manioc dough may be made into tortillas, an item introduced into the region only in recent years. Manioc is made into bread, which is baked in the open fire.

Numerous beverages are made of liana sap, maize, honey, green plantains, and the like. Some of these are made of a sour paste, which is diluted with water before it is eaten. Such food is usually carried while traveling. Alcoholic beverages are prepared in canoes (*Mosquito*) or log troughs (*Paya*) and stored in earthenware pots. Fermentation is hastened in various ways, notably by chewing uncooked or cooked maize or manioc and spitting it into the mixture.

Preserving and storage of food.—Fish is dried in the sun and meat is dried on a three-legged babracot. The *Mosquito* make a mixture of green bananas and pejibaye palm nuts which may be kept for 6 months or longer. It can be made into a beverage or baked as bread. The *Sumo* preserve boiled maize by steeping it in lye to remove the hull and then burying it. The *Sumo* also make up large parcels of maize or peeled bananas, which are placed in running water until partially fermented, then dried in the sun. Live turtles are kept in stockades in shallow water.

VILLAGES AND HOUSES

Mosquito villages (pl. 35, *bottom*) had between 100 and 500 inhabitants. *Sumo* villages appear to have been much smaller. Formerly, communal houses, called "palenques," had compartments for each family. Some were about 40 by 80 feet (about 12.5 by 25 m.) ; smaller communal houses were built by the *Mosquito*. *Sumo* houses had an elaborately carved central post. House plans were rectangular, the ends being rounded, elliptical (*Paya*), or circular (*Mosquito* of Honduras). At the present time rectangular houses with a hip roof used by single families are built. The steep roof, thatched with palm leaves, was supported on posts. All houses have walls about 4 feet (1.3 m.) high. Lofts for storing food and for sleeping are made by laying split bamboo sticks across the beams.

Household furniture consists of mattresses of bark or deerskin, platform beds (*Paya* and *Northern Sumo*), sitting hammocks, wooden chests, three- or four-legged stools, and a notched-post ladder. Fires are built of three logs on slightly raised mud platforms inside the houses. Stored near these are cooking pots, bamboo tongs used to remove food from the fire, gourd containers and colanders, wooden spoons, ladles, and sections of bamboo used to haul water and to store beverages.

DRESS AND ORNAMENTS

Bark cloth was formerly the most common fabric, but it is now being replaced by cotton cloth, usually obtained by trade. Native cotton cloth was used largely for ceremonial and festive occasions. The *Mosquito* made blankets and clothing of palm fiber.

The male costume consists of a breechclout and poncho. The latter is tied under the arms and secured around the waist with a belt. Everyone went barefoot, but occasionally *Paya* men wore tapir-hide sandals and *Mosquito* men moccasinlike footgear. Women wore a knee-length, wrap-around, bark-cloth skirt, but the upper part of their bodies was nude. Children went nude until they were 8 or 10 years old, when they adopted a breechclout (*Sumo, Mosquito, Paya*). *Sumo* chiefs used a long tunic and a sash, apparently made of cotton. It was dyed and embroidered with crane feathers. These costumes, or modifications of them, are still worn by the more conservative tribes, but commercial cloth is becoming more common and European styles are being adopted.

Men cut their hair short, but occasionally elder men left a lock at the back of the crown (*Mosquito*). In about 1850 the *Sumo* tied their hair into a queue, which was oiled or greased; at present they cut it short with bangs over the forehead. A crude comb was made of sticks tied together. Women cut the front hair in bangs allowing the rest to hang freely. The men attached feathers to their hair but women decorated theirs with flowers and colored bands. At time of mourning the hair is cut off short. Both sexes devote considerable attention to their hair.

Nose pins and lip and ear ornaments of gold or turtle shell were worn. The *Mosquito* hung shell or brass plates from the lower lip. Conical or bell-shaped lip or chin ornaments were worn by the *Kukra*. Wooden plugs worn in the ear lobes were common. On festive occasions the *Mosquito* and *Sumo* wore either a cotton headband decorated with feathers or a cap made of bamboo decorated with feathers and with long, painted, bark-cloth streamers. The *Mosquito* hung metal or shell plaques and ornaments made of bone and feathers about their necks. *Sumo* women wore tight cotton bands below the knees and above the ankles. Today woven bands of glass beads are worn around the neck, wrists, and ankles. Straw hats are decorated with feathers and jaguar teeth (*Mosquito, Paya*).

Black paint is smeared over the body by the men (*Sumo, Mosquito, Paya*) as a decoration and for protection from insects. Geometrical designs are drawn in red paint, mainly by the women. The *Sumo, Mosquito,* and *Paya* tattooed geometrical designs upon the face, arms, and breast. The *Sumo* men made ornamental scars on their faces and chipped their teeth. All *Sumo* tribes except the *Bawihka* practiced head deformation. During infancy a folding flap of wood at the top of the cradle was tied firmly to the crown of the head.

TRANSPORTATION

Loads are carried with a band passing over the head (women) or across the chest (men). Children are carried on the back in a blanket, the points of which are tied in front.

The country has hunting trails but no roads. Most travel is done in dugout canoes propelled with poles and broad-bladed paddles. Rafts are used for down-river traffic. Large keeled canoes, often equipped with a sail, are used at sea.

MANUFACTURES

Basketry.—Crude baskets, mainly of wickerwork, are made chiefly for storage bins. Bark and silk grass fiber bags are very common. Bark fiber is used also to make tumplines, hammocks, and such.

Bark cloth.—Bark cloth is beaten out of ficus-tree bark with a grooved wooden mallet.

Weaving.—Cotton is spun on a spindle, which has a whorl and is rotated in a gourd. Coarse-textured but soft cotton cloth is woven on a two-beam loom. Thread was formerly dyed and designs were woven in the cloth. Sometimes feathers, particularly a fringe of white Muscovy duck down, were incorporated into the fabric.

Ceramics.—Pottery making has been described only from the *Sumo* and *Paya,* although pottery was formerly made by all tribes. Women model small vessels out of a lump of clay but build up large ones with coils. They polish them with a pebble, dry them for several days, and fire them in the open. Pottery types include jars about 4 feet (1.3 m.) high, various types of jugs, water jars, small bowls, griddles, and tobacco pipes. All vessels have a convex base.

Miscellaneous manufactures.—Metates are still used by the *Paya* and *Sumo,* and they have recently been adopted by the *Jicaque,* but the *Mosquito* are said no longer to use them. Metates are flat-topped boulders, which only rarely have a trimmed surface. Manos are round pebbles.

Both the *Paya* and the *Northern Sumo* occasionally use elaborately carved metates and well-made manos obtained at ancient ruins. The *Mosquito* made large wooden mortars and single-ended or, more rarely, double-ended pestles.

Tools used for working wood and for fashioning many miscellaneous articles were: Scrapers made of fish teeth, turtle shells, or stone and knives made of split bamboo. Three-legged wooden stools were formerly richly carved, often having a bird or animal head. Spoons, ladles, cradles, and the like are also made of wood. Gourds are often engraved with simple geometrical designs (pl. 36, *bottom*).

Weapons.—*Mosquito, Sumo,* and *Jicaque* bows are 4 to 5 feet (1.3 to 1.6 m.) long, *Paya* specimens 6 feet (2 m.) long. They taper toward the ends and are rectangular in cross section. Killing arrows have a cane shaft and palm-wood foreshaft. Points of flint, obsidian, turtle shell, fishbone, and shark and alligator teeth were being replaced by iron ones as early as 1678 (Exquemelin, 1678). Arrows are not feathered. According to Exquemelin, the arrows used about the Laguna de Bluefields (*Kukra*) were 6 to 8 feet (2 to 2.6 m.) long with a flint tip and a wooden hook (possibly some type of barb?). Some arrows were weighted with pebbles. Stunning arrows have blunt knobs made of hard wood or beeswax.

The *Ulva* and *Paya* make blowguns, possibly only toys, from a reed 18 inches (45 cm.) long. These shoot wax pellets. The blowgun is, even among Hispanicized *Jicaque,* an effective weapon. It is bored from a branch of a certain tree, and clay pellets are carefully made by means of a gage (Von Hagen, 1943, pp. 50–52). The *Mosquito* and *Sumo* probably used the blowgun, but present information is not precise.

Arrow poison has been reported from some *Mosquito* tribes. Bancroft says that this was made from the juice of *Hippomane mancinella.* Conzemius did not observe this tree in the territory but mentions the possibility that the secretions from a frog (*Dendrobates tinctorius*) may have been used. The former poison is used by the *Carib,* and both types are used by the *Cuna* and *Chocó.*

POLITICAL ORGANIZATION

Little is known of the aboriginal organization of these tribes. Both chiefs and shamans had great power. Local governments now control the villages, but during the Conquest these tribes were organized for war in various ways. Chiefs were elected by the elderly men and their power was supreme. The office was not hereditary, but among the *Mosquito* a nephew or son-in-law of a chief might succeed him. The whole *Mosquito* tribe, under British guidance, was united and ruled by a "king" who carried as insignia a staff and a gold or silver breastplate.

Among the *Mosquito* and *Sumo* a man who has been wronged is considered a coward if he does not avenge himself. If revenge fails, both the offended man and the perpetrator of the offense are supposed to commit suicide. A thief, when caught, must return double the amount stolen. A creditor may help himself to his debtor's property, or he may destroy the property of a third person, in which case the debtor must pay the damage (*Mosquito*). An adulterous wife is beaten and forced to reveal the name of her lover, who is fined. A murderer is killed, unless he commits suicide, and his memory is dishonored. There is, however, no dishonor in poisoning an enemy, the method employed for most murders.

SOCIAL ORGANIZATION

A man and woman may agree to marry, or, more rarely, the girl's parents may make marriage arrangements without her consent. Child betrothals are common. Cross-cousin marriage is frequent, but marriage between parallel-cousins and closer relations is forbidden. *Mosquito* and *Sumo* chiefs and shamans have several wives, and the *Paya* of Río Platano and Río Paulaya practice polygyny, as do the *Jicaque*.

Before marriage a man must pass through various ordeals, pay the bride's family an agreed sum, and prepare a field for his prospective wife. The wedding is a simple ceremony. The levirate and sororate are practiced, and the many possible exceptions to this rule are adjusted by payments. A man may abandon his wife if she is barren. Divorce is accomplished by means of payments to the families of offended parties. The woman always keeps the children. Among numerous relationship taboos are the important mother-in-law taboo and the prohibition on a man's speaking to his sister-in-law and to other close female relatives by marriage.

LIFE CYCLE

Childbirth.—The *Paya* and *Mosquito* build special confinement huts; the *Sumo* partition off a corner of the house. During parturition the mother is aided by another woman who cuts the cord with a piece of bamboo. The afterbirth and umbilical cord are buried. Among the *Paya* a midwife is regarded by parents and child as a blood relative. This belief is said to have originated among the *Mosquito* and diffused to the *Sumo* and *Paya*. The second of twins and deformed children are killed (*Mosquito* and *Sumo*). Some female children were killed at birth.

Sumo and *Mosquito* women bathe immediately after bearing a child, *Paya* women on the third day. *Sumo* women take a steam bath but use no special structure; in other tribes they bathe in the river. This bath ends a period of ritual impurity. *Mosquito* women, however, are considered impure for one or two weeks. Women also observe a special diet. The return of the mother to the house is celebrated with a ceremony.

Among some tribes, this ceremony is repeated at a later date. The *Sumo* are said to have practiced circumcision. The couvade is general.

Individual names are derived from some peculiarity or mannerism. Such names were not used to address a person, especially older people.

Puberty.—Puberty ceremonies consist of tests, the details of which vary from tribe to tribe. *Sumo* boys receive serious military training at puberty.

Menstruating women are considered to be impure and are confined to a corner of the house (*Sumo*) or to a special hut (*Mosquito* and *Paya*). They are cleansed by bathing or, among the *Sumo,* by a steam bath.

Death.—Death is thought to be due to sorcery or to the machinations of evil spirits. People about to die are abandoned in the bush, or they may even be killed. If a person dies in a village it has to be abandoned. The dead are usually buried in the dwelling, which is abandoned (*Paya*), or, among some tribes, in a special hut. The corpse is placed in a coffin made of a canoe wrapped in bark cloth. Personal belongings, food, and a dog are placed in the grave. Among the *Mosquito,* corpses were sometimes sewed in a mat and placed upright in a grave, facing the east. Slaves, servants, and sometimes a shaman were killed and buried with *Mosquito* chiefs. Early reports of the mummification of chiefs appear to be exceptional and may refer to other tribes. Clay and gold masks of chiefs are reported from one locality, probably *Sumo.*

The dead were mourned in many ways. The relatives cut their hair short, wept, and fasted. A mourning ritual included attempts at suicide, which friends prevented. The women sang songs in praise of the dead. Anniversary ceremonies, held at varying intervals, were intended to appease evil spirits and to aid the soul on its long journey to the hereafter. Shamans invoke the soul in order to discover who was responsible for the death and to ascertain future needs. About a year after death the *Mosquito* hold an elaborate anniversary ceremony, in which face masks and other paraphernalia are employed. The *Sumo* have similar ceremonies which differ in detail. Formerly, a *Mosquito* woman exhumed the bones of her husband and carried them in a bag for a year, subsequently hanging them in the house. She might not remarry for 2 years.

According to Von Hagen (1943), *Jicaque* death and burial customs are a curious mixture of Christianity and their own beliefs. After some preliminary mourning the body, clothed in the garments in which the person died, is wrapped in cloth or bark cloth and buried in the cemetery. A small wooden cross is put at the foot of the grave, and a pot through which a hole is punched is laid at the head. The cemetery is an enclosure on a hilltop, which is walled off, as are Spanish cemeteries.

WARFARE

Most of the information concerning warfare pertains to the *Mosquito,* who were highly organized for this purpose. Undoubtedly much of this is an elaboration of aboriginal customs, encouraged by the English. Early records indicate that the *Sumo, Paya,* and *Jicaque* developed similar but perhaps less complicated organizations in order to resist the Spanish Conquest. Probably they too had waged war previous to the 16th century, but available data do not permit identification of aboriginal customs.

Among the *Mosquito* and *Sumo* all men were potential warriors. They were arranged according to military ranks, which were distinguished by feather insignia. The warriors, particularly of the *Sumo,* were subject to severe tests including dietary restrictions, and they celebrated various ceremonies. Women were not permitted to attend these ceremonies, and the warriors were not supposed to have any relations with women. Before a battle shamans were consulted. The warriors, painted black, usually attacked the enemy at night. The *Mosquito* took prisoners to be sold as slaves to the Whites. The *Sumo* killed as many of the enemy as possible. They mutilated the corpses and wore the teeth and fingernails as trophies. Some of the *Sumo* reputedly ate the roasted flesh of their enemies in order to inflict further insult upon them and to make sure that they were completely destroyed.

ESTHETIC AND RECREATIONAL ACTIVITIES

Dances and music.—All ceremonies are the time for much intoxication, dancing, and singing. On frequent occasions the *Mosquito* sing in groups or singly. There are many kinds of dances, some of them specially for women and others for particular ceremonies. There are two types of drums: a goblet-shaped drum used in funeral and memorial ceremonies and a drum of European origin which is used in some of the ceremonies and, perhaps, as a signal drum. Conch-shell trumpets and reed or bone flutes with one to four stops are blown. *Sumo* and *Mosquito* shamans use flutes 6 feet (2 m.) long. The musical bow, with or without a gourd sounding box, is played by women. Gourd rattles are also used.

RELIGION

The *Sumo, Mosquito,* and *Paya* believe in a deity, called "Our Father," who lives in the sky. He is little interested in mankind, is too far removed to be approached by humans, and has little influence upon human affairs. The sun, moon, and stars, especially the Pleiades, are considered to be supernatural beings. They figure in the mythology and are of some significance in the religious philosophy. Solar and lunar eclipses, thunder, wind, the rainbow, and other celestial phenomena are explained by myths. The last three are the agents of the major deities.

A *Sumo* creation myth recounts the activities of two brothers who made the animals out of maize cobs. People are believed to have been made from rays of the sun. The *Paya* believe that their god sowed men in the same way that manioc is planted. Some of the tribes recount a myth of a great flood. The *Jicaque* believe in two benevolent deities and a female god of evil. No offerings are made to the "good" deities, but attempts are made to placate the "evil" one, a female who is responsible for all misfortune and who causes death.

The *Sumo* and *Mosquito* and possibly the *Paya* believe that after death the soul makes its way eastward over a difficult route to a nether world of plenty and happiness. The description of the route traveled and the acts performed by the survivors of the deceased to aid the progress of his soul on this road differ from tribe to tribe. Under certain conditions the soul may remain about the house of the deceased and even occupy his former belongings, including domestic animals. For this reason these things must be destroyed.

The *Sumo, Mosquito,* and *Paya* believe that the world is populated with innumerable spirits. These haunt hills, caves, deep pools of water, and other places, and they are responsible for most misfortunes including sickness and death. A large part of the work of shamans is to placate these spirits, to drive them out of sick people, and otherwise to destroy them. Protection from the bad spirits is afforded by amulets and charms.

SHAMANISM

Most *Sumo* and *Mosquito* settlements have a shaman, who may take part in secular affairs but whose chief duty is to cure the sick. Shamans possess some spiritual power, but very little is known of the various rituals through which it is acquired. Sons and sometimes sons-in-law may succeed a shaman. Curing varies in detail according to the individual shaman and the spirits addressed. A shaman goes into a trance in which he contacts the spirits and, in one way or another, drives them out of the afflicted person. Curing rituals also include songs, dances, and the use of painted sticks, carved figures, and other paraphernalia. Some diseases are cured by the imposition of diets, the prohibition of sexual intercourse, and other restrictions. Complicated diseases or village-wide epidemics are isolated and receive special medical and ceremonial treatment. Infections, snake bites, and diseases such as malaria are cured by both shamans and laymen, the latter using infusions of herbs and a large number of native medicines. Steam baths followed by a cold plunge are also employed. Baths in hot springs and partial burial in hot sand are common practices, especially among the *Sumo.* When surgery is necessary a shaman employs knives made of obsidian, flint, bone, and such. Ashes, tobacco, wax, and resin are used as antiseptics.

A shaman may also prophesy the future or determine the route hunters should take in order to find game. By conjuring, a shaman may cause harm to come to people. A shaman may be retained by a person to eliminate an enemy.

PLATE 35.—**Sumo and Mosquito Indians, Nicaragua.** *Top: Sumo* man. *Bottom: Mosquito* village, Pearl Lagoon. (Courtesy American Museum of Natural History.)

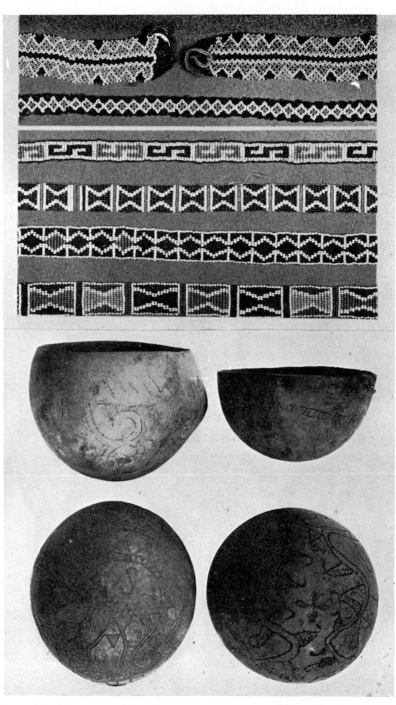

PLATE 36.—**Sumo manufactures.** *Top:* Beadwork. *Bottom:* Decorated gourd bowls. (Courtesy American Museum of Natural History.)

MYTHOLOGY

The literature, reported mainly from the *Mosquito* and *Sumo,* includes the many songs.   An extensive folklore includes stories of the chase, of fishing, and of war.   Quasi-historical tales speak of mysterious tribes who preceded the present inhabitants in the region.   A migration legend says that the former home of the *Mosquito* and *Sumo* was on the Isthmus of Rivas.   The *Sumo* version of a creation legend recounts the common origin of the *Mosquito* and *Sumo.*

LORE AND LEARNING

Rules of etiquette are elaborate even in everyday life.   Time may be measured by the number of knots on a string or by pebbles placed in a gourd.   The year was formerly divided into 13 months, the last of which was occasionally dropped in order to keep the months in adjustment with the seasons.   The *Mosquito* and *Sumo* employ a vigesimal numerical system.

BIBLIOGRAPHY

Conzemius, 1932; Exquemelin, 1678; Von Hagen, 1943.

THE CARIBBEAN LOWLAND TRIBES
THE TALAMANCA DIVISION

By Frederick Johnson

INTRODUCTION

Some tribes of the *Talamanca* Division became extinct and the remainder were modified by post-Conquest events, but the contemporary remnants are lineal descendants of the tribes that occupied the area at the Conquest (maps 2 and 5). Their culture may be considered as a unit, and early records may be compared with accounts made in modern times.

The following description of the culture of the *Talamanca* Division originates largely in studies of two tribes, the *Guaymi* (Johnson, field notes; Pinart, 1885, 1887 a, 1887 b, 1900; Peralta, 1890) and the *Bribri* (Gabb, 1875; Skinner, 1920). The culture of the closely allied central and northern Costa Rican Groups, though very inadequately known, differs from that of the *Bribri* only on some details. Sixteenth- and seventeenth-century data are assembled from miscellaneous observations of numerous tribes. Fragments of more recent information have been collected from remnants of several other tribes; the *Cabecar, Changuena, Dorasque, Terraba, Guatuso, Rama,* and others.

The *Guaymi* are divided into *Northern* tribes and *Southern* tribes. The former live in the Tropical Forest, and certain fundamental traits were superficially modified by it so as to contrast with the *Southern* tribes living in the Uplands of the Pacific coast. Other differences, though appearing in minor details, appear to be more deeply rooted.

CULTURE

SUBSISTENCE ACTIVITIES

Farming.—Descriptions by Columbus and other early explorers indicate that agriculture in the Tropical Forest was once more extensive than at present. Aboriginal crops are still staple foods, except where rice, plantains, and pigeon peas are grown in large quantities. (Cf. list below.) In the Tropical Forest hunting supplies nearly as much food as farming. Wild plants, though more important in the Tropical Forest, are collected by all tribes. Among the modern tribes, particularly the *Southern Guaymi,* farming is extremely important (pl. 37, *top*).

231

LIST OF FOODS MOST COMMONLY GROWN BY THE GUAYMÍ [1]

PLANTS OF AMERICAN ORIGIN:

Maize (*Zea mays*) : Several varieties of both flint and dent.

Beans (*Phaseolus vulgaris*) : Nine variants of this species were collected in 1932–33, seven of which were bush beans and two runner beans.

Lima beans (*Phaseolus lunatus*) : Five variants were collected.

Yuca, or sweet manioc (*Manihot utilissima* var. *aipi*).

Papaya (*Carica papaya*).

Alligator pear, or avocado (*Persea americana*).

Gourds: Vine and tree gourds of several varieties. Both edible gourds and those used for receptacles are grown.

Camote, or sweetpotato (*Ipomoea batatas*).

Cacao (*Theobroma cacao*).

Pejibaye (pejivalle) palm or peach palm (*Guilielma gasipaes*).

PLANTS OF FOREIGN ORIGIN:

Plantain: Several varieties.

Banana: Several varieties.

Pigeon peas (*Cajanus cajan*) : East Indian in origin, sometimes called "dahl." Introduced first into Africa and brought to America with the slave trade (pl. 37, *bottom*).

Gourds (*Lagenaria siceraria*) : Large "water bottles" are made of this gourd Probably of African origin but now grown generally in the American Tropics.

Name (*Dioscorea alata* or *D. batatas*).

Rice: A variety of Upland rice.

Hotöes: A tuber, identity not known.

Sugarcane.

A type of slash-and-burn agriculture is universally employed. Among the *Guaymí*, crops requiring different lengths of time to mature are planted at the same time in one or more plots, and harvesting continues on each plot over a period of several years. Each family owns a number of plots and clears new ones every year, so that planting, harvesting, and fallow periods rotate.

Clearing the fields and burning the slash are done by the men with simple ceremonies. Male relatives and friends gather to drink chicha at the house of the owner of fields. They sing songs and the owner encourages them to work hard and to be happy. The *Bribri* are said to dance to drums before clearing the fields, but the *Guaymí* dance only after the field has been cleared.

The *Guaymí* women do the planting, but among other tribes the men do this work. All tribes use a digging stick several feet long, sharpened to a chisellike edge (Gabb, 1875, p. 515). Skinner (1920) suggests that these implements may have once been used as clubs, perhaps being the quarterstaffs mentioned in the early literature. He says that the *Bribri* called the stick "macana," which he recognizes as a possible equivalent to the *Nahuatl* "macuahuitl." The term is used generally in South America for a flat wooden club.

---

[1] This list, obtained from the *Guaymí* in 1932–33, includes most foods grown by all tribes in the *Talamanca* Division. Some crops are not grown by certain tribes because of local conditions.

Salt was an important commodity obtained in trade by the people of the Tropical Forest from the *Boruca* and other tribes which owned natural salt pans.

Hunting.—Game is killed by stalking or by ambushing animals along their trails; frequently it is driven by small black dogs. Bows and arrows are still the important weapons, but a few Indians own guns. The blowgun is scarcely known to the *Southern Guaymí,* none of whom use it, but Tropical Forest tribes hunt with it, using a clay pellet rather than the dart (p. 243).

Traps are not adequately described. The *Guaymí* make baited box traps, sometimes strong enough to catch large cats. Snares, sharpened stakes in trails, and other types of traps are known. With the recent increase of economic difficulties, trails are sometimes guarded with bows and arrows and even guns to discourage theft and to prevent the uncontrolled movement of undesirable people in the region. It was impossible to discover whether this practice is aboriginal or not. The practice has been declared illegal by most of the tribal councils but had not been stopped in 1933.

Bees are not kept by these tribes, but wild honey is considered a special delicacy, and the larvae from the hives are eaten with a special relish. The *Guaymí* give most of the honey to the women and young babies but occasionally use it in making chicha.

Fishing.—Ferdinand Columbus says that nets and fishhooks were used to catch fish on the coast of Veraguas. People were also said to have lined up along the banks of a stream in order to frighten the fish and make them jump against mats set vertically in canoes.

During the dry season the *Southern Guaymí* catch small fish with their hands. The brooks may be temporarily dammed with stones and grass and the small fish driven into nets, which are fastened to hoops held in gaps in the dams. Small fish are also caught with spears made with sharpened pieces of wire 12 to 18 inches (30 to 45 cm.) long set into the end of a cane about 10 feet (3 m.) long. During the rainy season fish, lying in shallow water, are caught with similar but stouter spears.

People in the Tropical Forest shoot fish with the bow and single- or multiple-pointed arrow. The latter has at least three prongs. Single points with many barbs are reported from various tribes.

During the dry season the *Southern Guaymí* use a baited fish trap (pl. 38, *bottom*) operated by a man sitting behind a blind. When fish nibble the bait, causing dried leaves attached to a limber stick to rustle, he closes the gate. A conical trap, about 2 feet (60 cm.) in diameter at the open end and about 5 feet (1.5 m.) long (pl. 38, *top*), is used in seasons when the brooks rise and fall with some regularity. The trap is placed in an opening at the downstream apex of a **V**-shaped dam. Some dams zigzag across a stream so as to accommodate several traps.

Domesticated animals.—There are early references to a few domesticated animals. Dogs, tamed tapirs, and wild peccaries (zahinos, *Tayassu tajacu*) are mentioned by Ceballos (1610). People in the Tropical Forest now have dogs, a few cattle, and poultry. They also keep tame parrots and small native mammals.

Many *Southern Guaymí* families have cattle and a few horses, the introduction of which, about 1900, caused and is still causing rather extensive changes in the economy. An added stimulus to cattle raising came during the first World War, when a scarcity of grazing land developed in the Republic of Panamá. Now a few corrals are maintained, and such things as lassoes, whips, and saddles are used when they can be obtained from the Panamanians. It has been necessary to fence cultivated land and to make other adjustments. Some folklore connected with ranching has been added to native traditions, and a set of laws and other social regulations governing range areas, inheritance, cattle stealing and such are being developed in the tribal councils.

Food preparation.—Most foods are boiled. Meat, when not eaten immediately, is salted and smoked. Maize is hulled in a mortar, boiled, and then ground on a metate. The resulting mush may be eaten fresh or allowed to ferment. It may be formed into cakes, wrapped in husks, and steamed.

VILLAGES AND HOUSES

In the early chronicles the habitations of the *Talamanca* Group are called "palenques," but no detail is available. A palenque was, apparently, a large dwelling, perhaps a group of dwellings, usually fortified by means of a stockade. The term has been applied also to unfortified hamlets of several houses. Villages were located on the islands at the mouth of the Laguna de Chiriquí and in river valleys some distance from the coast. Early descriptions of house furnishings are singularly absent.

Modern houses in the Tropical Forest are grouped in small communities. Sometimes the houses are close together, but frequently they are scattered, those of the *Southern Guaymí* being one-quarter mile to several miles apart. Most families have a single house, but large ones may occupy two houses, in which case the second usually serves as kitchen and as the home of the older people.

Among the *Southern Guaymí* one man or the family he represents may own several house sites, even though they use but one. Each site is recognized as a separate parcel of land and is inherited, usually through the male line. The distribution of house sites bears no spacial relation to the farmland owned by a family. Modern houses last about 5 years.

They are seldom repaired; instead, a new house is built upon an unused site and the family abandons the old house.

The *Guaymí* build three types of houses; rectangular, square, and round. None of these has a specialized use. The square and round houses are more common among the *Northern* tribes. The rectangular

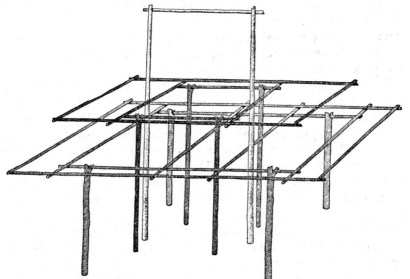

FIGURE 50.—Fundamental framework of *Southern Guaymí* hip-roofed house.

house, having a hip roof, is built almost exclusively by the *Southern Guaymí*. The framework is illustrated in plate 39, *bottom,* and figures 50 and 51. Grass is used as thatch by the *Southern Guaymí* and split palm fronds by the peoples in the Tropical Forest, the fronds being sewn to

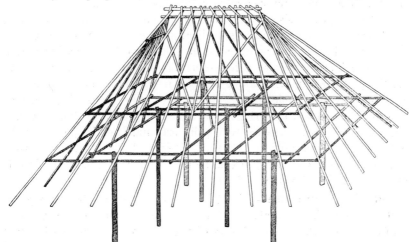

FIGURE 51.—Framework of *Southern Guaymí* hip-roofed house with rafters added.

rods attached to the rafters. In exposed places crotched sticks may help secure the thatch. Outside walls (pl. 39, *top*) are made of vertical poles lashed to the primary horizontal framework. Lofts are made inside the houses by lashing horizontal poles to the upper, secondary framework.

The square and round houses, characteristic of all the Tropical Forest tribes, are believed to be the older types. The construction of these is similar to that illustrated (pl. 39). The apices of the pyramidal and conical roofs are covered with large open-mouthed pots, e.g., broken iron pots. Most *Guaymí* houses have walls.

Various semipermanent shelters (pl. 40, *top*) provide additional living space or temporary shelter from the elements while traveling. Simple windbreaks may be the only shelter used for several weeks at a time.

The modern palenques built by the *Bribri* and, apparently, by the *Cabecar* and *Terraba* are circular or square in plan or, more rarely, have straight sides and rounded ends. The older ones are said to have been very large. The houses are conical or pyramidal, the roof coming down to the ground. The construction is of poles bound with vines (Gabb, 1875, p. 514; Skinner, 1920). These houses are distinctive in having pots to waterproof the apices of the roofs and a shedlike entry to prevent the rain from coming in the single door. Angulo (1862, pp. 153–154) notes that many families may live in the same house, each with its separate property and cooking fire. Other sources note that these houses were inhabited by groups of related families.

Today there are very few if any of these palenques in use. Modern *Bribri* houses are rectangular or oval in plan, with a hip roof and no vertical walls. *Cabecar* houses are now simply a shed roof, sloping in one direction and open at the front and sides. *Terraba* houses are "el" roofs raised on short poles and open all around below the eaves.

Guetar villages consisted of a few communal houses. The *Suerre* house was "shaped like an egg, in length about 45 paces, and 9 in breadth. It was encircled with reed, covered with palm branches remarkably well interlaced; there were also a few other houses but of a common sort" (Lothrop, 1926 b, p. 23, quoting Benzoni). *Guatuso* houses were scattered over a considerable area. "The houses are low, consisting of a roof pitching both ways from a ridge pole, and resting on very short but very thick posts. This is thatched with palm leaf and is entirely open at the ends and sides, under the eaves" (Gabb, 1875, p. 485). Tree houses were built by the aboriginal occupants of the region, according to Padre Zapada (Bancroft, 1883–90, vol. 8, p. 755).

Household furniture.—The *Guaymí* build platform beds along the walls. Other tribes pile plantain leaves on the floor in addition to using platform beds. Benches consisting of two horizontal poles or of a split log run around the walls. Stools are made of a single block of wood and are rectangular, with a **V**-shaped hollow as the seat (fig. 52, *a*) (*Guaymí*) or are carved with two or four legs. Skinner (1920, pp. 52, 55) says that frequently the *Bribri* carved these stools to represent tortoises. Hammocks, used for lounging but rarely for sleeping, are hung about the houses.

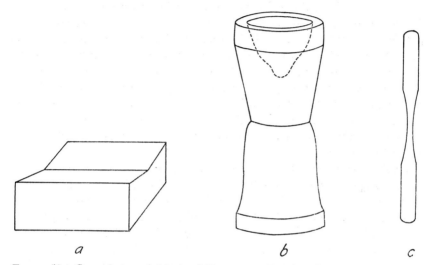

a   *b*   *c*

FIGURE 52.—*Guaymí* household furnishings. *a,* Wooden bench with concave **V**-shaped seat; *b, c,* wooden mortar and pestle.

The center of the floor of a *Guaymí* house is usually occupied by a large log trough in which chicha is made. Troughs are hewn into several forms: Some are canoe-shaped with pointed ends; some have square ends; others have a lip or flange on the ends. The sides are simply the surface from which the bark has been peeled.

Grain is stored in house lofts in cylindrical bins of bark, in baskets and such. The *Bribri* are said occasionally to build outdoor granaries. Miscellaneous property is hung about the houses in string bags and gourds and sometimes in baskets. Bows, blowguns, and arrows are hung in crude racks or stuck in the thatch. Sometimes, particularly in the Tropical Forest, poultry and even swine are confined in pens inside the house.

The fireplace is inside the house, usually opposite the door, if the house is walled, and its vicinity is cluttered with culinary acticles, such as metates and large chicha jars, the latter propped up with sticks and stones. Metates, however, may be in a separate shelter. *Bribri* houses may have floors about 4 feet (1.2 m.) from the ground (Skinner, 1920, p. 48); these cover only part of the area of the house. Floors and lofts are reached by a short notched-log ladder.

CLOTHING AND ORNAMENTS

The aboriginal man's costume was a breechclout, a narrow strip of bark cloth, some 6 feet (2 m.) long, passed between the legs and wound around the body. It was usually supported by a belt. The women wore the breechclout and a knee-length, wrap-around skirt. Both sexes frequently wore nothing above the waist, but in most tribes they might use a short jacket "so scant that it shows the entire breast." Near Herradura the people were said to wear bark-cloth mantles having a hole in the center for the head. Men and women occasionally wore, either with or without a skirt, a "blanket which covered the head and fell to the feet" (*Terraba, Boruca*). Girdles (*Changuena* and the Tropical Forest of Costa Rica) and feather-decorated aprons (*Guaymi*) are mentioned but not described. Some bark-cloth garments were decorated with painted designs. Feathers attached to the head in an undescribed manner are mentioned by the earliest explorers.

At the present time the more conservative people wear the breechclout about their houses and cover their shoulders with strips of cloth or rarely with short, shirtlike jackets. Sometimes the bark-cloth breechclout is covered by a second one of cotton cloth (Pittier de Fábrega, 1938 b, p. 11). A poncholike shirt, consisting of a wide strip of bark cloth with a hole for the head, is worn by both men and women. This is tied under each arm with a piece of string or a belt. In all tribes boys go practically naked until puberty, but girls are clothed when they are very young.

At the present time the less conservative *Guaymi* men wear shirts made with a neckband about 1 inch (2.5 cm.) high and cut to open at the back. The bosoms of the shirts are frequently outlined with strips of appliqué and are often decorated with geometrical designs in appliqué (pl. 45, *top, right*). Rawhide sandals are sometimes worn. These are attached to the foot by means of a lace running between the first and second toe and over the instep to a second lace attached to the heel and tied around the ankle.

Straw hats, a recent innovation, are made exclusively by the men. Straw is braided into plaits, and the plait is sewn in a spiral beginning at the center of the crown. The hat is shaped as it is sewn.

The modern *Guaymi* women wear a cotton or bark-cloth breechclout supported by a belt and a dress with sleeves and an extremely full skirt. The dress reaches from the neck to the ground (pl. 46, *top, right,* and *bottom, left*) and is slit in front nearly to the waist or has a round neck-opening. Appliqué decorations are frequently added about the neck and, more rarely, around the lower part of the skirt. The women's costume is completed with quantities of bead necklaces and strings of teeth and shells.

Guaymi ceremonial costumes are simply elaborations of ordinary clothes. The men's shirts have elaborate appliqué designs on the bosoms; the outside of the trouser legs is also decorated (fig. 53). Various types of headdresses are worn: a conical cap of fiber or bark cloth (pls. 45 and

46) ; straw hats, commonly decorated with a circlet of feathers attached to the crown, which corresponds to the circlets of brilliant feathers formerly worn; and sometimes a square piece of cloth folded diagonally and wrapped about the head. Men also wear an elaborate bead collar (pl. 45, *bottom, right*). Women's ceremonial clothing differs from their ordinary attire in the great amount of appliqué decoration and in the use of quantities of necklaces. It often includes straw hats.

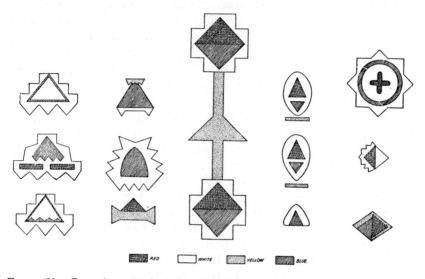

FIGURE 53.—*Guaymí* appliqué clothing designs. From trouser legs of men's ceremonial costumes.

For the balsería and the secret ceremonies *Guaymí* men carry on their backs stuffed animals decorated with beaded collars, ribbons, and bells. The front paws rest on the shoulders and the head sticks straight up (pl. 45).

Some people still wear headdresses of feathers set vertically into a tape which extends from temple to temple (Gabb, 1875, p. 19; Skinner, 1920, p. 80, and illustrations). Some headdresses are made of bands of decorated cloth. Beaded collars and necklaces are also worn.

Chiefs and other officials formerly wore special ornaments, apparently identifying insignia. Most frequently mentioned at the time of the Conquest were gold ornaments, which now are extremely rare. Chiefs also carried a decorated staff (Gabb, 1875, p. 520; Skinner, 1920, p. 89).

In the 16th and 17th centuries all the people of the region were said to have gold ornaments hung about the neck or fastened to the clothing or to the arms and legs. These were described as zoomorphic figures, such as eagles, lizards, toads, and spiders, and mirrors, golden medals, plates, and plaques. Necklaces of various types were also very common.

In the vicinity of Cartago the men tied a few threads of cotton about the prepuce.

The people of mixed ancestry living in the eastern section of the Pacific slopes, west of the Panama Canal, make a bark-cloth mask in which a deer skull with horns is frequently incorporated. These are used in ceremonies connected with Catholic holy days, which are observed in former mission towns. This custom is rapidly dying out.

Men cut their hair off just above the nape of the neck or sometimes clip the back and sides up to a line near the top of the ears. They wear bangs. Occasionally the hair is allowed to grow long, either hanging loosely or being plaited, bound with bark cloth, and coiled at the back of the head. Women's hair hangs freely and is tied with a ribbon about the top of the head, or it is divided into two plaits or rolled up at the back of the neck.

According to Ferdinand Columbus, "The people [probably *Guaymí*] were all painted on the face and body in divers colors, white, black and red." Urcullu (1763, p. 488) describes scarification or tattooing. The same source mentions bone nose and lip plugs and an earplug decorated with feathers. Pinart (1887 b, p. 119) says that the *Dorasque* scarified the body with sharp pieces of stone and also painted the body. The *Guetar* and the *Guatuso* also decorated themselves with paint. Gabb (1875, p. 519) says that the *Bribri* painted their faces with parallelograms or squares and that the *Terraba* formerly tattooed small patterns on the faces and arms. Painting has died out.

Guaymí men paint their faces at all times, but women rarely do so except during ceremonies. A man has his own set of geometrical motifs and applies them in any combination that suits his caprices. The *Southern Guaymí* do not now paint their bodies.

Some of the *Guaymí*, usually younger men, mutilate their teeth, a custom that probably was recently adopted. The corners of the upper and lower incisors are chipped off, usually to produce a sharp wedge-shaped point or what could be described as "needle" teeth. This custom is most common among the mixed Panamanian-Indian groups and among the *Guaymí* who have been in closest contact with the Panamanians. It is not characteristic of the conservative *Guaymí* and has not been reported among the *Talamanca* Group. The custom may be of African origin (Stewart, 1942).

TRANSPORTATION

Loads are carried in net bags or bundles equipped with a tumpline. Horses and, more rarely, bulls and steers are used as pack animals.

Dugout canoes are used where possible on the ocean and along the quieter, lower reaches of the rivers. They are paddled in the aboriginal manner, but some have a small sail and a fixed rudder. Small dugouts are used on the rivers. During high water the mountain people, who rarely have canoes[1], use logs or makeshift rafts to cross the rivers.

MANUFACTURES

Basketry.—For baskets, rough splints are woven in an octagonal openwork twill. Baskets vary from cup size to 3 feet (0.9 m.) high and some 2 feet (0.6 m.) in diameter.

Cordage.—All string is made either from majagua, a bast fiber, or from pita, a fiber obtained from cactus leaves. Both fibers are twisted by rolling them on the thigh.

Netting.—Hammocks and numerous bags (pl. 41) are made with a technique called "coiled netting." (Cf. Lothrop, 1937, fig. 82, p. 111.) Innumerable variations of this technique are possible and are employed at the discretion of each individual. The bags are decorated by employing dyed string. The finest and most highly decorated bags are made of pita fiber by *Guaymí* women, who work several colored threads into complicated geometrical designs by means of the simplest stitch.

Weaving.—Native woven cloth is being supplanted by modern European cloth. The *Guetar* were formerly famous for their cloth. Gabb (1875) describes a two-bar loom used by the *Bribri* men who wove locally grown cotton. Skinner (1920) visited the same people and found that weaving had disappeared, though he collected some old pieces of native cloth. Among the *Southern Guaymí*, in 1933, there was but one woman in several hundred families who knew how to weave. She used a two-bar loom (pl. 40, *bottom*) and wove with thread spun from wild tree cotton on a drop-spindle which had a disk-shaped wooden whorl.

Ceramics.—Pottery is made by all tribes, but details are available only for the *Guaymí*. Large, pointed or round-bottomed jars with restricted necks are general, but other types have been reported only for the *Guaymí*. The most conservative and inaccessible *Guaymí* groups are said to use slips and other methods of decorations, but most of their pottery is unadorned. Pottery is made by only a few women in each local group.

Pottery clay is kneaded with the hands and is fine grained; clean sand is added. A small lump of prepared clay is molded to a cup or dish shape and rolls of clay about 15 inches (38 cm.) long and less than 1 inch (2.5 cm.) in diameter are added to its edge as concentric rings to form the body of the vessel. The rolls are pinched together with the fingers and smoothed with the hands and with pieces of gourd. Necks of jars, rims, lug-handles, and such are added in much the same way (pl. 42, *top*).

---

[1] Large wooden troughs found in many *Guaymí* houses have been called canoes (e.g., **Pinart,** Peralta). The natives distinguish between canoes and these troughs, which are **not seaworthy.** On the coast, where canoes are used, the *Guaymí* also have troughs. It is possible that a canoe might be used as a trough when an exceptionally large quantity of chicha is to be made.

After the jars have dried for a few hours the surface is rubbed smooth with a wet tool. Several days later vessels are set on the ground and a fire is built about them. There are six fundamental forms of vessels (pls. 42, *bottom;* 43, *top;* fig. 54), some of them similar to the products of the modern Panamanian industry and others possibly resembling the basic forms of the more highly decorated prehistoric pottery.

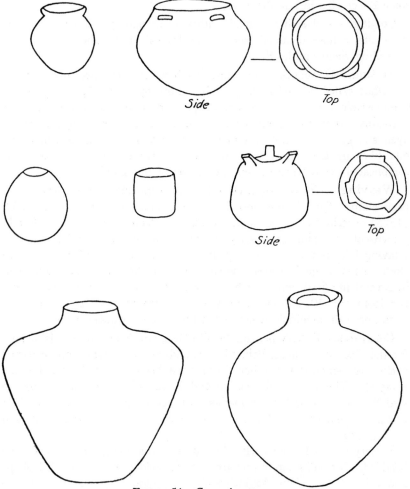

FIGURE 54.—*Guaymí* pottery.

Pottery ocarinas resemble gourd ocarinas, being round or egg-shaped with a protruding mouthpiece. Some have two stops arranged on each side of the center line; others have two or rarely three stops on the center line. A variant, usually smaller than the first two, is pear-shaped with two tubular stops rising above the surface of the ocarina about half an inch (1.3 cm.), one on each side of the center line.

Weapons.—Bows are 4 to 5 feet (1.3 to 1.7 m.) long, less than 1 inch (2.5 cm.) wide, and about half an inch (1.2 cm.) thick. The best bowstrings are made of pita fiber. Arrows are made of cane and are 4 to 5 feet (1.3 to 1.7 m.) long. Stunning arrows, used for small game, have blunt, knobbed heads made of deer antler, hardwood, or cow horn (Skinner, 1920) set into the larger end of the cane, bound with cord, and sometimes covered with pitch. Killing arrows are tipped with a piece of hardwood which has a rudimentary tang and is set in a deep notch of a wooden foreshaft. Only one reference to poisoned arrows has come to light. These were said to have been used in battle by the *Boruca.*

Gabb (1875, p. 516) describes a blowgun, or pellet gun, bored from one piece of wood, fitted with a double sight, and covered with pitch. "The missles are clay balls. These . . . are carried in a little net, with them are two bone implements. One, simply a straight, heavy piece of bone used to drive a ball out of the tube by its weight, in case of sticking. The other is similar in appearance, but the end is worked into a round pit with sharp edges, for trimming the balls to the proper size and shape."

Woodworking.—Woodworking is confined to hewing with machetes and small adzes and finishing with smaller tools and with certain kinds of leaves which are used as sandpaper. *Guaymí* wooden articles are illustrated in figure 52. *Bribri* articles are illustrated by Skinner (1920).

Stone industry.—No cutting tools are made of stone at the present time. The grinding surfaces of manos and metates are flattened and prepared by pecking with another stone. Whetstones are cut from deposits of soft sandstone or volcanic rock.

The *Guaymí* possess some stone tobacco pipes, which they highly prize. These are said to be made by the people living in a locality where a special kind of rock is obtainable. These pipes vary from the simple elbow variety, undecorated except for a small conical point at the bottom of the bowl, to those carved with conventionalized faces. Other varieties are decorated with small round lugs near the rim of the bowl, or rarely, with incised geometrical designs (fig. 55).

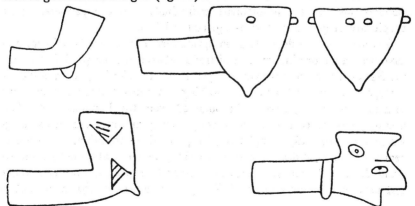

FIGURE 55.—*Guaymí* stone tobacco pipes.

Fire making.—Fire was formerly made with the hand-twirled drill, the tinder being cotton or shredded bark. Ceremonial fires, particularly of the *Talamanca* Group, are still lighted in this way. Fire is also made by striking a machete against a stone and catching the sparks on tinder, but no special strike-a-lights are used. Fire is seldom allowed to go out, being kept smoldering in punky wood or punky fiber hung in a protected place. Firebrands are carried when traveling.

Beadwork.—Necklaces of bone beads and perforated teeth are very rare at present. Beads of European origin are strung into necklaces and woven into collars. The *Guaymí* make collars with designs of various colors, the beads being strung on pita fiber thread (fig. 56).

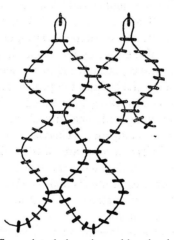

FIGURE 56.—*Guaymí* technique in making beadwork collars.

ECONOMIC ORGANIZATION

The majority of the *Guaymí* produce a surplus of food, but some people have insufficient land or other resources, such as labor, to supply themselves with enough to eat. In addition, there are orphans, disinherited families, and certain unfortunate individuals who are paupers. Such people are largely absorbed as agricultural labor.

Guaymí economy depends upon agriculture, but remnants of what may have been an aboriginal system of trade between the Tropical Forest and the Savanna may be observed in operation. In addition, commodities of European origin, such as cattle, clothing, machetes, fishhooks, sugar, and to some extent salt, have to be obtained from the Panamanians. This necessity has forced the people to adopt money and methods of exchange which are apparently completely foreign to their tradition. In spite of nearly 400 years of dealing with Europeans, the *Guaymí* do not yet understand the use of money. The less conservative groups, who have vague and usually erroneous ideas of European practices of exchange, obtain articles of European origin and trade them in the *Guaymí* country, following more or less the aboriginal barter system. This procedure results in the utmost confusion. A deal, even if initially of the simplest sort, usually becomes hopelessly complicated and ends up, sometimes after several years, in the council, where the governor makes an arbitrary and not always popular solution.

The influx of cattle, particularly since 1914, has interrupted the economic life to some extent. The principle effect has been to take the men off the land for a portion of the year, leaving more work for the women to do. In some cases this results in hardship for it reduces the normal supply of food. Cattle are so precious that they are rarely slaughtered and thus do not replace the agricultural losses.

Wealth is usually measured in terms of the productivity of one's land and the number of one's cattle. It is expressed not only directly but in terms of what the crops, particularly the surplus, can buy. Thus, a wealthy man may be the head of a family having a well-equipped house or he may be the owner of a large supply of some commodity such as cloth or salt.

SOCIAL ORGANIZATION

The whole social structure of the *Guaymí* is now being modified. Present rules are often contradictory and result in much disagreement among the people. The fundamental *Guaymí* unit is the family, which consists of a man, one or more wives, and their children. Occasionally this unit includes the first wife's mother and father and sometimes the parents of other wives. A man usually formally marries his first wife. He may marry or purchase subsequent wives. Divorces are illegal but frequent. A woman may leave her husband for another man, but the latter must pay the husband. The *Guaymí* have a clanlike organization which appears to be exogamous, but the details are unknown. All tribes are polygynous.

Descent among the *Guaymí* is reckoned through the female line, but property may be inherited through both the male and female lines. As a rule, land, cattle, and other property are held in the names of the men and boys. Women own a little land, many cattle, and all the household goods. Claims arising from this complicated system, which at present does not work well, are adjusted by the tribal council upon the order of the governor.

Pittier de Fábrega (1895) notes that the *Bribri* had exogamous matrilineal moieties, which were divided into clans. A *Bribri* man purchased his wives. Information from other tribes is extremely scarce, but it suggests that analogous systems were in vogue. Inheritance was apparently similar to the *Guaymí* system (Gabb, 1875, p. 496). At the time of the Conquest the *Guetar* were divided into three classes: nobles, commoners, and slaves, the last being women and boys captured in war. Captive men were sacrificed.

POLITICAL ORGANIZATION

Evidence from the early documents and from some more recent sources indicates that these tribes existed under a number of feudal governments. There were probably at least three feudal states—the *Guaymí*, the *Talamanca* Group, and the *Guetar*. During the wars with the Spaniards each government was rapidly welded into a strong unit. When these were broken up by the Conquest, realignments were attempted. At the present time these systems have broken down, and most of the surviving tribes are governed by heads of local groups.

The titular head of the *Guaymí* lives in the Miranda Valley and rules only by reputation. The local governors still have considerable authority. Each usually inherits his position, being, theoretically, the oldest surviving son of the first marriage. A governor rules over clanlike divisions. His authority depends upon the prestige of his office, his ability, and, to some extent, upon the support of a loosely organized council made up of influential members of the group.

The social and political organization of the *Guaymí* is in a state of transition. The people on the fringes of Indian territory are becoming closely associated with the neighboring Panamanian towns and districts and heed some of the orders of the Panamanian officials, especially those that are to their advantage. The infusion of Panamanian ideas is breaking down former ideas of family relationships and the inheritance of property. The resulting complication often becomes intolerable, and a *Guaymí* family group may break up and join the Panamanians or it may move farther back into the mountains and in turn upset the local social, political, and economic situation there. The position of some governors is not an enviable one.

Among the *Bribri* and related tribes the situation seems to differ only in detail. The *Bribri* conquered the *Terraba* after a war at the beginning of the 19th century (Gabb, 1875, pp. 488–489), and the *Bribri* chiefs now control the *Terraba* chieftaincy. In addition, the *Bribri* are the political superiors of the *Cabecar,* and the *Bribri* dialect has survived at the expense of the other dialects. The full powers of *Bribri* chieftainship rest in a single family, which does not observe unilinear succession but selects its most eligible member to succeed a deceased chief. The chieftaincy carries some social prestige, but the authority depends upon support of the Costa Rican Government, which has now gained control of it.

All the tribes were more or less warlike. The early sources emphasize the idea that the wars were for the purpose of obtaining captives for sacrifice (particularly in central and northern Costa Rica). It is probable that economic, political, and territorial difficulties also were involved. The Spaniards had considerable difficulty in conquering some of these tribes not only because of the environment but also because the tribes quickly formed alliances against the common enemy. They were, however, sometimes able to play one tribe against another. Nothing is known of the way in which the *Guaymi* organized for war. The *Bribri, Cabecar,* and *Terraba,* among others, had war chiefs who were usually elected and who exercised absolute power over the tribe. The warriors belonged to a special class and were frequently given special burials.

LIFE CYCLE

Childbirth.—During pregnancy the women of most of these tribes practice simple sympathetic magic in order to impart desired attributes to the expected child. A woman gives birth in a little house built for the purpose at some distance from the dwelling. She is assisted by her mother or by some elderly midwife. The umbilical cord is cut with a special bamboo knife. As soon as the child is born it is washed, the placenta is buried, and both mother and infant are ceremonially washed in a river. The woman returns to the house but may not enter it until she has been purified by a shaman, who blows smoke all over her. The details of this purification ceremony differ among various tribes. (Cf. Pinart, 1885, p. 444; Gabb, 1875, p. 494; Pittier de Fábrega, 1938 b, p. 23; Angulo, 1862, pp. 153–154; etc.)

The only naming ceremony reported is that of the *Guaymi,* who usually combine it with some other affair, such as clearing the land, which is attended by a number of people. The child's father swings it through the smoke of a fire and names it. Other men also swing it through the smoke. Names so given are used until the puberty ceremony, when new names are given.

Boys' puberty.—A secret puberty ceremony, called in Spanish the "clarido," is celebrated by the *Guaymi.* Certain male members of a local group instruct the boys, while designated women act as aids or servants. The leaders paint their bodies and appear in masks. The boys are taught to paint their faces, and, in some sections, their teeth are chipped. They receive an official but secret name, and, following the ceremony, they may take their first wives.

Death customs.—There are conflicting and confusing accounts of customs connected with death and the disposal of the dead. It is probable that each tribe buried in various ways, the method depending upon the deceased's social position. The *Southern Guaymí* bury after the corpse has hung in the house during a few days of mourning and ceremonial observances (pl. 44; fig. 57). The dead are not exhumed. Pinart

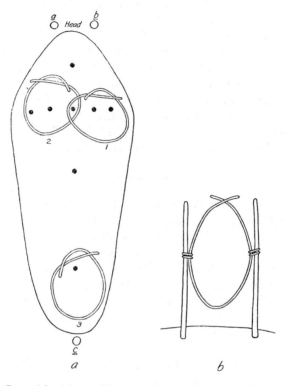

FIGURE 57.—*Guaymí* burial. *a*, Diagram of mound constructed over burial which was oriented with the head of the corpse to the west. Numbers 1, 2, and 3 are bejuco hoops which were laid over crosses located by black dots. *a*, *b*, and *c* indicate the location of small holes in which chicha in two small iron pots and articles such as mirrors, combs, a bit of face paint, etc. were buried. *b*, Sketch of gate or exit made of two upright balsa poles to which a loop of bejuco was lashed. The gate was located on the eastern edge of the cemetery. This was constructed while the grave was being filled. Everyone at the burial services passed through this exit at the end of the ceremony.

(1885, pp. 445–446) says that the *Guaymí* (probably the *Northern* tribes) wrap the corpse and leave it in a special place until the flesh has rotted off, when the bones are collected and buried with great ceremony. Inhumation and varieties of secondary burial are reported for several other tribes. The remains are put in the ground or hung in the houses. Among the *Guetar* embalmed bodies are put in mortuary buildings. All funeral ceremonies are long and complicated.

ESTHETIC AND RECREATIONAL ACTIVITIES

Musical instruments.—The *Guaymí* make conch-shell trumpets by grinding off part of the whorl and molding a mouthpiece of pitch. Cowhorn trumpets made of the horns of longhorn cattle or of several sections of short horns stuck together with pitch and equipped with a wooden mouthpiece are now replacing these.

Whistles or endflutes with three and four stops are made of bone, wood, and reeds. Each whistle is made to play a certain tune composed by its maker. Double-reed whistles with no stops are also made.

Pottery ocarinas have been described (p. 242). Ocarinas are also made of gourds or are molded of pitch. Rarely, turtle shells are suspended from the shoulders by a string and played by rubbing the hand over the edge of the shell.

A few drums are made by the present-day *Northern Guaymí*. Some have double heads tightened over a hollow log by means of hoops and lashings; others have no hoops. These drums are beaten with the hand or with two sticks. *Bribri* drums are made of a tapered hollow log and have a single head (Gabb, 1875, p. 517; Skinner, 1920).

The *Bribri* make an instrument of armadillo skin, which is rubbed with a beanlike seed. Gourd rattles and a xylophonelike instrument made by hollowing a chunk of wood are also mentioned.

Alcoholic beverages.—Many beverages or chichas are made, most of them fermented and some intoxicating. Most commonly, maize is used. It is partially ground on a metate or simply crushed in a mortar, and it may or may not be cooked before it is poured into a trough to ferment. A type of chicha, highly desired because of its alcoholic content, is made of maize, much of which is partially chewed by the women and spat into a trough. Other beverages may be made of yuca or of combinations of various kinds of fruits. Such beverages were first described by the conquistadors, and one account mentions a drink made from a tree of the "copal" species. It was said to resemble turpentine and to have been used also to embalm the dead!

Narcotics.—In discussing Ferdinand Columbus's descriptions of the natives (*Guaymí?*) encountered on the north coast of Veraguas, Lothrop (1937, p. 17) notes that in the land of the Cacique Urira the people were accustomed to chew a dried herb mixed with some sort of powder and suggests that this refers either to tobacco chewing or to coca chewing.

RELIGION

Early accounts of religious activities are confined to passing mention of priests who were usually also secular officials. By means of ceremonies these men cured the sick, prophesied the future, and such.

Modern references describe the remnants of religious concepts which must have had considerable influence upon everyday life. The *Guaymí* now speak of a God with attributes similar to the Christian God. They also have shamans and sorcerers who prophesy the future and placate various evil spirits. Ritual is now restricted to very private ceremonies held at night. Other ceremonies also have a certain religious background.

Accounts of the *Bribri* describe a formal priesthood usually made up of *Bribri* but ruled by a single priest chosen from the *Cabecar* tribe. In addition, a certain group of laymen is officially recognized as sorcerers and shamans. The *Guetar* had an organized priesthood, and they sacrificed human beings at every moon and at burial feasts.

The people have a well-developed theology which includes a Supreme Being and a multitude of lesser deities, both benevolent and malevolent. The bad spirits must be constantly placated in order to ward off sickness, death, and all kinds of misfortune. They are exorcised by the religious officials in various ways.

These tribes have concepts of various degrees of spiritual cleanliness of both human beings and inanimate objects. An object which has not been used for some time may become unclean and must be spiritually cleansed before it is serviceable. Some degrees of uncleanliness are conceived to be of a serious nature. (For further details, cf. Gabb, 1875, p. 188, pp. 503–504; Pittier de Fábrega, 1938 b, pp. 16–19; Skinner, 1920, pp. 46–47.)

CEREMONIES

Only the more important of the many ceremonies reported during the past centuries are now celebrated. All these have a religious background, and all characteristically involve varying degrees of drunkenness and brawling. Some are primarily of a social nature, such as the *Guaymí* "chichería," during which the men and women dance in a circle to a single song that everyone sings interminably. The dancing may last for several days. Upon occasion this ceremony is considered to be a memorial to the deceased rather than a social gathering.

One of the important *Guaymí* ceremonies is called in Spanish the "balsería." It is connected with agriculture, particularly the planting of crops, but no clear statement of the details has yet been obtained. Outwardly, the ceremony is a large social gathering in which there is some formalized competition between regional and relationship groups. These groups are perhaps extended families, possibly even clans, each of which occupies a certain region and owns a number of the ceremonial grounds. The balserías are held at a different location each year. A group of the *Northern Guaymí* occupies a special place on the program of the ceremony. In the principal activity, which lasts one day, two groups throw balsa-wood sticks at each other (pls. 46 and 47). These contestants belong in different classes, which are determined by either a family relationship or by region. In some instances men may wager property and even their wives upon the outcome of the "stick play."

For descriptions of ceremonies among the *Bribri*, see Gabb (1875).

BIBLIOGRAPHY

Angulo, 1862; Bancroft, 1883–90; Ceballos, 1610; Gabb, 1875; Lothrop, 1926 b, 1937; Peralta, 1890; Pinart, 1885, 1887 a, 1887 b, 1900; Pittier de Fábrega, 1895, 1938 b; Skinner, 1920; Stewart, 1942; Urcullu, 1763.

PLATE 37.—**Guaymí farming and foodstuffs.** *Top:* Fenced farmland on which yuca and pigeon peas are raised. *Bottom:* Pigeon peas being dried in the sun. (Courtesy Frederick Johnson.)

PLATE 38.—**Guaymí fish traps.** *Top:* Abandoned trap and stone dam. *Bottom:* Trap in working order. (Courtesy Frederick Johnson.)

PLATE 39.—**Hip-roofed house of the Guaymí.** *Top:* Completed. *Bottom:* Framework. (Courtesy Frederick Johnson.)

PLATE 40.—**Guaymí shelter and loom weaving.** *Top:* Flat-roofed shelter. *Bottom:* Beating down woof with sword batten in weaving. (Courtesy Frederick Johnson.)

PLATE 41.—**Valienti (Guaymí ?) bags, Panamá.** (Courtesy American Museum of Natural History.)

PLATE 42.—**Guaymí pottery making.** *Top:* Adding clay ring to form rim.
Bottom: Small jar before firing. (Courtesy Frederick Johnson.)

PLATE 43.—**Guaymí utensils.** *Top:* Large pottery jar. *Bottom:* Uncommon shape of mortar. (Courtesy Frederick Johnson.)

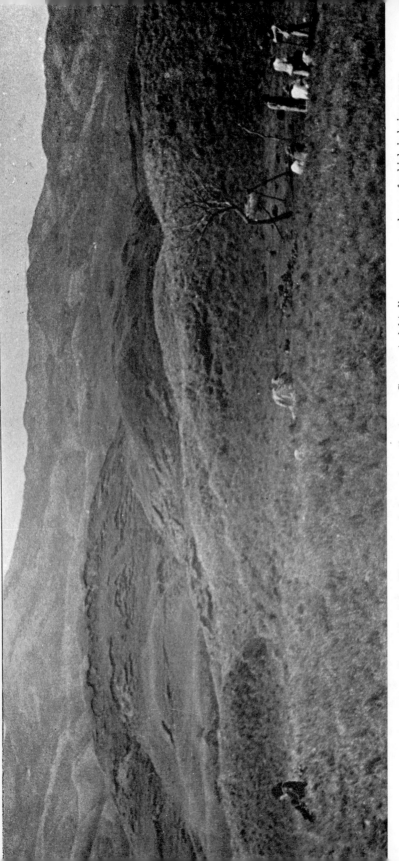

PLATE 44.—**Southern Guaymí burial.** The corpse is hung from the tree. Group at right digs grave, one phase of which is being super-intended by a woman relative of the dead. Mourning women sit at left while the pregnant widow sits outside the cemetery limits. (Courtesy Frederick Johnson.)

PLATE 45.—**Guaymí men in ceremonial costumes.** (Courtesy Frederick Johnson.)

PLATE 46.—**Guaymí ceremonies and ceremonial dress.** *Top:* (*left*) Balsería ceremony. Man pointing pole at his opponent. *Top* (*right*) and *bottom* (*left*): Women in ceremonial dress. *Bottom* (*right*): Man in ceremonial dress. (Courtesy Frederick Johnson.)

PLATE 47.—Guaymí balsería ceremony. *Top:* Man throwing pole at his opponent. *Bottom:* Rack of balsa poles prepared for balsería ceremony. (Courtesy Frederick Johnson.)

PLATE 48.—**Guaymí man.** Wearing "working" or everyday clothes. (Courtesy Frederick Johnson.)

THE TRIBES WEST AND SOUTH OF THE PANAMA CANAL[1]

By Samuel K. Lothrop

INTRODUCTION

The tribes west and south of the Panamá Canal appear to have been fundamentally similar culturally to those of the *Talamanca* Division, but 16th-century data reveal certain differences that warrant their separate treatment (maps 2 and 5).

Beginning with the first Conquest of the Panamanian Savannas (Espinosa, 1514, 1516, 1519; cf. also Oviedo y Valdés, 1851–55), Spanish writers made clear statements that the region was inhabited by peoples speaking languages which were mutually unintelligible. Some must have spoken *Chibchan;* others perhaps did not. That the indigenous population was practically obliterated before the end of the century, and that as early as 1600 enclaves of people speaking *Guaymí* and other dialects were moved into the area by the Spanish administrators, are reasons for seriously questioning whether the tribal identities of recent groups and of neighboring enclaves are any indication of the affinities of the population of the 16th century. In view of certain characteristics of their culture, these people are tentatively considered as a larger unit in a general *Guaymí* group.

CULTURE

SUBSISTENCE ACTIVITIES

Apparently the food supply was plentiful and the people cultivated and preserved maize, peppers, manioc, sweetpotatoes, calabashes and gourds, and possibly squashes and other plants.

Meat, preserved by smoking, was supplied by hunting deer, peccaries, iguana and other lizards, sea turtles, curassows, ducks, and small mammals. Game and fish were taken with nets made of various kinds of fiber or of hide thongs. The game was driven by dogs into these nets or sometimes into pits. During the dry season the grass was occasionally fired and a great number of animals were driven down upon a line of hunters armed with darts or bows and arrows. Birds were shot over

---

[1] A more complete summary of these data may be found in Lothrop (1937).

decoys or caught in nets. Fish occupied an important place in the diet, and shellfish were eaten.

Salt was not used in cooking but a lump was licked between mouthfuls of food. It was an article of commerce. Chicha, a beer made of maize or fruit juices, was the principal drink.

VILLAGES AND HOUSES

The people lived in towns which the Europeans named after the principal chiefs or caciques. Some of the towns had as many as 1,500 people. They were compactly built and often fortified. The log palisades or fences, which usually sprouted and grew into high dense hedges, were said to be intended to keep out wild animals, but the Spaniards found them effective barriers to military operations.

Oviedo y Valdés reports round houses with vertical walls and a conical roof. Chiefs' houses were of great size and were divided into many rooms. Espinosa states that he fed his expeditionary force for 4 months on the provisions discovered in the residence of the Chieftain Natá. These stores included the smoked carcasses of 300 deer, dried fish, and fowl.

Houses were furnished with hammocks or low benches which were used as beds. The beds were made up with cotton blankets or possibly sheets of bark cloth. Baskets with lids, a great variety of pottery, gourds, metates, and possibly wooden log mortars were part of the equipment of every house.

CLOTHING AND ORNAMENTS

It is probable that the common people went naked or nearly so. The caciques and other influential men were dressed in cotton cloaks studded with gold plaques. Archeological evidence adds small decorated aprons to the list of garments. The women wore a cotton skirt or apron, reaching at least to the knees. Information from eastern Panamá suggests that possibly longer skirts were worn by women of rank.

Except for the bearded warriors of the town of Escoría, both sexes everywhere removed all the facial and body hair. Everyone painted and tattooed himself. Tattooing indicated rank, and each chief had his own device, which was likewise used by his subjects. There were also special marks for slaves. Outstanding articles of personal adornment were various types of jewelry and precious stones, helmets of gold, greaves, circlets, feather headdresses, nose plugs, stone, bone, and gold ear spools of several types, necklaces, and pendants of metal, stone, and carved bone. Apparently some of these ornaments were worn only by persons of rank as both insignia and identifying ornaments.

MANUFACTURES

All industries were well developed, and the people had a plentiful supply of cloth, baskets, carved wooden tools and ornaments, pottery, and such. Metalworking was very highly developed, and many techniques of casting, plating, soldering, and cold-hammering were known and used in making the most intricate ornaments.

Fire was made with three sticks, two of which were lashed together and placed on the ground. The point of the third stick or drill was set in the notch between the two and rotated between the palm of the hand.

SOCIAL AND POLITICAL ORGANIZATION

Native communities were divided into four social classes. The supreme chiefs, such as Parita, Natá, and Escoria, exercised despotic authority and lived in great luxury with many wives and retainers. They were surrounded by a nobility, who won their titles in battle or inherited them if they dedicated themselves to war. These men had subjects and property of their own, often living in their separate villages, subject to the call of their head chief. Of the common people little is known except that they were allowed to marry into the nobility. Slaves were prisoners of war. Their faces were either branded or tatooed, and a front tooth was often extracted. In spite of its complexity this society seems to have been less developed than the most advanced cultures in South America and Meso-America.

WARFARE

War was a recognized activity of a large portion of the male population, and all the towns supported a permanent army. Weapons were bows and arrows, darts, and spears. Statements that the arrows were not poisonous are direct and precise. Spear throwers to project darts are recorded from Darién (Oviedo y Valdés, 1851–55) but curiously not from the Savanna. As they occur in the protohistoric graves, it is possible that the 16th-century Indians knew and used them. Clubs are illustrated in the gold figures from the region, but the Spaniards make no specific reference to them.

BALL GAME

These Indians had a native ball court (juego de pelota), which, however, definitely was not of Mexican or Central American type, for it was compared to the *Arawak* ball courts seen by the Spaniards in the West Indies. a type which differs radically from those of the mainland. In Panamá the ball court was reported from the base of the Asuero Peninsula, in the land governed by Cacique Jabraba.

CEREMONIAL LIFE

Of ritual associated with such functions as birth, puberty, marriage, divorce, dances, games, war, and religion little can be said except that no detailed account has come down to us. The complex symbolism found on archeological objects together with the meager observations of the Spaniards, however, suggests a rich development.

BURIAL

No descriptions of the disposal of the corpses of common people have come to light. Burial in the ground was a right which may have been confined to the chiefs, nobility, and their wives and retainers. In 1519 the Spaniards discovered and described the body of the Cacique Parita prepared for burial in sumptuous array, including gold ornaments which weighed 355 pounds. The most famous burial ground, today known as Sitio Conte, is situated on the Río Grande de Coclé. Here the graves of important men in protohistoric times have been exhumed. (See Lothrop, this volume, p. 147.)

BIBLIOGRAPHY

Espinosa, 1514, 1516, 1519; Oviedo y Valdés, 1851–55; Lothrop, 1937.

THE CUNA[1]

By DAVID B. STOUT

CULTURE

SUBSISTENCE ACTIVITIES

Farming.—Agriculture, almost exclusively men's work among the *San Blas Cuna,* is carried on by slash-and-burn methods in which a dibble is used. The modern crops grown are bananas, plantain, corn, rice, yams, sweet manioc,[2] sweetpotatoes, sugarcane, peppers, tobacco, and pineapples. In addition, coconut, cacao, orange, lime, mango, papaya, avocado, and coffee trees and bushes are tended.

Hunting.—Hunting, now a distinctly secondary activity and not engaged in by all the men, was once the object of expeditions composed of men and some women, who traveled in search of game for varying lengths of time. Peccaries are hunted by individuals or by the surround method, and pitfalls are occasionally built near the fields to catch tapirs. Other quarry consists of agoutis, iguanas, squirrels, two species of monkeys, deer, and several species of birds. Dogs are sometimes used as a hunting aid. The weapons employed are bows and arrows, blowguns, spears, and shotguns.

Fishing.—Fishing is done with nets, spears, bows and pronged arrows, and weirs and harpoons, the last probably borrowed from the Negroes. Decoys are used in catching the sea turtles in stationary nets (fig. 58).

FIGURE 58.—*Cuna* sea turtle decoy. (Approximate length 32 cm. (12½ in.)). (After Nordenskiöld, 1938, fig. 31.)

---

[1] See maps 2 and 5. The cultural data here refer to the modern *Cuna* unless an earlier period is indicated.

[2] Poisonous manioc was reported for the *Cuna* in the late 17th century but without details of the method used in pressing the poison from it.

Domesticated animals.—Dogs, pigs, chickens, and cats are the only domesticated animals. Pigs and chickens are kept more for trade purposes than as a direct source of food. Some individuals keep captive birds and monkeys for pets.

Food preparation.—Bananas, plantains, sugarcane, fish, corn, and rice are the principal items. Fish, bananas, and plantains are usually boiled, separately or together, as a mush, which is seasoned with salt and lime juice. Bananas, plantains, and the tuberous foods are also baked. Meat is roasted or, if there is a surplus, smoked. Fish also is smoked. One unfermented beverage is composed of sugarcane juice, roasted corn meal, cacao, and water; another, of mashed plantains or bananas, cacao, and water. These gruels form the usual breakfast and serve as snacks during the day and around nightfall. The principal meal of the day is taken in the early afternoon, when the boiled, roasted, or smoked foods are eaten.

VILLAGES AND HOUSES

The *San Blas Cuna* live in compact villages composed of regular rows of houses along one or more streets. The *Mainland Cuna* live in smaller villages along the riverbanks. The houses are rectangular with thatched roofs and palm-wood slat or cane walls. Most are built directly on the ground, though some at the eastern end of the *Cuna* territory are raised on piles. Many contain a loft reached by a notched-log ladder. Every dwelling has a smaller cook house, constructed either separately or as an extension of the main house.

Interior furnishings of the dwellings include hammocks, low, 1-piece wooden seats (pl. 49, *a*, *b*), looms, and a storage platform. Temporary partitions are constructed for ceremonial purposes, and permanent ones are found in the dwellings of the shamans. The central feature of the cook house is a 3-log fireplace, around which are kept the cooking utensils.

DRESS AND ORNAMENTS

Clothing.—Clothing at the time of the Conquest consisted of penis cover of shell, reed, or gold and, for the women, a cloth skirt extending to the knees or ankles. Late in the 17th century the men were described as wearing the penis cover and also a loose cloth garment containing neck and arm holes. This was put on over the head. Since then, particularly since about 1870, men have adopted European-style shirts and trousers, and women have added a trade-cloth blouse (pl. 49, *d*, *g*) made with appliqué techniques of intricate design. Of the feather girdles or aprons and feather-decorated crowns of the late 17th century, only the latter are still in use. These are composed of a basketry band with four upright tufts of feathers and a brim of shorter feathers. They are worn by the ceremonial leaders (pl. 50, *a*).

Tattooing and painting.—Tattooing, now no longer practiced, once was used to indicate status. Slaves were tattooed with a property mark. Face and body painting late in the 17th century was described as a woman's art. It was elaborate and included the use of red, yellow, and blue pigments. Warriors painted their faces red. Now only a few simple dots and lines are worn by women on their noses and faces. All the *Cuna* paint red spots on their palms, soles, and cheeks.

Miscellaneous ornaments.—The*Cuna* used nose and ear ornaments, breast pendants, gold cuffs, greaves, headdresses, and helmets. None of these have been found archeologically in the *Cuna* or *Cueva* area, though it seems very likely that they were similar in design to those found at Coclé (Lothrop, 1937). The men's large gold nose plates and ear plates and the women's gold nose rings described late in the 17th century survive in part in the nose rings and disk-shaped ear pendants worn by women of the present time. Likewise, the many-stranded necklaces of animal teeth (including those of the jaguar) and shells described for the same period are still used, but on a much smaller scale. They have been largely replaced with heavy necklaces of coins and glass beads and are now worn only by the women. In recent years the women have taken to wearing constricting rows of beads around the ankles, above the calf, around the wrist, and just below the elbow.

TRANSPORTATION

Canoes.—The *San Blas Cuna* oceangoing dugout, equipped with jib and triangular mainsail, is a post-Columbian development of the aboriginal long, narrow dugout with platform ends. This latter type is still used by some *San Blas* individuals when ascending the rivers of the mainland and is universal among the *Mainland Cuna* groups. It is propelled with crutch-handled paddles and with poles.

Carrying devices.—Articles are transported in large baskets slung on the back with a tumpline. Also, balanced loads are placed on opposite ends of a fore-and-aft carrying pole, which rests on the shoulder. Such poles are occasionally used in pairs.

MANUFACTURES

Bark cloth.—Bark cloth, though known to the *Cuna,* seems never to have been used extensively.

Weaving and cordage.—Until recently one of the major feminine occupations has been the manufacture of cordage from several bast fibers combined with cotton. Cotton cloth is woven on the vertical (*"Arawak"*) type of loom. Hammocks are still woven but now almost exclusively with trade string.

Basketry.—Basketry techniques are used in making fire fans, trays, telescoping envelopes, and many sizes of hemispherical and cylindrical containers. The weaves employed are twilling and wickerwork, often with one series of elements colored black (pl. 49, *f*). A coiled basketry technique has also been reported but is seldom used.

Gourds and calabashes.—Containers made of calabashes are employed as food dishes, cups, and water vessels and for storage of clothing and ornaments. The orifice of storage gourds is closed with a smaller inverted calabash held in place with strings. These calabash articles were formerly painted in several colors.

Ceramics.—Nothing is known of the aboriginal pottery of the *Cuna*, and no archeological specimens can be definitely assigned to this tribe. At present pottery techniques are used only in making anthropomorphic and zoomorphic figurines and braziers (pl. 49, *c, e*) used in the various ceremonies and in conjunction with medicine chants. This pottery is coiled; it is coarse and unevenly fired. The *Cuna* obtain large pottery chicha jars by trade from Colombia.

Rubber.—It is very doubtful whether the aboriginal *Cuna* ever used rubber.

Metallurgy.—Nothing is known of the techniques employed in making the gold ornaments described in the 16th and 17th centuries. The present-day gold ornaments are obtained from traders.

Stone objects.—No objects are made of stone, though many households possess a simple stone metate and mano which have been found on the old village sites or cemeteries.

Weapons.—Bows and arrows are used, the latter unfeathered and having a blunt, single or composite point. Spears and, recently, single-barrel shotguns are also used. If the *Cueva* are taken to be ancestral to the *Cuna*, then the spear thrower was also once a major weapon, though it has not been described for the *Cuna* area since early in the 16th century (Oviedo y Valdés, 1851–55, vol. 3, pt. 29, ch. 26, pp. 127, 129). The blowgun with poisoned darts does not appear to be aboriginal among the *Cuna*, but rather to have diffused to them from the neighboring *Chocó* during the historic period.

SOCIAL AND POLITICAL ORGANIZATION

The kinship system is bilateral and descriptive, with added age refinements.

Marriage is now almost exclusively monogamous, though polygynous marriages are allowed. The early accounts frequently noted that polygyny was usual among the leading men. There is very little intermarriage between the *Mainland* and the *San Blas Cuna*, but within each of these subdivisions marrying in or out of the village or island is determined less by definite endogamous or exogamous rules than by convenience and other circumstances. In all cases marriage residence is matrilocal; thus each house contains a household composed of one or more conjugal family units related by marriage to a lineage of women.

The oldest male in each household is its head, and younger men who have married his daughters or granddaughters are subject to his authority. Any tendencies to tyranny in this system are counterbalanced, however, by the fact that no payment is made in contracting a marriage and no penalties are levied if divorce occurs. The wife of the household head exercises a small degree of authority over the other women—daughters and grandaughters—and through her husband considerable authority over the sons-in-law. Upon the death of the household head the oldest of his sons-in-law succeeds to authority if the several families remain under one roof. However, being free from service to their father-in-law, some or all families may set up separate establishments, usually in the same village. Should a man's wife die, he is free to leave his father-in-law's household and remarry elsewhere. Until he is remarried he usually spends the interim in his own father's household. The house itself is inherited in the female line. Croplands and personal possessions are inherited from parents to children and between siblings but never between spouses.

The organization of the *Cueva* and other Darién tribes was described in the 16th century as strongly stratified, the classes being chiefs, nobles, commoners, and slaves. This system has long since been altered, and today there are two loosely defined strata, between which there is considerable mobility. These strata are differentiated largely by degree of economic possessions and, among the *San Blas Cuna,* by degrees of conservatism and adherence to the older customs. Political power is now vested in village chiefs, who are elected by the men of the village. Each chief is assisted by two second chiefs and by several sherifflike officials who act as his messengers, agents, and official greeters for the village. The chief presides over meetings held every several nights, when he chants a sermon which contains many references to the mythology and legendary history. These serve as precepts for proper behavior or allegorical parallels drawn with reference to misdemeanors occurring in the village. Other village officials are the adviser, a treasurer, and several men in charge of ceremonial preparations.

The island villages of the *San Blas Cuna* are members of either of two political parties, each headed by a high chief, who is selected from among the village chiefs. Upon death of such a high chief the office shifts to another island with the election of his successor. Some of the *Mainland Cuna* villages are also affiliated with these two political parties. All this political organization has its roots in aboriginal practices, though some aspects of it, such as the treasurer and perhaps the sherifflike officials, have been added or at least intensified through contact with the early Spanish missions.

LIFE CYCLE

Childbirth.—Birth takes place within an improvised enclosure in the house, from which men and children are excluded. A midwife assists the laboring mother, and the child is born into a water-filled canoe placed beneath the hammock in which the mother lies. Outside of the enclosure a shaman sings the childbirth chants and supplies various medicines to the midwife according to her reports of progress. In addition to several food taboos observed by both husband and wife during pregnancy, the couvade is in force for 3 days after birth. Albino children have, in the past, often been killed at birth.

Albinos, who constitute about 0.7 percent of the *Cuna* population, are not permitted to intermarry, and many of them have difficulty in finding mates among the brown members of the tribe. They are looked upon as weak and incapable of the full duties of adulthood, although they are thought to be more intelligent and to possess the power of driving away, with a small bow and arrow, the demons that devour the sun or moon during eclipses.

Puberty ceremonies.—There are no puberty ceremonies for boys, but for girls there are two. At the first, held at the onset of puberty, the girl is placed in an enclosure for 4 days, during which her female relatives and their women friends pour great quantities of water over her, her hair is bobbed, and she is painted black. Chicha is brewed during the next several weeks to be drunk ceremonially with rum when a dance is held in her honor.

The second ceremony, held a year or more after puberty, is actually a debut, for it serves as formal notice that the girl is now marriageable. It is a 4-day ceremony, during which the girl is kept in an enclosure and her hair is cropped. For this ceremony her parents accumulate large quantities of food and the materials for making several large jars of chicha. The ceremony itself is composed of many episodes, chief of which are those devoted to making the rattles and flageolets and other ceremonial equipment, such as painted balsa-wood planks (fig. 59), which

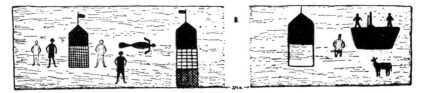

FIGURE 59.—*Cuna* painted balsa planks, which serve as mnemonic devices for leaders in girls' second ceremony (length 1.26 m. (4 ft. 1¼ in.)). (After Nordenskiöld, 1938, fig. 12.)

serve as mnemonic devices for the ceremonial chanters. The entire ceremony is under the direction of a leader whose position is achieved after years of training and assisting in ceremonies. It is his duty to sing the long chants relating to the origin of the debut ceremony. While doing so he lies in a hammock suspended in the center of the ceremonial house. The ceremony ends with a dance.

Two items occupy very prominent positions in this and the puberty ceremony: long cigars and the braziers (pl. 49, c, e) in which cacao beans are burned. The braziers are kept in constant use and are tended by assistants. Each step of the ceremony is punctuated with chicha drinking and with use of the cigars, which are placed with the lit end in the mouth and blown so that the smoke passes over the face of the various leaders and their assistants. This use of cigars was first described in the 17th century (Wafer, 1903, pp. 102–103).

Burial customs.—At death the deceased is sewn up in a hammock. Close relatives and friends mourn for a day and a night. A chant by a special chanter is often sung to insure safe journey to heaven. On the second day the body is carried to the cemetery—on the mainland in the case of the *San Blas Cuna*—and is there mourned over all day while two men dig the grave. Then the hammock is slung on two stakes in the grave, personal possessions are placed with the body, and the grave is filled in. Food, utensils, and furniture are placed on top.

WARFARE

Little is known of the warfare of the *Cuna* or their ancestors in the early period. The chiefs and nobles were the warriors and one object of waging war was evidently to take slaves. One middle-17th-century source (Requejo Salcedo, 1908, p. 128) credits the *Cuna* with the practice of killing enemy males whose blood was believed to be drunk by the sun. A special title was accorded men who had killed 20 such victims. A late-17th-century account describes a war house in the center of each village. This was strongly built to withstand siege, for it had loopholes in the walls. That the *Cuna* were a warlike people is attested by the fact that neighboring groups, such as the *Chocó* and *Catío,* have a number of legends recounting skirmishes with the *Cuna* and by the numerous records pertaining to *Cuna* alliances with French and English pirates during the 17th and 18th centuries.

ESTHETIC AND RECREATIONAL ACTIVITIES

Art.—Present-day art is almost entirely limited to the basketry designs, the fetishes carved by the men, the mnemonic picture writings, and the elaborate multicolored appliqué designs on the women's blouses.

Games.—There are no organized competitive team games, and the play of the children evidently has always been largely an imitation of adult activities.

Dances.—There are ritual dances, most of which are imitations of animals, performed by individuals or small groups as episodes of the two ceremonies for girls. Group dances in which anyone may participate are held at the end of ceremonies. No singing or instrumental music accompanies the former type, but the ceremonial leader sometimes plays his flute or other men may play panpipes for the group dances.

Musical instruments.—The 16th-century sources ascribe large hollow-log drums and smaller skin-headed drums to the *Cueva* and others of Darién, and late in the 17th century the *Cuna* were described as having bamboo drums. All these have dropped out of the culture since then. Instruments still retained are calabash rattles with deer-bone handles (fig. 60, *d*), panpipes, simple end-blown flutes (fig. 60, *c*), flutes with an attached air duct made of a bamboo tube to which a quill mouthpiece is fastened with a black wax (fig. 60, *a*), sets of single pipes of varying lengths played individually (fig. 60, *b*), bird-bone plug-flutes worn as necklaces, (fig. 60, *e*), and flutes made of an armadillo skull and bird bone (pl. 50, *b*). Most of these instruments are made in two styles, one for individual playing and the other in pairs of different pitch which are played in duet. Much of the music played on these wind instruments is antiphonal.

Alcoholic beverages.—Chicha, one of the central features of the girls' ceremonies, is made from fermented maize or plantains mixed with sugar-cane juice. It is made and drunk only at ceremonies but is greatly enjoyed. Both sexes become quite intoxicated, and the women take considerable pains to revive their drunken husbands by swinging them in a hammock and sprinkling water on them.

RELIGION AND SHAMANISM

Everything in nature and all people are believed to have an indwelling spirit or soul. Souls of human beings are spoken of in both the singular and the plural. It is the abduction of one's soul that causes illness. Upon death the soul journeys to the afterworld. A second attribute of all animate things is a life principle, which leaves upon death. Some persons also ascribe this quality to certain inanimate objects, such as water, metal, and rocks. It is thought to have departed when these things boil away, rust, or are broken. A third attribute assigned to humans, animals, and evil spirits and demons is a power which manifests itself in sexual potency, braveness, and industriousness and which can be increased or decreased with medicines. Finally, all humans are thought to possess a varying number of predilections, faculties, abilities, and talents which are localized

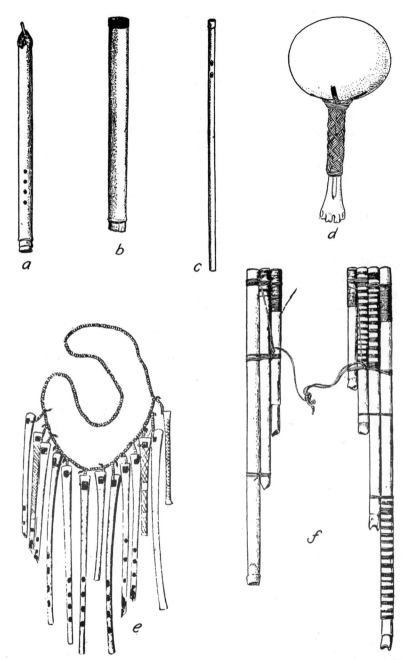

FIGURE 60.—*Cuna* musical instruments. *a,* Flute with attached air duct of bird quill. *b,* One of a set of single pipes, played in sets, one to a person. *c,* Simple end-blown flute used in ceremonies. (After Nordenskiöld, 1938, fig. 10.) *d,* Rattle used in girls' ceremonies. *e,* Necklace of plug-flutes made of a bird bone. (After Izikowitz, 1935, figs. 44 and 219.) *f,* Panpipes. (After Nordenskiöld, 1938, fig. 11.)

in the brain and which can be increased or decreased with medicines. Individual differences in skills and the sexual division of labor is rationalized on the basis of this fourth attribute.

The union of God and God's wife is the source of all things. A third deity, female in character, is in charge of the formation of human fetuses and endowing them with their attributes. These deities are never supplicated but are only addressed as creators in the various chants. God is omnipotent and omniscient, unforgiving, and stern of character. Death is predestined. It is still uncertain to what degree these conceptions of God and the supernatural world, the wooden fetishes, and the beliefs in predestination and punishment for sin are syncretisms of aboriginal, Catholic, and Huguenot beliefs. The design of the fetishes may possibly be ascribed to Negro influence.

The world is thought of as a plane beneath which there are eight layers of the underworld and above which there are eight layers of heaven. The fourth layer of the underworld is the abode of the chiefs of the evil spirits, and it is through this layer that the souls of dead persons journey on their way to heaven. Heaven now has special places in it for albinos and for brown Indians. There are special places for people who have died from various causes (Requejo Salcedo, 1908, pp. 132–133). The sky is thought of as hemispherical and is pierced at one point. Through this hole a legendary shaman once crawled and consequently became bald. The cosmography also includes a sun ship and moon ship which traverse the sky daily carrying certain evil spirits and demons.

Shamanism.—Shamans are of three sorts. The first and most numerous, to which both sexes may belong, are those who have learned the chants and medicines for curing specific illnesses. In most cases curing involves the recovery of the patient's soul, which has been abducted. The recovery is effected by means of a wooden fetish (pl. 51, a–e), the soul of which is addressed in a chant and instructed to retrieve the patient's soul from the evil spirit. These fetishes are named according to the kind of wood from which they are carved. Different illnesses are cured by specific woods. The design of the fetishes is incidental, though stereotyped. Pepper pods and cacao beans are burned in braziers during the chants. The shamans often use mnemonic picture writings to assist them in learning the chants. Many also carry a staff surmounted with a fetish figure (pl. 50, c).

The second type of shaman is much less numerous and specializes in curing whole villages stricken by epidemics. The evil spirit causing the epidemic is exorcised in a ceremony lasting for 8 days. The medicine man chants instructions to the souls of many large wooden fetishes (pl. 51, f, g). Braziers and long cigars are also used.

The third type of shaman is born to his status. He is usually a man, though a woman may attain this status if the proper signs (including a caul) are present at her birth. In any case, a long course of training is necessary to validate this position. It is also possible to vitiate these powers in a child by administering certain medicine. The abilities of this third type center about their close rapport with the supernatural world, particularly the evil spirits, enabling these persons to prognosticate, to find lost or stolen objects, and to diagnose illnesses with much greater accuracy than the lesser shamans. Their essential link with the supernatural world is the fetishes used either in dreams or while awake.

Nearly all medicinal and magical practices are beneficial. The few sorcerers in the population are either of the first or third type of shaman, who overdevelop their abilities and talents with medicines. By so doing they become unwitting agents of the evil spirits.

Evil spirits are everywhere in nature, and they cause all misfortunes. However, under some conditions the shamans may learn some cures from them. They are, like everything else in the world, the creation of God and serve as His agents of punishment as well as acting on their own accord.

MYTHOLOGY

The mythology, aside from the stories chronicling the creation by God, tells of how God destroyed the world by fire, darkness, and flood because the people sinned. The flood occurred 800 years ago, and after it there appeared a great personage who came to earth on a plate of gold and taught the people how to behave, what to name things, and how to use them. He was followed by a number of disciples who spread his teachings, and who, in turn, were followed by 10 great shamans, one of them a woman. These shamans had great powers over the elements. They investigated the underworld and heavens and discovered many medicines. These exploits grade into accounts of legendary chiefs and heroes who led the *Cuna* in their wars with the Spaniards and who led whole villages of the *San Blas Cuna* down from the mountains and out onto the islands.

Combined with the myths are a number of tales in which animals are involved. One of these recounts the felling of the World Tree at the behest of one of the principal culture heroes. The people attempted to cut it down, but each time they left it a giant frog healed the cut overnight. After two such attempts the culture hero bade his brother to kill the frog, whereupon the tree was felled and from its top came fresh and salt water, croplands, plants, reptiles, mammals, fishes, and birds. Other animal tales involve pairs of adversaries, one of whom wins out through trickery.

LORE AND LEARNING

Knowledge of the medicines and medicine chants, the girls' ceremony chants, and the mythology is in the care of the various types of medicine men and the ceremonial leaders. It is all passed on to their pupils during long courses of training for which the pupils pay in labor or goods. Familiarity with this body of knowledge brings considerable prestige and is prerequisite to being elected chief or second chief. The picture writings (pl. 52) in which some of the mythological motifs are recorded and which serve as mnemonic devices for the medicine and ceremony chants may be a survival from aboriginal times. Nowadays they are made with colored crayons on paper. They are not standardized, for most men cannot read another man's picture writings. Some symbols stand for whole lines of the chants, others for single words or names of plants, animals, or objects. The medicines, most of which are made from plants or stones mixed with water, are administered internally or by bathing in them. They are usually based on a sympathetic or imitative principle They are prescribed and sold by the shamans and are used in connection with the curing chants or at intervals after such chants. Surgery is not practiced. In the 17th century, venesection bows were used (Wafer, 1903, p. 54), but this practice has disappeared.

The numerical system is decimal-vigesimal, there being a separate name for each unit up to 10, then 10 plus 1, 10 plus 2, etc., up to 20, which is named "tule" (human). Thereafter, units and 10's plus units are suffixed to 20; 40 is reckoned as two 20's, etc. The present-day numerical system has undoubtedly been expanded through the necessity for counting large numbers of coconuts. In measuring small spaces, hand span, arm length, etc., are used. Croplands are estimated in terms of the number of banana plants they will hold.

BIBLIOGRAPHY

Andagoya, 1865; Gassó, 1910–14; Krieger, 1926; Lehmann, 1920; Linné, 1929; Lothrop, 1937; Nordenskiöld, 1928 a, 1928 b, 1938; Oviedo y Valdés, 1851–55; Requejo Salcedo, 1908; Stout, MS.; Wafer, 1903; Wassén, 1934, 1937, 1938, 1940 a, 1940 b.

PLATE 49.—**Cuna artifacts.** *a, b*, Wooden seats. *d, g*, Women's appliqué blouses. (After Krieger, 1926, pls. 4 and 26.) *c, e*, Pottery braziers used in ceremonies (height of *e*, approximately 16 cm. (6¼ in.).) (After Nordenskiöld, 1938, figs. 13 and 14.) *f*, Basket with one series cf elements colored black with a wax (height, approximately 22 cm. (8⅝ in.).) (After Nordenskiöld, 1928 a, pl. 145.)

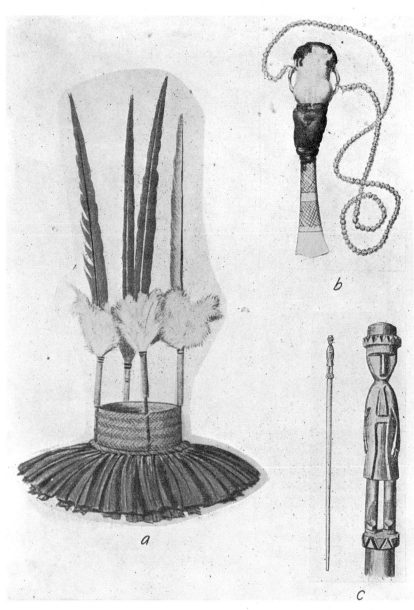

PLATE 50.—**Cuna ceremonial objects.** *a*, Leader's feather headdress (height, 90 cm. (35¼ in.)). (After Wassén, 1938, pl. 1.) *b*, Flute of armadillo skull and bird bones. (After Izikowitz, 1935, fig. 134.) *c*, Shaman's tutelary staff (drawing at left, 1 m. (3 ft. 3 in.) in height). (After Nordenskiöld, 1938, fig. 29.)

PLATE 51.—**Cuna wooden fetishes.** *a–e*, Fetishes used to recover souls (respective heights: 22 cm. (8⅝ in.), 32 cm. (12½ in.), 22 cm. (8⅝ in.), 24 cm. (9½ in.), 30 cm. (11¾ in.)). (After Nordenskiöld, 1938, figs. 25 and 26.) *f, g*, Fetishes used in mass curing ceremony or village exorcism (respective heights: 1.63 m. (4 ft. 7½ in.) and 1.73 m. (4 ft. 11¾ in.)). (After Wassén, 1938, fig. 26.)

PLATE 52.—**Cuna mnemonic picture writing.** Section of a manuscript made by a shaman. It illustrates the beginning of a fever-curing chant in which certain stones are the curing agent. (After Nordenskiöld, 1938, pl. 7.)

THE CHOCO[1]

By David B. Stout

CULTURE

SUBSISTENCE ACTIVITIES

The relative importance of agriculture and hunting and fishing varies with the environment in which the several *Chocó* groups live. Agriculture is limited to food crops—plaintains, bananas, sweet manioc, sugarcane, maize, and several fruit trees. No tobacco or cotton is grown.

Deer, peccaries, armadillos, agoutis, monkeys, and several species of birds are hunted with the bow and arrow and blowgun, and fish are caught with nets, spears, bows and arrows, and poisons.

Domestic animals are dogs, pigs, chickens, and ducks.

VILLAGES AND HOUSES

Dwellings are erected on piles and are scattered along the rivers. These houses are round and lack walls. The apex of the roof is often surmounted with a clay vessel (pl. 53, *a*). Several platforms for sleeping and storage are raised above the floor level. Hammocks are used only for children. Adults sleep on a pallet of bark cloth with their heads on wooden pillows. Other furniture includes 1-piece wooden seats (fig. 61) and mosquito nets.

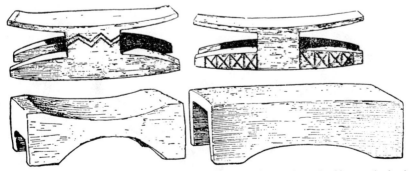

FIGURE 61.—*Chocó* wooden seats and headrests. (Approximately ⅛ actual size.) (After Wassén, 1935, fig. 10.)

[1] See map 6. The cultural data refer to the present day unless an earlier period is indicated.

DRESS AND ORNAMENTS

Women wear a wrap-around skirt; men, a loincloth held in place with a string. On occasion men also wear broad glass-bead girdles, crossed sashes of glass beads on their chest, necklaces of teeth or silver beads, silver earplugs (fig. 62, *c*), ear pendants, and sometimes silver cuffs and headbands. Silver nose ornaments are only occasionally worn now, though once they were common adornment of the men. Women wear necklaces of teeth but few or no silver ornaments. Both sexes wear flowers in their hair on festive occasions and frequently paint themselves with solid colors (fig. 62, *a*) or with red and dark blue designs applied with a 3- or 4-tined wooden fork (fig. 62, *b*) and with carved wooden

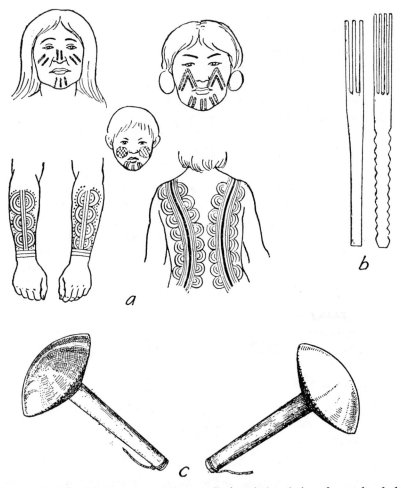

FIGURE 62.—*Chocó* body ornamentation. *a*, Body painting design; *b*, wooden forks for applying body paints (½ actual size); *c*, wooden earplugs covered with silver (½ actual size). (After Wassén, 1935, figs. 15, 14.)

stamps (pl. 53, *c*). Feather ornaments are not used. During ceremonies the *Northern Chocó* and *Catío* men wear woven crowns decorated with upstanding, painted strips of wood (pl. 53, *b*).

TRANSPORTATION

Most traveling is done in long, narrow dugout canoes which have platform ends. The *Chocó* move about considerably within their territory, seeking new sites for their fields or performing obligations incurred by marriage between distantly located families. Men, particularly the shamans, travel great distances, even visiting the *Cayapa* in Ecuador.

MANUFACTURES

Bark cloth.—Until recently, bark cloth was beaten out of bark with a grooved mallet (pl. 53, *d, e*) and decorated with painted designs.

Basketry.—Basketry is of many types and designs, most of it being of twilled (pl. 54, *e, f*) and wicker technique (pl. 54, *d*), though coiled varieties are also made (fig. 63).

Weaving.—Weaving has not been reported from the *Chocó* during the past several hundred years.

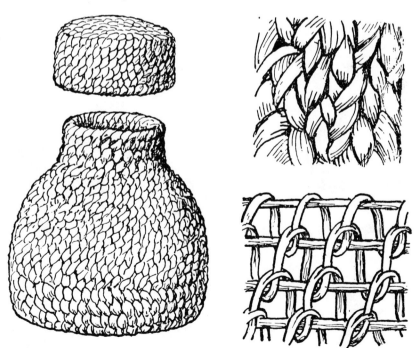

Figure 63.—*Chocó* coiled basket. Technical detail at right. (Basket is slightly enlarged; detail approximately 3 times actual size.) (After Wassén, 1935, fig. 22.)

Calabashes.—Calabashes, frequently decorated with incised geometric and realistic designs, are used for storage and as dishes (pl. 54, *c*).

Ceramics.—Coiled pottery is made in a variety of shapes, often of anthropomorphic or zoomorphic design (figs. 64 and 65).

Metallurgy.—Some of the silver ornaments are cold-hammered from coins or from silver obtained from traders.

Weapons.—Bows and arrows are used. The latter are unfeathered and fitted with single or multiple points or with blunt heads. Blowguns are made of two grooved strips of wood wound with bast fiber and fitted with a sight. The poison darts are carried in a bamboo quiver to which is attached a calabash stuffed with light, fluffy fiber to be twisted on the dart shaft. Two poisons are used: (1) a vegetable poison, with a spe-

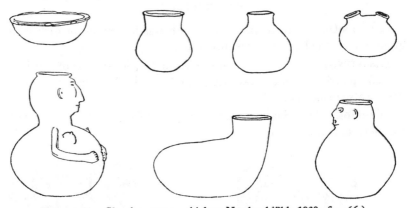

FIGURE 64.—*Chocó* pottery. (After Nordenskiöld, 1930, fig. 66.)

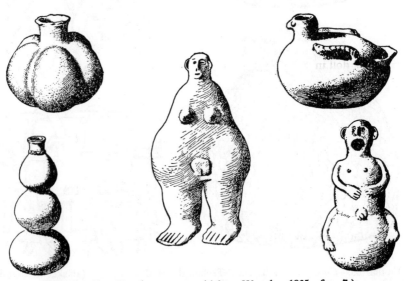

FIGURE 65.—*Chocó* pottery. (After Wassén, 1935, fig. 7.)

cific cardiac effect, the first to be reported for the New World[2]; and (2) an animal poison, made by heating the exudation of the skin of a certain species of frog, which evidently paralyzes the respiratory muscles (Wassén, 1935, pp. 90–108).

SOCIAL AND POLITICAL ORGANIZATION

All three groups of *Chocó* appear to be exogamous, though to what extent is not known. Aside from this exogamy, there is also obligatory exogamy in reference to patrilineal lineages which may be clans.

Playful fighting between father-in-law and prospective son-in-law and between bride and groom appears to be the extent of marriage ceremonies. Marriage residence, ideally patrilocal, actually is alternately patrilocal and matrilocal, for women have ownership rights in some of the agricultural plots; consequently they and their husbands periodically return to the woman's parents' house to work her land. Thus each household, composed of several conjugal family units, has a constantly shifting membership. Monogamy prevails but polygyny is permitted. The oldest male in a household is regarded as its head and spokesman and may even direct community activities. There appears never to have been permanent chiefs wielding political power over large numbers or over large areas. The war leaders of former times seem to have been simply temporary leaders chosen for their prowess.

LIFE CYCLE

Childbirth.—Childbirth takes place in the forest. Men may not be present. No particular ceremony surrounds it among the *Northern* and *Southern Chocó*, though the *Catío* mother takes a series of four baths beginning the fourth day after parturition. Some days after birth the child is painted entirely black. A year or so after birth a ceremony is held in which the shaman procures a guardian spirit for the child and gives it a doll in which the spirit lives (fig. 66, *c, d*).

Puberty.—There is no puberty ceremony for boys. At their first menstruation girls are secluded in the house. They must observe food taboos and must not scratch their heads with their fingers but instead use a short stick.

Death.—Burial practices have not been described for the *Northern* and *Southern Chocó*, but the *Catío* place their dead in a horizontal chamber reached by a vertical hole in the earth (Severino de Santa Teresa, 1924, p. 113).

ESTHETIC AND RECREATIONAL ACTIVITIES

Art.—Much of *Chocó* art is religious or magical in nature, for the bulk of it occurs in the pottery and numerous wooden objects used in the

---

[2] The South American curare poisons differ from the poison of the *Chocó*. The latter contains a glucoside as its active ingredient.

various ceremonies. The elaborate designs painted on the body (fig. 62, *a*) are used particularly at ceremonies. Some of the sculptured wooden fetishes are very similar to those of the *Cuna*.

Games and toys.—Games and toys include simple tops, musical tops, wooden dolls, bull-roarers, and buzz disks (fig. 66, *b–f*).

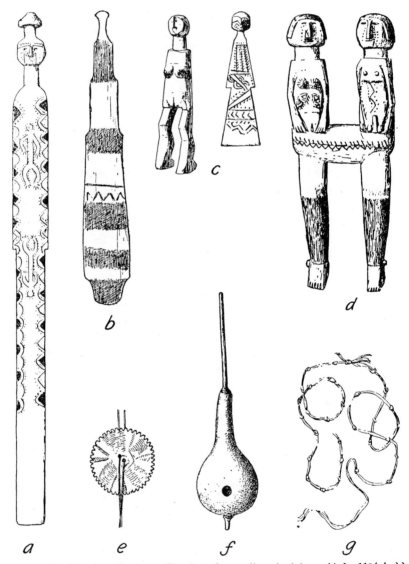

FIGURE 66.—*Chocó* artifacts. *a*, Tutelary figure (length, 1.6 m. (4 ft. 11½ in.)); *b*, bull roarer (length, 32 cm. (12½ in.)); *c, d*, children's dolls containing tutelary spirits (⅛ actual size); *e*, buzz-disk; *f*, musical top (both ¼ actual size); *g*, quipu—the closely spaced knots represent knives, the others hatchets (¼ actual size). (After Wassén, 1935, figs. 33, 12, 11, and 35.)

Musical instruments.—Musical instruments include panpipes, end-blown flutes, simple pipes blown individually by several men at once, single- and double-headed skin drums, and canoe-shaped wooden gongs (pl. 56, *left*) suspended at one end and beaten with two short clubs.

Drinks and narcotics.—Chicha is used in the ceremonies. A drug, made probably from *Datura sanguinea*, is used to induce dreams (Wassén, 1935, pp. 101–102).

RELIGION

The religion embraces a godlike culture hero, who is, however, not supplicated and has little concern with the daily affairs of the people. There are also a great many good and evil spirits. Some of these spirits are the souls of the good and bad persons who have died. Everyone is thought to have two souls; one goes to heaven and the other remains on earth.

Shamanism.—Shamans are important in the religious life. They pass through a period of training, during which they make wooden ships (pl. 55, *b*) on which are placed numerous sculptured figures representing various spirits. These are quite similar to the *Cuna* sun and moon ships. They acquire a helping or guardian spirit which dwells in a fetish-staff. The shamans cure the sick and practice various types of witchcraft.

Sick persons are believed to be possessed by evil spirits. A patient to be cured is placed in a little hut made of wooden slats (pl. 55, *a*). Representations of the evil spirits are painted on his back and on wooden slats hung nearby (pl. 55, *c*). The shaman exorcises the evil spirits with the aid of chants and the spirit dwelling in his fetish-staff. During these incantations, as well as those used when a tutelary spirit is obtained for the infants, chicha stored in zoomorphic and anthropomorphic jars is drunk. An important episode in the ceremonies is the consecration of the chicha by the shaman. The chicha drinking does not, however, have the character of a drinking bout.

MYTHOLOGY

The *Chocó* and *Cuna* have a creation myth in which the World Tree is cut down. The tree is the source of much in the world. There are myths and legends recounting *Chocó* skirmishes with the *Cuna* (Wassén, 1935, pp. 122–123, 125–128), in which mention is made that the *Chocó* once had thorny palisades around their houses. In addition, there are several legends pertaining to the time the *Chocó* were enslaved by the Spaniards, and one tale, in which balsa rafts are mentioned, recounts some fighting with tribes to the south (Wassén, 1935, pp. 142–145).

LORE AND LEARNING

Simple quipus are used to keep count of days and months and for recording quantities of small objects (fig. 66, *g*).

BIBLIOGRAPHY

Krickeberg, 1922; Krieger, 1926; Lehmann, 1920; Nordenskiöld, 1928 a, 1929; Severino de Santa Teresa, 1924; Wassén, 1933, 1935, 1940 b.

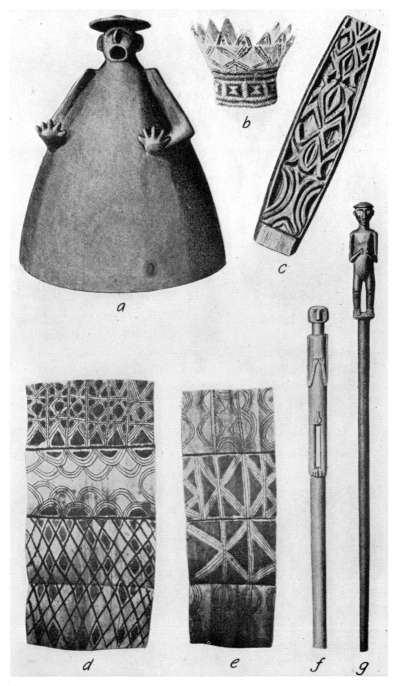

PLATE 53.—**Chocó artifacts.** *a*, Pottery roof-apex cap (height, approximately 1 m. (3 ft. 3 in.)). (After Nordenskiöld, 1928 a, pl. 96.) *b*, Shaman's crown of painted wood and basketry. (After Krieger, 1926, pl. 23.) *c*, Wooden stamp for applying body paints (height, approximately 26 cm. (10¼ in.)). (After Nordenskiöld, 1928 a, fig. 35.) *d*, *e*, Painted bark cloth. (After Kreiger, 1926, pl. 19.) *f*, *g*, Shaman's fetish staff (*f*, incomplete; *g*, length, 47 cm. (18½ in.)). (After Wassén, 1940 a, fig. 1.)

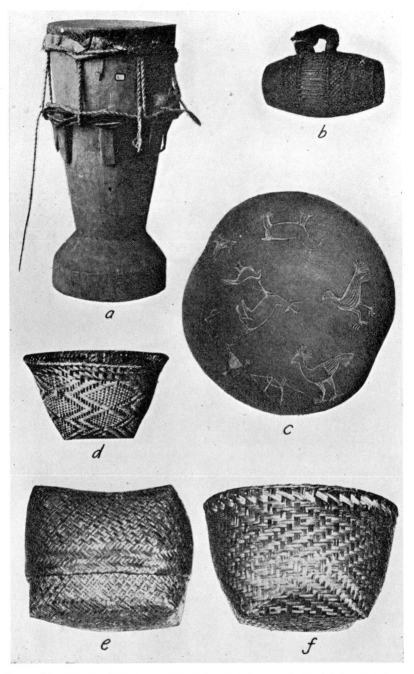

PLATE 54.—**Chocó artifacts.** *a*, Single-headed drum. *b*, Double-headed drum. (After Krieger, 1926, pl. 7.) *c*, Incised calabash (diameter, approximately 35 cm. (13¾ in.)). (After Nordenskiöld, 1928 a, fig. 22.) *d*, Wickerwork basket (height, approximately 15 cm. (6 in.)). *e*, *f*, Twilled baskets (height of each, approximately 13 cm. (5¼ in.)). (After Wassén, 1935, figs. 19, 20.)

PLATE 55.—**Chocó artifacts.** *a*, Curing hut (height, approximately 1 m. (3 ft. 3 in.)). (After Nordenskiöld, 1928 a, pl. 52.) *b*, Shaman's wooden model ships with spirits aboard (length, approximately 50 cm. (19½ in.)). (After Wassén, 1935, fig. 34.) *c*, Painted slats of wood used in curing ceremonies (length, approximately 40 cm. (15¾ in.)). (After Nordenskiöld, 1928 a, fig. 53.)

PLATE 56.—**Chocó Indians.** *Left:* A canoe-shaped wooden gong. (After Nordenskiöld, 1930, fig. 15.) *Right:* Harpooning a manatee. Harpoon has a balsa float. Río Salaqui, Atrato drainage. (Courtesy John Verrill by permission of the Bureau of American Ethnology, Smithsonian Institution.)

THE CAYAPA AND COLORADO

By John Murra

INTRODUCTION

The *Cayapa* and the *Colorado* are the last surviving Indian groups in the lush western lowlands of Ecuador (maps 1 and 6). Once an area of extensive Indian occupation, western Ecuador is now inhabited by a Spanish-speaking population of mixed Indian, Negro, and white ancestry, known as montuvios. The *Cayapa* and *Colorado* have precariously managed to hang on to their jungle homes. Speaking closely related if mutually unintelligible languages of the *Barbacoan* division of the *Chibchan* family, they represent the southernmost extension of that major division. Comparative studies with other *Chibchan*-speaking groups in Highland and eastern Colombia, with *Quechua*-speaking Indians in Highland Ecuador, and with various Montaña groups should prove of considerable culture-historical interest.

THE CAYAPA

The *Cayapa* are a riverain people inhabiting the lowlands of northwestern Ecuador. Sprinkled through the jungles of Esmeraldas Province, an area of difficult colonization and control, they managed for centuries to avoid the enslavement suffered by their Highland neighbors or the ethnic annihilation of most Coast aborigines. Only in the past few decades have their settlements been pushed back into the hills by Spanish-speaking montuvio and Negro homesteaders. World War II requirements in balsa wood, rubber, and other tropical commodities have accelerated this process of displacement and acculturation.

The Cayapa River and its affluents, from the mouth of the Anzole to the foot of the Andes, are the main area of *Cayapa* settlement. Barrett (1925) found three concentration spots: Punta Venado, Sapayo Grande, and San Miguel, corresponding to three political, tribal divisions, which might since have shifted or amalgamated. In addition, small groups of *Cayapa,* in various degrees of acculturation, are found in the Santiago Valley and along the coast into Colombia. Estimates of their numbers vary but hover around a mean of 2,000.

The chief source and authority on the *Cayapa* remains S. A. Barrett's monograph (1925). Barrett visited them in 1908–9, long enough to bring back an exhaustive account of their subsistence pattern and material culture as well as considerable data on religion and ceremonial life. According to modern interests, the report is weak in life-cycle data and economics, and a serious drawback is the almost complete lack of comparative considerations. Moreover, it describes a culture with marked European influences. Nevertheless, at this writing, it remains one of our most complete accounts of an aboriginal South American group. The remaining titles in the bibliography refer to linguistic treatises, hearsay accounts, and phantasies of hurried travelers.

The inaccessibility of their habitat facilitated the *Cayapa's* survival into the 20th century, but it also prevented most chroniclers from visiting their land. Early references to naked and painted Indians living along the Patia River in large houses on tall poles and wearing gold ornaments might refer to the *Cayapa* or to some other *Chibchan* people. Jijón y Caamaño (1940–45, vol. 2) has reproduced fragments from an unpublished Cabello Balboa chronicle discussing the people of Esmeraldas Province during the 16th century. Among the peoples figuring prominently in Cabello Balboa's report are the *Nigua*, an Indian group inhabiting traditional *Cayapa* territory. Jijón y Caamaño's suggestion (1940–45, vol. 2) that the *Nigua* and *Cayapa* are one people seems tentatively acceptable.

Both peoples claimed to have descended from the Andean Highlands, though it is unclear if they were refugees from the *Inca* or Spanish invasions. As reported by Barrett, this tradition is very strong even now, four centuries after the Conquest, permeating various divergent activities of the *Cayapa*, who date many techniques and artifacts in terms of pre- or post-migration practices. In 1907 Beuchat and Rivet had pointed to toponymic and archeological similarities between Esmeraldas Province and the *Cara* country in the Highlands. Later work by Jijón y Caamaño (1912, 1919, 1940–45, vol. 2) has strengthened the case for *Chibchan* affiliation of the *Cara* language and given a measure of confirmation to native tradition.

CULTURE

SUBSISTENCE ACTIVITIES

Agriculture is the main occupation of the *Cayapa*, although fishing and hunting supply a large percentage of their food. Each house is surrounded by clearings and fields, and additional clearings are customarily made away from the river, in the bush. Most families have fields of plantains, bananas, sugarcane, coca, and sweet manioc (yuca) ; in addition, cotton, tobacco, maize, yams, and pineapples are frequently cultivated. Many wild plants are encouraged through weeding and other care.

Plantains (pl. 60, *bottom, right*) form the staple food of the *Cayapa*, and each family will have several acres planted to this perennially ripening fruit. Bananas are fed to the hogs and cover an acreage almost as large as that of the plantain. Almost every family owns its cane mill and distillery, which are supplied by the omnipresent canefields.

With all this emphasis on agriculture, the *Cayapa* are, nevertheless, a jungle people, skilled hunters of many species of rodents, deer, felines, peccaries, armadillos, and birds. Life at the riverside encourages and is encouraged by dependence on fish, crustaceans, shellfish, and crocodile eggs. Under aboriginal conditions the *Cayapa* were probably never hungry.

Hogs and chickens are now kept everywhere. Dogs are not conspicuously reported.

Food is mostly boiled, though frequently meat will be broiled or baked. Surpluses are dried and smoked.

HOUSES AND VILLAGES

Though maps traditionally locate *Capaya* "villages," these are nothing but agglomerations of three or four houses and a church. The houses stand empty most of the year and are used only at holidays when the priests visit the *Cayapa*.

The actual habitations of the people are spread through the jungle, always at riversides (pl. 57, *top*) and usually isolated from one another by fields or even uncleared stretches. The houses stand on high poles 6 to 12 feet off the ground and are reached by removable ladders. The roof is thatched with palm leaves (pl. 57, *center*), and the rectangular house is virtually unenclosed. Sometimes the house floor is separated into two parts, one for cooking, the other for sleeping and eating. One chief had a large house (pl. 57, *bottom*) which could seat 40 people and which had more than two "rooms." The furniture is scanty: hammocks are used for sitting and sleeping, and wooden seats are sometimes found. An attempt by Barrett to correlate these seats with the famous stone seats of Manabi (Handbook, vol. 2, p. 780) seems very inconclusive.

In addition to permanent houses, small temporary ranchos are sometimes built when people are far from home. The houses in the "village" are standard structures, but the church follows Spanish ways: it rests on the ground and has walls.

CLOTHING AND ADORNMENT

Although *Cayapa* tradition records a period when the people wore blankets and even ponchos, today their clothes are scanty (pl. 59, *bottom*). The men wear a tight, small, white garment, made like bathing trunks, and a thin gaudy shirt of calico, with short and very tight sleeves. On festive occasions vests of European cut and manufacture are frequently donned over the shirt, and so are felt fedoras.

Women wear a long skirt of native cloth, girded with a narrow fringed belt. As in the Highlands, several skirts of different weights are sometimes worn. Head, shoulders, and chest are usually left bare.

Children wear no clothes at all until they are 6 or 8.

The hair is worn loose, long, and flowing by the women but is clipped above the ears by the men. Both sexes wear necklaces and wristbands of glass and porcelain beads, coins, seeds, and beetle wings. Only women wear earrings.

The traditional *Chibcha* custom of frequently painting body and face is found among the *Cayapa*. Red, yellow, and black are used, and the designs are very numerous. Barrett reproduces many of the motifs and insists that there is no special significance attached to any of them, nor is there any age, sex, or property correlation.

TRANSPORTATION

Watercraft.—A large part of every *Cayapa's* life is spent on the water fishing and traveling. Canoes are built with great skill and care. They can withstand not only fluvial but also maritime travel and are routinely sold in the "civilized" coast towns. They are dugouts, usually 10 to 12 yards long but sometimes much larger. Balsa-wood logs are sometimes used as outriggers.

MANUFACTURES

Details of *Cayapa* manufactures are contained in Barrett's work, which describes and illustrates finished products and minutely discusses the techniques of preparation.

Woodworking.—Woodworking includes house building, making deadfall traps, and carving seats and children's dolls.

Weaving and basketry.—The women weave cotton cloth on a narrow native loom, and the men do the sewing. The men also weave the fishing nets and hammocks. Barrett's discussion of *Cayapa* basketry is outstanding. The *Cayapa* make many kinds of baskets, mats, and fans of bark and of various roots.

Pottery.—Pottery is crude and undecorated. It is used particularly for storage. Tradition claims that in their old Highland habitat the *Cayapa* made better pottery but that calabashes have since largely replaced ceramics.

Stonework and metalwork.—Stonework is limited to the metates used in grinding corn and plantains. Although in aboriginal times Lowland Ecuador was a famous area of metallurgy, there is no evidence that the contemporary *Cayapa* practiced it.

Weapons.—The weapon most widely used today is the muzzle-loading shotgun. The blowgun was important in the past, but today its use is restricted to boys, who shoot poison darts while playing at hunting. Hardwood lances are being given up, and the bow and arrow is said not to be mentioned in *Cayapa* tradition. The steel machete is ubiquitous.

ECONOMICS

The *Cayapa* economic unit is the virtually self-sufficient, one-family household. Land is owned and worked familially, and there is as much land to be had as the family can clear. If any special rules govern distribution and inheritance, they are not reported by our sources. Also, there seem to be very few provisions for interhousehold cooperation: men will help a neighbor bring down a tree trunk from the hills, but all other activities are evidently left to individual enterprise.

This self-sufficiency does not apply to all spheres of activity. Machetes and rifles are essential in jungle life, and most families make at least one trip a year to the coast for trading and social purposes. In the small Ecuadorean and Colombian towns they find a ready market for rubber, tagua nuts, and other forest products. Cocoa is grown specifically for this trade. There is also a limited market for some of their manufactures: canoes, mats, fans, and other basketry. In exchange, the *Cayapa* want metal goods: axes, machetes, shotguns, fishhooks, fish spears, and copper tubing for their distilleries. But they also like beads and mirrors, pearls, vests, and old derby hats. In recent years machine-made muslins and calicoes have been edging out native-made cloth.

The *Cayapa* are not yet incorporated in Ecuadorean economy. Their need for metal goods and trinkets has not yet forced them to work on plantations or in placer gold mines. Their own supply of rum has helped them avoid debts contracted for alcohol, and they have usually retreated into the forest when their self-sufficiency has been menaced. It is improbable that this selective acculturation can last very long.

SOCIAL AND POLITICAL ORGANIZATION

The basic *Cayapa* social unit is the household. Though there is no definite indication as to size and composition, it appears to be an extended family including normally no more than 10 to 12 people. Chief Antonio Napa's house at Punta Venado could seat some 40-odd people at a feast, but it was unique in size, and the Napa household according to Basurco (1894) had only 8 to 10 members.

Barrett (1925) presents a detailed chart of kinship terms used by the *Cayapa*. We unfortunately know nothing about the behavior that goes with the terms or about marriage rules. On the face of it the system is a "lineal" one—collateral relatives are separated from lineal ones but are not differentiated among themselves. Thus, the term for uncle applies to both paternal and maternal ones. All terms are highly descriptive. There is no evidence of reciprocal use of terms, but Barrett's chart is not really complete. The system is quite unique and interesting.

The lineal and descriptive nature of the kinship system emphasizes the bilateral character of the *Cayapa* family. There is no clan organization. The extended family household is the truly basic social unit. There is some evidence of patrilocality, which might be reflected in the closer grouping of terms for fraternal nephews and great-nephews. But the patrilineal bias does not seem very strong. Within the family, men do all the fishing and hunting, the women all the food gathering, cooking, child rearing, and weaving. Men always do the sewing. Women make baskets, mats, and all the pottery. The two sexes cooperate in agriculture, the men clearing the fields, their wives tending the crops and harvesting. They also cooperate in the distillation of rum and the paddling of canoes while on trips.

Politically, the *Cayapa* tribe is divided into three parts: Punta Venado, Sapayo Grande, and San Miguel. Each has its chief (gobernador) and a full complement of Spanish-titled officials: secretario, teniente político, alcalde, comisario, capitán, and sargento. The governor carries a cane of black chonta wood with a silver head symbolizing his authority. Barrett feels that in most cases Spanish nomenclature was imposed on aboriginal positions. All offices are hereditary in the patrilineal line, but the new job holder needs the confirmation of the priest. The main duties of this leadership deal with the enforcement of law and order and the dispensation of justice.

None of these positions is a full-time duty, and there is no material compensation for exercising them. The chief has the largest house along the river, where he holds court and supervises punishments. He is quite responsive to public opinion and enjoys considerable prestige.

WARFARE

The *Cayapa* pride themselves on their peaceable relations with their neighbors. Tradition records no war since the mythological Indios Bravos were defeated and driven from the country. Lances and blowguns were used principally for war.

LIFE CYCLE

Childbirth.—There are few restrictions placed on the mother at childbirth. Heimann's (1931–32) report of the couvade is specifically contradicted by Barrett. Godparents baptize the infant, who takes their name. Children are never punished, and even the universal annual ceremonial whipping omits the young. Extremely friendly relations between siblings seem to be the rule. When very young, both boys and girls begin to help in adult activities or to engage in them playfully with diminutive tools. Canoeing, farming, and baby tending are all mastered before the child is 10 years old.

Puberty and marriage.—Barrett could find no puberty rites for either sex. He suggests that courtship was left to the young people. The chief marries them at a feast, where they are lectured and whipped. Like succession in political office, marriage must be confirmed by the priest.

Death.—Death is not considered to be a natural phenomenon but is attributed to the presence of malevolent spirits in the body. A dead man's soul hovers around his house, which is usually abandoned, though it may be dismantled and sold. The corpse is buried in a coffin in a Catholic-style cemetery near the church. The dead man's possessions are usually given away, but it is not known who inherits his fields and clearings.

ESTHETIC AND RECREATIONAL ACTIVITIES

Art.—The great range of designs used by the *Cayapa* in their face and body painting has already been mentioned. There is a similar variety in the geometric figures used to ornament their canoes. There are no design names, nor is there any apparent significance in their variation. Animals are sometimes painted on canoes destined for the market, but only geometric designs satisfy the native consumer.

Textile decoration, particularly on women's skirts, differs from canoe and body painting in its emphasis on realistic motifs. Men, mammals, reptiles, birds, fishes, and parts thereof are frequently woven into the cloth. Interestingly enough, in both design and execution this ornamentation resembles very closely the decoration used by Highland Indians on their belts (fajas).

Calabash dishes frequently have an incised design below the rim.

Canoe paddles and wooden seats are sometimes ornamented with carved images, and children usually play with carved wooden dolls.

Music and dancing.—Holidays, weddings, and other feasts are accompanied by much dancing and drinking. As elsewhere along the coast, the European marimba is widely used, as are panpipes, flutes, drums, and rattles. In recent years the Highland San Juan dance has been gaining in popularity. Also of immediate Highland provenience may be the small European wooden harp with palm-fiber strings.

Toys.—Children's activities are usually imitative of adult pursuits. Complete sets of diminutive artifacts are made for the children. Blowguns are given the boys. Only dolls and tops seem to be specifically children's toys.

Alcoholic beverages.—There is no evidence of the use of narcotics. Guarapo, the fermented juice of sugarcane, and rum, its distilled byproduct, are both made and liberally drunk by the people at appropriate occasions.

RELIGION

Native *Cayapa* religion has blended with many Roman Catholic practices. Baptism, marriage, and political office must be confirmed by the priest. Masses are told for the souls of the dead, and Easter and Christmas are celebrated whenever the priest happens to visit the community.

But the soul is believed to linger after death, and the methods used to encourage its departure are strictly aboriginal. A young couple's marriage may not be consummated until solemnized by the visiting padre, but the admonitions of the village chief to both bride and groom reinforce the authority of native jurisdiction. The annual Easter whipping of the whole community is also native.

Barrett could find no clear-cut creation story. The universe is believed to be made up of three superimposed worlds, with human life centered on the middle one. Men share this middle world with many spirits, some malevolent and other benevolent, all of whom are busy affecting human happiness and goals.

Sometimes the spirits must be exorcised, as when they cause illness. For this a shaman is called, and, with the cooperation of neighbors, he drives out the spirits amid much singing, smoking, and sprinkling. The shaman also may suck out the cause of illness.

Almost anyone can become a shaman by undergoing intensive training and acquiring a set of spirit helpers. There seems to be no "predestination" for this career, though Barrett was apparently unable to get enough information on this point. Like the chief, the shaman is not a full-time professional.

Because of his magic control of spirit powers, the shaman can be a force for evil as well as for good. It is he who causes illness and eventually death. There is a great deal of similarity between the behavior and the paraphernalia of the *Cayapa* shaman and that of the Highland medicine man.

THE COLORADO

The *Colorado*, or, as they prefer to call themselves, *Tsatchela* or *Tatchila* Indians, share with the *Cayapa* the distinction of being the last surviving aboriginal group in the Lowlands of western Ecuador. The two groups know about each other and even occasionally visit back and forth; but they speak mutually unintelligible languages, and their ways of life are quite distinct.

In contrast to the *Cayapa*, the *Colorado* are rapidly disappearing. Their territory and their numbers have been shrinking constantly, and one can easily foresee the time when the group will become extinct. They have not been able to withdraw before the pressure of "civilization," and they have been incorporated to a large degree into the Highland plantation system known as concertaje. The area they occupy on the upper reaches of several affluents of the Esmeraldas and Daule Rivers in the western part of Pichincha Province has been an area of heavy colonization in recent decades. During World War II an all-weather road was opened which increased the area's accessibility to colonization from the Highlands.

PLATE 57.—**Cayapa houses and village.** *Top:* Typical dwelling along river.
Center: Unfinished house showing roof structure. *Bottom:* Chief's house at
Sapayo Grande. (After Barrett, 1925.)

PLATE 58.—**Colorado houses, early 20th century.** (After Rivet, 1905, opp. pp. 192, 190.)

PLATE 59.—**Colorado and Cayapa Indians.** *Top: Colorado,* early 20th century. *Bottom: Cayapa,* same period. (After Rivet, 1905, opp. p. 186, and Barrett, 1925, p. 23.)

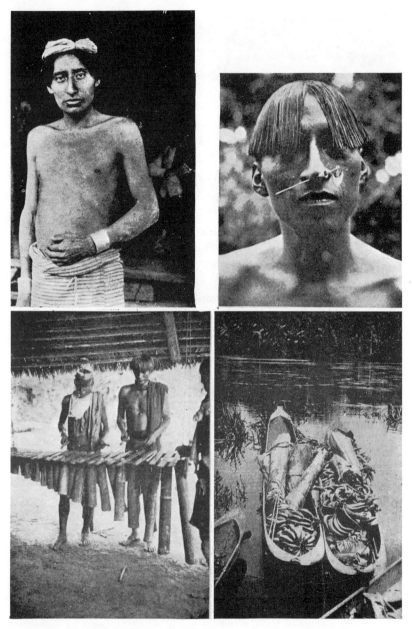

PLATE 60.—**Colorado and Cayapa Indians.** *Top (left): Colorado* man, early 20th century. *Top (right):* Tsátchela (*Colorado*) man wearing silver nose ornament. *Bottom (left):* Tsátchela (*Colorado*) men playing marimba. *Bottom (right): Cayapa* harvest of plantains. (After Rivet, 1905, opp. p. 178; after Von Hagen, 1939, pls. 7, 10; and after Barrett, 1925, pl. 60.)

Santo Domingo de los Colorados and San Miguel are the two centers of *Colorado* life. There are only about 300 *Colorado* left today. There is some evidence that their numbers were much larger in the past and that their territory extended considerably farther south along the Daule Valley. One of Buchwald's (1924) informants mentioned Babahoyo as the southern limit of the tribe's wanderings.

Tradition brings the *Colorado* from the Highlands. They speak a dialect of the *Barbacoan* division of the *Chibchan* family and are presumably related to the *Cara*, a Highland *Chibchan* group. Jijón y Caamaño (1940–45, vol. 2) has identified them with the *Campaces* who, according to 16th-century chroniclers, inhabited the Daule Valley. This identification is quite suggestive. According to Cabello Balboa, they were a warlike people, lacking chiefs and being very idolatrous. Cieza de León (1932) described a group of hill people (*Serranos*) who preferred hunting to agriculture, practiced frontooccipital skull deformation, and blackened their teeth. These people have also been suggested as the ancestors of the *Colorado*, the last two practices being common to both.

Whatever their ancestors or their location at the time of the Conquest, the *Colorado* were met in about their present location by the Jesuits toward the end of the 17th century. In the 18th century they took part in a rebellion along with several other Lowland groups. The opening of the 19th century found them 3,000 strong in about their present location. They were numerous enough then to support a full-time priest.

In recent decades they have been visited and described by two ethnologists and one naturalist (Rivet, 1905; Karsten, 1924; Von Hagen, 1939). While none of these descriptions or even the three combined give an adequate account of *Colorado* life, they are enough to stimulate our interest in this small but ethnologically significant population.

CULTURE

SUBSISTENCE ACTIVITIES

The *Colorado* are a forest people, but their hunting and fishing interests are backed by a well-developed agriculture. Houses are surrounded with fields, and each household clears and plants several more fields in the jungle. Here, as in the *Cayapa* country, the plantain is the staple crop, and each family has a few thousand trees. Yuca, yams, peppers, and cacao also grow in the immediate neighborhood of the house. The more distant fields are planted to maize, rice, manioc, sugarcane, pineapples, oranges, and lemons, as well as to medicinal plants and fish poison.

Fishing is intensively practiced with nets, traps, and hooks, but particularly with barbasco, a native plant, the roots of which contain a drug which stupefies the fish, after which they float and may be easily collected. Hunting is not very productive in this long-inhabited area, but deer,

monkeys, and agoutis are frequently bagged. The muzzle-loading shotgun is now the chief hunting weapon. At the opening of the century
Rivet still saw several blowguns in use. Clay pellets (not darts) were
used in these weapons.

Pigs, chickens, guinea pigs, and dogs are the domestic animals.

The diet of the *Colorado* reflects the fact that their area now has far
less game than that of the *Cayapa*. It is chiefly vegetal, plantains in their
many varieties being the staple, with rice, yuca, and maize supplementing
the menu. Food is steamed, boiled, and broiled.

HOUSES AND VILLAGES

Like the *Cayapa*, the *Colorado* have no real villages. The church and
the abandoned house of the priest mark the theoretical location of the
village, but the Indians live dispersed through the forest, each house
separated from the next by clearings or even by jungle.

Colorado houses are not mounted on poles, but architecturally they are
otherwise of a general *Chibcha* type. They are really large barns, without
walls, covered with a palm-thatched roof supported by chonta posts (pl.
58). Frequently the house has two sections, one of which, being used
for sleeping, is sometimes walled in. People sleep on balsa-wood beds
which stand a foot off the ground. A circular enclosure is usually provided near the house for the pigs.

CLOTHING AND ADORNMENT

In 1810, *Colorado* men are reported to have worn the short, tight
"swimming trunks" or drawers worn also by the *Cayapa*. A century
later they were wearing a cotton cloth with blue and white stripes wrapped
around their hips and reaching to their knees (pl. 59, *top*). A red cotton
belt kept the cloth in place. Their shoulder garment, a small square of
cotton cloth, remained the same since Stevenson's (1825) visit. This
diminutive poncho covered only the shoulders and chest, not the arms
or stomach.

Men's hair is cut at ear length, parted, and combed sideways. Adult
males keep it in place by wearing in it a crown of white cotton thread
(pl. 60, *top*, *left*). In Stevenson's time they wore a silver lace fillet.
Various Ecuadorean Highland and Coast tribes wore such hair decoration
at the time of the Conquest. Until today men wear silver bracelets, which
have to be bought in Quito. A nose plug of wood is worn under ordinary
circumstances and an ornate one of silver (pl. 60, *top*, *right*) on festive
occasions.

No changes seem to have occurred in women's fashions since Stevenson's visit in 1810. Women still wear a long wrap-around skirt made of
the same material as men's skirts. Chest and arms remain bare, although

many men now wear a colored calico shawl thrown over their shoulders and tied in front at the neck.

The hair is allowed to grow long and is worn parted in the middle and thrown back over the shoulders. Many rows of glass-bead necklaces are worn, replacing and sometimes coexisting with earlier adornment, which included sheaths of vanilla beans, seeds, armadillo tails, and other forest products. Bracelets and ankle beads are also frequently worn.

The *Colorado* ("red" in Spanish) receive their name from the profusion of red paint with which they cover their bodies at all times. The paint is applied from head to foot, the hair receiving a particularly liberal application. Although the *Cayapa* and many other groups in the mountains paint their bodies and faces, none carry it to the extreme of the *Colorado*. This group believes that contacts with forest and stream and their spirits require the magical protection of red paint. As all life is spent in the jungle, the practice is logical enough. The pigment comes from the seed of cultivated achiote or bixa. Women paint only their faces, and, on festive occasions, both sexes use black-line drawings made on this red base for special ornamentation. Teeth are also darkened with a black pigment.

Frontooccipital skull deformation is not now practiced, but in 1903 Rivet could still see numerous individuals so adorned.

MANUFACTURES

The opening of roads to the Highlands has accelerated the introduction of many articles which are replacing native manufactures. Nevertheless the *Colorado* still weave baskets and mats, make large pottery vessels in which to ferment cane juice, and weave the cotton cloth used in both men's and women's skirts. Pottery pipes are also made, but most containers are of calabash. No native metallurgy is practiced, and the native weapons, blowguns and bows, have been replaced by the muzzle-loader. Hollow treetrunk mortars are used for pounding plantains and maize, and a sugarcane press is owned by most families. The *Colorado* do not build canoes.

ECONOMICS

Our sources neglected data on economic phenomena beyond immediate subsistence. Some interhousehold cooperative effort was apparently involved in the clearing and preparation of fields, but what obligations this in turn created remain unknown. Fish poisoning is a group activity, and its products are divided equally among participants. Otherwise, each household seems self-sufficient.

In recent decades there has been a growing emphasis on production for the market. Rubber, balsa wood, jaguar skins, and other forest products find a steady market, while cacao has been grown for some time even though it is not consumed by the people. In exchange, the *Colorado* want

machetes, shotguns, axes, fishhooks, combs, beads, bracelets, cabuya fiber
for nets, and recently shawls and cotton yarn for women. According to
Buchwald (1924), arrow poison was much in demand in the old days,
and *Colorado* crossed the Andes to obtain it from the *Canelo* living in the
eastern lowlands. Store bread is considered a delicacy, and a trip to Quito
did not seem too far to go for it in Rivet's time.

The coming of Ecuadorean colonization in the 20th century created a
need for labor which the *Colorado* have been induced to supply. Plantations of cacao, rubber, and sugarcane have utilized the Indian's need for
store goods, ornaments, and liquor to attach him permanently to the
hacienda labor force and maintain him in debt. Nor has there been any
attempt to protect the Indian lands which are now incorporated in Ecuadorean holdings. An Indian attached to a plantation is known here as in
the Highlands as a concierto and owes as much as 15 days of work a month
to his creditors.

SOCIAL AND POLITICAL ORGANIZATION

The household is the basic social unit as well as the almost self-sufficient
economic one. We have mentioned above the few data available on interhousehold cooperation.

Social relations within the household were not studied by our observers,
who spent only a very short time in the area. We know that a male child
inherits his father's surname and a girl that of her mother. But we do
not know the extent of the exogamous unit nor any further restrictions
on marriage partners. Wiener (1882) states that orphans could choose
anybody for a mate.

Men and women cooperate extensively in cultivation and harvesting as
well as in the transportation of various products to market. In addition,
men clear the fields, hunt, fish, and make nets, while women cook, tend the
offspring and the domestic animals, and weave. The two sexes eat sepa-

The small size of the present-day *Colorado* community has obliterated
any political organization that might have existed earlier. In 1903 Rivet
found a gobernador who exercised much the same authority as the *Cayapa*
governor: he performed marriages and insured the preservation of law,
order, and morality. In 1936 Von Hagen found that leadership had shifted
to the shaman, who now exercised authority, civil and spiritual alike. This
shift of authority, if it be real and not due to faulty observation, would
make an interesting subject of further study.

In the town of Santo Domingo de los Colorados, which is now an
Ecuadorean town and is not inhabited by any *Colorado,* the Federal Gov-
ernment maintains a teniente político whose duties are manifold and vague.
They do not include the protection of the Indian or his land.

Childbirth.—*Colorado* women take childbearing easily, lying down only at delivery and returning to their duties the next day. Both parents observe a few food taboos for several days until the navel of the child has healed. There is a set of godparents for each child, and they baptize the infant. The hacienda owners frequently act as godparents in modern times.

Children grow up in a very permissive environment. Rivet saw a 3-year-old still nursing.

Puberty and marriage.—Boys undergo a nose-piercing rite at 10 or 12 years of age. The shaman perforates the nose from septum to right nostril and eventually introduces a permanent wooden nose plug in the aperture. At this time the boy begins to paint his body and face, as well as to wear the cotton-fiber "crown" in his hair. He also drinks nepe (a narcotic with medicinal and magical properties) for the first time. Our observers record no puberty ceremonies for girls.

Marriage takes place soon after puberty for girls, somewhat later for boys. Von Hagen "gathered" that the swain had to help his potential father-in-law, but we have no details on the extent or importance of this bride service, which is important elsewhere is South America. Marriage is now performed by the shaman but was once the "governor's" job. It is an occasion for a great feast with much drinking, music, and dancing. The man wears his silver nose plug instead of the wooden one for this occasion. The marriage is, nevertheless, not considered final until confirmed by the Dominican padre who sometimes visits the settlement.

Death.—At death the body is clothed in the best finery. The relatives guard the body for a day, weeping, crying, drinking, and, according to Weiner, even dancing. Special games with rubber balls or burning balsa wood are played at burial feasts to help the mourners stay awake. This will prevent the spirits that cause disease and death from molesting the survivors. Similar deathbed games are played by Highland Indians.

The body is buried in a shroud under the house floor. The dead man is lifted off the ground on several short poles and has a platform covering him. He thus does not touch earth either above or below. A string is tied around the deceased's neck and connected with the roof of the house. The belief is that this string will facilitate the departure of the soul.

At this point the house is abandoned, the relatives leaving only a candle and some food. At full moon the oldest relative might come back and gingerly touch the string. When it is rotten enough to break at the touch, the soul is gone. According to Karsten, who visited the *Colorado* in 1917, the dead are not buried in the house but outside in the forest. A small rancho is erected over the tomb and the string attached as above. Even so, the house is abandoned.

ESTHETIC AND RECREATIONAL ACTIVITIES

Art.—With the increased use of objects of foreign manufacture, *Colorado* art work has been seriously reduced. Cotton cloth is woven in blue and white without any particular ornamentation. Most of the jewelry comes from the outside.

Music and dances.—Colorado music and musical instruments have been affected by both the Lowland Negro and the Highland Spanish and *Quechua* influences. The two-man marimba is widely used (pl. 60, *bottom, left*), along with the Highland three-string violin. Flutes, balsa-wood drums, and rattles are also used. The dances today are of Highland inspiration.

Alcoholic beverages.—The *Colorado* prepare several fermented drinks of sugarcane juice and mashed banana, manioc, or maize. Guarapo and malakachisa are both made of cane juice and are considered indispensable at feasts and holidays. The *Colorado* do not distil their own rum and have come to depend on outside sources for it. This dependence has been the chief mechanism of the extension to the area of Highland debt slavery.

In addition, the *Colorado* use nepe (cayapi), the narcotic infusion of a local vine (*Banisteriopsis caapi*). Its effects include mild stupefaction, and it is used in curing and ceremonial life.

RELIGION

Religious life, like other aspects of *Colorado* culture, shows three different influences: aboriginal *Chibcha,* Highland *Quechua,* and Spanish Catholicism. The last is most pronounced in formal observances.

The *Colorado* community can no longer afford the services of a full-time priest as they could in 1810. Nevertheless, the attachment of the people to Catholic ritual and observances is very great. No baptism or marriage is definitive until the native ceremony has been confirmed by the Dominican priest who visits the community. Masses for the souls of the dead, prayer meetings, and the circulation of images all take place at this time at enormous expense to the Indians.

Nevertheless, Catholic beliefs and ceremonies have not obliterated native notions about the supernatural. The soul of the dead might go to heaven, but it does so along the string attached to the roof from the dead man's neck.

Cotopaxi and Chimborazo, the two snow-covered volcanoes high up in the Andes, play an important role in the native creation story, just as they do among Highland Indians.

There are many spirits, some benevolent and others revengeful and malicious, who roam the earth. The latter can cause disease and thunder, and they multiply jaguars and the venomous snakes. Shamans are necessary to handle these spirits and to invoke the counteroffensive of the benevolent ones.

The shaman, particularly in recent times, is a very powerful man. The reputation of *Colorado* shamans has spread even to the Highlands, and they frequently are brought up to ply their trade. Nor is their clientele always Indian.

Curing is the main activity of the shaman. Diseases are due to witchcraft, sharp chonta spines being sent into the sick man's body. The native narcotic, nepe, is drunk by both curer and patient, and, after much drinking of brandy, beating of rattles and drums, and dancing in a trance, the chonta spine causing the ailment is extracted for all to see.

BIBLIOGRAPHY

Barrett, 1925; Basurco, 1894; Beuchat and Rivet, 1907 (also see Rivet and Beuchat, 1910); Buchwald, 1908, 1918, 1924; Cabello Balboa, MS. (see Jijón y Caamaño, 1940–45, vol. 2); Cieza de León, 1932; Heimann, 1931–32; Jijón y Caamaño, 1912, 1919, 1940–45, vol. 2; Karsten, 1924; Rivet, 1905 (also see Beuchat and Rivet, 1907; Verneau and Rivet, 1912–22); Rivet and Beuchat, 1910; Seler, 1885, 1902; Stevenson, 1825; Verneau and Rivet, 1912–22; Von Hagen, 1939; Wiener, 1882; Wilczynski, 1888.

ANTHROPOLOGICAL NEEDS AND POSSIBILITIES
IN CENTRAL AMERICA

By Wm. Duncan Strong and Frederick Johnson

In evaluating the present status of anthropological knowledge concerning Central America it is impossible not to repeat the fact that the present corpus of material is utterly uneven and inadequate.[1] This deplorable and, in considerable part, unnecessary condition cannot be overemphasized. There is little advantage to be gained in lamenting the large amount of cultural materials in the area that have been lost forever through the ravages of time, looting, and indifference in recording. It is of more value to point out that there still remains in the region a great amount of such materials that can be revealed and integrated whenever Central American anthropology is made the subject of coordinated and persistent research. Since the region is not only scientifically important in its own right, but also holds the key to much of our potential understanding of adjacent cultures of both North and South America, it is desirable that the reasons for the present sorry state of anthropological knowledge in Central America be analyzed and the condition remedied so far and so soon as may be possible.

A review of the foregoing articles will show that one of the greatest obstacles to integration in regard to any study of native Central American civilization is the extreme unevenness of the anthropological and historical data. If, as is the case in only a very few instances, an adequate archeological sequence has been established, it is usually found that the historic, ethnological, and linguistic materials[2] available at present are confused and inadequate. Where history is most specific, or ethnology fairly adequate, it will often be found that the only available prehistoric data consist of speculations based on selected art objects dug up by looters and collectors. Finally, any attempt to correlate the products of men's hands and minds with the human beings who created them, whether in prehistoric or historic times, meets with complete failure at the start, for practically no anthropometric material on either the living or the dead is now available. It can fairly be asked, therefore, whether this sad state of affairs

---

[1] For other analyses, see Kroeber, 1939, p. 109, and Strong, 1940, pp. 377–385.
[2] The deplorable and misleading condition of historical linguistic studies in Central America has been stressed elsewhere; see Strong, op. cit., and Kroeber, 1940, pp. 463–470.

is entirely due to the impossibility of gathering such data because of its nonexistence or destruction, or whether the scientist may not be equally to blame for not securing much that is still available while there is time.

In regard to the historic approach to Central American problems it seems highly probable that much archive material is extant which has not yet been utilized. It is significant that every new archeological advance, as at Coclé, has drawn forth considerable amounts of historical data previously unknown or unappreciated. This lack of knowledge or appreciation of obscure but available historical documents particularly marks most modern North American investigators who, with a few shining exceptions, are not very familiar with such materials. Since the ordinary field archeologist or ethnologist can hardly be expected to be also a competent archival historian, this points up another issue. That is the fact that there is a great need for up-to-date compilations and revisions of such historic materials. Those available for Central America go back several generations to Squier, Bancroft, Brinton, and others, and even these are too little used by modern field men. Lothrop's brief summary (1926 b) of the ethnography of Costa Rica and Nicaragua at the time of the Conquest and Beals' similar ethnography of northern México (1932), based largely on the sources used by Bancroft in his somewhat hit-or-miss compilations, are shining exceptions. Beals' work is invaluable on the ethnographic level and, as archeology commences in that region, will be equally important in that regard. It is essential, not only for anthropology but also for history and the social sciences in Central America, that the continuity of the human record in this area be presented in the most complete form possible. Here the work of anthropologist, historian, and sociologist blends and each is dependent on the other. It would appear that no such unity of effort has yet been achieved.

In regard to ethnology, this lack is well illustrated by the fact that in the previous articles information from the 16th and early 17th centuries, the period of first contact, has barely been touched upon except in the area lying between the Panamá Canal and southern Nicaragua. Most of the information on the extremely important Meso-American tribes was brought to light by Squier, with some additions by Lothrop. Additional searches will undoubtedly reveal additional information. Modern studies are very few and often out of date and incomplete. We are forced still to rely on Gabb (1875), Pinart (1885), et al. for southeastern Costa Rica, and on Conzemius (1932, etc.) for the *Mosquito* and *Sumo*. The descriptions of various tribes in Nicaragua and Honduras are, perforce, based on Squier's researches (1858, etc.). Additions to such data may be found in a number of other descriptions, all of which are incomplete and sometimes not to be trusted. The principal problem of the moment is to obtain sound information concerning both the ancient and modern inhabitants of the region. Before satisfactory interpretations for any anthropological purpose can be made, experienced investigators must be sent into the region and given the opportunity to work out the details which we must have.

One of the most perplexing of the ethnographic problems is the full understanding of modern Indian culture and also the presumably indigenous culture traits which are found in the modern, outwardly Spanish, civilizations. Early European descriptions provide glimpses of highly organized indigenous civilizations. In some cases, such as in Panamá and Costa Rica, it is possible to block out several important phases of the evolution of present-day culture. Similarly, certain features of the Hispanization of the Meso-American tribes and, to a lesser extent, some of the peoples in the interior of Honduras and Nicaragua are known. For example, Stone's discussion of the *Lenca* (p. 61) emphasizes the intermediate position which this large and important group has occupied for a lengthy period. These people were in direct contact with the highly developed *Maya* civilization and with the curious combination of advanced and "primitive" cultures which appears to be characteristic of peoples to the south. The history of the tribes in the Caribbean Lowland can hardly be written. In this region the impact of European cultures has apparently had the most unfortunate results, for here there are indications of sometimes extreme degeneration. Even so, it is certain that they have not always been such; in fact, it is possible that civilizations of a high order, well adapted to life in the Tropical Forest, once existed. Adequate archeology is essential here as elsewhere.

The significance of the foregoing remarks ranges over a wide field. From a purely anthropological point of view there is interest in culture history and in purely theoretical studies of culture development under conditions which prevailed. In addition, such anthropological data are essential to the solution of modern political, social, economic, and geographic problems. The expansion of transportation facilities, the improvement of communication, and the development of natural resources have brought or very soon will bring the modern world into intimate contact with even the most conservative and isolated groups of Central American Indians. The effect of this upon these people and other less conservative groups will be most profound. Anthropological studies which provide not only analyses of present conditions but of the events which led up to these are essential. Surveys of the incomplete data suggest, for example, that the background and point of view of people whose culture is rooted in South America is vastly different from those of Meso-American tradition. Further, the different environments of various sections of Central America condition the human existence in various ways. It is essential to understand the relationship between different kinds of aboriginal culture as well as the modern cultures descended from them and the several environments.

A final note is concerned with the European background. The Spanish, English, and other nations which imposed their culture upon aboriginal Central America utilized various approaches. In addition, these approaches varied through the years. In tracing the evolution of culture from the time of the Conquest to the present, the character of the relationship between the European and the aborigine is of great significance. There are no Indian groups in existence, so far as known, that have not experienced the consequences of the impact of European culture. The social organization has been modified, religious concepts have changed, and many features connected with technology and economics have been adapted to the changing conditions. The character of this change and its effect upon ideas of people differed with the particular history of each region. Knowledge of this is fundamental to an understanding of the present-day culture, be it in an isolated Indian village or in the largest of the Central American cities.

BIBLIOGRAPHY

Beals, 1932; Conzemius, 1932, etc.; Gabb, 1875; Kroeber, 1939, 1940; Lothrop, 1926 b; Pinart, 1885; Squier, 1858, etc.; Strong, 1940.

Part 2. The Cultures of Northwest South America
SUB-ANDEAN TRIBES OF THE CAUCA VALLEY

By Gregorio Hernández de Alba

INTRODUCTION

The Sub-Andean cultural area extends from the eastern slopes of the Cordillera Occidental (long. 2°40′ west of the Bogotá meridian) to the western slopes of the Cordillera Central (long. 1° west of the Bogotá meridian) and from the region of Cali in the south (lat. 3°20′ N.) to the Sierra de Abibe and the headwaters of the Sinú and San Jorge Rivers in the north (about lat. 7°20′ N.). The Cauca River, earlier called the Río Grande de Santa Marta, crosses this zone. It emerges from the deep broad valley in the region of Armenia and flows northward alternately through deep canyons and narrow valleys, with a multitude of tributary rivers descending from cordilleras enclosing this zone. In addition to the Cauca and its tributaries, this territory, with its narrow valleys and steep slopes, is drained by the Nechi River and its affluent, the Porce, which flow toward the northeast, the Río Sucio running northwest, the Murrí, which joins the Atrato River in the west, and the Samaná and Nare Rivers, both tributaries of the Magdalena River to the east.

An exception must be made of the region which today is embraced by the Department of Valle del Cauca and the Departments of Caldas and Antioquia, which complete this zone. This region is predominantly mountainous with small mesas, terraces, hills, peaks, slopes, and depressions which so complicate the topography that an author of the ancient State of Antioquia stated, "The mountains form an almost indefinable ensemble, the description of which, even with a compass in hand, would require much time and study to be done satisfactorily" (Uribe Ángel, 1885). From the perpetual snows on the summits of peaks, such as Ruíz in the Cordillera Central (5,590 m., 18,339.9 feet), to the hot climates, there is every gradation of temperature from 5° to 6° C. (41° to 43° F.) on the Mesa de Herveo at 3,170 m. (10,400.2 feet) above sea level, to 27° C. (80.60° F.) in the low valleys, as at Zaragoza, 205 m. (672.57 feet) altitude. The altitude and mean temperature of the territories occupied by the peoples mentioned subsequently vary from south to north as follows: Cali, 1,046 m. (3,431.78 feet) and 22° C. (71.60° F.) ; Buga, 1,001 m. (3,284.08 feet) and 24° C. (75.20° F.); Cartago, 979 m. (3,211.93 feet) and 24° C. (75.20° F.); Anserma, 1,790 m. (5,872.7 feet) and 17° C. (62.60° F.); Nueva Caramanta, 2,107 m. (6,932.67 feet) and 17° C. (62.60° F.); Arma, 2,210 m. (6,922.6 feet) and 18° C. (64.40° F.); Concordia, 1,900 m. (6,233.6 feet) and 19° C. (66.20° F.); Ebéjico, 720 m. (2,362.2 feet) and 23° C. (73.40° F.); Antioquia, 572 m. (1,876.66 feet) and 27° C. (80.60° F.); Buriticá, 1,650 m. (5,413.4 feet) and 20° C. (68° F.); Cañasgordas, 1,490 m. (4,888.4 feet) and 20° C. (68° F.); and Ituango, 1,530 m. (5,019.7 feet) and 21° C. (69.80° F.).[1]

Typical of the Tropics, the natural flora and fauna vary with altitude and climate. The presence, absence, and nature of many cultural features, such as dress, habitations, sources of food, and food preparation, are conditioned by the natural environment. A general Sub-Andean culture, however, predominates; it is adapted to a region with a temperate climate (mean temperature of 18° C. or 64.40° F.), a broken terrain, considerable rain-fall, and forests. The altitudinal variations in natural resources of flora and fauna have been outlined previously by the author (Handbook, vol. 2, pp. 916–918). Foods obtained through farming, gathering, and hunting will be mentioned subsequently.

At the beginning of the 16th century a large number of peoples inhabited this region. According to the incomplete and biased accounts which the first chroniclers wrote of their contacts and wars with the Spaniards, they were similar to one another in some respects and different in others, and they constituted a mosaic of different nations and even of different languages. Uribe Ángel (1885, pt. 3, ch. 2), who first undertook to classify the more than 50 nations of native peoples listed by the chroniclers as inhabitants of the present Departments of Antioquia and Caldas, reduced them to three main groups: Catío, Nutabe, and Tahamí. These are not necessarily cultural divisions. Jijón y Caamaño (1936–38), using Robledo's information, describes the peoples of Nori, Caramanta, and Cartama as having a uniform language and dress, and classes the language of the Carrapa and Picara with Quimbaya. Following Cieza de León (1932, pt. 1), who states that the Pozo and Arma had the same language, Jijón y Caamaño gives the following linguistic groupings: Urabá and Catío (Chocó family); Arma and Pozo; Quimbaya, Carrapa, Picara, and Paucura; Chanco and Chocó of the Pacific Coast. He groups as culturally similar the Nutave, Tahami, Cenufana, Murgia, Ancerma, Gorrón, and Buga. The Caramanta understood the language of the Encerma, which was different from the languages of the other provinces. The Lile Yolo, Jamundí, Timba, etc., belonged, with Cuna and Barbacoa, to a group of Chibchan languages (Jijón y Caamaño, 1936–38, vol. 2, app. pp. *111–*112, *184, *189). Rivet 1943, pp. 55–87), using a linguistic argument

---

[1] The geographical data are from Uribe Ángel (1885), Arenas Paz (1922), and Hermano Justo (1943).

but taking into account the extension in the Cauca region of the custom of deforming the arms and legs with ligaments, sees four groups in the Cauca Valley that belong to the *Chocó* language, which he classes in the *Carib* family. From these he excludes the *Lile, Gorrón,* and *Chanco* of the broad valley and the *Dabeiba* and *Catío* of the mountains to the north.

In the present article we shall use the few available cultural data in an attempt to ascertain the tribes and subtribes which have the culture elements characteristic of the Sub-Andean area. This must be considered merely as a preliminary and tentative essay, as it was prepared in a very few weeks at the request of the editor of the Handbook and is intended only to sketch briefly the salient traits of certain tribes which it had previously been impossible to cover in the Handbook.

HISTORY

After 1501, when Rodrigo de Bastidas discovered the coast of Cartagena and Alonso de Ojeda arrived at the Gulf of Urabá, the conquistadors attempted repeatedly to penetrate to "tierra adentro." They were lured by the discovery of mines whence had come the quantities of gold which they found worn as ornaments by the living Indians of Darién or Cenú, whom they killed for their riches, or which was obtained from the graves of dead Indians. But instead of the coveted gold these expeditions found mainly hardship, caused sometimes by poisoned arrows but more often, as in the case of the expedition of Pedro de Heredia in 1534, brought on by the cold and impenetrable country they had reached above Zaragoza and Remedios in the Department of Antioquia. The greed for gold outweighed the death of soldiers, however, and Alonso de Heredia repeated the attempt in 1535, reaching Ayapel, near the Cauca. In 1536, the conquistador Don Pedro went up the Darién River to seek his fortune. The next year Francisco César left San Sebastián de Urabá with a large company and, passing through the difficult hills of Abibe, reached the Cauca Valley, where he fought the cacique Nutibara and returned defeated. Simultaneously with these attempts to penetrate the country from north to south, Spanish incursions were made from south to north. They started in 1535 from Quito under the commands of Sebastián de Belalcázar, Pedro de Añasco, and Captain Juan de Ampudia. Añasco and Ampudia passed through Popayán, crossed the Jamundí River, and arrived in *Gorrón* territory, where they founded Villa de Ampudia. They went on through the region of the *Lile,* where they met Belalcázar early in 1536. Cali was founded in *Lile* territory in 1537 by Captain Miguel Muñoz, after which Villa de Ampudia was gradually abandoned.

Thus from the beginning the coast and interior competed in the discovery of the lands between the Atlantic and Perú, and both accomplished it. These expeditions are the main source of information on the tribes they found between the Magdalena, Cauca, and Atrato Rivers. They founded the first cities so as to exploit the land and the gold sands, they initiated the extinction of the Indian and the importation of African slaves, which resulted in the extension of the Negro population, and they laid the foundation for the riches of the present Departments of Caldas and Antioquia. From antiquity the chroniclers of the Conquest couched the details as in the following from Castellanos (1847):

> In canyons, rivers, waterholes
> And wherever one seeks,
> Is manifest sources of gold
> To delight the avaricious breast,
> And the diligence of the miners
> Finds the washing-trough well filled.[2]

The principal object of the settlements in the territory of Antioquia was the exploitation of mines. The most important of the cities of the Conquest was "Real de Minas de Santa Fé" or Santa Fé de Antioquia, which was described by Cieza de León (1932) as follows: "There are very rich mines near this city in the Río Grande de Santa Marta which flows near it. In summer, the Negroes and Indians take vast riches from its beaches." This remark reveals that from the beginning of colonization the Spaniards established Negro slaves in the mines, for already the Indians had been largely exterminated and the few remnants had migrated to the wilderness of the mountains to escape subjugation through the encomienda and the "mita," which had forced them to work in mines far from their tribal lands. Vicente Restrepo (1937) has written an important study on the historic role of mining in this territory.

Another industry, and one which greatly endangers archeology, is the search for graves rich in gold ornaments. This originated in Conquest times, when the Spaniards forced the Indians to reveal the graves of their chiefs. "They energetically put all hands to work at disinterring the dead, opening the sepulchres . . . They found them so rich that they took out thirty thousand pesos, twenty thousand, twelve thousand, six thousand, and down to fifty, the least find" (Simón, 1882–92, pt. 3, Primera Noticia, ch. 21). This industry, which continues in vogue among the people of Antioquia and is called "guaquería," removes pieces of gold from the ancient sepulchers without regard for the less precious objects, the skeletal material, or data essential to archeological investigations.

In the present Department of Valle del Cauca, which was so densely populated at the Conquest that Castellanos said that "in more than 30 leagues of road there is someone every step of the way" (in Acosta, 1901,

[2] Porque quebradas, ríos, vertederos
y cualquiera lugar que se catea,
manifiestan auríferos veneros,
con que el avaro pecho se recrea,
y la solicitud de los mineros
saca bien provedia la batea.

ch. 9, p. 114), the native population disappeared culturally, and the few survivors of the cruel Spanish epic are mixed with European or African blood, giving rise to the Mestizo and the mulatto or zambo, which forms the mass of the population of the Department. In Caldas and Antioquia, as well as in the neighboring territory of the *Chocó* to the west, a few groups of natives more or less pure in race and culture, or else much acculturated, have succeeded in surviving the persecution and despoliation. But it must be noted that before the arrival of the Whites, wars and cannibalism had annihilated some peoples, of which Tulio Ospina cites an example: "The meseta oriental, Rionegro, Concepción, etc., had been depopulated by attacks of the cannibal Nutabes." Robledo states: "On through the sierra there are many depopulated towns, wide roads, and ditches made by hand, and seats of great populations all already destroyed." Robledo continued to the pueblo of Tamí, "And here the chief came out peacefully. From him, the Captain endeavored to obtain information about the land and about those ancient structures which he had been finding in the Province of Aburrá. The former replied that once there had been a great population and that the people of the Provinces of Nutabe and Urezo, where the Señor was, had destroyed those very ancient things." (Ospina, 1905, pp. 145–164.)

An example of the depopulation in post-Conquest times is the following note: "The native population of more than 600,000 souls, the equivalent of 120,000 Indian laborers (fighters and miners), in the middle of the 16th century, were entrusted to the cruel encomenderos. Fifty years later there remained only 1,500" (Ospina, 1918, pp. 413–414, from the Relación of the visit of the Oidor Herrera Campuzano in 1616). The census of the same territory for 1778 gives 49,445 inhabitants for all the Province of Antioquia, of which 10 percent were slaves, according to Ospina's investigations. In 1581 there were the following settlements: Arma, Caramanta, Antioquia la Vieja, Santa Fé de Antioquia, San Juan de Rodas, Valdivia, Cáceres, San Jerónimo del Monte, Zaragoza, and Remedios (Uribe Ángel, 1885, p. 761). In the middle of the 19th century the few Indians of the territory were located in Caramanta, Murrí, Chontaduro, Juntas, Musinga, Uramá Grande, Uramita, Pital, Ríoverde, and Monos, the greater part toward the northwest and in the Districts of Urrao, Frontino, and Cañasgordas (Uribe Ángel, 1885, p. 520). Later the penetration of Whites and Mestizos had dislocated the Indian element farther toward the jungles of the Chocó and the Atrato Rivers, or up toward the Sinú River and its tributaries (Laura de Santa Catalina, 1936, p. 136). The territory today occupied by the Department of Caldas first had typical Spanish pueblos or municipios at Santa Ana de los Caballeros de Anserma (1539), Cartago (1540), and Victoria (1553). According to López de Velasco (1916), Santa Ana de Anzerma had 30 Indian villages with 5,000 tributaries and more than 1,000 Negroes to mine the gold. Arma had 27 Indian villages with 17,000 tributaries. The Indians became fewer daily. Today, García (1937, pp. 228–236) gives a total of 10,294 Indians in the census of 1918, 2.4 percent of the total population, these Indians being in the Municipios of Ríosucio, Quinchía, Guática, Mistrató, and Pueblorrico. He writes, "The native family sows secret places between the bushes, gives his share of work on the farms, and lives in permanent migration. Lacking money, he pays with his work. But his nomadism at least prevents his debts becoming hereditary. Not mixing with other ethnic elements, he preserves his customs and language. Hunting and fishing entice him to the valleys of the Suarraga, Taibá, Amurrupá, Guarató, San Juan and Chamí Rivers."

Of the many native gold ornaments taken by guaqueros, or treasure hunters, some pieces from this territory have been preserved intact in museums, such as the London Museum, the Brooklyn Museum, the American Museum of Natural History in New York, the Museum of the American Indian, Heye Foundation, New York, the University Museum in Philadelphia, and, in Colombia, in the Museo Arqueológico Nacional. Today, the Museo de Oro del Banco de la República de Colombia is assembling private collections, especially from Medellín and Manizales, and now has a collection which for both size and importance is unequaled, surpassing the so-called "treasure of the Quimbayas" in the Museo de Madrid in Spain.

The only scientific archeological research carried out in this region is that done in *Gorrón* territory west of Buga by Henry Wassén in 1935, by the author in 1937, and in Valle del Cauca by Wendell C. Bennett and James A. Ford for the Institute of Andean Research in 1941–42. Luis Duque Gómez worked in the Department of Caldas, especially at Zupía, in 1942. For a long time the name Quimbaya has been used generally to designate the civilization which produced the greater part of the goldwork and ceramics taken from graves in Antioquia, Caldas, and the region of Quindío. Various authors have studied Quimbaya archeology, the most outstanding being Restrepo Tirado (1929) and Posada Arango (1875). (See also Handbook, vol. 2, pp. 838–841.)

The archeology of this zone presents many problems. There is need to establish typology, distributions, and cultural sequences and to identify the Sub-Andean cultures archeologically so as to verify or modify the very inadequate ethnological picture, which has been reconstructed from fragmentary data in old chronicles or gleaned from strongly acculturated modern peoples.

TRIBES OF THE UPPER CAUCA RIVER

TRIBAL LOCATIONS

The *Jamundí* (*Xamundí*) lived on the Xamundí River, which enters the Cauca below Popayán, and in the territory toward the Cordillera

Occidental. They adjoined the *Aguale*, who are not precisely located by the historians but who Cieza affirmed had the same customs as their neighbors, i.e., the *Lile*. North of these tribes, toward the Mar del Sur, lived the *Timba*, who spoke the same language as the people of Valle Lile and "the small valleys of the Cordillera Occidental" (Jijón y Caamaño 1936–38, vol. 2, app. p. *185; Cieza de León, 1932, ch. 28, p. 94). Closer to the valley lived the *Atunceta*, adjoining the *Lile*. The latter were occupants of the Valley of Lile or Lili to the west of Cali (which took its name and corrupted it) and of surrounding territory extending northward to the *Gorrón* and eastward to the *Guambía* and *Buga*. The *Gorrón* lived on the slopes of the Cordillera toward the valley, north of Lile. Their territory extended through the mountains to adjoin the *Barbacoa;* to the northeast it reached to the *Chanco,* who separated them from the *Ancerma;* and to the east it was bounded by the Cauca River, which divided them from the *Buga*.

Linguistic studies are very deficient, being based on a very few words transmitted through a foreign tongue, Spanish. Because of cultural similarities, the *Gorrón* are placed with the *Buga, Chanco,* and *Ancerma,* and the *Lile, Timba,* and *Jamundí* are put in the *Chibchan* family (Rivet, 1943; Jijón y Caamaño, 1936–38, vol. 2, app. p. *189). According to this, the *Gorrón* and *Chanco* spoke the same language as the *Chocó*.

CULTURE

SUBSISTENCE ACTIVITIES

These tribes practiced farming, which was greatly favored by the local environment. The *Lile* had plantations of maize and manioc, and many fruit trees, including bananas, guayavas, guamas, granadillas, zapotes, papayas, starapples (caimitos), vocados, and guanábanas (Guillén Chaparro, 1889), as well as palms, called "pixivaes" by the chroniclers, which were very useful for both food and drink. The extensive use of fruits is shown by the way in which the Indians around Cali, especially the women, brought them by the basketful to the expeditionaries of Ampudia.

The *Gorrón* cultivated much maize and, like the *Lile,* hunted deer, guadaquinajes, and birds native to the region. But they were outstanding as fishermen, and they received their name from the cry by which they announced to their new customers, the Spaniards, that they had fish to sell. They lived in the mountains but came down to the banks of the Cauca to fish and at the same time to cultivate small parcels of land. Their fisheries were in front of Buga, where they constructed a special pond which yielded quantities of fish each summer when it became dry.

Concerning food preparation we know only that the *Lile* roasted or boiled maize (Pascual de Andagoya, *in* Jijón y Caamaño, 1936–1938, 2: 55) and that the *Gorrón* smoked their fish, having no salt in which to preserve it (Cieza de León, 1932, ch. 26, pp. 79–81).

VILLAGES AND HOUSES

Lile houses were large, high, circular in ground plan, walled with thick, erect poles, and covered with broad grass. The dwelling of a chief, according to Cieza, had a door in the center and four tall windows; inside, running across it, were benches on which were trophy corpses of slain enemies. The villages were "large and beautiful," with the houses placed near one another.

The tribes living in the Cordillera, toward Buenaventura, made smaller houses, covered with palm leaves and enclosed with thick poles. One author, however, claims that the *Lile* had palisades or forts in the sierra, where they remained part of the year, and temporary houses for fishing in the plains. *Gorrón* houses were like those just described, and the villages were large, the houses being in groups of 10 or 15, tables always in the sierras. Inside the house there was always a storage place for dried fish.

Among household objects must be mentioned tables (the trophy corpses were seated on tables), stone metates for grinding maize, and, in dwellings of principal men, gold plates.

The only noteworthy engineering work is the artificial lake which the *Gorrón* constructed to raise fish (Sardilla, 1891–94, vol. 2, p. 392).

CLOTHES AND ADORNMENT

The *Lile* wore a small apron in front and another hanging behind, those of the women being of cotton and hung from a belt. The *Gorrón* wore cotton clothes, of very beautiful appearance. Men wore "maures," or breechclouts, and women heavy blankets 3 varas long and 2 wide (a vara is 80 cm. or about 32 inches). The *Chanco* dressed only in "maures" made of "crushed" tree bark, probably bark cloth, but not of woven cotton. These were 1 vara long and 2 palms wide.

The neighbors of the *Lile* gathered up the hair and adorned it with fillets of gold and with bone or shell beads (chaquiras). They wore crescentic gold nose ornaments, or "caricuríes." Ear ornaments made of rings of twisted gold, fine necklaces with gold figures, and "long strands of small white and colored bone beads which they call 'chaquira'." Chaquiras were an item of women's adornment. The *Gorrón* used the same kinds of jewels and ornaments.

TRANSPORTATION

As the Cauca River in the country of the *Lile* and *Gorrón* is broad and tranquil, these Indians were able to travel on water by canoes, some of which Cieza noted 5 leagues from Xamundí. They also used the curious method of straddling a bamboo trunk, carrying their loads of objects and provisions in a basket on their heads, and even spinning while crossing the river, as observed near Cali. The *Lile*, or closely related groups living in the sierra toward Buenaventura, were employed by the conquistadors and colonists to carry cargo and passengers on their shoulders between Cali and this port on the Pacific. To transport the Spaniards, they used chairs made of branches, probably litters. So difficult was this trip for the Indians that, according to Cieza, "when they arrive near the city of Cali, where they entered the plains, they were footsore and walked with great pain, which profited them nothing," for "all they gained and all the encomenderos gave these miserable ones they had carried with them" (Cieza de León, 1932, ch. 29).

MANUFACTURES

Spinning and weaving.—The *Chanco* made breachclouts of bark cloth, but the *Lile* and *Gorrón* practiced weaving. The women spun the thread, even while crossing a river with cargo on their heads. This custom of performing some task while going from one place to another persists among the modern rural peoples of Colombia, especially among women, who spin as they walk.

Cotton was woven for blankets and "maures," or breechclouts. Some blankets were 3 varas (2.4 m., or 8 ft.) long and 2 varas (1.6 m., or 5 ft., 4 in.) wide.

All these tribes made cordage. To wrap funeral bundles the *Gorrón* made three-ply cords more than 200 brazas (fathoms) long (Cieza de León, 1932, ch. 26).

Ceramics.—Pottery is scarcely mentioned among these tribes, but it is known archeologically. There are characteristic types and features, such as the use of human figures and faces as adornos, and particularly the well-known "caricuri," which is in the form of a twisted nail with enlarged extremities (Bennett, 1944, and Ford, 1944).

Metallurgy.—The *Gorrón* and *Lile* as well as the other tribes of this area worked gold, either pure or alloyed with copper, the latter being called by the chroniclers, "low gold" ("oro bajo"). They made objects of personal adornment, described above, among them "caricuris," and the chiefs or principal men had gold plates among their household utensils.

Stonework.—Historical sources mention polished stone knives and stone metates for grinding maize. In addition, archeology has revealed the use of stone axes and celts (Wassén, 1936, pp. 30–67; Bennett, 1944, and Ford, 1944; Hernández de Alba, 1938).

Preparation of skins.—There is no mention of the preparation of hides, but the *Lile* and *Gorrón* flayed the corpses of slain enemies and stuffed the skins with wood ashes, the potash of which preserved them for some time.

SOCIAL AND POLITICAL ORGANIZATION

Lile territory was divided into six "cacicados" or subtribes, each governed by its own chief (cacique), who had little power, as Cieza remarks "they counted for little with the Indians".[3] There seems, however, to have been some tribal organization or federation under a single head, for Petecuy was, at the time of the discovery, the most powerful chief.

There was an aristocratic class, the members of which received tribute from their subjects and were buried in a special grave. Inheritance, at least in this class, passed to the son of the principal wife, a fact which also indicates polygyny.

Economic activities.—Chiefs received tribute from their subjects, a prerogative which passed to the son, perhaps the oldest, of the principal wife. The chiefs likewise contracted with the Colonial Spaniards to have goods transported from the coast to Cali, their subjects performing this task.

The *Gorrón* carried on more organized commerce, trading dried, smoked fish and oil extracted from these fish with the peoples of the Province of Cali. They stored surpluses of dried fish taken in summer from their special pond at Buga to eat or sell during the rainy season.

LIFE CYCLE

Nothing is known of customs pertaining to childbirth, and initiation rites are not mentioned.

Polygyny was practiced, at least by the chiefs. Chiefs always married their nieces, or, sometimes, their sisters, suggesting endogamy of a ruling class.

A sexually inverted man was derisively called a "woman."

The *Lile* treated sick people with baths and with herbs, the curative qualities of which they knew well. Chiefs were interred in their own houses, in large, deep graves; food, weapons, and gold ornaments were placed with the corpse. The *Gorrón* adorned a deceased person with his precious ornaments, wrapped him in many cotton blankets, which were tied with bast cord, and buried him.

WARFARE

In great wars with their neighbors, these tribes fought with darts, lances, and macanas, or thick wooden clubs, and defended themselves with painted wooden shields.

They flayed their enemies, stuffed their skins with wood ashes, and modeled wax features on the skulls. They put weapons in their hands and exhibited them in their houses. Even detached hands and feet were

---

[3] "Eran tenidos en poco de los indios."

kept as trophies. The *Lile* and *Gorrón* made great use of such trophies to ornament their houses, and they even kept intestines stuffed with ashes. The place of honor was inside, over the door.

Cannibalism was also practiced, for after flaying the corpses they ate the flesh, a ritual that was carried out in a special house. In the village of Petecuy the Spaniards found a hut with a "great quantity" of pieces of corpses, heads, and bones.

So developed was the spirit of warfare among these tribes that *Gorrón* women went to war with their men, carrying arms, fighting, and taking trophies.

ESTHETIC AND RECREATIONAL ACTIVITIES

Art forms are known only from specimens of ceramics and goldwork. There is no record of music, musical instruments, or dance forms.

A social game or contest was practiced by the *Lile* as an annual mourning ceremony. Thirty to fifty persons from each of two villages would assemble, each group under the leadership of its chief. After eating and drinking in a common feast the groups would confront each other and fight by hurling darts, which they warded off with shields. Many would emerge wounded and some were killed, but this did not cause enmity between the two villages (Pascual de Andagoya, *in* Jijón y Caamaño, 1936–38, vol. 2, doc. 2). A similar contest was held by the *Páez* of the Cordillera Central (Hernández de Alba, Handbook, vol. 2, p. 952).

RELIGION

Cieza found no idols, temples, or special places of worship among these tribes. There were, however, priests or shamans, who communicated with the divinities, which the historians called "demons." The shamans practiced divination, witchcraft, and magic, for purposes both of protection and of vengeance.

Soon after the Conquest these Indians, who were treated as people who were "simple and without malice," became Catholics, adopted European shirts, and were wholly assimilated.

TRIBES OF THE NORTH COLOMBIA HIGHLANDS

The ethnology of the peoples who occupied the territory which, at the time of the Conquest, was called "between the three rivers"—the Magdalena, Cauca, and Atrato Rivers—will be treated in three divisions. The first includes the tribes of the right bank of the Cauca River, the *Quimbaya, Carrapa, Picara, Paucura, Pozo,* and *Arma.* The second division includes several tribes from the *Ancerma* to the *Abibe,* between the left bank of the Cauca River and Atrato River, which was formerly called the San Juan River and the Río Grande del Darién. The third comprises the *Aburrá* (*Avurrá*), *Nutabe, Urezo, Tahamí,* and *Yamicí* of the Province of Aburrá.

Almost without exception these tribes speak dialects of the *Chocó* language (Jijón y Caamaño, 1936–38, vol. 2; Rivet, 1943). In 1551, Asensio (1921) made the same claim, without naming the language, when he stated, "They have their own language, although it is somewhat different among the Indians of Cartago, Encerma, Arma, Charamanta, Sante Fé de Antioquia."

We have assembled ethnographic data on 21 provinces, tribes, or groups of Indians who lived in this portion of the Sub-Andean area. There are many ethnological references for some tribes, but very few for those which were seldom visited by the conquistadors. Agriculture, hunting, simple huts, and ceramics were common to all these Indians. In all, 43 culture elements are mentioned in the sources: agriculture, hunting, fishing, domesticated animals, pile dwellings, communal houses, hammocks, roads, irrigation ditches, bridges, fences, woven blankets, bark-cloth garments, gold mining, goldworking, featherwork, body painting, basketry, marriage with consanguineous relatives, polygyny, slavery, intertribal trade, villages, isolated dwellings, desiccation of corpses, cremation, arrows, darts, lances, spears, macanas or clubs, slings, spear throwers, stone missiles, harpoons, boiling water and deadfalls or pitfalls used as weapons, war banners, stone knives, cannibalism, coca, human trophies, shamans, temples, and idols.

Of these elements, the *Arma* had 25, the *Pozo* 16, and the *Picara* and *Paucura,* 11. The *Carrapa* had 9 and the *Quimbaya* 16 plus 2 peculiar to themselves, cremation of corpses and the use of shields made of their own hair. The *Ancerma* had 25, the *Toro* 5, the *Caramanta* 13, the *Buriticá* and *Antiochia* 19, the *Evégico* 11, and the *Catío* 18.

The most common elements were agriculture, hunting, woven blankets, goldwork, cannibalism, human trophies, body painting, arrows, lances, and macanas. The least common were fishing, pile dwellings, hammocks, bark-cloth garments, feather ornaments, corpses dried over a fire, cremation, shields, pitfalls used in warfare, and domesticated animals. On the basis of such limited material, the characteristics of the cultures are sketched in the following pages.

TRIBES EAST OF THE CAUCA RIVER

TRIBAL LOCATIONS

The *Quimbaya* lived between the Cauca River to the west and the high peaks of the Cordillera to the east. According to Restrepo Tirado (1929), they were bounded on the north and south, respectively, by the Tacurumbi and Zegues Rivers, but Jijón y Caamaño (1936–38, vol. 2) gives their boundaries as the Chinchiná and Paila Rivers. On the north they adjoined the *Carrapa* and the *Pozo,* the latter being nearer the Cauca River. North of the *Carrapa* lived the *Arbi* and *Picara;* the latter dwelt west of the former and were eastern neighbors of the *Pozo.* The *Pozo* extended west of the Cauca River, east to the territory of the *Picara* and *Carrapa*, and north to that of the *Paucura*. The *Paucura* lived in the Pácora River Basin, south of the *Arma*. The *Arma* were located "from the cordillera which separates the Pueblanco and Piedra Rivers, both tributaries of the Arma, to the basin of the Pácora River, from the cordillera central" (Jijón y Caamaño, 1936–38, vol. 2). The *Cenufana* (*Cenufama, Cenufara*) lived to the north of the *Arma*.

CULTURE

SUBSISTENCE ACTIVITIES

All these tribes were good cultivators of maize, sweet manioc, and beans (*Phaseolus vulgaris*). They grew various fruits, especially palms called "pixivaes" or "pijivaes," and pitahayas and paltas, but they also collected wild fruits. They raised cotton (*Gossypium arboreum*) and coca (especially the *Arma* and *Quimbaya*).

The animals most commonly hunted were rabbits (*Sylvilagus fulvescens*), deer (*Odocoileus virginianus columbicus*), and guadaquinajes. The sources do not mention fishing, but it must have been practiced, especially by the peoples along the Cauca and other large rivers.

HOUSES AND VILLAGES

Quimbaya, Picara, Paucura, and *Pozo* houses were rectangular (Robledo, *in* Jijón y Caamaño, 1936–38, vol. 2). Cieza describes *Quimbaya* houses as small ones, made of cane. The *Pozo* houses were large and round, with a circular ground plan. They were protected by palisades of thick canes and had elevated, mat-covered platforms which served as watch-towers and were also dedicated to human sacrifice.

Arma houses were large, with a circular plan, and the frame consisted of large poles arched across from the sides. They were covered with thatch, and the interiors were divided into compartments by means of mats, providing accommodations for many occupants. The houses were fortified with palisades, or rows of verticle bamboo trunks, forming streets. In the center of each village was a platform or gallery provided with stairs. It was dedicated to sacrifices. The habitations of the *Picara* and *Paucura* had enclosures fenced with thick canes on which were kept trophy skulls.

Of furniture, we know only that these tribes had mats, which served as house and wall covers, hammocks (*Quimbaya*), pottery vessels, and metates without legs, with two legs at one end so as to tilt them, or with three or four legs. Goldwork was represented by spoons, small jars, and plates.

CLOTHING AND ADORNMENT

All these tribes used woven cotton garments, but only as breechclouts (maures). The *Arma*, however, also made breechclouts of bark cloth.

The *Quimbaya* had head bands (monteras) of woven cotton, which fitted closely over the forehead with one or two quadrangular bands hanging down behind. The *Arma*, said Cieza, went to war "dressed or armed with gold from head to foot."

Personal adornment in all the tribes included gold crowns, nose ornaments, earrings, necklaces, and bracelets. The *Quimbaya* wore bands around the knees and anklets, both as ornaments and to constrict the legs. Common people cut their hair, but chiefs wore theirs long as evidence of status. Body hair was pulled out with special depilatory pincers of gold.

The *Pozo* and *Arma*, especially the chiefs, painted themselves, preferably with yellow, blue, and black on the face, and anointed their bodies with an odorous resin over which they painted red, bixa. These tribes also perforated the lower lip with spines and wore gold labrets through the holes. The labrets hung down in such a manner that the Spaniards called them "beards" (Robledo, *in* Jijón y Caamaño, 1936–38, vol. 2). For warfare, the Indians wore a feather headdress (Cieza de Léon, 1932).

The *Quimbaya* and perhaps the *Pozo* deformed their skulls.

TRANSPORTATION

The *Quimbaya* made bridges of creepers. The *Arma* constructed large roads which ran as far as the Province of Cenufana.

MANUFACTURES

Weaving and cloth.—The *Arma* made bark coth, and they and the other tribes produced finely woven cotton cloth.

Basketry and pottery.—In addition to mats, frequently mentioned in the sources, these tribes made baskets for storing and transporting objects. Their pots included vessels for ordinary use, large receptacles for holding objects of gold, jars for boiling salt, and beautiful painted ware. The last are not mentioned by the conquistadors, but archeological material shows that they were finely polished and were painted with negative designs or with effigies. (See Handbook, vol. 2, p. 839.)

Metallurgy.—A characteristic industry was goldworking. The metal was melted in crucibles, hammered, and beaten into sheets. It was mixed with different proportions of copper, melted and cast, or else worked by repoussé. Gold objects included spoons, knives, plates, and, in the words of the first Spaniards who saw these Indians, "flyingfish, eagles, guans, vampires, pincers, everything that is seen they had in jewels." (For illustrations of *Quimbaya* goldwork, see Handbook, vol. 2, pl. 170.)

The Indians obtained the gold from placer sands or from mines, extracting it from the latter with a short sharp-pointed stick.

Salt working.—The industry of extracting salt from saline water was perhaps expedited by the availability of metal for making evaporating vessels. The *Quimbaya,* instead of using pottery vessels, as was common among many Colombian tribes, such as the *Chibcha* and *Páez,* used copper kettles. When the salt water began to thicken, "They removed it and mixed it with more salt water, and boiled it again until it began to crystallize into grains, not a lump, when they took it out and made it into a loaf and compressed it between cold ashes so that it came out very white" (Simón, 1882–92).

The *Arma* extracted salt and traded it for gold.

SOCIAL AND POLITICAL ORGANIZATION

Polygyny was practiced, especially by the headmen. Among the *Carrapa, Picara,* and *Paucura,* the chiefs married their sisters and nieces to perpetuate their aristocracy, though the *Arma* prohibited marriage with siblings. The *Arma* did not require that women be virgins at marriage.

Inheritance was from father to son and, lacking a son, to the sister's son. Among the *Carrapa,* if the chief died without sons the principal wife inherited his authority and possessions, and when she died the chief's sister's son inherited them, as elsewhere.

The *Quimbaya* consisted of a confederacy of six subtribes, governed respectively by the following chiefs: Tucurrumbá, or Tacoronvi, Yanva, Zazaquavi, Via, and Pindana. The *Carrapa* chief was Irrua, who fought and vanquished the *Quimbaya.* Pimana was chief of the *Picara.* The *Arma,* from whom were derived the *Pozo,* accorded their chief special treatment, the people building his house, working his fields, giving him women, and providing him with gold as an offering and a tribute.

LIFE CYCLE

A woman bore her child unaided in a hammock, as shown by a representation on a *Quimbaya* gold ornament. Afterward, she bathed in the river. No diet or confinement is reported.

Until they were 12 years old children were under the complete care of the mother and aided her in her tasks. After this age the boys were under their father's care.

Nothing is known of girls' or boys' puberty observances.

Sick people were treated by shamans, or witches, or, among the *Quimbaya,* they were cured with baths in the river and with herbs.

At the death of a chief the *Quimbaya* spent a night of vigil, weeping, drinking intoxicating chicha, and singing. The following day the body was burned and the ashes were placed in a gold receptacle, which was buried at great depth. In other cases, the deceased was clothed, provided with food and weapons, and buried with his slaves and wives, who were given a stupefying drink called "tonga" before being interred alive. The *Carrapa* and *Pozo* buried a dead man in a deep grave in his own house, accompanied by food, drink, his possessions, and some women.

These tribes were extremely warlike, and *Arma* subtribes even fought among themselves. The main enemies of the *Arma*, however, were the *Quimbaya, Putimá, Carrapa,* and *Pijao.* The *Picara* fought the *Pozo* and *Carrapa,* and the *Carrapa* warred with the *Picara* and *Quimbaya.* The *Pozo* engaged the *Carrapa, Picara,* and *Paucura.* In these wars, as well as those against the White invaders, the Indians fought with darts, bows and arrows, spear throwers, slings, and flint knives. The knives were used to cut open and flay the dead for cannibalistic purposes. The *Arma, Pozo,* and *Carrapa* carried banners of woven cotton decorated with stars and figures of gold. The *Quimbaya* carried shields made of their own hair, while the *Arma* used a kind of protective armor of gold. There is archeological evidence that the *Quimbaya* had helmets of gold, as illustrated in the collections of the British Museum in London.

Cannibalism must have been a feature of most of the warfare, for the warriors often carried special ropes to tie up their prisoners and flint knives to quarter the dead. The *Arma, Picara,* and *Paucura* kept their prisoners in enclosures, where they were fattened until the tribe ate them. Cannibalistic ceremonies were accompanied by special festivities. Of the *Arma,* López de Velasco states (1916, pp. 193–208), "Brother eats sister, husband eats wife, and father eats son; they fatten prisoners and have festivities and dances when they consume the living, limb by limb," an opinion shared by Cieza (1932) and Robledo (*in* Jijón y Caamaño, 1936–38, vol. 2). Although cannibalism of enemies cannot be doubted, it is wholly unlikely that endocannibalism was simultaneously practiced, and this statement illustrates the extravagant and indiscriminative claims often made by the early chroniclers.

These tribes displayed trophies of their sacrificial victims. The *Picara, Paucura,* and *Pozo* placed trophy skulls on the tops of bamboo posts in front of their houses. The *Pozo* also kept skulls and bones inside their houses and placed corpses on large poles to face the rising sun.

ESTHETIC AND RECREATIONAL ACTIVITIES

Art.—The highest expression of art was unquestionably in goldwork. It was manifest in the selection of decorative motifs and particularly in the sculpture of the molds, or of the positives for making molds, which took the form of very perfect and realistic, though miniature, figures.

Games.—The *Quimbaya* had a special contest in which a line of women and another of men and boys faced each other. They assaulted each other with weapons, such as spear throwers, shouting "batatabati," meaning "Look, we are playing!" This usually resulted in several people being wounded or even killed. (Cf. this with the *Páez* contest, Handbook, vol. 2, p. 952, and that of *Lile,* this volume, p. 307.)

Dancing, singing, and musical instruments.—Singing and dancing were common, but the dances were not recorded, and only the songs used at a chief's death are described. These songs related to the chief's deeds and to his and his ancestors' exploits.

Music accompanied attacks in warfare as well as peaceful songs and dances. Among instruments were membranophones, such as drums, and aerophones, such as cane flutes, pottery ocarinas, gold whistles, and trumpets. In the lower portions of the cane posts sustaining war trophies, the *Picara* and *Paucura* made holes in which the wind made a sound.

Narcotic and intoxicating beverages.—These tribes cultivated coca and, therefore, must have used it as a narcotic. They made fermented chicha, which the *Quimbaya* and *Carrapa* served in gold cups. On solemn social or religious occasions, they became drunk on chicha.

RELIGION AND SHAMANISM

Some variation is evident in religion. The *Quimbaya* had a temple dedicated to the god named Nabsacadas. Here, they made offerings of bags of maize and of an unfermented maize drink (massato) to their gods, which the Spaniards as usual called "demons." Inside the temple was a painted stool placed over a mat decorated with colors, and there was an offering of 14 cotton blankets. War captives were dedicated to the divinities, and, according to Robledo, one was sacrificed each day. The *Quimbaya* believed in metempsychosis, or the transmigration of souls, and in resurrection after death.

The *Carrapa*, who had no temples, worshiped the sun. They believed that their god could appear before them, and when sick they made offerings to him. The *Pozo* made sacrifices to the gods before war expeditions. Their gods were represented by wooden idols, with human skulls, which had features modeled in wax. The idols were painted, decorated like chiefs, and kept in the houses. Every week the *Picara* and *Paucura* sacrificed two men to their gods. The sacrifices were made on platforms in the dwellings, and the victims were offered to the god. The *Arma* had mat-covered and well-ordered altars placed on high platforms in their dwellings. Here they made human sacrifices and burned fragrant incense in pottery censers before their idols.

TRIBES OF THE CAUCA-ATRATO REGION

TRIBAL LOCATIONS

From south to north, between the left or western bank of the Cauca River and the Atrato River, were the following tribes: The *Ancerma* (*Anzerma, Anserma*), who were called *Umbra* by the local Indians, extended westward to the territory of the *Cima* in the Cordillera Occidental, eastward to the *Cartatama* on the Cauca River and beyond the river to *Pozo* territory, and northward to the *Quinchía* and *Zopía*. They were also bordered by the *Tabuya* and *Guatica* (Fernández Piedrahita, 1881). Toward the Province of Chocó were the *Toro*. The *Quinchía* and *Zopía* (*Soppia, Supía*) were bounded on the south by the *Ancerma* and the *Cartatama* and, across the Cauca River, by the *Pozo*. The *Caramanta* were the next tribe to the north and extended to *Buriticá* country. On the south they must have adjoined the *Ancerma*, in part at least, for these tribes had formed an alliance. Their neighbors to the east were the *Cartama*. North of the *Caramanta* were the *Buriticá-Antiocha,* who abutted the *Pequi* on the east and the *Evéjico* on the west. The *Nutibara, Nore,* and *Guaca* were identified with them. The *Evéjico* (*Hevégico*) occupied the province surrounded by the *Penco, Pequi, Porruto,* and *Buriticá*. The *Catío*, located by Castellanos (1852) between the Nechi and Porce Rivers, adjoining the Province of Darién, were probably situated, as Uribe Ángel (1885) has pointed out, "between the western bank of the Cauca, the course of the Atrato, the Atlantic coast, and the serranía de Abibe."

The *Guazuzú*, of the Province of Arriba, lived between the *Abibe* and *Urabá,* adjoining the *Antiocha* (*Antioquia*). The *Abibe* inhabited the mountains of that name, and extended north to the *Cenú*, east to the *Guazuzú,* and west to the *Chocó* and *Cuna*.

SUBSISTENCE ACTIVITIES

All these tribes occupied mountainous, temperate regions. The early historians noted that the *Ancerma* were outstanding farmers. They mention that the following plants were cultivated: Cotton, maize, ají (*Capsicum annuum*), coca, root crops such as sweet manioc, sweet-potatoes (*Ipomoca batatas*), a saffron called "rumi" in Antiochia, and kidney beans (*Phaseolus vulgaris*). Common fruits included guayavas, palm fruits which were eaten cooked, quinces, guamas (*Inga* spp.), sour-sop (*Annona muricata*), nisperos or medlar (*Achras zapotilla*), guabas, a palm called pixivaes or pijivaes from the palmito or heart of which they made a kind of bread and a drink, avocados (*Persea americana*), and pineapples (*Ananas sativus*).

Animals hunted included the iguana, fresh-water turtle, deer (*Odocoileus virginianus columbicus*), peccary (puercos), otters (*Lutra annectens*), tapir (*Tapirus roulinii*), ant bear (*Tremarctos ornatus majori*), oppossum (*Caluromys philander*), rabbit (*Sylvilagus fulvescens*), partridge (*Colinus* sp., or *Odontophorus* sp.), turkeys (*Penelope*), turtle doves (*Columbidae*), guans (*Crax alcetor*), and duck (*Anas*).

The Indians cooked vegetables in many ways, and used both salt and pepper as condiments. They ate fruits, sometimes cooked, and, in

Antiochia, according to Castellanos (1852), they prepared maize in various ways, including a thick gruel, now characteristic of the Departments of Antioquia and Caldas, and tortillas.

HOUSES AND VILLAGES

Houses were built of wood, and most of them were fortified with a stockade of thick poles or canes. Dwellings built on platforms or piles, which are characteristic of the Pacific coast, were also found here. In addition to pile dwellings, the *Toro* built houses in trees. *Antiochia* houses accommodated more than 200 persons and were reached by ladders. *Catío* houses had floors more than four estados (an estado is 1.85 yards) above the ground, and they were enclosed by thick poles which reached to the thatched roof. There were loopholes for shooting arrows in case of attack, and heavy, loose pieces of wood that could be dropped down as deadfalls. To store water, the *Catío* made gutters of half-bamboos, which collected rain and conducted it into large wooden vessels or pottery jars. The *Ancerma* used floor mats and elevated, mat-covered beds.

Special temples were built by the *Ancerma, Caramanta, Nutibara, Nore,* and *Guaca*. Those of the *Ancerma* were built on hilltops, reached by bamboo stairs. The *Ancerma* and *Caramanta* had bamboo enclosures at the village entrances, where they kept trophy skulls. Among the *Antiochia* there was a large village, divided into wards (barrios). The *Toro*, however, lacked villages, their houses being dispersed.

ENGINEERING WORKS

From Ancerma to Cali ran a native road. The *Catío* had roads leading up to their fortified houses; these roads were protected with pitfalls. The *Abibe* built roads along the sides of their mountains, and they constructed bridges of vines that were anchored to trees and were floored with strong cross poles.

CLOTHING AND ADORNMENT

Clothing was commonly made of woven cotton cloth. *Ancerma* men wore a breechclout (maure), which passed between the legs with the ends, front and back, hanging down over a band a palm wide made of thin shell beads (chaquiras) and gold. These breechclouts were adorned with paintings. Women wore painted blankets (mantas) hanging to their feet. Chiefs wore breechclouts and a large robe or blanket, called "nagua," which was decorated with paintings and circular and star-shaped ornaments in gold leaf. The robe hung from the shoulders to the feet and was constricted at the waist with a belt. Chiefs' wives wore similar blankets. *Caramanta* men wore a breechclout supported by a cord around the waist, and women wore a blanket covering them from the breast to the feet. Such garments were common to the other tribes, except the *Catío*, who had more luxurious dress, similar to that of the *Ancerma*, and the *Toro*, who wore bark-cloth garments, called "amahaguas," similar to those of the *Arma* and *Chanco*.

The hair was generally worn long, especially by chiefs among the *Ancerma*, *Nutibara*, *Abibe*, and *Catío*, but the last cut it short when going to war. The *Toro* cut their hair short, plucking it out so as to form a crown, like that of the friars, hence their name, "*Coronado*." The *Ancerma* wore garlands and crowns of feathers, nose ornaments (caricories), four or five pairs of earrings, necklaces of beads (chaquiras) with gold figurines, especially in the form of frogs (chiefs' necklaces were entirely of gold), and ligatures made of strands of chaquiras below the knees. In addition, the chiefs wore their fingernails long and painted their faces in various designs and colors. The *Buriticá* and *Catío* also painted themselves and like the *Evégico*, wore gold ornaments.

TRANSPORTATION

Among the *Ancerma*, *Nutibara*, and *Abibe*, chiefs were carried in hammocks or litters. Transportation of objects and merchandise was by human carrier over the mountainous country, but devices used are not mentioned.

MANUFACTURES

Ceramics.—The only mention of pottery is food containers placed in graves and water vessels. Ceramics are known principally from objects taken from graves.

Basketry and weaving.—Bark cloth is accredited to the *Toro*. Of basketry, the only mention is of matting, which was commonly used, especially by the *Ancerma*. Cordage was generally made and served for belts, hammock making, necklace strings, and the like. All tribes but the *Toro* wove cotton textiles, which they painted and made into clothing.

Skin preparation.—There was no skin preparation, except in making trophies of slain enemies, whose bodies were flayed and the skins stuffed with ashes (see below).

Metallurgy.—Metallurgy was as important as among the tribes east of the Cauca River, for the chroniclers speak of the abundance of gold. The chief of the *Caramanta* "took out what he wanted." The *Buriticá* mined gold with sharp sticks and smelted it with forges, furnaces, and crucibles. This industry was common to all the tribes, except the *Guazuzú*, who obtained their gold through trade.

SOCIAL AND POLITICAL LIFE

Polygyny is reported for the *Ancerma*, *Caramanta*, *Guazuzú*, *Nore*, and *Guaca*, *Catío*, and *Nutibara*. The *Ancerma* were also exogamous by village. An *Ancerma* man, especially a chief, had as many wives as he could support, taking each, regardless of whether she were a virgin, without ceremony. The first to bear a son was considered the principal wife. These women came from other villages, and, when they were five months pregnant, they returned to their native village, presumably to remain until the child was born. Among the *Catío,* who were reported to have as many as 20 wives, a wife was purchased through the offices of a go-between. In matrimonial relations the man might make no advances to his wife until she gave a special sign, but there was great fidelity. Adultery was severely punished, and a woman's husband and parents guarded her closely. The *Zopía,* on exceptional occasions, practiced some form of marriage with close relatives.

Among the *Ancerma,* possessions and authority were inherited by the eldest son, or if he had died, by the next son. Lacking sons, the daughters inherited. Succession among the *Zopía* and *Nutibara* passed to the oldest son of the principal wife, and, in default of such a son, to the son of the man's oldest sister. The *Catío* present a curious case, if the sources are interpreted correctly, for the slave who had worked longest for his master inherited his master's goods, wives, and sons.

Political authority was in the hands of chiefs, and in some cases there were several chiefs in one tribe, showing an organization into subtribes. Eight chiefs are mentioned for *Ancerma* territory: Ocusca, Humbruza, Fanfarrones, Guarma, Chatapa, Umbría, Riterón, and Ciricha. Cauroma was chief of the *Caramanta,* and Zuzaburruco ruled the *Antiochia.* Nutibara was the main chief of the *Nutibara* and *Abibe* but governed the latter through his brother, Quinuchi. Nabonuco was chief of the *Nore* and *Guaca,* and Zuzabunuco of the *Evégico.* The *Catío* had several chiefs, but their subtribes had formed a confederation, especially for warfare. Their main chief was Tone. Among the *Guazuzú* a chief controlled about 10 houses, each house sheltering 8 to 10 families.

Most of these chiefs, as among the *Ancerma* and *Nutibara,* enjoyed special privileges and etiquette. For example, they went forth carried in hammocks or litters, the latter decorated with plates and ornaments of gold.

The *Ancerma* punished thiefs by making them slaves and eventually selling them to another tribe, presumably to compensate the robbed party with the price received.

These tribes also kept prisoners of war as slaves. The *Ancerma* sold captives taken from the *Caramanta* and *Antiochia.* Among the *Nore* and *Guaca,* slaves were married to tribal members so that their offspring might be sacrificed in cannibalistic feasts. The *Catío* made their slaves farm their lands or else ate them. The *Guazuzú* sold their slaves to the *Antiochia,* or kept them to perform labor, and buried some of them with a chief when he died.

ECONOMIC FEATURES

Gold and slaves were the main objects of native trade. Slaves were sold from tribe to tribe, especially by the peoples practicing cannibalism, and were given in exchange for gold or food. Gold objects were the main item of exchange among *Ancerma,* who traded with the *Pozo,* or who carried on intratribal trade at periodic markets ("tianquez"). The *Antiochia* traded mainly with the *Nohava.* With their gold the *Buriticá* purchased foods, while the *Evégico* bought "cerdos monteses" (peccaries?) and other things. The *Guazuzú* exchanged fine, painted, cotton cloth, which they manufactured, and slaves for gold objects, which they did not make.

LIFE CYCLE

Observances at sacrifices, marriages, birth, initiation, and the like, though involving ceremonies and constituting the heart of the culture of each group, passed largely unnoticed by the chroniclers, who, however, frequently mention practices at death because of the gold interred with the deceased.

These tribes were evidently very fertile, for Robledo observes that an *Ancerma* woman had a child each year.

At the death of a chief the *Ancerma* placed the body on a platform or grill between two fires until the corpse had dried; then they buried it either in a deep grave on the top of a hill or under the floor of the house, accompanied by food, ornaments, weapons, and some of the man's wives. *Caramanta* burial was like that of the *Ancerma,* except that they put the body at the door of the house in a deep hole with an opening toward the east. The *Nore* and *Guaca* wept many days for a chief and cut the hair of the wives and those who were closest to him. The deceased was placed in a mound, with a paved floor and an opening to the east, and was wrapped in blankets, adorned with ornaments, equipped with his weapons, and accompanied by women and servants, who were buried alive. The *Catío* and *Guazuzú* buried in the same manner.

WARFARE

Two features are of special interest: the boiling water which the *Antiochia* hurled at their enemy from their pile dwellings, and the pitfalls filled with sharp stakes which the *Catío* and *Evégico* concealed in trails. Otherwise, the common weapons were darts, bows and arrows, lances, spear throwers, slings, and macanas (clubs).

The *Nore* and *Guaca* fought among themselves and against the *Buriticá* and made slaves of their prisoners. The *Evégico* fought in ordered formations, and their main enemies were the *Pequi.* When the Spaniards slept or camped in *Evégico* houses, the Indians burned the houses afterward, possibly because of some magical belief. The *Catío* fought frequently against the *Antiochia,* hiring neighboring Indians to accompany their war parties and making slaves of their prisoners. They had forts, such as one called Nobobarco, on the summits of hills. So brave were these Indians that when the conquistadors brought a bulldog to tear one of them to pieces the Indian said, without fear or sign of pain, "Hurry, eat, eat."

The *Ancerma* made war trophies of human skulls, which they painted vermilion, and of arms, legs, and skins stuffed with ashes, and placed them on tall bamboo poles in their village plazas. The *Caramanta, Antiochia, Nutibara, Nore, Guaca,* and *Catío* exhibited their trophies over the doors of their houses.

CANNIBALISM

Simón (1882–92) ascribes cannibalism to the *Ancerma,* but López de Velasco (1916) denies it, and Robledo, whose word carries more weight as he was one of their conquerors, states that they practiced little cannibalism but ate game animals. It is possible that these Indians were cannibalistic only on ritual occasions and that their practices corresponded to Simón's statement that "they held that those who ate the flesh or drank the blood of the vanquished would become superior to him."

The *Caramanta* bought Indian slaves from the *Ancerma* in order to eat them. The *Antiochia* did likewise, and, according to Simón, they held their slaves over a special stone where they cut open their breasts and removed the fat to make torches to illuminate their mine tunnels. They ate the flesh of these victims and also sold it to others. Descobar (*in* Jijón y Caamaño, 1936–38, vol. 2) claims that they fattened their sons— perhaps referring to the sons of slaves—and ate them during feasts. The *Buriticá, Nutibara, Catío,* and *Abibe* ate only their enemies. The *Nore* and *Guaca* ate the sons of slaves taken in war as well as captives and old male slaves.

ESTHETIC AND RECREATIONAL ACTIVITIES

On the subject of art nothing can be added to the statements made concerning the tribes east of the Cauca River (this volume, p. 307).

The *Ancerma* gathered with their principal men in the houses of their chiefs, and for 3 or 4 days and nights danced, sang, and drank chicha until they were drunk; then they brawled, wounding and even killing each other. Chicha was generally used, being drunk as an intoxicant during communal religious and social feasts. To become drunk the *Ancerma* mixed an herb, called "tabaque," with chicha or with other drinks. In addition to chicha the *Nore* and *Guaca* made an intoxicating drink of certain roots.

RELIGION AND SHAMANISM

The *Ancerma* had wooden idols, the faces of which were painted various colors. On a hill, called Buena Vista by the Spaniards, they had a large sanctuary to which only the chiefs and priests had access. The main god was called Xixarama, and the sun and moon were his children. The sun and moon were supplicated for rain to water the crops. The *Ancerma* sent two virgins to a high hill, where Xixarama was thought to have intercourse with them.

The *Ancerma* also had priests or shamans, who cured by means of herbs as well as by passing their hands over the patient, massaging, sucking with the mouth, and blowing the supposed cause of the sickness into the air. When the sky darkened and rain threatened, they blew and spit upward, gesturing the rain away.

The *Caramanta* kept idols of wood and gold, some in their houses and others placed between bamboo posts at the entrances of their dwellings. They had temples in which they sacrificed Indians, cutting out the heart and parading with it while executing "areytos" or dances. To obtain water or sunshine necessary for their farming, they made sacrifices.

Among the *Antiochia* there was a "demon" cult. Old men spoke with this divinity and communicated their replies to the faithful. The demon or god of the *Nutibara*, called "Guaca," was represented as a jaguar. Its temple, a hut with the entrance facing east, was filled with gold offerings. The *Nore* and *Guaca* also had temples. The *Evégico* did not worship idols but had priests who spoke with the divinity. The *Catío* lacked temples, but worshiped two deities, Avira, the benevolent god—the Spaniards were called "Aira," the son of God—and Cunícuva, the evil god. They also worshiped the stars, had a legend of the flood, and believed that the souls of the dead were transformed into jaguars, pumas, and other animals. The *Toro* and *Zopia* were said to worship a "demon."

LORE AND LEARNING

These tribes had extensive knowledge of curative plants, and the *Toro* drank the juice of "bencenuco" against serpent bites.

Measures and weights were used by the *Catío* and *Evegico* in trade. The *Antiochia* used the balance beam, with gold weights.

Simón and Castellanos claimed that the *Catío* had a form of writing, which consisted of inscribing their histories in hieroglyphics painted on their cotton blankets. (Cf. with the *Cuna*, this volume, p. 268.)

THE INDIANS IN 1880

Uribe Ángel (1885, pp. 520–524) sketches the picture of the Indians who, in 1880, survived in the northeastern part of the State of Antioquia, near the Province of Chocó. Because of its climate and diseases, such as malaria, this region was infrequently penetrated by Whites. The Indians described by Uribe Ángel must have been predominantly though not entirely *Catío*.

The Indians practiced little agriculture, which was restricted to small plots of maize, sugarcane, and bananas. Hunting and fishing had assumed greater importance than formerly, and the Indians were provided with firearms and iron fishhooks. They slightly roasted maize and ground it, both for ordinary consumption and for a ration taken on trips. They became intoxicated frequently by drinking the traditional chicha, made of fermented ground maize, and modern aguardiente (hard liquor), and they used considerable tobacco.

Houses were still built on platforms. The Indians buried their dead under the house and abandoned it to build another some distance away. They were very clean, habitually bathing in the river each morning before breakfast and again during the day. They decorated themselves with red (bixa), applied to the face, arms, and legs, and with drawings done in a blackish pigment made from a fruit called "jagua." They dressed in bark cloth (corteza "mahagua") and a mantle of commercial cloth worn as a cape. Around their necks they wore strings of beads (cha-quiras), which included small glass beads and pieces of vanilla wood and sweet basil, which they called "yerba del buen querer" ("pleasing herb").

Women performed domestic chores, cared for the children, and trans-ported burdens while traveling. Men cleared the forest for farm plots and hunted and fished, foraging with their blowguns, firearms, and fishhooks.

A girl had an initiation feast, after which she married the first man she met. A boy had to show his skill with his blowgun by shooting a maize grain thrown into the air.

These Indians were ruled, according to the Colonial system, by a gov-ernor and a group of captains and judges, that is, by a cabildo or council of Indians.

The native religious cult had disintegrated, and the Indians had acquired some Catholicism, though they still believed in the gods, Cala-gavi and Antomiá.

THE TWENTIETH-CENTURY CATÍO

Between 1916 and 1922 an intelligent missionary, Mother Laura, made interesting observations on several Indian groups, including those of the banks of the Río Sucio and the Tuguridó and Murrí Rivers, those in Antadó and Chimiadó, and even some *Catío* in the jungles of the Sinú to which they had fled, pressed by modern colonists, from the mountains of Antioquia and Chocó. The subsequent ethnographic data are taken from her account (Madre Laura de Santa Catalina, 1936). New linguistic data on the *Catío* are supplied by Fr. Pablo del Santísimo Sacramento (1936).

These Indians still resist cultural change, clinging to their native customs and disliking to adopt modern clothing and rules. Distrust and suspicion are their defense against foreigners, and they do not wish to submit to the jurisdiction of Colombian laws. They settle injuries and wrongs by payments, after which disputants remain friends as if nothing had happened.

CULTURE

SUBSISTENCE ACTIVITIES

Each family has a small parcel of land on which it cultivates maize, yuca (sweet manioc), arracacha, mafafa, sugarcane, and a perennial species of bean called "vida." Groups assist each other in farming, singing to the rhythm of their work. The *Catío* gather a fragrant wild root, called "jaramalí," which they greatly relish.

Game animals include deer, opossums, guagua, and rabbits. The skulls of slain animals are hung from the roof beams of the huts. The Indians now raise pigs, chickens, and dogs. Fishing is very important. The Indians stay in caves on the riverbanks, where the men fish at night with hooks, while during the day the women show great skill in catching by hand fish called "cuere cueriar" ("cuere" means "fish" in *Catío*) that live under rocks.

Meals consist of ground maize, roasted bananas which take the place of bread and accompany all meals, roasted or broiled game in a state of decomposition, and boiled birds and fish, both of which are eaten bones, entrails, and all. They occasionally obtain beef, and, though little acquainted with sweets, they use chocolate.

HOUSES

The *Catío* still live in huts elevated on platforms about 2 m. (6 feet) above the ground and reached by a wooden ladder. These huts are circular, about 2.4 m. (8 feet) in diameter, and roofed with thatch. Inside, there is a shelf holding calabash cups, pottery cooking pans, and ollas. The fireplace is in the center and over it hang the skulls of wild animals and some bones.

CLOTHING AND ADORNMENT

Men wear a breachclout (ambura) 1½ varas (about 48 inches) long, which is usually made of linen and sometimes is decorated with bone beads (chaquiras). Women also wear a cloth (jampurí) covering the genitals. It is twice as long as the men's ambura and is made of flowered, or striped, modern, commercial printed cloth in various colors, except green and yellow, which they do not like. Over these, both sexes wear a mantle about 4 m. (13 feet) long. Men wear theirs so that it somewhat covers the face, and the end falls behind to the ground. Women's are worn over the shoulders, with one end wrapped around behind so as to cover the left hip. Everyone adorns his body with figures painted black or red. Women comb their hair to fall over the shoulders and wear chaquira necklaces (ocamá) which hang down to the breast. Young women wear roses around their necks and, if they can obtain it, a red scarf, which they all desire. Men have long hair hanging down behind, chaquira necklaces, and, if unmarried, a garland of roses. Chiefs wear a garland of leaves, and shamans (jaibaná) one of feathers.

MANUFACTURES

The modern *Catío* make pottery water jars, ollas, and plates, calabash drinking cups, and a variety of baskets. They also make blowguns but purchase firearms, machetes, and axes from the Whites.

SOCIAL LIFE

Marriage is very brittle, and woman's position is inferior. Upon marriage the woman goes to the house of her husband or father-in-law to become her husband's faithful servant in farming, running the household, and carrying goods. She may be thrown out and replaced by another woman when the husband wishes, even if she has small children, merely because "he is tired of her." She may not take anything from the household with her. She accepts her fate, saying, "If you are a woman, what can you do? It is the Indian law." A married woman may even be turned out by her own father.

Children are cared for by their parents until they can shift for themselves, and they are readily abandoned. The attitude toward children is shown by the common remark, "My son went away" or "My daughter left the hut. It was good of her." Few know much about their own parents, and they take whatever name they please.

The Indians are being dispossessed of their lands by the Whites, as happened in Murrí, where they had to yield lands to which they had held title for more than 50 years. Every 6 months the men go to work in the harvest on the civilized, neighboring haciendas.

There is no more warfare.

SICKNESS AND DEATH

When a person is sick his relatives call a shaman (jaibaná); if he becomes worse he is abandoned in a corner of the house on the belief that nothing can be done, and the family continues normal life.

At death, the relatives sing sad songs. They place many specially purchased mantles on the corpse, which they bury, afterward burning the house. "Tobo" or "moindú" leaves are placed at the foot of the ladders of other houses to prevent the soul from entering a place it likes, for it would go into a house which lacked such leaves and remain there forever.

Decorative art is influenced by the Indian's dislike of certain colors. They not only lack native terms for some colors, but they assured Madre Laura that "it is not easy for an Indian to distinguish green, blue and yellow; they are all the same color."

Drums, trumpets always worn suspended from the neck, and modern stringed instruments or small guitars comprise present-day musical instruments. The *Catío* sing melancholy and soft songs in the native language, especially when drunk. Rhythmical singing to the tempo of work plays an important part in their communal farming labor.

The Indians dance when they have gathered together and become drunk, or on religious occasions. Dancing is not done in pairs, but in groups, each person performing individually, even in the modern churches.

The Indians make intoxicating chicha of maize, fermentation of which is started by the addition of some grains that have been chewed. They also like modern hard liquor.

RELIGION

The god most frequently worshiped and feared today is Antomiá, who gives shamans their power. The Indians living in Uré believe that another god, Caragabí, had married in Quibdó, now capital of Chocó, but, when his wife was unfaithful, he transformed her into a bird as punishment and went to the sky with a sister or sister-in-law of his mother. The origin myth of the creation and manner of living of the Indians is given below.

SHAMANISM

Shamanism is of great importance and virtually dominates the activities of the *Catío*. A few old Spanish elements may have entered the pattern. The shaman or witch (jaibaná) has magical power, which Antomiá gives him when his initiation is concluded. He is both feared and sought, as he may cause as well as cure disease.

The confirmation of a shaman is celebrated with intoxicating drinks, while an older shaman performs the initiation rites. The neophyte is put in a trance, and the master speaks in a low voice, then whistles three times to the god Antomiá, and hangs a bunch of wooden figurines and a mirror, the insignia of the profession, around the neophyte's neck. When the young man awakens, the ceremony is completed. Henceforth, the new shaman may perform cures and ask payment for his services, usually one or more deer, or the equivalent.

Both men and women may be shamans, and some persons are destined before birth to take up this profession. In such cases, a practicing shaman performs rites over the mother's belly, and from time to time after the child is born nocturnal ceremonies are held with dances and drinking, while the child is bathed in water of "anamí," after which the master sings and passes his magic stick over the child's body.

In case of sickness the shaman fasts during the evening, and that night he dreams what he must do. Next morning he goes to the patient who must be purified of all contact with or influence by Catholic religious objects. He blows tobacco smoke over the ailing place or over the whole body and passes his idols (jai) over the body. He has various idols, one for each sickness and one that is larger and more powerful than the others. He is aided by a young woman, who must have her teeth and fingernails painted to the end with "jampurí" and who wears bunches of herbs (anamí) around her neck. The woman kills a chicken, boils it, and throws the cooking water into the river without spilling a drop lest the jai be annoyed and not complete the cure. At the curing altar nine jai hang from a pole to the left of the snake jai, or cross (a small tablet of white balsa wood painted with red and black zigzag lines). A small calabash cup of hard liquor is placed at the foot of each jai, and the cooked chicken is located so that its odor will please them and make them cure better. The shaman prays to each jai, which he takes down to wet the end of it in the liquor. He finishes off the liquor in each cup, then massages the patient with chewed tobacco, blows on the person's fingertips and crown, and rubs him with a narrow piece of new cloth. In the cup of liquor poured for the snake jai he places three iron nails and then puts one end of this jai in the patient's mouth and the other end against the mirror which every shaman carries around his neck. After this he gathers up the chicken and the liquor with the nails in it, and the female assistant casts them into the river, for these are left-overs of what the jai ate or drank, and the sickness adheres to them.

A shaman has the power of causing disease, and only a more powerful shaman can cure it. He may make a child sick with his breath, causing an obstacle to become lodged in its throat. This causes death if another shaman does not cure it. The Indians distinguish natural death from that caused by witchcraft. In the latter case the identity of the evil sorcerer is ascertained by covering the face of the deceased with ashes, then washing them off when the face will resemble that of the witch.

In addition to shamanism, curing is accomplished with various herbs. Chewed tobacco leaves are rubbed on the stomach for colic. For diarrhea and dysentery a large quantity of bees' honey is drunk.

MYTHOLOGY

The following legend, collected by Madre Laura de Santa Catalina, combines native myth with historical tales and even has traces of Christian influence:

When God created the world, the Indians were people, not animals, and knew a great deal. But one Indian woman was deceived by the very poisonous serpent of the kind called birrí, and married him, hiding the fact from her father. To conceal her serpent husband, the woman placed him under a tree and covered him with firewood she had brought for the house. When the wood was nearly used up, she brought more. After a while she gave birth to a serpent son. The serpent mother-in-law with many members of her species attended the birth to see her grandson. When the serpents had gone, the Indian woman's father returned, and, smelling the odor of birrí or of their excrement, he removed the firewood and found the serpent husband and the little serpent grandson underneath it. He understood what had happened. In a fury he whipped his daughter and killed the serpent and his grandson. At this, the serpent mother-in-law returned to revive her son, but the body turned into a soldier, called "Spaniard." Full of fury, the soldier made war on the Indians and drove them to the mountains. Then the Indians became fools and animals, and did not again turn into people. They would not become people again, because the serpent soldier would return and finish them.

Another story related that Dabeiba was formerly a cold land, but a shaman stood on an eminence on the right bank of the Río Sucio and blew tobacco smoke over it, making it a warm country. Since then Dabeiba has been unhealthy for children.

TRIBES OF THE PROVINCE OF ABURRÁ

TRIBAL LOCATIONS

The province of the *Aburrá* (*Avurrá*) was the territory between the Magdalena and Cauca Rivers, east of Cartama. The *Nutabe* and *Urezo* lived east of the Cauca River, between it and the Nechí River. The *Tahami*, who were related culturally to the *Nutabe*, occupied the same area. The *Yamicí* were located between the Nechí and Porce Rivers. Thus, all these tribes inhabited the northern portion of the Sub-Andean culture area and adjoined the culture area of Darién or Cenú, i.e., the North Colombia Lowlands.

CULTURE

SUBSISTENCE ACTIVITIES

Ethnographic information is scant, but it shows that these tribes practiced agriculture, cultivating maize, beans, sweet manioc, sweetpotatoes, yams, and cotton.

Among animals hunted were peccaries, which ran in large herds in this territory. The *Yamicí* captured and raised the young ones, which they fattened, as the *Aburrá* fattened mute dogs.

The *Aburrá* made loaves of salt, in the same way as the tribes farther south, whereas the *Yamicí* used salt water from springs, without crystallizing or cooking it. The *Aburrá* had storage places in their houses for foods, such as maize and manioc, and the *Yamicí* preserved fish, making it into meal.

HOUSES, VILLAGES, AND OTHER STRUCTURES

These tribes built large houses. In the territory of the *Nutabe* and *Urezo* the Spaniards found large, ancient structures which had been destroyed.

The *Aburrá* made aqueducts for water and very wide roads. The *Nutabe* and *Urezo* also made wide straight roads, and, over the Cauca River, bridges of woven vines, three palms wide, with hand rails.

CLOTHING AND ADORNMENT

The *Yamici* wore virtually nothing but adorned themselves with feathers, ornaments, breastplates, and diadems of gold, all finely worked and well burnished or hammered. The *Nutabe* and *Urezo* dressed in white cotton cloth, ornamented with colors, and adorned themselves with plumes, gold crowns and armor, and red paint (bixa). The *Aburrá* clad themselves in a blanket, 1½ varas long and 1 vara wide (about 48 by 32 inches), and the men held the penis up by means of a white or colored thread affixed to the belt and tied around the prepuce. They wore a crown of feathers, gathered the hair up on the head, had a nutria pelt hanging down the back, and painted themselves with bixa.

MANUFACTURES

The *Nutabe* and *Urezo* were good weavers and builders, and the *Yamici,* like the tribes farther south, were gold miners and skilled goldworkers.

For hunting and warfare they used darts with fire-hardened palm points, spear throwers, macanas, slings, bows and arrows, stone axes, and maces.

SOCIAL FEATURES

The *Nutabe* and *Urezo* carried on trade with the *Tahami,* but the *Yamici* fought with the people on their frontiers, the *Patángoro, Aburrá, Guamoco,* and even the *Malebú* of Mompox. The *Yamici* enslaved their prisoners but did not sacrifice or eat them.

BIBLIOGRAPHY

Acosta, 1901; Andagoya (*in* Jijón y Caamaño, 1936–38, vol. 2); Arena Paz, 1922; Asensio, 1921; Bennett, 1944; Castellanos, 1847 (1852, 1874); Cieza de León, 1932; Cuervo (see Sardilla, 1891–94, vol. 2); Descobar (*in* Jijón y Caamaño, 1936–38, vol. 2); Fernández Piedrahita, 1881; Ford, 1944; García, 1937; Guillén Chaparro, 1889; Hermano Justo, 1943; Hernández de Alba, 1938; Jijón y Caamaño, 1936–38, vol. 2; Laura de Santa Catalina, 1936; López de Velasco, 1916; Ospina, 1905, 1918; Pablo de Santísimo Sacramento, 1936; Posado Arango, 1875; Restrepo, 1937; Restrepo Tirado, 1929; Rivet, 1943; Robledo (*in* Jijón y Caamaño, 1936–38, vol. 2; also see Sardilla, 1891–94, vol. 2); Sardilla, 1891–94, vol. 2; Simón, 1882–92; Uribe Ángel, 1885; Wassén, 1936.

TRIBES OF THE NORTH COLOMBIA LOWLANDS

By Gregorio Hernández de Alba

INTRODUCTION

A group of Tropical Forest tribes, which differed culturally from their neighbors, the Sub-Andean peoples of the Cauca River (this volume, p. 297) and of the mountains extending north to the Sierra Nevada de Santa Marta (Handbook, vol. 2, p. 867), occupied the tropical rain forests between the lower Magdalena River and the Atrato River. Their territory comprised nearly all the present Department of Bolívar and, in the extreme west, part of the Department of Antioquia in the region of the Gulf of Urabá. More precisely, this area was bounded on the south by the northernmost Sub-Andean tribes (the *Nore, Guaca, Evégico,* and *Remedio*), on the west by the Atrato River, formerly called the Darién, on the north by the Atlantic Ocean, once known as the Mar del Norte, and on the east by the Magdalena River. The country in general is composed of low, swampy areas alternating with elevations that mark the extension of the Cordillera Central, and its climate is hot, about 27° to 30° C. (80.6° to 86° F.).

Among the tribes living in this area at the time of the Conquest were the *Calamari, Turbaco, Tolú, Urabá, Cenú* (and its subtribes, the *Fincenú, Pancenú, Cenufana*), *Utibara, Yapel, Mompox* (*Malebu*), *Tamalameque, Bonda, Buritacá, Pacabueye, Pemeo, Yamici,* and *Zendagua.* These tribes soon became extinct, and there is insufficient record of them to indicate their cultural and political relationships to one another. Of the tribes just enumerated, we have ethnographic data only on the first ten; the *Bonda, Buritacá,* and others were not described.

Jijón y Caamaño (1936–38, vol. 2) gives evidence that the *Urabá Yapel, Cenú, Fincenú,* and *Catío* spoke the same languages. As *Catío* belongs with *Chocó,* so must those related to it (Jijón y Caamaño, 1936–38, vol. 2; Rivet, 1943).

TRIBAL DIVISIONS AND LOCATIONS

The *Calamari,* and several tribes culturally similar to them, occupied the coast 'and small islands of the Atlantic from the Magdalena River west to the *Urabá,* who lived on the Gulf of Urabá (or Darién), and south to the various *Cenú* subtribes. The center of *Calamari* territory was the present city of Cartagena, which was formerly called Calamari or Calamar, the native name for crabs, which were abundant on its beaches

(Peredo, 1919, pp. 450–480). Other tribes listed here were the *Carex* (on an island), *Turbaco* (*Turuaco*), *Caron, Bahaire, Cospique, Cocon, Caricocox* (*Coricocox*), *Matarapa, Zamba, Mazaguapo, Guaspates, Turipana, Mahates, Cipacua, Oca, Tubará,* and *Cornapacua* (Castellanos, 1852, pp. 365–462; Simón, 1882–92).

Simón states that all these people were known as *Mocana* and that they claimed to have originated from groups that came by canoe along the coast from *Maracapana* and *Caracas* territory in Venezuela. Next to the southwest, on the coast, were the *Tolú* (*Tulú*), and then the *Urabá*. The *Urabá* had fled from the Spaniards to the Atrato (Darién) River (Cieza de León, 1932).

Inland were the *Cenú* (*Zenú*), whom the conquistadors divided as follows: *Fincenú,* occupying all the Sinú River Basin; *Pancenú,* the region east, toward the San Jorge River; and *Cenufana* (*Senufana, Cenúfama, Cemefana, Cenufara, Cermefama*), where Zaragoza and Remedios are now situated, in the vicinity of the Nechí River and its affluents, in the Department of Antioquia (Acosta, 1901, ch. 7, p. 84; Mesa Jaramillo, 1905). East of the *Tolú* lived the *Yapel* (*Ayapel*), and east of them the *Mompox,* more properly known as the *Malibúes* (*Malebúes*) (Asencio, 1921), and the *Xegua* and *Tagua* (Heredia, 1916, pp. 59–63). The *Tamalameque,* adjoining the *Pacabueyes,* lived east of the Ariguani, on the right or southern bank of the Cesare (Zezare, today César) River (Rebollo, 1919).

HISTORY

Rodrigo de Bastidas reached the coast of this area in 1501, but the true Conquest was begun in 1510 by Alonso de Ojeda, Nicuesa, and Juan de la Cosa, when Ojedo founded the first settlement, San Sebastián de Urabá, at the northeast extremity of the Gulf of Urabá. Some months later the Indians besieged and destroyed this town, and the Spaniards, under Nicuesa's direction, founded a second settlement, Santa Maria la Antiqua del Darién, on the Atrato River, but it suffered the same fate as the first. Twenty-three years later Heredia founded Cartagena at the Indian port of Calamari. This settlement was destined to become the principal port of ingress and supply for a large portion of South America, especially the Pacific countries, as there was no other route across the continent north of the great road from Argentina to Chile.

Ojeda carried an edict that the Indians should become Christians and subjects of the King of Spain, because the Pope had given these Spaniards charge of their lands. This edict was read to the Indians, who did not understand it, but those who grasped its point replied "that one god seemed all right, as they did not wish to argue or to give up their religion, but it was necessary to be very frank about this stranger, the Holy Father, who gave away lands that were not his own; and as for the King, he must be very poor, as he coveted, from such a distance, the little they had, and very bold, as he threatened those he did not know" (Gómara, 1901, p. 20).

The result of the Indians' resistance in this region was their progressive decrease in numbers and their replacement by Negro slaves. In the Province of Cartagena there were 83 towns in 1772, with 13,993 Christianized Indians, but a few years later only 7,000 or 8,000 Indians tributaries remained in 100 repartimientos (López de Velasco, 1915). The proportion of Negro slaves in 1772 is illustrated by the section of Turbaco, which had 571 Indians and 537 slaves, and by Tolú, with 1,093 Indians and 260 slaves (Piñeres, 1917).

In 1542, Heredia gave his soldiers the first encomiendas, each with its Indians and chiefs, in the Uraba regions—Chuchyraly, Queyva, El Tuerto, Carcate, and Olla (Heredia, 1915 b). At San Sebastián de Urabá, 729 natives remained in 1772 (Peredo, 1919). The region of Urabá became the objective of the Spaniards on the one hand and of the English, Dutch, and even French on the other. The famed riches of the region of Darién led to the formation in Scotland of the Darién Company or the Scotch Company, and the first immigrants or colonists arrived in November 1698. The few who remained a year later were pushed out by the Spaniards (Arévalo, *in* Cuervo, 1891–94, vol. 2). The Indians of the town of Urabá continued to resist subjugation, taking up arms against the neighboring people of Santa María la Antigua in 1724 and again in 1750. In 1750 the Governor, Don Joaquín Valcárcel de Miranda, counted 5,000 families of Indians (Cuervo, 1891–94, vol. 2, p. 373). In Cenú, the Sinú River section, there were 4,580 natives and 244 Negro slaves in 1772 (Piñeres, 1917). Around San Nicolás there were 521 Indians, and at Cereté, formerly called Mocari, were 518 Indians, who cultivated their fields on the Sinú River and spoke Spanish in addition to their native language (Peredo, 1919). Soon after the Conquest some slaves escaped and established their own village near Mompox. Here they were served by the Indians, being much afraid of the Spaniards (Andagoya, *in* Jijón y Caamaño, 1936–38, vol. 2, doc. 2). At the time of writing his account, López de Velasco (1915) stated that there were 2,000 Indian tributaries in 26 repartimientos around the main city of Santa Cruz de Mompox, which Heredia had founded. Other cities were Tamalameque, founded in *Tamalameque* territory, and Chiriguana, but the former did not survive.

The valor of these Indians was the trait that impressed the chroniclers most. The *Calamari* were described as astute, brave on land and sea, clever in their maneuvers, and resourceful. The *Urabá* hated Criollos and colored people, whether Negroes, mulattoes, or zambos, because the conquistadors had used the Negroes from the very beginning in their wars against the Indians.

All the native peoples of the Colombian Atlantic littoral, except the *Cuna, Chocó,* and *Goajiro,* have disappeared culturally and been absorbed racially. Joaquín Acosta states (1901), "Degradation, servitude, and intermixture have destroyed the rest."

CULTURE

The coastal tribes of the North Colombia Lowlands are distinguished culturally from their Sub-Andean neighbors to the south in Antioquia and Caldas by lacking cannibalism and by using feather ornaments, poisoned weapons, and sleeping hammocks, but the interior tribes of this area share cannibalism, human trophies, and woven cotton garments with the Sub-Andean tribes. For 8 tribes studied, the historical sources mention the occurrence of culture elements with the following frequencies[1]: Agriculture, 6 times; hunting, 5; fishing, 5; woven cloth, 5; feather ornaments, 4; body painting, 2; temples, 4; bridges, 1; hammocks, 5; canoes, 3; mound burial, 2; idols, 2; quivers, 1; balsa rafts, 1; shamanism, 3; polygyny, 3; marriage with a consanguineous relative, 1; prostitution, 1; sexual inverts, 1; poisoned arrow, 5; cannibalism, 2; human trophies, 1. These 22 elements were reported among the tribes (who, it must be remembered, were little studied by the historians) with the following frequencies: *Calamari,* 14; *Cenú,* 14; *Urabá,* 8; *Tolú,* 7; *Yapel,* 5; *Mompox,* 4; *Turbaco,* 4; *Tamalameque,* 2.

SUBSISTENCE ACTIVITIES

All these tribes practiced farming, supplementing it with hunting and, along the coast and in the rivers and swamps, with fishing. Castellanos (1852) mentions the following fruits: Caimitos (star apples, *Chrysophyllum cainito*), guanábanas (soursop, *Annona muricata*), anones (sweetsop, *Annona squamosa*), hobos (hog plum, *Splondias lutea*), guayabas (guava, *Psidium*), papayas (*Papaya carica*), mamones (genip, *Melicocca bijuga*), pineapples (*Ananus sativus*), and bananas. Simón lists (1882–92) the following crops: Maize, sweet manioc (yuca), sweetpotatoes, kidney beans, and others. Cotton was cultivated for its fibers. The main *Turbaco* crops were maize, manioc, and cotton (Peredo, 1919). Heredia (1916), saw many cultivated fields among the Indians and noted that those of the *Tolú* were especially large. The *Cenú* had houses full of maize.

Hunting yielded rabbits, guinea pigs, iguanas, peccaries, guaquiras, guaratinagas, various tortoises or turtles, and such birds as parrots (papagayos), catarnicas, perdices, wild turkeys (pavas), and guans (paujiles). The *Urabá* caught and raised young peccaries and when they were fat ate them. In addition to other wild animals, the *Cenú* ate caimans.

A special food, particularly of the *Turbaco,* was manioc loaves or tortillas, called "cazabe." The *Tolú* ate bees' honey. The *Cenú* espe-

---

[1] All *Cenú* subtribes are counted as *Cenú.*

cially the *Cenufana,* preserved meat smoked on babracots. As condiments the *Cenú* used salt, which they manufactured locally, and ají (chili pepper.) Simón (1882–92) accredits the *Yapel* with using pepper to preserve fish.

HOUSES AND VILLAGES

These peoples lived in large villages. *Turbaco* villages were enclosed by two or three fences of trees. The "court" of the female chief of the *Cenú* consisted of 20 houses, each surrounded by three or four small storehouses or granaries. The village was protected with a stockade. *Yapel* villages had plazas and well-laid streets. *Mompox* and *Tamalameque* settlements were on the banks of the Magdalena River. The principal *Tamalameque* town was divided into three wards (barrios), each triangular in plan, with a central plaza and a strong defense.

Houses were built of poles and thatch, but sometimes they were constructed of poles, mud, and grass, e. g., those of the *Turbaco,* which had two doors and were conical (beehive), the thatched roof reaching to the ground. The *Cenú* built a temple, more than 100 paces long, with its interior divided into three naves. It was probably rectangular, for Simón (1882–92) likened it to Spanish buildings.

A sleeping hammock was used by the *Calamari, Cenú, Tolú, Turbaco,* and *Urabá.* These tribes used cooking pots, and the *Calamari* also had large jars for storing water. The *Cenú* used boxes ("habas") for storing articles of personal adornment.

Outstanding structures were the *Calamari* wells and *Urabá* tombs. These tombs were enclosed in mounds, which were paved with carefully laid slabs. The vault inside was reached by descending stairs of well-dressed stones (García Carbonell, 1918). Across the Magdalena River, the *Mompox* laid "bridges," consisting of vines more than 150 fathoms long (Heredia, 1916).

CLOTHING AND ADORNMENT

The lack of clothing was general, owing to the hot climate, especially on the coast. *Calamari* men wore a fringe of fine gold tubes covering their genitals. This tribe was unusual in wearing deerskin sandals (abarcas) tied with cords. *Turbaco* and *Tolú* women wore a white or painted cotton skirt (manta) from the belt to the feet. Among the *Urabá,* men covered their genitals with a fringe of gold tubes or of snaillike ornaments (caracoles) attached to the belt, while women wore a cotton manta covering them from the breast down and, sometimes, another mantle over it for protection. *Cenú* women also wore cotton mantas, "curiously worked," i. e., decorated with colored drawings.

As adornments, particularly for warfare, feather crowns were worn by all but the Magdalena River tribes. Body painting was practiced by the *Calamari* and *Yapel.* Common gold ornaments included diadems, pectoral plates (chagualas), earrings, loop-shaped nose ornaments (cara-curis), finger rings, and strings of bone beads (chaquiras) and gold beads which were worn around the neck, the arms, and the ankles.

TRANSPORTATION

These tribes traveled the rivers and the ocean in canoes propelled by paddles. The *Cenú* went down the river in balsa canoes to the markets, where they abandoned them, being unable to return against the current (Striffler, 1920, 1922).

Chiefs' litters are mentioned for the *Cenú*.

MANUFACTURES

Bark cloth was not made in this area, in contrast to the middle Cauca River, and cotton weaving was the main industry. The coastal Indians made textiles mainly for trade with the *Cenú* and other inland tribes, and they excelled in manufacturing hammocks woven of cord.

Ceramic products included cooking vesels and, in the regions of few springs, large water-storage jars. Containers were made also of cala-bashes.

Other industries mentioned, though not practiced by all tribes, were salting fish, manufacturing of dugout canoes, making poison for arrows and other projectiles, and the decoration of calabash cups with special pitch or resin. The last was a specialty of the *Urabá*.

Goldwork gave Darién, or Cinú, such fame that a saying of early Cartagena was, "Misfortune to Perú if they discover Cenú." The *Fin-cenú* were the main gold producers and outstanding goldsmiths.

SOCIAL AND POLITICAL ORGANIZATION

These people were divided into villages or groups, each with a chief (cacique) and subchiefs. Among those mentioned were: Chief Carex of the *Calamari* whose captains or subchiefs were Piorex and Curixix; Duhoa, chief of the *Bahaire;* Tocana, of the *Mazaguapo;* and Cambayo of the *Mahates.* There were also dependencies. For example, the *Oca* were a dependency of the *Cipacua,* who were enemies of the *Mahates.* The *Tubara* were governed by the chief Morotoava, and his nephew, Hare. *Tolú* divisions were each under minor chiefs, and each *Urabá* group or village had its chief. The *Yapel* had a principal chief named Ayapel. The chiefs of the two groups of *Mompox* living on opposite sides of the Mag-dalena River in 1541 were friends and relatives (Heredia, 1915 a). The three divisions of the *Cenú* were united under related rulers, for the prin-cipal chiefs of the *Fincenú, Pancenú,* and *Cenufana* were brothers. The following legend recounts the origin of this government:

There were three gods (demons) who, in ancient times, were the chiefs and head men. The principal one was Zenufana, who took the richest lands for his dominion while his sister ruled the lands of Finzenú. He was so fond of this sister that he desired that all his own vassals and those of the other two Zenú divisions accord her the same reverence that he himself received. To this end he ordered that all the head-men of the other two Zenús be buried in the Zenú of his sister, with all the gold that could be collected at the time of death, according to the custom, or at least that they be placed in the cemetery of the great temple and house of the Devil which stood in this Finzenú, where the Spaniards found it; or, if they wished to be buried not in this cemetery but in their own lands, that they send one-half the gold assembled at the time of death that it might be buried in their stead in the cemetery, an unbreakable law that no one dared disobey. [Simón, 1882–92, vol. 4, pt. 1, ch. 19, p. 26.]

The main village of the *Fincenú* was governed by a female chief and her husband, and she was more respected than the chiefs of the other two *Cenú* subtribes. She had female servants who carried her on their backs to her hammock, which was more beautiful than those of common people, and the floor of her house was covered with grass, like a tapestry. The chieftainness at the time of the discovery was called "La Tota." The chief of the *Cenufana* was Utibara, son of Anunaibe. His brother, Quinunchú, ruled the mountains of Abibe and his people paid him tribute in smelted gold, textiles, animals, etc. When he went to war or to visit his subjects, Utibara was accompanied by squads of Indians, who carried him in a gold-adorned litter.

Marriage among the *Calamari* was arranged by the couple's parents, the young man sending the young woman one hammock while she sent him two. The union was celebrated in the bridegroom's home by the couple's relatives and friends, who drank chicha from a calabash cup. In a cup of chicha for his father-in-law, the young man had to place grains of gold. This ceremony was repeated three times daily for the next 15 days and at the birth of his first child. As the *Calamari* were polyg-ynous, the feasts were held at each of a man's marriages. Premarital sexual freedom was allowed women, but both parties to adultery were punished by death. Some chroniclers, exaggerating the sexual license permitted, claim that fathers had relations with their daughters, and sons with their mothers.

The aristocratic class of the *Urabá* were polygynous, and they practiced marriage between a man and his sister's daughter, who became his prin-cipal wife. With inheritance passing to their son goods were thus retained in the family.

The *Cenú* were also polygynous, and a man married as many wives as he could support.

TRADE

In their trading the coastal peoples specialized in textiles, fish, and hammocks. The *Calamari*, for example, traded these items with the *Cenú* for gold. The *Cenú*, especially the *Cenufana*, traded gold for salt, ham-mocks, textiles, and food. The *Mompox* acquired canoes from the *Tolú* on the Cauca River and carried them 9 leagues to the Magdalena River. The *Urabá* traded salt, fish, and specially raised and fattened peccaries to the interior tribes, and calabash vessels decorated with resin, their specialty, to people in Cartagena. The *Tamalameque* gathered with members of other tribes in the plazas of their main centers to hold markets.

It appears that some chiefs received tribute from their own subjects or from federated tribes. This tribute consisted of gold, manufactured products, and plant and animal foods. The Spaniards used these tributes as the basis for the much greater taxation, which they made the Indians of each encomienda and Church division pay to the encomenderos and priests.

Among the *Urabá* the sons of the principal wife were a man's heirs, the remaining sons receiving nothing. Among the *Cenú*, who had female chiefs, the sons were also heirs.

BURIAL CUSTOMS

At a death among the *Urabá* many people assembled in the house of of the deceased. That night they drank chicha and lamented in the darkness, then buried the deceased with his weapons, cherished possessions, food, jars of chicha, and living women, for they believed in life after death. The graves are described above. *Cenú* and *Yapel* graves, much sought by the conquistadors for the famed riches they contained, were marked by mounds, which the Spaniards called "mogotes." The body was placed facing east in a deep hole and was accompanied by the dead man's weapons and ornaments, and by jars of chicha, maize, and stone metates. Several women and servants, who had first been made drunk, were interred with the deceased. The grave was covered with red earth, which the mourners brought from a distant place. The ceremony lasted as long as there was chicha to drink, so that the size of the mound depended on the available quantity of chicha. At the *Fincenú* temple site, where all the *Cenú* chiefs were traditionally buried, each grave was marked either by a specially planted tree with a gold bell hung from it or by an earth mound.

WARFARE

The *Calamari, Tamalameque, Tolú, Turbaco,* and *Urabá* used poisoned darts or arrows, which they kept sheathed for their own protection in quivers. Other weapons reported were lances, spears, harpoons, macanas, and slings. The *Cenú* hurled gold (headed?) darts at the Spaniards. The *Urabá* bow was made of black palm wood and was a fathom or more long.

Probably none of these tribes, except perhaps the *Cenufana*, practiced exocannibalism (see below), and Simón probably confused the *Urabá* with the *Chocó* or *Catío* when he accredited them with eating human flesh.

These Indians were valiant warriors, even the women. In one battle an 18-year-old girl killed eight Spaniards with her arrows. Women customarily went to war, some of them to pass weapons to their men and others as regular soldiers. The latter were young girls or virgins, and they were privileged to participate in the drunken, communal feasts, carrying their bows and arrows, when the Indians were not able to carry arms, as Heredia observed among the *Calamari* and *Turbaco*. Fighting was accompanied by cries and the sound of trumpets and other musical instruments. The *Tolú* fought in formations, orderly disposed in files. The *Cenú* chief preceded his warriors into battle, carried by his subjects on a litter decorated with gold, as among the *Chibcha* of Tunja and Bogotá.

CANNIBALISM

The *Cenufana*, or subjects of Utibara, ate human corpses, according to one chronicler. It is uncertain whether they consumed their own dead, but a suggestion of exocannibalism, i. e., of enemies, is seen in the custom of placing human trophies over the house doors. Farther south, in the Sub-Andean zone, this custom is associated with exocannibalism. The *Urabá* seem to have practiced endocannibalism, cooking their own dead on babracots and eating them (Simón, 1882–92).

ESTHETIC AND RECREATIONAL ACTIVITIES

Art work was practiced in connection with the decorative drawings on textiles, ceramic designs, gold objects in zoomorphic and anthropomorphic forms, idols, and resin-decorated calabashes.

Musical instruments included drums, conch-shell trumpets (caracoles), trumpets, and whistles.

Chicha, made of fermented maize or yuca, was in general use as an intoxicating drink.

RELIGION AND SHAMANISM

The *Calamari, Cenú, Cenufana,* and *Urabá* had temples for their gods. The great temple of *Fincenú* accommodated 1,000 persons, and contained 24 tall wooden idols covered with gold leaf and crowned with a tiara. For each, a hammock hung from a stick served as a receptacle for offerings. Around the temple were the graves of important persons, each covered by a mound or marked by a tree from which hung a gold bell. Another temple, divided into three naves, had a highly decorated hammock suspended from a cross pole resting on four supports in human form, two men and two women. Above the hammock, in which the god was supposed to repose, were two boxes for offerings. The temple was guarded so that common people might not enter. The *Fincenú* believed that their god, or "demon" as the Spaniards called him, appeared to them and spoke with the priest-shamans, who, like the present-day *Goajiro* shamans, were called "piaches." The most important idols in Cipacua and Cornapacua were a peccary (puerco espin) and eight gold ducks. The Indians believed that the god appeared in the form of animals, especially as a jaguar, which suggests a jaguar cult like that which was so widespread in South America.

Among the *Tolú* and *Calamari,* shamans (mohanes) interpreted the gods' replies to the people, practiced magic, and cured the sick. Shamanism was inherited. Among the shaman's paraphernalia were pebbles kept in a pottery olla in the temple. To learn from the god, Buziraco, which herbs he should use to treat an illness, the shaman removed the pebbles from the olla. In one of the ceremonies, the shaman, accompanied by old men and women, entered the temple at night. The women threw their ornaments into the pottery vessel, which contained the pebbles, tobacco leaves, and some water, while the shaman held a quantity of pulverized tobacco. He moved the pebbles in the water, and everyone looked and listened for the god in the water. Then the shaman took the tobacco powder in his mouth and blew it over everyone present, after which they did the same to him. Finally, the old women took their ornaments from the jar and carried the water away to purify their houses.

MYTHOLOGY

In addition to the myth of the origin of the three *Cenú* rulers (above), the chroniclers recorded origin tales of the *Calamari* and *Tolú.* These Indians were said to have come from a man, Mechion, and a woman, Maneca. The woman had only one breast, where she concentrated her milk with greater abundance and strength than in two and thus gave her sons greater fortitude. These tribes related that once there were giants in their territory, people guilty of the heinous sin of being sexual inverts. The giants associated with women only for the purpose of having children, and when these were girls the midwives killed them. The giants were finally killed by lightning (Simón, 1882–92, vol. 3, pt. 1, ch. 8). Possibly this legend was intended to explain the existence of sexual inversion, represented among the *Calamari* by the female warriors and by men who impersonated women and went from village to village selling their services like the ordinary prostitutes among them.

LORE AND LEARNING

The *Calamari* had a system of reckoning the time for planting and for harvesting maize, manioc, sweetpotatoes, and the like. Of the *Mompox,* Heredia said, "they are smarter than the peoples of the other provinces . . . because they handle weights and measures" (Heredia, 1915 a).

BIBLIOGRAPHY

Acosta, 1901; Andagoya (*in* Jijón y Caamaño, 1936–38, vol. 2; English version, 1865) ; Arévalo (*in* Cuervo [Sardilla], 1891–94, vol. 2) ; Asensio, 1921; Castellanes, 1852 (1874) ; Cieza de León, 1932; García Carbonell, 1918; Gómara, 1749 (*in* Acosta, 1901) ; Heredia, 1915 a, 1915 b, 1916; Jijón y Caamaño, 1936–38, vol. 2; López de Velasco, 1915; Mesa Jaramillo, 1905; Peredo, 1919; Piñeres, 1917; Rebollo, 1919; Rivet, 1943; Simón, 1882–92; Striffler, 1920, 1922.

PATANGORO AND AMANI

By Paul Kirchhoff

INTRODUCTION

In the dense forest of the eastern slope of the Cordillera Central, the monotony of which is only very rarely broken by small patches of savanna, two remarkable tribes have been described by Pedro de Aguado (1916–17) on the basis of information given to him by men who conquered this region between 1557 and 1561. No later data are available on these tribes, who seem to have disappeared rapidly (map 6).

The *Patángoro* (*Pantágoro, Pantágora, Palenque, Coronado*) seem to have included the *Zamaná, Punchiná,* and *Marquesote.* The *Amani* evidently were a *Patángoro* tribe that had been profoundly influenced by tribes of a different culture, probably those of the Cauca Valley. Aguado, our only source, states that they resembled the *Patángoro* in those aspects of culture that he did not describe. At least two other tribes, the *Panche* and *Muso* (*Muzo*), and the several subdivisions of the latter, may have resembled the *Patángoro* in the same way as the *Amani.* Thus, the *Patángoro* culture was the basic type, and the *Amani, Panche,* and *Muso* cultures represented special developments that were caused, at least in part, by outside influences. The culture of the *Patángoro,* and, to a large extent, that of the other three tribes, presents a striking contrast to that of all other areas of western Colombia.

All these tribes are said to have spoken similar languages of the *Chibchan* family.

CULTURE

SUBSISTENCE ACTIVITIES

Farming.—Maize was the most important food, but sweet manioc, auyama, beans, avocado pears, and guavas were also cultivated. In cultivating only two fruit trees these tribes were unique in western Colombia, where many different fruit trees were grown. The *Patángoro* were also exceptional in caring little for chili peppers, and it seems that they did not cultivate them, though the *Amani* did.

Twice every year, in December and in August, men cleared new patches of forests felling the trees with stone axes and burning the underbrush and branches. A man's sisters (not his wives) sowed his fields, at least the maize and beans, using planting sticks. No piece of land was sown twice, for otherwise the weeds would kill the crops.

The agricultural calendar was regulated by the movements of two constellations. A certain position of the Pleiades was interpreted as the constellation's having begun the planting season in Heaven, and men had to follow suit by cutting and burning trees. This first part of the task had to be finished before Castor and Pollux, sisters of the Pleiades, had reached the zenith at midnight, when they were thought to begin sowing, inviting the men's sisters to do the same. An alternative signal for the beginning of sowing was the arrival of certain migratory birds. During the second planting season, in August, every detail was guided by the blossoming and development of a certain tree.

Domesticated animals.—The dog is not mentioned. Guans (paujies) and possibly other birds were taken from the nest and raised in the house.

Hunting and fishing.—The forests inhabited by these tribes harbored almost no animals or birds. It is specifically stated that the only meat eaten by the *Patángoro* was that of rats. The *Marquesote* also ate monkeys and certain birds.

Fishing seems to have been important, at least in some parts of the area, but no data are available on methods used.

Food preparation.—No bread was prepared, either of maize or of manioc. Maize was eaten in the form of tamales or a sour dough made of maize flour mixed with manioc flour and consumed diluted in water, i. e., a food similar to the South Mexican and Guatemalan pozole, except for the addition of manioc flour. The more well-to-do carried lumps of this dough wrapped in leaves when they went to work in the fields.

The two daily meals, one in the morning and the other in the evening, consisted of auyama leaves, wild amaranth and other unspecified "greens," and a few handfuls of maize flour all boiled together in a pot. Sometimes a few auyamas were added as a special feature. This dish was taken with maize and manioc beer. The only other dish mentioned is the leaves of certain unnamed wild plants, broiled between bigger leaves.

The larger part of the maize and manioc harvested was consumed in liquid state, as fermented drinks.

The *Marquesote* dried food, e.g., fruit, small fish, birds, rats, and monkeys, for preservation.

Salt was unknown. As a substitute salty water was drunk. It was brought from springs in sections of giant bamboo. Chili pepper was little or hardly ever used by the *Patángoro* but was important among the *Amani*.

The only tribe in the area that ate human flesh was the *Amani*. They boiled or barbecued it, or, as a specialty, toasted and ground it into powder, mixed it with chili pepper, and drank it in maize or manioc beer.

Hands, feet, and bowels were considered special delicacies. Large stores of human flesh, prepared in any of these ways, were found in most of the *Amaní* villages.

HOUSES AND VILLAGES

Patángoro villages were located in high places. In the villages of every tribe, there was a special building for ceremonies and festivals. Some *Palenque* villages had more than 50 houses, and those of the *Amaní* had an average of 80 or 90, built close together along regular streets. The villages of the *Patángoro,* who were simpler folk than the *Amaní* or *Palenque,* may have been smaller, and they are said not to have followed the same orderly plan.

The most distinctive feature of *Palenque* and *Amaní* villages was a palisaded fortress ("palenque") of heavy logs, provided with loopholes.

The method of house construction is not known, but building materials included bamboos (guadua), 7 feet (about 2 m.) long and as thick as a man's thigh, and bihao leaves.

The only piece of furniture mentioned is the platform bed ("catre" or "barbacoa").

DRESS AND ORNAMENTS

Men went completely naked, but if their bodies bore some ugly scar they covered it with a piece of skin. Young girls wore an apron of loose strings of agave or cotton thread reaching almost to the ankles. At marriage they changed it for a small apron of cotton cloth; they always sat down in such a way that the apron covered their private parts.

Men cut their hair at a level between the ears and shoulders. For an act of bravery they were tonsured ("coronado"). Women wore the front portion of their hair, from the ears forward, loose, while the rest was woven with lianas into two braids wound around the head.

Heads were deformed in such a way that the forehead was broadened. No ear, nose, or lip ornaments or other kind of bodily decoration are mentioned. Ornaments consisted of feather crowns, white beads, and some apparently rare gold jewelry.

TRAVEL AND TRANSPORTATION

Liana bridges were used throughout the area. Canoes are not mentioned, possibly through a mere oversight.

MANUFACTURES

Pottery was apparently made. Gold was not worked. For weapons, see Warfare below.

POLITICAL ORGANIZATION

Each village seems to have been autonomous. Among the *Patángoro* and *Amaní* the village headman was usually the oldest man with the largest family and the most outstanding personal qualities. Except during war the *Patángoro* chief's authority was small. The *Amaní* headman, who was elected by all the townspeople, had considerable authority.

No exchange of goods whatever was carried on between villages or tribes.

SOCIAL ORGANIZATION

Marriage.—Among all tribes of the area, a man acquired a wife by giving a sister to the brother of his bride-to-be. A man, therefore, generally had as many wives as he had sisters. In the case of several brothers and sisters, the oldest brother allotted the sisters to his brothers, so that they might exchange them for wives. A man who had no brothers but many sisters might distribute some of them among close clansmen who had no sisters. If a girl had no brothers and her mother were a widow, she disposed of her sisters, but if a girl without brothers had lost her mother, her mother's brother or nearest male relative made the marriage arrangements.

Most men had several wives, who often were sisters. In any case it was considered correct for a man to have intercourse with all the sisters of his wife or wives. The widow became the wife of the dead man's brother or closest relative, lest she be lost to his village and return to her own.

Marriages were easily dissolved. The woman abandoned her husband whenever her brother or nearest clansman told her to. As a consequence, her brother also lost his wife, who, being the abandoned husband's sister, likewise returned to her own village. Both women would take their children with them. A husband could also discard his wife whenever he wished, but at the same time he sent for his sister who had married his brother-in-law. It is even said that at the death of one wife all others would go home unless her brother could fill her place with another of his sisters.

A man's wives all lived together in one house without any jealousy or quarrels. The husband slept every night with a different one. When a wife's turn came, it was she who cooked for him; when he returned from the field or the warpath, she handed him a drink of maize beer, after which he went down to the river to bathe. Next, she covered his body with artistic designs. They then ate and retired.

When a wife was visiting her mother, her husband was not allowed to have intercourse with her in the mother's house but called her with certain whistling sounds to join him in the fields.

A son-in-law and mother-in-law were never permitted to look at each other and had to look away if they ever met by accident. In some villages there were special pathways and roads where sons-in-law could be sure of not encountering their mothers-in-law.

A woman abstained from any intercourse during her menstruation and while she was pregnant or was nursing a child.

Patrilocal residence was the rule. A widow with daughters but without sons would not permit her daughters' lovers to take the girls home to their villages, though she allowed them to have intercourse near, though not inside, her house. These lovers had to prepare her a maize field.

Wives were expected to obey their husbands lest they be sent home for good. Among the *Patángoro,* however, wives enjoyed great sexual liberty and were never restrained by their husbands, who always feared desertion. *Amaní* wives had much less freedom. An adulterous wife was put into a dark room in the building where the wedding had taken place and kept there by special guards. Here, day after day, all men of the village who wished could have intercourse with her. If, after a specified time, she survived this treatment, she was starved to death. No husband could save his adulterous wife from this fate. If he should attempt to do so, he would lose his public standing and even risk being killed by his own relatives. In any case he could not take another wife. The adulterous woman's lover was also killed. Instead of burial, the couple's bodies were left at some frequented place outside the village to be eaten by carrion birds, and a conspicuous mark was left there which would last a long time. Here, at short intervals, a man specially appointed for the task delivered a long sermon before a big crowd including even people from other towns. He explained the crime and the punishment commemorated at the place, dwelling on the shame brought on all of the delinquents' descendants, and admonished everyone to lead a clean and decent life, "something certainly never before heard of among savage peoples," adds our chronicler.

Among the *Amaní* an unmarried girl who gave herself to a man was condemned to perpetual celibacy and had to submit to the control of her parents or close relatives. The man was condemned to 6 months in the communal ceremonial building, during which he had to keep it clean and was not allowed to leave it for any reason.

In all these tribes men sometimes exchanged wives.

Among the *Patángoro* the wedding celebration lasted 7 days. On the first day the bride-to-be painted her future husband black, red, and other colors. During the first 6 nights the couple slept together without having intercourse, which was impossible because many boys and girls joined them every night. On the seventh night both were led to the bed, he by an old man of his clan and she by her brother; maize grains were placed at the head of the bed, and the bridegroom and bride threw them at each other. Planting-sticks were placed on both sides of the bed and weapons hung up high to signify that the husband would provide his wife with food and shelter and defend his family.

Among the *Amani* 4 months had to pass between the preliminary agreement and the actual wedding. During this time the prospective bridegroom and bride investigated each other's qualities. If both were satisfied, the wedding took place in the public building with all the husband's clansmen participating in the celebration. The young couple lived for some time in this house, where a man had the special assignment of counseling the wife daily to be faithful to her husband, to serve him willingly, and to rear their offspring properly. The husband was told to treat his wife well and not to have intercourse with her when she was with child.

Clans.—All tribes were divided into exogamous matrilineal clans. Because marriage was patrilocal, members of different clans were found together in the same villages. The rules of exogamy were strictly observed, but in the very rare cases when they were broken the guilty persons were killed with clubs and sticks, and it was believed that they would forever wander around without heads, suffering and doing penance.

Throughout life a man's relations with his sisters were closer or at any rate more permanent than those with his wives. It was a man's sister, not his wife, who constantly helped him in the field. The wife had only to prepare his meals, paint his body, and spend the night with him whenever her turn came, but sometimes she helped in the fields. When a husband fell ill, especially for a long period, the wife returned with her children to her brother's village, and her brother's wife, the sick man's sister, returned to her village.

In all these tribes certain men posed as women and lived with men. Their status seems to have been publicly accepted.

WARFARE

These were warlike and cruel tribes. Local groups, although connected by marriage bonds, were at continuous war with one another. Prisoners, including small children, were killed immediately. In fact, few prisoners were taken, for foreigners were killed at once. Children, even though still nursing, were taken to the corpses and given a little stick with which to touch the dead man's wounds so that they might become brave warriors. When a group of Indians met a beautiful woman from another village, they first raped her and then killed her, considering this an insult to her relatives. All who took part in such an assault thenceforth wore their hair tonsured.

Weapons used in this area were long bows and arrows, some of which were poisoned, clubs, and stone axes, but the use of axes in war may have been only incidental. Lances were noted only among the *Palenque*.

The poisoned arrows bore finely incised lines and had a small notch about 3 inches from the tip, so that it broke off in the wound. The poison was prepared by old women, who were tired of living. The fumes of their poisonous concoction usually killed them. Into a big vessel they threw all the snakes they could find, many red ants, scorpions, spiders, and other poisonous animals. To this they added menstrual blood and, if they could be had, men's testicles. They kept a number of frogs for a few days in a vessel without food and then tied each by its legs to four stakes over a bowl and beat it with small sticks so that it exuded a poison which dripped into the bowl. They added this poison and the whitish juice of certain trees to the animals and other ingredients, which by now had putrified, and mixed the whole. Whenever this poison lost its strength, they added a little of the juice of the same trees and of manzanillo, which, among neighboring tribes (none of which used frogs, except the far-distant *Chocó*), was the basic ingredient of their arrow or dart poison.

Villages, and often individual houses, were protected by trenches 14 feet (4 m.) deep, filled with pointed stakes, long and sharp enough to pierce a human body lengthwise. These trenches were carefully concealed with a covering of earth. Whether the stakes were poisoned is not clear. To lure the enemy, game was placed over these excavations; sometimes the defenders were stationed behind them.

The palenques or palisades, particularly those of the *Amani*, were extremely strong and were built in almost inaccessible places. At vulnerable places there were two palisades, the outer more than 20 feet (6 m.) high, the inner 7 feet (2 m.) high, with the intervening space filled in to the height of the latter, except for a trench 7 feet (2 m.) deep. The trench was filled with water, which was carried over extremely difficult mountain trails from considerable distances. In addition to the palisades the easier slopes leading up to the fortification were protected with sharply pointed stakes.

One palenque, manned by 4,000 warriors and provisioned with ample supplies of human flesh preserved in different ways, had to be besieged by the Spaniards for 40 days before it was taken. The defenders not only showered the attacking enemy with innumerable arrows but also threw large stones, great quantities of water, and burning torches down upon them. A special feature of some palenques was heavy wooden trap doors. Heavy logs, placed close to forest trails, were arranged to fall on anyone who touched a trip-cord tied across the trail.

Warriors wore crowns of feathers and painted their faces and bodies. Shouts, noises, and vituperations against the enemy were considered indispensable features of battle. One palenque had a special tower from which during the night a defender launched insult upon insult on the enemy outside.

On one occasion a group of young warriors accompanied by women and children tried to enter a Spanish encampment under the pretext of delivering building materials. Each man carried a giant bamboo in which he had a swordlike club and had a stone ax fastened to a string around his waist. The women and children carried smaller clubs hidden under bundles of bihao leaves.

LIFE CYCLE

There are no data on birth or puberty. In view of the fullness of data on other aspects of native life, this would seem to mean that these tribes had no puberty ceremonies.

Death.—A corpse was prepared for burial by the deceased's sisters and other clanswomen. The big toes and the legs above the knees were tied together. The whole body was painted with the most artistic designs; in addition to colors used on other occasions the Indians employed white and yellow, which were restricted to corpses. The body was adorned with white beads and a great number of feathers, and it was wrapped in a mat. The deceased was bemoaned and praised for a long time, then carried to the grave. Before burial an elder member of his family pierced the body three times with an arrow on the lower lip, on the shoulders close to the neck, and on the thighs, then left the arrow stuck between his belly and the mat. This was done to assure him good treatment in the other world.

The brief reference to burial—"they bury him in a grave and cover the body with earth"—does not seem to describe the deep-level graves typical of most western Colombian tribes.

RELIGION

Major deities.—The *Patángoro* believed that a windlike being called Am lived in the skies, but, in keeping with their general lack of formalized religion, they did not worship him. Regarding the sun and moon and another deity called Chusman or Chanzan, two different opinions are said to have existed. According to one, the sun and moon were both deities, and only they and Am were in heaven. Chusman was a rather malignant deity who, though evidently not living in heaven, sent terrible frightening visions, diseases, famine, and thunder and lightning. According to those who did not worship the sun and moon, Chusman lived with Am in the skies, was well disposed toward mankind, and expressed his will through shamans; he was also lord of the nether world.

The afterworld.—It was said that dead persons returning to visit their living relatives described the afterworld as a place of plenty and happiness. The Indians were so sure of its attractiveness that at different times, including the period of the Spanish Conquest, many of them hanged themselves so as to go there more quickly. Some believed that it lay in the east, on the banks of the Magdalena River; others imagined it to be in the west. The part of a man which went to the afterworld was an airlike substance called tip, similar to man but intangible, which resides in the heart and leaves it upon death.

Magic and shamanism.—If a boy of 5 or 6 had certain visions of human beings, birds, or other animals, he hurried to tell his mother his terrible experience. She would counsel him not to be afraid and to be prepared for further visions, for they meant that he had been chosen to be a shaman. To strengthen such a boy the mother would call other children to beat him with sticks at certain hours and on certain days. It is not stated how long such preparation lasted. At the end of it the boy was considered a full-fledged shaman. If, as only rarely happened, a long time elapsed during which no boy received the visions necessary to become a shaman, a close relative of a dead shaman was asked to be his successor.

The shaman cured wounds simply by washing them with warm water and putting his hand over them; for head wounds the hair was parted and tied. In cases of wounds from poisoned weapons all the flesh affected by the poison was cut away with a stone knife. For pains and diseases the affected part was rubbed, sucked, and blown. The shaman would draw blood from his gums and spit it out to demonstrate that the malady had been extracted.

Among the *Patángoro* but not the *Amani*, if the patient died, his relatives killed the shaman.

Shamans as well as ordinary people warded off rainstorms by blowing.

Among the *Amani*, village "principales" and shamans would assemble in the ceremonial building and, seated on their stools, question one of the shamans regarding war, weather, cases of adultery, the number of children people would have, and the number of years they would live. The shaman answered from outside the house, through a special little window or loophole, or from a structure built near the ceiling.

MYTHOLOGY

According to the *Patángoro* flood myth, everyone was drowned by the flood except one man, to whom Am gave a stick wrapped up in a mat, a hollow bamboo, and a vessel. From the stick he made himself a little hut to live in. When he awoke the first morning the bamboo had been changed into a woman, who took the vessel and went for water. After this Am returned to heaven, and a horrible snake appeared to the couple telling them not to answer Am's calls lest they too be transformed into snakes. They followed the snake's advice and as a result remained forever naked and in need of many things. The possible Christian elements may have been brought into the story by Rufo or Aguado; its basic native features can, however, easily be discerned.

LORE AND LEARNING

The numeral system seems to have been decimal, for the Indians counted up to 10. Beyond 10, however, they called everything "much."

The tribes of this area had developed a whole set of combined whistling sounds for long-distance communication.

Antidotes against animal poison consisted, whenever possible, of certain parts of the animal in question and, only in cases when this could not be had, of herbs and bark. All such remedies were taken internally.

THE NORTHEASTERN EXTENSION OF ANDEAN CULTURE

By Alfred Métraux and Paul Kirchhoff[1]

INTRODUCTION

Although *Chibcha* (*Muisca*) culture is, in spite of its obviously Andean character, curiously isolated geographically, cultures of a more or less Andean or at least semi-Andean type continue toward the north and northeast of it for a considerable distance (map 6).[2] At the time of the European Conquest they extended as far as the mountain ranges con-nected with, or easily accessible from, the Andean system. Exactly like these mountain ranges, the chain of Andean or semi-Andean cultures bifurcated at some distance northeast of the *Muisca,* one branch follow-ing the Venezuelan Andes or Sierra de Mérida, the other following the Sierra de Perijá to the Sierra Nevada de Santa Marta. At an earlier period Andean cultural influence must have reached even farther to the northeast, for archeology reveals it especially around Lake Valencia and in the plains south of the Venezuelan Andes, and ethnology shows that scattered Andean elements occurred within the eastern portion of the Colombian-Venezuelan coast and even beyond in the Antilles. The Andean culture elements encountered in the region around Medellín (the old Province of Aburrá) appear to be geographically isolated, although future archeological investigations in the area between Bogotá and Medellín may bridge this gap, adding thus a third, northwestern, branch to the two already mentioned.

Most of the tribes with this culture live in higher altitudes, but there are some tribes who have a large number of Andean culture elements, in certain cases with a culture that is markedly Andean or at least semi-Andean in type, and who live in the foothills or even in the hot valleys and plains within or close to high mountains.

Information regarding most of the tribes of this area is extremely scanty. Some tribes are included here not only because they occur within the general area but also because they have a few elements—often the only elements recorded—that are obviously Andean. Other tribes, such

---

[1] The material on the *Chaké* is by Métraux; the Introduction and the information on the other tribes are by Kirchhoff.

[2] The tribes of this article appearing on map 6 are principally those appearing in the text.— Editor.

as the *Lache,* the tribes of the *Timotean* family, and the *Arhuaco,* fortunately are better known, so that their inclusion in this area is beyond doubt. These and probably other tribes, such as the *Corbago,* have not only characteristically Andean traits but also a cultural level comparable to that of many less advanced Andean tribes in Ecuador and Perú. However, the inhabitants of the region around San Cristóbal—the *Zorca, Quenaga, Sunesua,* and probably many others, and the *Chaké,* as Jahn (1927, p. 80) calls the Highland tribes of the so-called *Motilones* group in contrast to the *Mape* or lowland *Motilones*—are characterized not only by considerably fewer Andean traits but also above all by a definitely lower cultural level. These peoples give the impression of having come under Andean influence only relatively recently, for they still retain much non-Andean culture.

Although the basic culture of this area, as manifested by the *Chaké,* is found also among a number of other tribes around and to the east of Lake Maracaibo (see p. 469) in the territory of the *Mape,* the *Chaké* and *Mape* probably do not have a sufficient number of specific traits in common to warrant their being grouped together as *"Motilones."* In the 16th century only the *Mape* were called *"Motilones"* (in Spanish, "those with cut hair"). Since the disappearance of the other tribes of this region the term *"Motilones"* has become practically the equivalent of "wild Indians," first to the white settlers and then to anthropologists. The name *"Motilones,"* therefore, is not used in this article, except in the section on history.

The *Mape* in no sense belong to this culture area, but at the coming of the Spaniards there existed a number of tribes in the region inhabited today, and very probably then also, by the *Mape,* whose culture, to judge by the scanty information at our disposal, was Andean or at least semi-Andean (the *Tayatomo, Corbago,* and *Araucana*). Geographically these tribes link the *Chaké* and other tribes to the north of them with the more southern members of this culture area, forming a chain broken only by the *Mape.*

The *Arhuaco* tribes of the Sierra Nevada de Santa Marta, whose culture is on the whole very markedly Andean (though resemblances with the culture of the Colombian-Venezuelan coast are not missing), are treated elsewhere (Handbook, vol. 2, p. 868).

Some Andean elements have found their way to the *Tairona* and the *Goajiro,* who are respectively the northwestern and northeastern neighbors of the *Arhuaco,* but these tribes are strikingly different culturally from each other and both are markedly non-Andean.

Enough Andean elements to give the local tribal cultures a distinctly Andean flavor are encountered in a curiously isolated region: the so-called Province of Aburrá around Medellín in the upper Porce Valley (this volume, p. 326). Although the Porce and Cauca Valleys are con-

MAP 6.—The native tribes of Venezuela and Lowland Colombia. Heavy lines segregated areas treated in Volumes 2 and 3. (Prepared with data furnished by Paul Kirchhoff and Gregorio Hernández de Alba.)

(Face p. 350)

nected by an easy mountain pass, their cultures seem to have had little in common. The Andean elements found in or near Aburrá seem, however, to be attributable to an ethnic group different from, and probably exterminated by, the Indians encountered there by the Spaniards.

The linguistic affiliation and even the language of most tribes in this area are unknown. The peoples of the Venezuelan Andes seem to have spoken related languages, this linguistic family being somewhat arbitrarily called *Timote* by Jahn (1927, p. 334). To judge by tribal and place names, the only linguistic data available, some of the tribes farther to the southwest possibly also belonged to this family, which to date must be considered as isolated. The *Chaké* tribes, and probably some of their immediate neighbors to the south (*Carate*) and northwest (*Coanao, Itoto,* and *Cariachil*), belong to the *Cariban* family. Most *Carib* tribes living in this part of the continent form part of the neighboring culture areas (e. g., the *Carare, Opón, Bubure-Pemeno,* and *Kirikire*). The *Arhuaco* tribes belong to the *Chibchan* family.

All the tribes treated in this chapter except the *Chaké* disappeared long ago, although in the Venezuelan Andes they have left traces of their culture among the local Mestizos. Their culture is known almost exclusively through the accounts of the conquerors, as no missionaries worked among them. The most important sources are Oviedo y Valdés (1851–55), Castellanos (1874), Aguado (1916–17), and Simón (1882–92).

HISTORY

The historical data referring to the *Chaké* are not easily separated from those referring to the *Mape,* because these tribes have for some time past been lumped together as "*Motilones.*" Between 1779 and 1792, both the "*Chague*" (i. e., *Chaké*) and "*Motilones*" (i. e., *Mape*), in some cases together with the *Sabril, Coyamo,* and *Aratomo* (tribes that no more belonged to this area than the *Mape*), were collected by the Capuchins of the Provinces of Navarra and Cantabria in small settlements in the region of Perijá and along the Catatumbo and Escalante Rivers. A census taken in 1810 gives for these 10 missions a total of 1,190 Indians of the tribes named above. The first "*Motilones*" vocabulary, collected around 1738 by Father Francisco de Cartarroya but now lost, may have been taken among either the *Chaké* or the *Mape*.

Relations between the Whites and *Motilones* (apparently both *Chaké* and *Mape*) deteriorated completely after 1836, when the Indians were cruelly provoked. From then to the present many tribes have constantly maintained a hostile attitude and have attacked all who entered their territory or settled nearby. Several employees of the Caribbean Petroleum Co., which has many oil wells on the Venezuelan side of their territory, were killed by them. Since about 1915, however, relations between certain

tribes and the Whites have improved. The Capuchin missionaries at La
Granja, on the Colombian side of the Sierra de Perijá, have established
friendly relations with many villages, and, on the Venezuelan side, members of the *Tucuco* tribe (who are *Chaké*) come to work on farms near
Machiques. When Dr. and Mrs. Bolinder (1937) crossed the Sierra de
Perijá from west to east in 1936–37 they were amiably received by several
tribes. The *Yasa* (a *Mape* tribe) remain intractable, however, and are
feared by the other tribes of the region.

TRIBAL DIVISIONS

The following six groups of tribes are provisionally included in this
culture area, largely because of their geographical location and because of
the similarity of tribal and place names. Their inclusion is based on
cultural features only in the few cases where data permit.

(1) The *Lache* on the slopes of the Nevado de Chita differ both
linguistically and culturally from the following groups.

(2) The *Tequia* (*Cercada*) to the northeast of the *Lache* are practically unknown but were stated to differ both linguistically and culturally
from their neighbors.

(3) The *Chitarera* (*Chitarero*), including the *Chinácota*, lived in the
region of Pamplona. The *Cúcuta* and the inhabitants of the towns of
Loma Verde (La Guazábara) and Zamia may all or in part have been
merely subdivisions of the *Chitarera*, in the district around Cúcuta.

(4) A number of tribes to the northeast of the *Chitarera* are practically unknown both linguistically and culturally, except for some cultural
data on the *Chinato, Zorca, Quenaga* and *Sunesua*. Among this group
of tribes were:

the *Azua* and *Cazabata;*

the *Táriba, Aborotá, Toituna, Guásimo, Tononó, Sirgará, "Barbillos," Simaraca, Tucape, Tamoco,* and *Tirapara;* the *Chucuri*
and *Cuite;*

the *Burgua,* on the Burgua River;

the *Chinato* and *Lobatera,* in the mountains northeast of San Cristóbal, and along the Zulia River:

the *Capacho* (*Capucho*), between the latter and the *Chitarera;*

the *Táchira, Tote,* and *Tocó,* on the Táchira River;

the *Tororó* (*Auyamas*), in the lower Torbes Valley;

the *Mocoipó, Guaramito, Peribeca,* and *Carapó;*

the *Oriquena* and *Cacunubeca,* in the upper Torbes Valley;

the *Umuquena,* on the Umuquena River;

the *Venegara, Bocaquea, Babiriquena, Tucapuya, Nebica, Buriquero,
Mancueta, Burumaquena, Huria,* and *"Piaches,"* in the Uribante
Basin;

the *Seburuco,* around Seburuco;

the *Zorca,* in the Santiago (today San Cristóbal) Valley;

the *Quenaga* and *Sunesua,* in the Espíritu Santo Valley, near San Cristóbal;

the *Susaca,* in the Corpus Cristi Valley, near San Cristóbal;

the *Burba* and the inhabitants of the town called Arcabuco (*Corrales*)

the *Humugria* and *Cariquena,* in La Grita Valley;

the *Quenemari* (*Quinimari*) ;

the *Guaraque,* around Guaraque; and

the *Cabaria* and *Mesoy.*

(5) A number of tribes grouped together linguistically by Jahn as *Timote:*

the *"Bailadores"* and *Mucuti* (*Mocoti*), on the Mucuties River :

the *"Estanques,"* *Carigri,* and *Iricuye,* on the Chama River from Estanques to the beginning of the plains (the *Guaruri,* said to be linguistic relatives of the last three tribes, are not likely to have belonged to this culture area, since they lived at the mouth of the Chama River) ;

the *Chiguará,* on the slopes north of Lagunillas; ethnographically unknown but important because of being mentioned in the traditions of the ruling family of the *Caquetio* of Coro, who claimed to have come from this region;

the *Jají, Capáz* (*Capás*), *Tucani, Escaguey,* and *Torondoy,* on the wooded slopes watered by the Capáz, Tucaní, and Torondoy Rivers (the *Torondoy,* at least those who used blowguns as did the *Pemeo,* on the southern shore of Lake Maracaibo, probably did not belong to this culture area) ; the *Torondoy,* like the *Chiguará,* are mentioned in the traditions of a *Caquetio* group, far to the northeast, in this case those of Yaracuay;

the *Quinaró,* including the *Jamú* (*Jamuene*), *Orcasé,* and *Casé,* around Lagunillas and on the Mesas de Caparú; in the same neighborhood probably the *Quirorá;*

the *Isnumbi,* around Pueblo Nuevo;

the *Miguri* (*Barbados*), including the *Tiguiñó, Mucuñó, Camucuay,* and *Mocochopo,* around Acequias; to the south of them the *Macaria;*

the *Mirripú,* including the *Mucujebe* (*Mucujepe*), *Mucumbi,* and *Mucuguay* (*Mocobay*), on the Nuestra Señora River; in the same neighborhood probably the *Mocoabá;*

the *Tucuo,* in the Quebrada de González; in the same neighborhood the *Guaimaro;*

the *Guaque,* around Ejido and in the Pedregosa Valley; in the same neighborhood the *Curo;*

the *Tatui,* around Mérida;

the *Tabay* (*Tapay*), around Tapay; in the same neighborhood the *Cacute*; these two tribes may have been either the last of the lower altitude tribes or the first of the higher altitude tribes.

the *Caraguá, Mucuchay, Mucutubiri, Caparó, Aricagua, Michay, Ticoporo,* and *Curvatí* (*Curbatí*), on the southern slopes, from Canaguá in the upper Mucuchachi Basin to the upper Curvatí River; neighboring on them the *Tiruaca, Moquinó* (*Qinó*), and *Judigua* (*Judigüe*);

the *Mucujún,* including the *Mocanarey* and *Mocaquetá,* on the Mucujún or Alisares River; the *Mucurubá,* around Mucurubá; in the same neighborhood probably the *Mucumanó;* and the *Mucuchí,* including the *Mocao, Misteque, Misintá, Mosnachoa, Musiquea* (*Misiquea*) and *Mucuchache,* around Mucuchies; i. e., all these tribes on the upper Chama River;

the *Mucubají* (*Carboneros*), on the upper Santo Domingo River; the *Aracay,* on the Aracay River; and the *Pagüey* (*Pabuey*) and *Pescahuey,* on the upper Pagüey River; the *Barinao,* on the middle Santo Domingo River may also have belonged to this culture area, although around Barinas tribes of other culture areas are mentioned, e. g., the *Jirajara* and the *Achagua* (see pp. 469 and 399);

the *Tostó,* including the *Tostó, Estiteque, Guandá, Misquichá,* and *Niquitao,* on the upper Boconó and its tributary, the Burate or Oburate; to the southwest of them, on the Tucupido, the *Tucupí;*

the *Timote,* including the *Timote* (and their subdivision, the *Esnujaque*), *Miquimboy, Jajó, Quindorá, Chachopo, Mocotapó,* and *Mucujurape,* on the upper Motatán;

the *Tirandá,* including the *Tirandá, Chachú, Estiguati, Curandá, Bombá, Bujay, Tonojó,* and *Misisí,* on the Jiménez, Castán, and middle Motatán Rivers;

the *Escuque,* including the *Escuque, Isnotú, Betijoque, Quibao, Pocó,* and *Mosquey,* on the Pocó River, and around Escuque, Betijoque, and Isnotú; the *Coromocho,* either to the north of them, or possibly identical with one or several of these tribes;

the *Cuica,* including the *Monay, Siquisaye, Burbusay, Cabimbú, Chejendé, Carache,* and *Cuica,* around Monay, Burbusay, Carache, and Cuicas; and

the *Umucaro* (*Humucaro, Umacaro*), on the upper Tocuyo.

(6) A number of tribes in the northern part of the Cordillera Oriental and its northern continuation, the Sierra de Perijá, the majority of them belonging to the *Cariban* family:

the *Carate,* around Ocaña;

the *Tayatomo,* not precisely located;

the *Corbago,* in the Sierra de Mene, situated probably farther to the south than the mountain range of that name shown on modern maps;

the *Xiriguaná*, on the slopes down to the Magdalena River;

the *Araucana*, to the northeast of the *Corbago;*

the *Chaké* group of tribes, including, from north to south, the *Aguas Blancas, Cunaguasata, Tucuco, Sicacao, Pariri, Chaké, Yasa, Macoita,* and *Macoa,* on the eastern side of the Serranía de los Motilones, and the *Socomba, Casacará, Milagru, Togaima,* and *Tolima,* on the western side of the Serranía de los Motilones;

the *Coanao* (*Guanao*), *Itoto,* and *Cariachil,* in the western foothills of the Serranía de Valledupar and on the upper César;

the *"Coronudos,"* possibly identical with the *"Coronados,"* i. e., the *Burede,* a subdivision of the *Bubure* (who do not belong to this culture area, but were neighbors of the *Arhuaco,* who are the northwesternmost tribes with an Andean culture, Handbook, vol. 2, p. 868).

Grubb (1927, p. 58) calculates the total number of the modern *Motilones* at about 5,000.

PHYSICAL APPEARANCE

Many *Chaké* are diminutive in stature, and they appear almost pygmoid, to judge by Bolinder's photographs (1937, p. 56). According to De Booy's measurements, *Macoa* men average 5 feet 1 inch (1.55 m.) in height; women, 4 feet 8 inches (1.42 m.).

CULTURE

SUBSISTENCE ACTIVITIES

Farming.—This area has two groups of cultivated plants: those characteristic of the surrounding low country or Tropical Forest and those of the higher altitudes of the Andes. Only the first group, which includes sweet manioc, sweetpotatoes, yams, maize, beans, auyama or uyame (*Curcubita pepo*), gourds, malanga (*Xanthosoma sagittifolium*), algarroba, papaya, pineapple, tobacco, urucú, and cotton, was known to such tribes as the *Zorca* and *Chaké.* The tribes of the *Timotean* family grow these and fruit trees, such as the avocado, guava, guaimaro, star-apple, spondias, pejivalle palm, and pitahaya. Plants of the second group include *Ullucus tuberosus, Oxalis tuberosa, Solanum tuberosum,* ocumo, churí, celery, aniana, icoraota, and zapayo.[3] The only surviving Indians of this area, the *Chaké,* also cultivate plantains, a few bananas, and some sugarcane, but their staples are manioc and maize.

Farming techniques show the same contrast, although the dividing line is not so much that of altitude as of cultural level. The *Chaké* have a semimigratory type of cultivation; they open large clearings along the wooded mountain slopes, today using axes traded or stolen from the

---

[3] See Handbook, vol. 2, p. 5, for list of Andean cultivated plants.

Whites. The *Timotean* tribes had permanent, fields, often terraced, and for irrigation they employed either storage tanks or ditches. The tribe called *"Los Estanques"* had a tank or reservoir next to every house. The *Miguri* tribes in the valley called "Acequias" ("irrigation canals") and the *Coronudo,* to the northwest of the *Chaké,* had ditches. The *Timotean* tribes cut irrigation ditches through hills and rocks and conducted the water onto terraces (catafós) that were 2 to 3 rods wide and had retaining stone walls. These may still be seen. It is not clear whether these terraces were made only for irrigation or whether they were intended also to check soil erosion.

It would be expected that this higher Andean type of farming was in the hands of men, but our sources are silent on this point. Among the *Chaké* men clear the field and plant; the women harvest. Among the *Lache* the women did the work in the fields.

The *Chitarera* stored maize in underground bins ("silos"), which in one village were so conspicuous that it was called the "Pueblo de los Silos."

Hunting and fishing.—The *Chaké* are good hunters. They shoot game and birds from small blinds built on the ground or in trees. In certain localities fishing is particularly rewarding. The Indians shoot fish with bow and arrows, drug them, or seize them by hand in small ponds made by damming rivers.

Food preparation.—In the Venezuelan Andes the beans of the wild cacao tree were ground on a grinding stone and made into a drink called chorote. Chorote is made today. The "butter" which formed on the top of cooled chocolate was, together with the beans, the most prized religious offering.

The *Chaké* usually roast meat on the babracot. These tribes eat maize on the cob or grind it on a slab with a stone mano (pl. 67, *top*), wrap the meal in leaves, and cook it. They pound manioc, mix it with water, and heat it in a calabash placed among hot stones until it coagulates.

Maize was used by the *Timotean* tribes to prepare an unfermented drink (mazato or masato) and a fermented drink (chicha). Only the latter is mentioned among the *Chaké.* (See p. 366; pl. 62, *top, left.*)

The tribes of the Venezuelan Andes had to import their salt from the lowlands near Aricagua. The *Chaké* have no salt and shun condiments; today they use only a mixture of ashes and lemon juice. The *Coanao* produced and traded salt.

The Indians living at Lake Jurao in the Venezuelan Andes cut through two layers of deposits in the lake bottom to obtain chunks of sodium carbonate (jurao). They used it as a salt substitute on food, they mixed it with coca (?) in place of lime, and they made it into a paste which they licked. They traded it to distant tribes, including the peoples of Lake Maracaibo, the Tocuyo region, and the Venezuelan llanos.

Captive and domesticated animals.—In enclosures close to their houses the *Jamú* kept paugies(?), guans, turkeys, turtle doves, and several other kinds of birds. (See *Macoa*, pl. 64, *bottom, right.*) The *Chaké* have no dogs today, and our sources do not mention dogs among other tribes except the *Aburrá*, who had mute dogs.

HOUSES AND VILLAGES

The distinction between the two types of culture within this area— both in cultural level and in the number of Andean traits (pp. 349–351)— is seen clearly in the dwellings. Large towns are mentioned among the *Lache*, the *Timotean* tribes, and the *Corbago*. The *Lache* town of Cocuy consisted of some 800 stone-wall houses. The valleys and slopes of the Venezuelan Andes were covered with a great number of settlements, and the Spaniards were astounded by the size of buildings and towns—one source says there were "as many houses as in Rome"—and by their orderly appearance, always with a temple in the center of town. There were few *Corbago* towns, but each was large, the principal settlement having about 800 houses. The *Jamú* settlements at Lagunillas were divided into quarters and were embellished by ornamental trees, in addition to the groves of fruit trees, and by enclosures full of birds. At Estanques a water tank was found next to every house.

The modern house has a circular ground plan and a wall of stones joined with clay, which, however, is of no structural importance as the roof rests directly upon a wooden framework.

Chitarera, Zorca, and *Chaké* settlements (pl. 61, *top*), and probably those of the majority of the remaining tribes, are villages rather than towns. The size of only one *Chitarera* settlement is known; it had 20 houses. Subterranean storage rooms for maize were a conspicuous feature of the *Chitarera* village called "Pueblo de los Silos." *Zorca* villages were composed of 8 to 10 or at most 20 houses, the walls of which were formed of vertical sticks with the interstices filled in with straw and *Speletia* leaves. The *Chaké* villages visited by Bolinder (1925) consisted of very rudimentary structures: either simple lean-tos, supported by a transverse bar resting on two vertical posts, or huts formed by double lean-tos with both ends closed and a small porch along the front. These huts were flimsy and gave little protection against cold and rain. The floor was covered with ferns and small mats on which the Indians slept.

The *Chaké* lack hammocks and wooden benches. The absence of hammocks, nowhere mentioned, seems to be one of the negative characteristics of this area.

The houses of *Tequia* chiefs were, like those of the *Muisca* chiefs, surrounded by palisades, for which reason they were called "Los Cercados." The houses of the *Timotean* Indians called *Los Valientes* were provided with loopholes.

Causeways, which are such a conspicuous feature in the archeology of the plains south of the Venezuelan Andes, have also been reported from *Los Valientes*. Causeways built of slabs and described as similar to those of the *Muisca* and "wider than in Cuzco" were found by the Spaniards in the Province of Aburrá. At intervals of about 2 leagues, they had wayside shelters filled with provisions and surrounded by fields. Although these causeways seem to have been in use at the time of the Conquest, being routes of trade with tribes farther east, they were evidently not built by the Indians encountered here by the Spaniards but by an earlier people, who had also left behind many ruined cities, apparently of stone. According to local tradition, these cities were destroyed by the *Nutabé*, a people of Colombian-Venezuelan coast culture, and by the inhabitants of the otherwise unknown "Province of Urezo."

DRESS AND ADORNMENT

Despite frequent lack of details there is no doubt that dress in most of this area was distinctly Andean, being characterized by garments, usually of cotton cloth, that covered more than the sexual organs and in some cases included a covering for the head, also of cotton.

Lache dress is unknown, but warriors of this tribe are said to have fought "naked." The *Chitarera* wore "cotton blankets." From the *Zorca* to about where the boundary between the Venezuelan States of Mérida and Trujillo crosses the Venezuelan Andes, women wore a tunic, described as a long, tight, sacklike garment, or they simply wrapped a blanket around the body and tied it over one shoulder. The blanket was gathered around the waist with a belt in such a way that the upper part hung over loosely and could be used to carry all kinds of objects. Both tunics and blankets were woven of agave fiber in the western portion of this region but were of cotton in the eastern. In contrast to women, men went naked, with the prepuce tied to a string worn around the waist. Among the *Quenaga* and *Sunesua*, however, men wore tunics of agave fiber, apparently identical with those worn by the women, except that they were provided with shoulder straps. Among some of the tribes in the valleys east of Mérida, as far as the *Timote,* the men wore cotton tunics extending below the knees; in others, however, men perhaps went completely naked. Women in this region wore a big cotton blanket gathered at the waist with a belt and held together over the left shoulder with a wooden or golden pin, which often had a hollow head containing one or several tiny pebbles. Their arms and legs remained bare. Until the beginning of this century, *Mucuchí* women wore a dress composed of two such blankets, one white, the other with colored stripes; they wore one over the other and fastened the upper one with a pin. An Andean type dress, described as a baglike garment which was painted, as among the *Muisca,* with leaf and curvilinear motifs, occurred eastward to Guanare River, in the foothills of the Venezuelan Andes, i. e., probably among the *Tucupí*. Among the *Cuica*, who are the northeasternmost *Timoteans*, the dress of both sexes was non-Andean, being identical with that of some of their neighbors of the adjoining culture area. Men went naked except for a gourd penis cover, while women wore only a multicolored cotton apron ("bayo") not wider than a hand. Here cotton blankets are mentioned only as religious offerings. The inhabitants of the town called "Las Tapas" (probably *Tucaní*) made tight capes of interwoven palm leaves that covered a man from head to foot. These capes are seemingly an isolated occurrence.

Following the other branch of this Northern Extension of Andean culture, we find again that a number of tribes characteristically have complete and Andean type dress. *Tayatomo* women wore one-piece tunics that reached to the ground and were provided with cowls. Among the *Corbago* and *Xiriguaná* both sexes wore painted blankets. In an unnamed tribe nearby cotton tunics painted with curvilinear and leaf motifs are mentioned. A *Chaké* man wears a long cotton tunic decorated with brown stripes or ribbons, and on his head a cotton cap, a wide woven head band which the wealthy decorate with seeds (among the *Macoa* the extremities fall down the back), or a straw hat with a conical crown trimmed with bunches of feathers (pl. 63, *bottom;* pl. 64). Women use a small cotton loincloth, and in cold weather they throw a cotton mantle over their shoulders and tie it under the chin. Children and even young unmarried girls go very scantily dressed or else completely naked (pl. 65, *top*). Babies wear a long shirt which may be used to carry the child on the mother's back. The *Coanao* wore cotton blankets.

For the inhabitants of the Province of Aburrá we have conflicting reports, which may refer to two different ethnic groups, one of which may be either an ethnic remnant of the builders of the causeways found in this region or else people who inherited their culture. One authority speaks of breachclouts, 1½ yards long by 1 yard wide. The breachclout is characteristic of the Cauca Valley tribes across the mountains. Robledo (1864), on the contrary, states that the men went naked, with the prepuce tied to a hank of red or white thread wound around the waist. This custom, though not typically Andean, is found also among tribes which belong both culturally and geographically in the Andean area. (See above.)

The most frequent and usually the only personal adornment are necklaces of colored seeds (the *Chaké* use seeds of *Abrus precatorius* and *Coix lacryma-jobi*), jaguar and other animal teeth, tufts of small feathers, and, especially characteristic of this area, carved bone beads. In addition, the *Timoteans* use white and green stone beads (*Jamú*) and very thin shell disks (chaquiras). Whereas these tribes usually employed but one material at a time, such as stone, shell, or bone (e. g., the *Jamú*), the

Chaké seem to prefer a combination of several materials in one string, which they wear tightly (men) or loosely (women) around the neck, or over both shoulders and under the opposite arm.

Mucubuy men wore many gourds tied to their waist, apparently as part of their war make-up.

Breastplates of bone were worn by the *Jamú*. Very thin stone breastplates representing a highly stylized bird, possibly an eagle with outstretched wings, are frequently found archeologically in the Venezuelan Andes. Breastplates have not been reported among the *Chaké,* but the *Coanao* to their northwest wore eagle-shaped gold plates.

Deformatory ornaments are only mentioned twice: bone nose ornaments in the Venezuelan Andes and golden earrings among the *Coanao.* Their rarity may be one of the negative characteristics of this area.

Whereas bone is the most characteristic material used for personal adornment in this area, gold (probably guanin) seems to have been but rarely employed, the only two known occurrences being in the Venezuelan Andes and among the *Coanao.* It is probable, though not certain, that the *Timotean* tribes did not manufacture the few golden objects they used. The *Coanao* are definitely known to have acquired theirs in exchange for salt, probably through some neighboring tribe, from the *Tairona* or the *Pacabuey,* both belonging to the Colombian-Venezuelan coastal culture area.

Red and black are the most common colors used for face and body painting. The *Mucubuy* painted their faces and bodies black all over, for which reason the Spaniards called them "Carboneros." The *Macoa* paint their faces with intricate designs of stripes and dots in black, brown, and scarlet (pls. 67, 68, 70, for example). The Colombian *Chaké* use urucú.

From the region of the *Zorca* to about Mérida, the hair was worn long. The *Zorca* wound it around the head, which was covered with certain broad leaves. From Mérida eastward the hair was cut at ear level. The *Timote* wore little pigtails close to the ears. Feather headdress has been reported only in this region. Among the *Macao* both sexes cut their hair short.

The *Miguri* tribes, who seem to represent one of the highest cultural levels within the *Timotean* family, wore beards and were consequently often called *"Los Barbados."* The *"Barbillos,"* to judge by their Spanish nickname, may have done the same. A man with a painted mustache and beard was observed among the *Macao.*

TRAVEL, TRANSPORTATION, AND TRADE

No means of transportation is mentioned except the carrying baskets of the *Chaké* (pl. 63, *top;* pl. 64, *bottom, left*). Babies were carried on the back, in special slings (Venezuelan Andes) or by means of the long shirt the child wears (*Chaké*). To cross gorges the tarabita (a rope bridge) is used today in the Venezuelan Andes and may be pre-Columbian. Articles of trade were salt (Venezuelan Andes and *Coanao*) and jurao (Venezuelan Andes). Balls of cotton thread and strings of tiny shell disks were used as media of exchange in the Venezuelan Andes.

MANUFACTURES

Division of labor.—Little is known about this subject. Among the *Lache* the women worked in the fields. Among the *Chaké* men build the huts, do basketry work, knit bags, clear the forest, plant and sow, and make their weapons and clay pipes, while women spin, weave, and make pots.

Textiles.—The *Chaké* spin cotton threads with a drop spindle (pl. 67, *bottom*); the thread passes through a ring hanging from the roof. Agave fibers are made into strings by rolling them on the thigh.

These Indians make looped or netted bags identical to those of their *Arhuaco* neighbors, from whom they probably borrowed the technique and the ornamental motifs. Among the *Chaké,* bags are knitted by men, not by women. To loop the cotton threads they use wooden needles without a hole.

Cotton fabrics (tunics, loincloths, bands) are woven on the vertical loom (pl. 64, *top, right;* pl. 68, *top*).

Basketry.—The *Chaké* are good basketmakers. Their carrying bags, satchels, telescope boxes, quivers, and fire fans are produced in the same twilled and hexagonal weaves as in the Guianas, but the specimens collected by Bolinder are plainer than those of the more eastern *Cariban* tribes. In our area the strands are not stained, but decorative effects are achieved by alternating strips with the rough side out and the smooth side out.

Ceramics.—To judge by the rich archeological ceramics in the Venezuelan Andes, this area must have had good potters. Our sources only rarely mention that the tribes of the *Timotean* family made vessels and other objects of clay, among them censers and idols. The tribes with comparatively few Andean traits and with a low cultural level (p. 350) used gourds and calabashes to a far greater extent than clay pots. The *Chitarera* even received their name from their extensive use of calabashes as receptacles. The clay vessels of these tribes are described as course or crude. Those of the *Quenaga* and *Sunesua* were about three fingers thick at the rim and were used only for cooking. All *Chaké* pots characteristically have a pointed bottom and four ears. They are unpainted but sometimes are decorated with finger impressions.

Weapons.—The tribes of this area fall into two groups according to whether the bow is absent or is the main or only weapon, though a number of tribes are intermediate. The two groups seem to coincide more or less with the two types of cultures found here.

The bow was absent among the *Tequia* and the *Aburrá,* both of whom used spear throwers, and, judged by somewhat inconclusive evidence, some *Timotean* tribes lacked it. For warfare, tribes without bows used clubs (the tribes around Mérida), clubs and slings (the *Coromocho*), or lances, spears, and clubs (the *Cuica*). The remaining tribes of this area, including some of the *Timotean* family, used the bow. The bow occurred mainly among the marginal southwestern peoples, who possibly belonged to another culture (the so-called *Valientes,* the *Mucuchachi,* the *Aricagua,* and the so-called *Bailadores*). The *Chaké* seem to use only the bow (pl. 70, *top, right* and *bottom, left*), but the other tribes apparently, always preferred clubs, slings, spears, or lances. Among the *Lache* at one extreme of this area and the *Itoto* and *Cariachil* at the other, bows are not mentioned, but it is not certain that they were lacking. *Itoto* and *Cariachil* warriors are described as carrying long lances.

Blowguns occurred only among the marginal *Torondoy* who, though linguistically members of the *Timote* family, may not have belonged to this area culturally.

Shields were used from about Cúcuta in the south to the *Itoto* and *Cariachil* in the north, being apparently absent among the *Timotean* tribes and the *Chaké*.

These weapons are rarely described. Clubs, always called "macanas" and often described as long, seem to have been of the cutting variety (sword-clubs). Those of the *Lache* were provided with a "bannerlike" adornment made of the feathers of guacamayas, parrots, etc., or of fine straw. In the Venezuelan Andes, where the use of wrist guards has been reported, bows are said to have been long, while those of the *Corbago* were so small that they were carried in the quiver, together with the arrows. *Chaké* bows are of palm wood, with an elliptic or lozenge-shaped cross section and a length of 1.2 to 1.5 m. (4 to 5 feet). *Macoa* bows average 1.92 m. (6 feet 4 inches) in length. The *Chaké,* like the tribes of the Colombian-Venezuelan coast, frequently use their bow staves as clubs and can inflict heavy wounds with the sharp edges. The bowstring is of vegetable fibers.

Only the *Chinato* are said to have used arrow poison, a characteristic of the Colombian-Venezuelan coast. *Chaké* arrows lack feathering. Arrows have reed shafts into which are fitted points of various types, the most common now being a wooden foreshaft tipped with an iron blade (pl. 71, *top, left*). The bindings form various designs named after animals or designs like those on serpents. Hunting and fishing arrows are tipped with a barbed wooden rod, with two wooden rods, or with a wooden rod and four points diverging from its base. Harpoon arrows are also used for hunting game. Arrows are kept in a quiver, which the *Chaké* make of basketry.

Shields used by warriors were, to judge by the terms used by our sources (adarga and pavés), oval or oblong, and large enough to cover almost the whole body. The *Corbago* made them either of deerskin or of bark. Offensive weapons were bows, clubs, spears, and lances.

POLITICAL ORGANIZATION

Political fragmentation seems to have been characteristic of this area; tribal organization and chiefs were unknown. Among the *Lache* there were fist fights between certain subdivisions ("parcialidades"), probably of a local character. These were usually accompanied by many casualties.

Little is known of the nature of chieftainship, which probably differed considerably in the two types of tribes. In some tribes the chief evidently ruled over a whole valley, while in others he was simply the village headman. Thus in the region just west of Mérida in the Venezuelan Andes chiefs were called cepo and apparently wielded considerable authority, while among the *Zorca* the local headman was usually the man with the biggest family and the largest fields. He had little authority and did not intervene in disputes among his people, a thief being punished, often killed, by his victim.

There is no evidence of social stratification, even among the more advanced tribes, except that one reference states that war leaders were selected from the local noblemen ("principalejos") in the Venezuelan Andes.

SOCIAL ORGANIZATION

Marriage.—Among the *Zorca*, parents betrothed their children at birth. The children grew up and slept together in the house of the girl's parents, having their first intercourse at the time of the girl's first menstruation. A house was built for the new couple and the wedding celebrated with drinking, singing, and dancing.

A wife apprehended in adultery remained with her husband and was not punished, provided her brothers or nearest kin killed her lover. Otherwise she was sent home to her parents or brothers, her offense being considered a great disgrace.

Among the *Chaké,* monogamy seems to prevail. Important *Macoa* men may have two wives (pl. 61, *bottom*), but the second has a far lower status and is regarded as a servant. Child betrothal is said to be common, but marriage takes place only after puberty.

Among the *Zorca,* parents are said to have been so domineered over by their children that the latter had the right to punish them.

Homosexual relations.—The *Lache,* in contrast to all the other tribes of this area and almost certainly through the influence of their neighbors and friends, the *Arawakan Caquetío,* publicly recognized male homosexuals, whom they married and buried as if they were women. Women who bore five male children consecutively were permitted to rear one as a woman.

The majority of the tribes of this area seem to have been warlike, though some were more so than others. In the 16th century all the Indians encountered by the Spaniards attacked in orderly formation, with much shouting and noise (which caused the valley inhabited by the *Humugría* and *Cariquena* to be named "La Grita"). To annoy and provoke the enemy, warriors in the Venezuelan Andes danced around with wild movements and made faces; hence came Spanish names such as *"Los Locos"* and *"Los Bailadores."* Near Cúcuta (Loma Verde) we hear of warriors drinking chicha before going into battle, just as in the Colombian-Venezuelan coastal culture. In the tribe called *"Los Bailadores"* the warriors carried into battle heavy ropes wound around their waists. These were used to tie prisoners.

Pointed stakes hidden in tall grass were used in an unnamed village near Cúcuta. Fortifications of palisades and moats with drawbridges seem to have been adopted in the Venezuelan Andes during the wars against the Spaniards, when some tribes lived exclusively in fortified settlements. These were located in inaccessible places from which the inhabitants rolled big boulders down upon the attacking Spaniards. Whether any of these military techniques were known in pre-Colombian days is uncertain.

Childbirth.—*Chaké* women give birth in the forest without assistance. The baby is bathed, after which girls and women of all ages perform a dance during a feast. Only two men assist, one holding panpipes in one hand and weapons in the other. After the dance, which is extremely slow, the men shoot their arrows to the ground in front of them.

Puberty.—At the appearance of her first menses a *Chaké* girl runs away but is pursued and caught by an old woman who shuts her in a small cabin, like those used by hunters, where she remains for 10 days. She must turn her back to the opening, through which food is given to her, and she receives a drug which is supposed to stop the flow of blood.

Burial customs.—The *Zorca* placed their dead horizontally in graves just big enough to accommodate the body. A deceased widower (or widow) was not allowed to wash himself nor touch any food with his hands for 10 months. Other people had to feed him; if he were alone he had to lift the food to his mouth with his wrists.

In the Venezuelan Andes, to judge by archeological finds, the body was placed in a stone tomb (called to this day "mintoy," i. e., "cave"), closed with a stone slab. To prevent the corpse from touching the walls or roof it was either seated (on a stool?) or placed squatting on its heels. Sometimes the dead were buried in natural caves. Maize, "roots" (probably manioc), chicha, clay figures, and weapons (for men) or a grinding stone

PLATE 61.—"**Motilones**" (**Macoa, i. e., Chaké**) **village life.** *Top:* Village scene. (Courtesy, University Museum, Philadelphia.) *Bottom:* Family group. (After De Booy, 1918 b.)

PLATE 62.—"Motilones" Indians. *Top (left):* Making chicha. *Top (right):* Group at Maracá. *Bottom (left):* Woman, Department of Magdalena, Colombia. (Courtesy Batista Venturello.) *Center:* Chicha trough (hollowed log) of the *Perija. Bottom (right):* Temporary camp on Río Negro at foot of Perija range. (Courtesy American Museum of Natural History.)

PLATE 63.—"Motilones" (Macoa, i. e., Chaké) carrying devices. *Top:* Tumpline carrying basket and gourd. *Bottom:* On the trail, wearing tunics, straw hat, and carrying packs. (Courtesy University Museum, Philadelphia.)

PLATE 64.—"**Motilones**" (**Macoa, i. e., Chaké**) **Indians.** *Top* (*left*): Man playing an ax-flute. *Top* (*right*): Weaving. (After De Booy, 1918 b.) *Bottom* (*left*): Tumpline basket. *Bottom* (*right*): Man with parrot. (Courtesy University Museum, Philadelphia.)

PLATE 65.—"**Motilones**" **costumes.** *Top:* Women and children, Colombia.
(Courtesy Batista Venturello.) *Bottom (left):* Men from Río Yasa. Garment
of native-grown cotton. *Bottom (right): Perija* Mestizo man with haircut
and costume typical of Sierra de Perija country, Venezuela. (Courtesy
American Museum of Natural History.)

PLATE 66.—"**Motilones**" **weaving.** *Top:* Cotton cloth on a vertical loom. (Courtesy University Museum, Philadelphia.) *Bottom:* Twining a reed mat. (After De Booy, 1918 b.)

PLATE 67.—"Motilones" (Macoa, i. e., Chaké) crafts. *Top:* Grinding meal for chicha. (After De Booy, 1918 b.) *Bottom:* Spinning cotton. (Courtesy University Museum, Philadelphia.)

PLATE 68.—"Motilones" (Macoa, i. e., Chaké) musical instruments and fire-making. *Top* (*left*): Man playing a flute. *Top* (*right*): Using a fire drill. *Bottom:* Blowing on the sparks to start the fire. (*Top* (*right*) after De Booy, 1918 b; others, Courtesy University Museum, Philadelphia.)

PLATE 69.—"Motilones" Indians. *Top* (*left*): Bone platform used by the *Perija*, a "*Motilones*" subtribe. Human bones are dried in these platforms and then thrown into a cave. (Courtesy American Museum of Natural History.) *Top* (*right*): "*Motilones*" from Department of Magdalena, Colombia. *Bottom* (*left*): "*Motilones*" group from same region. (Courtesy Batista Venturello.) (*Bottom* (*right*): "*Motilones*" on log-bridge trail. (Courtesy American Museum of Natural History.)

PLATE 70.—"Motilones" (Macoa, i. e., Chaké) Indians. *Top (left):* Woman dressing child's hair. (After De Booy, 1918 b.) *Top (right)* and *Bottom (left):* Men with bows and arrows. *Bottom (right):* elderly woman. (Courtesy University Museum, Philadelphia.

PLATE 71.—"Motilones" (Macoa, i. e., Chaké) Indians of the Sierra de Perija. *Top (left)*: Warrior with arrows. *Top (right)*: Old man playing a musical bow and youth with panpipes. *Bottom (left)*: Burial practices, involving the disinterring of the remains of a chief. *Bottom (right)*: Woman with a basket. (Courtesy Gerard Reichel-Dolmatoff.)

(for women) were placed close to the corpse, together with beads of a reddish quartz, which are frequently found today in the graves, usually in a pottery vessel.

In the houses of the *Corbago* the Spanish conquerors found heads, arms, and legs stuffed with straw. Since war trophies are reported nowhere in this area, these remains may have been the deceased of this tribe.

The body of a deceased *Chaké* is kept for 2 days in his hut and then taken to an isolated cabin where it is placed on the floor and covered with grass. (Formerly the corpse was deposited on a platform (pl. 69, *top, left*).) Food, drinks, and the deceased's weapons are left by the corpse. After a month the Indians collect the bones and sew them up in a piece of cloth. They carry the bundle to the dance ground while men shoot arrows into the air and women pelt each other with liana leaves. They drink and dance for 2 or 3 nights during which two of the deceased's closest relatives dance and play the flute, carrying the funerary bundle on their backs. After the feast the bundle is suspended from the hut roof for 2 or 3 years (pl. 71, *bottom, left*).[4] If for some reason the bones are not available, pieces of wood are substituted. These are painted with red figures and bound together. Finally the bones are carried to a cave in the mountains. Whoever has touched the bones may not touch food with his hands but must use leaves to handle it. He is also prohibited from going to the fields, lest he spoil the maize.

ESTHETIC AND RECREATIONAL ACTIVITIES

Musical instruments.—Shell trumpets are mentioned among the *Chitarera,* the tribes of the *Timotean* family, and the *Chaké.* The last also have side-blown cow-horn trumpets (post-Conquest), bone quenas or end flutes with a single stop (pl. 68, *top, left*), and panpipes (pl. 71, *top, right*) of eight tubes bound with a simple ligature. These Indians have a unique type of flute with a lateral air duct placed at right angle to the air chamber. The projecting part of the mouthpiece is wound around with cotton thread and the rest is covered by a large lump of wax (Izikowitz, 1935, p. 375). This contrivance gives it the appearance of an ax, hence its name, "the ax flute." Its length is about 1.1 m. (3 feet 8 inches) and its diameter 5.5 cm. (2.2 inches) (pl. 64, *top, left;* fig. 67).

Drums and rattles, reported from the Venezuelan Andes, are unknown to the *Chaké.*

---

[4] Some additional details are given by Wavrin (1937, pp. 453–462). The body is forced into a fetal position. The mother or wife of the deceased weaves a special blanket in which to carry the bones. The woman who crushes the maize for the chicha consumed during the feast of the transport of the bones observes chastity. The march to the tomb is preceded by a ceremony in which two men play bone flutes while others dance. Women also dance or play panpipes. On the way back from the grave, men open a new path in the bush. The bones are kept in the hut only for two days and are then carried to an ossuary.

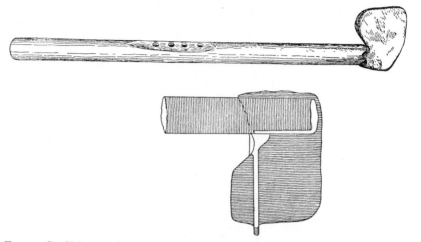

FIGURE 67.—"Motilones" ax-flute. Cross section of head below. (Redrawn from
Bolinder, 1917, fig. 29, *a, b.*)

Dances.—*Chaké* dances follow a simple pattern: Men dance in pairs, each resting his bow or his hand on his partner's shoulder, while they walk forward and backward, stamping the ground and singing a monotonous song.

Sports and games.—The *Lache* of different groups, probably local, indulged in fist fights, which usually resulted in many casualties. In a favorite *Chaké* game boys shoot at each other with arrows tipped with corncobs. In another game a ball is caught in a kind of basket affixed to the end of a pole. String figures are also popular.

Alcoholic beverages.—The *Chaké* prepare chicha with young fresh maize, which is ground and boiled, then mixed with old chicha to hasten the fermentation. They do not add saliva to obtain this result.

A particularly strong chicha is made of crushed maize wrapped in leaves to make small bundles and cooked for about an hour. The maize pellets are then dried in the sun until they develop a covering of fungus through partial fermentation. The day before the feast the pellets are placed in a hollow log, the "kanoa," together with crushed ripe bananas, yuca, and sweetpotatoes. Water is poured on this mixture and fermentation commences immediately. (De Booy, 1918 b, p. 202; Wavrin, 1937, p. 456.)

Stimulants.—Coca was used by the *Timotean* tribes. Some *Chaké* groups use it today but only for medicinal purposes. In the Venezuelan Andes tobacco was and still is consumed in the form of a jellylike preparation called mo or chimo. The *Chaké* are passionate smokers. They know how to make cigars but prefer to smoke pipes, which consist of a clay bowl and a wooden stem and resemble those of stone which have been found in the *Tairona* region. These pipes are manufactured locally.

RELIGION

The *Lache* venerated stones, believing that the dead became stones, that all stones had originally been men, and that at some future date they would turn into men again. They also considered shadows as "gods," which the sun gave to men and objects. The "House of the Sun" was an important religious center and burial place, not only for the *Lache* but also for many of the *Chibcha* (*Muisca*). It was built facing the rising sun on the eastern slope of the Andes, facing out over the plains. It was evidently visible from a great distance, especially when the sun was reflected from the golden objects placed outside it. Inside were many suspended strings of beads, sea shells, and chests of gold placed on racks. The location of the *Lache* "House of the Sun" and its place in *Chibcha* culture were similar to those of the Temple and Convent of the Virgin of the Sun found to the east of the *Chibcha*, in the plains farther south in *Guayupé* territory (see p. 385), and to the causeway which is said to have descended all the way from the *Muisca* town of Sogamoso to the eastern plains. The latter was built in commemoration of Bochica's disappearance.

The tribes of the Venezuelan Andes believed in a supreme being (ches), who lived on the highest mountain peaks and in lakes. The temples that stood in the middle of every town were places of worship, although certain rituals seem to have been performed directly on mountaintops, in caves, etc. Idols were made of cotton thread, fired clay, wood, or stone. Offerings consisted of the heads, antlers, or bones of deer, balls of cotton thread, small cotton blankets, anthropomorphic figures of clay, wood, stone or cotton thread, strings of stone beads of many colors or of tiny shell disks, green stones, painted bones, salt, cacao beans, cocoa butter which was burned in tripod censers, and the flesh of deer killed and burned within the temple.

The most famous temple in the Venezuelan Andes was devoted to a female deity called Icaque. Located in Escuque, it was a place of pilgrimage for people from far and wide. The building consisted of three parts ("naves"). It contained many figures made of cotton thread and filled with offerings of greenstone beads and tiny shell disks. It also had boxes full of bones, semiprecious stones, and a few pieces of guanin breastplates. The walls of another temple were covered with skulls. The only persons permitted to enter this temple (and probably others as well) were priests, who made offerings and communicated with a deity from whom they learned about the future. If anyone else entered it the earth was expected to tremble and to swallow the trespasser.

The *Jamú* sacrificed children to a water god by throwing them into the lake. Before planting trees the *Miguri* celebrated a ceremony at night called "the coming down of the ches." This included a mimicry of sowing and harvesting. In another ceremony the participants held a rattle in their left hand and a whip in their right with which they beat each other.

After a crushing defeat by the Spaniards the men and women of the tribe called *Los Valientes* committed mass suicide. This, as well as the individual suicide of many *Aburrá* men when the Spaniards were first sighted, may be connected with certain ideas regarding the hereafter which were found here and there in northwestern South America.

The religious system of the *Chaké* still remains unknown except for a few practices. According to De Booy (1918 b, p. 208), the *Macoa* believe in a supernatural being which they call Kioso. When it thunders they look up and say, "God is angry."

Bolinder (1925, p. 237) speaks of duels fought during drinking bouts, when people castigate one another and visitors with bow staves.

After the maize harvest, men and women dance in separate groups until the men suddenly discharge their arrows toward the sky. Often the dancers are wounded by the falling arrows. In order to dispel a storm, the Indians threaten the clouds with their weapons, make noise, dance, and drink.

Several taboos have been listed. Fire and maize must be kept apart; for this reason nobody may cross a maize field while smoking, and maize is never roasted. Nobody may eat the game he has killed, lest his marksmanship deteriorate.

MYTHOLOGY

"Motilones" myths recorded by Wavrin (1937, pp. 600–603) come either from the *Chaké* or the *Mape*. At the beginning of the world there existed four murderous giants who were invulnerable. Finally, having committed incest and lost their power, they could be slain by men. Yuca was owned by Zamuro, the black vulture. It was stolen by the Vulture's son-in-law. Fire was owned by Toad and was stolen by Stars, who put it into several kinds of wood. Sun is a cannibal who attempts to devour a man whom Moon saves. Moon's arrows are snakes.

LORE AND LEARNING

In the Venezuelan Andes the year was divided into lunar months. When necessary, as in the case of the restrictions imposed upon widows and widowers, the months were counted by knots in a string.

BIBLIOGRAPHY

Aguado, 1916–17; Bolinder, 1917, 1925, 1937; Castellanos, 1874; De Booy, 1918 a, 1918 b; Ernst, 1887 a, 1887 b; Febres Cordero, L., 1918; Grubb, 1927; Ibi, 1919 a, 1919 b; Izikowitz, 1937; Jahn, 1927; Nicholas, 1901; Oviedo y Valdés, 1851–55; Robledo, 1864; Simón, 1882–92; Wavrin, 1937.

THE GOAJIRO

By John M. Armstrong and Alfred Métraux

THE REGION

The Goajira Peninsula, projecting as part of Colombia northward into the Caribbean Sea, contains an area of about 5,000 square miles, bordered on the east by the Gulf of Venezuela. The broad level plain known as Lower Goajira occupies the base of the peninsula, while the northern extremity is known as Upper Goajira and is characterized by three distinct ranges of hills. These hills have a maximum height of 2,600 feet (about 780 m.) and are separated from each other by two broad plains which run from sea to sea. The country is dry and infertile, the vegetation consisting of divi-divi, cactus, pricklypear, and other xerophitic plants. Even these are absent where bare rock and stone slides preclude vegetation. Rivers are almost nonexistent, the country being cut in all directions by shallow, dry, sandy water courses which drain off rain as it falls. In the south and west, on the treeless prairies or savannas, the land is more hospitable. Here the Indians do most of their stock raising.

LOCATION AND HISTORY

The pastoral *Goajiro* who inhabit this peninsula (map 6) differ profoundly from the agricultural forest-dwelling *Motilones* and *Arhuaco* to the south. Juan de Castellanos, in his "Elegías de los Varones Ilustres" (1874), is the first to allude to these Indians, though he calls them *Cosina*. He states that in his time, about 1550, cattle were already abundant in the area. It seems that the adoption of pastoral life by the *Goajiro* took place soon after the Spanish settlement of that part of the continent. The name *Goajiro* was, however, already known in the 16th century and was applied first by Pedro Simón (1882-92). The first reliable ethnographic information about the *Goajiro* goes back to José Nicolás de la Rosa (Nicholás, 1901) and Antonio Julián, who both visited these Indians in the 18th century. Jahn (1927, pp. 119-136) has gathered the few data concerning the *Goajiro* which he found in the early literature. A short summary of the first description of these Indians is given by Hernández de Alba (1936, pp. 8-12).

369

During the Colonial Period, the *Goajiro* were hostile toward the Spaniards. After 1830, however, as a result of better treatment from the Whites, thanks in part to the efforts of Juan MacPherson, they become more friendly. Present authorities in the *Goajiro* region merely regulate frontier traffic.

The attempts by the Capuchin Fathers to alter their ways of life have been unsuccessful. Except for the thin Catholic veneer, noticeable in baptismal rites and Spanish names, *Goajiro* social life seems to have been little affected by centuries of contact with Hispanic culture. Foreign influence is more apparent materially in iron implements, utensils, guns, textiles, and ornaments. All the domestic animals are of Spanish origin.

As a result of tuberculosis, smallpox, and venereal disease, the *Goajiro* are gradually dying out, and the population estimates found in the literature have become smaller and smaller, the most recent indicating a scant 18,000.

PHYSICAL APPEARANCE

The *Goajiro* are usually described as aggressive and untrustworthy, of medium or small stature (cf. J. A. Mason, 1926, pp. 39, 52), copper colored, with jet-black hair, dark eyes rather obliquely set, a broad and blunt nose, and a large mouth (pl. 72, *bottom, right*). Within the tribes there are physical differences which seem to correspond with social status, the lower classes being smaller and more Indian in appearance, while those of higher rank are more often of a greater stature, with curlier hair and larger noses.

LANGUAGE

The *Goajiro* language belongs to the *Arawakan* family. There is, however, no good analysis of it. A grammar, "replete with errors" according to Simons, was published by Rafael Caledon in 1878. Various word lists have been published from time to time.

CULTURE

SUBSISTENCE ACTIVITIES

Farming.—The *Goajiro* have a poor opinion of agriculture, and only the poorer sibs practice it. The one fertile part of the peninsula is near Punta Espada. Here the land is well cultivated, and plantains, maguey, onions, coca, sugarcane, and grain are grown. Tobacco, bananas, maize, gourds, manioc, sweetpotatoes, millet, beans, and watermelons also are raised. Those who own cattle grow only small patches of quick-maturing corn for the purpose of making chicha beer.

Hunting, fishing, and gathering.—Hunting, fishing, and gathering occupy a minor place. Deer, armadillos, land tortoises, and rabbits are the chief game. The *Goajiro* who live near the coast sometimes catch fish (with hook and line), lobsters, mollusks, and crabs.

Cattle raising.—The *Goajiro* are primarily nomadic cattle raisers and, consequently, depend upon the water supply. In the rainy season they seek natural depressions, which they sometimes enlarge artificially, where the water may gather. In case of drought they wander toward the sea, where wells 30 to 40 feet (9 to 12 m.) deep are dug.

Besides cattle the *Goajiro* keep sheep, goats, horses (pl. 72, *bottom, left*), mules, pigs, and domestic fowls, which they take with them wherever they go. An estimate gives them 100,000 cattle, 200,000 sheep and goats, 20,000 horses and mules, and 30,000 donkeys. As cattle are a measure of wealth, the Indians are reluctant to kill them for food, but they utilize the milk or export the animals to Curaçao and Aruba in exchange for textiles and corn. Each tribe has its own cattle brand, and the annual round-up and branding is an occasion for great festivities. Horse races and other sports take place, and large quantities of food and drink are consumed.

Food preparation.—*Goajiro* diet consists almost entirely of meat and milk products. Goats and sheep are killed every day or two for meat, and the milk of the cows is made into butter and cheese. This diet is supplemented by yuca, cactus fruit, sugar, rice, and plantains, the last three obtained from Colombian and Venezuelan traders in exchange for skins. Meat that is not immediately consumed is suspended from tall poles, and skins are pegged to the ground and salted in preparation for sale. Butter is made by stirring the cream with a fluted stick in a calabash or wooden bucket. To make cheese, rennet is added to skimmed milk in a trough, and the curds are put in a primitive wooden cheese press, which is weighted with a heavy rock.

HOUSES AND VILLAGES

Although the *Goajiro* are of a common origin, they are divided into sibs ("castes" or "tribes"), each living within a rather limited area (Simons, 1885, p. 796). The sibs are split into local groups, which occupy extended villages or rancherías, each with 2 to 50 houses (ranchos) and 10 to 250 or more Indians. Houses are always within gunshot distance of one another and so disposed that surprise attacks would be difficult. If a village is at all permanent, a protective cactus hedge surrounds it.

Goajiro nomadism makes elaborate houses unnecessary. Dwellings are mere lean-tos, arbors, and temporary gabled roofs supported on poles. Thatch is made from the core of the cactus, split lengthwise. Rough tables, chairs with rawhide seats, and benches are often used. The hammock is always present. House walls are often lacking, but a corner of the hut may be closed off for a girl's puberty seclusion. When migrating from one locality to another the *Goajiro* generally dismantle their houses and take them along, piling the poles and thatch on the backs of burros. Sometimes, however, they leave them for their own or some-one else's use in the future.

DRESS AND ADORNMENT

Goajiro dress has changed little since the time of Nicolás de la Rosa (18th century). Men normally wear only a breechcloth, a necklace, and a head band with feather attached (pl. 72, *top*) ; but when traveling, paying visits, or receiving company they wear a large loincloth with many folds, a mantle (nowadays of bright colors), and an immense sash, in which they carry their arrows. A knitted string bag is hung from the waistband. In towns trousers and shirts are worn. The women wear a cotton dress, sometimes made like a simple sack with holes cut for the head and arms. The puna—long strings of beads passing over both shoulders, crossing each other on the breast and back and held in place by a sash or belt of beads (the sirapo)—is placed on a female child a few months after birth and gradually augmented according to the parents' wealth and the child's age. Black beads are generally used for the sirapo, colored ones for the puna. A married woman wears the puna until her first confinement. After her seclusion at puberty, a robe, sometimes containing 8 or 10 yards of embroidered material, is also worn by a *Goajiro* woman, but the loosely folded cloth which was her sole covering before puberty is still worn beneath it. Women, unlike men, are modest and avoid being seen naked.

Some young girls have as many as 100 turns of beads around their waists, as well as many around their wrists and ankles. Red coral is preferred, but most beads are made from seeds or coconut shell and are cut out by means of a hollow metal reamer twirled rapidly between the palms. The perforated shell may then be used as a colander. Glass and porcelain beads and earrings are also worn. The most prized orna-ments are the tumas—polished and perforated stone ornaments found in some of the old graves. On dress occasions necklaces of beads and gold ornaments are worn. These, found in *Tairona* graves, are fashioned in the form of tiny animals, frogs, turtles, etc.

The men, except the medicine men, wear their hair short, kept back by a ring or crown made of plaited straw, or of wool with a tassel behind. Often the two are combined and adorned with a couple of feathers in front; or the whole may be made of feathers. For protection against mosquitos and sun both sexes paint their skin with powders made from rotten wood, a black stain made from a wild nut, and another color ex-tracted from leaves and mixed with fat. After puberty women cut their hair short, keeping the shorn tresses in a bag hung from the roof; hence-forth they never let it grow beyond the neck. They make designs on their skin with black stain and tattoo themselves, especially on the arms and legs, with charcoal dust pigment. At least one of the marks is the same as the tribal brand.

MANUFACTURES

Women have a rather definite daily routine. They arise before daybreak, milk the cows, and prepare the morning meal for the men, who then go off to fish, hunt, fight, or merely loaf and drink chicha. They fill their jugs at the water hole and then spend the rest of the day collecting wild cotton, spinning, weaving, making ropes, grinding corn, making butter, cheese, and chicha, and performing other household duties. They milk again in the evening.

Textiles are probably the best *Goajiro* manufactures. Their other products are pottery (which is the virtual monopoly of a few sibs), bows and arrows, and saddles and harnesses.

Spinning and weaving.—Wild cotton is collected, the seeds removed by hand, and small wads are rolled around a thin stick to form small tubes about half an inch (12.5 mm.) in diameter and 6 inches (15 cm.) long. These tubes are then spun into thread with the use of a spindle, one end of which rests in a calabash bowl on the ground. Yarns are colored with vegetable dyes, especially divi-divi.

Almost every household owns a loom, before which the women sit for hours weaving hammocks and bright-colored belts for men and horses. The warp is made from one long continuous thread wound around two thick horizontal poles, the upper one firmly attached to two uprights, the lower one hanging loose and maintaining the tension. As the work progresses, the cloth is moved forward around the poles, so that an endless strip of cloth is produced, which is then cut. Shuttles are passed through by hand, the warp being shifted by means of a threading arrangement which takes hold of alternate strands. On a piece of cloth about 2 yards wide an inch of weave every three hours is considered very fast work.

Containers.—Most cooking utensils are made of crude earthenware by a few tribes in the vicinity of the Teta, a peak near the middle of the peninsula. Spoons and forks are cut out of calabashes. Some Indians possess enameled mugs and pots obtained from itinerant traders.

Weapons.—Almost every man possesses a good rifle. Cartridges are scarce and expensive and must be smuggled in. Firearms are consequently reserved mainly for warfare, and the bow and arrow is the everyday weapon.

The bow is made from the hard, springy wood of the black palm. It is almost round in cross section, 5 to 6 feet (1.7 to 2 m.) long, and strung with a special sisal cord. The end which rests on the ground is protected by an empty cartridge case, to which a metal ring is sometimes attached, giving a musical note with every shot.

Feathered arrows show many designs. Bird arrows may be tipped with cartridge cases or with large, rounded, wooden knobs about 1 inch (2.5 cm.) in diameter. Heads made from nails are used for small game. Serrated metal-tipped arrows are used in warfare; but the most dangerous arrow is pointed with a sting ray tail, sharpened to a fine needlelike point and fitted into the hollow end of a light cane shaft about 4 feet (1.2 m.) long and three-eighth inch (9 mm.) thick.

To prepare arrow poison, scorpions, centipedes, and poisonous spiders are mashed, snake venom is added, and the mixture is allowed to putrefy for several days. The poison will retain its potency for six months. It is kept in a short section of bamboo, which is carried around the waist, together with the arrow points, each in a hollow reed. Before shooting, an Indian dips the point into the poison and inserts it in the shaft.

A decorated leather wrist strap is worn as a bowstring guard.

Fire making.—Fire is made by twirling an arrow on a cactus hearth; the spark is caught in dry grass.

TRADE

There is considerable trade between the *Goajiro* and foreigners. Firearms and ammunition, cloth, beads, blankets, rum, cutlery, corn, crude sugar, rice, plantains, and tobacco are imported in exchange for salt, cattle, cheese, milk, hides, pearls and pearl shells, logwood (*Haematoxylon campechianum*), and divi-divi (*Caesalpinia coriara*).

During the salt season the Indians of the interior flock to Manaure, where they are paid for loading sacks of salt into the warehouse and onto ships. Both men and women take part in the work, the men filling the sacks and the women carrying them.

SOCIAL ORGANIZATION

The *Goajiro* are subdivided into 30 odd matrilineal sibs ("castes" or "tribes"), each identified with an animal. Some of the larger and more important sibs are split into smaller groups, each with a special totem. (See Simons, 1885, p. 796, and Weston, 1937, p. 139, for a list of the various sibs, together with the totem animals and the locality which they inhabit.) The members of any sib are more widely spread throughout the peninsula than previously thought, although in some localities, one sib may be found to the exclusion of all others. Each "caste," according to Petrullo (1937, p. 155), "holds sovereignty over a well-defined territory." The sib which is largest and wealthiest in livestock is that of the Urianas. It has many subdivisions, such as Uriana jaguar, Uriana rabbit, Uriana paularate (a song bird), and Uriana gecko (a lizard). The

Urianas are connected by marriage with the Pushaina, another wealthy "tribe" of the *Goajiro*.

Each extended village (section or ranchería) consists of related sib members who are bound by close ties and who unite against outsiders if one of them is wronged. Intermarriage among the sibs is common.

The role of the maternal uncle in *Goajiro* culture is of great importance. Santa Cruz's detailed study of it (1941) will be summarized here. Types of behavior, both prescribed and unformalized, vary, not only according to the seniority of either uncle or nephew but also according to that of the nieces. The maternal uncle must leave all his property to his oldest sister's oldest son, the other nephews receiving nothing. In practice the maternal uncle transfers most of his property to his own children, and after his death little if anything remains for the nephew. The attitude of a senior nephew toward his senior maternal uncle largely depends on what inheritance he expects from him. If the nephew marries a girl from a wealthy family and has, therefore, to pay a high bride price, the senior maternal uncle is expected to make a donation to meet the price. The uncle has no authority, however, in the selection of the bride.

Etiquette requires that in company the nephew must always remain silent if his senior maternal uncle is speaking; if the nephew wishes to speak he must first ask his uncle's permission. The nephew must always show respect and conduct himself with propriety. On the other hand, a senior uncle should not criticize or laugh at his senior nephew. No such behavior is prescribed between father and son or between other uncles and nephews. Public opinion castigates any deviation from this behavior between uncle and nephew.

The relationship between a maternal uncle and his niece is just the reverse of this, for the uncle is the recipient of benefits. He receives the bride price paid for the niece, and he contributes nothing toward the dowry for the bridegroom. The maternal uncle, however, is empowered to accept or reject a prospective bridegroom, and the girl has no recourse in the matter. A girl is respectful and considerate, although less rigidly formal, toward her senior maternal uncle. Her behavior toward her other uncles depends solely on her regard for them.

POLITICAL ORGANIZATION

There is no central government uniting all the sibs, but each sib or subdivision thereof has its chiefs who inherit their position matrilineally. The oldest chief has greatest authority and may carry a knobbed stick as symbol of his authority. He is generally the wealthiest and has most retainers. Hereditary status is very important, and a man born poor may never achieve a high position, even though he acquires much wealth. He may, however, marry a woman of high rank and his children will inherit her rank. Chiefs are polygynous and have many daughters, for whom very high bride prices are paid—sometimes thousands of animals, worth $6,000 to $10,000. Such rich chiefs take great pride in their daughters, dressing them in fine silken robes and necklaces of gold and pearls and providing them with personal servants.

There is a class of slaves who are beneath the chiefs' retainers in the social hierarchy. It consists of people born into this status and of captives.

PROPERTY

All cattle, though individually owned, belong in theory to the local group as a whole and are worked for the common benefit of all. For example, the cattle paid as a bride price when a girl marries within her own sib go to a new owner, but the milk, butter, cheese, and hides from them continue to be shared by everyone in the sib. When a woman receives cattle as a bride price for her daughter any new stock born to them belongs to the daughter's husband and his sons, and when the animals are rounded up for the annual branding each son is allowed to brand a certain number of them.

ETIQUETTE

The *Goajiro* are in general unfriendly to strangers but have a well-established code of hospitality. Strangers calling at a house must wait until invited in. Inside a house a bowl of chicha or rum (coffee when available) is the first gift offered the visitor, who is thereafter given a hammock and treated as a member of the family. A special feast may be arranged if there are many guests. A guest of high rank is feasted, and some of the young girls of the house may be placed at his disposal.

LAW AND ORDER

The chiefs have little power outside their own local group, where they settle minor disputes. The solution of many disputes and transgressions of custom are left to the parties concerned. The laws of group responsibility and group retaliation lead to frequent intertribal feuds. A person without a strong sib to protect him is helpless, for others may use any act which may conceivably be interpreted as harmful as pretext for demanding indemnity. For example, a person injured while intoxicated may demand payment from the person who sold him the rum, or a person injured by a borrowed animal may demand payment from the owner of the animal; a thief who hurts himself when trespassing on the property of his intended victim will demand compensation of him; and anyone aiding a sick or wounded person who subsequently dies incurs a liability.

If a person injures himself he must make an expiatory gift to the members of his own sib and a lesser gift to his father's relatives. If a child dies when under the care of one parent, this parent must reimburse the other.   Many other cases indicate the absolute nature of *Goajiro* law and the refusal to recognize extenuating circumstances.

Murder is a very serious crime, and the victim's family immediately demands blood money to the amount of 200 or more cattle.   For failure to pay, a member of the murderer's sib of the same rank as the victim must forfeit his life.   If payment is not forthcoming retaliatory raids are made.   As the defenders generally lose more people than the attackers, the feud may continue indefinitely until all the members of one sib will consider themselves at war with the members of the other, thereby spreading the war throughout the peninsula.   If a feud should develop between the sib of the husband and that of the wife, the latter, with her children, will return to her own group until the trouble is over.

A person who has received a deadly insult from another is baited and chided until he takes revenge by killing the offender, in proof of which he removes the victim's viscera and takes them home.   This act also prevents the victim's soul from bothering him.   If unable to accomplish this he may commit suicide.   Suicide is also sometimes a means of vengeance, a person feeling that he will suffer less than those who caused him to commit the act.   Thus a wife who is not allowed enough freedom may hang herself.

Next to murder, one of the most serious offenses is to mention a person's true name (given at birth?) or to mention a person's name after his death.   This has caused many tribal conflicts.

The value of the compensation demanded in disputes varies directly with the social rank of the offended party.   In some cases a repeated offender may be killed by his own sib members.   Sometimes, rather than to continue the warfare, hostile sibs may confer under the auspices of an outsider, such as a Capuchin monk, and draw up peace terms.   In personal quarrels or minor brawls women often step in and enforce peace.

WARFARE

Wars between the *Goajiro* and outsiders are rare, but any White man may be held liable for the offense done by another, as all Whites are thought to belong to the same sib.   Sometimes the few civilized people living in the peninsula take vengeance on the Indians, which leads to further reprisals by the latter.

At the time of De la Rosa, war was declared by sending to the other tribe an ambassador who, in a public speech, asked indemnities for damage previously done.   If these were not conceded war was declared, but a brief truce was observed in order that preparations might be made.   In battle each group of opposing warriors formed a semicircle and tried to surround and destroy the other.   In individual encounters a *Goajiro* rode out on a horse, but, upon seeing the enemy, he dismounted and shot his own horse with an arrow to show his confidence and willingness to fight on equal terms. He then approached the enemy from the left while making quick movements, jumps, and turns, with his legs apart and his knees bent. More recently, according to Ernst (1887 c), war is not declared, attempts being made to take the enemy by surprise.

Wars last indefinitely, sometimes being broken by a peace brought about by an influential "civilizado" or the Capuchin monks, the latter sometimes paying the retribution demanded out of their own pockets. Some tribes, such as the *Cosina* of Serranía Cosina (actually a conglomeration of outcastes rather than a sib), make their living almost entirely by robbery and pillage, destroying houses, stealing cattle, and killing or enslaving their enemies.

LIFE CYCLE

Birth and childhood.—During pregnancy a woman continues to do her heavy work up to the very hour of delivery. At childbirth, the shaman pronounces various spells over the patient and applies poultices made of dried flowers, roots, etc. A large, heavy stone placed over the womb and vigorous massaging bring about the birth. If the placenta is not soon expelled, the woman drinks a medicine concocted by the medicine man. As soon as the child is safely delivered the father serves rum and chicha to all his relatives. If the pains of childbirth appear when the sib is on the march, the woman mounts and rides ahead so that when the sib catches up the event is practically over. The husband cuts the cord with his machete and cauterizes its ends with a glowing ember. The woman then continues on the march with the child in a sling on her back. When the permanent camp is reached she washes herself and the child.

Baptism is a Christian ceremony which the *Goajiro* have adopted, and most of the Indians are called by Spanish names, as their real names may not be mentioned. Teknonymy is practiced; a parent is addressed by its child's name plus a prefix, nushi or sushi for the father, ni or si for the mother. Thus, a father may be called Nushijuan after a son or Sushijuana after a daughter.

At 6 or 7, girls learn to grind salt, pick cotton, and tend the smaller animals; the boys imitate their fathers.

Parents are said to show little affection for their children, sometimes selling them at Sinamaica. They receive $10 or $15 for a child of 8 or 9 years. The purchaser becomes the child's guardian, teaches him the Catholic faith, and keeps him until he is 17 years old. These children rarely return home. Abandoned children are taken to the San Antonio orphanage, where the girls continue to wear their *Goajiro* dress, but the boys are put into jackets and pants.

Girls' puberty.—At her first menstruation a girl is isolated in a small dark hut and stripped of all her ornaments. She lies in a hammock, sometimes hoisted near the roof. For the first 2 days she drinks no water but is given an herbal purgative. Her hair is cut short. Generally several of her relatives stay around the door of the hut, and strangers and men with an eye to matrimony may look in. During this period the girl is taught the duties of married life and such skills as weaving, sewing, and making hammocks. When she emerges, stout and bleached, a special festival is held, when she resumes her ornaments and puts on the adult clothes that she has made during her confinement. She is now considered marriageable. The length of her confinement depends on her status, though theoretically it lasts until her hair again reaches the nape of her neck. Poor girls are secluded only a few weeks, rich girls up to 2 years.

Sexual life and marriage.—Little is known about the sexual life of the *Goajiro*. A certain amount of promiscuous love making occurs among the young people at the biweekly festivals. Dances also provide an opportunity for sexual advances.

There are some male transvestites who carry on only female activities and are ridiculed by the men.

When a man desires to marry he sends his father or uncle as intermediary, then pays a bride price which has been set by the girl's relatives. The payment is usually in cattle, but goats, pearls, liquor, cotton cloth, and gold ornaments also are used. The father retains the purchase price only when his first daughter marries; the income of subsequent marriages goes to the girl's senior maternal uncles. The mother also receives part of the income. A son obtains the cattle for the bride payment from the increase of his father's herds.

Intermarriage between the sibs is frequent, and many of the *Goajiro* give their daughters to "civilizados" from Maracaibo and Río Hacha, who pay higher prices and find such a tie with the Indians useful in their trading relations.

The marriage ceremony consists of a series of feasts and exchanges of presents between the two families. The wedding night is spent at the ranchería of the bride's mother, but the nuptial hammock (specially woven by the female relatives of the bride) is hung from a tree some distance away from the house. For a period of days and even months the bridegroom leaves his bride at dawn and returns only after sunset. In this way the groom shows respect to his mother-in-law.

Polygyny is general. The number of wives depends on the economic status of the husband, some men having as many as 20. Each wife lives in her own house, where her husband occasionally visits her. The man, as head of the polygynous household, supervises the daily slaughter of animals and the distribution of meat and corn to each household according to the number of its members.

If a wife shirks her domestic duties she may be divorced and her husband may claim the return of the bride price cattle, plus their increase and minus an amount considered equivalent for the sexual right he had exercised. If a woman dies in her first childbirth the husband may demand the full return of the bride price (Simons, 1885, p. 792, however, states that the wife's relatives demand compensation from the husband). Adultery entails divorce with full return of the bride price. It rarely occurs, however, as the wife will be treated badly by her own relatives. At his death a man's wives are inherited by his brother, and next by his sister's sons; the women may avoid this by making a payment equivalent to their bride price. If he is of the Catholic faith his children may claim to be his legal heirs, which leads to conflict with the maternal nephews. (See Social Organization, p. 374.)

The influence of women in political affairs is sometimes noticeable. There are cases of female chiefs, and women are respected enough so as to be able to intervene and stop brawls.

Death.—Funerals are accompanied by festivities which last days or even weeks, according to the wealth of the family. There are some differences in the funeral ceremonies which are apparently associated with the particular sibs. These funeral feasts afford the best opportunity for display of wealth, and more than 1,000 head of livestock may be butchered. Every mourner who comes to the feast contributes animals for slaughter and continues to do so as long as he cares to remain. After the mourning period, marked by weeping and lamenting interspersed with drinking and feasting, the corpse, which has lain in a hammock slung from the rafters, is sewn up in hides by the women (men may not touch a dead body) and carried to the cemetery of the tribe. For a year or so, the body may be temporarily consigned to a shallow grave marked by a pile of stones. Food and drink are often placed in the grave, and, if the deceased had been a warrior, his bows and arrows are put in. A year or two later the bones are exhumed and reburied in a large urn. The exhumation is generally done at night and is accompanied by a feast. The remains are carried in a funeral procession to the dead person's birthplace, where they are buried in the family's own cemetery. The funeral urn is placed in a vertical position with the narrow neck of the jar protruding above ground to permit the free entry and exit of the spirit and to allow the remains of other members of the family to be added from time to time. A cactus hedge surrounds the cemetery, and in wet weather half a calabash is placed over the opening of each jar to keep out the rain. Whenever two relatives of a recently deceased person meet, they bow to the ground, shouting and groaning, for several minutes. (For a slightly different account of the burial of a rich man, see Simons, 1885, p. 792.)

If a person is stricken with smallpox the whole tribe moves away, only the family of the sick person remaining. When the death occurs they bury the body below the floor and burn the hut over the grave.

PLATE 72.—Goajiro Indians.   (Courtesy American Museum of Natural History.)

The *Goajiro* believe that after death the deceased in ethereal form wander about the country, their favorite meeting place being in the vicinity of Bahía Honda in the extreme north of the peninsula. There is some evidence that the Indians look forward to a happier existence after death. From this belief in the afterlife stems the practice of mutilating the body of a slain enemy, for once his body is broken and scattered it is not possible to reassemble his soul, and the slayer is protected from a vengeance-seeking spirit.

The dead are highly respected or feared; consequently, it is a serious offense to mention a dead person by name.

ESTHETIC AND RECREATIONAL ACTIVITIES

Games.—The *Goajiro* have various athletic sports, such as horse racing, wrestling, and archery. Contestants shoot at a skin ball or a fruit tossed into the air or at targets; they are very accurate up to 125 yards. Tournaments are held in which the contestants pair off, the victor of each round winning an arrow and continuing to compete.

Feasts and dances.—The *Goajiro* are fond of feasts and hold them whenever opportunity offers—at funerals, when they have received their pay for loading salt, at baptisms, or when a person completes his training as a medicine man. Weston (1937) describes a festival held on the last-mentioned occasion. For 2 days the big drum was sounded by relays of players, spreading the news. The dance, practiced beforehand, took place in a circle some 25 feet (7.5 m.) in diameter around which some 200 Indians gathered. A man, nude except for his waist cloth and head band with ornamental plume, with his face painted red in a crisscross pattern, danced backward from a girl dressed in a voluminous robe and wearing a large red handkerchief on her head. The girl attempted to overtake and head off the man, who retreated before her in a circle with a peculiar double step, almost a hop and a skip. As one pair tired another took its place, the dance continuing indefinitely.

Musical instruments.—*Goajiro* musical instruments are few. A calabash filled with stones or peas serves as a rattle for dance accompaniment. The clarinet is about 2 feet (0.6 m.) long, made of telescoped (?) sections of reed with a bell consisting of calabash and a vibrating reed in the mouthpiece. It is side blown. The large drum is carved from a hollow section of tree, 15 inches (38 cm.) in diameter and 24 inches (60 cm.) long, and has both ends covered with sheepskin. It is slung from the rafters, a branch, or from the player's neck. Singing among the *Goajiro* is virtually nonexistent.

Narcotics and stimulants.—To make chicha beer, maize may be masticated by the women and spat into a large earthenware bowl, with water and crude sugar added. After 3 days it is strained and drunk. By another method the maize is finely pulverized by hammering on a flat stone, instead of being masticated. Beer is drunk in large quantities, as is rum received by trade.

Both sexes commonly smoke long narrow cigarettes, which the women make of bundles of 8 or 10 leaves. Formerly, at least in the western portion of the country, the *Goajiro* chewed coca (hayo) with lime, which stained their teeth black. Coca is still grown, but there is no mention of this custom in recent times.

RELIGION

Goajiro religion is imperfectly known. Mareigua (Maleiwa) seems to have been the Creator and Culture Hero. He caused the first *Goajiro* to emerge from the ground and taught the tribe how to produce fire with a drill. He saved them during the flood by raising the Cerro Pororo where they had taken refuge and by driving the jaguars away. As a Supreme Being he shows some moral preoccupation, in the past having punished those who lived in incest. He sends rain and all the good things which the *Goajiro* expect from nature (Hernández de Alba, 1936, p. 44).

Yoluha (Yorja) has been thought to signify the god of thunder, lightning, and drought, but the term probably does not designate a single deity but bad spirits or ghosts in general. These are feared at night when the sky is clouded; to prevent their inroads the *Goajiro* stretch a thin cord between two poles reaching above the roof. They attach to this cord, at regular intervals, fishhooks which serve to entangle the Yoluha and make their stay unpleasant. Sometimes when sounds coming from the bush are thought to have been made by spirits, the Indians light embers and throw stones at them.

The *Goajiro* give considerable importance to dreams. A dream may cause the desertion of a camp, a war, or a consultation with a shaman. The *Goajiro* carry charms which they buy from shamans.

SHAMANISM

Goajiro shamans (piache) are of both sexes. Aside from their long hair shamans differ little in external appearance from ordinary persons, but their power is reputed to be considerable and people avoid offending them. They are said to cause the heart of a person to stop beating unless they are paid enough.

A shaman keeps his cures secret and divulges them only to a successor, who undergoes a long period of training and who pays his instructor a certain number of cattle. When the training is complete, there is a public initiation with dancing and drinking, at which the novice is seized by fits as demonstration of his new power. The instructor chants spells over the novice as he (or she) lies in the hammock twisting and groaning as his spirit takes possession of him, imparting knowledge and power.

In attempting to cure, a shaman often causes greater injuries to the patient; permanent blindness may result from his effort to cure eye injuries with caustic powders or to remove foreign substances with horse-hairs or cactus spines. Tuberculosis is treated by inducing expectoration and prescribing a meaty diet. Dysentery is cured with herbal medicines. Well-chewed tobacco or tobacco-laden spittle rubbed over a painful area is a common method of therapy. If the medicine man effects a cure, which he frequently does, he is rewarded with gifts of cattle, rum, etc. No attempt is made to treat smallpox, the victim often being abandoned to his fate.

Some practitioners who are not exactly shamans divine by burning a bundle at the end of a stick or by examining the bottom of a bottle, i.e., by crystal gazing (Hernández de Alba, 1936, p. 42).

BIBLIOGRAPHY

Brettes, 1898; Castellanos, 1874; Celedon, 1878; Ernst, 1870, 1872, 1887 c; Hernández de Alba, 1936; Jahn, 1914, 1927; Kirchhoff, 1931; Kohler, 1887; Mason, Gregory, 1940; Mason, J. A., 1926; Nicholas, F. C., 1901; Nicolás de la Rosa, 1739 (see Nicholas, 1901); Petrullo, 1937; Santa Cruz, 1941; Sievers, 1898; Simón, 1882–92; Simons, 1885; Weston, 1937.

THE GUAYUPE AND SAE

By Paul Kirchhoff

INTRODUCTION

In the southernmost section of the Venezuelan-Colombian llanos, the so-called Llanos de San Juan, the German and Spanish Conquerors (Speyer, Federman, Hutten, Pérez de Quesada, Avellaneda) encountered a series of tribes which they did not always mention by name and whose culture they described only briefly (map 6). Of these tribes only the *Guayupé* (*Guaypí*) and the *Sae* have been described by the chroniclers of these expeditions (Castellanos, 1874; Oviedo y Valdés, 1851–55; Simón, 1882–92; and Aguado, 1916–17) in sufficient detail to reveal that they had a culture with distinctive characteristics, and to suggest that the remaining tribes, little as they are known, shared this culture. Tentatively, we may also assign to this group the *Eperigua* (*Operigua*), about whose culture nothing is known but whom the *Guayupé* considered to have the same origin as themselves and the *Sae*.

At least one of these tribes, the *Guayupé*, lived not only in the llanos (which resemble the other Venezuelan and Colombian llanos) but also in large part also inhabited the dense rain forests of the Andean slopes. The *Guayupé* villages that directly adjoined the *Chibchan Muisca* even extended beyond the rain forest into the marginal sections of the Bogotá Highland.

Language and relations with other tribes.—Of the languages spoken by these tribes, only a few words, mainly personal names, are known. These suggest an *Arawakan* speech.

The *Guayupé* and *Sae* had relations with the *Caquetío* to the north (Speyer came to the *Guayupé* with a *Caquetío* interpreter) and the *Chogue* to the south, whom they dreaded as cannibals. They also knew quite well the *Muisca* on the Bogotá Highland, who came down into their territory to purchase cotton in return for gold objects, and they even knew of Highland tribes farther to the south and gave news of their vessels of silver and gold and their llamas. In fact, their relations with the more southerly tribes may have been even closer than with the *Muisca*, for from them they obtained 22-carat gold in thin leaves and sheets, jewels, and silver bells.

CULTURE

SUBSISTENCE ACTIVITIES

Farming.—The products of their fields included: manioc (seemingly both the sweet and bitter varieties), maize, sweetpotatoes, beans, peanuts, chili peppers, and some unnamed "vegetables"; also cotton and tobacco.

Fishing and hunting.—Fishing was an important source of food for all tribes. Hunting was absolutely undeveloped by the *Sae,* who ate no meat whatsoever, while the *Guayupé* would eat no fowl, hunting only quadrupeds, such as deer and peccaries. Peccaries were important game in most of the area.

Food preparation.—Manioc and maize were both used for making bread and a drink (undoubtedly fermented) of rather thick consistency; in fact, they were used mainly for the preparation of such drinks.

Domesticated animals.—That the dog is nowhere mentioned may be a mere accident. The only reference to domestic animals is in a curious passage about "domestic animals of strange nature," which may, however, refer only to tamed animals. Birds seem to have been kept in captivity, since Pedro Simón credits the tribes of the Llanos de San Juan with the knowledge of how to change the coloring of the feathers on the living bird, sometimes even producing feathers of different colors on one bird. They plucked the feathers of young birds and filled the holes with a paste which contained, in addition to the coloring matter, some kind of poison similar to that put by other tribes on arrows. This poison is said to have made the flesh of birds thus treated inedible.

HOUSES AND VILLAGES

The houses were built around a plaza on which there was a special building used for ceremonial purposes. Houses were kept very clean, and their inhabitants went to the river to defecate.

Few details of *Guayapé* house construction are known. The roof sloped to the ground, there were two doors facing each other, and houses were so big and long that many families lived in them. Hammocks were used for sleeping.

DRESS AND ORNAMENTS

Throughout the area men went completely naked. In most tribes women also went naked, but among the *Guayupé* they wore in front a pointed piece of bark (apparently not bark cloth), hanging from a string tied round the waist. Cotton blankets were made, but their use is not mentioned. Feather blankets were part of the chief's regalia.

Of exceptional interest are deer-hide moccasins that covered the foot to the ankles and leggings made of the fiber of the leaves of a tree called palmicha, both worn for protection against the hard, high grass that covers the llanos.

Men wore their hair long, usually falling down the back to the waistline, but sometimes they braided it with white cotton ribbons and tied it back "like a rose." The front part of the hair was shorn, and immediately behind it was shaved into artful designs. On the Meta River women shaved their heads completely.

One group of warriors was encountered with their faces and the upper halves of their bodies painted black, the lower halves red. They wore showy headdresses of guacamaya feathers to the tips of which rattles of rattlesnakes were fastened.

No ear, nose, or lip ornaments are mentioned, but the *Guayupé* said that a tribe farther south, probably outside of this culture area, wore wooden earplugs, because they had no gold. Golden ornaments as well as strings of shells were typical of the area, but it is not known how either was worn.

TRAVEL AND TRANSPORTATION

Canoes were used for river traveling. No data are available regarding land travel, except that the high, hard llanos grass was burned several times every year to make walking easier.

POLITICAL ORGANIZATION

Headmen seem to have controlled only individual villages. Among the *Guayupé* their successors were not necessarily, and possibly only rarely, close relatives. They may have been chosen by general agreement of the old men, who seem to have been important and may have had special status, as they are spoken of as "principals."

When a *Guayupé* headman died his body was cremated in a hollowed-out log. The ashes were put into one vessel and the bones were ground to powder and placed in another. The remains were kept in these vessels until the deceased's successor or some close relative had accumulated enough beer to entertain the people of his own and neighboring villages at a ceremony in his honor. The two vessels were bedecked with the deceased's gold and shell ornaments and feather blankets and placed on his ceremonial stool. Then two or three of his closest relatives, followed by all persons present, danced around with these objects on their shoulders, first inside the house and then outside, circling it to enter again through the opposite door. Inside, they sat down in silence, while the pretender to the deceased's position arose, lance in hand, and challenged anybody claiming a better right than he to take it away from him. When nobody accepted the challenge, an old man arose and declared the speaker to be the legitimate successor of the dead headman.

After this challenge and confirmation had been repeated thrice, the new chief sat on the stool where the ashes of the dead man had been and invited the latter's closest relatives to sit on his right and left. The old man who had spoken before recommended these relatives to his care. The men who had danced with the deceased's ashes now danced carrying the new headman, seated on the ceremonial stool, on their shoulders, while everyone present followed, dancing as before.

After a period of wailing, directed by a special leader, the new chief was given the ashes of the dead man to drink. In this way the former headman was believed to come to life again. The chief shared this drink with other important persons, lest any of them feel slighted. The drink was prepared, therefore, in sufficient quantities, and any left over was given to the lesser people. To conclude the ceremony all men danced holding their bows and arrows.

No other prerogatives of the headman are mentioned except that he received half of the bride price that any man paid for a wife. Stools and feather blankets were among his regalia.

In addition to the main headman and the "principals," there may have been special "war captains." An army led by 14 such captains was once encountered.

Waifs were permitted to go around every 8 days or so to beg for food.

SOCIAL ORGANIZATION

Marriage.—Among the *Guayupé,* a husband-to-be negotiated with his future wife's parents or brothers and paid them for her. Half of the payment, however, went to the headman. The wedding consisted simply of the usual dancing and drinking.

Among the *Sae,* many men had several wives. Wives were chosen by two methods. By the first, married and single people gathered annually in a special building to dance, sing, and drink, after which there was general sexual intercourse. Married people slept with their own spouses, while unmarried people paired with their future wives or husbands. By the other method, a girl indicated her choice of a husband at the public celebration which terminated her 3 months' puberty confinement by giving a man a basketful of food. This did not bind him to become her husband, but he often acceded.

Sae women might leave their husbands at any time, especially if they were not pregnant after a year. Some women changed husbands several times until they became pregnant.

Among the *Sae,* marriages seem to have been contracted only with people of the same village.

WARFARE

All the tribes of this area were very warlike. For offense they used short hurling spears of a wood called pipiri, long lances, likewise thrown, three-edged clubs tied to the wrist, bows and arrows, and, in some tribes, slings. Spears, arrows, and clubs were ornamented with feathers. For defense they had great round shields, big enough to cover a man completely, made of a single piece of tapir or manatee hide, and a head protection of strong hide, decorated with feathers. Some warriors hung a kind of trumpet from their necks. The Indians of this area attacked in orderly formations, with the usual shouting and noise.

Some tribes built palisades of wooden posts tied closely to each other with lianas.

LIFE CYCLE

Childbirth.—A *Sae* woman delivered alone in the bush, then left the child there to inform her husband or some other relatives, who brought water so that she could wash herself and the child. If the father showed signs of sadness because of the new child, the mother immediately buried it alive or threw it into the river; otherwise they went home together to celebrate the occasion.

Among the *Guayupé,* the first child, boy or girl, always was buried alive or thrown into the river. The reason given was that firstborn children are naughty and disobedient. Of subsequent children, girls were sometimes also killed. As a rule, however, the birth of a second child occasioned great rejoicing and many ceremonies. The father was confined for a month (according to tradition, in former days for 3 months or until the child started crawling around) in a special hut where every 5 days he was given a piece of cassava and a fermented drink made of cedar bark. When entering the hut many men lashed him with bundles of nettles; then 12 old men pushed him and plucked as much of his hair as they could. After his confinement they tied these tufts of hair to lances, and, accompanied by other old men, they put them into the ground on the plaza and sat down in silence. The shaman arrived, took one of the lances and challenged anyone to take it away from him. The father, now released from his confinement, made a show of trying to do so, but the shaman struck him heavy blows with a thick cord and nettles. Having withstood this test, the father was anointed all over with a chili-pepper solution. It was believed that the child would die if the father did not undergo these ordeals.

Puberty.—When a boy reached puberty his father invited many guests to a ceremony during which the headman and other old men repeatedly jumped through a big fire. After that the headman whipped the boy with nettles and pricked him with lances, the points of which had been heated, to make him a good warrior.

At their first menstruation *Sae* girls were confined for 3 months in a dark room or hut. After that the father invited everyone in the village to a celebration. The girl's hair was cut all around slightly above ear level, her body was painted black, and she was adorned with all the family heirlooms. The women danced around her while four women held a tambourine-shaped basket full of all kinds of food over her head. During the singing and dancing the girl picked the man she liked best and handed him the basket. He had to accept and sleep with her at least once. Often the two became husband and wife.

During menstruation a woman might not go close to a maize field which was being sowed or harvested. Chili pepper had to be sowed by a young girl.

Death.—The *Guayupé* had a tradition that formerly they buried their dead but that they were instructed by their gods to burn them, grind the bones into powder, and drink both ashes and powder. A detailed description of the funeral of a headman has been given under Political Organization (p. 387). It lasted 3 or 4 days, i.e., until all the drinks had been consumed. At intervals, after every five or six rounds of dancing, the people stopped with loud whistling, shouting, and weird movements of the body, sat down to drink, broke into wailing, directed by a leader, who praised the deeds of the dead man, and finally started dancing again.

Among the *Sae,* a corpse was half cooked over a wooden frame and cut into pieces, which were divided among his closest relatives. The more important and richer people made the burned and pulverized ashes into a beverage, which they drank during a ceremony, whereas poorer people, who had insufficient drinks to serve guests, ate the flesh at once, accompanying it with so many drinks that they fell down unconscious. This was the only time the *Sae* ever tasted meat.

ESTHETIC AND RECREATIONAL ACTIVITIES

Dances.—Evidently only men danced. The only form, which is repeatedly described, is that in which each man put his hands on the shoulders of the one before him. The dancers sang, keeping the rhythm with their steps. No musical instruments are mentioned in connection with dances and ceremonies.

Narcotics.—Coca (yupa) was taken, and tobacco was smoked through the mouth or nose in order to provoke visions; whether this was limited to shamans is not stated. What people saw under the influence of these stimulants provided them with an unbreakable rule for action.

SUPERNATURALISM

Major deities.—In *Guayupé* belief the sun and moon are husband and wife. The sun sends heat and dryness; the moon, the rains. When there is an excess of one or the other the sun intervenes with the moon, or the moon with the sun, on behalf of mankind. A complete circle surrounding the moon is considered a sign of fertility and prosperity, while a broken or half circle is a sign of impending calamities which the people try to ward off by blowing toward the moon and by fasting. Against earth-quakes, which are caused when God (the sun?) goes to sleep, a 7-day fast is necessary. The moon has eclipses when it is attacked by dead people looking for food and drink. The living frighten them away by showing their strength in a display of their lances and other weapons; having achieved their purpose, they celebrate their victory by a drinking bout.

Another deity may have represented the evil principle, although in this respect our main source, the missionary Pedro de Aguado (1916–19), may not be trusted. This "devil" took the form of jaguars, bears, and certain other wild animals, which were never to be killed.

The *Guayupé* believed that they, the *Sae,* and the *Eperigua* all descended from one couple, and that at some future time they would disappear, after which God (the sun?) would descend from heaven to create new men.

Shamanism and sorcery.—Shamans could take the form of jaguars, bears, and other wild animals. For this reason they were highly esteemed and at the same time feared. They could ask any man for his daughters. People helped them in their fields, gave them presents, etc. Their sons succeeded them in their profession.

Their curing methods depended upon the nature of the ailment. They tried to cure wounds and leprosy with herbs. Swellings were considered due to some object, such as herbs, thorns, or worms, having been placed in the body by witchcraft. The cure consisted of sucking out the object. In more serious diseases, especially fevers, the patient was placed in his hammock between two fires and kept there until he got better or died, some magic formula being the only additional treatment given him.

Ritual numbers.—The numbers 3, 5, 7, and 12 are mentioned. All of them are, in fact, of ritual importance in one or another of the neighboring areas.

BIBLIOGRAPHY

Aguado, 1916–17; Castellanos, 1874; Oviedo y Valdés, 1851–55; Simón, 1882–92.

THE BETOI AND THEIR NEIGHBORS

By Gregorio Hernández de Alba

TRIBAL LOCATIONS

The extensive llanos in eastern Colombia comprise a submountainous territory which is crossed by several large rivers, such as the Orinoco, Vichada, Guaviare, and Meta. It was described by the first explorers and by the Jesuit missionaries of the early 17th century as a region of forests and great mysteries, inhabited by various tribes and peoples. This region, called Ayrico (Airico), was bounded by the Guayabero and Guaviare Rivers on the south, the Uva or Vua River on the northeast, the Manacacías and Vichada Rivers on the north, and the eastern slopes of the Cordillera Oriental of the Andes on the west. Today it embraces almost all the Province of Meta in Colombia. A large number of rivers and streams cross it from west to east, among them the Duda, Cabra, Guejar, Cunumio, San Vicente, Pororio, and Ariarí; the last, which flows through the center of the region, is the most important.

In the days of the Conquest the region of Ayrico was occupied by the *Airico* and *Curicuriveni.* Farther north, living near the last foothills of the Cordillera Oriental in an environment similar to Ayrico, were the *Anabali* and *Jirara* (*Girara*) on the upper Arauca and Tame Rivers and near the Girara River, the *Lolaca, Atabaca* and *Situfa* (*Cituja*) on the plains of the Sarare River, the *Lucalia* on the banks of the Arauca River, and the *Betoi* (*Betoy*) in a region bounded on the south by the Sarare River and on the north by the Uribante (Uribán) River, a region today embracing parts of the Departments of Santander, Boyacá, and Arauca, where Colombia and Venezuela meet (Gumilla, 1745; Rivero, 1883; Salas, 1920). The most important and most numerous of these tribes was the *Betoi,* whose widespread language was formerly designated as the *Betoya* linguistic family but today is called *Tucano* (Castellví, 1934).

LANGUAGE

Gumilla (1745) states that all these peoples and several others, who are unknown ethnographically and may be subdivisions of those mentioned above, spoke the same language though possibly different dialects. He writes that the languages of the "Betoy and the Jirara, although the latter has few 'r's' and the former too many, must be related and

393

from them were derived the languages of the Situfa, Ayrica, Ele, Luculia, Fabúe, Arauca, Quilifay, Anabali, Lolaca, and Atabaca" (Gumilla, 1745, vol. 2, p. 38). Rivero (1883, p. 339) finds that "Betoy is similar to that of the Giraras." Salas (1920, p. 121) and Rivet (cited by Pericot García 1936, p. 597) follow Gumilla in every respect, except that Rivet changes the name of *Lucalia* to *Buculia* and *Fabúe* or *Jabué* to *Jabrie*, and classes these two tribes as *Chibchan*. Castelleví on the other hand, includes the *Tama* and *Airico* in the *Tucano* (formerly the *Betoya*) family.

HISTORICAL SOURCES

The most important and authoritative chroniclers of the Conquest and of the attempts to colonize this zone were unquestionably the Jesuit missionaries, such as Fathers Gumilla (1745), Rivero (1883), and Oviedo y Baños (1824, 1932, 1935). The contemporary Venezuelan author Salas based his studies (1920) on these classic authorities. Very few modern ethnographers have made field studies of the small remnants of the once numerous native tribes of eastern Colombia and western Venezuela. Koch-Grünberg (1917–28, vols. 2, 3, 4) made some important scientific observations but unfortunately did not visit all the tribes of the Orinoco and Amazon regions.

CULTURE

SUBSISTENCE ACTIVITIES

The natural fertility both of flora and fauna of this mountainous, warm, humid, and well-watered region afforded ample resources to its native inhabitants, who were gatherers of wild fruits, cultivators, hunters, and fishers. The most important native crops were manioc and maize; fruits, such as pineapples, and condiments, such as pimientos and ají or chili peppers, supplemented the diet. Bananas were adopted after the Conquest. Hunting, carried on with the bow and arrow, yielded tapirs, peccaries, deer, bears, jaguars, and pumas. The *Jirara* and *Airico* ate snakes after cutting off their heads and the ends of their tails.

VILLAGES AND HOUSES

The tribes of this region apparently did not have large villages with many houses built in any one place, but lived in small communities (caseríos or rancheríos). The *Betoi*, the most populous people, had the following villages or subdivisions: *Betoi* proper, *Guanero, Agualo, Guaracapón, Situja (Situfa?), Quilifay, Aibali,* and *Mafilito* or *Isabaco* (Rivero, 1883, p. 348). The typical habitation was the "caney," a communal house sheltering an extended family. It was built of poles and had a roof thatched with grass or palm leaves. Among the *Jirara* and *Airico*, it was 200 feet (about 60 m.) long and 30 feet (about 9 m.) wide and had small doors in its ends. In 1759 the *Jirara* and *Airico* of the

Girara River had 18 communal houses sheltering 450 people, an average of 25 persons per house (Rivero, 1883, p. 77). A *Betoi* village also had a community clubhouse which was used for festivals and for the accommodation of guests.

CLOTHING AND ADORNMENT

Nudity was characteristic of these tribes, although *Betoi* headmen or chiefs used some kind of bark-cloth garment, and *Jirara* and *Airico* women wore a leaf genital cover. The climate rendered clothing unnecessary, but these Indians painted their bodies not only as decoration but also as protection against the sun and the bites of mosquitoes and other insects. The most common ornaments were crowns of colored feathers, necklaces of snail-shell beads (quiripas), and red or vermilion body paint in the form of rays and other figures. As evidence of mourning the relatives of the deceased painted themselves black with "jagua" (*Genipa*).

TRANSPORTATION

For river travel these Indians made dugout canoes which were hollowed by means of fire. On land they carried goods on their backs.

MANUFACTURES

Pottery cooking vessels were probably made by all the tribes. The *Betoi* made bark cloth for garments. The *Anabali* wove mats. The *Betoi* and probably the other tribes made calabash containers.

SOCIAL AND POLITICAL ORGANIZATION

The *Betoi* were organized into locally exogamous groups, each under the leadership of the most distinguished elder. "They obey the oldest man," wrote Rivero (1883, p. 348), which suggests that the occupants of the communal house, or caney, comprised a pater familia or group of relatives with the oldest man as chief.

Among the *Jirara, Airico,* and perhaps the other tribes men periodically held festivals in the community clubhouse, drinking chicha and playing musical instruments. The celebrants sat in two lines facing each other, each man holding his weapons. The chicha jar was in the center.

Marriage was forbidden with relatives to the fifth degree, a restriction which perhaps applied mainly to the local, exogamous group. There was little polygyny because female infanticide caused a shortage of women. The *Betoi* practiced infant betrothal when the boy and girl were only a year old, but a man might later repudiate the agreement. Marriage was celebrated by a drinking festival, the betrothed being first carried to the house by their friends and relatives and left there. After the death of a spouse, a year of chastity had to be observed. To obtain a new wife, a widower made presents of birds, game animals, and fish to the girl until she accepted him.

The *Jirara* and *Airico* celebrated a wedding with a community banquet. The parents of the betrothed hunted and fished in advance in order to accumulate the necessary provisions. The father or some other relative of the young man took him to the girl's house, where the girl and her mother met them at the door and they exchanged presents of strings and beads (quiripas), which had great economic importance in the region. The girl's mother put a necklace of these beads on her son-in-law and the boy's father placed one on his daughter-in-law. The newly wed couple then sat down, and the girl's mother placed a jar of chicha at the feet of her daughter. While her husband sat solemnly with folded arms, the girl served the chicha, meat, and fish to the people of the village.

ECONOMIC LIFE

As these tribes depended greatly on hunting and fishing and were semi-nomadic, owing to the custom of abandoning a house at the death of an occupant, they had only a simple economic life. Among the *Betoi,* men hunted, fished, and cleared the fields that were to be cultivated. Women planted, weeded, and harvested these fields, carried the produce to the house, and prepared the meals and drinks.

An interesting feature of this area was the use of strings of snail-shell beads as money (quiripa). The beads were small, perforated disks made from shells obtained in the rivers. The points were cut off and the shells ground down. Value was proportionate to the length of the string. This money was used in trade with neighboring tribes, and among the *Airico* the most distinguished or powerful persons used them to pay servants or workmen of their own group for their labor.

There appear to have been no restrictions on hunting rights, and game probably belonged to the hunter just as farm produce belonged to the cultivator. The *Jirara* and *Airico,* believing that sickness and death contaminated things, abandoned crops, the house, and the personal goods of the deceased at a death.

LIFE CYCLE

A *Betoi* mother buried a newborn daughter alive unless prevented by her husband or relatives. The reason given the conquistadors for this was that a woman's life was very hard and painful. The *Betoi* practiced the couvade. At childbirth the father took to his bed and his wife took care of him in the belief that if he walked about he would step on the child's head, if he cut wood he would cut the child's head, and if he shot an arrow at a bird he would shoot the newborn.

At death the *Betoi* buried the corpse and the dead man's utensils, weapons, and ornaments in the portion of the house used for cooking. The night after the burial the relatives of the deceased held a funeral ceremony in the communal house. The men sat on one side of the house and the women on the other, all playing musical instruments. The widow recited sad laments to which the others responded in chorus. The *Betoi* believed the house site to be contaminated and moved the habitation to another place. The custom of abandoning a house and cultivated fields at a death was general among these tribes.

Among the *Jirara* and *Airico,* mourners painted themselves black, the amount of paint depending upon their relationship to the deceased. The widow, children, and brothers painted their entire bodies. Slightly more distant relatives, such as cousins, aunts, and uncles, painted their legs, feet, arms, hands, and part of their faces. The remaining relatives painted only their hands and feet and put spots on their faces. A year of widowhood was required before remarriage. The chroniclers (Gumilla, 1745; Rivero, 1883) called attention to the great sorrow exhibited by the deceased's women and children. The widow, painted entirely black and her hair cut, spent 9 days weeping for her husband at the arroyo or river nearest the village. The *Anabali* covered the grave with many mats and abandoned the house and fields, but after the Conquest they merely burned the house as the Spanish missionaries and encomenderos would not permit them to move away.

WARFARE

While attacking in battle the Indians uttered so many shouts that the Spaniards referred to their attacks as "shouts." Weapons included bows and arrows, macanas of hard palm wood, lances, and axes. The *Lucalia* used arrow poison, especially against their neighbors and enemies, the *Chinato* (Rivero, 1883, p. 139).

The *Jirara* apparently did not poison their arrows, but a person who wished to kill someone brewed a poison called "irruquí alabuquí" and mixed it with his chicha. This poison was made by boiling a certain species of ant and skimming off the poisonous grease, which was kept in an animal bone (Gumilla, 1745, vol. 2, p. 165).

ESTHETIC AND RECREATIONAL ACTIVITIES

Music, which accompanied community gatherings, dances, and funerals, was played on such instruments as "fotutos" and flutes. The "fotuto" consisted of a calabash resonator fitted to a hollow cane about 2 varas (5 feet) long, which was blown at the free end producing a raucous sound. The special instrument of this area was the hollow-log drum, which was made by burning out a log 2 varas (1.6 m.) in circumference and 3 varas (2.4 m.) long. The drum was suspended above the ground and struck with two wooden clubs on one side over slots.

Chicha, an alcoholic drink made principally of fermented manioc, was used on all social occasions—meetings, weddings, burials, and religious rites.

RELIGION AND SHAMANISM

The *Betoi* regarded the sun (Es) as the creator and protector and a being called *Memelú* as an evil spirit which caused the death of children. The *Jirara* and *Airico* had no idols, but believed in two gods who were brothers. The older created everything but destroyed it with a great flood, after which the younger made people and ruled over them. The latter causes earthquakes by moving his arm. (The *Chibcha* or *Muisca* similarly ascribe earthquakes to a god named Chibchacúm). These brothers now live in the stars and are very fond of drinking chicha. When drunk, they spill it and it falls on the earth as rain. These tribes also believe in an evil spirit which has charge of the peccaries. In the religion of these tribes recorded by Father Rivero (1883, p. 116) there may be a trace of Christian belief introduced by the missionaries.

Beliefs in shamanism and magic were very extensive. Evil was associated with the place where a death occurred, and the place was abandoned. The *Betoi* believed that the soul of the deceased remained at the house site.

The shaman could both cause and cure illness. While the *Betoi* shaman performed a cure, the patient and his relatives had to fast. To cure or to foresee the future, the *Jirara* and *Airico* shaman took a narcotic snuff of "yopa" or "yopo" powder. He also blew it slowly over a patient's body to counteract the illness. He had the power to send several demons or spirits, which became visible, to the sick man to perform the cure. In women's breasts a shaman could place a charm called "moján," which the child took with the milk. At the entrances to their villages the *Anabali* built little towers of branches in which a spirit, moján, stayed to protect the houses against human and invisible enemies, while the people confidently went away on hunting and fishing expeditions.

At a moon eclipse, which the *Lolaca* and *Atabaca* greatly feared, the women hurried to cover their cooking fires and utensils with earth, a practice prompted by the belief that if the moon died all fire would die with it except that which was buried for protection, and if, as is natural, the buried fire died, the moon would continue to live (Gumilla, 1745, vol. 1, p. 315). The *Betoi* attached special meaning to the cries of the birds and wild animals in the mountains, and deduced from them what would happen. The *Betoi* believed that spirits made revelations in dreams. An individual's power was increased by scarification: to obtain fish, he wounded his legs with the spine of a ray fish; to insure hunting luck, he scratched his right arm with a peccary bone and his left with a bird's femur; and to be brave in warfare, he cicatrized his entire body. To avoid bites from poisonous snakes, he painted snakes on his legs so that the poison of the painted ones would drive away the living. *Betoi* accredited men with the power to send snakes to bite other men.

THE ACHAGUA AND THEIR NEIGHBORS

By Gregorio Hernández de Alba

TRIBAL LOCATIONS

The *Achagua* were widely distributed in Venezuela and eastern Colombia. Rivero, apparently exaggerating their extent, assigned them a habitat which extended from near Barinas, southeast of Lake Maracaibo, to the now abandoned city of San Juan de los Llanos east of Bogotá in Colombia. Farther south there were several isolated groups near the Province of Popayán. In addition, there were the following scattered groups: One distributed from the Casanare River to the Ariporo River and the banks of the Meta and embracing more than 20 "nations or provinces with the same Achagua language"; another which included 21 groups or peoples between the banks of the Vichada River and the mouths by which the Guaviare River enters the Orinoco River; another along the Guaviare River; another with *Achagua Catarubén* on the Orinoco, above the island inhabited by the *Adole;* and one on the Aritagua and Onocutare Rivers (Rivero, 1883). In terms of modern political divisions, Salas (1920) locates the *Achagua* in the Venezuelan states of Bolívar, Guárico, Zamora, and Bermúdez. They lived at the confluence of the Meta and Orinoco Rivers, between the Apure, Meta, and Orinoco Rivers and between some of the tributaries of the Meta, especially the Uribante and Arauca, and on the south side of the Guaviare adjoining the *Guahibo* and *Sáliva.* In modern times Fabo (1911) places the *Achagua* in Colombia on the Maní River, not far from the Orocué River, and Codazzi (1889) locates them on the right side of the Muco River, where they are supposed to be survivors of the old Jesuit missions. Caulín (1841), an important source, divides the *Achagua* into the following subtribes: *Chiricoa, Taparita, Otomaco,* and *Yaruro.* Groups mentioned by Rivero are the *Catarubén, Barria, Ucataquerri, Quirruba, Lizarva,* and *Abani.* Gumilla (1745) divides them into the *Aycubaverrenay* and *Univerrenay.* Salas (1920) adds the *Amarizán* and the *Issirriberrenai.*

The *Guaiqueri* (*Guayqueri, Guayquiri, Guajqueri, Guajkeri*) occupied the country around Cumaná, the islands of Margarita, Coche, and Cubagua, and part of Trinidad. They were essentially coastal and insular.

Farther south or southwest of Cumaná were the *Palenque* and *Piritu* (*Piritu, Pirichu*). The Spaniards called the territory of these tribes the "Misión" or "Provincia" of the *Piritu*. The name comes from a local species of cane of which the Indians made tobacco pipes. The *Piritu* were divided into two subtribes, the *Piritu* proper and the *Chacopata*.

The *Caberre* (*Cabre, Cavarri, Cabritu*) occupied part of the region of the Inírida (Inirria, Inirricha) River, especially its confluence with the Nooquéne, and groups of *Caberre* held a portion of the banks of the Atavapo River (Caulín, 1841, p. 230). Salas places this tribe on the southern side of the Orinoco, from the Caura to the Caicara River.

The *Puinave* (*Puinabe, Puinabi, Puinabo*) were neighbors of the *Caberre* in the region of the Nooquéne and Inírida Rivers, and, together with the *Guaipunabis* (*Guipunabis*), they extended through the mountains of Mabicore and the Raudal de Maipures.

The *Sáliva* (*Sáliba, Saliva*) occupied the Orinoco River at and downstream from its confluence with the Meta, the banks of the Guaviare, Vichada, and Meta Rivers, and the western margin of the Carichana River. Salas (1920) includes the *Piaroa, Adole, Maipure, Duniberrenai,* and *Yaruro* (*Yuro*) as cultural and linguistic relatives of the *Sáliva*.

The *Piapoco* inhabited the territory drained by the María and Cuinacía Rivers (Fabo, 1911).

Other tribes in this area are little known culturally and linguistically, and remain ethnographic riddles. Among them are the *Tamanaco, Maipure,* and *Abani* of the territory between the Apure and Meta Rivers.

The *Pareca* lived along the Caviari, Muruparu, Cururuparu, Luyeme, and Sacure Rivers, all affluents of the Orinoco.

The *Mapoye, Totomaco,* and *Toto* lived on the headwaters of the Sibápuli, Urupére, Suapure, Auyacoa, and Paraute Rivers, i.e., east of the *Sáliva*.

HISTORY

The Jesuits, accompanied by military escorts, began the subjugation of these tribes at the end of the 16th century. They assembled a large number of Indians in the "reductions," i.e., settlements, and in the missions. The natives who survived the wars of the Conquest, the slavery on Spanish settlements, and the missions began to migrate to new areas where they could preserve their customs, religion, and language. The *Achagua, Guaiqueri, Palenque,* and *Piritu* went especially to the banks of the Meta, Guaviare, and Casanare Rivers, and the *Caberre, Puinave, Sáliva,* and *Piapoco* went to the Macuco, west of Orocué. The tribal remnants which survived in the Oriente continued to shift their habitat as white or civilized people penetrated their lands to exploit rubber, chiclé, and other products, to establish cattle ranches, and to carry out political objectives, such as the protection of frontiers.

Among the Jesuit settlements were San José on the Aritagua River, an affluent of the Casanare, and San Salvador del Puerto on the Casanare and Onocutare Rivers, which enter the Meta from the north. The missions of the Province of Piritu had 34 villages with nearly 12,000 persons; these included 13 *Carib*-speaking villages (Caulín, 1841).

The *Caberre* went to Orocué in the middle of the 19th century, and a little later they migrated farther up the Meta River. In recent times Fabo found them where the San Juanito River enters the Meta.

The Jesuits founded missions among the *Sáliva* at Carichana and elsewhere. At the beginning of the 17th century Nuestra Señora, San Miguel de Guanapalo, Beato Regis, Santa Teresa de Jesús, and others were flourishing missions.

The Jesuit missions founded in the Guianas, the Amazon, and the Orinoco region seem to have been succesful from a social point of view, for they evidently made the new converts into prosperous peoples, who lived on large cattle ranches with a communal system of property. From the beginning, however, the strife between the Jesuits and the Spanish lay population was notorious, and the fathers accused the expeditionaries, merchants, and even the civil authorities of exploiting and maltreating the Indians who had been "reduced," or appropriated, to their settlements. For example, Father Rivero said of the *Achagua*, "They are made to groan under the tasks and work, and, moreover, they are sold as slaves," especially those of Santiago de la Atalaya. Thus the Spaniards increased the number of "macos," a word used throughout the region of the great rivers for "Indian slaves." The civil authorities, on the other hand, believed that the region should be developed by no one but themselves. They organized against the Jesuits, and the order was finally expelled by Carlos III in 1767. The Indians were taken over by other religious orders; their government became mixed in method and purpose, being part Spanish and part Indian. Communal work and property was replaced by individually owned haciendas, and at best the missions were badly administered by the new missionaries. The wealth in cattle was lost, and so many of the animals ran wild that by the time of the wars of Independence Bolívar's and Santander's troops were able to live on them.

The cattle industry of eastern Colombia and of adjoining Venezuela which began with the Jesuits' attempts to develop socialism has vanished. The only remnants of the Jesuit missions today are ruined buildings and cattle corrals. It is interesting to note the inventory which the Jesuits made for the conveyance of the *Achagua* mission of Surimena to the Recoletos de San Agustín. The inventory was made in the presence of the Indians—a lieutenant, a chief, a captain, and two others. It lists the mission house, dispensary, school, carpentry shop, blacksmith shop, church, and herd. The herd consisted of 400 horses and 4,000 head of cattle (Ganuza, 1921).

In the *Piritu* region the missionaries, hoping to facilitate their work, brought together people of various tribes and languages and endeavored to make the *Cumanagoto* language a lingua geral, comparable to *Quechua* in the Andes of southern Colombia and Ecuador.

CULTURE

Most of our cultural information concerns the *Achagua, Piritu,* and *Sáliva,* and, unless stated to be otherwise, the following description applies to these tribes.

SUBSISTENCE ACTIVITIES

In addition to the major plant foods listed by Kirchhoff (p. 355), the *Achagua* ate the following: The fruit of a vine gathered in summer and prepared like green broadbeans; "camuirro," a grapelike palm fruit; and "emau," a fruit the size and shape of a billiard ball. The farms, cultivated mainly by women, were divided into individual plots marked by stakes.

Among the *Sáliva,* men cleared the fields of trees and brush and women cultivated them. Before the work of clearing was begun, the older men lined up the younger and ceremonially whipped them so that they would not be lazy. *Sáliva* crops included sweet manioc, maize, ají or chili peppers, and, after the Conquest, bananas.

Animal foods included birds, wild rats, iguanas, monkeys, deer, tapirs, turtles, turtle eggs, ants, and even grubs. Fish were taken with bows and arrows, harpoons, nets, cane traps, and a drug, barbasco, which the *Achagua* call "cuna." The *Piritu* apparently used fishhooks.

These tribes prepared a maize dough which they carried as a ration on trips; it was mixed with water when eaten. Sweet manioc was roasted or boiled in water. Bitter manioc was grated on a board studded with small pieces of stone affixed with resin, and the poison was removed by squeezing the pulp in what, to judge by Rivero's detailed description, was the typical tipití. It was then washed, put through a basketry sieve, and made into cakes, cassava, which were baked on a pottery plate (budare) supported over a fire by three stones. Foods were seasoned with ají, for these tribes used no salt.

HOUSES AND VILLAGES

Each village was enclosed by a palisade of poles and earth. The entrance was very high and could be defended against attack. Inside the palisade were the dwellings and a special building which served as the men's clubhouse and where festivals and gatherings were held and guests accommodated. The *Achagua* called such a building "daury." The houses were large communal dwellings which could hold a considerable number of people; Chief Irrijirre's had a capacity of 500. The occupants of each house comprised what the chroniclers called a "parentela," that is, probably a sib (see below). The dwellings were circular, except among the *Piritu,* who made them long and rectangular.

There were apparently separate cook houses. Household furniture and utensils included pottery vessels, half-calabash drinking cups (totumas), stools covered with the skins of jaguars, tapirs, and other animals, and sleeping hammocks (chinchorros) below which fires were built at night.

CLOTHING AND ADORNMENT

Garments were limited to women's skirts, which were apparently plaited of very flexible fiber cords. The cords were probably of maguey or hemp. These skirts were about 1 vara (80 cm. or 2 feet 8 inches) long and three-quarters of a vara (60 cm. or 2 feet) wide and were held up by cords passing over the shoulders. Men wore a small breechclout (guaruma).

The principal ornaments were various designs painted on the body, black (genipa, "jagua") stain on the hands, feathers glued to the body with resin, feather tufts, necklaces of snail-shell beads (quiripas) or of pearls (which the *Piritu* called "thenocas"), men's pearl ear and nose ornaments, women's silver lower lip ornaments made in semilunar and other shapes, and metal and coral pins. The *Achagua* tattooed children around the mouth, puncturing the skin with a fish tooth and rubbing genipa in it to make black marks. The hair was worn long and was painted red or anointed with oil (*Achagua*). Beards were plucked with wooden tweezers.

TRANSPORTATION

These tribes traversed their many large rivers in dugout canoes propelled with paddles and on pole rafts.

MANUFACTURES

True weaving has not been reported. Fish nets and hammocks were knotted or netted.

Basketry and matting were well developed. Among the products were the finely woven, flexible women's skirts, manioc squeezers, carryingbaskets (called "camayas" by the *Piritu*), manioc sifters, and light, flexible shields of cane (*Achagua*).

Women made pottery ollas, plates, cook pots, and containers. Containers were also made of calabashes and drinking cups (muriques) of half calabashes.

Wooden products included stools, dugout canoes, weapons, and large hollow-log drums.

The *Sáliva* had an adhesive (peramán) made of black wax and vegetable resin prepared with heat. They used it to glue arrow points to the shafts and, according to Gumilla (1745, vol. 2), even to mend broken bones!

SOCIAL AND POLITICAL ORGANIZATION

The *Achagua* were seemingly divided into patrilineal sibs or gentes. Local exogamy is attested by Rivero's statement (1883, p. 326) that they had to "go to distant villages to marry," and some evidence points to patrilocal residence. The *Achagua* had totemic groups; e.g., Aycuba-verrenais, children of the trunks; Univerrenais, children of the rivers; Amarizán, descendants of the serpent, "amarizán"; Isirriberrenais, descendants of the bat; and others connected with the jaguar, fox, and other animals and birds. It is not stated that these totemic groups coincided with the communal house (which perhaps usually constituted a village), the village, or a larger group; perhaps they were not localized at all. The data, however, strongly suggest totemic, exogamous, patrilinear sibs, and the pattern may have resembled that of the *Tucanoan* tribes to the south (Handbook, vol. 3).

Evidence of sibs among the other tribes is less clear. Possibly some groups designated as tribes, such as the *Caturubén, Barria, Ucataquerri. Quirruba, Lizarva,* and *Abani,* were really sibs, but their totems have not been recorded.

The *Achagua* were polygynous. Every man endeavored to have three or four wives, each of whom had equal rights and obligations and cultivated her own fields, which was marked by stakes. Either the husband or wife could dissolve the marriage.

Among the *Guaiqueri,* women about to be married were confined for 40 days, during which their daily diet was about 3 ounces of cassava, 3 "muriche" fruits, and a jar of water. Gumilla explains this on the basis of woman's malevolent influence: "Our old people believe that whatever . . . menstruating women step on will dry up; if a man steps where a woman has set her feet, his legs will swell up . . . To prevent their bodies being poisonous [women] are made to fast forty days. Thus they dry up well and are not dangerous; at least not so much so as in ancient times." On the eve of the marriage, all the Indians adorned themselves with paint and feathers, while some old women dressed up the girl. The ceremony was held in the dance house and was presided over by the chief, who sat on a stool. At sunrise the participants, dancing and making music, arrived at the girl's house, which they encircled. An old woman appeared at the door and presented them a plate of food, which they took to the nearest woods and threw away, saying, "Dog demon (?), take this food and do not come to disturb our festival." Crowned with flowers and holding a bouquet in the left hand and a rattle or jingles in the right, to mark time to the music, the dancers returned to the girl's house with the boy dancing in the center of the group.   The girl now came forward accompanied by the old woman, who wept while uttering special chants.   Then everyone feasted on cassava, turtle, fish, and other food.

Among the *Piritu* a youth's parents selected his bride.   The wife had to give her husband strict obedience.   In some cases a newly married man had to serve his father-in-law for a certain period.

Each *Achagua* communal house or village had a chief, whom the chroniclers and missionaries called a "cacique."   The *Piritu* group or house chief had to prove his fitness for the office by observing a long fast, after which he drank a cup full of water and dried pepper (ají), and by lying in a hammock filled with stinging ants.   If he endured these ordeals quietly and bravely without showing pain, he was confirmed as chief. The *Sáliva* imposed similar tests.

Among the *Achagua* and *Piritu* was a group of young girls who were not only a kind of vestal virgins, but who might be taken for sexual purposes by the chiefs.

Men's gatherings.—*Achagua* men had a special clubhouse (daury), from which women were barred.   Each afternoon they lounged in their hammocks in this house and discussed matters of current interest.   Here also they occasionally held drunken festivities (chubai).   After preparing a great quantity of chicha in wooden troughs, the men would paint their bodies with various designs in the morning and go to the clubhouse. They squatted while the chief sat on a stool.   Loquacious with the chicha, which servants passed around in bowls, everyone sang to the accompaniment of musical instruments and made much noise.

Punishment.—*Achagua* law permitted personal revenge or punishment of a wrongdoer.

Etiquette.—The *Achagua* received visitors with a solemn ritual, which Father Rivero described.   The rite was called "mirraye" from the verb "numerraidary," which means "to make a speech."   First, seated in the clubhouse with their weapons in their hands, the men rose and, standing in line one behind the other, they greeted their guest saying, "mude," which means "cousin," to which he replied, "cha," meaning "alright."   The men sat down again and the women passed the drinks, whereupon a long speech was begun by an orator who had committed it to memory. The orator sat on a stool or squatted on his heels, his elbows resting on his knees, his left hand grasping his right arm, and his right hand free.   After he delivered the long address in a serious and monotonous voice, the guest responded.   The orator then continued the second part of his oration which, says Rivero, might last an hour and a half or longer.

The *Piritu* accorded great respect to old men.   At festivals, young people were not permitted to stand in their presence.   Also, young people had to serve their elders food and drink, and women were not allowed to sit down and eat with their husbands. Guests received a special greeting and were invited to sit down and drink, but there were no long speeches like those of the *Achagua*.

ECONOMIC LIFE

Among the *Achagua*, men made baskets, mats, and articles of wood, cleared the fields for farming, assisted in gathering wild foods, and hunted and fished. Women made cords, hammocks, nets, and pots, fetched firewood and water, cultivated the fields, cooked, prepared cassava, and painted their husbands' bodies and groomed their hair.

Private property existed in the form of the cultivated fields, but some economic activities of major importance to the group, such as hunting and fishing, may have been done communally, for they were preceded by community ceremonies. The *Guaiqueri* sense of economic and social solidarity was shown in the custom of dividing game among all families, regardless of who killed it, and of helping one another in farming activities.

Trade.—Two articles of commerce were especially important to the *Achagua*. The first was an oil which the subtribe *Becirri* produced and sold. It was made from a fruit called "abay" and was used for anointing the hair and for illumination. The second, of greater importance, was strings of shell beads which served as money in all kinds of transactions in the Orinoco area and which were also worn as necklaces. This money, called "quiripa," was obtained from the *Betoi* in the vicinity of Casanare to the west (p. 396). Rivero (1883, p. 157) says of this money, "With it they carry on their trade and conclude their deals and obligations; it is the national money, and it is highly valued in the Guianas and even on the Island of Trinidad . . . they do not make it but they get it from the port of Casanare where it is worth a string of pearls long enough to encircle a man's girth, the equivalent of two silver reales, or, in the city of the Guianas, four, and on the Island of Trinidad, eight." The *Puinave*, who were given to much travel and trade, also used this money.

The *Guaiqueri* fished for pearls and traded them to other tribes. On the Islands of Cubagua and Margarita, the conquistadors forced them to dive for pearls.

LIFE CYCLE

The couvade was practiced among most of these tribes (Karsten, 1926, p. 543).

In the case of twins, the *Sáliva*, believing that only one could be the father's child and that the other must have been sired by another man, killed the first born. Both the *Achagua* and *Sáliva* killed the first-born daughter, perhaps to make sure that the oldest child, who inherited the father's rights and privileges, would be a son. These tribes circumcized infants of both sexes 8 days after birth. Some of the Indians on the tributaries of the Meta River merely drew blood from the genitals, but, when a boy was 10 or 12 years old, they intoxicated him to the point of insensibility so that he might withstand the loss of blood and then scarified his body and arms (Karsten, 1926, p. 177).

From early childhood boys were taught to use weapons, starting with small bows and arrows. The *Piritu* were very fond of their children and seldom punished them. When boys were 12 or 14 years old they began to make trips and to learn men's tasks; by 16 or 18 they were ready to marry. At her first menstruation, a girl was confined to the house, where she had to fast. She remained in an elevated hammock, in which stinging ants were placed. Thus purified, she was able to fulfill the obligations of marriage. During a dancing festival after her confinement the girl was given in marriage.

When an *Achagua* became dangerously ill, his weapons were placed beside him so that he could defend himself against death. As great care was devoted to one's hair, a dying man's widow or oldest daughter groomed him. When he expired everyone wept, and one person went to the entrance to the enclosure to announce the death in a loud voice so that the people could foregather for the funeral observances. For 3 or 4 days the participants drank chicha from calabash cups, and each had to make a speech about the deceased, describing his deeds and attainments. The grave was dug in the center of the house and the body buried with weapons, food, ornaments and a hammock. The mouth of the sepulcher was filled with packed earth, and each day any holes were stopped with clay to keep out ants.

When a *Piritu* chief died his body was kept 8 days or longer while the people sang his prowess, accompanied by funeral flutes and other instruments. The grave was lined and covered with cane mats or thin planks. Convinced that a dangerous spirit which had caused the death now lurked in the house, they abandoned the place. A year later the relatives of the deceased returned, gathered up his remains, and carried them in a procession to another place, where they burned them and threw the ashs into the air. They believed that the deceased, pleased with the ceremonies in his honor, would turn the ashes into rain.

The *Sáliva* celebrated a death with the usual chants and eulogies of the deceased. They prepared the grave in the center of the house, and beside it on columns they placed feather crowns, imitation birds, and masks. The funeral dancers wore feathers and played musical instruments, including special trumpets, which Gumilla (1745) illustrates. At the end of the ceremonies the dancers threw the grave ornaments and trumpets into the river and purified themselves by bathing. Rivero describes a disinterment ceremony held later. The participants feasted on chicha,

game, fish, maize, cakes, and cassava cakes. They placed the disinterred
bones in the center of the house, and for 3 or 4 days they sat around
lamenting, chanting, and, at intervals, drinking and dancing. The ceremonies were concluded when the bones were cremated and the ashes drunk
in chicha. In doing this they believed "that they drink all the valor and
qualities of the deceased."

WARFARE

There is a tradition that the *Achagua* fought with the Amazons, the
mythical tribe of women who were alleged to live on a kind of island formed
by the Meta and Orinoco Rivers. The particular enemies of the *Palenque*
were the *Chaima* and *Tapacuare*. The *Caberre* fought especially against
the *Carib,* whom the *Caberre* chief, Macapú, was engaging when the conquistadors first came. They also attacked the *Sáliva* in order to take captives (macos or macus), whom they sold or traded to the Dutch of Guiana.
Although sometimes taking the initiative in warfare, the *Achagua* were
more often victims, both before and after the Conquest. The *Chiricoa,
Guahibo,* and *Carib* tribes of the interior attacked them and took them as
slaves; the *Chibcha* captured them for sacrificial victims (mojas) in their
religious cult; and the Spaniards made them the object of repeated attacks
and depredations. In spite of this, the Indians received the Spaniards
peaceably, as in 1606 when more than 4,000 *Achagua* accepted and submitted to the expedition of Capt. Alonzo Jiménez, which had come to their
territory via the Meta River.

The *Achagua* arranged the entrances to their palisades so that missiles
could be discharged at attackers from above. To conclude a peace, a
group of *Achagua* met a group of the enemy in mock battle while the
women shouted; afterward everyone sat in a circle and drank chicha.

Before a battle the *Piritu* took a strongly intoxicating drink to make
themselves braver and more insensitive to wounds. Some of the groups
would leave behind two youths whom they tortured to insure success of
the battle. Whipped with the inner shoots of palms while seated on stools,
the young men had to show fortitude so that the warriors would be brave
in battle. Then one was placed high in a hammock from which he shot
arrows at a target near the house roof; each hit meant that the warriors
would hit one of the enemy. Victorious warriors returned with their
enemies' arm and leg bones, which they made into flutes. Played in
future battle, these flutes would insure victory. The *Piritu* dried and
powdered the enemies' hearts and mixed the powder with their drinks in
order to make themselves braver.

Weapons.—The principal weapon was the bow and arrow. The
Achagua sometimes poisoned their arrows with "curare" and the *Piritu*
with a mixture of woman's menstrual blood and vegetable and animal
poisons. The *Piritu* bow was 1.9 m. (about 6 feet) long, thick at the

grip, and slender at the ends.   The wooden club or macana was also commonly used.   The *Achagua* used a basketry shield made of thin, flexible canes woven together.

Poisons.—In addition to arrow poison, the *Piritu* used a poison to kill personal enemies.   Made of the skin of a certain snake, it was put secretly in the victim's food or drink, causing him to vomit blood until he died. The *Caberre* were the principal producers of "curare," which they sold to other tribes at annual markets.   True curare, which has been studied chemically and medically, is made of a species of *Strychnos*.   The *Caberre* "curare" was made of a certain swamp plant.   The root was mashed and slowly cooked under the supervision of old women, who usually died from the fumes.   To test the poison the chief took a small amount of it on a stick and held it near an open wound of another Indian without touching him.   If the wound stopped bleeding, the poison was ready.

ESTHETIC AND RECREATIONAL ACTIVITIES

Art.—Manufactures such as basketry and pottery were mediums for art, but styles are not known.

The *Sáliva* explained pictographs in their territory to Humboldt by saying that in times of high water their forefathers had arrived at these places and painted the rocks.

Music.—The *Achagua* are accredited with cane flutes which were played individually.   The *Piritu* and neighboring tribes used tambourines(?), flutes of various lengths up to 2 varas (1.6 m. or 5 feet 4 inches), trumpets (fotutos), and instruments called "purmas" made of a length of cane and two calabashes.   An important instrument, used especially by the *Sáliva,* was the hollow-log or signal drum (maguaré).   A large log was hollowed out by means of fire, and, to give it resonance, a stone was cemented inside in the middle with an adhesive called "peramán."   The drum was suspended by vines from a scaffold of poles, and it was struck with wooden sticks covered with resin (currucay) on the side where it was cut with slots so as to leave tongues.   The drum served not only as a musical instrument but as a kind of telegraph, as it could be heard at a great distance.   The *Sáliva* also made two kinds of trumpets, one with a cane stem and a pottery bell, the other consisting of a series of two or more joined and intercommunicating pottery spheres with several openings along its length.

Narcotics.—The *Achagua* used a snuff made of the narcotic powder of certain leaves called "niopa" or "yopa."   Two Indians took this snuff simultaneously; with two crossed bird bones, each blew it into the other's nose.

Intoxicating drinks.—The main intoxicating drink, "berria," was made of cassava fermented with honey and water in a calabash vessel.

Maize and fruits, however, were also used for fermented drinks. These drinks were drunk during religious ceremonies, funerals, public gatherings, and merrymakings.

RELIGION

Several *Achagua* gods are recorded: Tanafimi and Tanasurú, whom the Spaniards identified as "demons"; Cuaiguerry, the principal god who saw everything; Gurrana minari, god of cultivated fields; Baraca, god of riches; Pruvisana, who holds up the earth and causes earthquakes when he shifts it from one shoulder to the other; Achacato, god of fate and of madness; and Cuisiabirri, god of fire. The *Achagua* also worshiped lakes. Idols were not used, but supernatural beings were represented by masks or costumes (chuvay) during dance festivals which men held at fixed times. Women were excluded from these ceremonies lest they die. Available data do not permit a full analysis of these ceremonies, but they suggest the *Tucanoan* cult in which the sib ancestors are impersonated by masked men (Handbook, vol. 3).

The *Piritu* worshiped the sun and moon as gods and believed that eclipses were caused by their anger. When an eclipse occurred the men played musical instruments and prepared their weapons as if for combat, while the women tossed maize grains into the air and lamented, promising to cease being lazy. The end of the eclipse was celebrated with a general dance. Some of the groups (or sibs?) worshiped frogs as lords of the water and would not kill them, perhaps because they were totems, but in the dry season they kept frogs under ollas and whipped them with thin sticks. One of their religious ceremonies was a dance, accompanied by musical instruments (purmas). The purmas were carried between two small images to which they sang reverently. In another religious dance in celebration of the yield of their fisheries, the performers carried imitation fishes. The *Piritu* made sacrifices to the water by throwing fish into it; they sacrificed beads from their necklaces to the earth in payment for good harvests.

The *Palenque* believed that in life after death people stayed in cultivated fields (conucos), but some of the groups thought the dead went to a lake from which they were carried in the belly of a monstrous snake to a delightful land where people danced and feasted all the time.

The *Sáliva* creator god was Purú; he made all good things. His daughter killed the serpent that had been destroying the Indians, but from its body came worms, which turned into the *Carib*, the enemies of the *Sáliva* (Gumilla, 1745, vol. 2). (The *Catío* have a similar legend, except that the worms turned into Spaniards. See this volume, p. 326.) At fixed times, possibly at each moon, religious ceremonies were celebrated in honor of Purú. The sun and moon were also *Sáliva* gods; they were thought to cause eclipses. The main indication of a priest-idol cult was among the *Sáliva,* who had artistically made sculptured figures representing "demons," whom priests consulted as oracles, receiving answers to their questions (Rivero, 1883; Karsten, 1926, p. 260).

SHAMANISM AND MAGIC

The shaman ("piache") not only cured by both supernatural and natural means and acted as diviner and magician, but among the *Sáliva* he served as priest or intermediary between the people and their gods. Every person in the tribe, however, also could divine, prognosticate, and harm victims through witchcraft.

The *Achagua* foretold future events from the songs of birds and from encounters with terrestrial animals. To prognosticate the outcome of an undertaking, they took "yopa" snuff: A nasal secretion from the right nostril signified success, from the left meant failure, and from both was an indeterminate sign. From the first fish caught they predicted their general fishing success. In this connection they held a ceremony (chaca) at the beginning of the fishing season. It was a blessing of the fish. All the people foregathered at night and threw various fish into a large olla. Among these were small fish, also called "chaca." While the fish were being cooked on the fire, the shaman blew the smoke from several cigars over them and over cassava cakes which had been prepared. To eat this purified food immunized one against sickness. For example, children who were just beginning to eat solid food would never in their lives be harmed by eating fish, and girls would not become too fat when they were adults. The *Achagua* also believed that dreams foretold events, and each morning, starting with the chief, the people sang their songs of the night before in a sad, melancholy, singsong voice.

In addition to killing an enemy with a poison made from snake skin, the *Achagua* and *Piritu* bewitched a victim by putting his hair, spittle, or something else from his body in "chicha," shaking it up, and putting it in a small calabash, which, with its contents, was called "carraje," "moján," or "camerico." The shaman carried this, uttering incantations, and the victim, thus bewitched, died no matter how far away he might be. This power of bewitching from a distance naturally caused much enmity, and the victim or his relative would seek out the witch to take revenge.

The *Palenque, Piritu,* and *Sáliva* shamans also used "yopa" for divination. To cure, they used such magical means as blowing, sucking (probably to remove the disease-causing object), and anointing, as well as certain medicinal remedies. They offered the smoke of cigars containing grains of a fragrant copal to the spirit which helped them. The shamans lived in remote places in the mountains where in the dark of night they held dances and invocations accompanied by music.

The *Piritu* also cured with herbs and roots and by bleeding the arms and other parts of the body.

The *Palenque* believed that a hunter could insure great hunting success by painting his face with the extract of a root called "parikchayepue." The extract was carried in small calabashes. To propitiate fish, the fisherman carried the horns of a certain beetle and fishbones. The *Palenque* did not kill animals that were not dangerous, believing that to do so would make their own children sicken and die. Upon killing a game animal they threw water in its mouth so that the animal's soul would tell the other animals of the hunter's kindness and these animals would come to him. To lure game animals the *Palenque* also had an old man drink a great quantity of intoxicating liquor; when he was disposed to vomit they took him through the plains to advise the animals that there was drink for all. Thus the animals did not wander off or flee.

MYTHOLOGY AND LITERATURE

The *Achagua* had the myth of the "Manoa," or the flood. A great flood drowned the people and animals, but some Indians escaped by climbing to the top of a high mountain. The waters covered the earth and formed a huge lake called "catena manoa" ("large lake"). The *Achagua* believed that beyond their territory there was a lake in the center of which was an island with a prodigious city of high, gilded buildings, the residence of King Paititi.

The *Piritu* had the tradition of a great earthquake which had occurred before the Conquest.

The *Sáliva* had, in addition to the legend of the snake which turned into *Carib* Indians, another which recounts that the earth germinated men and women. Other groups, which are not identified except that they were related to the *Sáliva,* explain that the creation was accomplished by certain trees which produced men and women like fruits and were their ancestors. Still other groups held that the sun was their father and creator. The *Mapoye* stated that they originated from a large stone on the top of a hill called "Uruana" and for this reason they liked to be called "Uruan-ayes" (Karsten, 1926, p. 338).

LORE AND LEARNING

The *Piritu* and *Sáliva* reckoned time by the stars, especially by the position of the Pleiades. Their year began when the Pleiades were first visible after sunset. The *Piritu* also had lunar months, and they reckoned time during the day by the sun

THE ARCHEOLOGY OF VENEZUELA

By Alfred Kidder II

INTRODUCTION

Few American scholars, either North or South American, have concerned themselves seriously with Venezuelan archeology. The area is east of the Andean-Central American axis of the great early American civilizations, and the generally unspectacular nature of archeological remains has attracted few field workers to what is, nevertheless, an important and interesting region, particularly with respect to the problems of the peopling of the Antilles.

Venezuela, lying between Colombia, on the west, and British Guiana on the east, and north of Brazil, is a nation of sharp geographical and climatic contrasts. Foothill valleys of the cold, barren Andes are pleasant and healthful. The heavy tropical forests of the Maracaibo Basin give place to the dry, inhospitable, scrub country of much of the northwestern coast and interior. The great expanse of plain and forest of the Orinoco River and its tributaries, which drain the greater part of the country, reaches the little-known Guiana Highlands in the east. Archeologically most of the area is imperfectly known, and intensive controlled excavation has been limited to a few sites on the Orinoco, the Lake Valencia area, and the foothills of the Andes in the northwest. Scattered finds have been made in many localities, although there are large, and often easily accessible, areas from which there is no archeological information whatsoever.

The early Venezuelan Indians left simple cultural remains, by no means uniform, throughout the area.

Village sites, some low earth mounds and earth causeways, shell heaps, burial caves, open cemeteries, and petroglyphs in some mountainous areas complete the general list.

Perishable remains are almost never found; recoverable material culture is limited to some few wooden house posts, pottery varying from the crude and drab to the excellent and decorative, and the usual array of stone, bone, and shell tools and ornaments characteristic of neolithic cultures the world over.

Fabric impressions on pottery and historical accounts indicate the use of basketry and cotton textiles. Gold ornaments were used but have so far not been found in recorded archeological diggings. Simple American tropical agriculture, combined with hunting and fishing, provided food for most of the Indians, although hunting and gathering alone probably supported some of the people in pre-Columbian as well as in recent times.

Cultural changes in time have been noted in a few sites but, however striking, do not necessarily indicate more than changed preferences in burial customs and ceramic styles. No fundamental changes in the aboriginal way of life are inferrible from the archeological record, nor is it yet safe to attribute stylistic changes to shifts in population. There are no remains of demonstrably great antiquity. Absolute chronologies have not been developed; probably some of the earlier remains were left prior to A.D. 1,000, but there is as yet no evidence to indicate an occupation of Venezuela before the beginning of the Christian Era.

SOURCES AND HISTORY OF INVESTIGATIONS

A number of short papers by Ernst (see Osgood and Howard, 1943, and Kidder II, 1944, for bibliography), published in the 1870's and 1880's, are the first important recordings of prehistoric sites and artifacts, chiefly from western Venezuela. For many years archeological activity was limited almost entirely to the Lake Valencia area, first intensively excavated by Marcano in 1887 (Marcano, 1889). Later papers on the mounds and the village and burial sites of this region are those of Von den Steinen (1904) covering the work of Jahn, Requena (1932), and the detailed reports of Bennett (1937), Osgood (1943), and Kidder II (1944).

Until recently, investigation has been sporadic in other areas. Among the more important contributions by Venezuelan authors are those of Briceño-Iragorry (1928, 1929) on the Andean region, Oramas (1917) on the llanos sites, and Nectario María (1933, 1942) on central Lara. Short studies of the archeology of Margarita Island (De Booy, 1915–16) and Falcón (Nomland, 1933, 1935) are useful sources, as are the briefer descriptions of material from the Apure Delta (Petrullo, 1939 b) and the Goajira Peninsula, obtained by Korn (Bennett, 1936). Survey has been limited to that of Spinden (1916), Kidder II (1944) in parts of the northwestern area, and Osgood and Howard (1943). The last-mentioned investigation, undertaken as one of the projects of the Institute of Andean Research in 1941, covered a great part of the northern area from the Orinoco River to the Colombian border and resulted in the first comprehensive summary of Venezuelan archeology (Osgood and Howard, 1943). As a part of the same project, Howard (1943) carried out an intensive excavation of the Ronquín site on the middle Orinoco.

REGIONAL PRESENTATION OF CULTURES

The basic data of Venezuelan archeology are here presented regionally, since the shortness of historical perspective precludes a description of the materials by periods. Osgood and Howard (1943) have described archeological materials by political divisions (states and territories) and have tentatively classified the prehistoric cultures on the basis of the McKern system (Midwestern Taxonomic system[1]). The geographical terms used to designate the major divisions (Phases) of this classification, with some others, are here used simply to designate somewhat arbitrary areas (map 7) as a basis for regional presentation of the data. The size of such areas depends largely upon the amount and kind of information available, but their designations are without classificatory or chronological implications. The writer has used fewer and more general regional terms and a cultural classification for the Lake Valencia area and part of the northwestern area different from that of Osgood and Howard. An attempt is made below (see chart, p. 432) to correlate previously published classifications temporally and spatially.

LOWER ORINOCO RIVER

The area comprises the Delta of the Orinoco and the Barrancas area in the State of Monagas (map 7). No sites in the Delta have been noted by archeologists. In 1941 Osgood and Howard (1943) excavated the village refuse site of Los Barrancos on the north bank of the river and tested several other localities in the vicinity. No house remains or burials were found. A humus stratum 0.75 cm. thick, overlying sterile sand, produced quantities of sherds of a colorful and highly distinctive ware. No significant changes in style throughout the refuse layer can be discerned. Most Los Barrancos sherds have a slip varying in color from glossy browns and blacks to reds and orange; yellow shades predominate. Decoration in addition to the solid slip color occurs on over a quarter of the sherds, and consists primarily of broad, smooth incision, done with a blunt tool. Shapes are chiefly plates and bowls, with the characteristic incision adjacent to the rims. Broad incised lines on the lips of rims are common. Complete designs are lacking, but sherds indicate that these were often complex, depictive, and highly conventionalized (fig. 68).

Incised rim lugs and realistic animal-head adornos (decorative applied elements, often biomorphic) are also characteristic (fig. 69). Annular bases, but no vessel legs, were found. Vertical handles are the usual form.

---

[1] This is a system of archeological culture classification used in the Midwestern States in North America. Its underlying methodology is based upon typological affinity. Excavated sites are arranged in an implicitly genetic scheme of categories, subcategories, etc., to show typological relationship. The factors of time and space are not considered in the system as it is expounded by McKern.

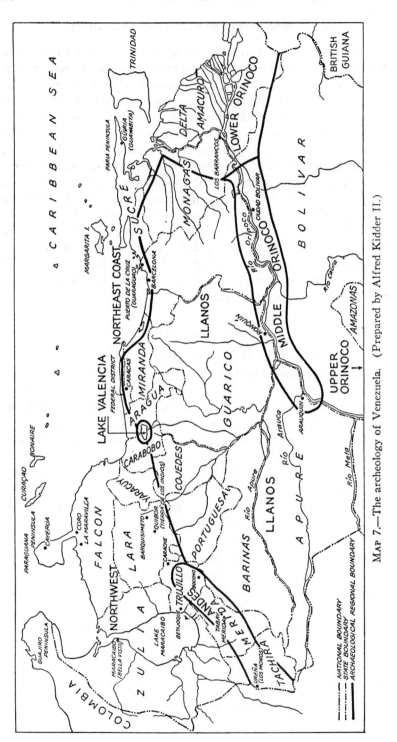

Map 7.—The archeology of Venezuela. (Prepared by Alfred Kidder II.)

FIGURE 68.—Incised pottery, Los Barrancos, Venezuela. (After Osgood and Howard, 1943, fig. 16.)

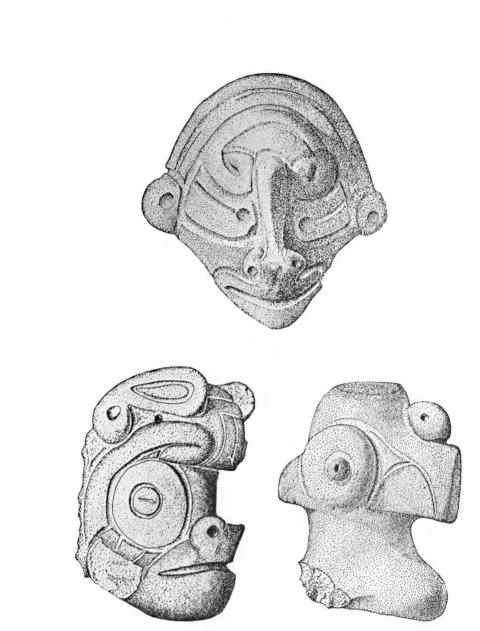

FIGURE 69.—Pottery adornos, Los Barrancos, Venezuela. (After Osgood and Howard, 1943, fig. 22.)

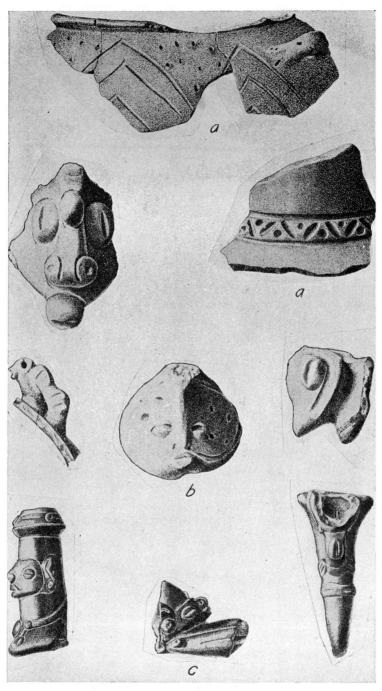

FIGURE 70.—Pottery from Lake Valencia, Los Tamarindos lower strata or La Cabrera Phase. *a*, Decorated sherds; *b*, adornos; *c*, pipe fragments. (After Kidder II, 1944, pls. 2, 3, and 4.)

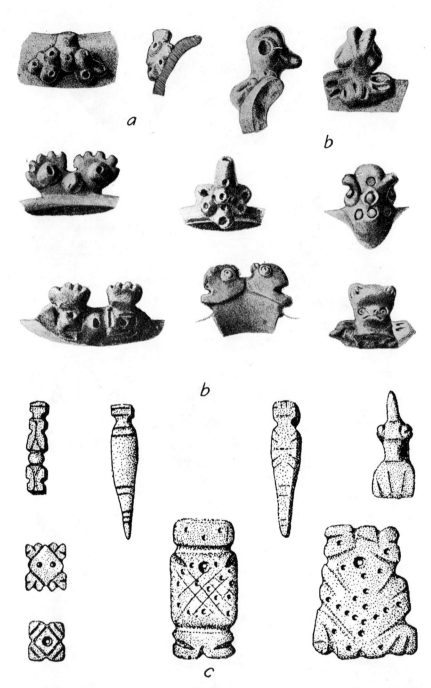

FIGURE 71.—Lake Valencia pottery adornos and shell objects, Valencia Phase, a, Handle adorno (½ actual size); b, adornos (½ actual size); c, shell beads and pendants. (After Kidder II, 1944, pls. 8, 10, and 9; c, after Osgood. 1943, fig. 11.)

FIGURE 72.—Lake Valencia figurine, Valencia Phase.   (After Kidder II, 1944, fig. 32.)

Pottery griddles occur in the refuse with relatively very few artifacts of other materials, including some broken stone celts, grooved stones, apparently used as sharpeners or polishers, hammerstones, and a few simple bone awls.

MIDDLE ORINOCO RIVER

In this region are included the Arauca Delta in the State of Apure and low, flat land closely bordering the Orinoco both north and south of the river in the State of Guarico and Bolivar. The area cannot well be separated from the llanos on geographical grounds but is located separately for the sake of convenience and because some of the most intensive excavation in Venezuela was done in the Ronquín region of Guarico (map 7). Here Howard, in 1941, made excavations in the Ronquín site and tested three other sites (Howard, 1943). All are village refuse deposits located on dunes on the flood plain of the Orinoco. At Ronquín two cultures and periods of occupation, called Early Ronquín and Late Ronquín, are represented by groups of pottery largely concentrated in distinct sand strata, the latter overlying the earlier, and the two totaling about 2 m. (6½ feet) in thickness. Four post holes and a badly disintegrated burial were found, but no house type or burial customs can be inferred from these fragmentary remains.

Early Ronquín pottery is characterized by smooth or polished reddish surfaces, shallow, smooth incised designs, usually curvilinear, made with a wide, blunt tool (pl. 73, a). Biomorphic adornos (pl. 61, b) with the typical broad line incision are common. Red and white painted areal designs also occur (fig. 73).

Late Ronquín pottery contains sponge spicules in the paste. Surfaces are unpolished and generally buff colored; some sherds are covered with a maroon slip. Decoration (pl. 73, c) is much less common than in the preceding period. It consists typically of rectangular incision, for which a narrow tool was used, and crudely modeled biomorphic lugs. The pottery of the nearby sites tested by Howard belongs to this style. Sherds from both Ronquín periods are chiefly from bowls, although sherds from jars and bottle-shaped vessels do occur. Griddles are found throughout both periods. Stone artifacts are very scarce and are not diagnostic of either period.

Few other sites in the middle Orinoco have been found; none have been thoroughly excavated. Petroglyphs have been noted on various rocky points along the Orinoco but cannot be related to village sites. Sherds from the Caura River are closely comparable to those from the Late Ronquín Period.

From several localities in the Arauquín district, near the mouth of the Arauca, Petrullo (1939 b) collected red-slipped, narrowly incised sherds and modeled animal- and bird-head adornos (pl. 73, c, d), which show a general but clear stylistic relationship to Late Ronquín pottery.

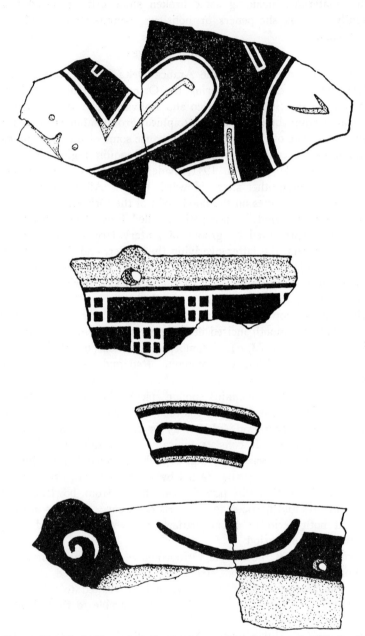

FIGURE 73.—Early Ronquín painted pottery. (After Howard, 1943, fig. 9.)

UPPER ORINOCO RIVER

The upper Orinoco includes the southeastern part of Venezuela, comprising the Federal Territory of Amazonas. Archeologically, information is limited to that obtained by 19th-century explorers, from the various sites along the river in the Atures region. Osgood and Howard (1943) include a complete summary of the recorded data on the burials in caves and rock shelters found in the area. Skeletons in the caves and shelters were found free, in baskets, wrapped in mats, or contained in urns. In some cases red paint on the bones indicates secondary burial. Other remains are partly preserved in resin, indicating primary burial. There is some historical and ethnographic evidence, as well as the presence of perishable materials in association with these burials, to indicate that many probably date from historic times.

THE LLANOS

The llanos are the great plains of Venezuela drained by the northern and western tributaries of the Orinoco, chief among which are the Apure, with its many northern tributaries, the Arauca, and the Meta. The area is flat, periodically inundated, and has probably always been relatively sparsely settled in comparison to the foothill valleys of the Andes and the Lake Valencia Basin. Archeological finds have been scattered; no planned survey or excavation has been undertaken in the entire region lying between the Colombian and Venezuelan Andes and the immediate flood plain of the Orinoco itself.

There are no archeological data whatever from the large area comprising the entire State of Cojedes and the State of Guarico, except for the immediate flood plain of the Orinoco (the Ronquín area). Most of the State of Portuguesa is similarly unknown.

Multiple secondary urn burials, in large drab urns, associated with fabric-impressed sherds, have been reported from the middle course of the Arauca River, and urn burial has been noted in a number of undesignated localities on the Portuguesa, Apure, and Arauca Rivers; clear descriptions and illustrations are lacking.

Mounds and causeways are reported from many places in the State of Barinas and in neighboring southern Portuguesa. All available data have been fully summarized by Osgood and Howard (1943). The causeways, or calzadas, are earth structures varying between 1 and 3 m. (about 3 to 10 feet) in height, 6 to 25 m. (about 20 to 82 feet) in width, and extending, in many instances, for several kilometers, often branching in different directions. In some cases these structures connect directly with conical earth mounds, some as high as 5 m. (about 17 feet), and 60 m. (about 200 feet) in basal diameter. Hollow, pear-shaped clay objects found in some of the mounds suggest vessel legs, but this is not possible to determine from the illustrated specimens. No burials have been found in the few mounds that have been excavated, and the purpose both of mounds and of causeways is a matter of speculation. It has been suggested that the causeways served as roads across the inundated plains, possibly leading as far as the high ground of the Andean foothills, from the upper and middle courses of the Apure River and its northern tributaries. It is also quite possible that the mounds served to elevate dwellings above the level of flood waters.

LAKE VALENCIA

The sites.—Lake Valencia (map 7), sometimes called Lake Tacarigua, lies in the center of an inclosed drainage system of the maritime Andes in the States of Aragua and Carabobo. The region is also commonly referred to as the Valley of Aragua. Archeological sites abound on the pleasant shores of the lake and on the lowland at one time covered by its waters. The immediate lake basin has been the scene of very considerable excavation, both unrecorded and scientific, but the hills, valleys, and coasts elsewhere in Aragua and Carabobo are still virtually unknown archeologically.

Mounds, village refuse deposits, and cemeteries containing urn burials are the three kinds of sites found singly but more often in combinations of at least two of the above elements. Mound groups are concentrated on the flatlands east of the lake, urn burials and village refuse sites on all sides.

The mounds have attracted many workers, beginning with Marcano and Jahn (Marcano, 1889). Jahn made further excavations in 1903 (Steinen, 1904; Jahn, 1932), and he was followed by Oramas in 1914 (Oramas, 1917). At about the same time a large private collection from the mounds was acquired by the American Museum of Natural History, in New York. Requena, in the twenties, had further excavations carried out (Requena, 1932), but it was not until 1932 that Bennett undertook the first scientifically controlled study in the area at the mound group called La Mata (Bennett, 1937). Osgood followed in 1933 with a similar detailed excavation and analysis of a mound in the nearby Tocoron group (Osgood, 1943).

Groupings of Lake Valencia mounds along the eastern affluents of the lake show considerable variations in size of individual structures and no apparent relationship in plan. They are low accumulations of clay and humus, seldom exceeding 3 m. (about 10 feet) in height, roughly round to oval in plan, measuring from about 10 to 30 m. (33 to 100 feet) in basal diameter. Larger ones, measuring over 100 m. (about 330 feet) in long axis, have been reported, and mounds with double eminences, or connecting mounds, are sometimes seen. From the recorded evidence it is apparent that not all mounds were built in exactly the same manner or used in the same way. All rise from the old lake bed, either as accumulations of refuse, possibly from pile dwellings over the shallow water, as sometimes indicated by post holes in the lower levels, or by artificial accumulations of clay and earth. Upper levels of humus often, but not always, contain urn burials and dwelling site refuse. It is apparent that the mounds served either as dwelling sites or cemeteries or combinations of both. Protection against inundation has been offered as a primary reason for their construction, which seems reasonable in view of the former extent of Lake Valencia and the proximity of the mounds to affluent streams.

Village refuse sites and urn-burial cemeteries have been noted at various places in the lake basin, but only one has been largely excavated. This is the Los Tamarindos site on La Cabrera Peninsula (pl. 76, a) on the north side of the lake (Kidder II, 1944). Here, on a slope leading to the water's edge, a humus cap, containing many urn burials and refuse, covers a thick series of lake-deposited gravels, sands, and clays, as well as stone slide material from outcrops on the slope. These water-laid deposits contain primary burials, as opposed to the urn burials of the humus cap, and quantities of potsherds and other village refuse. Pile dwellings may have been in use at the time these deposits were laid down, but no post holes were found at the site.

Materials from the Lake Valencia sites represent two primary cultural periods, related to the stratigraphy of the Los Tamarindos and mound sites.

The earlier, called the La Cabrera Phase (Kidder II, 1944), and included in the Los Tamarindos Aspect, Lower Orinoco Phase, by Osgood and Howard (1943), is represented in the lower levels of the lake deposits at Los Tamarindos and sparsely in the lower levels of mounds east of the lake. Much work remains to be done in the correlation of archeological materials with the rise and fall of the lake levels in this period. The later period, represented by materials from the humus levels of Los Tamarindos, the upper and middle levels of mounds, and the urn-burial cemeteries of the valley, has been called the Valencia Phase (Kidder II, 1944) and the La Mata Aspect, Valencia Phase, by Osgood and Howard (1943).

The early period.—The early period (La Cabrera Phase), is characterized by primary burial, in some cases covered by a stone slab or pottery vessel, but with few grave goods. Pottery is primarily a plain, gray unslipped ware. Large jars and double-spouted jars are common; bowls and griddles are rare. Decoration (fig. 70, a) is limited to broad incisions, punctation, and modeling. Adornos are relatively rare but are of distinct type (fig. 70, b). Horizontal handles are characteristic.

Less frequent is a polished gray ware, represented by bowls, often with low leg-ring bases (pl. 74, a), and many elbow pipes, both plain (pl. 74, *b*) and decorated (fig. 70, *c*) with modeling and broad incision, the latter sometimes filled with red paint. A third ware, with polished red slip, occurs in bowl forms decorated with broad incision, often on the tops of everted rims, and some low relief modeling.

Stone artifacts consist of large polished celts, some large stone pendants, a few of which are of the broad-winged type, and a few beads. Bone is confined to beads and gorge fishhooks. Shell beads occur, but flat shell pendants are very rare.

The late period.—The late period (Valencia Phase or La Mata Aspect) displays many marked contrasts with the earlier period in burial customs and pottery styles.

Secondary urn burial (pl. 76, *c*), single or multiple, was the usual method; primary burial (pl. 76, *b*) is rare. Grave furniture is frequently abundant, in the form of vessels, figurines, beads, and food offerings. Most of the thousands of specimens in the large collections representing this period are from urn burials.

Pottery varies in color from drab gray to brick red, produced by a slip characteristically containing mica flakes. Specimens from the mound sites tend to be grayer than those from Los Tamarindos. A large variety of jars is found, varying in size from the large, flat or round-bottomed urns (pl. 74, *c*) to small bottles and jars with bulbous necks, upon which faces were frequently modeled (pl. 74, *d*). Double-spouted jars are rare. Bowls (pl. 74, *e*) are very numerous, as are griddles. Hollow rims are found in the mound sites but are lacking from the Los Tamarindos collection. Vessel bases are nearly all flat, although annular bases occur. Small, horizontal adorno handles (fig. 71, *a*) are characteristic.

Decoration (fig. 71, *b*) consists of highly varied modeling, adornos of many types, including mammal and bird heads, and conventional knobs, often in combination with thin-line incision.

Typical of the area and of the late period are the numerous female figurines of the same drab or red slipped ware as vessels. These are either standing (fig. 74) or sitting (fig. 72) figures, varying in size and head form, and often grossly exaggerated in style.

Animal figurines of the same ware are less frequent but none the less typical in style of modeling.

Stone objects consist of small petaloid celts, very few large celts, many beads, and various miscellaneous objects. Broad-winged ornaments occur but rarely.

Bone artifacts are not numerous. Simple points, awls, gorge fishhooks, and tubular beads are found. A very few end flutes, including several elaborately carved specimens, have been found in the valley.

Shell artifacts (fig. 71, *c*) are numerous in collections from this period. Many burials contain necklaces consisting of single or varying types of shell beads, often combined with others of stone. Tubular, discoidal and elongated, incised shell beads are usual, as are "tinklers" of *Oliva* shell. Pendants of cut shell, plain or carved as conventionalized frogs and turtles, are found separately or with necklaces. Miscellaneous carved shell objects of uncertain use have also been found in many urn burials.

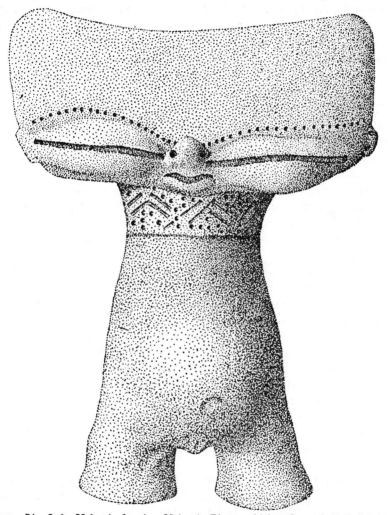

FIGURE 74.—Lake Valencia figurine, Valencia Phase. (After Osgood, 1943, fig. 13.)

Comments on the sequence.—The two major Lake Valencia cultures outlined above appear to have merged without a clean break, although this question requires further analysis. No stylistic changes within the early period (La Cabrera Phase) have been noted, although it is highly probable that such did occur during the time period, certainly at least several centuries in length, required for the deposition of the lake deposits from which specimens have been excavated.

Subperiods within the late period (Valencia Phase or La Mata Aspect) have been tentatively defined on the basis of correlation of mound stratigraphy and isolated horizontal distribution with minor variants in shape and decoration of the late pottery and figurines. These are discussed fully by Osgood (1943), Osgood and Howard (1943), and Kidder II (1944). The Lake Valencia sequence as a whole is still capable of very considerable refinement, with many detailed problems of cultural and geological correlation within the immediate area awaiting investigation.

NORTHEAST COAST

The area comprises the Caribbean coast from the Orinoco Delta to the Federal District, including Margarita Island (map 7). The eastern extension of the maritime Andes leaves little coastal plain throughout the area; in many places the hills rise sharply from the sea, limiting the areas suitable for habitation. The interior of the States of Sucre and Anzoategui are virtually unexplored archeologically. No information is available from the State of Miranda, and none from the Federal District beyond the fact that one coastal site has been found.

The few coastal sites reported are small village refuse and shell-heap deposits.

At Guayabita, near Guiria on the south coast of the Paria Peninsula (map 7), Osgood and Howard (1943) tested a shallow shell midden in which no cultural change could be correlated with depth. Pottery is a drab gray to brown ware, sometimes slipped in buff or brown. Sherds indicate open bowls, wide-mouth jars, vessels with annular bases, and griddles. Decoration is limited to less than 1 percent of the material

Crude modeling and incision are present on a few sherds. Two specimens of linear painting in red on buff and one of yellow on red are probably trade sherds.

Nonpottery artifacts are limited to a few small stone celts, hammer and milling stones, and a few pieces of worked shell and bone. No artifacts of *Strombus* shell occur, although unworked food shells of other species are common in the middens.

Margarita Island was explored by De Booy (1915–16), whose work has been summarized by Osgood and Howard (1943). Excavation was confined to the Gire-Gire shell heap, but surface collections were made at various other localities. Again no cultural depth is apparent. Pottery is largely drab and undecorated. Painted pottery is exceedingly rare and, as at Guayabita, may be the result of trade. D-shaped handles, decorated with small modeled heads, and some modeled adornos from vessel walls or rims are found. Griddle fragments were absent at Gire-Gire, but present at other localities.

Stonework included petaloid celts, some "Guiana" axes, with notches near the butt, hammerstones, handstones, mortars, and rubbing stones.

Worked shell is apparently rare. Several crude broad-winged ornaments of conch shell were found.

In the vicinity of Barcelona, in Anzoategui, Osgood and Howard (1943) found a number of small village and shell-heap sites. The Guaraguao Hills, near Puerto de la Cruz (map 7), produced the bulk of the material from this area. Surface sherd collections consist of preponderantly undecorated brownish-yellow and yellowish-gray pieces, from wide-mouth jars and open bowls, some of which had low annular bases. Only one handle, a D-shaped specimen, was collected. No sherds are definitely identifiable as griddle fragments. Linear painting in red or dull yellow is more frequent here than at Guayabita or Margarita Island. Designs (pl. 74, *f*) are parallel or oblique line arrangements, spirals, triangles, and concentric circles. Modeling, incision, and punctation on applied strips and necks occur relatively rarely in crude designs, indicating faces with doughnut or punctate nub eyes and mouths (pl. 74, *g*).

Stone objects are limited to hammer grinders and a few fragments of miscellaneous artifacts, including flint flakes. Celts are absent in the collection.

Implements of *Strombus* shell are common here, in contrast to Guayabita and Margarita. These consist of cups, tips, plates, lips, and one gouge. *Oliva* shell beads, of the familiar "tinkler" shape, also are relatively frequent. Osgood and Howard (1943) regard the similarity of the *Strombus* shellwork to that of the Cuban Ciboney sites as probably coincidental.

THE NORTHWEST

The area lying west of Lake Valencia, north of the llanos and the high Andes, is included in the northwest region (map 7). Climate and topography are varied. Forests cover most of the western and northern Maracaibo Basin and parts of Yaracuy. From the Andean foothills dry hills and well-watered valleys lead to the eroded, cactus-covered low hills and flats of the States of Lara and Falcón (pl. 76, *d*).

The State of Yaracuy is archeologically unknown, as is the greater part of the Maracaibo Basin. Several sites in central Falcón, one in foothill Trujillo, and several in Lara have produced surface collections or have been briefly excavated.

In the vicinity of Barquisimeto, Nectario María (1933, 1942) excavated a number of primary burials containing vessels, broad-winged ornaments, stone and shell beads, and pendants. Pottery includes plain-ware bowls with leg ring, annular and tripod bases, some painted ware, the decoration of which is not clear from the published illustrations, and two plain elbow pipes.

Two village refuse sites (pl. 76, d) near Quibor, in Lara, were visited by Osgood and Howard (1943) in their survey. These produced no burials or house remains, no shell or bone artifacts, little stonework, but numerous sherds. Plain red and linear painted sherds, primarily from bowls, hollow legs, probably from tripod vessels, and horizontal handles are characteristic. Some annular bases occur, but leg-ring bases are very rare. Unpainted sherds show some examples of applied punctate strips and nubs, some incision, and a few corrugated rims. Painted ware is relatively frequent, in one to three colors—red, black, and white—on orange, white, or gray. Designs (pl. 74, h) are complex arrangements of straight and curvilinear lines and dots, in which the "comb" motif predominates.

Two sites near Carache, in northern Trujillo (Kidder II, 1944), produced pottery closely related to that of the Quibor area. Burials are primary, sometimes covered by a stone slab but without grave goods. Plain red sherds, chiefly from jars, some from bowls and griddles, and plain, small, compact tripod vessels with solid legs, called incensarios, were found. Large horizontal handles are common. Bases are annular or plain. Applied punctate strips and small pitted nubs are sometimes used to decorate the unpainted ware. Painted decoration is (fig. 75) limited almost entirely to open bowls, with high leg-ring bases or hollow tripod legs. Colors are red on a plain red surface, or red on white slip. Design, as at Quibor, is in combinations of linear elements, which at Carache include the spiral, arranged in bands and panels. Many specific design elements are shared with Quibor.

Stonework is limited to a broken oval pendant and some pencil-shaped objects. One amulet of human skull bone was found, but no shell artifacts.

Village sites and shell heaps on the Falcón coastal plain are recorded from Coro and to the west (Nomland, 1933, 1935), and on the Paraguaná Peninsula (Osgood and Howard, 1943). The general relationship of the culture of this area to that of Quibor and Carache, as well as to that of Curaçao, Aruba, and Bonaire, the Dutch islands off the Falcón coast, is obvious, although differences in detail and in frequency of certain traits are apparent. Secondary urn burials, from near Coro, for example, are in contrast to the primary burials of Carache and central Lara.

Plain ware is commonly incised at Coro, much less frequently so at other Falcón sites. At the Cayerua site on Paraguaná Peninsula, pottery marked by impression of knotless netting showed a marked increase in the upper level of a shallow excavation, with a proportionate decrease in linear painting.

Bowls and jars with corrugated necks (fig. 76, a) are characteristic of this area; hollow rims also occur. The linear decoration of painted ware is strikingly similar in style to that of Quibor and Carache but occurs on double-spouted jars (fig. 76, *b*) in the north coastal area as well as on bowls and plain jars.

Stonework from the area includes celts, rough axes, hammer grinders, round hammerstones, mortars and pestles and grinding stones, and miscellaneous objects.

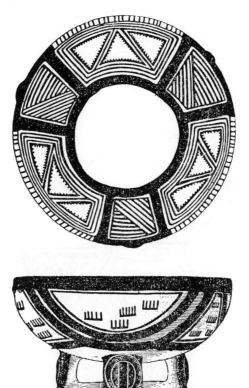

a

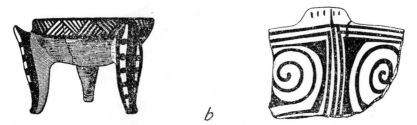

b

FIGURE 75.—Carache painted pottery.   *a*, Interior and exterior red on white ware. *b*, Red on red ware. (All ⅓ actual size.) (After Kidder II, 1944, figs. 47, 46, and 45.)

a

b

c

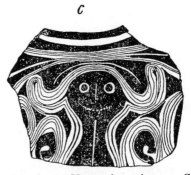

FIGURE 76.—Pottery of the Northwest Venezuela region. *a*, Corrugated rim jar
(½ actual size) ; *b*, spouted jar (⅜ actual size) ; *c*, painted ware from Betijoque.
(After Kidder II, 1944, figs. 51, 54, and 57.)

PLATE 73.—**Early and late Ronquín pottery, Venezuela.** *a*, Early Ronquín incised; *b*, Early Ronquín adornos; *c, d*, Late Ronquín (not all to same scale). (After Howard, 1943, pls. 3, 4, 6, 2, and 7; *c* (bird's head) and *d*, after Petrullo, 1939, pls. 31 and 32.)

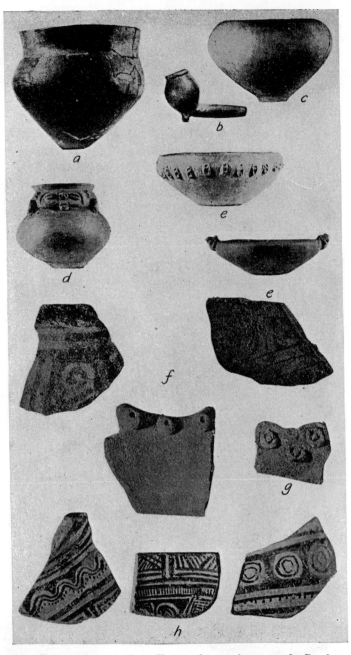

PLATE 74.—**Pottery from various Venezuelan regions.** *a*, *b*, Bowl and pipe from Lake Valencia, Los Tamarindos lower strata (La Cabrera phase). *c*, *d*, *e*, Burial urn (diameter 60 cm. (23¾ in.)), jar (⅙ actual size), and bowl (⅙ actual size) from Lake Valencia (Valencia phase). *f*, Painted pottery, Guaraguao, Northeast region. *g*, Modeled pottery, Northeast region. *h*, Painted pottery, Quibor area, Northwest region. (*a–e*, After Kidder II, 1944, pls. 5, 6, and 7; others after Osgood and Howard, 1943, pls. 4, 5, and 8.)

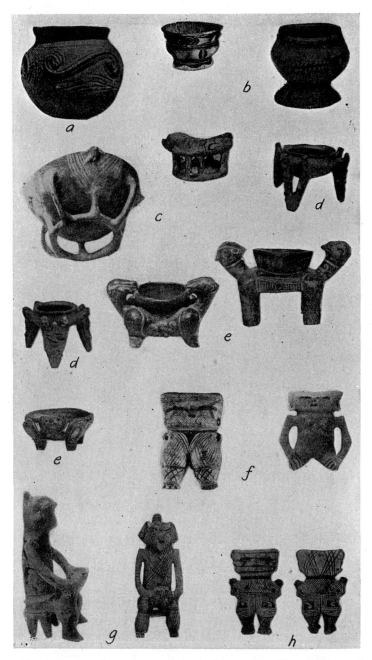

PLATE 75.—**Pottery and stoneware of the Andean region, Venezuela.** *a*, Incised jar (⅙ actual size); *b*, annular base bowls (⅛ actual size); *c*, leg-ring base bowls (1/15 and ⅛ actual size); *d*, tripod bowls (¼ actual size); *e*, tetrapod bowls (⅙ actual size); *f*, female figurines (⅛ and ⅕ actual size); *g*, male figurines (¼ actual size); *h*, stone figurine (¾ actual size). (After Kidder II, 1944, pls. 16, 14, 15, and 17; *a*, after Osgood and Howard, 1943, pl. 3.)

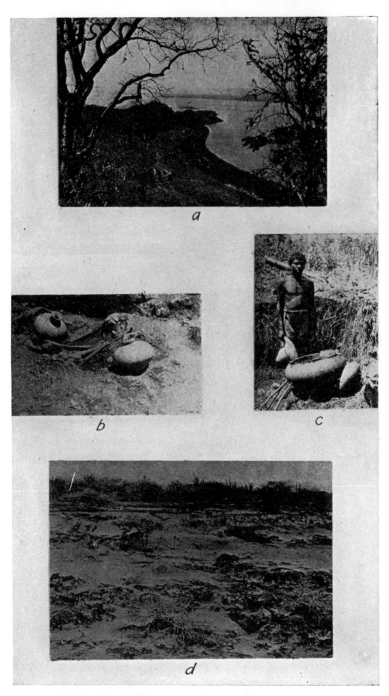

PLATE 76.—**Venezuelan archeological sites.** *a*, Lake Valencia, La Cabrera Peninsula; *b*, Lake Valencia primary burial, Los Tamarindos; *c*, Lake Valencia urn burial, Los Tamarindos; *d*, Tierra de los Indios site, Quibor area, Northwest region. (After Kidder II, 1944, pl. 1; *d*, after Osgood and Howard, 1943, pl. 1.)

Bone artifacts are rare, one bone point and a carved pendant having been found in the Cayerua site.

Shell, lacking at Quibor and Carache, occurs in the Coro district in the form of beads and pendants, and Cayerua produced beads, a *Strombus*-shell ax, and *Strombus* tips.

Secondary burial in globular urns with annular bases, and covered by inverted bowls, is reported from the Bellavista and Punta de Leiva sites in the vicinity of the city of Maracaibo (Osgood and Howard, 1943). Decoration sometimes occurs on these and associated vessels, one of which is a spouted jar (fig. 76, *b*). A very few black-on-orange and black-on-white sherds (fig. 76, *c*) bearing striking curvilinear designs, found near Betijoque, Trujillo, near the eastern shore of Lake Maracaibo, are the only further specimens reported from the immediate lake basin (Kidder II, 1944). Simple secondary urn burials and secondary urn burials, covered by bowls, have been found on the Goajira Peninsula by Korn (Bennett, 1936). In some of the latter the bones are painted red. Surface collections from the Goajiro area include red and brown ware, decorated by incision, relief and modeling, and painted ware.

THE ANDES

The western Highlands of Venezuela in the States of Táchira, Mérida, and Trujillo are an extension of the northeastern Andes. Peaks of 15,000 feet (about 4,500 m.) rise above barren plateaus and temperate subtropical valleys.

Formal archeological survey has been limited, but collections from the area are relatively large, particularly from the Bocono area of Trujillo. Much of the collected material is from cave sites, variously reported to be burial places or deposits of ceremonial objects. Rock-lined tombs and hill terraces with stone retaining walls have been found also. There is no evidence that caves were inhabited; undoubtedly more adequate survey would lead to discovery of open village sites.

The collections from caves and tombs represent a highly selected sample, consisting primarily of decorated pottery vessels and figurines, many stone and shell broad-winged ornaments, and small human and frog figurines of stone.

Pottery vessels occur in a variety of shapes and wares, with little associational data. Simple, unfooted bowls are absent from the collections. Globular jars, profusely incised (pl. 75, *a*), were found at Tabay, Mérida, by Osgood and Howard (1943) but have not been noted elsewhere. Other shapes noted in collections from the Trujillo and Mérida Highlands include bowls and jars with annular bases (pl. 75, *b*), bowls with leg-ring bases (pl. 75, *c*), tripod jars, and, much more frequently, small tripod bowls with solid legs (pl. 75, *d*) and simple or effigy tetrapod bowls with hollow, often mammiform, legs (pl. 75, *e*).

Decoration of unpainted ware (pl. 75, *a, b, d*) from Trujillo and Mérida is limited to incision, crude punctation, and some application and modeling on jars and tripod vessels. Profuse modeling and the use of adornos are not characteristic. Knotless netting impression occurs on some sherds from the Los Moños site near Urena on the Colombian border (Osgood and Howard, 1943).

Painted decoration is chiefly black on white or unslipped surfaces. Spirals and curvilinear motifs (pl. 75, *c, e*) predominate in designs, with an emphasis on the production of thin lines from thick ones. Various arrangements of lunate forms also occur (pl. 75, *b*). These designs are confined to bowls with annular or leg-ring bases.

Human figurines of pottery form the most numerous class of objects in Andean collections (Kidder II, 1944). Males, females, and individuals of uncertain sex are represented, in plain ware, unslipped ware with dark paint, black-on-white slip, and black and red on white. Characteristic types are small, simple, usually plain ware figures (fig. 77, *a*), standing or seated female figures (pl. 75, *f*), and males, often holding bowls, seated on four-legged stools (pl. 75, *g*). Head forms and other details are variable; painted designs are predominantly simple linear patterns, although a few bearing curvilinear designs, similar to those on vessels from the same area, have been noted.

Stone broad-winged ornaments (fig. 77, *b*) of the forms illustrated, varying in detail of shape and ranging in length from 3 to 75 cm., are numerous in Andean collections. Not all are pierced for suspension. They are said to occur in caves in association with small tripod vessels and figurines, although this has not been verified by excavation. Small stone figures, often green in color, representing humans (pl. 75, *h*) and conventionalized frogs (fig. 77, *c*), are also characteristic of the Andean area, and stone beads were made. Stone tools are rare, probably because village sites have not been excavated. A stone celt, a hammerstone, and a milling stone were found at Tabay, Mérida.

Shell broad-winged ornaments (fig. 77, *d*), much less frequent in collections than those of stone, have been found in the Andes. Some have incised designs. Other shell specimens have not been reported.

SUMMARY AND CONCLUSIONS

The foregoing regional summary of Venezuelan archeology as known in 1945 provides an outline of spatial distribution of recorded sites and associated artifacts and notes what few temporal sequences have been discovered in stratified sites. The regional presentation is without chronological or classificatory significance.

Ideally, the archeology of an area is presented as a historical record, correlating changing or static cultural conditions reflected in material remains with an absolute or relative time scale. Although more stratified

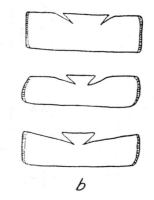
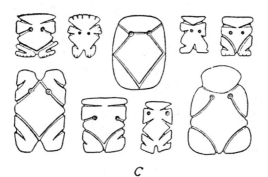
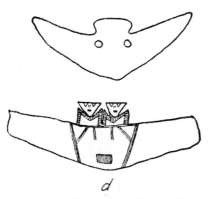

FIGURE 77.—Artifacts of the Andean region, Venezuela. *a,* Plain ware figurine
(½ actual size); *b,* broad-winged stone ornaments (common scale); *c,* stone
figurines (½ actual size); *d,* broad-winged shell ornaments (ca. ⅓ actual size).
(After Kidder II, 1944, figs. 58, 59, 60, and 61.)

Venezuelan Archeology in Space and Time

(O&H = Osgood and Howard; K = Kidder. Temporal sequence is not implied unless space is left between lines.)

Lower Orinoco	Middle Orinoco	Upper Orinoco	The Llanos	Lake Valencia	Northeast Coast	The Northwest	The Andes
The Conquest	Late Ronquín Aspect, Middle Orinoco Phase —O&H (Ronquin). Arauquin Aspect, Middle Orinoco Phase—O&H (Arauquin sites).	? Cave Burials— Atures Area	Mounds and Calzadas sporadic urn burial	La Mata Aspect, Valencia Phase —O&H. Valencia Phase— K. (La Mata, Tocoron, Los Tamarindos, Upper Strata and other late Lake Valencia sites).	Guaraquao Aspect, Coastal Phase—O&H. Guayabita Aspect, Coastal Phase—O&H. ← ? Gire-Gire Aspect, Coastal Phase —O&H. (Gire-Gire site, Margarita Island).	Bellavista Aspect, Northwest Phase— O&H (Bellavista and Punta de Leiva sites, Maracaibo area). Betijoque site, Trujillo State. Tierra de los Indios Aspect, Northwest Phase—O&H (Quibor area sites, Lara State). Mirinday Aspect, Northwest Phase—O&H; Carache Phase —K. (Carache sites). La Maravilla Aspect, Northwest Phase— O&H (La Maravilla and related sites, Falcón State). Coro Aspect, Northwest Phase—O&H (Coro site, Falcón State).	Cave sites and graves, Mérida and Trujillo States. Tabay Aspect, Andean Phase —O&H (Tabay site, Mérida State). Los Monos site, Táchira State.

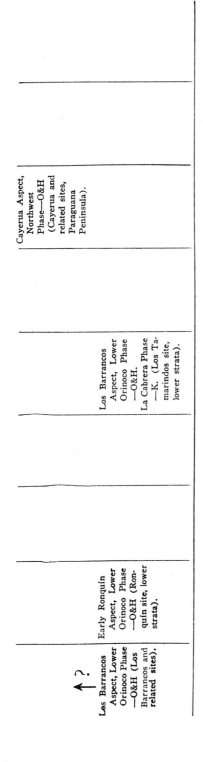

sites have been reported from Venezuela than from many large regions of South America, historical perspective for the area as a whole is lacking.

Cultural change is correlated with depth in three areas. At Ronquín, on the middle Orinoco, an Early and a Late culture are represented by contrasting pottery styles. In the Lake Valencia Basin one group of material (Valencia Phase or La Mata Aspect) from mounds, villages, and urn burial cemeteries shows gradual change presumably ending at the time of the Conquest. This is preceded by a period, undoubtedly capable of subdivision, marked by distinctive pottery styles and the lack of secondary burial. Lastly, the Cayerua site on Paraguaná Peninsula shows an increased relative frequency of fabric-impressed sherds and a decrease in linear painting in a total depth of 50 cm. (about 20 inches). Lack of significant change in shallow deposition has marked all other excavated sites; such conditions will probably obtain in most of those yet to be discovered.

Lack of historical perspective emphasizes the value of spatial relationships of trait complexes and cultural classification. Osgood and Howard (1943) have compiled a table of selected, general traits, pointing out, at the same time, the over-all inadequacy of the data. Other studies of trait distribution directly or indirectly concerned with Venezuela are those of Linné (1929), Palmatary (1939), and Kidder II (1944). Cultural classification is rendered difficult by incomplete representation from most of the archeologically surveyed areas, and the dangers of comparing collections variously composed of carefully excavated village refuse, surface sherd collections, grave goods, or highly selected specimens from ceremonial deposits.

Osgood and Howard (1943) have developed a tentative cultural classification of sites, setting off six focal centers in sharp contrast to one another, in terms of diagnostic characteristics of typical sites within each, and relating other sites or groups of materials to the six centers in a classification following the Midwestern Taxonomic System. In such a classification geographical designations of divisions (phases and aspects) refer only to cultural types, without regard to their actual distribution in space, although frequently a phase or aspect may be known from the area from which it takes its name. No other over-all classification has been attempted, but Kidder, following a different system, has used some of the same terms to designate cultures found in certain localities. In order to correlate the cultures as variously classified with the regional presentation above, and to show what is known or guessed as to their relative temporal relationships, a summary chart is herewith presented. This visually emphasizes the lack of sequence in most areas but indicates cultural relationships between certain areas. Without detailing the evidence, these connections are reviewed in terms of important diagnostic traits; significant external relationships are briefly noted.

The earlier cultures, grouped by Osgood and Howard in the Lower Orinoco Phase, are found on the lower and middle Orinoco and in the Lake Valencia region. Important traits found at Los Barrancos, Ronquín (lower strata), and Los Tamarindos (lower strata) are pottery in solid colors with polished surfaces, decoration in conventionalized designs rendered in broad-line incision, lips of bowls bearing encircling broad-line incision, and realistic biomorphic adornos. There are also significant differences. At Los Barrancos and related sites incised decoration is distinctive and more elaborate than at the other centers. Vertical handles predominate on the Orinoco and horizontal handles at Los Tamarindos, while the elbow pipes and leg-ring bases characteristic of Los Tamarindos are absent at Ronquín and Los Barrancos. The presence of red and white painted ware in the Ronquín lower strata led Osgood and Howard to classify Early Ronquín as a separate aspect.

In spite of considerable differences in detail, the relationships of the three earlier manifestations are clear. All are relatively early, but the presence of some attributes of Late Ronquín culture at Los Barrancos suggests a somewhat later position of that site in absolute time than that of the lower levels of Ronquín and Los Tamarindos.

Osgood (1942 b) has discussed the correlation between Los Barrancos culture and that of the West Indies, particularly Trinidad. Added to similarities in vessel form, style of modeling and incision, and the use of vertical, D-shaped handles, the discovery of red and white painted pottery at Ronquín strengthens the relationship of early Venezuelan cultures with similarly relatively early Antillean cultures, including those of Trinidad, many of the Lesser Antilles, and the Crab Culture of Puerto Rico.

For lack of evidence for absolute dating, the stratigraphically relatively late cultures, and those found in shallow, superficial deposits, and hence of short duration, are shown in the accompanying chart as not greatly antedating the Conquest. Some may be considerably earlier; others, in part, historic. In Osgood and Howard's classification they are grouped in five phases, from which certain poorly represented manifestations are omitted.

The Late Ronquín Aspect, represented by Ronquín upper strata and several related sites, contrasts with Early Ronquín and other earlier aspects in the use of unpolished pottery in few and simple shapes, decorated with narrow-line incision and punctation, and some use of modeled lugs and adornos. To this is related the small sample of material from the Arauquín sites in the Apure Delta area, classified as a separate aspect by Osgood and Howard on the basis of a greater profusion of adornos and the formalization of narrow-line incised design. In general these wares resemble those of the late period at Lake Valencia and certain combinations of traits of pottery decoration suggest connections with sites on the Amazon.

Late Lake Valencia culture, represented by mounds, village refuse, and urn burials, displays a wide range of drab or red pottery vessels, decorated typically with relief modeling, particularly in the form of highly conventionalized adornos. Female figurines are distinctive in style. Certain elements of modeling resemble some of those from Late Ronquín, and there are general resemblances between late Lake Valencia pottery and specimens from the Venezuelan coast from the Paraguana to the Paria Peninsulas. As a whole the Valencia Phase is a typically Venezuelan manifestation, unrelated as a complex to anything outside the country, although some of the vessel and figurine shapes and decorative motifs have a wide South American distribution.

The Northwest region is represented by a number of aspects in the Osgood and Howard classification. Characteristic of the Lara and Falcón sites, and Carache, in Trujillo, are shallow tripod bowls, linear painting in one to three colors, and horizontal handles. The Quibor sites (Tierra de los Indios Aspect) and the Carache sites (Mirinday Aspect) are closely related in painted design, which occurs in one color only at Carache. There is a high proportion of leg-ring bases at Carache, in contrast to the Lara sites, but corrugated rims found at other sites in the area are lacking. The La Maravilla Aspect is set off from the Coro Aspect on account of the preponderance of incised, as contrasted to painted, decoration at the Coro site, and the Cayerua Aspect is distinguished by the presence of fabric impression, occurring with relatively greater frequency in the upper level of the Cayerua site.

Primary burials at Carache contrast with secondary urn burials, found on the Falcón coast, the Goajira Peninsula, and at the two Maracaibo sites (Bellavista Aspect). The last two are related to others in the area by the presence of linear painting and corrugated rims. Double-spouted vessels have been found only in sites of the La Maravilla and Bellavista Aspects.

Betijoque, in the southeastern Maracaibo Basin, has produced too little to be included in the Osgood and Howard classification. Linear painting and tripod bowls indicate a relationship with other northwestern cultures. The culture of the area as a whole, but particularly the La Maravilla and Cayerua Aspects, is chiefly related to that of the Dutch West Indies, just off the coast of Falcón. Linear painting occurs sporadically along the north coast of Venezuela to the east. The painted designs of the Quibor and Carache areas particularly are strikingly similar to some of those of Coclé and Chiriquí Provinces in Panamá, indicating a probable but distant connection.

The northeast coast region is characterized by predominance of plain, drab pottery and rarity of handles and of decoration. The Guayabita Aspect is set off from the Guaraguao Aspect on the basis of the complete lack of handles and shell implements in the former. Such linear painting as does occur, chiefly at Guaraguao Aspect sites, is clearly similar to that of the Falcón coast and the Dutch Islands of Curaçao and Aruba. The general similarity of northeastern coastal modeled decoration to that of the Valencia Phase has also been noted.

Margarita Island drab pottery is similar to that of the northeastern coast of the mainland, but the Gire-Gire Aspect is separately classified on the basis of several polychrome sherds, **D**-shaped handles, some broad-line incision, and notched stone axes, indicating a connection with the Orinoco, the early West Indian cultures, and Trinidad. These traits may be the result of trade or of raiding parties. The evidence suggests a somewhat earlier position for Margarita Island culture than that of the northeast coast in general, as indicated tentatively in the accompanying chart. It is quite possible, however, that a sequence of pottery styles exists and that wares related to those of the Orinoco and West Indies were followed by the plain wares characteristic of the northeast coast region generally.

The little-known Andean region is represented by one aspect, the Tabay, of the Andean Phase, in Osgood and Howard's classification. The lack of associational data on collected material makes further classification useless at this time. Important diagnostics for the area as a whole are globular vessels with incised designs, tetrapod vessels, unpainted tripod vessels with solid legs, effigy vessels, cursive painted design on bowls with solid leg-ring and annular bases, figurines, usually painted in linear designs, representing standing or sitting females, and males seated on tetrapod stools, and the stone broad-winged ornament. Although many of the single attributes of Andean style are widely distributed, typical combinations, such as female figurines with linear painting, or leg-ring base vessels with cursive painted design, occur in other parts of Venezuela only as apparent trade objects. Such traits as the male figurine seated on a stool, tetrapod vessels and bulbous or mammiform legs, and the broad-winged ornament suggest general relationships with Colombia.

The Los Moños site in western Táchira is not included in the Osgood and Howard classification. It produced no distinctive traits other than fabric impression, suggesting a relationship with the Cayerua site, possibly indicative of a continuous distribution of this form of decoration across the Maracaibo Basin.

Too little material is available from remaining areas to attempt classification or to suggest meaningful relationships. The upper Orinoco cave burials, of which some are probably post-Conquest, are isolated. The mounds and calzadas of the llanos have produced no associated artifacts accessible for examination.

FUTURE FIELD WORK AND PROBLEMS

Further field work should be directed toward filling the gaps in regional knowledge, clarifying the relationships between known remains, and establishing chronological sequences. The Orinoco Delta, nearly all the llanos, the upper Orinoco, and the States of Miranda and Yaracuy are virtually unknown archeologically. A survey of the coast from Falcón to the Orinoco should clarify relationships along the Caribbean littoral and of the coastal areas with central Venezuela, including Lake Valencia. Margarita Island offers little depth of deposit, but careful excavation might serve to isolate some material on an early chronological level. A detailed stratigraphic study of the Lake Valencia Basin, emphasizing the correlation of archeology and lacustrine geology, might lead to the establishment of an absolute dating system and would certainly serve to refine the known sequence. In view of the relationship between early Lake Valencia and Orinoco cultures, and the bearing of these on the early history of the Antilles, any additional chronological evidence would be valuable.

The Maracaibo Basin, both east and west of the lake, should be surveyed to connect the known northwestern sites with those of the Andes and Colombia. Such sites as Betijoque should be explored, and numerous new sites would undoubtedly be found. In the Andes there is need of location and excavation of village sites, as well as cemeteries and cave sites, in order to provide representative samples in place of selected, unassociated objects.

BIBLIOGRAPHY

Bennett, 1936, 1937; Booy, 1916; Briceño-Iragorry, 1928, 1929; Howard, 1943; Jahn, 1932; Kidder II, 1944; Linné, 1929; Marcano, 1889; Nectario María, 1933, 1942; Nomland, 1933, 1935; Oramas, 1917; Osgood, 1942 b, 1943; Osgood and Howard, 1943; Palmatary, 1939; Petrullo, 1939 b; Requena, 1932; Spinden, 1916; Steinen, 1904.

THE OTOMAC

By PAUL KIRCHHOFF

INTRODUCTION

In the Venezuelan Llanos, between the Orinoco, the Apure, and the Meta Rivers, lived the *Otomac* and the related *Guamo,* whose culture differed so strikingly from their neighbors' that they must be considered to have formed a separate cultural group in spite of their small geographical range (map 6). The culture not only differs sharply from that of neighboring tribes, but also it definitely seems to have been derived originally from one of the high culture areas toward the west. But more surprisingly, resemblances in general flavor and in specific traits are not with Perú or Colombia, but with Middle America. A further striking fact is that the *Otomac* Indians seem to have been aware of the uniqueness of their culture within the area and, as foreigners in a new country, to have developed special means of keeping alive its essential features. Their daily routine of life reminds one of White settlers among jungle tribes who symbolize their intention of maintaining their cultural heritage by dressing every evening for dinner.

The *Otomac* Indians were discovered and converted to Christianity in the 18th century. Their missionary, José Gumilla, is our main source on their culture. It is evidently no longer possible to recover further information from the few survivors. Gumilla's account (1745) is tantalizingly short, failing to touch upon many important questions and treating others in a short sentence. Nonetheless, his data, supplemented by two other missionaries, Gilij (1780–84, vol. 3) and Bueno (1933), and by Humboldt, reveal a remarkable chapter in the history of human culture.

The culture described below was shared in part, at least by several neighboring tribes—the *Guamo, Taparita, Pao, Saruro,* and *Paranoa.* The *Guamo* and *Taparita,* both food gatherers, were closely related linguistically to the *Otomac,* and some of the *Guamo,* through intermarriage with the *Otomac,* had borrowed much of the latter's culture, including farming, while in turn influencing it. (The nonfarming *Taparita* and *Guamo* are described in "Food-gathering Tribes of the Venezuelan Llanos," p. 445.) The *Pao* and *Saruro* cultivated the same variety of maize as the *Otomac.* Carvajal (1892) stated that the *Paranoa* and *Otomac* were closely related, even being divisions of the same people, but his cultural data for the *Paranoa* are very different from those for the *Otomac.*

CULTURE

SUBSISTENCE ACTIVITIES

Farming.—The following plants were cultivated: Only one variety of maize, which developed in 6 months and therefore yielded two crops every year (this variety was known also among the neighboring *Yaruro* and *Pao* but nowhere else); several kinds of calabash; sweet manioc; apparently a considerable number of other, unspecified "roots"; and pineapples. In Gumilla's time plantains, sugarcane, and watermelons had already been added.

In their farming these tribes did not waste an inch of soil; every field had a basic crop of maize, with other plants sown between. They cultivated clearings and the ground surrounding the many lagoons of the Orinoco and its tributaries, taking advantage of the annual rise and fall of the rivers to sow the areas fertilized by the inundation.

In striking contrast with all surrounding areas, *Otomac* and *Guamo* farming lay exclusively in the hands of men.

The harvests were not stored, except for sowing purposes. No domestic animals are mentioned.

Hunting and fishing.—Few details are known. The peccary and the manatee are mentioned as animals of the chase. They may have been hunted with bow and arrow. To take turtles a man swam behind them, turned them on their backs, and thus brought them to the riverbank. Their eggs were collected and eaten. To catch caimans men worked in pairs, armed with a long manatee-hide rope with a noose at the end. After putting the noose around the animal's nose, they pulled it out on the bank and struck it between the eyes.

The *Otomac* and *Guamo* are said to have been expert fishermen, better than their neighbors, but no technical details are given.

Food preparation.—Turtle eggs were eaten raw, or they were smoked in baskets to be preserved. There are no data on the preparation of fresh meat or fish for eating. To preserve fish it was dried in the sun or by a fire.

These tribes made flour of cultivated and wild plants. To prepare a "bread" of maize they buried a mixture of maize and other kinds of flour in the ground for a few days until it was about to become sour; then they strained it, added a good quantity of turtle and alligator fat, made it into loaves, and put them into an oven, which is not described.

These tribes, especially the *Otomac,* ate ¾ pound of clay daily when food was scarce.

A fermented chicha was prepared of maize, manioc, and palm fruits.

DRESS AND ORNAMENTS

Among the *Otomac,* both sexes wore a belt and apron.

Men had the outer edge of their ears separated by an incision, in which they often kept small objects which they did not want to lose or to carry in their hands.

These tribes wore feather headdresses, necklaces of monkey teeth, and strings of beads. In Gumilla's time glass beads were already in use.

The feature that distinguished them most from neighboring tribes was the beard.

VILLAGES AND HOUSES

A village consisted of a number of palm-leaf sunshades built on the river bank and each inhabited by a considerable number of people.

People slept on the ground (*Guamo*) or half buried in sand brought from the river banks, each family covered by mosquito nets (*Otomac*).

TRAVEL AND TRANSPORTATION

These tribes used canoes, which must have been of great importance in view of the location of villages on the riverbanks and of the importance of fishing.

MANUFACTURES

Women made a coarse, black pottery. Plates and pots are the only shapes mentioned. Of the fiber of the muriche palm women made baskets, mats, bags, and blankets, and of palm leaves they made a kind of mosquito net big enough to cover a whole family. They probably also wove the belts men wore.

POLITICAL ORGANIZATION

Each village seems to have been autonomous, but no village headman is mentioned. The only authorities described are the chiefs ("capitanes") of the inhabitants of a certain number of houses, who constituted an independent economic unit and cultivated their fields collectively. These chiefs probably acted in mutual agreement, thus constituting a kind of village council. No data are given on the method of their election or appointment. Their authority and functions, however, are clear. They controlled and directed every single activity of their people to the extent that a village seemed more like a military establishment than a community of free farmers and fishermen. The democratic character of the arrangement is nonetheless unmistakable. Nothing is said of the chief's role in warfare. Whereas fields were tilled collectively by the men of each group led by a chief, hunting and fishing grounds belonged to the village as a whole. The animals hunted and fish caught were distributed among these groups.

SOCIAL ORGANIZATION

There is absolutely no information on the kinship status of spouses and their children or on courting and marriage. The only relevant data are that young men had to marry old women, so that they might learn the secrets of married life; widows were given by their chief to the young men. As only elderly men were allowed to take young girls, women, like men, started their married life with much older partners. This system seems to have been combined with frequent *Otomac-Guamo* intermarriages. Older men often had several wives.

WARFARE

The *Otomac* were continuously at war with the *Carib*, who raided their territory. They fought with bows and unpoisoned arrows and with clubs. Unlike most South American tribes, they attacked without bragging and shouting. The women accompanied the men into battle in order to recover the enemy's arrows which had missed their mark.

Before entering battle men took coca and bled themselves with sharpened bones.

LIFE CYCLE

At childbirth, one of the parents pierced his tongue and spat on the newborn. The *Otomac* and *Guamo* practiced circumcision.

Upon reaching old age an *Otomac* dug his own grave. The dead were buried with bread and chicha for use of the soul during its voyage to the other world. It is not clear in which part of the body the soul was thought to reside or to what extent, if any, this part was involved when the skulls were unearthed a year later and carried to a hill called Barraguan or "grandmother" and deposited in caves in the shadow of a rock believed to be their grandmother. In these caves the skulls were thought to be transformed into stones.

ESTHETIC AND RECREATIONAL ACTIVITIES

Music and dances.—Every evening from about sunset to midnight the whole village disregarded the house groups and everyone danced together. Men, women, and children formed three concentric circles, the men inside, the women next, and the children outside. Everybody danced and sang in unison, directed by a leader who stood in the center. No musical instruments were used during these ordinary daily dances.

On special occasions trumpets 2 m. (6 feet) long were used, always in pairs. Those who served the drinks were accompanied by two such trumpet players. Such festivities were held in specially constructed huts or sheds made of freshly cut branches. Men would drink chicha and become intoxicated by taking coca (yopa) through the nose. The women took care of them while they were in this state (*Otomac*). The participants drew blood from their temples and foreheads with fish teeth and pointed bones (*Guamo*).

Ball game.—Every village had special grounds for the ball game, which was played with a big rubber ball that was propelled only with the right shoulder. In the morning only men played. They divided into two bands of 12 each and wagered baskets full of maize and strings of beads. The spectators took sides and also made bets. When the sun began to rise the players started to draw blood from their legs, thighs, and arms with pointed bones, without interrupting the game. With rapid movements they also threw handfuls of a certain kind of earth into their mouths.

At noon women entered the game. Twelve of them, the wives of the players, joined each side. They used paddle-shaped ball sticks (possibly simply ordinary canoe paddles) with a round blade and threw the ball with such force that it was received by the men with the full back. During the whole game old men served as umpires.

Bueno (1933) reports a ball game which differs in detail from that just described.

THE DAILY ROUND

Long before the sun rose the people started their daily crying for the dead. When the sun appeared the chiefs selected those who should fish and those who should work in the field. Any men remaining in the village started playing with the rubber ball, while all the women spent the morning weaving or making pots. At midday the women entered the ball game. Around 4 o'clock the groups of men sent out in the morning returned to the village. Both the agricultural produce and the result of their hunting and fishing were distributed by the chiefs according to the number of mouths to be fed in each family. The fishermen left their fish in the canoes, and women and children took them out and piled them up. At this time the only meal of the day was eaten. Afterward everybody went to the river to bathe and to eat a certain kind of clay to be found near it, and then, divided into families and led by their family heads, they went to the bush to defecate in excavations made with a digging stick. Upon their return to the village they started a dance which lasted until midnight. After a few hours of sleep they started the following day before sunrise exactly as the previous day.

RELIGION AND SHAMANISM

Religion.—No special deity is mentioned, but the moon may have been regarded as a supernatural being. Women were thought to have a special relationship with the moon. During an eclipse the men struck their bows

and arrows together, scolded the women for their faults which had supposedly caused the eclipse, begged them to supplicate it to return, and
finally showered them with gifts of strings of beads in order to gain their
cooperation. The women left the house so as to greet the moon after it was
fully visible again.

The *Otomac* believed that they were descended from stones, i.e., that
their forefathers had been transformed into stones which may be seen to
this day on the Barraguan Hill on the banks of the Orinoco. Their oldest
forefathers they saw in two rocks, one called "grandmother" on the summit
of this hill and another called "grandfather" on a nearby hill.

According to Gilij (1780–84, vol. 3), the *Otomac* believed themselves
descended from jaguars. It was thought that *Otomac* and *Guamo* shamans
could transform themselves into jaguars.

Shamanism.—When a child became sick its mother pierced her tongue
with a pointed bone and smeared the blood over the child's body. The
headman drew blood from his own body for every one of his people (apparently with the exception of children) who fell sick and smeared the
blood upon the person's chest. During epidemics this procedure must
have been very hard on the headman.

Diseases were thought to be caused by what Gumilla, without explanation, calls "the devil," who placed little stones in the patient's body. The
task of the shaman was to suck them out. There were, however, other
diseases, probably those accompanied by high temperature, which the
shamans cured by throwing cold water over the patient.

Otomac shamans, under the influence of ñope, predicted the future.

BIBLIOGRAPHY

Bueno, 1933; Carvajal, 1892; Gilij, 1780–84, vol. 3; Gumilla, 1745; Humboldt, 1860.

FOOD-GATHERING TRIBES OF THE VENEZUELAN LLANOS

By Paul Kirchhoff

INTRODUCTION

The scattered food-gathering tribes of the Orinoco Basin (map 6) stand in striking contrast to the horticultural tribes of the Amazon-Orinoco area. The culture of these hunters and gatherers is not uniform. All of them hunt and gather vegetable food, but, to some of them, this is the principal subsistence activity, whereas others depend primarily on fishing and on gathering shellfish in rivers and lagoons. These differences in subsistence activities are correlated with other cultural differences, indicating that there was not one basic culture type but two, the Hunting Culture and the Fishing Culture. Each in turn was divided into at least two subtypes.

Without further comparative research, it is impossible to say whether these subtypes were simply local variants of the two basic types or whether they too sprang from different origins. In any case it is highly significant that these food-gathering tribes formed an important link in the now-broken chain of food-gatherers that at one time must have stretched from Alaska to Tierra del Fuego, and that, like the tribes of the southern part of South America, they were divided into people who were mainly hunters and people who were principally fishermen and shellfish gatherers.

The territory occupied by these food-gatherers is very much larger than had been recognized previously. Whereas to the southeast, food-gathering tribes, like the *Shirianá* and *Waica,* appear as isolated remnants in an area characterized by horticulture, food-gatherers predominated and farmers were the exception in an almost uninterrupted area north and west of the Orinoco River, stretching from the delta of that river (see the *Warrau,* Handbook, vol. 3, p. 869) to the foothills of the Venezuelan Andes in the west and the Vichada River in the south.

A considerable number of specific traits, such as the *Gayón* earth oven, linked these tribes with the food-gatherers of North America and with those farther to the east and south in South America. A few elements must have been borrowed from neighboring cultivating tribes, and portions of certain food-gathering tribes had even adopted farming. (The farming *Guamo* are treated in the article on the *Otomac*.) There was a small but significant number of traits—for example, *Guahibo* and *Chiricoa* rafts and *Guamo* vessels with two spouts—which seem to indicate that some of these tribes had been in contact with the Andean civilizations, though most of them are now separated from Andean tribes by peoples with a Tropical Forest culture of the Amazon-Orinoco type. The *Guamo* and *Taparita* tree-dwellings, on the other hand, may date from a time when these tribes were in contact with the *Chocó* and the *Barbacoa* of western Colombia, or, they may be links in the chain of tree-and-pile dwellings that stretches from western Colombia and the pile-dwellers of Lake Maracaibo to the *Warrau* of the Orinoco Delta and to several horticultural tribes of the Guianas.

The data on the majority of the food-gatherers of the Venezuelan Llanos are unfortunately so scanty that the present cultural grouping is only provisional.

Hunting Cultures

THE GUAHIBO AND CHIRICOA

INTRODUCTION

The immense savannas or llanos, covered with hard grass growing higher than a man, that stretch from the Meta River to the Vichada River, and the narrow strips of forest which separate the savanna from the river are inhabited by a number of nomadic tribes. The culture of these tribes differs as markedly from that of the sedentary tribes surrounding them on all sides as the country inhabited by them differs from the Tropical Forests. However, some traits in the culture of these nomads· were undoubtedly taken from the nearby farmers. For the most part, the nomadic groups are confined to the savanna country, which is unsuited for Tropical Forest horticulture. There are also a few representatives of the nonfarmers just beyond the limit of the savanna, in the forests lying to the southwest. Interestingly enough, the latter, although considered to be related to the *Guahibo*, differ from them in some traits (such as permanent settlements and shields used in warfare). This marginal group of the forest is called by a name composed of *Guahibo* and the name of an *Achagua* subtribe from which they may have taken these elements.

Of other Indians still farther south, the first explorers say that they spoke a language similar to that of the *Guahibo* but that they differed from the *Guahibo* culturally, above all in being farmers. Thus it may be that the *Guahibo* and related tribes originally were forest dwellers, or inhabitants of both the forest and the savanna, being driven out from the former and into the latter by the advance of agricultural forest tribes. The invaders may have been the *Arawakan Achagua*, who seem to have had the closest relations with and influence upon these nomads.

HISTORY, SOURCES, AND DEMOGRAPHY

The first expedition to meet a tribe of this group, the *Guahibo* (*Guaibo*), was that of Federmann in the 16th century. Missionary work began early in the 18th century. It never met more than temporary success and was practically abandoned before the end of the century. This explains our lack of early references dealing with these tribes. Still, our most important sources are those of Jesuit missionaries—Casani (1741), Gumilla (1745), Rivero (1883), and Gilij (1780–84, vol. 3). Among later sources the possibly none-too-trustworthy Marcano (1889) deserves mentioning.

The early sources agree in detail, giving a consistent although far from complete picture of *Guahibo* and *Chiricoa* culture of the 18th century. Later sources, among them Marcano (1889), describe a culture profoundly altered, probably not so much by direct European influence as by neighboring sedentary tribes which the white man was dislodging from the llanos. As a result of this, *Guahibo* and *Chiricoa* culture today is, at least superficially, much less sharply set off from the culture of the surrounding horticultural tribes.

All early sources remark upon the great numbers of the *Guahibo* and *Chiricoa*. In raiding the villages of the sedentary Indians, they always had superior manpower. A few data given in the following pages (the description of a band on march and the fact that in most groups there was a surprisingly great number of invalids) bear out the truth of this observation. According to Bolinder, present-day local estimates put the number of the *Guahibo* as high as 20,000.

LANGUAGE

Two of the Savanna tribes, the *Guahibo* (*Goahibo, Guaiba, Guahiba, Guaiva, Guahiva, Guahiba, Goahivo, Guagibo, Guajivo*, etc.), and the *Chiricoa*, including the *Sicuane*, speak closely related languages or possibly only dialects of one language. These two tribes, which are said to be culturally indistinguishable, are practically the only ones on which there is ethnographical data. The *Maiba* probably belong to this group of tribes, and possibly also do the *Bugí* and the so-called *Rancho*.

Culture

SUBSISTENCE

The *Guahibo* and *Chiricoa*, and probably all the other tribes enumerated above, depended principally on hunting land animals and on gathering vegetable food. The hunting of river animals and fishing apparently took a secondary place.

Hunting.—Except for a pointed stick used by some of the *Guahibo* and *Chiricoa* to get armadillos out of their dens, the only hunting weapons were bows and arrows. Of dubious importance, and not mentioned by some sources, were darts which were kept in quivers. It is nevertheless possible that the so-called darts (occasionally called lances) were in reality arrows. No technical descriptions of any of these weapons are extant. Poisoned arrows were mentioned once with reference to a *Chiricoa* subtribe or band, the *Sicuane*. It is not clear whether these were used for hunting or only in warfare. The blowguns now used by these tribes consist of an *Arundaria* cane inserted in a scooped-out palm stem. They are never mentioned in the earlier sources and are today imported from neighboring sedentary tribes.

The most common method used to take deer, peccaries, "zorras" (skunks?), jaguars, pumas, and other animals is a communal hunt in which the men advance in a crescent-shaped line, closing the circle when they get close to their prey, which they then shower with arrows and darts. Deer are also stalked by hunters whose heads are concealed behind branches and whose chests and part of whose arms are covered with a rosin, called mara. The rosin attracts the animals so that they can be killed from a short distance. Armadillos, the most important and dependable food animals, are simply driven into their dens by setting fire to the savanna grass and then taken out with a pointed stick. Savanna grass close to the rivers is often burned off so that the fresh sprouts may attract deer and other animals. The flesh of large water snakes and manatees, though disdained by the *Achagua*, is highly esteemed by the other tribes. Manatees are shot with "harpoons," barbed on one or both sides (Gilij, 1780–84, vol. 3).

Fishing.—The only fishing method described is one generally used among and probably borrowed from the surrounding sedentary tribes. Fish are shot with bow and arrow after being drugged by a mascerated root (called cuna by the *Arawakan Achagua*) which has been thrown into stagnant water. "Harpoons," unfortunately not described, are substituted sometimes for arrows. It is possible that, previous to their contacts with the sedentary tribes, these people lived only by hunting and by gathering vegetable food and not by fishing.

Collecting wild foods.—As soon as the band arrives at a river the men spend their time hunting or fishing while the women gather vegetable foods, principally roots and palm fruit. The roots, especially those the Indians call guapo and cumanapana and the wild pineapple, are simply pulled up. The digging stick is not mentioned and was probably unnecessary. That the guapo root is the mainstay both of these tribes and of peccaries gives the sedentary tribes occasion for rather derisive comparisons. The datelike fruit of a palm called becirri by the *Arawakan Achagua* and the olivelike fruit of the cunama palm are brought down in a manner that is not stated. From April until June the Indians travel from palm grove to palm grove. They return with their bodies filled out, having eaten as much as their stomachs would hold. These palms, each yielding up to 50 pounds (2 arrobas) of fruit, loom large in the thought and conversations of these Indians, and the palm-fruit season is the happy time of the year. During the remaining months they must rely on the guapos and other roots.

By Marcano's time the *Guahibo* had taken to the cultivation of bitter manioc and cotton.

Food preparation.—Meat is roasted in or over the fire. Intestines are eaten uncleaned, and even those left by members of a sedentary tribe are greedily devoured. Meat and fish are preserved by smoking. How roots are prepared for eating is not stated. Palm fruits are roasted in or over the fire, cooked in vessels (presumably of pottery), or consumed in the form of a liquid the appearance of which is described as similar to beaten eggs. Wooden mortars, though actually mentioned only in the process of extracting oil from the fruit of the cunama palm, are probably used in the preparation of vegetable food as well. The *Guahibo* and *Chiricoa* extract from palm trees (apparently the corozo palm) a juice which they allow to ferment in a manner similar to that described for the *Warrau.* (See Handbook, vol. 3, p. 871.)

The use of salt is unknown.

DWELLINGS

These nomadic peoples never spend more than 2 or 3 nights in the same place. Consequently, dwellings are either completely lacking, as among the

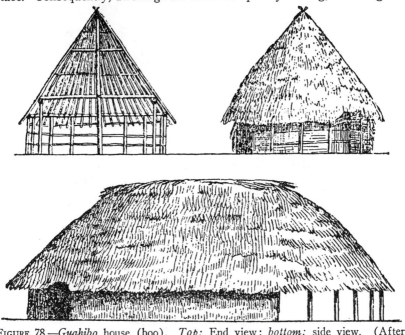

FIGURE 78.—*Guahibo* house (boo). *Top:* End view; *bottom:* side view. (After Stradelli, 1888.)

Guahibo and *Chiricoa,* or they are portable and are made of palm "straw" (probably mats woven of this material). The *Guahibo* and *Chiricoa* simply sling their hammocks between trees in the open air or sleep on the bare ground. Pedro Simón's report (1882–92) of Federmann's trip of 1538 referring to portable huts of "heavy cotton cloth" used by the *"Guaigua"*

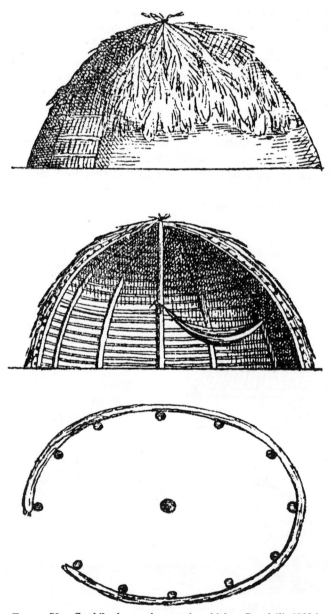

FIGURE 79.—*Guahibo* house (sorueto). (After Stradelli, 1888.)

of the Meta River south of the Pauto River is likely to be the result of a misunderstanding.

Both the *Guahibo,* who lived outside the savanna and were culturally half *Achagua,* and those, described by Marcano (1889), who lived in the savanna near the cataracts of the Orinoco and had already become much acculturated, had permanent houses (figs. 78 and 79).

The hammocks of the *Guahibo* and *Chiricoa* were netlike (chinchorros) and were made by the women from thread extracted from the heart of the quitebe palm. In Marcano's day they were made of cotton.

DRESS AND ADORNMENT

Among the *Guahibo* and *Chiricoa* all men and the majority of women went naked. Some women wore, *Achagua* fashion, little aprons made of quitebe-palm thread. By Marcano's time the *Guahibo* made cotton loincloths. Among the *Guahibo* and *Chiricoa* both sexes wore their hair cut very short (or shaven?). Facial hair was pulled out. In warfare the face was painted black and red. In one case a war party aiding some *Achagua* against another band is said to have smeared their bodies with white clay, allegedly to distinguish themselves from their tribesmen on the other side. No ornaments or deformations are mentioned by writers who report them among neighboring sedentary tribes.

TRANSPORTATION

Women carried loads in baskets on the back. Men occasionally carried loads (pl. 77) and always carried any sick members of the band. Usually though, they carried only their weapons, hammocks, and a shell filled with parica. The women carried the main part of the belongings of the band, especially all the vessels, the wooden mortars, etc. Children were carried by both men and women, by the former on their shoulders and by the latter either on top of the baggage or clinging to their breasts.

Rivers were crossed or traveled downstream with the aid of rafts described as trough-shaped, made of bamboo logs tied together or of bundles of savanna grass. Both men and women were excellent swimmers.

MANUFACTURES

The early sources mention weapons, hammocks, mortars, rafts, garments, and dwellings (which were rather exceptional), calabashes varnished black inside, baskets, and, surprisingly, cooking vessels which must mean clay pots. Today the *Guahibo* make pots that are often beautifully painted and basketry that is said to resemble that of sedentary tribes farther south. The older sources mention small and large carrying baskets (the latter big enough to seat a person!) made of palm leaves, and tubes 6 feet (2 m.) long made of flexible cane strips. The latter seem to have been similar to the tipití of horticultural tribes, but the *Guahibo* and *Chiricoa* used them to extract oil from the cunama palm fruits that had been mashed in wooden mortars. The oil was collected in small calabashes and bartered to other tribes, especially the *Achagua*, who used it on their hair. The *Guahibo* and *Chiricoa* did not use this oil, and the stimulus for it may have come wholly or partially from a foreign group, probably the *Achagua*. The *Guahibo* and *Chiricoa* made snail-shell disks (chirípa) which are used by many of the neighboring sedentary tribes as a medium of exchange. It is likely that this industry, too, was due to foreign stimulus.

At the time of Marcano's visit cotton was spun and woven by the *Guahibo*.

Fire was started with a wooden drill. A piece of cotton, kept in a wooden box covered with a piece of skin, served as tinder. Torches consisting of a bark tube filled with tacama resin were used at night Marcano, 1889).

TRADE

Commercial relations with their sedentary neighbors are important in the life of these tribes. The *Guahibo* and *Chiricoa* trade cunama palm oil, palm thread, palm-thread hammocks, receptacles made from calabashes (or the calabashes themselves?), "iguana stones" (?), and, most important of all, slaves captured or stolen from other tribes. In return they receive chica (achiote), tobacco in powder form, snail shells, and glass beads. Agricultural produce is perhaps not mentioned among the goods received by the *Guahibo* and *Chiricoa* because these tribes combine extensive begging and stealing with their trading expeditions into the villages of the sedentary tribes. Upon leaving a village laden with goods either received in trade or given them in order to get rid of them, they fall like locusts on the fields. These simple and trusting Indians, however, can often be sent away with mere promises.

The exchange of news seems to be as important as the exchange of goods. In fact, these Indians spend the first few hours before trading starts (the begging and stealing follow at the end) telling the villagers all that they have seen or heard in their wanderings since their last visit. They insistently ask questions which the villagers have to answer to avoid scenes. For this news exchange, and probably for the subsequent exchange of goods, the visitors break up into small groups, certain individuals or families evidently always pairing off.

All sources mention the insolence of these Indians, made bold by their usually superior numbers, and their attemps to deceive their customers. For example, they half fill with water the calabashes in which they sell cunama palm oil.

SOCIAL AND POLITICAL ORGANIZATION

The unit of political organization is a local subdivision of the tribe which we may call a band. Spanish sources call it a "parcialidad." It is led by a chief, who is succeeded in his office by his son. The tribe itself does not seem to be a functioning unit. The band, in turn, is divided into subgroups, probably on the basis of kinship, although we have no data on this point. These subgroups are led by headmen whom our sources call "captains." Although these subgroups separate for hunting, they often cooperate under the command of the band chief in attacks on other tribes. On such occasions the chief addresses the headmen in a formal manner, reminiscent of the "mirrayes" of their sedentary neighbors. In the only case where figures are given, the subgroup controlled by a headman consists of 6 or 8 families, with a total of about 30 people. The bands themselves are usually much larger, powerful units, quite capable of inflicting serious damage on their sedentary neighbors.

A division of the band on the basis of age and sex, possibly reflecting a more permanent organization, may be seen in a description by Gumilla (1745) of a band on the march. Marching in Indian file and extending sometimes over several miles ("una legua"), it was composed of six well-defined sections. At the head marched the unmarried young men, their weapons ready for any emergency. The first section had the difficult task of opening a path for those following; when the leading man tired, his legs bleeding from the hard savanna grass, he was replaced by the next young man, and took his place in the rear of the entire band where the walking was easy. The second section consisted of the married men, carrying their weapons. They also carried on their shoulders some of the children not yet able to walk. Old men and women, as well as the physically weak of both sexes, followed next. The fourth group consisted of the married women, each buried under a load of domestic utensils, usually with one child on top of this load and another clinging to her breast. Children big enough to walk formed part of this group. Next followed a curious group, a walking hospital. The strongest men of the band carried the sick and aged of both sexes on their backs in big carrying baskets. (See basket, pl. 77, *bottom, left*.) A case has been described of an aged *Guahibo* woman being thus carried around for years. The rearguard was formed, like the vanguard, by a group of warriors, increased now and then by a young man from up front who had worn himself out opening a path for the others.

On kinship we have no data whatever. Reports regarding the prevalence of polygyny are conflicting. Rivero (1883), in opposition to Casani (1741), speaks of the frequency of polygynous unions. He affirms that those remaining without women indulged in homosexual relations. Homosexuality is denied by all sources for the surrounding sedentary tribes but was quite a common trait farther to the west.

WARFARE

It is not clear whether in aboriginal conditions warfare was of importance among the *Guahibo* and *Chiricoa*. In mission times some bands, under capable chiefs, displayed a knowledge of tactics which may have been due to contact with Spanish military expeditions. They attacked under the command of the chief of the whole band, with a perfect cooperation between the various subgroups led by their respective "captains."

Weapons included the bow and arrow (pl. *77, top, left;* pl. *78, left*), somewhat doubtfully the dart or lance (p. 448), and sword clubs, the last probably borrowed from their sedentary neighbors. As a matter of fact, all their weapons are stated to have been "like those of the other Indians." However, shields of the type used by some of the sedentary tribes, though mentioned in the description of a sham battle with the *Achagua* and in a peace ceremony in the form of a sham battle with the same tribe, seem to have been used by the *Guahibo* and *Chiricoa* only in these ceremonies. It is likely that the ceremonies were of foreign, possibly of *Achagua,* origin. Only in one group, now outside the savanna and half *Achagua* in culture as their very name indicates (pp. 446, 451), were shields employed in actual warfare. They were used together with a weapon called caporano and described as similar to a butcher's knife. The caporano is not known from the *Arawakan Achagua,* but possibly it is related to the otherwise unique weapon of the *Carib Oye.*

The *Sicuane* and possibly some other *Chiricoa* and *Guahibo* used poisoned arrows, apparently only in warfare. The *Sicuane* also placed sharpened and poisoned sticks along trails and covered them with grass, a custom totally isolated in this region but well known among some of the tribes of the upper Magdalena Valley.

The fear of enemy attacks induced the *Guahibo* and *Chiricoa* to allow the fire used for the evening meal to continue burning while they stealthily retired to another place for the night.

Whether the capture of slaves for sale, practiced by the *Guahibo* and *Chiricoa,* was a pre-Contact custom we have no means of knowing.

LIFE CYCLE

Women, who frequently gave birth while the band was traveling, washed themselves and the child in the first stream they encountered.

If a sick *Guahibo* or *Chiricoa* died on the march, he was superficially buried by the man who had carried him, aided by the two last men in the rear guard. No observers seem actually to have seen such a burial. On the other hand, human skulls and bones frequently found on the surface of the ground seem not to have been buried.

ESTHETIC AND RECREATIONAL ACTIVITIES

Musical instruments.—Marcano mentions rattles, cane flutes, and panpipes for the *Guahibo*.

Stimulants.—*Guahibo* and *Chiricoa* men invariably carried a shell or a jaguar bone containing parica. These tribes were said to carry the habit of parica snuffing to extremes not found among the neighboring tribes. Parica was used in connection with their "superstitions and telling of the future" and generally before going into battle in order to enrage themselves.

RELIGION AND MEDICINE

Nothing whatver is known regarding the religion of these tribes, except that the *Guahibo* believed in a supernatural being, the devil, called duati.

Sick people running a temperature were buried up to their necks in fresh clay or water, a treatment that caused many a death. When bitten by a snake, especially while taking an armadillo out of its den without using a stick, the Indians immediately cut off the hand or foot, so that in every "capitanía" there were 40 or 50 people with only one hand or foot.

BIBLIOGRAPHY

Casani, 1741; Gilij, 1780–84, vol. 3; Gumilla, 1745; Marcano, 1889; Rivero, 1883; Simón, 1882–92.

THE GAYON

The *Gayón* and the *Cumatigua, Atarigua, Quibor,* and *Barquisimeto* (these last four possibly local subdivisions of the *Gayón*) lived in the dry plains and hills around Barquisimeto and Bobare. They seem to have depended on vegetable foods to a much greater extent than the *Guahibo* and *Chiricoa,* but unfortunately our knowledge of their culture is too scanty to be sure about this point. Their most important plant foods were agaves and palm fruits; deer and rabbits were the principal game animals. They cooked their food in earth ovens covered with bihao leaves. Animals were eviscerated, but put into the oven unskinned. The skins were removed after the animals had been cooked for about 2 hours and were ready to be eaten. In the same ovens the Indians cooked the agave hearts, which they then chewed in order to extract the sweet juice.

These tribes seem to have had no dwellings whatever. Their netlike, agave-fiber hammocks, a variety called chinchorros, were simply slung under trees. No watercraft is mentioned.

BIBLIOGRAPHY

Altolaguirre y Duvale, 1908; Herrera, 1729–36; Rionegro, 1918, 1926; Simón, 1882–92.

Fishing Cultures

THE YARURO

INTRODUCTION

The *Yaruro* appear to be the last representatives in this area of a type of culture different not only from that of their horticultural neighbors but also from the savanna-dwelling tribes of hunters. In contrast to the savanna-dwelling *Guahibo, Chiricoa,* and related tribes, which live largely by hunting land animals, the *Yaruro* live on sandy river banks and are mainly fishermen and hunters of river animals. While the former usually travel by land and have only wooden rafts for crossing of rivers and occasional downstream travel, the *Yaruro* are expert canoe men and spend much of their time on the river.

While there exist cultural differences as to both details and basic features between the *Yaruro* and the *Guahibo–Chiricoa* group, the nature of the sources and the kind of data they give probably exaggerate these differences. For the *Guahibo* and *Chiricoa* we depend almost exclusively on relatively early sources (18th century). On the other hand, practically all we know about the *Yaruro* is derived from a single recent source (Petrullo, 1939 a), which deals with entirely different aspects of culture than that treated in the early sources, making it difficult to compare the data.

As with the *Guahibo-Chiricoa,* the *Yaruro* have important cultural features, such as matrilineal moieties, which are isolated in the region of the Venezuelan-Colombian Llanos and are rare among or atypical of food-gatherers in general. The best explanation of their presence among the primitive *Yaruro, Guahibo,* or *Chiricoa* is that they are hold-overs from earlier contacts with western cultures, probably *Chibchan* tribes. These relationships were later obscured when the hunting and fishing peoples were surrounded by tribes with an Amazonian type of culture.

The original habitat of the *Yaruro* or *Pumeh,* as they call themselves, is not well known. Today some 150 of them are found on the banks of the Capanaparo River, and others are said to live on the Sinaruco River.

The first missions were established among them in 1739 by the Jesuits.

Culture

SUBSISTENCE ACTIVITIES

Farming.—According to Gilij (1780–84, vol. 3), they grew maize only on a very small scale and ate it green, as so many food-gathering tribes do when they first take to farming. Petrullo (1939 a) does not mention farming at all.

Hunting.—Animals hunted are, more or less in order of importance, crocodiles (*Crocodylus*), turtles (terracais, matamatas, galápagos, and tortoises), iguanas, manatees, chiguires (capybaras), deer, and armadillos. According to Petrullo, the *Yaruro* have practically stopped hunting land animals, and it is possible that they originally lived not only along the sandy riverbanks but also in the savanna. He reports, however, a definite aversion for hunting inland and a decided preference for hunting river animals, chiefly crocodiles. This would indicate a specialization of long standing.

The crocodile is hunted every day and is eaten in its entirety. Deer (rarely hunted) are usually stalked by a hunter who camouflages his body with white paint and feathers pasted on it, and by wearing a jibaro-stork mask and imitating the movements of this bird. The arrows used for this hunting are so heavy that they can be shot only from a short distance. The armadillo, the basic food of the savanna-dwelling *Guahibo-Chiricoa*, is seldom obtained by the *Yaruro*. Animals not hunted because they are believed to be related to man are the caiman, the tonina, and the howling monkey.

The bow and arrow seems to be the only weapon used in the hunt. Bows are 5 to 6 feet (1.5 to 2 m.) long, with a planoconvex cross section and a string made from the fiber of the macanilla palm. Arrows differ in material and construction according to their use. Harpoon arrows with a barbed head (today, of iron) tied to the shaft with a 30 foot (9 m.) string, are used for hunting crocodiles and turtles.

Crocodiles are also hunted with hard sticks sharpened at both ends and attached to a rope or, today, wire. They are baited with a large piece of meat. Chiguires and manatees are caught with hooks made of strong wood or iron.

For birds, which are but rarely hunted, arrows with bone points or wooden knobs are used.

Fishing.—The Yaruro met by Rivero (1883) near the *Achagua* village of Onocutare and those known by Forneri (Gilij, 1780–84, vol. 3) lived mainly by fishing. According to Petrullo, the present-day *Yaruro* of the Capanaparo River resort to fishing only when neither crocodiles nor turtles are to be had. Apparently all available species of fish are caught, including the electric eel. Men fish in pairs from a canoe, but sometimes they take a boy along. Fishing is done mostly with the bow and arrow, the fisherman standing in the prow of the canoe. Fishing arrows consist of a reed shaft into which a bone point has been inserted, its proximal end often protruding sideways through the shaft so as to form a barb. Three feathers and a notched piece of wood are inserted in the butt end of the shaft. Hooks of wood, bone, or iron are also used for fishing.

Collecting wild foods.—Women go out in canoes to collect turtle and crocodile eggs. Men also may collect these eggs during their hunting expeditions. Women also go inland to dig up roots (changuango, barbaco, guapo, yam) with a digging stick or to gather the seeds of the chigua. The hearts and fruits of palm trees (macanilla and moriche) are usually gathered by men.

Domesticated animals.—These tribes have the dog today; nothing is known of its use.

Food preparation.—Crocodile and turtle eggs are sucked out raw, roasted on hot coals, or boiled in pots. Roots are roasted in the fire. Chigua seeds are crushed, toasted on flat earthenware dishes, and pounded into flour in a trough-shaped wooden mortar. Any ordinary hard stick is used as a pestle. Crocodiles and turtles are placed in the fire until their skins or shells can be cracked open. Afterward the meat is cut into pieces and stuck on spits to be heated rather than boiled. Fish is also eaten half raw. Food is rarely boiled in pots; meat and turtle eggs are most frequently cooked in this fashion. Wooden ladles are used in cooking.

Food is placed in calabashes in the center of the family circle and is picked out with the fingers. Only one meal is eaten a day.

The use of salt is unknown. Instead, salty clay is either eaten (as stated by early sources) or merely chewed (Petrullo, 1939 a).

The only vegetable foods stored, and these only for a couple of days, are the root of the changuango and the crushed and toasted seed of the chigua. Live turtles are kept in shallow water for future use. Their hind legs are tied to the front ones, or they are fastened to canoes by means of strings which pass through holes drilled in their carapaces.

DWELLINGS

Camps are located on sandy riverbanks or, in the interior, near water holes. During the dry season they are usually occupied only for 2 or 3 days and consist simply of some leafy branches thrust vertically in the sands. For longer periods, or during the rainy season, the *Yaruro*, especially those living on the islands at the mouth of the Capanaparo River, build low hemispherical structures. These consist of poles stuck into the ground and connected by horizontal sticks. They are covered with palm leaves which reach down to about 2 feet (0.5 m.) from the ground. Hammocks are used mainly as cradles for children and for certain ceremonial purposes (couvade, female shamans). During the day people sit with their legs doubled under them. At night they prefer to protect themselves from the cold and from mosquitoes by sleeping in pits dug in the sand. People rise only after the sun has risen.

DRESS AND ADORNMENT

The original clothing of men consisted of a breechclout, held in place by a hair rope tied around the waist, and wide fiber belts. Both breechclouts and belts were made of moriche palm-leaf fiber, dyed red. They were woven by the women. The women's original garment was a girdle consisting of a bundle of loose fiber, about 2 feet (0.5 m.) long. It was fastened together at the back in a big knot and held by a hair rope tied around the waist. The whole mass of fibers was then passed between the legs, brought up in front in triangular fashion, and tucked in the rope belt. No body decoration has been reported for men.

Women wear a narrow string below the knees and above the ankles and necklaces of carved asabache figures. They drill several small holes through the lower lip for bone pins. As many as 13 pins have been so observed.

A lancet-shaped delousing tool, made by men but used exclusively by women, has a serrated end used as a comb to expose the lice. The lice are then seized in the fingers and crushed between the teeth. This same delousing tool has a pointed end used to crush blisters raised by mosquito bites.

TRANSPORTATION

Loads are carried by men and women in nets suspended by a tumpline. Women use baskets suspended similarly when on food-gathering expeditions. Babies are carried in a sling or simply sitting astride their mother's hips. A man carries turtles and crocodiles hanging from the ends of a balance pole placed on one shoulder.

Dugouts are usually 18 feet (5.5 m.) long. Paddles have a crutch and differently shaped blades for bow and stern paddling. A *Yaruro*, if alone, paddles seated in the bow.

MANUFACTURES

Basketry and netting.—Basketry has a simple weave, either three-over-three or two-over-two. The former is for baskets to be used only once or twice; the latter, for fire fans, mats, hunting pouches with flap and handle, and small baskets (with or without handles) in which to carry or store food or miscellaneous objects. The material used is the inner cortex of the moriche palm leaf. Simple baskets are sometimes woven of a single palm leaf.

Hammocks are made of strings from the moriche palm leaf. They are made with a "knotter's netting technique," on a loom consisting of two upright poles to which crosspieces are fastened at top and bottom. Carrying nets are of the knotless variety.

Pottery.—The *Yaruro*, like the *Guahibo* and *Chiricoa*, though nomadic, make pottery. The clay is tempered with ashes from the bark of the mecla tree. Vessels are coiled and smoothed by hand or with a piece of shell. After drying in the sun for 2 days, the pots are baked in the fire for 2 hours, producing a rather porous ware. The upper part of water jars is decorated with red paint. Two other forms mentioned are bowls (used as cooking pots?) and flat plates used for toasting seeds, both undecorated.

Miscellaneous.—Realistic figures, birds (mostly ducks), fish, and other animals and geometrical designs are carved from asabache with a knife.

Fire is drilled with two laurel sticks.

Division of labor.—Men hunt, fish, and make camp. They collect honey, crocodile and turtle eggs, and probably also palm fruits and hearts. They make weapons, implements, string, hammocks, canoes, wooden stamps, and the delousing tools, and carve asabache figures. Women gather roots and seeds, prepare the food, and make pottery, basketry, and clothing.

While there is a marked separation of the sexes in daily life, there are also many instances of close interdependence. This is seen both in small matters and in ritual. For instance, women roll cigars for their men, or the wife of a shaman will assist him in his performance.

Usually everybody leaves the camp during the day to hunt, fish, and gather vegetable food. Boys accompany their fathers in the canoes, while the little girls, each carrying a basket and her little digging stick, accompany the women on their inland trips. Only the very old and those fatigued from a strenuous hunt the day before stay behind.

TRADE

In Rivero's time the *Yaruro* exchanged fish for tobacco and arrow cane with the *Achagua*.

SOCIAL AND POLITICAL ORGANIZATION

The basic social and economic unit is the extended family, generally matrilocal, except, as it seems, for the headman.

The kinship terminology seems to belong basically to the type in which parallel relatives are equated with immediate relatives and distinguished from cross relatives.

Marriage today is usually monogamous, but polygynous and polyandrous marriages are also found. Polyandry is of the fraternal type (including parallel cousins). Both levirate and sororate are practiced.

The relations between a man and his sister's son are very close. The young man helps his uncle in hunting throughout his life, especially in his old age. Relations between grandparents and grandchildren are also said to be rather intimate.

Young men of different moieties (see below) address each other as "brother-in-law." In a more limited sense this term is applied only to one's mother's brother's sons, while another term is used for one's mother's brother's daughter. Petrullo (1939 a) states that marriage with one's father's sister's daughters are excluded because they belong to one's own moiety, which is not the case. A myth explains the origin of marriage with the mother's brother's daughter. A number of cases of marriage with other relatives have been reported: Father's sister, father's mother, daughter's daughter. In view of the reduced numbers of *Yaruro* today, it cannot be said whether these are exceptional cases or are instances of preferential marriage.

Certain relations between mother-in-law and son-in-law, who usually live together, and between father-in-law and daughter-in-law, who rarely live together, are tabooed. A son-in-law is obliged to supply his mother-in-law with food, firewood, and basketry material and to gather delicacies, such as honey, for her. The mother-in-law will often prepare food and make pouches for him or show him other favors, but the two must never have any direct relations with each other. They may not address or look at each other, eat or perform their personal toilet in each other's presence, or sing or dance close together. When forced to be in close proximity, they turn their backs or sit apart, as in the stern and bow of a boat.

The discovery of matrilineal moieties by Petrullo (1939 a) is of great theoretical significance. Unfortunately, a number of the details he gives about their functioning, especially about their influence upon marriage, suggest theorizing rather than a description of actual facts. The two moieties are called Itciai (Jaguar) and Puaná (Snake). A legend explains that they originated from two young men who, finding no marriageable girls, mated with a jaguar and a snake, respectively. The moieties not only regulate marriage through their exogamy, but in ceremonies the moieties are separated, the members of each standing or sitting together near their shaman. In a certain ceremony the members of one moiety sleep in sheds erected by the other (Petrullo, 1939 a). Each moiety has a chief who is always a shaman. The Puaná moiety takes precedence over the Itciai moiety, and its chief is considered the chief of the *Yaruro* tribe as a whole.

Succession to the post of a chief-shaman ideally is matrilineal, but actually the individual fitness of the candidate is taken into account.

LIFE CYCLE

Birth and puberty.—Two shelters are built when delivery is imminent, one for the prospective mother, built by members of her moiety, and another for the father, built by his moiety. Both parents are tended and brought food by members of their respective moieties. Both abstain from eating fish, turtle, and crocodile for a full month after delivery. During delivery and for the first 10 days after it the husband lies in a hammock and engages in no physical activity.

During her first menstrual period a girl's face is covered with a piece of cloth.

Death.—A corpse is washed by the women (of the deceased's moiety?). It is wrapped in a hammock and carried to the grave by the brothers and uncles (on the mother's side?). The body, together with the person's belongings, is buried, wrapped in the hammock, with the head toward the east. The parents do not accompany the body to the grave, but the wife does. The night after the burial a feast takes place in the camp, during which, however, no fish may be eaten. All fires are extinguished and fresh ones are kindled. The widow goes on a diet, first for 4 days and then for a whole month. On the fourth day the widow and the two men who buried the body bathe and abstain from all food during the following day. That night the shaman ascertains from the nether world if the dead person has arrived there.

A widow may not remarry for a long time, lest her new husband die of the same sickness as the former.

RELIGION

Cosmology.—The sun appears to play no important role in *Yaruro* religion, but Kuma, his wife, seems to be basically a moon goddess. On the shaman's rattles she is represented as a human being with raised hands. Both sun and moon travel over the skies in canoes. Kuma created the world, but she had the assistance of two brothers, the water snake (Puaná) and the jaguar (Itciai), who created earth and water, respectively. The first people created (seemingly directly by Kuma) were the *Yaruro,* and the last the *Guahibo.* In the versions of the creation myth given by members of the Puaná moiety (the only versions known) Puaná teaches Kuma's son, Hatchawa, many arts, including fire making, bow and arrow making, hunting, and fishing. Hatchawa, in his turn, passes this knowledge on to mankind, which he has brought up through a hole in the ground by means of a rope that breaks when a pregnant woman tries to climb out. Kiberoth, a female evil spirit, rules over the races of the underworld which were not liberated by Hatchawa. The caiman is one of these, and because of his relationship to mankind he is not hunted.

Kuma rules the afterworld, located in the west, a land of happiness in which for every species of plant and animal there exists a gigantic counterpart. The stars are the ancestors of the *Yaruro.* According to Gilij (1780–84, vol. 3), the Little Dipper had one of his legs bitten off by a crocodile in the Meta River. Falling stars are messengers sent by Kuma to her people, the *Yaruro.* Another contact is established through the shaman.

A great flood was sent once by Kuma when men turned to evil ways. The howling monkeys are subhuman survivors. The human survivors, after a period of brother-sister marriage, started the institution of cross-cousin marriage between the "watersnakes" and the "jaguars."

SHAMANISM

There are both male and female shamans. Little is known about the latter. The former, in the course of several years, learn from an old shaman tribal traditions and the songs to be used in their performances.

Finally, they see the land of Kuma in a dream or vision. Before they may represent their vision on a rattle, which, together with a special breechclout and headdress, they use from now on, the vision is reviewed and criticized by other shamans. A shaman is usually succeeded by a close relative, usually a nephew (or niece) or a son (or daughter).

During a shamanistic performance the first songs describe the voyage made by the shaman's soul to the land of Kuma, when the shaman shakes his rattle violently. Subsequent songs describe this land. The spirits of the different gods or dead ancestors now enter the shaman's body and talk to the people through him. The next day the shaman does not remember anything that happened in the trance.

The shaman faces the east, in front of a pole around which the people dance, men and women in separate circles. Whereas male shamans sing only at night, seated or dancing, female shamans sing only during the day, sitting in a hammock.

Sickness is caused by Kiberoth, who enters the body of a person; only Kuma, through the aid of a shaman, can help him. The sick person is laid on the ground, with his head to the east, while the shaman stands to the north of him, singing and shaking his rattle. The rest of the people dance forward and backward. Nobody is allowed to pass by the head of the sick person, and no menstruating woman may be present. If the person does not recover during the night's performance, a woman shaman, lying in a hammock with her head toward the east, continues the singing during the following day. If the sick person be a woman in her menstrual period, a male shaman may not sing to her and she is cared for by a female shaman.

During their performances male shamans consume enormous quantities of various narcotics: Cigars made of several strips of tobacco leaf wrapped in a green leaf from a tree, the narcotic tcuipah root, and fermented crushed maize (or manioc). Sometimes the latter is taken before fermentation. According to Petrullo (1939 a), about 100 cigars, together with 6 inches (15 cm.) of the tcuipah root, and 2 quarts of fermented maize were taken in a single night.

Sickness.—The skin disease called pinto, or carate, is very common among the *Yaruro* today.

THE GUAMONTEY, GUAMO, TAPARITA AND ATURE

INTRODUCTION

An important group of fishing and shellfish-gathering tribes, not previously taken into account in modern ethnographical literature, stretched all the way from the *Warrau* to the southern foothills of the Venezuelan Andes, thus bridging the gap which formerly was thought to exist between the *Gayón* and the *Warrau, Yaruro, Guahibo,* and *Chiricoa.*

"*Guamontey*" and "*Guamo*" seem to have designated whole groups of tribes. Some sources called the *Guamo*, both in the east and the west, *Guaikerí* (*Guayquirí, Gaiquerí, Guaycarí*), but there can be no doubt that both names refer to the same people. (The name *Guaikerí* occurs also outside of our region as a designation of tribes that live exclusively or largely by fishing.)

The territories occupied by the *Guamontey* and the *Guamo* stretched from the eastern to the western extreme of our area, in two wide, parallel bands. The *Guamontey* were found along the lower Orinoco and the Apure River to its junction with the Zarare, and on the Guanare River. The *Maiba* (*Amayba, Amayva, Amaygua, Amaiba*) and the *Guaypura* were found camping with the *Guamontey* and may have been related to them. The *Guamo* lived more to the north of the latter, principally on the Portuguesa, Pao, Cojedes, Guanare, Guanaparo, and Acarigua Rivers. The *Dazaro,* on the Guanare River, seem to have been closely related to the *Guamo.* The *Taparita,* on the Arauca, stand culturally somewhat apart from both the *Guamontey* and the *Guamo,* although linguistically they were closely related to the latter (but also to the horticultural *Otomac!*). The *Guárico* lived between the Guárico, Portuguesa, and Apure Rivers. They were enemies of the *Atature, Masparro,* and *Colorado,* on the Portuguesa, Sarare, Colorado, Boconó, and Masparro Rivers. These last four tribes are nearly unknown culturally. but seem to belong to this culture area. The *Zavire,* on the Capanaparo River, are known only by name, but are included in this area on the basis of their geographical location.

The physical appearance of the *Guamontey* and the *Guamo* is surprising. Our sources stress that they were taller and better built than other tribes (the comparison is probably with their sedentary neighbors) and describe them as markedly dark-skinned (Federmann, 1840; Castellanos, 1852; Gilij, 1780–84, vol. 3), Federmann saying "black as coal" and Castellanos "black as a raven."

The two groups of the *Guamo,* that near the junction of the Apure and the Orinoco Rivers and that north of the junction of the Apure and Sarare Rivers, maintained close relations with neighboring horticultural tribes, the *Otomac* and the *Caquetío,* respectively. The first was not only linked to the *Otomac* through constant intermarriage, but had learned from them a certain measure of cultivation. The two tribes had so influenced each other that these *Guamo* are described in the chapter on the *Otomac* (p. 439). The westernmost *Guamo* (Federmann's *Guaycarí*) had retained their fishing culture, but their settlements were intermingled with those of the *Caquetío,* who seem to have been their overlords, and these tribes carried on an active exchange of their respective products.

The few demographic data our sources provide give the impression that these tribes, or at least some of them, were as numerous as the *Guahibo* and

Chiricoa. The *Guamontey* were estimated to have numbered 30,000. According to Federmann (1840), 70,000 *Guamo* were observed in one single war party, and 15,000 were said to have crossed a river at one time.

Culture

SUBSISTENCE ACTIVITIES

Hunting.—Although fish or shellfish was undoubtedly the most important food to these tribes, and occasionally a tribe was said to have lived "only on fish," all them probably did some hunting. Animals living in the rivers and lagoons, especially manatee, may have been more important, especially to the *Guamo,* than land animals, among which tapirs, peccaries, and deer are mentioned. Most tribes are said to have eaten all nonpoisonous animals. The bow and arrow, which apparently was never poisoned, is the only hunting weapon mentioned by most sources, but Castellanos (1852) states that the food-gatherers encountered by Losada and Reynoso used darts and lances. The *Guamo* caught caimans by the same method used by the *Otomac* (p. 440).

Fishing and shellfish-gathering.—The *Guamontey* and the *Guamo* seem to have been true fishermen, the latter specializing in the catching of large fish, whereas the *Atature, Masparro,* and *Colorado* are accredited with the gathering of shellfish. The *Guamontey* used bows and arrows and "fisgas," the latter either three-pronged spears or harpoons. The *Guamo* used ropes to haul big fish and aquatic mammals from the rivers and lagoons.

Gathering of vegetable food.—All these tribes probably dug roots, including caracaras and guapos, the latter an item in *Guahibo* and *Chiricoa* diet. They also gathered fruits, especially palm fruits. Collecting wild honey was of special importance in the west, between the Barinas and the Apure Rivers, a region which is described as "one great bee-hive."

Cultivation and domestic animals.—Except for the *Guamo* who had come under *Otomac* influence, these tribes knew nothing of cultivation. Castellanos (1852, p. 85) relates that when the Spanish conquerors showed grains of maize to the *Guamo* and *Guamontey* of the lower Orinoco, the Indians "sniffed at them as something strange." Castellanos (1852, p. 136) reports that the food-gatherers, whom Losada and Reynoso met between the "province of Catapararo" and the great causeway near Buena Vista, cultivated a root called "lerene," but he insists that these people did not cultivate maize.

No source mentions dogs among any of these tribes.

Food preparation.—Dried fish and roots were ground, the latter in deerskins, in holes that were dug for that purpose and trampled smooth. Fish and root meal were also mixed together and made into tamales or mush. When the land was flooded, meal was stored in calabashes or baskets. Jerked meat, preserved in lye made of a salitrous plant, called coa, was stored in the same way.

Intoxicating drinks, prepared from fruits and possibly from roots, were of great importance, at least among some tribes.

INDUSTRIES

Most tribes seem to have used only calabashes and baskets for the storage of food. Among the eastern *Guamo,* the women manufactured double-spouted jars, apparently of baked clay. These were much coveted by neighboring, sedentary tribes, being used to keep water cool. Although this unusual trait may indicate *Otomac* influence, it is curious that the latter did not make these jars.

DRESS AND ADORNMENTS

Men generally went naked. In the east, *Guamo* men wore only woven belts, which, in Gumilla's time, were so finely woven of cotton thread that the Spaniards used them as neckties. Originally, the belts may have been made of some other material. In some tribes, both sexes, or possibly only women, wore small aprons woven of moriche palm fiber or grass. The *Taparita* were named after their men's calabash penis covers (tapara). Hats, perhaps only for men, were woven of thin lianas and lined with cachipo leaves; these served as a protection against rain. They seem definitely to be a pre-Columbian trait. *Guamo* men wore long beards. Deformation of the body seems to have been rare or entirely absent among most tribes, except that the *Guamo* separated the outer edge of their ears by an incision in which they kept small objects that they did not want to lose or to carry in their hands.

DWELLINGS

Dwellings and mode of life differed completely in the wet and dry seasons. During the latter, the Indian often traveled more than 20 leagues before striking camp. They either built no huts at all, sleeping on the bare ground (the *Guamo* of the lower Apure) or on a bed of leaves (*Taparita*), or they constructed simple huts made of or covered with palm leaves or grass, which one source describes as "movable," as if they were carried along from camp to camp. On the lower Orinoco, people slept in such huts on deerskins. During the long months when the whole country was flooded, the Indians had to travel by canoe, and their camps seem to have been more permanent. They lived either on sand banks that rose above the water level, possibly in the same type of dwellings as in the dry season, or, more typically, they made tree-dwellings, which are described as "interwoven," i.e., probably made of wickerwork.

The western *Guamo,* who lived in the same territory as that of their *Caquetío* overlords, though in separate settlements, seem to have had permanent villages. The *Guamo* of the lower Apure, when settled in regular villages by the missionaries, continued to build simple structures of freshly cut branches for festive occasions.

TRAVEL AND TRANSPORTATION

The only watercraft known to these tribes were dugouts, which were used for both fishing and hunting. The craft were so well made that the Spaniards used these Indians as boat builders. For caiman and manatee hunting, the *Guamo* of the lower Apure used a special, rectangular, coffin-shaped dugout, which other tribes ridiculed because of its clumsy appearance.

SOCIAL AND POLITICAL ORGANIZATION

A camp might consist of as many as 25 families, who were usually related to one another. Chieftainship is said to have been weakly developed, but family and kin cohesion was strong. In at least some tribes men had several wives, often two sisters, or a woman and her daughter by a previous marriage. One source mentions homosexual relations between men.

Frequently, several tribes, or bands belonging to different tribes, were found camping together.

WARFARE

Wars between different tribes or between local bands of the same tribe seem to have been frequent, and most sources stress the warlike character of these Indians. To steal women and children is said to have been a frequent purpose of warfare. Bows and arrows were evidently the only weapons, but poisoning and sorcery were also employed against enemy groups. Arrows were both poisoned or unpoisoned. The nature of the poison is not known, except that the *Taparita* used curare. To judge by the case of a Spanish horse that died 6 days after being shot, though showing no characteristic symptoms, the more northern tribes may have used the coastal type of poison, which led to death only after several days.

The *Taparita* placed quivers full of poisoned arrows in places where they expected enemy attacks. While one source states that some of these tribes ate human flesh, the *Taparita* clearly were not among them; they killed all their captives and burned them to ashes.

The western *Guamo* painted themselves before going to war.

BURIAL

The *Guamo* buried their dead in the ground. The *Taparita* roasted the deceased and placed them, covered with bark, in tree dwellings, which apparently they abandoned after a death.

SUPERNATURALISM

We know little of the religion of these tribes. *Guamo* shamans were accredited with the faculty of transforming themselves into tigers. Among the *Guamontey,* the shamanistic cure of a chief is recorded. The shaman placed a garland of certain herbs on the head of the sick chief and anointed his body with an extract made of certain other herbs. On his own head he placed another garland, already withered, into which he had stuck a sting ray spine. A cotton thread was attached to the spine. The shaman thrust the spine through the head of his penis, pulled the prepuce over it, and tied it with another string. Bending over the sick man, he suddenly cut the string and let the blood that had gathered in the meantime cover the patient's chest and abdomen. Lowering himself and muttering certain words, he anointed the chief's body with more herbs until the chief fell asleep, to awaken 2 hours later completely restored. The shaman subsequently joined a fishing party, seeming not to have suffered from the effects of his ordeal (Carvajal, 1892, pp. 351–352).

BIBLIOGRAPHY

Bueno, 1933; Carvajal, 1892; Castellanos, 1852; Federmann, 1840; Gilij, 1780–84; Gumilla, 1745; Rionegro, 1918, 1926.

PLATE 77.—**Guahibo Indians.** *Right* and *bottom:* Carrying baskets. *Left:* Man with bow and arrows. (*Left* and *bottom,* courtesy Batista Venturello; *right,* courtesy Llewelyn Williams.)

PLATE 78.—**Guahibo Indians, Sikuani tribe.** *Left:* Young man stringing a bow, Río Tuparro, Llanos Orientales of Colombia. *Right:* Mother and child, Río Tuparro, Llanos Orientales of Colombia. (Courtesy Gerard Reichel-Dolmatoff.)

TRIBES OF NORTHWESTERN VENEZUELA

By Gregorio Hernández de Alba

TRIBAL LOCATIONS

At the time of the Discovery, three important tribes living east of Lake Maracaibo were the *Quiriquire* (*Quiriquide, Kirikire, Guiriguiri*), *Jirara* (*Jirajara*), and *Caquetío* (*Caiquetío, Caiquetia*). The *Quiriquire* occupied the territory extending eastward from the lake to the region of the *Teque*, southwest of the Caracas Valley (Simón, 1882–92, 1:37), but originally they lived on the western shores of the lake (Febres Cordero, T., 1920). Salas (1920) places the *Quiriquire* in the drainage area of the Tuy River south of their neighbors, the *Mariche*. The *Jirajara* lived west of the *Caracas*, near Barquisimeto in the mountainous part of the present Venezuelan State of Falcón and the neighboring Venezuelan States of Lara and Zulia (Simón, 1882–92, vol. 1; Pericot, 1936, p. 634). The *Caquetío*, northern neighbors of the *Jirajara*, must have occupied the Atlantic Coast, especially the Peninsula of Paraguaná and the Islands of Aruba, Curaçao, and Bonaire. On the west they were bounded by the Coculza River, on the south by the Tocuyo and Baragua Rivers, and on the east by the Gueque River (Salas, 1920). Pericot García (1936), a modern author using earlier documents, assigns the *Jirajara* not only the islands previously mentioned but also the Venezuelan coast from Lake Maracaibo to the Yaracuy River and the inland territory south to the Ele River, where the *Achagua* call them the *Tamud*.

LANGUAGE

The *Quiriquire*, together with their neighbors the *Mape, Motilones*, and *Zaparas*, belong to the *Carib* linguistic family, but the *Jirajara* and *Caquetío* speak an *Arawakan* language (Oramas, 1916).

HISTORY

The riparian tribes near Lake Maracaibo were first discovered by Juan de Ampués, who arrived in the region of Caquetia in 1527, followed by Ambrosio Alfinger a year later. Because of its lake dwellings, the region was called Venezuela, "little Venice." There followed the rapid decline of the native population in the vicinity of the lake. The Indians who were not killed in the wars of the Conquest, in which they strongly resisted the Spaniards, were so rapidly decimated by the slave trade that Simón (1882–92, 1:372) states that in his day there remained only four small villages near Carora and Trujillo in the eastern side of the lake— Paraute, Misoa, Coro, and Mopico. In being enslaved, these Indians were treated as *"Caribs,"* that is, as cannibals. They were "marked with a **C** (Carib) branded with a hot iron and sold to dealers. Thus, Lake Maracaibo was depopulated" (Salas, 1920). The *Quiriquire* and *Jirajara* stubbornly resisted the Conquest and slavery, and they came out at various times to attack the Spanish ships, which hastened their own destruction and ruin. The *Caquetío,* on the other hand, were more pacific, and they fled from the conquistadors to take refuge in the jungles of the interior in the region of the Ele River.

CULTURE

SUBSISTENCE ACTIVITIES

Although these tribes preferred to live on the shores of the lake, they cultivated maize, manioc, and sweetpotatoes in plantations in the interior, the *Caquetío* and *Jirajara* being the most intensive farmers. The Indians near Barquisimeto had an irrigation system in which water was diverted from the rivers and conducted to the fields.

The *Caquetío* and *Jirajara* also ate cactus fruits or "datos" and tender cocuy leaves (*Agave cocui*). They prepared maize in various ways, including a boiled soup, called "caza," which was seasoned with ají or chili pepper. Fish, taken with a drug, barbasco (*Lonchocarpus* sp.), provided the staple food of the *Quiriquire,* and deer, tapirs, and other game, killed with the bow and arrow or surrounded with fire, constituted an important portion of the diet of the *Jirajara* and *Caquetío*.

HOUSES AND VILLAGES

The *Quiriquire* lived on the shores of the lake or sometimes in the interior. After their migration from the south, they established the four villages named above near Carora and Trujillo. One of these, Mopico, was also called Barbacoas (Simón, 1882–92, vol. 1, p. 37), a name which the Spanish gave various Indians such as the *Chocó, Catío,* and *Barbacoa* of western Colombia, who built pile dwellings over the water or land. To explain the custom of building pile dwellings over the lake the chroniclers say that, although there was sufficient territory away from the coast to avoid the numerous and annoying mosquitoes of the hot sections, they probably chose the lake for such reasons as the greater security against enemies and the greater ease of procuring fish and shellfish. The lake dwellings were reached by channels hidden in the rushes and aquatic plants, and the Spaniards had great difficulty in finding and destroying them. The Spaniards, however, sought them out with great perseverance and eliminated nearly all the Indians of old "Venezuela." The *Paraujano*, whom the present author visited in 1935 on the northwestern side of Lake Maracaibo near the *Goajiro* (Hernández de Alba, 1936), are, however, survivors of these Indians. The *Jirajara* must also have used piled dwellings, for a Spanish town built in the beginning of the 16th century in the territory of the *Curarigua*, a *Jirajara* subtribe in the central part of the area east of the lake, was named San Felipe de Barbacoas (Salas, 1920, p. 229).

Villages in the interior had the houses arranged in rows, facing each other on opposite sides of a wide street. The *Jirajara* and *Caquetío* grouped their houses in two's or four's, preferably by their cultivated fields, in order to protect them against dangerous animals (Descripción de la Ciudad . . . , 1579). The houses were rectangular huts of poles, vines, and grass, and there was a separate house for the shaman (piache) (Antolínez, 1943). A letter written in 1546 by the Licenciado Juan Pérez de Tolosa to the King of Spain states that the *Caquetío* built poor houses and slept in hammocks.

CLOTHING AND ADORNMENT

The only garment of the *Quiriquire* was a genital cover consisting of a small apron which hung down from the belt (Simón, 1882–92, vol. 1, p. 38) or a calabash penis cover suspended from the belt by a cord called "bayoque" (Salas, 1920). Oviedo y Valdés (1851–55) says that men tied the prepuce with a thread by which the penis was fastened up to the belt, for they believed that this preserved their virility, and that women hung a cotton string from the belt and attached another string to it so that it fell down in front and passed between the legs, ending in a knot which was held between the buttocks. They were greatly ashamed when this string was not in place. *Jirajara* men wore a garment called "guayuco" or "guaruma," and women a kind of very short skirt. *Caquetío* men wore calabash penis covers, and women wore genital covers that were evidently woven ("de manta").

Body ornamentation usually consisted of red and black paint, the latter of a pigment called "onoto" and of a fruit called "jagua" or "buxera" (*Genipa*). The paint was mixed with a resin (Castellanos, 1852). Other ornaments were tufts of feathers, facial designs, diadems for chiefs and nobles, gold earrings, and, especially among the *Caquetío* of the maritime region of Paraguaná, pearl bracelets.

TRANSPORTATION

These Indians were excellent navigators of the coast and lake, traveling and carrying their goods in dugout canoes that could accommodate three or four persons. After the Conquest they became handlers of cargo and were engaged by the Spaniards to transport goods from the coast to Barquisimeto and Nueva Segovia.

Paths or roads connected the villages with one another and with the cultivated fields.

MANUFACTURES

These tribes seem to have done little weaving, for their clothing was minimal. Thread, made of cotton or other fibers and sometimes dyed red, was used only for genital covers, for hammocks, which were probably netted, for carrying-bags (mochilas), and for objects called "cataures."

Ceramic wares included cooking pots, jars for fermenting chicha, and storage vessels. Calabashes were used both as containers and as lids.

Salt was prepared in the *Caquetío* region, possibly by the evaporation of tidal water confined in the low portions of the beaches.

SOCIAL AND POLITICAL ORGANIZATION

The *Jirajara* were divided into subtribes (parcialidades), each under a chief, but at the Conquest there was also a tribal war chief named "Camisetano." Subtribes mentioned were the *Nirgua, Cuiba, Curarigua, Ayamán, Coyón,* and others. The *Caquetío* were likewise divided into various lesser "chieftaincies" but had a general chief, the Señor de Paraguaná, named Manaure (Oviedo y Baños, 1824, 1935), who was ceremoniously carried in a hammock which was decorated by the lesser chiefs or "diaos." He was attributed divine or magical power to control nature and to make the crops fertile. In addition to the chiefs there was a noble class consisting of distinguished warriors and another class of rich men. The *Caquetío* villages were Todaquiribo, Zacerida, Carao, Tamodoré, Gapatárida, Guaybacoa, Miraca, Hurraqui, Hurehurebo, Cacicare, Cacorida, and Sarasaragua, of which Miraca was the principal one. Among the chiefs mentioned by the Germans, who first contacted the tribe in the early 16th century, were Catimayagua, Categue, Geeoagúa, and Badurajara (Castellanos, 1852).

The only information on marriage is references to polygyny.

TRADE

The *Quiriquire* traded with the *Caquetío* and *Bubure,* exchanging fish for maize and other products. The *Caquetío* traded salt and tobacco to the *Curarigua, Jirajara,* and *Nirgua,* and obtained objects of gold from the last two.

WARFARE

Weapons were limited to clubs (macanas), and bows and arrows. *Jirajara* arrows (Salas, 1920) were about 85 cm. (33½ inches) long, tipped with a poisoned, harpoonlike bone point (of iron after the Conquest), and carried in quivers. These tribes fought other tribes before the Conquest and dominated Lake Maracaibo, which they crossed in their small, fast canoes. When the Spaniards came, they attacked their ships and colonies. The *Quiriquire* staged an uprising in 1580, leaving the servitude to which they had been subjected in Maracaibo and Gibraltar, and, after attacking Gibraltar, they migrated south, toward the mouths of the Cúcuta River, having allied themselves to the *Zapara, Alile,* and *Eneale.* They took with them three daughters of their encomendera, Doña Juana de Ulloa, and married them to three men of the tribe, by whom they had children. The mothers and children lived as Indians until they were rescued between 1610 and 1617. The *Jirajara* were belligerent from the time of their discovery by the German, Federman, in 1530; they staged a rebellion in 1610 and did not cease fighting until completely subjugated in 1614. In the Conquest, expeditions such as those of Jorge de Spier or Espira captured slaves to be sold to plantations or mines.

DEATH PRACTICES

At the death of a *Caquetío* noble, the people assembled in his village and spent the night lamenting his demise and praising his noteworthy deeds. The next day they desiccated his corpse on a babracot over a fire and cleaned his bones, which they ground and mixed with masato and drank. In the case of a chief, they put the desiccated corpse in a new hammock, beneath which they placed a wooden image or likeness of him and then abandoned the house. The son or successor of the chief renewed the hammock when it became old. When the bones of the corpse began to fall apart, the whole tribe was convoked. Painted with genipa and bixa and adorned with all their ornaments, the people spent 3 days consuming the powdered bones in masato and burning the wooden image, which had remained under the hammock.

ESTHETIC AND RECREATIONAL ACTIVITIES

Musical instruments reported are horns and shell trumpets. These accompanied songs, such as those eulogizing the deceased at funerals, and were played during attacks in battle.

The *Caquetío* shaman smoked tobacco together with various herbs which "robbed him of his senses."

The *Caquetío* made an intoxicating drink of maguey, or fique, which was probably very similar to Mexican pulque. During funeral ceremonies they also drank masato, which may have been a kind of chicha.

RELIGION AND SHAMANISM

The head chief of the *Caquetío* had great religious power, being capable of increasing the fertility of crops and of controlling natural phenomena. There were community temples (adoratorios), but each family also had its own idols. The principal gods were the sun and moon, to whom the shamans (boratios), acting in the capacity of priests, made offerings or sacrifices. Each village, or caserío, had its shaman or priest who made offerings to the deities, foretold the future, and predicted the outcome of battles.

The *Caquetío* and *Jirajara,* according to the account of the city of Nueva Segovia (Antolínez, 1943), offered a 10-year-old girl to the Sun as his wife in order to obtain rain for their fields. They bought the girl from her mother, decapitated her with a stone knife on the bank of a river, and offered her blood to the Sun.

To divine the future and the outcome of battles, the priest-shaman shut himself up for 3 days smoking tobacco and other narcotics, which made him insensible, after which he announced what he had learned from the spirits during the trance. He advised individuals on the outcome of projected enterprises by placing tobacco ash on a dried maize leaf. If the ash formed a curve, the enterprise would succeed, but if it remained straight, failure was certain.

To insure the success of a battle, the shaman required that people limit their diet to a daily meal of the soup called "caza."

In a shamanistic curing it is not clear whether spirit helpers were involved or whether the shaman supplicated the cult gods. At Nueva Segovia the *Caquetío* called the evil spirit "Capu," the same name given the Spaniards (Antolínez, 1943), and good and bad spirits were said to be supplicated by the shaman-priest to cure the sick. In any event the shaman required that his patient fast and that his patient's family limit its diet to a daily meal of "caza" soup. To effect the cure he passed his hands over the ailing place of the sick person to locate the cause of the trouble, then blew on it and sucked out the disease-causing object—a thorn, piece of stone, or piece of wood—which he spit out. The shaman was customarily paid for his services with gold ornaments.

Herbal curing was also practiced. For example, the Indians made a purgative of "piñón" fruits (*Jatropha curcas*) mixed with "cañafístola" (*Cassia fistula*).

LEARNING

It is probable that time, at least seasons of the year, was measured not in terms of astronomical phenomena but of the ripening of wild fruits, for the *Caquetío* would set a date by saying "when such and such fruits ripen."

THE TRIBES OF NORTH CENTRAL VENEZUELA[1]

By Gregorio Hernández de Alba

TRIBAL LOCATIONS

In a territory which, according to Oviedo y Baños, extended 40 leagues west from the port of Borburata and 20 leagues north to south were various tribes known by the general name of *Caracas* (Oviedo y Baños, 1935; Salas, 1920). Oviedo y Baños (1935, ch. 10, p. 74) gives the following list of tribes in this area: *Caracas, Tarma, Taramaina, Chagaragoto, Teque, Meregoto, Mariche, Arvaco,* and *Quiriquire.* Some of these, such as the *Quiriquire,* belong to the area of Northwest Venezuela, east of Lake Maracaibo. The *Caracas* gave their name first to a Colonial province and later to the modern capital of Venezuela, which, according to Salas, was previously named Mayo, Guairo, or Gaire, after the Guairo River, which crosses the valley in which Caracas is located. To the tribes listed above, Salas adds the *Tomuza, Mucaria, Aragua, Tacarigua, Naiguatáe,* and *Guaraira.*

The *Teque,* eastern neighbors of the *Quiriquire,* extended southwest to the Caracas or Guairo Valley. The *Mariche* lived east of Caracas in the plains of the Guairo River and the coastal mountains. The *Tarma, Chagaragoto,* and *Taramaina* adjoined one another in the mountains which run to the sea and on the headwaters of the Guairo and San Pedro Rivers. The *Arvaco* (*Arbaco*) were northeast of the last group, and the *Meregoto* were east of the *Arvaco.* The *Mucaria, Aragua,* and *Tacarigua* lived around Lake Valencia. The *Naiguatáe, Guaraira,* and other tribes occupied the coast from Cape Codera to the Yaracuy River.

The tribes occupying the Colonial Provinces of Maracapana and Cumaná more or less adjoined the *Caracas* group, of which they were an eastern extension. They also adjoined at least some of the tribes north of the Orinoco River (p. 481). In general, they lived inland from the portion of the coast around the port of Maracapana. As their limits are not exactly known and as some of the tribes, such as the *Cumanagoto, Piritu,* and *Pariagoto* (*Paragoto*), extended into the territory of and had cul-

[1] Dr. Hernández de Alba hurriedly prepared this article in the last weeks before volume 4 went to press in order to fill in gaps that still remained in the Handbook coverage. Time permitted neither the coordination of cultural data and tribal locations with Kirchhoff's material dealing with closely related tribes nor inclusion of the modern ethnology.—Editor.

tural influence on the other tribes, the present article must be considered as complementary to Kirchhoff's articles on "The Tribes North of the Orinoco River" (p. 481) and "Food-gathering Tribes of the Venezuelan Llanos" (p. 445), which overlap this area. Simón (1882–92)[2] lists the tribes of the Provinces of Cumaná and Maracapana, together with the following tribes or subtribes: *Cariaco, Chacopata, Chaigoto, Cherigoto, Pitagoto,* "and many others, which could never all be enumerated, that are named after their chiefs." Among these were the *Cumanagoto, Piritu,* and *Paragoto,* which Kirchhoff has described.

The present article gives only those cultural data which are not found elsewhere in the Handbook.

HISTORY

From the beginning of the Conquest all these Indians resisted enslavement by the conquistadors. To this end, outstanding leaders, such as Guaicaipuro, chief of the *Teque,* united all the other chiefs and subtribes (parcialidades) under their command. The principal confederated tribes were the *Teque, Taramaina, Arvaco,* and *Meregoto,* whose resistance to the conquistadors was well organized by 1561. By 1562, however, the first two Spanish colonies were established: Nuestra Señora de Caraballeda on the Atlantic coast, 2 leagues east of La Guaira, and San Francisco in the interior. The latter was founded by two Mestizo brothers, sons of the chieftainess of one of the subtribes. The continued attacks of the Indians forced the Spaniards to abandon these settlements after a few years, but in 1565 or a little later Capt. Diego de Lozada founded the cities of Santiago de León de Caracas in the Guairo Valley and Nuestra Señora de los Remedios. The Indians continued to resist the colonists, but in 1568 Guaicaipuro, chief of the federation, died, and soon the Spaniards executed 25 *Mariche* chiefs, thereby drowning these Indians in blood and exterminating them.

CULTURE

SUBSISTENCE ACTIVITIES

These tribes depended upon farming, hunting, fishing, and the gathering of wild fruits. *Caracas* crops included cacao, which was made into a hot drink, tobacco, cotton, agave (fique), sweet manioc, maize, and such fruits as genipa (mamón), cardones (datos), and cactus (tuna or comoho).

Animal foods included anteaters, deer, peccaries (zaíno or puerco montés), hares, mute dogs, tapirs, such birds as partridges, parakeets, and pigeons, and lobsters, which were roasted. The Indians used snares and pitfalls; in open country they hunted with bows and arrows. Chief Guaramental's people had a special lake for fishing, but shortly before the Conquest they relinquished it to another tribe.

---

[2] Kirchhoff did not have access to this source.

Domesticated bees, which were kept in calabash hives, were an unusual feature.

Dried meat and other foods were kept in well-stocked storage places for use during wars and times of scarcity.

CLOTHING

Caracas women wore a small cotton loincloth (bragas), about 2 palms wide. Held up by a cord around the waist, it passed between the legs, the back end falling down over the buttocks and the front end over the belly. "Virgins" (probably all unmarried women) also wore bragas but were distinguished by a cord worn around the neck and crossed over the breast with the ends tied on each side of the body to the belt and a second cord running vertically on the back from the first cord to the belt. Men usually wore only a penis cover, perhaps a calabash. They cut the hair at ear level all the way around the head, wore gold ornaments, painted their bodies, and tattooed themselves by rubbing finely ground charcoal into scratches.

Among the *Maracapana*, as among the *Carib*, young women wore cotton threads as ligatures above and below the knees; these made their legs bulge, a mark of feminine beauty.

MANUFACTURES

Cordage was made for women's belts and neck strings and for woven products. Weaving, though little developed, was practiced by the *Caracas*, who made women's loincloths and hammocks of cotton. The weaving technique is not known.

SOCIAL AND POLITICAL ORGANIZATION

The *Caracas*, an essentially warlike tribe, had a graded military class with rank indicated by special tattooing. For one triumph in battle the right arm was tattooed; for another the breast received a design which was sometimes similar to that on the arm; and for the third a line was tattooed from each eye to the ear. Men of higher grades were privileged to wear a jaguar-skin headgear or a necklace made of human bones or possibly of human teeth like those recently found archeologically in *Pijao* territory (Oviedo y Valdés, 1851–55, vol. 2, bk. 25, ch. 19).

The tribes or subtribes were ruled by chiefs, or caciques, and in case of war they formed a confederacy under a single leader, like that under the *Teque* chief, Guaicaipuro. The chief of the *Maracapana* appointed a special war captain and designated men to guard the village palisade. If these men were lax, their commander was punished with death and his wives and children were made slaves of the chief. A similar punishment was imposed on people who used the hunting and fishing places reserved for the sovereign, and the culprits' goods were confiscated. It was the chief's prerogative to be guarded by four Indians, who always stayed in front of him in battle.

Children captured in war were spared and became a special class of slaves.

Some men in these tribes were sexual inverts. They wore their hair shoulder-length, were sodomists, practiced transvestitism, avoided going to war, and carried on traditional tasks of women, such as spinning and weaving.

The *Maracapana* practiced polygyny. The principal wife governed the others, and her child inherited the father's goods and privileges. If the principal wife had no children, the children of the wife who took her place when she died received the inheritance. It was the youngest of the sons to whom the inheritance passed; there was no primogeniture, though it is common elsewhere. According to Simón, the newlyweds' house was built by the bride's father, the groom furnishing the materials. After a ceremony in which the men of the tribe danced with the groom and the women with the bride, the latter was given to the shaman, who initiated her in the nuptials and turned her over to her husband, warning her to be faithful because an adulterous woman would be returned to her father while her lover was punished.

WARFARE

The warlike nature of these tribes has been mentioned. No details of warfare can be added here except that the *Caracas* used bows and arrows, with and without poison, and clubs (macanas) of hardwood.

CANNIBALISM

The only mention of cannibalism is among the *Maracapana* under Chief Guaramental. After a victory, these Indians cut off the arms, legs, and other parts of a captive enemy chief, and, when he died, they opened his breast with a flint knife and removed the viscera, which were distributed among the people and eaten.

ESTHETIC AND RECREATIONAL ACTIVITIES

Among the *Maracapana* and *Cumaná* all festivals were accompanied by chants, some grave and solemn, others gay and jocular. To judge from an example given by Simón, these songs or ballads used a device of grammatical transposition: "Tenemos buen señor—señor tenemos bueno."

The *Caracas* made an intoxicating drink (comoho) of maguey, similar to Mexican pulque.

RELIGION

Before going to war or making sacrifices to their gods, the *Caracas* dieted for one day, eating only a soup called "mazamorra."

Shamans (piaches) are mentioned, but their practices are not described. They undoubtedly cured by supernatural means, but they also employed various materials remedies, including herbs, of which they had considerable knowledge. Their pharmacopoeia also included roots, which were administered cooked or uncooked and whole or ground, potions made of wood, e.g., guayacán, the fats of animals, birds, and fishes, and certain minerals.

THE TRIBES NORTH OF THE ORINOCO RIVER

By Paul Kirchhoff

INTRODUCTION

On the Venezuelan coast, from the Gulf of Paria to Cape Codera and south practically to the banks of the Orinoco (map 6), there is a series of tribes of an essentially similar culture. There are, however, local variations, and these are most striking between the damp coastal forest peoples and the dwellers of the more open country to the south. The inhabitants of the islands of Trinidad, Cubagua, and Margarita are considered as part of this culture area.

All tribes, with the exception of one town on the eastern fringe of the area, Aruacay, probably *Arawakan,* belong to the *Cariban* family. The main tribes were the *Pariagoto, Cumanagoto, Chaima, Palenque* or *Guarine, Core,* and *Tumuza.* "Provinces" mentioned, but not always coinciding with tribal areas, are Aruacay, Paria, Cumaná, Chiribichi, Piritú, Maracapana, Anoantal, Guacharuco, Paripamotú, and Curiana.

Christopher Columbus (1870), his son Ferdinand (1811), Amerigo Vespucci, Oviedo y Valdés (1851–55), Castellanos (1874), and Las Casas (1909) are our most important of the 16th-century sources. The Spanish missionary Ruíz Blanco (1892), of the 17th century, has added the only other important study. Since then the tribes of this area have lost their culture and themselves in the new Mestizo population.

CULTURE

SUBSISTENCE

Farming.—A rather advanced type of horticulture formed the main basis of subsistence. The following plants and trees were cultivated in the area as a whole, but not all of them by every tribe: Maize, bitter and sweet manioc, sweetpotatoes, ají, calabashes, chili peppers, pineapples, some unspecified "greens" and fruit trees, including the guava, guanabana, mamón, guamo, hicaco, hobo, and tuna. Bitter manioc was the staple. The most highly prized of the cultivated trees, which formed a conspicuous feature of *Cumanagoto* villages, was coca (hayo), which was grown for its leaves, not for its fruit. The trees were planted in regular rows and were watered by a system of canals and ditches. An unnamed tree was cultivated for resin, which was used as incense. It is not clear whether the fruit trees were planted and watered in a fashion similar to that applied in the cultivation of the coca. Other plants were not irrigated.

Every year new clearings were made by felling trees and burning off the branches. Fields were cleaned of weeds, but after 2 years it was considered more advantageous to abandon them for new clearings. The Spanish chroniclers praised the neat appearance of native fields. Maize was planted in the soft ground after the rains with the aid of a straight planting stick. Bitter and sweet manioc were planted from small cuttings, preserved fresh in moist places.

Aruacay crops were raised in soil enriched by inundations of the Orinoco.

Cotton seems not to have been cultivated but used only in its wild state.

Collecting wild food.—An apparently large number of wild fruits and roots were collected, especially in times of bad harvests. In the llanos of the interior, various palms were important sources of food. Along the coast and on the islands oysters were collected.

Hunting.—Hunting was an important source of food. The following animals are said to have been eaten: Tapirs, deer, peccaries (saguino), porcupines, anteaters, a kind of skunk (mapurichi), cuchicuchis (araguato), acuris, zapiguas, rabbits, squirrels, three different kinds of rats or mice, lions, jaguars, tortoises, and cachicans. The iguana was eaten in Chiribichi but not in Piritú. Birds hunted were pigeons, turtle doves, quails, partridges, ducks, and certain birds described as being like turkeys and chickens. The young of some other animals, mainly monkeys, were captured and kept as pets.

The only hunting weapon was the bow, with nonpoisonous arrows. Technical details of the bow are not given; it is described as long and straight, lustrous, and neatly carved. In the house the bow was unstrung; the material of which the string was made is not mentioned. Arrows were made of cane tempered in fire, or of wood, with points of stone, the infectuous bones of some fish, or the prong of the sting ray. Quivers are mentioned among the *Palenque*.

In hunting tapirs, after killing the first animal the hunters climbed the nearest tree, from which they shot its fellows, attracted by the moaning of the wounded tapir.

Other devices used in hunting were nets (for birds and small mammals, including the anteater), snares (for small animals), and bird lime. The tortoise was chased out of its hiding place in grassy plains by setting fire to the grass. The iguana was sometimes caught alive—probably to be eaten later. In the llanos animals were encircled by fire, and as many as 400 hunters, stationed at the only exit to the circle, killed them as they attempted to escape.

Amulets were worn for luck in hunting.

Domestic animals.—No source mentions the dog. In Paria, and apparently only there, a kind of turkey was bred. According to Petrus Martyr (Anghiera, 1912), the first Spaniards were given a number of male turkeys killed and ready to be eaten, as well as live ones for breeding purposes. In Curiana at least two kinds of domesticated ducks, or ducklike birds, were known, one of them possibly being the Muscovy duck.

People raised many animals in captivity. When young mammals refused to eat, women would feed them at their breasts.

Fishing.—Hunting was less important than fishing. There is no record of the fish caught. The mention of sharks being eaten by the *Tocuyo,* a tribe far to the west, suggests that they were not eaten within the area under consideration.

For fishing, bows and arrows, multipronged spears, harpoons, basket traps, nets, and hooks were used. At night fish were blinded by torches and killed from canoes with arrows or harpoons.

The most spectacular method was one by which a group of men swam shoreward in a half circle. By making a noise with their hands, one open, the other armed with a staff, they drove great masses of fish to the beach.

Food preparation.—The most common method of preparing food seems to have been to roast it, although undoubtedly other methods existed. Small wild bees were eaten raw, fried, or boiled. Salt and chili pepper were used for flavoring.

The most important foods were liquids—fermented drinks prepared of palms, of fruits, and (possible only among the *Cumanagoto*) of maize. Among the *Aruacay* maize flour was sometimes added to cassava beer to make it stronger.

The natives preserved maize for several months by smoking it, an indispensable technique in this humid climate. They salted fish, whole or in slices; dried it with the aid of fire; roasted it; or boiled it and made it into a paste. Both shrimp and fish were dried and ground into powder, which was taken in cassava wine.

DWELLINGS

In the 17th century, villages were small and were built on high and dry places. Before native culture broke down, they may have been much larger; that of the *Aruacay* on the lower Orinoco for instance, consisted in the 16th century of 200 large houses. Special buildings, used for ceremonies and dances, stood in every village on a central plaza.

Among the *Palenque* and the *Pariagoto* of the interior, villages were fortified with two or three palisades (palenques) of tree trunks. In the older palenques these had taken root again and were closely tied together with lianas. They were provided with loopholes. Castellanos (1874) describes the palenque of the cacique Guaramental, which was situated near the Unare River, as an enormous palisade surrounding a complex of buildings, with streets and plazas. Among its buildings were several storehouses and the cacique's harem of 200 women. Outside the palisade there were storehouses for food, among them one full of maize beer and pineapple wine.

Houses were always round, with a roof of bark, palm leaves, reeds, or straw which reached to the ground. They are described as shaped like a tent or haystack.

In the village of the *Paria* tasteful cotton blankets of various colors with little golden bells on one end were used for interior decoration. Sleeping hammocks, of two types, were tied to the house posts. One type consisted of a well-woven cotton blanket gathered at the two ends, which were decorated with a fringe; the other was netted and (possibly always) was made of agave fiber. Fires were kept burning underneath the hammocks at night. When the mosquitoes became unbearable, people half buried themselves in the ground, covering themselves with branches and grass. Wooden stools of a very black wood were carved with such excellence that they attracted the attention of the Spaniards.

DRESS AND ADORNMENT

There were two basic types of men's dress. *Cumaná, Chiribichi,* and *Curiana* men tied the prepuce to a string; wound it tightly with cotton thread; or, apparently more frequently, covered the penis with a calabash (provided with two little holes and tied to a string around the waist), a shell, or a golden tube. *Aruacay, Paria,* and *Piritú* men wore a cotton breechclout which reached to the knees; it passed between the legs and was tucked in front and back under a string tied around the waist. In one unnamed village close to the Orinoco Delta men wore a small apron in women's fashion.

Girls went naked. Married women wore either aprons, (usually just big enough to cover the sexual organs, but on the Paria coast, reaching halfway down the calf); among the *Cumanagoto* (Oviedo y Valdés, 1851–55) they wore, in men's fashion, a breechclout; or, in some tribes, they wore a garment described by various sources as a kind of shorts. On their breasts women wore tightly fitting plates of an unknown material. (Much farther west, in the North Colombia Lowlands near the Gulf of Urabá, these plates were of gold.) Below and above their knees women wore tight cotton bands.

Men wore their hair long in Trinidad and among the *Piritú,* but short, to about the height of the ears among the *Cumaná* and *Chiribichi.* They removed their beards with small pincers. *Piritú* women wore their hair long.

Men wore strings made of the teeth and claws of animals they had killed, especially jaguars. Men's nose ornaments—rings or half moons—were formerly of gold, but in Ruíz Blanco's time they were made of silver. When Gómara (1552–53) states that *Curiana* men wore golden rings he may refer to nose rings.

Both sexes wore necklaces, bracelets, anklets, and ear ornaments of gold, oyster pearls, coral beads, shells, bones, or clay. On gala occasions women wore a belt consisting of a number of strings of pearls, coral, and other beads, and men wore crowns of feathers or gold, garlands of flowers and shells, golden breastplates (often decorated with pearls and shaped as birds, fish, and other animals), and shell rattles on their legs.

They painted their body with bixa or covered it with resin (carapa), to which, on festive occasions, they glued feathers. The *Cumanagoto* was the only tribe that painted dark circles around the eyes ("alcoholados").

Teeth were blackened by chewing a powder or paste of coca leaves and lime. The lime was prepared by burning shells with a certain wood in a specially excavated hole. The *Cumaná* and *Chiribichi* traded a coca-lime paste far and wide. In other regions coca and lime were kept in separate calabashes and mixed only at the moment of use. According to one source, the natives (men only) chewed coca every day. According to another source, the blackening of the teeth was produced only once, at puberty. At this time young men abstained for several days from eating and drinking in order to allow the coca and lime to produce this effect. Contradictory sources leave doubt whether among the *Curiana,* in the west, the custom of blackened teeth prevailed, or whether, on the contrary, teeth were whitened by chewing some unknown substance.

A frontooccipital deformation was produced with the aid of two cushions made of cotton.

TRANSPORTATION AND TRADE

Canoes were made of hollowed-out tree trunks. When traveling by canoe, one man sitting in the bow sang to set the rhythm for the crew.

Chiefs were carried in litters.

Buyers of coca and fish came from distant areas to the coastal area of the *Chiribichi* and *Cumaná,* bringing maize, slaves, and guanin necklaces. The Araya Peninsula was a salt-producing center; the salt was traded in the form of bricks.

The *Curiana* obtained gold, in exchange for pearls, from a country 6 days' travel to the west, called Cauchieta. This region has not yet been located, but we know that it had a somewhat divergent culture (e.g., headhunting).[1] According to Gómara (1552–53), the *Curiana* used

---

[1] According to Petrus Martyr (Anghiera 1912), however, the *Curiana* were headhunters.

scales and weights in goldwork, but it seems more likely that these data refer to the people of Cauchieta.[2]

SOCIAL ORGANIZATION

Marriage.—There was no special esteem for virginity, although young girls are said not to have been promiscuous. On the other hand, girls (and perhaps also married women) frequently offered themselves to the Spaniards.

In most places only headmen and chiefs had many wives. The wives either lived together in one big house (*Cumaná*) or each had a special hut (*Piritú*). The chief, Guaramental, had a big harem composed of 200 women, sent to him from many different countries.

Widows were inherited by the dead man's brother. Older men often reared young girls in order to marry them later on. Marriage among cross-cousins seems to have been frequent.

For the wedding, bridegroom and bride dressed in all their ornaments; necklaces of stone beads are specially mentioned, and a young couple that had none would borrow them from their neighbors. Women guests brought food; men brought building materials and constructed a house for the young couple. According to one source, however, the bridegroom was obliged to build the house and prepare a field for his wife.

At the marriage ceremony the bridegroom and bride sat outside the new house, the former surrounded by dancing young men, the latter by dancing girls. A man cut the bridegroom's hair, and a women the bride's. Then the bride was handed over to the bridegroom, but she had to sleep the first night with the shaman.

A young husband served his father-in-law for 1 year.

Not only at meal time but also in all the ordinary occupations both sexes were systematically separated. Homosexual relations among men are said to have been very frequent and to have been publicly condoned.

Division of labor.—Men hunted, fished, and went to war. The *Cumaná* not only felled the trees and generally prepared the new fields but also did the sowing and weeding. This left to the women only the harvesting in which the men also helped. Among the *Aruacay,* however, women also planted the crops.

Men made wooden stools, baskets (including basketry traps for fishing), ropes, nets, hammocks of agave fiber, and weapons.

Women, in addition to raising the children, preparing the meals, and harvesting the fields, spun and wove cotton and made pottery. They also went to war with their husbands, handling bows and arrows as expertly as the men.

---

[2] In western Colombia, as far east as the *Pacabuey,* scales and weights were used.

Etiquette.—Visitors did not enter the house or speak to the women. Upon their arrival, food and drinks were at once brought out to them, and they were put up in a special hut. It was customary to offer one's wife to a guest who stayed overnight. In *Aruacay* women often followed the guest on his departure, and if she stayed with her husband, he was considered to be under special obligation toward her for not having gone away with the guest.

POLITICAL ORGANIZATION

Everywhere old men were highly respected, and young men would not sit down in their presence.

Chiefs seem to have been both elective and hereditary. In the village of the *Paria* there was a principal chief ("king") and five subchiefs. All of them were called "chiaconus" and were elected for a year. Among the *Piritú* the chieftainship was hereditary, descending to the eldest son. In one part of Trinidad the chief was succeeded by his nephew; whether brother or sister's son is not stated. The *Aruacay* had a principal chief and nine subchiefs, each of whom governed a barrio. The principal chief was distinguished by a beard.

Considerable pomp and ceremony surrounded some of the leading chiefs. Guaramental was carried in a litter of black wood, which was carved with animal figures and adorned with gold plaques. Ordinary people were not permitted to enter his palenque. His decrees were promulgated from the top of an artificial mound. He also possessed a harem, which was guarded by eunuchs, an institution not reported often in South America.

Generally, a chief's power was based on having a big family, possessing much gold and many canoes, being able to point to great deeds of his people and his forefathers, and having magical power. Often a man was both chief and shaman.

In most of the area chiefs seem not to have intervened in disputes of their people or to have punished crimes. Justice lay in the hands of the offended. For example, in cases of adultery, the husband punished the trespassing lover but not the wife. Certain chiefs, however, such as Guaramental and the chief of Anoantal, wielded great authority. In Anoantal a man who fished without the chief's permission was killed and eaten. Guaramental was surrounded by a group of elderly councillors who were also judges and who directed various henchmen. Gallows, for executions, are mentioned.

Slaves seem to have been common in the whole area and were traded or presented as gifts by one chief to another.

Fruit orchards were protected by a cotton thread or thin liana tied around them; trespassers, it was thought, would be struck by immediate death. Among the *Piritú* people inherited any part of a dead man's property by being the first to lay their hands on it.

LIFE CYCLE

Birth.—A woman gave birth without anyone's help. For a difficult delivery she went into the bush. The mother bathed herself and the newly born child in the river. During the first few days the father did not go to the bush to fell trees, lest the child be harmed and die. Small children were carried in a cotton sling. They were never punished, since otherwise they would die.

Puberty.—At puberty girls were secluded for 2 years in a dark compartment. During this time their hair must not be cut. At every menstruation a woman was confined and fasted for a few days.

Death.—People who were seriously ill were abandoned in the bush with a provision of bread and water.

The *Cumaná* dried the bodies of the dead on a barbracot over a fire fed with special herbs. The fat dripping from them was collected and the bones ground into a powder. The powder and fat were drunk by those present. Among the *Chiribichi,* the bodies of men and women of high social standing were desiccated and hung up in the house. A more common procedure, however, was to bury the dead (*Piritú,* after roasting them), outside of the house, in a seated position. Weapons, other belongings, and food and drinks were placed in the grave. The burial celebration lasted 8 days. The house in which a death had taken place was abandoned. After a year the body was dug up and the bones burnt. Among the *Cumaná* and *Chiribichi* the skull was given to the dead man's principal wife. *Piritú* burned the bones jointly for many dead, and threw the ashes into the air. Rain clouds were believed to be formed by them. The participants in this anniversary ceremony pulled their hair, then grabbed their feet with their hands, put their heads between their knees, and danced around in this position. Afterward they lay down on their backs with arms and legs stretched skyward, weeping and moaning.

The *Aruacay* buried the body inside the hut in a kind of tomb built of clay over a framework of posts, with a clay figure on top representing some deity. Cassava bread and a calabash of cassava beer were placed in the grave. Some time later a ceremony was held in commemoration of the dead, but it is not known whether the bones were burned.

The daily round.—People got up and went to bed early. They never started out for the fields before the day had warmed up. At dawn and sunset the people of the village greeted each other singing and playing various instruments. At night a guard stood on the roof of the highest hut and shouted at certain intervals, being answered by guards in other villages. This was done because of fear of night attacks by some enemy. Whenever one had to walk outside of the villages at night he carried a torch for fear of wild animals.

People bathed daily during the hot season before daybreak, and during the rainy season after sunset.

They squatted on their heels or sat cross-legged, although the latter position may have been used only in a certain ceremony.

A *Cumaná* chief desiring military allies sent one of his own arrows by messenger, and whoever accepted it thereby bound himself to take part in the war. A *Piritú* messenger shot the arrow into the midst of the village; the headman picked it up and shot it if he agreed to the alliance.

Weapons of warfare were bows and poisonous arrows which were kept in quivers (some men wore two quivers) and were provided with points of flint, sting ray spines, or shark's teeth. In addition, clubs of two types and large spears of fire-hardened palm wood were used. The *Aruacay* and the natives of Trinidad had shields, and in the former place a special helmet. Spear throwers seem to have been used only in Trinidad.

Before going to war people first tried to foresee the future by taking tobacco and coca, and then they became drunk.

Warriors everywhere wore showy headdresses. In Trinidad they painted themselves red and black from head to heel and wore a great variety of ornaments, including necklaces of human teeth, eagle-shaped gold breastplates, and jaguar tails. Some of the most distinguished warriors were clad in puma or bear skins, with the animal's mouth placed over the head.

Little boys practiced shooting with the bow, using arrows with blunt points of clay, wood, or wax. Women were as expert with the bow and arrow as their husbands and went to war with them.

The erecting of defense works was part of the art of warfare in Trinidad. The palisaded villages of some of the interior tribes have already been described. That of the chief Guaramental contained, in addition to other buildings, an arsenal filled with bows and arrows for 10,000 warriors, and others with a similar number of darts, lances, clubs, and slings. Six hundred young warriors at a time patrolled the palisaded area.

In an unknown place, quite some distance up the Orinoco, the Spaniards met a war party of a little over 70 men, traveling in orderly formation and carrying shell trumpets. Before them went two young men who carried bowls full of burning fire into which they threw pulverized chili pepper, so that the fumes were driven by the wind toward the Spaniards' camp. These people, however, may not have belonged to this culture area, since their war arrows were not poisoned.

The arrow poison was prepared among the *Cumaná* and *Chiribichi* by old women during a 2-day period. Gómara (1552–53) distinguishes between a "simple" kind and a "bad one." The former consisted of the blood of a certain snake (áspide), certain herbs, and the juice of the manzanillo tree. The "bad kind" is described as differing only in the addition of the heads of poisonous ants. If, after 2 or 3 days, the old women who cooked the poison had died, or at least fainted, the poison was praised; if not, they were scolded and the poison was thrown away. The death produced by this poison was not instantaneous; as an antidote the natives used the tail of a snake (Ruíz Blanco, 1892).

To eat slain enemies was a common procedure among the *Cumanagoto* and *Palenque* but seems not to have been a general practice in this area. Few data are available, but the cannibalism cannot have been highly developed. The only precise data refer to Cubagua Island, where human flesh was prepared in vessels that might not be used for any other purpose and was eaten only by certain persons, always outside of the house. According to Castellanos (1874), the inhabitants of this island did not enjoy eating human flesh; on the contrary, "it caused them much grief."

ESTHETIC AND RECREATIONAL ACTIVITIES

Dances.—Various kinds of dances were known. In the most common, people danced in a circle with clasped hands. When they dropped something they picked it up with their feet without unclasping their hands.

Musical instruments.—Wooden drums with a carved figure at each end, calabash drums, cane or deer-bone flutes, very large trumpets, and trumpets made of two calabashes were the musical instruments used. A unique reference speaks of a shell over the opening of which strings had been tied (Petrus Martyr, 1912). Shell rattles were reserved for shamans.

Drinking bouts.—Drinking bouts lasted up to 8 days. Men and young girls were the main participants. When drunk, older women cared for them. Men often became so drunk that they insulted each other and fought. Participants produced vomiting by taking certain herbs in order to be able to drink more.

There was a ceremonial way of drinking in which a man received a cup from a woman and then passed it on to all others.

People invited to a drinking bout arrived dancing and singing at the hut of the chief, who had had the road leading to it carefully cleaned of weeds and sometimes widened. Here they staged a sham battle and then entered the chief's hut, everyone dancing in imitation of a certain kind of animal. Then the singing ceased and one of the party made a speech in honor of the host.

The *Aruacay* performed an interesting ceremony. In the midst of about 150 big pots full of cassava beer, 2 still bigger vessels were placed. These had attached handles large enough to support a person. Two Indians stood on these handles, 1 of whom started bragging while the other 1 denied the truth of what he claimed and challenged him to resist 6 heavy blows with a whip made of lianas. If the first man could not withstand them another man took his place, and so on.

Tobacco.—Men inhaled tobacco smoke through their noses.

RELIGION

Major deities.—Sun and moon, considered husband and wife, seem to have been the supreme deities. Thunder and lightning were believed to be caused by the sun's anger. A lunar eclipse was also thought to be caused by the angry sun having wounded the moon. Sad songs about the latter's disappearance were sung. The *Cumaná* and *Chiribichi*, especially the women, fasted to ward off the danger to the moon. In addition, married women fought, scratched their bodies and pulled hair while young girls drew blood from their arms with pointed fishbones. No amusements were allowed during the lunar eclipse. The reappearance of the moon was greeted with shouting and merrymaking. All foods or drinks prepared before the eclipse had to be thrown into the sea or river. The *Piritú* took up weapons to defend the sun and moon. They threw maize toward them to placate them, and they promised to mend their ways and work hard, actually going to their fields to work.

Comets were thought to have an evil meaning; people tried to frighten them away by shouting, blowing on their trumpets, and beating their drums.

The *Piritú* believed that frogs were the representatives of the rain god. They were kept in the house under a bowl and were scolded when it did not rain.

An unusual feature was the use of the St. Andrew's cross, simple or enclosed in a square, to drive away spirits that roam about at night. This symbol was painted on newborn children.

The afterworld.—At death, a person's soul separated from the body. Some souls went to live in the deceased's fields, but the majority left for a lake called "Machira," where big snakes swallowed them and took them to a place of eternal dancing and merrymaking.

Ceremonies and miscellaneous beliefs.—On a certain day every year the *Piritú* held a ceremony at which people ate a roasted deer while standing and holding weapons in their hands. At another ceremony dancers carried fish representations carved out of wood.

When a hunter came home his wife put a drink of maize beer into the mouth of an animal he had slain so that its soul might tell the other animals how well it had been treated. Offerings of first fruits and of fresh fish together with strings of pearls, coral, or shell beads were made to the earth and ocean.

Whoever killed another person had to cleanse himself by fasting.

A newly arrived guest was not spoken to at once, in order to give his soul time to arrive.

SHAMANISM AND SORCERY

The shaman (piacheor piazamo) was the most important person in every settlement. Often a man became the headman of the village because he was such a powerful shaman. People would rise in the presence of shamans and were said to have treated them like gods.

As candidates, fathers selected those of their sons whom they considered predestined to become shamans. The boys, 10 to 12 years old, had to live for 2 years secluded in caves or in special huts in the bush, where they ate no meat, saw no other human beings, and did not think of women. The old shamans visited them at night and, while special guards watched the camp, taught them the magic formulae and curing methods.

Shamans wore a head band, bead bracelets, and thin plates of shell and carried one calabash filled with coca and another containing lime and a stick ending in a little monkey figurine, "which they say is their god" (Ruíz Blanco, 1892).

Shamans would never cure relatives, and, in general, men from distant regions were preferred. Shamans led a life all their own. They had their special ceremonies, and even when they went to some general festivity they kept apart from other people. They tried to renew their magic strength by getting drunk and by inhaling tobacco smoke and incense.

Some shamans transformed themselves into jaguars and other dreaded animals. They caused an enemy to fall sick by burying little figures of lizards or other animals along the trails he frequented or by poisoning him.

To cure slight sickness the shaman took certain herbs into his mouth, licked the patient, and pretended to suck the sickness-causing substance out, and then left the house with his cheeks inflated to show that he was carrying it away. In more serious cases, when the sick person was thought to be possessed by malignant spirits (iboroquiamo, in *Piritú*), the shaman first tried to call these spirits and pull them out of the body through the joints. When that failed he took a stick made of a special wood, which only he knew and which he had meanwhile placed in a bowlful of water, and forced it down the patient's throat until he vomited. The evil spirit was thereby believed to pass into the body of the shaman, who fell upon the ground, sweating, shaking, and screaming for 2 hours or more until completely exhausted. In this state he vomited a blackish substance surrounded by a mass of mucus. While the shaman was lying half dead on the ground, the relatives of the sick person took this blackish substance out of the surrounding mucus and threw it far away from the house, saying, "Go away spirit!" If the patient fell sick again the performance was not repeated, but herbal remedies were applied. Certain diseases were cured exclusively, or mainly, with raw, cooked, or ground herbs and roots and with the fat of certain birds, fish, and other animals. Immediately after the cure the shaman was asked the amount of his fee. If the patient died the shaman was killed.

Another function of the shaman was to foresee the future. On the request of a headman a shaman was taken at night either to a cave or into a secret chamber of the ceremonial hut that belonged to every village. Seated on a stool, he called a spirit with his rattle and with special invocations.   When this spirit appeared, the headman's representatives questioned the shaman about fishing, selling, good or bad harvests, eclipses, and comets.   Some shamans are said to have been able to predict lunar eclipses 3 months in advance.   For these consultations the shamans were also paid.

LORE AND LEARNING

The year was known to have been divided into lunar months.

In the field of practical therapy, the Indians bandaged their whole body tightly to counteract high blood pressure.

PART 3. THE WEST INDIES

THE WEST INDIES: AN INTRODUCTION

By IRVING ROUSE

The islands of the West Indies, stretching in a great arc between North, Central, and South America, fall into four groups: The Bahamas, a series of small coral islands southeast of Florida; the Greater Antilles, large mountainous land masses extending 1,000 miles (1,609 km.) eastward from Florida and Yucatán; the Lesser Antilles, tiny volcanic islands curving southward 800 miles (1,287 km.) from the last of the Greater Antilles to the coast of South America; and the three islands of Trinidad, Tobago, and Barbados, remnants of an ancient land mass that formerly lay just off the mouth of the Orinoco River (map 1; map 8).

The Greater Antilles are the most populous of these four groups. They consist of four large islands: Cuba, at the mouth of the Gulf of Mexico (pls. 80, 81, 82); Jamaica, south of the eastern end of Cuba; Hispaniola (divided between the Republic of Haiti and the Dominican Republic) (pl. 79), just east of Cuba; and Puerto Rico (pl. 83, *bottom*) east of Hispaniola. In the time of Columbus these islands were inhabited mainly by relatively peaceful Indians who spoke an *Arawakan* language and who had a single type of culture, characterized by agriculture, permanent villages, a well-developed aristocracy, an emphasis upon songs, dances, and ceremonies, and the worship of images known as "zemis." It is customary to call these Indians *Arawak,* after their language (map 8).[1]

The *Arawak,* although occupying the bulk of the Greater Antilles, were not the only Indians there at the time of the Conquest. In the extreme western part of Cuba, on the small group of keys off the north and south coast of that island which are known as Los Jardines de los Reyes, and on the long narrow peninsula of Guaicayarima, which forms the southwestern part of Haiti, the Spaniards encountered a more primitive population who lived in caves or open camps rather than permanent villages; obtained their food by hunting, fishing, and collecting rather than agriculture; and seem to have lacked the aristocratic and ceremonial aspects

---

[1] This term seems to have been introduced by Brinton (1871). The name *Taino* is sometimes used as a substitute, although it ordinarily is given a more specific meaning (see footnote 9, p. 521). To distinguish the *Arawak* in the West Indies from those on the mainland, Lovén (1935, p. 41) and others use the term "Island *Arawak*" or "Insular *Arawak*."

of *Arawak* civilization. Since the *Arawak* interpreters who accompanied Columbus and later explorers of Cuba were unable to understand these people, it has been inferred that they spoke a language other than *Arawak*.[2] No trace of this language has survived, but it is often given the same name as that of the people themselves: *Ciboney*.[3]

In historic times the limits of the *Ciboney* territory do not seem to have extended beyond the Greater Antilles. In the Bahamas were only *Arawak,* similar in language and culture to those of the Greater Antilles. The Trinidad-Tobago-Barbados group also contained mainly *Arawak* who, however, were somewhat different in language and culture from those of the Greater Antilles.[4] The Lesser Antilles, on the other hand, were inhabited by a third group of people, the *Carib*.[5]

The *Carib* language and culture, which have been given the same name as the people themselves, differ from those of the *Arawak* and the *Ciboney.* The *Carib* relied more upon fishing than upon agriculture; their villages were only semipermanent; they had more elaborate canoes; placed greater emphasis upon warfare, choosing their leaders by prowess in fighting rather than by inheritance; lacked elaborate ceremonies; had no worship of idols; and were cannibals. Periodically they conducted raids upon their more peaceful *Arawak* neighbors in Trinidad, along the Guiana coast of South America, and as far northwest as Cuba and the Bahamas in the Greater Antilles. It is said that they were gradually encroaching upon the territories of the *Arawak;* by the time of Columbus they had taken over the northwestern part of Trinidad and may have secured a foothold in eastern Puerto Rico.

---

[2] It is also possible, as implied by Stirling (1936, p. 335), that the people spoke a "primitive" form of *Arawak.*

[3] This term originated with Las Casas (*in* Fernández Duro et al., 1885–1932, vol. 6, pp. 7–8), who applied it to one of the two Cuban Indian groups which seem to have been non-*Arawak* at the time of historic contact. Harrington (1921, pp. 21–22) is responsible for expanding its meaning to include all of the non-*Arawak,* and he is followed here. Lovén (1935, p. 2) prefers to substitute the name *Guanahatabey,* which Las Casas (op. cit.) used for the other group of non-*Arawak* in Cuba. Pichardo Moya (1944, pp. 543–544) employs both terms, applying them to different non-*Arawak* cultures, as described in note 10 below. Ortiz Fernández (1943, pp. 5–6) uses the names *Guanahatabey* and *Aunabey* for these two cultures, shifting the term *Ciboney* to what is here called the sub-*Taino* group of *Arawak.* (See footnotes 6, p. 500, and 10, p. 521.)

[4] Some authorities believe that Tobago and Barbados had become depopulated by historic times (Fewkes, 1922, pp. 79–80).

[5] This is the name by which the *Carib* distinguished themselves from the *Arawak.* The linguistic usage of the name, and its extension to Indians of the mainland who speak *Carib* languages, are secondary. Because of the latter, the island people are now often called "Insular *Carib.*"

THE CIBONEY

By Irving Rouse[1]

INTRODUCTION

The three linguistic-cultural groups in the West Indies—*Ciboney, Arawak,* and *Carib*—may be conveniently discussed in that order, since that is roughly their distribution at the time of historic contact, going through the islands from North to South America. Moreover, it seems to be the order in which the three groups arrived in the Antilles.

That the *Ciboney* were the original inhabitants of the West Indies is suggested by their peripheral position during historic times (map 8). It is also indicated by the archeology, for traces of a preagricultural hunting and fishing population have been found throughout Cuba and in many parts of Haiti besides the peninsula of Guaicayarima, apparently at an earlier date than the *Arawak* population wherever the two happen to overlap (tables 1, 2.). There is little doubt that the *Ciboney* were more widely distributed during prehistoric than historic times and that they were pushed back into their historic position as a result of the advent of the more advanced *Arawak* and *Carib*.

It is commonly assumed that the *Ciboney* came into the West Indies from Florida.[2] Not only do they appear to have been limited during historic times to the parts of the Greater Antilles adjacent to Florida, but also no sure archeological traces of the *Ciboney* have as yet been found elsewhere in the West Indies. Some *Ciboney* artifacts do have resemblances with the Lesser Antilles rather than with Florida, but these may be the result of *Arawak* influence.[3]

ARCHEOLOGY

Although the number of known *Ciboney* archeological sites is large, particularly in Cuba, they are quite similar in type. Most are located near the shore, either along bays and streams or in other areas sheltered from the full force of the sea. Except for several cave burials in Cuba, all the sites are places of habitation, there being no ceremonial structures.

---

[1] Except for section on ethnography, as noted.

[2] Cosculluela (1922, p. 9) seems to have been the first to make the assumption, and it is generally held in the West Indian field today. Many Florida archeologists, on the other hand, follow Harrington (1921, pp. 422–425) in deriving the *Ciboney* from South America.

[3] In general, the stone artifacts, from *Ciboney* sites have the most resemblances with the Lesser Antilles (Rouse, 1947), while the shell artifacts are more like those of Florida (Osgood, 1942 a, pp. 39–45).

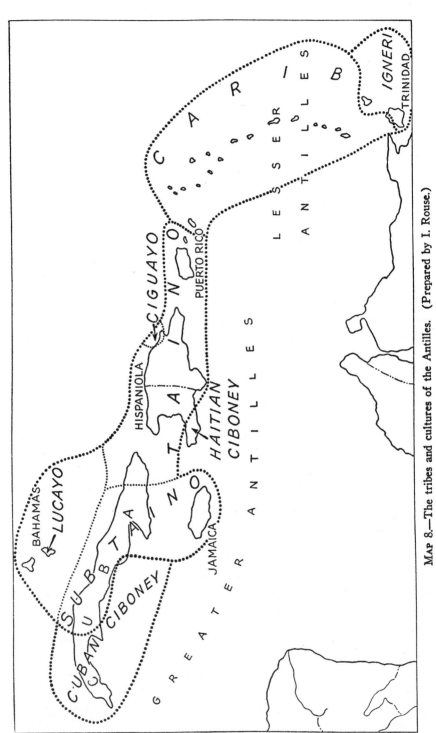

MAP 8.—The tribes and cultures of the Antilles. (Prepared by I. Rouse.)

Each site consists of a single heap of refuse (often called a "caney") containing shells, animal bones, artifacts, and in many cases burials. The largest of these middens are in swamps, but they occur also in smaller size in the open, on tiny islets offshore, and in caves—usually in areas favorable for hunting, fishing, and the gathering of shell food but not suitable for agriculture. One group of pile dwellings is known from Cuba (Harrington, 1921, pp. 76–79).

Ciboney burials have so far been found only in Cuba. As summarized by Royo Guardia (1940 a, pp. 39–42), the burial practices included inhumation, both primary and secondary, and cremation, either in the open or in caves. Most burials were in refuse, but several have been found instead in sterile soil in caves or sinkholes. At one site the bones were protected by stone slabs; at another they had been stained red with ocher. Only two of the burials known to the writer contained grave objects, and these were not ornaments or utensils; in each case one or more stone balls accompanied the body. In all *Ciboney* burials the skulls lack the deformation practiced by the *Arawak* and the *Carib*.

So far as artifacts are concerned, certain negative data characterize all *Ciboney* sites. Pottery is never present,[4] nor are the griddles on which the *Arawak* used to bake cassava. Except in a few sites, which seem to have been under *Arawak* influence, no traces have been found in the *Ciboney* sites of the elaborate ceremonial apparatus of the *Arawak*, such as bone spatulas for inducing vomiting, shell masks, and representations in stone, bone, and shell of the anthropomorphic deities which the *Arawak* called "zemis."

CULTURE SEQUENCES

Except for these negative characteristics, the artifacts found in the *Ciboney* sites vary from place to place, making it possible to formulate a series of different types of *Ciboney* culture (table 2).

Cuban Ciboney.—In the Cuban sites shell artifacts are the most characteristic. Gouges, made from the outer whorl of the conch, occur everywhere; there are also cuplike artifacts cut from the same type of shell, lips and tips from that shell, and plates consisting of the outer whorl of the shell (pl. 84, *l–o, q–s*). Hammerstones (pl. 84, *e–h*), many of them pitted, are common. Ornaments include crude stone pendants (pl. 84, *j*), made by drilling pebbles, and beads of bone and shell. No examples of art have yet been found.[5]

Divisions of Cuban Ciboney.—Cuban archeologists have tentatively established the existence of two different types of *Ciboney* culture in their

[4] The few pottery-bearing sites which Harrington (1921, pp. 177–181, 273–276, 308, 311–316) called *Ciboney* have since been shown to be *Arawak* (Rouse, 1942, pp. 161–163).

[5] Certain objects incised with geometric designs (Harrington, 1921, pp. 348–355, 398–399) and a group of painted pictographs (Herrera Fritot, 1939, pls. 1–3) may be *Ciboney*, but the identification is uncertain.

country, which have been termed the Caya Redondo and the Guayabo Blanco (Rouse, 1942, pp. 160–163).[6] In addition to the types of artifacts enumerated above, the former is characterized by stone balls and disks (pl. 84, *i, k*), peg-shaped ceremonial stones (pl. 84, *d*) called "gladiolitos," hammer grinders, and other evidences of stone-grinding and polishing, whereas the latter had only the battering of stone, as evidenced by the ubiquitous hammerstone. In addition, the Guayabo Blanco culture is characterized by a type of deep vessel made from the conch which is absent from the Cayo Rendondo culture.

Haitian Ciboney.—Most of the above types of shell artifacts are not present in the Haitian sites, the emphasis there being upon stonework. Large single- and double-bitted stone axes take the place of the shell gouge, and there are also hammer grinders, milling stones, stone balls, stone dishes, and gladiolitos, some of them engraved with complicated geometric designs (pl. 85). Rechipped flint blades, having the form of daggers, knives, and scrapers, are common.

The Haitian sites fall into three groups, Couri in the northern part of the country, Cabaret in the center, and Bay of Conch in the south.[7] The Couri sites have yielded all the artifacts listed in the preceding paragraph and in addition a stone knife, a shell chisel, a stone bead, and pendants of stone and shell engraved with straight parallel-line designs (Rouse, 1941, pp. 24–52). In the Cabaret sites have so far been found only daggers, knives, and scrapers of flint (Bastien, 1944). The Bay of Conch sites, finally, have yielded artifacts of the types listed in the previous paragraph and also pointed stones used for smoothing and polishing, mortars and pestles, and single-butted, eared stone axes, one of which is decorated with a complicated spiral design (Krieger, personal communication; Rouse, 1947).

Other West Indian nonpottery sites.—There are four other groups of nonpottery sites in the West Indies, which cannot as yet be definitely identified as *Ciboney.* Gabb (1881, pp. 146–147) and Krieger (1929, pp. 5–6) have each excavated an apparently preagricultural stratum underlying an *Arawak* one in caves near Samaná Bay in the northern part of the Dominican Republic. These strata contained crude unworked stone knives, hammerstones, and other artifacts of stone and shell which have not yet been described. Rouse (1945) has located another group of nonpottery sites in Puerto Rico, named Coroso. These sites are small shell heaps containing only irregular hammerstones, several possible milling and sharpening stones, flint chips, pieces of coral, plain and fractured shell tips, and

---

[6] Alternatives for the term Cayo Redondo, as used here, include *Ciboney* (Pichardo Moya, 1944) and *Guanajatabey* (Ortiz Fernández, 1943). In place of Guayabo Blanco are used Aunabey (Ortiz Fernández, 1943), *Ciboney* (Harrington, 1921), and *Guanajatabey* (Pichardo Moya, 1944). Many Cuban archeologists do not agree with the identification of the Cayo Redondo culture as *Ciboney* (in the sense in which that term is used in this article). Instead, they consider that the Cayo Redondo culture represents a separate ethnic group, comparable to the *Ciboney, Arawak,* and *Carib* (Royo Guardia, Morales Coelló, and Herrera Fritot, 1942; Pichardo Moya, 1944).

[7] An alternative name for the Couri group is "Flint" (Rainey, 1941).

PLATE 79.—**Landscapes of Hispaniola.** *Top:* Mountain forests of the Dominican Republic along the Santiago-Puerto Plata highway. (Courtesy Jacob Gayer and the National Geographic Magazine.) *Bottom* (*left*): The lower Yuna River, Dominican Republic. (*Bottom right*): The Savanne Diane east of St. Michel, Haiti. (Courtesy Alexander Wetmore.)

PLATE 80.—**Cuban landscapes.** *Top:* Savanna country of western Cuba. (Cour-
tesy H. H. Bennett by permission of the American Geographical Society.)
Bottom: Scene along road from Havana to Guanajay. (Courtesy Theodor
De Booy by permission of the American Geographical Society.)

PLATE 81.—The Maniabon hills, Cuba. (After Rouse, 1942, pl. 1.)

PLATE 82.—**Cuban landscapes.** *Top (left)*: Desert vegetation, Cape Maisi. *Top (right)*: Mouth of Bat Cave, near Pontales de Guane, Pinar del Rio. *Bottom (left)*: Mountain formations, near Vinales, Pinar del Rio. *Bottom (right)*: Tropical vegetation near mouth of Jauco River. (After Harrington, 1921, pls. 20, 40, 106, 18.)

PLATE 83.—**Antillean landscapes.** *Top:* St. Thomas harbor from a hill east of Charlotte Amalia. *Center:* Old saltponds, Mathew-Town, Island of Inagua, Bahamas. *Bottom:* Beach at Joyuda, Puerto Rico. (Courtesy Theodor De Booy by permission of the American Geographical Society.)

PLATE 84.—**Ciboney artifacts from Cuba.** *a,* Flint chips; *b,* coral rasp; *c,* stone mortar; *d,* ceremonial stone; *e,* irregular hammerstone; *f,* cubical hammerstone; *g,* discoidal hammerstone; *h,* rectangular hammerstone; *i,* stone ball; *j,* stone pendant; *k,* stone disk; *l,* shell gouge; *m,* shell cup; *n,* shell plate; *o,* shell pendant (?); *p,* milling stone; *q,* fractured shell tip; *r,* plain shell tip; *s,* shell lip. (Sizes very approximate: *c,* ⅛; *d* and *n,* ½; *f, k,* and *l,* ¼; *i,* ⅓; *j,* ⅕; all others, ⅖.) (*c, d,* and *m,* After Osgood, 1942 a, pls. 4 D, 6 E, and 3 F; others after Rouse, 1942, pl. 2.)

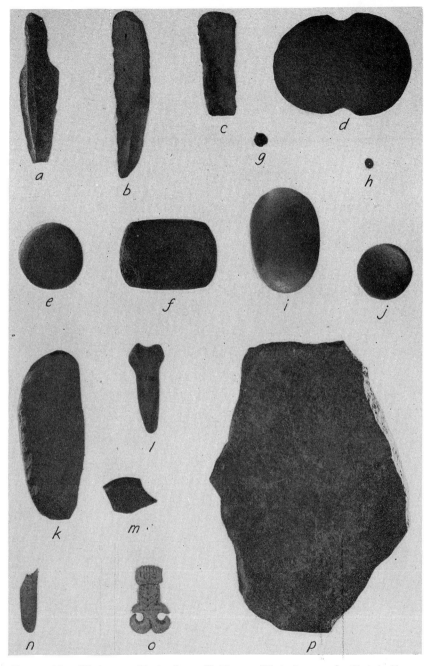

PLATE 85.—**Ciboney artifacts from Haiti.** *a,* Flint dagger; *b,* flint knife; *c,* flint scraper; *d,* double-bitted stone ax; *e,* irregular hammer-grinder; *f,* rectangular hammer-grinder; *g,* spherical stone pendant; *h,* stone bead; *i,* irregular hammer-grinder; *j,* stone ball; *k,* stone knife; *l,* ceremonial stone; *m,* fragment of a stone disk; *n,* shell chisel; *o,* shell pendant; *p,* milling stone. (All approximately ¼ actual size.) (After Rouse, 1941, pl. 1.)

shell plates. Hatt (1924, p. 31) has excavated comparable shell heaps at Krum Bay, St. Thomas, Virgin Islands, finding only long rectangular stone adzes, red ocher, scrapers made of clamshell, and a few surface potsherds. In Trinidad, finally, J. C. Carter (personal communication) has found only crude flint ships in the Savanetta site near Claxton Bay.[8]

Middle American contacts.—Because of the closeness of the *Ciboney* territory in western Cuba to Yucatán, several archeologists have searched there for remains of the *Maya*. Ries (1936) reports the discovery of two *Maya* sherds and a perfect obsidian blade, found on the end of the Peninsula of Guanahacabibes, the westernmost in Cuba. Although there are numerous *Ciboney* sites in the vicinity, these specimens were obtained on the surface and were not in association with any other Indian remains. A few metates and other carved stone objects of Central American types have also been found in Cuba and in the other islands of the Greater Antilles (e.g., Joyce, 1916, fig. 58), but these were probably introduced after the Conquest by Indian slaves from Central America.

Extinct faunal associations.—A number of *Ciboney* sites in Cuba have yielded bones of an extinct form of the ground sloth (*Megalocnus* sp.), comparable to those which in North America have been considered an indication of great antiquity. There can be no such antiquity in Cuba, both because the *Ciboney* are known to have survived into historic times and because some bones of the ground sloth have been obtained from the early *Arawak* sites (Harrington, 1921, p. 274). Nevertheless, a study of the distribution of the bones of the ground sloth in *Ciboney* sites might provide a good basis for the establishment of a chronology.[9] So far, it has been possible to show only by seriation that the *Ciboney* were earlier than the *Arawak* in the areas in which both occur (table 1).

HISTORY

When the Spaniards first arrived in Cuba they were told that the *Arawak* had taken away the most of the island from the *Ciboney*, enslaving the latter or driving them into isolated sections of the central and western parts of the island. The Spaniards mention five "provinces," or chieftainships, in the west, named from west to east Guanahacabibes, Guaniguanico, Marien, Habana, and Hanábana (map 9). It is not clear whether any or all of these were *Ciboney* at the time of the Conquest; the names are *Arawak* but only *Ciboney* sites have so far been found in these provinces.[10]

---

[8] The last three of these groups of sites, instead of representing separate cultures, may be secondary sites of the *Arawak*. Those in Puerto Rico and the Virgin Islands could have been places for opening shellfish; the Trinidad site, a flint-gathering locality.

[9] Another possibility would be to classify the sites according to the presence or absence of *Arawak* influences.

[10] Ortiz Fernández (1935, pp. 368–416) concludes that the *Ciboney* were still in possession of all the western provinces at the time of first historic contact. García Valdés (1930, 1936–37) argues on the contrary that the *Arawak* had driven the *Ciboney* out of all this territory except for the most inaccessible regions. Extensive archeological research in the western part of the island is needed to settle this controversy.

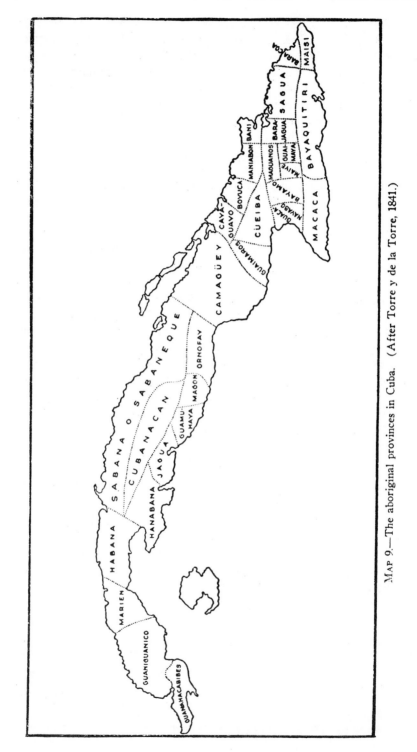

Map 9.—The aboriginal provinces in Cuba. (After Torre y de la Torre, 1841.)

In Haiti the bulk of the population was also *Arawak,* but there were said to be isolated groups of *Ciboney*-like Indians living on the long narrow Peninsula of Guaicayarima in the southwestern part of the island. As in Cuba, these Indians are supposed to have been driven into this peripheral position as a result of the *Arawak* migrations from South America.

With the exception of the province of Habana in Cuba (which may not have been *Ciboney*), the Spaniards rarely visited the inaccessible regions occupied by the *Ciboney.* The fate of those Indians is, consequently, unknown, except in the extreme western part of Cuba, where some are said to have survived until the Spaniards colonized that part of the island at the beginning of the 17th century. At that time the Indians attacked the cattle of the settlers with bows and arrows, and rewards had to be offered for their extermination. There are traditions that some of them survived until the middle of the 19th century.

SOURCES

The historical sources contain few references to the *Ciboney.* Isolated statements have been published by Gómara (1749), Las Casas (n. d.), Anghiera (1912), Oviedo y Valdés (1851–55), Torres de Mendoza (1864–84), and others. These sources have been summarized by Cosculluela (1922, pp. 8–9, 21–22), Fewkes (1922, pp. 243–244), and Lovén (1935, pp. 3–6). They can be supplemented with material from several reconstructions of *Ciboney* culture from the archeological remains, including for Cuba, Osgood (1942 a, pp. 50–52) and Santovenía y Echaide (1939, pp. 66–71), and for Haiti, Rouse (1941, pp. 50–52).

THE ETHNOGRAPHY OF THE CIBONEY

By Pedro García Valdes

LANGUAGE

Nothing is known of the *Ciboney* language beyond the fact that it was probably different from both the *Arawakan* and the *Cariban.* The word "Ciboney" seems to be derived from the *Arawak* siba, which signifies rock, and eyeri, man; it may have been given by *Arawak* who saw *Ciboney* people living in caves. The size of the *Ciboney* population is unknown, but it must have been small, since the people lived in isolated groups in inaccessible places.

CULTURE

SUBSISTENCE ACTIVITIES

The *Ciboney* have been considered fish eaters, because their sites contain the bones of fish and great quantities of shells, including clam, conch, mussel, oyster, and snail, many of which have been perforated to extract the meat. Land and sea crabs, the manatee or sea-cow, and the turtle also seem to have been eaten. The hutia, a rodent, and the almiqui, a small insectivorous mammal which formerly existed in great abundance in Cuba, the iguana or giant lizard, snakes, and birds were all probably hunted with special techniques. The people must also have nourished themselves with a number of native fruits, including the caimito, the corojo, the guanábana, the guayaba, the mamey, the manón or chirimolla, and the roots of various plants. According to the explorers, there were no cultivated crops.

The vegetable foods may have been prepared in mortars and on milling stones, of which a number have been found in the sites. They could then have been mixed in bowls of wood and stone, which are also known from the archeological remains. Since many of the sites lack traces of fire, the food may often not have been cooked. At some sites, however, there are layers of ash, and it may be suggested that the fish and shell food were roasted over the fire.

DWELLINGS

The evidences from both the archeological remains and the historical sources is that the *Ciboney* lived in rock shelters and caves. They probably dwelt also in the open, where it is doubtful that they constructed more than the simplest windbreaks of brush or palm thatch. Their villages were probably small and semipermanent; one might be justified in calling them camps.

DRESS AND ADORNMENT

According to the conquistadors, the *Ciboney* wore little clothing, perhaps only girdles or breechcloths made from vegetable fibers. The sites have yielded rough beads and pendants of shell and stone, with which the Indians must have adorned themselves. The presence of red and yellow ocher suggests that the *Ciboney* colored their bodies or faces, possibly during ceremonies or ritual periods. They did not deform their foreheads, as did the *Arawak*.

TRANSPORTATION

As an island people who placed great emphasis upon fishing, the *Ciboney* must have had some kind of boats, possibly the dugout canoe. On land it is likely that they traveled only on foot, since they could not have had either conveyances or beasts of burden. Although they may have moved from place to place when the wildlife became exhausted, it is doubtful that they undertook long journeys.

MANUFACTURES

The manufactures of the *Ciboney* were primitive. In all their sites are encountered specimens of primitive workmanship, including objects of stone, shell, bone, and wood. These indicate that the principal technological processes were battering with stone hammers, chopping with the shell gouges and (in Haiti) with stone axes, and cutting by means of flint chips. A few sites in both Haiti and Cuba have yielded also traces of the grinding and polishing of stone with combination hammer grinders of the same material. Sites in Haiti reveal a knowledge of the flaking and rechipping of flint blades. Bark cloth, basketry, and gourd containers may have been present, but no traces of them have yet been found in the sites.

SOCIAL AND POLITICAL LIFE

To judge from the nature of their sites and the utensils they have left us, the *Ciboney* must have had a primitive social organization. Each local group, consisting of several families living together, may have constituted an independent band.[11] At Cayo Redondo, one of the larger sites in Cuba, it has been estimated that the total population of such a band was 100. According to Oviedo y Valdés, each group of *Ciboney* in Haiti held all its property in common, but this may not have been entirely true, since some artifacts have been found in burials in Cuba. In any case, trade must have been rare, as few indications of it have been found in the sites.

Nothing is known of the life cycle of the *Ciboney* beyond the traces of their burials, which have already been described in connection with the archeology. When the Spaniards first encountered the Indians of western Cuba, the latter uttered war cries and fought with stones and wooden clubs.[12] In Haiti, the flint daggers which are common in archeological collections may have been used for warfare. The presence of stone balls and disks in many of the Cuban and Haitian sites suggests some sort of game, which may have had a ritual function, as indicated by the deposition of balls in some of the graves.

RELIGION

Perhaps the most significant statement that can be made concerning the *Ciboney* religion is that it was unlike that of the *Arawak*. There are none of the typically *Arawak* zemis in *Ciboney* sites. The gladiolitos, or ceremonial stones, however, may have had a religious function. The presence of stone balls in the burials, finally, may be considered an indication of a belief in life after death.

[11] The "provinces" which the conquistadors mapped on the western end of Cuba must have been either *Arawak* social units or else designations which the *Arawak* applied to *Ciboney* territory.

[12] The bows and arrows that the Indians used during the 17th-century colonization of western Cuba may have been a later addition.

THE ARAWAK

By Irving Rouse [1]

INTRODUCTION

It is generally agreed that the *Arawak* came into the West Indies after the *Ciboney* but before the *Carib*, as is indicated by the presence of *Arawak* archeological sites throughout *Carib* territory and also by the traditions of the *Carib*, who claimed to have conquered the Lesser Antilles from the *Arawak*. Unlike the *Ciboney*, the *Arawak* must have come from South America, for their language is Amazonian in type, and so also are the basic elements of their culture (agriculture, clothing, and shelter in particular). Presumably they entered the West Indies by way of Trinidad and the Lesser Antilles, sweeping the *Ciboney* before them when they reached Hispaniola and Cuba.

ARCHEOLOGY

Arawak sites are not difficult to distinguish from those of the *Ciboney*. They are located inland as well as near the shore, usually in the areas best suited for agriculture. As among the *Ciboney*, the most common type of site is the refuse heap, but it is often without shells. Some sites comprise only a single midden, no larger than those of the *Ciboney*, but most consist of a number of middens, which may or may not have coalesced into a single deposit. While some of these deposits are in rock shelters or in caves, most are the remains of villages built in the open.

Ceremonial structures are common in *Arawak* sites. Most of them consist of large flat areas alongside the refuse deposits, either circular, oval, or rectangular in shape and lined with embankments, faced in some cases with upright stone slabs (pl. 86, *top, center*). These are called "ball courts," although many of them may have served primarily as ceremonial plazas, and several are so long and narrow as to resemble roads. Some are accompanied by walks paved with flat stones and others by megalithic columns known as "pillar stones." Petroglyphs are common (pl. 86, *bottom, right*), occurring on the slabs lining the ball courts, on the pillar stones, on boulders near streams, and on the walls of caves. The caves containing petroglyphs, as well as a number of others from which have been taken wooden seats, pottery bowls, and images of wood, cotton, and

---

[1] Except section on Ethnography of Puerto Rico, as noted.

stone, were probably used as shrines. Several caches of ceremonial artifacts and ornaments are known also.

Burials.—*Arawak* burials have been obtained from the dwelling sites
(pl. 86, *bottom, left*) and from caves that were not inhabited. Burial
mounds and cemeteries in the open, away from the dwelling sites, have
also been reported but so far without verification. The typical burial
practice was inhumation, usually primary but occasionally secondary, in
the former case with the body either flexed or extended, on the side, on
the back, or in a sitting position. A few examples of primary and
secondary urn burial, usually of children, have also been encountered.
Grave objects are somewhat more common than in the *Ciboney* sites; they
usually comprise a pot, rarely ornaments.

Artifacts.—Almost all the *Ciboney* types of artifacts occur also in the
Arawak sites; many of them had presumably been taken over by the in-
vading *Arawak*.

Pottery.—The *Arawak* sites contain a large variety of other types of
artifacts, the most characteristic of which are potsherds. These are rarely
found in the form of complete vessels, but it is clear that they come principally from bowls, either round or boat-shaped (pl. 87). In addition,
one finds fragments of platters, jars, some water bottles, and many large
discoidal griddles which the Indians used in baking cassava. The techniques of decoration include painting in one, two, or rarely three colors,
sometimes positive and sometimes negative; incision; the application
of strips to the surface of the vessel; modeling; and the affixiation of
lugs and loop handles, often to the ends of the boat-shaped bowls.
The first three of these techniques were employed almost exclusively to
produce geometric designs; the modeled and affixed ornamentation, on
the other hand, is largely zoomorphic.

Utensils and ornaments.—Petaloid celts and chisels, made either of
stone or of shell, are also diagnostic of the *Arawak* sites (pl. 88, *c*; 89, *a*).
Other utilitarian objects include net sinkers, made of clay and of stone,
and awls, anvils, gouges, needles, picks, and spoons, made primarily from
the bone of the sea-cow, or manatee. Ornaments are made from clay,
stone, bone, or shell (see pls. 87, 88, 89); they include not only the simple
types made by the *Ciboney* but also elaborate beads, earplugs, masks, pendants, rings, and stamps for painting the body, many of which are carved
with complicated geometric and zoomorphic designs or are prepared for
the attachment of feathers, pieces of gold, or other bits of decoration.
Although the conquistadors imply that gold ornaments were common
among the *Arawak*, only three small fragments of that metal have yet been
obtained from the sites.

Ceremonial and problematical objects.—Ceremonial paraphernalia
are characteristic of many *Arawak* sites. They comprise idols of bone,
clay, cotton, shell, stone, and wood (pls. 87, *k*; 88, *p*; 89, *g, h, k*); eyes

and teeth of shell which were inlaid in the wooden idols (pl. 89, *d*);
seats of wood (pl. 89, *j*, *l*) or stone shaped for the most part like hammocks; and swallow sticks or spatulas used during the ceremonies to
induce vomiting (pl. 88, *o*). Trumpets of conch shell are common in
some sites, while others have yielded disks of bone, clay, shell, and stone,
drilled or undrilled (pl. 89, *e*). It has been suggested that the latter were
either spindle whorls or tokens used in some sort of game.

TABLE 1.—*Sequence of cultures in the West Indies*

Period	Location					
	Trinidad	Lesser	Virgin Islands	Eastern and northern Puerto Rico	Western and southern Puerto Rico	Dominican Republic
	Culture	*Culture* Antilles	*Culture*	*Culture*	*Culture*	*Culture*
IV	Late Erin Bay and Palo Seco (?)	Carib	Magens Bay-Salt River	Esperanza	Capá	Boca Chica
III	Late Erin Bay and Palo Seco (?)	Late Erin Bay and Palo Seco (?)	Magens Bay-Salt River	Santa Elena	Ostiones	Anadel
II	Early Erin Bay and Palo Seco (?)	Early Erin Bay and Palo Seco (?)	Coral Bay-Longford	Cuevas	Cuevas	Nonpottery strata (?)
I	Savanetta (?)	(?)	Krum Bay (?)	Coroso (?)	Coroso (?)	Nonpottery strata (?)

Period	Location—Continued					
	Haiti	Bahamas	Jamaica	Far eastern Cuba	Eastern and central Cuba	Southern and western Cuba
	Culture	*Culture*	*Culture*	*Culture*	*Culture*	*Culture*
IV	Carrier	Carrier (?)	Meillac (?)	Pueblo Viejo	Baní	Cayo Redondo or Guayabo Blanco (?)
III	Meillac	Meillac (?)	Meillac (?)	Baní or Meillac	Baní	Cayo Redondo or Guayabo Blanco (?)
II	Bay of Conch, Cabaret, Couri (?)	(?)	(?)	Guayabo Blanco (?)	Cayo Redondo or Guayabo Blanco (?)	Cayo Redondo or Guayabo Blanco (?)
I	Bay of Conch, Cabaret, Couri (?)	(?)	(?)	Guayabo Blanco (?)	Cayo Redondo, Guayabo Blanco (?)	Cayo Redondo or Guayabo Blanco (?)

Two groups of problematical stone objects are associated with the *Arawak,* although they usually occur as isolated finds rather than in the sites themselves. One group, obtained principally from Puerto Rico and the neighboring islands, comprises the so-called "stone collars" (pl. 88, *g*), "elbow stones" (pl. 88, *k*), and "three-pointed stones" (pl. 88, *i*), which are highly decorated with biomorphic as well as geometric designs and are believed to have had some function in connection with the worship of the *Arawak* idols or zemis. The second group of problematical objects, which centers in Guadaloupe and St. Vincent, includes crescents, artifacts shaped like hourglasses, and other peculiar geometric forms whose functions are not known (pl. 88, *n*).[2]

CULTURE SEQUENCES

The *Arawak* material just described varies considerably from site to site—and often also from stratum to stratum within individual sites. These differences make it possible to formulate a series of cultures based largely upon the pottery, the most frequent and most variable of the material (table 1).

Trinidad.—In Trinidad the cultural sequence is as yet poorly defined. Two strata have been noted at the Erin Bay and Palo Seco sites (Bullbrook, 1920; Osgood, 1942 b). Both strata contain a style of pottery characterized by elaborate figurine lugs and by geometric designs, executed in modeling and incision, often red- or black-slipped, and located typically upon a flange or outward extension of the rim. The bottom layer has in addition yielded red-slipped sherds bearing white-painted designs which appear to be from the outer walls of the vessels rather than from the rims. Both layers comprise shell deposits containing some burials but without the ceremonial manifestations of *Arawak* culture.

The white-on-red painted sherds limited to the lower levels at Erin Bay and Palo Seco resemble, on the one hand, the painted pottery obtained by Howard (1943) from the lower levels of the site at Ronquín in the middle Orinoco region and, on the other, the white-on-red sherds of the Cuevas culture in Puerto Rico. (See below, p. 511.) The modeled-incised pottery is more like some of the La Cabrera plain and polished gray ware obtained by Kidder II (1944) from the lowest levels at the Los Tamarindos site near Maracay, Venezuela. It also resembles the sherds obtained by Osgood and Howard (1943) at the site of Los Barrancos in the lower Orinoco region.

The Lesser Antilles.—Throughout the Lesser Antilles the archeology is known only from surface collections and from a few descriptions of

---

[2] It has often been assumed, for example by Fewkes (1922, p. 93), that these geometric objects were *Carib* rather than *Arawak.* They are associated, however, with single- or double-bitted stone axes of the types which have been found in the earlier *Ciboney* and *Arawak* sites of the Greater Antilles, at an age which would preclude a *Carib* origin (Rainey, 1940, pp. 29, 73; Rouse, 1941, p. 163).

shell heaps (Fewkes, 1922, pp. 88–166; Lovén, 1935, pp. 88–134). Both the white-on-red and the modeled-incised pottery are present, but it is not known what their association is with each other or with the geometrically carved stone objects of the Lesser Antilles. Petroglyphs and cave shrines are the only manifestations of ceremonialism yet discovered in the Lesser Antilles; there are no burial caves.

Only the white-on-red pottery is present in the Virgin Islands. In that country, Hatt (1924) found it in the first of two groups of *Arawak* sites, the Coral Bay-Longford, but it is absent from the second group, Magens Bay-Salt River (table 1). The Coral Bay-Longford seems to be a local variant of the Cuevas culture of Puerto Rico. Similarly, the Magens Bay-Salt River resembles the Santa Elena and Esperanza cultures in eastern Puerto Rico. (See below, pp. 511–512.)

Unpublished excavations by Josselin de Jong on the tiny Dutch islands of Saba and St. Eustacius between the Virgin Islands and the rest of the Lesser Antilles confirm this sequence, except that the pottery, ball courts, and problematical stone objects of the Esperanza culture are absent. This suggests, as Hatt (1924, pp. 40–41) has pointed out, that the Esperanza traits taper off as one goes eastward from Puerto Rico through the Virgin Islands into the Lesser Antilles.

Puerto Rico.—The Cuevas-Santa Elena-Esperanza sequence (table 1) is the result of recent excavations in eastern and northern Puerto Rico by Rouse (1945).[2a] The Cuevas potsherds are characteristically thin, hard, and finely constructed. Most are from bowls, but jars are also represented. The sides of the bowls typically slope outward and have thickened rims, which show in profile a bevel or a rounded lip facing inward. Ribbon handles are common; they are vertical, **D**-shaped, and do not extend above the rim. Although the white-on-red designs are the most striking elements of decoration, they are not the most characteristic, for they occur only on a few of the sherds and during the first half of the period of existence of the Cuevas types of pottery. The usual decoration is red or black paint, applied either as a slip upon all or part of the vessel surface or else in the form of crude geometric designs. Simple rectangular or semicircular lugs, formed as an extension of the rim, are also characteristic. Modeled and incised sherds are rare; a few examples which resemble the modeled-incised pottery of Trinidad and the Lesser Antilles may be trade objects.

Cuevas potsherds occur only in relatively shell-free refuse deposits located close to the shore. Rectangular stone adzes and cleatlike shell ornaments are the most typical of the associated artifacts; there are no

---

[2a] Work done since the above was written indicates that the Ostiones culture of western and northern Puerto Rico was also present in the eastern and southern parts of the island. In terms of table 1, the Ostiones culture now appears to have occupied the first half of Period III on the eastern and northern coasts, with the Santa Elena culture coming in (possibly from the Virgin Islands) during the latter half of the period.

traces of the usual *Arawak* ceremonial apparatus. The Cuevas culture, in this respect, is different from those found otherwise among the *Arawak* of the Greater Antilles.

Santa Elena sherds are cruder and thicker than the Cuevas, and they reveal a simpler shape and decoration. Bowls predominate to the virtual exclusion of jars. Their sides tend to be vertical rather than outsloping and convex rather than concave. The rim is typically thickened and cylindrical in cross section; most handles are vestigial. The painted decoration of the Cuevas sherds is largely replaced by simple designs incised, applied, and modeled on the outer wall of the vessel, the most typical being a series of vertical parallel lines bordering a ridge or covering a vestigial handle.

Santa Elena potsherds come mainly from the coast, but they have also been obtained from the mountainous interior of Puerto Rico. They are found not only in shell-free deposits but also in shell middens, in some ball courts, and in cave dwellings. The associated artifacts include petaloid celts of stone and shell; tubular pendants and beads of stone; tiny stone amulets carved in the shape of flexed human figures (zemis); and small three-pointed objects of stone and shell. These indicate that ceremonialism had begun to develop in the Santa Elena type of *Aarawak* culture.

Esperanza potsherds are thinner than the Santa Elena but are composed of the same crude ware. Bowls again predominate to the virtual exclusion of jars. Their sides are characteristically incurving rather than vertical, and their rims tend to be tapered and rounded inward. Decoration is confined to the shoulder formed by the incurving side. In most cases it consists of incised designs, especially two parallel lines in a semicircular or alternating oblique arrangement.

Esperanza potsherds have been found almost exclusively in shell heaps and in shell-free village sites along the shore. A few come from ball courts, but none so far from caves. They are accompanied by the usual *Arawak* utilitarian objects of stone, bone, and shell and by the simpler ceremonial objects.

The sequence in the western and northern parts of Puerto Rico has been worked out by Rainey (1940) and Rouse (1945). As in the rest of Puerto Rico, this sequence begins with the Cuevas culture (table 1). The latter is succeeded in turn by cultures called the Ostiones and the Capá, which replace respectively the Santa Elena and Esperanza cultures to the east.[3]

Ostiones potsherds bear a closer resemblance to the Cuevas than they do to the Santa Elena, for they are finely made and come commonly from jars as well as bowls. Although the sides of bowls tend to be vertical

---

[3] As originally formulated by Rainey (1940, pp. 107–110), this sequence was termed Crab-Shell-Problematical Recent. Site names have been substituted for the sake of consistency with the rest of the West Indies.

rather than outsloping, the rims are characteristically beveled inside. Most of the sides are convex rather than concave, and the handles are loop-shaped rather than **D**-shaped.

In the lower levels of the Ostiones sites, pottery decoration is almost entirely limited to painting like that on the later Cuevas sherds. Other modes of decoration make their appearance in the top levels. More complicated than on the Cuevas and Santa Elena sherds, they include horizontal incised lines situated on the bevel inside the rim and often ending in dots; modeled-incised lugs located on the ends of the vessel, which are called bat- or monkey-heads; and faces, limbs, or geometric figures executed in appliqué work on the outer wall of the vessel. These modes of decoration resemble designs on the earlier pottery of the Dominican Republic and may represent a diffusion from that country.

Ostiones potsherds have been found in shell-free deposits, in shell middens, and in association with ball courts. The accompanying artifacts include all the types listed above for the Santa Elena culture and also carved stamps of clay.

Capá sherds are among the crudest in the Antilles; many of them are sandy and crumble easily. Few jars are represented. The sides of bowls usually curve inward, they are convex, and they taper at the rim. Handles and painting are virtually nonexistent; the few lugs consist primarily of grotesque figures executed in modeling and incision. Incised designs, located on the shoulder formed by inturning the vessel wall, are characteristic of this pottery. More complex than on the Esperanza pottery, they each consist of a combination of several motifs, of which a circle with a dot in the center is typical. As Rainey (1940, pp. 109–110) has pointed out, both the incised designs and the lugs have resemblances with the later pottery in the Dominican Republic and Haiti.

Capá potsherds are characteristic of the ball courts in the mountainous interior of Puerto Rico. They have also been found in the top levels of some of the refuse deposits along the shore, with or without shells and usually in association with ball courts. Although a few occur in inhabited caves, they are more typical of the cave shrines. Associated with them are almost a complete complement of the other *Arawak* artifacts described above, including the biomorphically carved stone objects of the Greater Antilles. The Capá cultural complex apparently represents the height of *Arawak* ceremonialism.

Hispaniola.—Hispaniola divides into two areas, one comprising Mona Island and all except the northwestern corner of the Dominican Republic, the other the rest of the island, including Haiti (table 1). The first area is little known, for stratigraphical excavations have yet to be undertaken in the Dominican Republic. Two *Arawak* cultures seem to be represented, the Anadel and the Boca Chica. Anadel pottery has resemblances with both the Cuevas pottery of Puerto Rico and the later Boca Chica pottery of the Dominican Republic; presumably it represents a transition from the former to the latter. It is known from shell middens and from cave dwellings (Krieger, 1929, 1931).

Boca Chica bowl sherds are somewhat like the Capá in Puerto Rico, but they differ from the latter in having firm, well-polished surfaces, ridges outside the rim, vestigial handles, and large prismatic lugs modeled and heavily incised either biomorphically or geometrically. The jars characteristic of western and southern Puerto Rico are replaced in the Boca Chica complex by bottles. The complex is known from shell middens, shell-free refuse sites, ball courts, and possibly cave shrines (Krieger, 1929, 1931).

Two kinds of *Arawak* culture, the Meillac and the Carrier, are known in Haiti, and it has been possible to show by seriation that the former was earlier than the latter (table 1). Meillac potsherds are thin, hard, and fairly well made. They all appear to come from bowls rather than jars or bottles. Unlike the pottery of the Dominican Republic, the bottoms of the bowls seem to have been always round, never flat. Their sides typically turn inward, are convex, and have a ridge outside the vessel just beneath the rim. The latter is characteristically round in profile. Loop handles are common. The usual decoration consists of parallel straight-line incised designs made with a sharp tool, unpolished, and sometimes copied in appliqué work. These designs, of which the cross-hatch is typical, completely cover the shoulder of the vessel up to the ridge bordering the rim. They are said to resemble on the one hand certain decoration on *Ciboney* work in stone and shell and on the other hand pottery designs in the southeastern part of the United States (Rouse, 1940).

Additional modes of pottery decoration occur in the upper levels and at the later middens in the Meillac sites. These include horizontal incised lines on the ridge bordering the rim, and also faces, limbs, and geometric designs executed in appliqué work. They bear a striking resemblance to comparable elements of decoration on the Anadel pottery in the Dominican Republic and on sherds in the upper levels of the Ostiones sites in western Puerto Rico, despite the fact that the three types of pottery are otherwise quite different.

The Meillac pottery is known only from excavations in a few shell middens. The associated artifacts are similar to those in the Ostiones sites of Puerto Rico except for the presence of flint and stonework like those of the Couri type of *Ciboney* culture, and for the absence of tubular pendants and three-pointed objects. Since the ball court is also apparently absent, it may be suggested that ceremonialism was less developed in the Meillac type of *Arawak* culture than in the others from Hispaniola (Rainey, 1941; Rouse, 1941, pp. 54–112).

The Carrier pottery is known from ball courts and cave dwellings as well as from village sites. It is like the Boca Chica pottery of the Dominican Republic, except that the flat bottom is almost entirely absent, the prismatic lugs are more heavily modeled and less heavily incised, and the circular incised motif gives way to the ovoid, an oval line surrounding a straight line which ends in dots. In contrast to the Meillac pottery, the Carrier is characterized by a slight eversion of the vessel wall just beneath the rim, by a flat rim, and by broad incised lines made with a blunt tool, polished afterward, and curved as well as straight. There are no separate loop handles or simple face designs. The other utilitarian artifacts are similar to those in the Meillac culture. The ceremonial apparatus of the *Arawak* was probably also present, but the only example yet associated definitely with Carrier pottery is a carved shell figure (Rainey, 1941; Rouse, 1941, pp. 113–154).

Jamaica.—In Jamaica the sites consist of shell middens, of petroglyphs, and of caves used as dwellings, shrines, and burial places (personal communication from C. B. Lewis). The remains found are comparable to those of the Meillac culture in Haiti (De Booy, 1913 a).

Bahamas.—In the Bahamas, potsherds of both Meillac and Carrier types have been collected on the surface (table 1). It is not known how these sherds were distributed within the refuse deposits, which are either in the open or in caves. Petroglyphs and cave shrines are both present (De Booy, 1913 a, 1913 b).

Interest in the archeology of the Bahamas has centered upon certain resemblances with Florida. Holmes (1894) has shown that the designs carved on wooden stools from Turks Island are largely duplicated on stamped pottery from the mainland. In addition, it has been noted that a number of sherds from the northern Bahamas are fabric-stamped like mainland pottery. This recalls the statement of Martyr (Anghiera, 1912, vol. 2, p. 251) that the Indians of Florida used to visit the Bahamas in order to hunt birds.

Cuba.—A pair of *Arawak* cultures comparable to the Meillac and Carrier are present in Cuba; they have been named the Baní and the Pueblo Viejo (table 1). The former is best known from the Maniabón Hills in the east-central part of the island, where excavations have been concentrated in recent years (Rouse, 1942). The principal differences from the Meillac pottery are that the alternating-oblique-parallel-line design is more common than the cross-hatch, loop handles are rare, and the appliqué work is poorly developed. In the later middens at the Baní sites the pottery bears many additional designs otherwise characteristic of the Pueblo Viejo culture. Hilltop village sites, composed of a series of middens which contain few shells, are typical; in addition there are coastal shell heaps, burial caves, shrine caves, and in some places cave dwellings.

The associated artifacts include all those characteristic of the Cuban *Ciboney* cultures, plus the usual complement of *Arawak* tools and ornaments. Work in shell, which is probably the result of *Ciboney* influence, is outstanding, and there are many ceremonial objects, including swallow sticks and idols of clay, stone, bone, and shell.

The Pueblo Viejo culture, which is limited to the eastern tip of Cuba, is not well known. Its pottery resembles the Carrier pottery in Haiti, except for a certain lack of sophistication and a greater variation in design. The sites and the associated artifacts are similar to those of the Baní culture, with the addition of the ball court and the petroglyph.

Summary and reconstruction.—As shown on table 2, the cultures described above fall into three divisions: *Igneri, Taino,* and *Sub-Taino.*[4] The first of these divisions, the *Igneri,* is characterized by painted pottery, by the absence of most of the ceremonial aspects of *Arawak* culture, and possibly also by the presence of the geometrically carved problematical stone objects of the Lesser Antilles. The *Taino* Indians typically manufactured incised rather than painted pottery and biomorphically rather than geometrically carved stone objects. Their ceremonialism was the best developed and they were the only one of the three divisions to have ball courts. The *Sub-Taino* also made incised pottery but usually decorated it with simple, straight-line designs. They had no biomorphically carved problematical stone objects and, while they worshiped idols, they usually made no petroglyphs.

A tentative hypothesis concerning the prehistory of these three groups of people may be expressed in terms of four periods (table 1). Period I, before the arrival of any of them, represents the original *Ciboney* occupation of the West Indies. In Period II the *Igneri* are presumed to have entered Trinidad and the Lesser Antilles, spreading as far as Puerto Rico and possibly also into the Dominican Republic. Period III saw a twofold fission from the *Igneri:* of the *Taino* in the Virgin Islands, Puerto Rico, and the Dominican Republic; and of the *Sub-Taino* in Haiti.[5] During the same period the *Sub-Taino* seem to have spread into Cuba, Jamaica, and the Bahamas, driving the *Ciboney* into the isolated position which they occupied during historic times. Period IV, finally, was marked by the conquest of the remaining *Igneri* in the Lesser Antilles by the *Carib,* and by the encroachment of the *Taino* upon the *Sub-Taino* territories in the western part of the Greater Antilles. This produced the historic distribution of Indians within the West Indies. which is shown on map 8.

---

[4] These are the names of three of the groups of *Arawak* Indians living in the Antilles at the time of historic contact and are discussed as such below (pp. 521–522). They are here applied to the archeological divisions upon the assumption, adopted from Lovén (1935, p. vi, ff.), that the ethnographic groups correspond to the archeological divisions. An alternative, purely archeological terminology is that of Rainey (1940) and Rouse (1941), who substitute the name "Crab" for *Igneri* and "Shell" for the *Taino* and *Sub-Taino.*

[5] Rainey (1940) prefers to derive the *Taino* and the *Sub-Taino* (his Shell culture) from the mainland of South America rather than from the *Igneri* (his Crab culture).

TABLE 2.—*Classification of cultures in the West Indies*

CULTURES	DIVISIONS	GROUPS
Cayo Redondo Guayabo Blanco	Cuban Ciboney	Ciboney
Couri Cabaret Bay of Conch	Haitian Ciboney	
Dominican Nonpottery Strata Coroso (?) Krum Bay (?) Savanetta (?)	Other Ciboney (?)	
Early Erin Bay-Palo Seco Late Erin Bay-Palo Seco Coral Bay-Langford Cuevas	Igneri	Arawak
Magens Bay-Salt River Santa Elena Esperanza Ostiones Capá Anadel Boca Chica Carrier Pueblo Viejo	Taino	
Meillac Baní	Sub-Taino	
?	?	Carib

HISTORY

The *Arawak* were the first Indians to be encountered in the New World. Columbus made contact with them in the Bahamas, northern Cuba, and northern Hispaniola during his first voyage (1492–93) ; the fort he built at La Navidad in Haiti was destroyed by *Arawak* after his departure for Spain.

On his second voyage (1493–96), Columbus explored all the islands of the Greater Antillean area, including the Virgin Islands, which had then been occupied by *Carib*. He established the first permanent Spanish settlement at Isabela in the northern part of the Dominican Republic and pacified the Indians in the whole central part of the island, imposing upon each chief in that area a tribute of gold, to be collected every 3 months. By the end of his third voyage in 1500, the system of tributes had been extended to the Indian province of Xaragua at the western end of the island.

In 1500 Bobadilla replaced Columbus as governor of Hispaniola. Since the Indians were now unable to provide the proper amount of gold every 3 months, the new governor demanded that each chief contribute a certain number of Indians to work in the Spanish gold mines. Two years later Bobadilla's successor, Ovando, ordered all the Indians of the island (including those of the easternmost province of Higuey, which had never been conquered) to be used in this manner, thus establishing the dread system of repartimientos, the principal cause for the extinction of the *Arawak*. All available male Indians on the island were distributed among the Spanish colonists; they were to work in the gold mines or on the plantations of their masters for 6 or 8 months of the year. Each Indian treated in this manner received the name "encomendado"; if he worked as a house servant of his master, he was called instead a "naboria" (Wright, 1916, pp. 42–48).

In theory the system of repartimientos was to operate for the benefit of the Indians. It was intended to give them the opportunity to learn Spanish culture and the Christian religion, in return for supplying a moderate amount of labor. In practice, the system was badly abused. The Indians were overworked and ill-fed; many of them starved to death, others committed suicide. Mothers killed their children to spare them the lot of their fathers, and in addition hurricanes and smallpox decimated the population. By 1535, only 500 natives were left on the island; and the colonists were importing Negroes and Indians from other parts of the Caribbean to take their place.

The *Arawak* did not accept this treatment without a struggle, particularly in the extreme eastern and western parts of Hispaniola, where the Spanish control was still weak. The conquistadors, however, easily put down the rebellions, in many cases using great cruelty. The captured Indians were either massacred or branded and treated as slaves. Only in the southwest did the natives succeed in withstanding the Spaniards. There, after a struggle of 15 years, the cacique, Enrique, won an honorable peace and was allowed to establish a village of his own at Boya, 30 miles from what is now Trujillo City.

Between 1540 and 1550, when the gold of the islands had been exhausted and most of the colonists had turned to richer fields in México and Perú, the system of repartimientos was abolished, but the damage had been done. When Sir Francis Drake visited Hispaniola in 1585, he reported that not a single Indian was left alive.[6]

The fate of the Indians was the same in Puerto Rico and Jamaica, which the Spaniards settled in 1508 and 1509 after the conquest of Hispaniola had been completed. In the Bahamas, too, the Indian population was destroyed before 1600, as the result of slave raids undertaken by the

---

[6] Ober (1895, p. 289), however, notes that half-breeds still lived at Boya in 1798.

colonists of Hispaniola to replenish the diminishing supply of Indians on that island.[7]

In Cuba, on the other hand, the situation was different. Partly because this island was the last in the Greater Antilles to be conquered and partly because of its great size, the natives there succeeded in surviving the system of repartimientos. When it was abolished in 1550, there were still over 2,000 Indians in Cuba, as compared with some 700 Spaniards. They were set up in towns of their own near the principal Spanish towns and were allowed to own their own property and govern their own affairs.

The Indians prospered; they built up farms and established trade with outsiders. In the 18th century they founded at least one new town, Jiguaní, in the eastern part of Cuba. During the first half of the 19th century they were living in five towns in eastern Cuba (Yara, near Baracoa; Dos Brazos, between Baracoa and Yateras; La Güira, near Yateras; El Caney, near Santiago; and Jiguaní), in one town in the central part of the island near Camagüey, and in another at Guanabacoa across the bay from Habana. Contact with the Spaniards was constant; the Indians gradually intermarried with them and took over their culture. By 1900, although some 400 Indians still survived, mainly at Yara, Dos Brazos, and La Güira, almost all traces of the native mode of life had disappeared (pls. 96–97).

About the time of the discovery of America, or perhaps later, a group of *Arawak* from Cuba migrated to Florida in search of the fountain of youth. Under the leadership of the chief, Sequene, and of his son Carlos, they founded a town called Abaibo somewhere in southern Florida and established a semblance of control over the original inhabitants of the region, at the same time preserving their contacts with the country of their origin. These Indians had some relations with the Spaniards, but their fate is not known (Escalante Fontaneda, 1837–41, vol. 20).

At the other end of the Antilles, Columbus discovered Trinidad in 1498. The first attempt to found a colony was made by Spaniards from Puerto Rico in 1530 to 1540. After the failure of this attempt, the island was abandoned until 1584, when De Berros converted it into a base for his search for El Dorado on the neighboring mainland. As a result, the natives escaped the system of repartimientos. They did not avoid a decline in population, however. Many Indians died in resisting the attempts to found a colony. Others fell prey to slave raids. European diseases, too, swept the island. When the British took Trinidad from the Spaniards in 1797, only 1,082 Indians were left; 34 years later the population had declined to 726. At present, about 200 Indians live at Arima in Trinidad. Although called *Carib,* these natives are probably mainly *Arawak* (Hollis, 1941, p. 5; Bullbrook, 1940, p. 4).

---

[7] Culin (1902, p. 185), however, was told that Indians still lived in the unexplored parts of Little Abaco Island in his time. Similar reports are current in some of the other islands, but, except in Cuba, all appear to be unfounded.

SOURCES

The sources for *Arawak* ethnology fall unevenly into two groups. A majority of them are concerned with the natives of the Greater Antilles, while a few contain information on Trinidad. Most of the former date from the original colonization of the Indies, whereas the latter have arisen from the subsequent attempts of the English and the Spaniards to find El Dorado in the Guianas.

In the Greater Antilles, as one might expect, our data are richest for the island of Hispaniola, where the Spaniards first settled. The earliest anthropological research in the New World took place on that island when, during his second voyage, Christopher Columbus commissioned a friar named Ramón Pané to study the religion of the native *Arawak*. Pané's report has survived in three principal versions (F. Columbus, 1811; Las Casas, 1909; and Anghiera, 1912; compiled in Bourne, 1907). It is the only ethnographic source for the *Arawak*.

All the early historians provide some information on the life of the Indians of the Greater Antilles, most of them with special emphasis upon Hispaniola. The best information comes from writers who had lived in Hispaniola before the Indians there became extinct, such as Benzoni (1857), Christopher Columbus (1893, 1930, 1930–33), Ferdinand Columbus (1811), Las Casas (1909, n.d.), and Oviedo y Valdés (1749, 1851–55, 1906). Subsequent historians have depended for their data upon the original sources; they include Abbad y Lasierra (1866), Bernáldez (1870), Gómara (1749), Herrera y Tordesillas (1725–26, 1730), Irving (1851), Martyr de Anghiera (1912), Muñoz (1797), Scillacio (1859), and Tamara (1556).

In recent years most writers have turned their attention to summarizing the ethnographic data for particular islands. Charlevoix (1730–31), Cornilliac (1875), Edwards (1818–19), Featherman (1881–91), Jefferys (1760), Joyce (1916), Krieger (1930), Nau (1894), and especially Roth (1887) have done this for the island of Hispaniola; Fewkes (1907), Morales Cabrera (1932), Stahl (1889), and Tapia y Rivera (1854) have done it for Puerto Rico; Guiteras (1865–66), Santovenia y Echaide (1939), Torre y de la Torre (1841), and Wright (1916) have done it for Cuba; and Cundall (1894) has done it for Jamaica. Ober (1895) has made a brief survey of the ethnography from island to island, while Gower (1927) and Lovén (1935) have traced the distribution of *Arawak* culture traits. A few writers have concerned themselves only with special topics; for example, Roumain (1942) and Safford (1916, 1917) have discussed the ethnobotany of Haiti, and Bourne (1907) and De Hostos (1941) have studied *Arawak* religion. Bachiller y Morales (1883), Coll y Toste (1907), and Zayas y Alfonso (1931) have compiled lexicographies of *Arawak* words, principally from the sources on the Greater Antilles.

Nothing like this wealth of information is available for Trinidad. A number of the historians who came into contact with the natives, including Castellanos (1874), Dudley (1899), Scott (*in* Harlow, 1925), and Sir Walter Raleigh (1848), have provided scattered observations concerning the Indians, but we possess no well-rounded picture of their culture. Fewkes (1922, pp. 63–65) and Lovén (1935, pp. 32–42) have gathered together many of the observations, while Bullbrook (1940, 1941) has supplemented them with archeological information concerning the native customs. Most recent histories of Trinidad also contain brief references to the Indians.

In view of the great amount that has been written about *Arawak* culture as it was known at the time of historic contact, it is surprising that little has been done with the modern *Arawak* culture. Culin (1902) and Torre (1890) have published information on the modern Indians of Cuba, but no account is known to the writer of the Indians at Arima in Trinidad. A thorough study of the customs in these two places, westernized though they are, might reveal some survivals from prehistoric times.

ETHNOGRAPHY

Two systems exist for distinguishing among the *Arawak* who inhabited the West Indies at the time of historic contact. One system, based upon the aboriginal social organization, divides the *Arawak* according to islands and within each island according to their chieftainships (maps 9–11). The other, derived from the linguistic and cultural differences recorded in the historic sources, separates the *Arawak* into five groups (map 8). Three of these have already been defined archeologically (on p. 516). Ethnographically, they have the following characteristics:

IGNERI: The *Arawak* who survived the *Carib* migrations in Trinidad and the Lesser Antilles. More warlike than the rest of the *Arawak*, they apparently spoke a divergent dialect.[8]

TAINO: The majority of the inhabitants of Puerto Rico, Hispaniola, and the eastern tip of Cuba. These appear to have been the most typical of the *Arawak*, with the highest development of ceremonialism.[9]

SUB-TAINO: The Indians of Jamaica and the central part of Cuba. These people spoke the *Taino* dialect but do not appear to have been as highly developed culturally.[10]

[8] The term *Igneri* was originally used by the *Carib* to refer to their *Arawak* predecessors (Dutertre, 1667–71, vol. 2, p. 361). Rafinesque (1836, pp. 163–165) applied it, together with the name *Cairi*, to the language of the *Arawak* in the Lesser Antilles. Other ethnographic variants include *Ieri*, used by Hollis (1941, p. 6) for the Indians of Trinidad, and *Eyeri*, which Morales Cabrera (1932, p. 12) applies to an *Arawak* dialect in Puerto Rico.

[9] As a name, the term *Taino* is not aboriginal but was introduced, probably by Rafinesque (1836), to distinguish the *Arawak* dialect characteristic of the Greater Antilles from that of the *Igneri*. The term has since been used in many other ways. Fewkes, for example, applied it at first (1907, p. 26) to all the *Arawak* of the West Indies, but later he (1922, p. 56) restricted it to the inhabitants of the Greater Antilles. The meaning used above is from Harrington (1921, pp. 412–413).

[10] This term was coined by Harrington (1921, pp. 395–396) to apply primarily to the archeology. Ortiz Fernández (1943) substitutes the name *Ciboney*, upon the assumption that it originally applied more to the *Arawak* of Cuba than to the non-*Arawak* (see footnote 3, p. 496).

CIGUAYO: A small group in the northeastern part of the Dominican Republic, who had a divergent dialect and also seem to have been more warlike than the *Taino* and *Sub-Taino*.[11]

LUCAYO: The inhabitants of the Bahamas. These "people of the small islands" spoke the *Taino* dialect but are supposed to have been less advanced in culture. Their differences from the *Sub-Taino* have not been worked out.

Ideally, the following ethnographic data should be presented according to one of these two systems. In practice this is impossible because the conquistadors, not having had the knowledge of the modern investigators, did not record the data from the standpoint of these systems. Hence, the following account will conform to the usual practice of presenting the ethnographic data according to island except in the case of Hispaniola, where a distinction will be made between the *Taino* and the *Ciguayo*. The *Taino* in Hispaniola will be described in detail, since they are the best known, and the remaining *Arawak* will then be discussed in terms of their differences from the *Taino*. The period treated is circa 1510, when the Spaniards were in full contact with the Indians in the Greater Antilles.

THE ETHNOGRAPHY OF HISPANIOLA: TAINO

In prehistoric times the island of Hispaniola was called Aiti (mountainous country), Bohio (house), or Quisqueya (mainland). Its total population, including both the *Taino* and the *Ciguayo*, has been variously estimated from 100,000 to 6,000,000. The Indians were medium in height, broad-headed, strong-boned, and well proportioned. They had high cheekbones, high brows, flat noses with wide nostrils, thin to moderately thick lips, and generally poor teeth. Their hair was straight, soft, and black; their skin copper-hued; and their bodies lithe and supple. Although peaceful and lethargic, they possessed considerable intelligence and were quite emotional.

SUBSISTENCE ACTIVITIES

Farming.—Manioc (casavi) was the staple food of the *Taino*. They planted it twice a year, when the soil was damp. Every few years they changed fields, burning out a new clearing in the forests. The women heaped up small mounds and placed in them cuttings of manioc root, using a fire-hardened digging-stick (coa). They fertilized the mounds with urine and also included in them ash from burnt trees. Irrigation was extensively practiced in the southwestern part of the island.

In colonial times both the bitter and the sweet varieties of manioc were in use; the latter may have been introduced after the Conquest (pl. 91,

---

[11] The term *Ciguayo*, together with an alternative, *Maçoriges*, was used by the *Taino* for the above group. It refers to the fact that the *Ciguayo* wore their hair longer than the *Taino*. (Zayas y Alfonso, 1931, vol. 1, pp. 199–200.)

6, 7). The method of preparation was to scrape the skin off the root with a piece of flint, to shred the root on a board set with small pieces of flint, and to squeeze the juice out of the shreds in a woven basketwork or cotton tube. One end of the tube was hung from a branch; the other was weighted with a stone or else a woman stood on a cross bar attached to the tube. From the shreds she made a cake, baked it on a discoidal clay griddle (buren) set on three stones over the fire, and parched it in the sun. The ordinary cakes were coarse; those for a chief, however, were fine. They were often stored in dried leaves. The juice from the root was used in the pepper pot to be described below.

Corn was an important source of food, although apparently more so after the Conquest than before. It was always planted on the hillsides and without the benefit of the mounds heaped up for the planting of cassava. The ash from the burned forests was used as fertilizer, and the planting took place twice a year, during a new moon and after it had commenced to rain. Each planter carried the kernels in a bag around her neck. She dibbled four or five kernels in each hole, a pace apart, working the planting stick with a vertical motion. Birds were kept from the fields by the children, stationed on platforms in the trees.

From the absence of metates in prehistoric times, it has been assumed that the *Taino* then had only a soft variety of corn. They harvested it green and used it mainly in a soup. After the Conquest, at least, they made cakes, which were of two kinds, one for the commoners and the other for the chiefs. To produce the cake of the common people the women wet the grain and left it overnight. Then they ground it between two stones, or possibly in wooden mortars hollowed out of tree trunks, mixed it with water to form loaves, wrapped the loaves in leaves which had previously been moistened, and baked them in the fire. In making bread for chiefs, the process began in the same way, but the meal was washed, the husks removed, and the meal reground into flour before being baked into cakes, on clay griddles over the fire.

Corn meal was also used (after the Conquest at least) in the preparation of beer. The women put meal into large jars of water containing kernels of corn that had been warmed and chewed. They left this liquor to ferment, heated it for 3 or 4 hours, allowed it to cool, and then strained it through a cloth.

Other cultivated plants included the yahutia, the potato, the arrowroot, the bean, the pepper, and the peanut, most of which were mixed with water and with manioc juice in the pepper pot. This was a bowl left on the fire to boil continuously. From time to time the *Taino* ate from it or added new material to it. The potato and the arrowroot are also said to have been baked; the peanut was eaten with cassava.

Wild plants.—Several wild roots were mixed in the pepper pot. They included wild varieties of arrowroot, peppers, and a turnip. Most fruits, such as the alligator pear, the annona, the coconut, the guayaba, the mamey, and the papaya, were probably also gathered wild, although there is some mention of fruit gardens near the houses. Another food was guayaga, a root filled with larvae. When they had nothing better the natives consumed the sour fruit of the mangrove.

Hunting.—The *Taino* hunted mainly the hutia, a small rodent, and the iguana, or giant lizard. They also ate birds, snakes, and occasionally worms, spiders, and insects. The hunters drove the hutias into corrals, using torches and dogs to frighten the animals at night, or else burning the prairies. The corrals also served as pens for the animals. Hunters were able to pluck iguanas off trees, by first imitating their call to make the animals open their mouths and then stuffing something in them. They used tame birds to decoy wild parrots within reach, caught geese by hiding themselves in the water under one of several calabashes, and with their dogs chased other birds which could only hop off the ground, until they tired. Birds and other animals were dispatched with clubs, not with bows and arrows. The flesh was put into the pepper pot or roasted upon a spit, that of the iguana and a certain variety of hutia being reserved for the chief.

Domesticated animals.—The only domesticated animals were the dog and the birds which were used in hunting. The former, called alco, are said to have been mute.

Fishing.—Fishing techniques varied. There were nets made of cotton or fiber, fitted with wooden floats and stone sinkers and probably used for dragging. Hooks and lines, the former of one piece (either shell or bone), were common. The natives sometimes poisoned the water with a kind of vine. They also had many-pronged fish spears (the prongs being spines of fish bones), harpoons for taking manatees, baskets for fishing in rivers, and weirs for use in tidal waters. The last were employed both for fishing and for storing fish and turtles. Other sea food included crabs and many varieties of shellfish. Except for fish eyes, which were eaten raw, marine foods were boiled in the pepper pot or roasted on a spit over the fire.

Eating.—The people ate at least three times a day: morning, noon, and evening. A fourth meal, at night, is also mentioned, but this was probably only during festivals, for it was preceded by vomiting.

VILLAGES AND HOUSES

Settlements.—The *Taino* settlements were located without particular regard for the nature of the site. They are said to have varied in size from a single dwelling, containing several families, to as many as 1,000 houses, having a population of 3,000. These houses were irregularly arranged except in one village on the eastern end of the island, which had a pair of streets intersecting at right angles. Every village contained one or more ball courts, each of which was a flat, rectangular area lined with an embankment and sometimes also with upright stone slabs. The chief's dwelling was always alongside one. of the courts, often at its end. Some chiefs had additional buildings outside the village, one a storehouse and another a temple to house his idols (zemis). Other chiefs stored such possessions in their own houses, like the ordinary people.

Houses.—The *Taino* dwellings were of two kinds, bohios and caneyes. The former, which were large, rectangular, and gabled, were occupied by the chiefs (pl. 90, *10*); the latter, small, circular, and provided with a conical roof, were for commoners (pl. 90, *9*).[12] The houses of both kinds had only a single room despite the fact that each was shared, in the case of a chief, by all his wives, in the case of a commoner by several different families. Each had a single low doorway and perhaps also windows but was without a smoke hole.

To construct the rectangular house the people set heavy posts in the ground five to six paces apart, following the line of the wall, and braced them at the top with wooden poles, corded together with rope vines. The central posts at either end were taller; to them was attached a ridge pole. Other poles were laid on as rafters, and the roof was thatched with straw, the tops of canes, and palm leaves. The floor was of dirt, but the builders filled in the walls with thick canes, set on end in the ground, and bound them together with rattan. In case the house was exposed to the wind, a series of forked posts were run down the center of the building to give strength to the roof. The circular dwelling was constructed in a similar manner, except that it lacked the ridge pole and had only a single post in the center. Both types are said to have been so well constructed that they rarely had to be rebuilt.

Household furniture.—Most of the Indians slept in hammocks (hamaca), made of cotton netting and hung by cords between two of the house posts (pl. 90, *8*); some chiefs used raised platforms instead. Carved stools, made of wood or stone, were common among the people of higher class, being used principally during the religious ceremonies. Gourds and baskets hung from the ceiling; hunting, fishing, and cooking gear lined the walls. Every house contained one or more idols (zemis). In addition there is mention of platforms set on four posts and used to store food, particularly manioc cakes. It is not known whether these platforms were in the dwellings, in the chief's storehouse, or were provided with roofs of their own.

DRESS AND ADORNMENT

Clothing, hairdress, and toilet.—Most *Taino* men went naked before the arrival of the Spaniards. Afterward, they assumed a genital

---

[12] There is some question whether both of these house types were prehistoric. Lovén (1935, pp. 340–341) concludes that the rectangular house was introduced by the Spaniards. It is still in use today in Hispaniola.

covering of cotton (pl. 91, *4*). Girls who had passed puberty, on the contrary, even in prehistoric times wore a net over their genitals; when they married they exchanged this for an apron of cotton, grass, or leaves which they bound around their hips. The length of this apron seems to have been a sign of rank; upper-class women wore it down to their ankles.[13] To keep off the rain the people covered themselves with the fibrous sheaths off palm shoots (yagua), just as the modern inhabitants do.

Both men and women originally wore their hair in tufts, between which the head was shaved. After the Conquest the custom (for adults, at least) was to cut the hair at the neck and fasten it with a band. The men were beardless, except for a few straggling hairs.

Washing was a common custom, both for the sake of cleanliness and as a preventative against sickness. The *Taino* used an aromatic fruit to form a lather in the water.

Painting, tattooing, and deformation.—Both sexes painted themselves, some red, others white, black, yellow, or a combination of colors. The occasions varied, but usually painting was done mainly in preparation for festivals and warfare. Men painted their bodies more than women; men favored the red color, women the white. The materials used were vegetable matter, mixed with a resinous gum. Warriors were accustomed to paint their whole bodies red; other persons often painted themselves with figures of their zemis.

The figures of the zemis were tattooed as well as painted, sharpened reeds being used for the purpose. The mothers flattened the foreheads of their children, a high one being considered ugly. They also pierced the ears and the nasal septum for the insertion of pendants.

Ornaments.—Ear and nose ornaments were of gold, silver (?), stone, bone, or shell and were hung on cords. Many were carved in the shapes of zemis. No mention is made of earplugs, but some clay heads bear ear disks that have concave sides.

Necklaces were common, the beads being of stone, bone, shell, clay, or gold. They belonged principally to the upper classes, who prized them highly. Each family handed down its beads from generation to generation, giving them to children who were about to be married. Most beads were discoidal; some were cylindrical and pierced transversely for the insertion of feathers. Armlets and leg bandages were made either with beads or from cotton

When they went into battle the warriors wore on their foreheads little stone figures of men, flexed and with prominent penises. During dances and upon ceremonial occasions feathers were inserted in the hair, and many people wore masks of wood or shell, often inlaid with gold. Other

[13] Authorities disagree concerning this apron, some failing to specify that it was the married women who wore it. Others have not noted the distinction between short and long aprons. Charlevoix (1730–31, p. 37) states that the unmarried women wore the short aprons, married women the long. Still other authors fail to mention the net worn by unmarried women.

ornaments included plates of gold suspended on the forehead and girdles of cotton interwoven with small beads of fishbone or with pieces of gold. Occasionally these girdles were decorated with tiny masks.

As a symbol of their rank, the chiefs wore suspended from their necks a pendant of gold, alloyed with copper. This pendant, called a guanin, was apparently imported from South, America. Chiefs are also said to have had gold crowns and feather headdresses; their women, gold wreaths and turbans. Gold objects, it appears, were a sign of high rank.

TRANSPORTATION

The *Taino* had dugout canoes (canoa) made from the cedar and cottonwood (*Ceiba*) trees. They burned a ring around the tree to kill it, felled it with fire, and hollowed the log by alternate burning and chopping. The ends of the canoe were square (pl. 91, *1*). The larger canoes, some of which could carry 70 or 80 men, belonged to the chiefs; they were the only ones painted. There were no sails, the only method of propulsion being paddles, spade-shaped with cross-bar handles and very long blades. Bailing was done with gourds.

The canoes were used not only to coast the shore of Hispaniola but also to travel from island to island. Single men were not afraid to set out on long trading voyages, carrying only food and a gourd of water.

Travel by land was not common. There were paths, but they were just broad enough for a single man to pass at a time. The chief traveled in a litter, the chief's son rode on the shoulder of a retainer, and the chief's brother walked, supported beneath the arms by two men of upper class. The people originally carried burdens only in baskets on the back. After the Conquest the balance pole came into use (pl. 91, *8*).

MANUFACTURES

Basketry and weaving.—The *Taino* apparently possessed neither mats nor bark cloth. They wove some baskets from biheo leaves and maguey fiber (pl. 91, *8*). The technique is not known, but an impression of twilling has been found on a griddle sherd excavated in Haiti. Baskets used for storage of trinkets had a double wall and a cover, which made them waterproof. Other baskets may have been open, since they were used variously to carry salt and to bring offerings to the idols.

Cordage made from native hemp, from maguey fiber, from a certain brown grass, and from cotton, was common (pl. 91, *9*). There is no proof that cotton was woven into cloth. It is mentioned in connection with the manioc squeezer and the fabrication of bags, hammocks, and aprons; but the technique may have been netting rather than weaving. Drilled pottery disks, perhaps spindle whorls, have been found in some archeological sites, but these prove only the making of cotton cord.

The lack of large land mammals precluded the working of skins.

Pottery and gourds.—Pottery was common. The potter built up the vessel with the coiling technique and fired it in an open hearth. Shapes include bowls used for pepper pots (the boat-shape is characteristic), platters, spherical bottles, and flat griddles for baking cassava.

The Indians also made gourd containers used mainly for carrying drinking water.

Stonework.—A few stone bowls have been found in Hispaniola, some sculptured with zemilike designs. Hammer-grinders and pestles of stone are common; mortars are rare. These, too, are sometimes sculptured. The *Taino* of the northwestern part of the island made daggers and knives of flint; elsewhere only flint chips seem to have been used.

Celts were either of stone or shell. They were petaloid in shape, the pointed butt being inserted in a cleft in the handle and bound with a cord (pl. 90, *12*). Picks were of shell or manatee bone; there were also chisels of shell or stone and wedges of shell.

Woodwork.—The inhabitants of the western part of Hispaniola, particularly on the island of Gonave, were excellent woodworkers. They made well-polished bowls, hollowed out with fire, and stools, the latter often being carved with zemis. Other articles of wood included digging sticks with fire-hardened points and the fire drill. The latter was a stick, twirled between the hands and resting either upon a softer stick or upon two lighter sticks tied together (pl. 91, *2*).

Metallurgy.—The *Taino* washed gold from the mountain streams or dug it out of sedimentary deposits, particularly river beds that had dried up after the rainy season. They knew how to beat the metal upon pieces of stone but not how to smelt it. There are a few references to copper and silver, which may have been imported from South America. The ornaments of metal have already been described. Metal was employed only for ornaments.

SOCIAL AND POLITICAL ORGANIZATION

On Hispaniola the Spaniards observed five provinces, or chieftainships, not counting that of *Ciguayo,* which will be discussed below in connection with those people. These provinces are shown on map 10. Magua, in the northeastern part of the island, was the most populous. The wealthiest and most aristocratic was Xaragua to the southwest; it was the model of refinement in customs and manners. As shown on map 10, each province had its own chief, called a "cacique." In addition, there are said to have been some 30 subchiefs in control of local districts within each province and 70 to 80 headmen in charge of the villages of the province.

Each chief, subchief, or village headman seems to have governed the village in which he resided. He organized the daily routine or work, arranging for hunting, fishing, and tilling the soil. He was also respon-

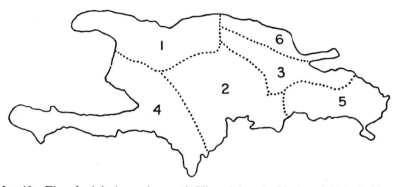

MAP 10.—The aboriginal provinces of Hispaniola. 1, Marien (chieftainship of
Goacanagaric); 2, Maguana (chieftainship of Caonabo); 3, Magua (chieftainship of Guarionex); 4, Xaragua (chieftainship of Behechio); 5, Higuey (chieftainship of Cayacoa); 6, Ciguayo (chieftainship of Mayobanex). (After
Charlevoix, 1730–31.)

sible for the storage of extra provisions and for their ultimate distribution
among the villagers. His was the largest canoe in the village and he
probably directed transportation. He acted as host to visitors and conducted relations with other villages, through their chiefs, subchiefs, or
headmen. He was the leader at feasts and dances, and, having learned
the songs by heart, he also directed the singing. His were the most
powerful zemis in the village, and he organized their worship by the
villagers. His authority is said to have been despotic; he could order
the death of his subjects, and they had to obey his commands to the letter.

The authority of the headman apparently extended no farther than his
own village, but the subchief also had a certain control over the other
villages in his district, while the chief's authority extended over the entire
province. The chiefs and subchiefs exacted no tribute from their sub-
ordinate villages, but they had the power to requisition agricultural or
military services. This power may have been quite nominal and dependent largely on the personalities of the chiefs and subchiefs, for there is
some evidence that it shifted considerably from time to time.

Each chief was always addressed in full by a set of some five titles
which he inherited with his office. He was also entitled to special food,
special houses, special dress and ornaments, and the special modes of
transportation already described. At least one of the chiefs, Goacanagaric,
spoke to his subjects only through two old men.

These prerogatives were inherited matrilineally. They went first to
the eldest son of the eldest sister; failing sister's sons, they passed to a
brother; and only failing these did the chieftainship pass to a son. Women
relatives were also allowed to inherit the position. In absence of any
relatives, the people chose as chief the most worthy and powerful man.

Beneath the set of chiefs was a hierarchy of other social classes which the Spaniards called nobles, commoners, and slaves. The nobles (nitaynos) acted as the chief's assistants; for example, they supervised communal labor. Only they and the chiefs attended the cahoba meetings at which snuff was taken to decide matters of village policy, such as war or peace. They also had certain unspecified judicial functions. The commoners, for whom no native name is given,[14] did the actual work of the village. In this they were assisted by the slaves (naborias), whose exact status is not known. They seem to have been dependents of the chiefs and nobles. There is some indication that all of these classes tended to be endogamous.

Crimes were judged by the chief, who imposed punishments. In the case of theft, the penalty was death, the guilty person being impaled on the branch of a tree and left to die. Adultery, too, was punished by death.

Etiquette.—The *Taino* were a hospitable people. The chief of each village acted as host; he went out to receive the traveler, brought him into his house, seated him on his stool, and provided him with food. The other people of the village sat on their heels around the visitor; if they wished to honor him, they placed their hands on his head. It was the custom to offer women from the village for sexual intercourse and to give feasts for important people. At a feast for the Spaniards, the chief's wives danced and there was a gladiatorial contest, in which several men were killed with the bow and arrow. To show friendship the *Taino* would exchange names or presents with their visitors.

Economic organization.—The extent of private property is not clear. Pané (*in* Bourne, 1907, p. 323) quotes a myth implying that each man inherited his family's agricultural land. Personal property, including beads and other ornaments, was inherited matrilineally, as in the case of the chieftainship, or else it was transmitted in the form of gifts at the time of marriage or death. House owners laid canes across the door to prevent entrance and theft of personal property.

On the other hand, the mention of communal agricultural and hunting activities, and of the communal storehouse controlled by the chief, suggests that food and perhaps other materials were held in common. Many writers refer also to a general lack of acquisitiveness; the *Taino* were generous in giving away their possessions.

Despite a lack of markets, trading was common. For this purpose individuals or groups of Indians traveled from one village to another, sometimes overland and sometimes by canoe, from province to province or from island to island. Manioc, pepper, stools, wooden bowls, pottery,

---

[14] Several sources mention a term "guajiro." This may have applied to the common people; Las Casas, however, lists the guajiros before the nitaynos, thus suggesting that they were of higher rank.

gold, and carved stone objects were the principal objects of barter. Certain places specialized in different products; e.g., Gonave Island off the west coast of Hispaniola was noted for its woodwork. Hispaniola as a whole had a reputation throughout Cuba and the Bahamas for its gold.

The plates of guanin (gold and copper alloy) must have been traded in from South America, probably before the arrival of the *Carib* in the Lesser Antilles.

LIFE CYCLE

Birth and childhood.—There is no record of birth customs. Immediately after delivery, the mother washed the baby in the sea or in a river. Upon the birth of a chief's son the villagers congregated to salute the child, using his titles. The chiefs gave their children to the wise men to be taught the origin myths and the recitation of the deeds of their ancestors.

Chastity was not valued; it was considered desirable for a bride to have had sexual experience. Incest was unknown. Continence is reported to have been observed only during the 20-day period when the men were gathering gold (p. 532). There were said to have been berdaches, who dressed as women.

Marriage.—The tendency was to marry a person of one's own rank. Marriage with a sister or the daughter of a sister was prohibited. The prospective groom had to pay a bride price; if he were poor he could work it out by service to his future father-in-law. A chief who wished to marry opened negotiations by sending one of his principal men to obtain the consent of the prospective bride's father, sometimes carrying a gift of food. Then the chief himself visited the father and arranged for the bride price, which consisted of plates of guanin and strings of stone beads, to be paid in daily installments during a month. Throughout the month the future bride remained in seclusion in a hut, seeing no one but the girls who brought her food. Then her hair was cut to signify her new estate, and the marriage was celebrated with dancing and a feast, at which time the father-in-law gave guanin and beads to the bridegroom, apparently in exchange for the bride price.[15]

Residence seems to have been patrilocal, despite the matrilineal inheritance. Polygyny was prevalent but only among people who could afford it. It was largely limited to chiefs; at the time of the Conquest, 1 chief had 30 wives. One of the wives was always considered the principal one; authorities differ as to whether she had control over the rest. All the wives lived, ate, and slept together in the same house. Several Spaniards looked for evidence of divorce but were unable to find it.

Division of Labor.—Columbus observed that women worked more than men. They cultivated the crops, prepared the food, brought water, cared for domesticated animals, and wove the basketry and cloth (if any).

---

[15] Some sources say these gifts went to the daughter rather than to her husband.

The men hunted and fished, cleared the fields, helped women harvest crops, and taught the children customs and rites. They collected gold, forming expeditions which had to remain away from the women for 20 days.

Death and burial.—When it became apparent that a chief was about to die, he was strangled. This was also done to commoners upon the order of the chief. The dying person might, instead, be driven out of the house by his relatives or he might be abandoned in his hammock with food and water nearby.

The methods of disposing of the body varied. If the deceased had been abandoned before death, the people returned later to collect and bury his bones. If he had died in his house, the building might be burned with the body inside. Often the corpse was flexed, wound with cotton, and placed in a prepared grave, which might be lined with sticks. Another method was to deposit the corpse in a cave. If the deceased were a chief, his body was sometimes disemboweled and dried over the fire, apparently to be kept as a fetish (zemi). The heads of both chiefs and commoners were similarly treated and kept in baskets in their children's houses.

Grave objects were sometimes placed with the corpse: a bowl of water and some bread, the deceased's personal ornaments, and, in the case of a chief, the stool upon which he had sat. Several of a chief's wives were often buried alive with his body.

A ceremony is mentioned only in connection with the burial of a chief. The dead chief's followers and his neighbors came together, divided up his personal property, composed chants to commemorate his reign, and danced and sang for 15 or 20 days. The chants composed at this ceremony were sung throughout the reign of the chief's successor.

WARFARE

The *Taino* were a relatively peaceful people and had little success in defending themselves against *Carib* raids. They sometimes fought among themselves to avenge murders, but most of their wars resulted from disputes between the chiefs, e.g., over hunting or fishing rights or the refusal of one chief to deliver his daughter to another who had paid the bride price. All men took part in the fighting, but only the chiefs and nobles attended the meeting at which snuff was taken and warfare was decided upon. One of the chiefs was elected to lead the attack; the nobles acted as bodyguards for the chiefs.

Warriors kept their weapons at home. These included the spear thrower, or atlatl (a staff with fishbone peg and a braided-cotton loop for the fingers), the javelin (sometimes pointed at the end and hardened in the fire, otherwise provided with a stone point or with one to three bone spines), clubs (often digging sticks wielded with two hands), and stones. The distribution of the bow and arrow was intermittent; they were com-

PLATE 86.—**Arawak sites in the West Indies.** *Top:* Ball courts at Capa, Puerto
Rico. *Center:* Walls of a ball court at Capa, Puerto Rico. *Bottom (left):*
Burial from El Mango near Banes, Cuba. *Bottom (right):* Petroglyphs on
St. Vincent. (*Top* and *center,* after Mason, 1941 a, pl. 2, fig. 1, and pl. 15,
fig. 2; *bottom (right)* after Joyce, 1916, pl. 28, fig. 1.)

PLATE 87.—**Arawak pottery from the West Indies.** *a*, Modeled-incised vessel from Trinidad; *b*, white-on-red painted bowl of Cuevas type, Puerto Rico; *c*, unpainted bowl of Cuevas type, Puerto Rico; *d*, red-painted bowl of Ostiones type, Puerto Rico; *e*, unpainted bowl of Collores type, Puerto Rico; *f*, incised bowl of Boca Chica type, Dominican Republic; *g*, spindle whorl, Dominican Republic; *h*, stamp, Dominican Republic; *i*, incised bowl of Meillac type (reconstructed), Haiti; *j*, water bottle of Carrier type (reconstructed), Haiti; *k*, idol, Cuba; *l*, griddle (reconstructed), Haiti. (*b*, *c*, and *e*, approximately ¼ actual size; others, size unknown.) (*a*, After Fewkes, 1922, pl. 3, *c*; *c*, *f*, *g*, and *h*, after Kreiger, 1931, pls. 43, left; 34, top: and 35, fig. 2; *i*, *j*, and *l*, after Rouse, 1941, pls. 6, fig. 1; 26, fig. 2, and 26, fig. 3.)

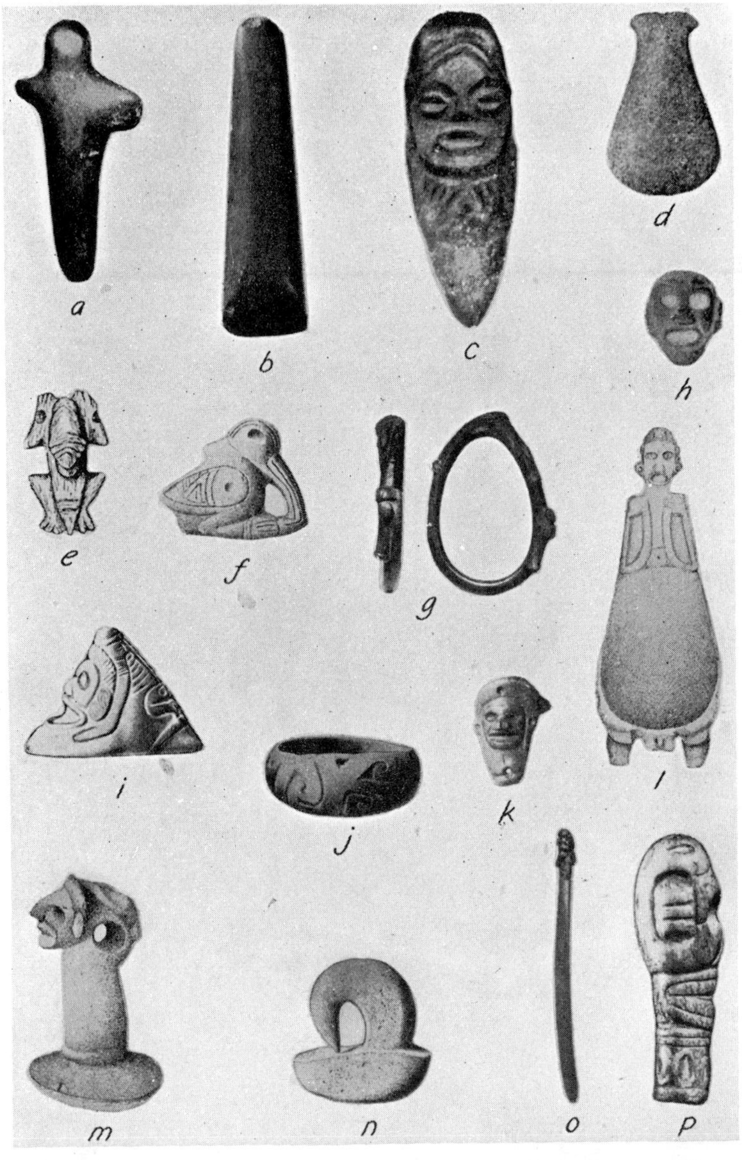

PLATE 88.—**Arawak stone and bonework from the West Indies.** *a*, Monolithic stone ax, Dominican Republic; *b*, rectangular stone adze, Puerto Rico; *c*, petaloid stone celt, Dominican Republic; *d*, eared stone ax, St. Vincent; *e*, zoomorphic stone pendant, Haiti; *f*, stone bird, Puerto Rico; *g*, stone collar, probably Puerto Rico; *h*, stone bead, Puerto Rico; *i*, three-pointed stone, Puerto Rico; *j*, stone mortar, Puerto Rico; *k*, elbow stone, Puerto Rico; *l*, stone seat, Puerto Rico; *m*, stone pestle, Dominican Republic; *n*, problematical stone, Guadeloupe; *o*, bone swallow sticks, Puerto Rico; *p*, bone idol, Cuba. (Approximate sizes: *a*, 1/5; *c*, *k*, and *m*, 1/7; *d*, 1/9; *e*, 4/5; *h*, *j*, and *l*, 2/5; *i*, 1/4; *n*, 1/6; remainder unknown.) (*a*, *c*, *f*, *k*, *l*, *m*, and *o*, After Fewkes, 1907, pls. 14, *a*; 15, *a*; 25, *b*; 69, *b*, figs. 40; 7; and pl. 2, *e*. *d*, *g*, and *i*, After Joyce, 1916, pls. 24, fig. 3; 18, fig. 2; and 17, fig. 3. *e*, After Rouse, 1941, fig. 7. *j* and *n*, After Fewkes, 1922, pls. 112, *c*; 81, *c*. *p*, After Rouse, 1942, pl. 6, n.)

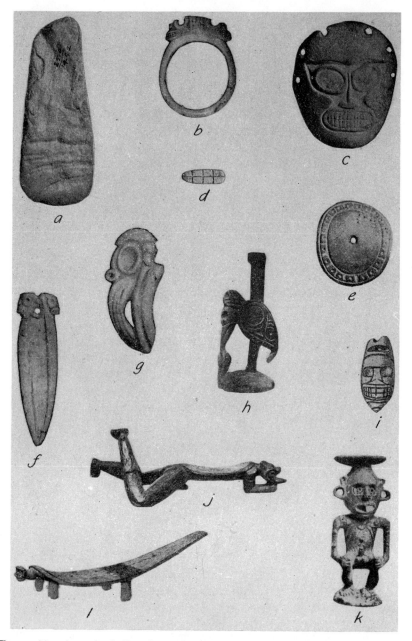

PLATE 89.—**Arawak shell and woodwork from the West Indies.** *a*, Shell celt, Puerto Rico; *b*, shell ring, Cuba; *c*, shell mask, Cuba; *d*, shell teeth, Cuba; *e*, shell disk, Cuba; *f*, shell pendant, Cuba; *g*, shell bird, Cuba; *h*, wooden idol, Greater Antilles; *i*, shell pendant, Cuba; *j*, wooden seat, Dominican Republic; *k*, wooden idol, Puerto Rico; *l*, wooden seat, Bahamas. (Approximate sizes: *d*, ⅖; *h*, 1/14; *i*, ⅘; *j*, 1/11; *k*, 1/18; *l*, 1/15; remainder unknown.) (*b*, *d–g*, and *i*, After Rouse, 1942, pls. 8, *a*, *h*, *e*; 7, *q*; 8, *d*; and 7, *p*. *h* and *j*, After Joyce, 1916, pls. 21 and 22. *k* and *l*, After Fewkes, 1907, pls. 90, *c*; 93, *d*)

PLATE 90.—**Arawak history and ethnography in Hispaniola.** *1*, Coat of arms of
Christopher Columbus; *2*, southern cross, as used for navigation by the conquistadors; *3–6*, *Taino* drums, showing the varieties of gonglike openings;
7, tube used by the *Taino* for sniffing cohoba snuff; *8*, *Taino* hammock, as
set up while traveling; *9*, circular house (caney) used by *Taino* commoners; *10*,
rectangular house (bohio) used by *Taino* chiefs; *11*, genital covering worn
by *Taino* men before the coming of the Spaniards; *12*, stone ax used by the
Taino in hollowing out canoes. (After Oviedo y Valdés, 1851–55, vol. 1,
pl. 1.)

PLATE 91.—**Arawak ethnology and plants in Hispaniola.** *1, Taino* canoe, showing manner of paddling; *2*, fire drill, as used by the *Taino*; *3*, gold torque found
as an archeological specimen in Asturias, Spain; *4, Taino* mining gold for the
Spaniards with native bowls of wood; *5*, the cut used for emeralds in the
Mediterranean world; *6–7*, leaves of the bitter manioc; *8, Taino* carrying two
baskets by means of a balance pole; *9*, the maguey plant, from which the
Taino made cordage; *10*, the pineapple. (After Oviedo y Valdés, 1851–55,
pl. 2.)

PLATE 92.—**Arawak dance to the earth goddess.** (After Picard. Reproduced from Fewkes, 1907, pl. 10.)

monest in *Ciguayo* territory on the eastern end of the island and nobles used them more than commoners. The arrows seem to have been made in the same manner as darts; they were featherless and bore poison only in the vicinity of the *Ciguayo* territory.

Warriors practiced dodging missiles. Before going into battle, they painted their bodies red, hung little stone images of the zemis on their foreheads, and danced. They did not use feathers and had no martial music. They attacked from ambuscades and attempted to surprise the enemy. No mention is made of the treatment of prisoners or of cannibalism, but a victory dance is recorded.

ESTHETIC AND RECREATIONAL ACTIVITIES

Art.—The *Taino* had developed stone carving to a greater extent than any of the other Indians of the Tropical Forests. They also carved well in wood, bone, and shell. Their modeling in clay, however, was poor. No examples of painting, which was done principally on the human body, have survived.

The overwhelming art motif was the zemi, represented as a grotesque anthropomorphic being, usually with the arms and legs flexed and with prominent male or female genitals (p. 535). This occurred as petroglyphs, in the form of idols, and upon secular implements and utensils. A cruder, geometric type of design was also produced, the principal motif being an oval line enclosing a straight line ending in dots.

Games and sports.—The Indians were fond of various athletic contests, including running, wrestling, fighting, and, above all, a ball game. The last was played in a rectangular court, which formed part of each village. As many as 20 persons participated on a side. They used a rubberlike ball made from the gum of a tree. The players had to keep it in the air without crossing a line, knocking it out of the court, or touching it with their hands and feet. Each time one of the sides failed to do this, its opponents scored a point. The spectators sat around the court on slabs of stone, the chiefs on their carved wooden stools.

Both men and women played this ball game, but never together (except that the young men of the village occasionally opposed the young women). Often village played village, using the large courts outside the villages. The chiefs sometimes offered prizes.

The ball games and other contests were accompanied by dancing, which also took place upon ceremonial occasions, such as the marriage or death of a chief, before and after victory in battle, and during the autumnal festival in honor of the chief's zemis (pl. 92). The more solemn dances were organized by the chiefs, who sent messengers to inform the people; the more jocular ones, however, took place without authority. Sometimes the men and women attended together; sometimes they had separate dances.

Dances.—Dances were usually held at night, when it was cool. In preparation, the *Taino* bathed, decorated themselves, and vomited, using an emetic made of the paste from an herb (see below).

Men and women, if both were present, sometimes danced together or separately. They stood opposite each other or formed a ring, sometimes placing their arms on each other's shoulders. The leader (a chief) began, and then the dancers repeated his motions. Often violent, these consisted of a series of steps or else of pantomime. In one case the women are said to have carried branches of trees. In historic times, at least, the dancers were liberally supplied with corn beer and usually became quite drunk. Some took snuff and became unconscious. An unconscious chief was put to bed, but ordinary people were left on the ground. The dance lasted until the people became exhausted.

Such dances were accompanied by singing, the two together being termed an areíto. The leader of the dance also led the singing; he sang a phrase in a medium voice, and then it was repeated in a higher tone by the dancers. Only the chief and nobles could act as leaders; they learned the songs by heart in childhood. Each song lasted 3 or 4 hours, and it dealt with one of the following topics: Warfare, mourning, love, the power of the zemis, and the history and deeds of ancestors. In particular, there were songs celebrating the events of the previous chief's reign, composed at his funeral and sung throughout the reign of his successor.

Musical instruments.—Three kinds of musical instruments were used to accompany the songs and dances: drums, rattles, and a kind of castanet. The drums were actually gongs hollowed out of logs (pl. 90, *3–6*). Like modern matracas, the rattles consisted of gourds filled with stones; those of shamans had split handles. For castanets the *Taino* used little plates of metal, attached to the fingers. Only the chiefs and principal men were accustomed to play these instruments, but the ordinary people wore strings of snail shells on their arms and legs while dancing, to give a rattling sound.

Stimulants.—Tobacco was native to Hispaniola. The *Taino* made it into cigars (tabaco), wrapping the dried leaf in a corn husk. This smoking was apparently secular; for religious purposes the natives prepared snuff (cahoba) from the *Piptadenia* plant, grinding the seeds in mortars, carrying the powder in calabashes suspended around their necks, and sniffing it through forked tubes (pl. 90, *7*). During the ceremonies they also pounded up and drank the leaves of an herb (gioia), which may have been either coca or a plant resembling it, in order to induce vomiting.[16]

---

[16] There is considerable difference of opinion concerning these uses of narcotics. Roth (1887, p. 258) follows Oviedo y Valdés in assuming that the sniffing through tubes was of tobacco smoke rather than a powder. Lovén (1935, pp. 388–394) concludes that snuff was used but that it was made from tobacco leaves rather than *Piptadenia* seeds. Roth (1887, p. 259) has likewise suggested that the leaves taken to induce vomiting were of tobacco rather than coca. The version presented above is taken from Safford (1916. 1917) and Roumain (1942).

RELIGION

Spirits.—The *Taino* believed in the existence of spirits or souls, not only in their own bodies but also in some trees, rocks, and other natural phenomena. The spirits of nature are not named, and our sources do not describe their character. The spirits of living people were called "goeiz"; those of the deceased "opia." Even during life the goeiz could leave the body; after death they went as opias to an earthly paradise called Coaibai, which was said to be a remote valley in some part of Hispaniola. At night the opias sometimes returned to visit the living and to obtain a certain kind of fruit of which they were fond. They were apparently considered malevolent, for people traveled in groups at night to avoid them. A woman always felt for her partner's navel before having sexual intercourse for fear that a spirit without a navel was attempting to rape her. There is some indication that dreams and nightmares were considered the work of the spirits; a man, for example, would sometimes fight with an opia and then find that he had got hold of a tree, or he would think he was lying with a woman and then find that no one was there and, presumably, that he had been tricked by a spirit.

Zemis.—The *Taino* believed that by obtaining control over the spirits of nature and of their ancestors they would gain supernatural power. They did this by constructing idols of wood, stone, bone, shell, clay, cotton, or gold as places for the spirits to reside. These idols were called zemis; each person had at least one and often as many as ten zemis. The chief often kept his in a special house built for that purpose on the outskirts of the town; the ordinary people had theirs in their homes. Zemis were also placed in various sacred caves, some being carved on the walls in the form of petroglyphs. The rock carvings in the open in various parts of the island may also have been zemis. People painted images of their zemis on their bodies, carved them in jewelry, and decorated many of their utensils with them.

Most zemis were in the shape of grotesque human beings, often with prominent male or female sexual organs. There were also animal and vegetable forms, including turtles, lizards, frogs, birds, leaves, manioc, and potatoes. Some zemis were geometric; these included the three-pointed stones and possibly the collars and other problematical stone carvings found in the Antilles. The stones which the shamans "removed" from the bodies of sick persons were also considered zemis, as were the bones of the deceased which some Indians kept as fetishes. Those of a dead chief were often encased in a wooden image of the chief; others were kept in the house in baskets.

Some zemis, such as the bones of an ancestor, seem to have required no special preparation. Others were apparently constructed in response to dreams or to other visionary experiences. The cotton zemis, e.g., are said to have been representations of images seen during dreams. Those of wood or of stone were made in the following manner: When a *Taino* was going through a forest, he might discover by an unusual movement of a tree that he was being accosted by a spirit. He would ask the spirit for its command and would be told to fetch a certain shaman. After arriving at the tree, the shaman would take snuff in an apparent effort to induce visions of the spirit and would "converse" with the latter. If the spirit so instructed, the shaman would cut down the tree and carve from it a zemi in the form ordered by the spirit. He would bring this zemi, with the spirit inside it, to his house or temple and there worship it.

The zemis were highly regarded because of the powers they were thought to give to their owners. Each *Taino* boasted that his were the best. We hear of attempts by one person to steal the zemis of another and of the transfer of zemis from one person to another—whether by trade or by inheritance is not stated. It would seem that the chiefs depended for their power on the superiority of their zemis. This is revealed by the experience of the Spaniards when they discovered that a chief had constructed a speaking tube between his zemi and a hidden corner, where a confederate spoke into the tube, making it appear that the zemi was talking. The Spaniards threatened to expose this deception, whereupon the chief begged them not to, saying that it would undermine his authority over his subjects.

Each zemi had its own name, and there was a story concerning its origin, its personality, and its powers, often set forth in song. Many zemis had supernatural characteristics, such as the ability to regrow legs that had been burned off or the strength to break cords with which they were bound, but otherwise they were believed to act as in natural life. The zemis in human shape, e.g., would eat the food offerings set before them. One male zemi is said to have been a philanderer; a female one was supposed to have had two attendants. Another zemi in the form of an animal was believed to run away into the forests at night, and parties were organized from time to time to search for it.

The powers of the zemis varied. Some were believed to influence the weather, some to foretell future events (particularly victory or defeat in warfare), some to regulate crops, some to improve hunting and fishing, some to produce wealth, and others to help women during childbirth. The stones "removed" by shamans from the bodies of the sick were considered the best for the latter purpose. Three-pointed stones had the most power over crops.

Each zemi was set up in a niche or upon a table, with a smaller table or bowl containing snuff in front of it. When the owner wished to utilize the powers of his zemi, he would place some of the snuff on top of its head (which was often carved flat for the purpose) and would sniff it through a forked tube, thereby inducing visions and learning the will of the zemi. Some people fasted 5 days before communicating with their zemis; some vomited first in order to purify themselves, using either a stick or the paste made from an herb. It is said that some worshipers, weakened perhaps by fasting, became unconscious when they took the snuff.[17]

It was believed that if a zemi were not supplied with food it would cause its owner to become ill. Therefore, the owner gave it food from time to time or rubbed it with cassava. Each fall the whole village brought offerings to the chief's zemis, this being the occasion for an elaborate ceremony organized by the chief. The ceremony began with a procession of the villagers, dressed in their best ornaments and singing songs about the zemis. The chief led this procession, beating on a drum; he was followed by men and women carrying baskets of manioc bread, decorated with flowers. The chief seated himself at the entrance to the temple, still beating the drum, while the rest of the people entered. Within, the chief's attendants dressed the zemis. Each of the villagers presented himself before the temple, pressed a stick down his throat, and vomited in order to purify himself. Then the worshipers sat back upon their heels and sang more songs. The women brought their bread to the attendants to be presented to the zemis. Dancing followed, and the people sang the praises of the zemis and of their former chiefs, also offering prayers for the prosperity of the village. Finally the attendants broke up the manioc bread and distributed the pieces to the heads of families. These fragments were preserved all year as a protection against accidents.

SHAMANISM

It is not clear whether the chief and his attendants (the principal men of the village) were also shamans. The latter had a special name, bohuti. They wore the figures of their zemis on their bodies, communicated with the zemis or with other spirits of the dead at public séances, and had enough position to refuse to accept the poorer people as patients. When curing a sick person they worked only in the presence of the principal men and received gifts of cassava in payment.

Before the shaman visited a sick person both he and his patient fasted. The shaman then took snuff in order to learn the cause of the disease from his zemi. He blackened his face with soot and proceeded to the sick person's hut. There he swallowed an herb called gioia, which induced vomiting (p. 534). He lighted a torch, took a certain kind of juice, and began to sing, accompanying the song with his rattle. He approached the patient, sucked his body, grimaced as if he had discovered something disagreeable, and drew off an imaginary object, going to the door and throwing it outside.

The shaman sometimes sucked out a stone, a piece of flesh, or a bone object (secreted on his person for the purpose). This was considered the cause of the disease; often the shaman would put it in a small basket, give

---

[17] See footnote 16 above for a discussion of the nature of the snuff and paste taken during ceremonies and for the possibility that tobacco smoke was absorbed.

it to the patient after his recovery, and tell him to treat it as a zemi. He might explain that the person had swallowed it, thereby causing the disease, or he might say that the patient's own zemi had put it in his body, making him sick because he had neglected to care properly for the zemi.

If the patient died and his family was powerful enough to oppose the shaman, they might blame the latter for the death. Before doing this they attempted to learn from the deceased himself whether the shaman had been negligent in his curing ceremony or had caused the death in some other manner. Making juice from the gioia leaf, they mixed it with the nails of the deceased and with hair from his forehead pounded between two stones, poured the mixture down his throat and nostrils, and asked him to say whether the shaman was the cause of his death. Another method was to place the corpse on live coals, covering it with earth; in this case the deceased could answer 10 questions, and smoke from the fire might reach the shaman, causing him, if he were guilty, to break forth in sores.

Having learned that the shaman had caused the death, the family waylaid and beat him. This never killed the shaman, however, as his zemis, taking the form of snakes, licked his injuries and helped him to recover.

The shaman and certain old women knew various herbs and infusions for treating disease. The only one mentioned by name is guayacan (made by boiling the wood of a tree), which was used to cure pimples. The patient took this for a period of 20 days, during which he had to abstain from meat or fish. Baths and purgatives were considered treatments for disease; some women used an aphrodisiac. No cure is mentioned for syphilis, but it may have been prevalent.

MYTHOLOGY

In response to questions concerning a supreme deity, the *Taino* mentioned an immortal invisible being called Jocchu Vague Maorocon, who lived in the heavens. This person had a mother with five names (Attabeira, Mamona, Guacarapita, Iiella, and Guimazoa) and a maternal uncle, Guaca.[18]

The Indians believed that the sun and moon came out of a cave called Giououcua, in which they were accustomed to worship at the time of the Conquest, and that their ancestors had emerged from two other caves in Hispaniola called Cacibagiagua and Amaiuua. The first people to come out were changed by the sun into stones, trees, and animals.

A man named Guaguiona persuaded the women and children to abandon this cave life in Hispaniola. He took the women to the island of Matinino (sometimes identified with Guadeloupe) and the children to Guanin, where they eventually turned into small animals (particularly frogs) from lack of food. Guaguiona himself returned to Matinino and had many experiences with the women, including an attack of syphilis.

---

[18] These names vary greatly in the sources. Bourne (1907, p. 318) gives a detailed synonymy.

Meanwhile the rest of the men, left alone on Hispaniola, had to find a substitute for the women. They discovered a group of neutral beings hidden in a tree, and had woodpeckers fashion female genitals in them.

The origin of the sea was attributed to a man Giaia and to four brothers born to a woman who died at their birth. The man Giaia slew his son, placed the bone in a gourd, and kept the gourd in his hut. When later he examined the gourd, the bones had turned to fish. He left them there, but one time the four brothers came into the hut in his absence and upset the gourd, causing the waters of the sea to pour forth.

Several other myths explain how the four brothers, one of whom was called Caracarocol because he was scabby, obtained manioc and tobacco from people whom they visited. These stories are said to have been put to song.

LORE AND LEARNING

The *Taino* could count only to 10. As already mentioned, they kept a record of their immediate past in song. Their only tradition of the far past was that they had originally lived in Martinique and had abandoned that island because of quarrels with the rest of the population. They had no writing, and there is no information as to how they kept time.

THE ETHNOGRAPHY OF HISPANIOLA: CIGUAYO

In the northeastern part of Hispaniola, principally along the north coast and on the Peninsula of Samaná, was a small tribe of Indians who spoke a somewhat different *Arawakan* dialect from the *Taino* (map 8).[19] As they also had a number of peculiarities in customs they have been classed as a separate cultural group, under the name *Ciguayo*.

Some idea of the population of the *Ciguayo* may be obtained from the statement that they were able to muster as many as 15,000 warriors. They wore their hair longer than other people and painted their bodies completely black. Feather headdresses were more common among them than among their *Taino* neighbors. They made fewer aristocratic distinctions. In historic times they had a chief named Mayobanex, but he may have been under the domination of the neighboring *Taino* chief, Guarionex (map 10).

The *Ciguayo* were the most warlike Indians of the Greater Antilles, and in this respect they have been compared with the *Carib*. They were particularly skilled in the use of the bow and arrow; their bows were larger and stronger than those on the other islands. Except for their *Taino* neighbors in the province of Higuey, they were the only *Arawak* of the Greater Antilles to use poison arrows. They were also the only Indians to attack Columbus without warning when he first explored the coasts of Hispaniola and Cuba.

---

[19] Lovén (1935, pp. 46–47) believes that they also represent a separate migration from South America.

THE ETHNOGRAPHY OF PUERTO RICO

By Adolfo de Hostos

POPULATION

Two different peoples—the *Arawak* and the *Carib*—were found in Boriquén (or Borinquén) by the discoverers. The *Arawak*, in permanent possession of the lands, formed the great bulk of the population, scattered throughout the island in the coastal settlements as well as in the mountainous interior and along the valleys of the larger streams. The *Carib,* evidently newcomers, had fought for and gained isolated footholds, mainly along the eastern and southern coasts.[20]

Seventeenth-century estimates as to population, made by Spanish observers living in Puerto Rico, vary from 600,000 at the time of discovery to 20,000 during the Indian rebellion of 1511 (Abbad y Lasierra, 1866, pp. 279, 290). The difference between these figures is too wide to permit their acceptance. According to Oviedo y Valdés (1851–55; Abbad y Lasierra, 1866, p. 63), 11,000 Indian combatants gathered at Yagüeca in 1511. If we suppose that this number represents the maximum manpower available at that time, and that the proportion of the male adults who could bear arms in a relatively feeble-bodied and short-lived population was approximately 5 percent of its total, then it may be surmised that the island had about 200,000 inhabitants 3 years after the Spanish occupation. This is substantiated by the remarkable abundance of prehistoric sites and remains in Puerto Rico.

Most of what is known about the Indians of Puerto Rico concerns the *Arawak*. These Indians, often called *Boriqueño* after their name for the island, appear to have been similar both in language and in culture to the *Taino* of Hispaniola.[21] As a result, Fewkes (1922, p. 169) has placed them in the *Taino* cultural division.

CULTURE

Unlike the rest of the *Arawak* in the Greater Antilles, those in Puerto Rico cultivated pineapples, which they exported to the neighboring islands (Lovén, 1935, p. 406). To judge from the archeology, ball courts were more numerous in Puerto Rico than in Haiti. The stone carving, too, was the best in the Antilles, stone collars, three-pointed or mammiform

---

[20] This is the opinion of Fewkes (1907, p. 219). Lovén (1935, pp. 53–58) cites contrary historical evidence that no permanent *Carib* settlements were ever established in Puerto Rico. None have appeared in the archeology.—Irving Rouse.

[21] Reports that the *Eyeri* dialect of the Lesser Antilles also existed in Puerto Rico are probably unfounded (Morales Cabrera, 1932, pp. 12, 332–333).

idols, and elbow stones being particularly common. Recent research has
shown that these objects, of high artistic excellence, are related to agricultural practices, especially to the supposed "fertilization" of staple food
products by means of certain practices of sympathetic magic. This involves the representation, both direct and symbolical, of certain natural
agencies (entomogamous animals) or mythical concepts (rain- or sun-
procuring deities) incised or carved on the fetishes (Hostos, 1941, pp.
108–132, 146–174).

Upon landing on the island in 1508, Juan Ponce de León found regional
authority vested in certain chieftains, or caciques. Whether these chiefs
exercised authority over the members of a clan, a moiety, or a tribe the
author has been unable to ascertain. Agüeybana, or Güeybana, is often
mentioned by some 16th-century chroniclers as the island's principal
cacique, but in most cases they fail to state whether this appellation is
given him by reason of the extent of his territory, the number of its inhabitants, or the fact that it comprised other tributary caciquedoms.
Oviedo y Valdés (in Tapia y Rivera, 1854, p. 15), on the other hand,
refers to the "principal lord" of Boriquén (whose name he omits) and
states that he was "obeyed by many other caciques." There is a hint here
that the Boriquén *Arawak* constituted a tribe, divided into groups whose
exact nature no one, perhaps, would venture to define on the strength
of the available data.

The names of some of the caciques ("régulos," i.e., chiefs of small
states) simultaneously ruling over certain island districts has been preserved. From them a reconstruction has been made of the distribution
of the chieftainships, as shown on map 11.

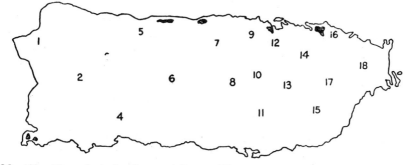

MAP 11.—The principal villages of Puerto Rico and of their chiefs. 1, Aymaco
(chief Aymamon) ; 2, Yagueca (chief Urayoan) ; 3, Guajataca (chief Maboda-
maca) ; 4, Guaynia (chiefs Agueybana 1 and 2) ; 5, Abacoa (chief Arasibo) ;
6, Otoao (chief Guarionex) ; 7, Sibuco (chief Guacabo) ; 8, Jatibonico (chief
Orocobix) ; 9, Toa (chief Aramana) ; 10, Guaynabo (chief Mabo) ; 11, Guayama
(chief Guamani) ; 12, Bayamon (chief Majagua) ; 13, Turabo (chief Caguax) ;
14, Cayniabon (chief Canobana) ; 15, Guayaney (chief Guaraca) ; 16, Jaymanio
(chieftainess Yuisa) ; 17, Macao (chief Humacao) ; 18, Daguao (chief Daguao).
(After Coll y Toste, 1907.)

The Puerto Rican *Arawak* were more warlike than the other *Taino,* perhaps because of their greater exposure to *Carib* raids. The warriors were led into battle by people blowing on conch-shell trumpets. They were expert in the use of the bow and arrow, although they employed no poison. Cannibalism was not practiced.

From information available in the texts of some of the early chroniclers (F. Columbus, 1811, pp. 133–141; Casas, n. d., pp. 523–550; Martyr de Anghiera, 1912, pp. 167–176), which, although meagre, is sufficiently revealing, and from references as to the functions of some of the Indian artifacts and their possible connection with biological phenomena, it appears that the *Arawak* of Boriquén based their agricultural practices on animistic conceptions of plant life, although in some respect they were certainly developing more rational ideas.[22] It has been demonstrated, for example, that fertility idols, commonly called three-pointed stones, were employed in an effort to control certain natural agencies (insect pests, rainfall, germination processes, etc.) through the efficacy of magico-religious practices based firmly on animistic reasoning (Hostos, 1941). Idols embodying the stylized form of certain edible roots, or some of their parts, further strengthened with representations of animals beneficial to plant life or with symbols of rain or bud germination, were generally utilized in conjunction with formulas of specific magic to promote plant growth (Hostos, 1941).

THE ETHNOGRAPHY OF CUBA

POPULATION

The name for the island of Cuba is aboriginal; its etymology is not known. Archeological and historical research has shown that the inhabitants, sometimes called *Cubeño,* fall into three culturally distinct groups (map 8). As already described, the western tip of the island and certain isolated places elsewhere were occupied by *Ciboney.* On the eastern tip were *Taino,* who are said to have migrated from Hispaniola only 50 years before the Conquest. The remainder of the island was inhabited by *Sub-Taino,* who are also believed to have come into Cuba from Hispaniola, after the *Ciboney* but before the *Taino* (Rouse, 1942, pp. 30–33). The population of all three groups, taken together, has been variously estimated from 16,000 to 600,000; this would indicate that the island was more sparsely settled than either Hispaniola or Puerto Rico.

CULTURE

The differences in culture between the two *Arawak*-speaking groups (*Taino* and *Sub-Taino*) are difficult to determine from the sources, for most of the early explorers did not distinguish between them. From the

---

[22] Soil fertilization mainly by means of sympathetic magic coexisted with certain practical means of fertilization, such as irrigation and the application of organic matter to the soil.

standpoint of archeology, however, the *Taino* had essentially the same culture as their namesakes in Hispaniola, and therefore it may be suggested that most of the features in which the culture differed from Hispaniola apply to the *Sub-Taino*.

The *Arawak* of Cuba used the suckerfish (*Remora*) to catch turtles and other fish, attaching its tail to a line and float. They snared parrots with nooses fastened to the ends of rods, which were manipulated by children hiding in blinds. More improvident than the *Taino* of Hispaniola, they are said to have had at any one time only enough food to last 4 to 8 days. Cotton was particularly common, but gold was rare. The villages were located in high areas along the coast and inland. One pile dwelling is mentioned.

The *Arawak* of Cuba were most peaceful. They had neither the bow nor the arrow. Their chieftainships, although numerous, were smaller· than in Hispaniola (map 9) and were apparently not divided into districts ruled by subchiefs. There is some indication, too, that the power of the chief was not so great as in Hispaniola. The jus primae noctis seems to have been peculiar to Cuba.

Some archeological data from the *Sub-Taino* sites may help to fill out this ethnographic picture. The *Sub-Taino* had a preference for locating their villages on hilltops. They built no ball courts, nor did they carve petroglyphs, as did the *Taino*. They were particularly fond of shell ornaments and made a simpler pottery than is found in the *Taino* sites. Three-pointed stones, collars, and many other typically *Taino* representations of zemis are absent from their territory, but they did construct many idols of clay, bone, shell, and stone, most of them simpler in conception than the *Taino* zemis.

THE ETHNOGRAPHY OF JAMAICA

The term "Jamaica" is an Indian one and has been said to mean fertile land. According to one estimate, the aboriginal population numbered slightly more than 60,000; according to another it was 600,000. Like the Indians of central Cuba, those of Jamaica have been classed in the *Sub-Taino* cultural group (map 8), on the basis of archeological reports that they lacked the ball courts, wooden stools, elaborate stone zemis, and (except in one case) petroglyphs of the *Taino*.

As in Cuba, fishing was done with the suckerfish (*Remora*). The bow and arrow were absent, and there was apparently little gold. (It did not occur naturally on the island.) Cotton was unusually common. Feather caps and capes, women's aprons embroidered with stone beads, a gold pendant in the form of a fleur-de-lis, and other ornaments like those in Hispaniola were observed by Columbus.

It has been established that there were 8 or 10 chiefs on the whole island, at the time of historic contact, but the names of only 2 along the northeastern coast have survived: Ameyro and Huareo.[23] The people were gentle and peaceable and at first received the Spaniards with hospitality. A chief who met Columbus was accompanied by a "standard bearer" and by attendants with wooden drums and with trumpets (which may have been batons). A number of wooden idols have been found in the caves of Jamaica.

THE ETHNOGRAPHY OF THE BAHAMAS

The *Arawak* name for the inhabitants of the Bahamas was *Lucayo* (map 8). Their population has been estimated at 40,000, which is probably an exaggeration. These Indians had the same dialect as on the other islands, but their culture was simpler. Because of the relative infertility of the soil, fishing predominated over agriculture. The *Lucayo* had the bow and arrow but used them only for fishing. The parrot was the only domesticated animal. *Lucayo* villages were small, comprising on Long Island not more than 15 houses, and lacked ball courts. Feather mantles and pearl beads are mentioned; also rafts made by binding sticks together. Gold was rare, as it had to be imported.

Each village had its own chief, who seems to have been independent. Class distinctions were not so far developed as in Hispaniola and Puerto Rico. The people were peaceful. They traded largely in balls of cotton, parrots, and tobacco leaves. They made petroglyphs and had the *Taino* style of cooking pottery. Although they lacked stone collars and three-pointed stones, they had other idols comparable to those of the *Taino*.

THE ETHNOGRAPHY OF THE VIRGIN ISLANDS

It is generally assumed that the Virgin Islands, as well as the small neighboring islands of Vieques and Culebra, which are now under the jurisdiction of Puerto Rico, were inhabited during historic times by the *Carib*. Hatt (1924, pp. 41–42), however, could find no archeological traces of the *Carib* in the Virgin Islands and therefore suggests that at least the island of St. Croix still belonged to the *Arawak*.

The ethnographic data are little help in settling this problem. The inhabitants of St. Croix, the largest of the Virgins, are said to have practiced cannibalism and poisoned their arrows, like the *Carib*. The fact that they attacked the Spaniards without warning also suggests that they were *Carib,* although this was likewise a custom of the *Arawak*-speaking *Ciguayo*. On the other hand, the St. Croix people seem to have had chieftainesses and female warriors, both of which are *Arawak* rather than *Carib* traits, and they called their island Agay, apparently an *Arawak* term.

---

[23] Several sources claim that these two chiefs ruled over the whole island and were chronologically rather than geographically distinct. According to this version, Ameyro and Huareo were the last of a dynasty begun in 1420 and including Beroica, Bemberoica 1, and Bemberoica 2 (also called Abemberoica).

According to the archeological evidence, the latest prehistoric inhabitants of the Virgin Islands belonged to the *Taino* division of the *Arawak* cultural group. They constructed ball courts, carved petroglyphs, and had most of the elaborate zemis characteristic of Puerto Rico. An example has been found of a funnel leading through a stone slab to a carving of a zemi, perhaps comparable to the tube described above (p. 536), in connection with the *Taino* religion in Hispaniola (Hatt, 1924, pp. 36–37).

THE ETHNOGRAPHY OF THE LESSER ANTILLES

The *Carib* name for the *Arawak* whom they conquered in the Lesser Antilles was *Igneri*. A variant of this term, *Eyeri* is often used for the distinctive *Arawak* dialect of the Lesser Antilles, and the name *Igneri* is applied also to their culture. Only a few traces of this culture have survived in the archeology and in the history or can be inferred from the customs which the *Carib* are likely to have adopted from their *Igneri* predecessors. As in the Greater Antilles, the Indians apparently cultivated manioc, lived in brush huts, carved petroglyphs, and set up idols of cotton in the caves. There was frontal deformation, and the women wore skirts. The bow and arrow were present; burial was either primary or secondary.

On the other hand, ball courts are not represented in the Lesser Antilles. The pottery styles appear different from those of the Greater Antilles and there are not elaborately carved idols. It may be inferred that the priesthood, and therefore probably also chieftainship and the social hierarchy, were less developed among the *Igneri* than among the *Taino*.

THE ETHNOGRAPHY OF TRINIDAD

The *Arawak* of Trinidad are generally included within the *Igneri* cultural group of the Lesser Antilles (map 8). Unlike their neighbors in the latter region, they survived the effects of the *Carib* migration except in the northwestern part of the island, where the *Carib* are said to have seized control.[24] Since the early explorers failed to distinguish between *Arawak* and *Carib* customs, our ethnographic information is probably a mixture of both. In the following account the data may refer either to the *Arawak* or to the *Carib*, unless otherwise stated.

The *Arawak* name for Trinidad was Cairi, meaning island. The inhabitants seem to have spoken a different dialect from that in the Greater Antilles, but it is not known whether it was the same as the *Eyeri* dialect of the Lesser Antilles. Their bodies are said to have been lighter and better proportioned. They had, however, the same general food habits,

---

[24] According to Scott (*in* Harlow, 1925, p. 120) there were three ethnic groups in Trinidad at the time of the discovery: *Carib* in the north, *Arawak* in the south, and a group in the center who were variously called *Napoyes* and *Sepoyes*. Lovén, (1935, p. 41) concludes that the latter group was also *Arawak*. Fewkes (1922, pp. 64–65) argues that all three were *Arawak*.

except that deer, which were absent elsewhere in the West Indies, were available to them. Their houses, which they moved frequently, were large and bell-shaped; each local group, comprising as many as 100 people, lived in a single house. As among the *Carib*, the Indians had both pirogues and canoes, some with a house structure in the center.

The **Trinidadians** went naked, except for girdles and head bands of many-colored cotton cloth. They wore their hair long and parted it in the middle, as among the *Carib*. They painted their bodies red and used feather decoration. The chiefs had gold crowns and eagles of gold for their heads. There were beads of stone and bone (some of the latter were human), as well as small carved stone amulets. Guanin (the gold-copper alloy), stone beads, and pearls were obtained from South America in exchange for tobacco and the greenstone used for making axes. Until recently the Indians of the lower Orinoco River used to make regular trips to Trinidad to obtain articles of trade.

Five "nations," probably equivalent to the chieftainships of the Greater Antilles, are mentioned in the sources.[25] The southeastern corner of the island around Point Galeota was occupied by the *Arwaca*. North of them along the east coast of the island were the *Nepoio*. The northwestern section, centering in Port of Spain, was inhabited by the *Carinepagoto*. South of the latter along the central part of the west coast bordering the Gulf of Paria, were the *Iaio*. The southwest corner, particularly the western part of the south coast which seems to have been the most thickly populated section of the island, was inhabited by the *Saluaio*.[26]

These "nations," which seem to have been ruled by chiefs called acarewanas, sometimes formed alliances against one another during warfare. Men fought with darts, thrown from atlatls having hooks on the extremities of their back sides, with sling stones, and with the bow and arrow. The last, which were carried in quivers, were feathered, tipped with bone, and poisoned. Warriors also used a round or square shield, as on the mainland. War parties signaled with drums and had shell trumpets. Burial was in the ground or in caves, the bodies being flexed horizontally and sometimes accompanied by pottery. The shamans took snuff to communicate with the spirits, as in the Greater Antilles.

---

[25] These names vary from source to source. The version presented here is that of Raleigh (1848, p. 4), who states that the list is not complete. See the preceding note for another version.

[26] It is agreed that all these chieftainships except possibly that of the *Carinepagoto* were *Arawak*. Raleigh's description of their location, upon which the above account is based, may be interpreted in a number of different ways depending upon how one matches his geographical terms for different parts of the island with the modern terms. The above version is based upon a comparison of the terms of Raleigh (1848, p. 4) with those upon the map of Trinidad in Dudley (1899, back cover), which also bears several of the tribal names mentioned by Raleigh. Somewhat different versions are presented by Lovén (1935, pp. 40–41) and Schomburgk (in the notes to Raleigh's account (1848, p. 4) and on the folding map in front of that book).

THE CARIB

By Irving Rouse

INTRODUCTION

The *Carib*, like the *Arawak*, were South American in origin. According to their traditions, they came into the West Indies no more than a century before the arrival of Columbus; by his time they had succeeded in conquering all the Lesser Antilles and probably also the northeastern part of Trinidad, exterminating the *Arawak* men who formerly lived there and taking their wives as slaves. They were conducting raids upon the *Arawak* of the Greater Antilles, but there is no confirmation of reports that they had settled anywhere in that territory, except possibly in spots on the eastern end of Puerto Rico.

ARCHEOLOGY

Very little work has been done on *Carib* archeology. Some writers, however, have assigned to the *Carib* all the archeological remains in the Lesser Antilles described above as *Arawak*. In view of the shortness of the time during which the *Carib* inhabited the Lesser Antilles, this is not likely. The only possibly authentic *Carib* site known to the writer is the place at Banana Bay on the small island of Balliceaux to which the English moved the *Black Carib* in 1797. Fewkes (1922, p. 89), who made a study of this site, has not described the material found.[1]

Additional *Carib* sites will undoubtedly be found in the future, but it should be difficult to identify them because of the fact that the *Carib* wives were often captive *Arawak* women, who probably made the pottery and other objects which survive in the sites according to their own customs. A study of the location of the historic *Carib* sites may perhaps help to overcome this difficulty.

HISTORY

Columbus first made contact with the *Carib* during his second voyage, in 1493, when he purposely sailed farther south in order to investigate these fierce savages of whom he had heard in Hispaniola. His first landing place was a small uninhabited island near Dominica; from there he went to Guadeloupe and discovered a *Carib* village. The men being absent on a raid, he was able to receive on board six captive *Arawak* women from

[1] Lovén (1935, p. 545) believes that even this site is *Arawak*.

Puerto Rico. He then proceeded to St. Croix, where *Carib* warriors savagely attacked the expedition before it departed for the *Arawak* island of Puerto Rico.

The Spaniards made no attempt to settle the Lesser Antilles. There was no gold there, and the agricultural potentialities did not compensate for the difficulty of subduing the *Carib*. The colonists did, however, make numerous slave raids against the islands taking advantage, after the prohibition of such raids elsewhere, of a provision permitting attacks on cannibals.

In 1623 the British and French settled St. Kitts, driving the *Carib* from that island with great cruelty. In rapid succession the British then colonized Nevis, St. Lucia, Barbados, Montserrat, and Antigua; the French settled Guadeloupe, Martinique, Désirade, Marie-Galante, St. Lucia, and Grenada; and the Dutch occupied Montserrat and Antigua. By the end of the century the *Carib* had been driven from all the important islands except Dominica and St. Vincent, and on those islands they were being buffeted between the British and French, each of whom obtained the aid of the savages in attacks on the other.

French missionaries made many attempts after 1650 to convert the *Carib* to Christianity, but with little success. The missionaries began to reside among the Indians, to study and speak their language. Fathers like Raymond Breton and Phillipe de Beaumont remained 25 years in Dominica, but the *Carib* gave only lip service to the Christian religion. About 1706 the missionaries abandoned St. Vincent entirely because of a plot of the *Carib* to kill all of them.

In 1675 a cargo of Negro slaves was shipwrecked upon St. Vincent, and they intermarried with the Indians. This *Carib*-Negro mixture became most hostile to the Europeans, and so in 1795 the English moved them from St. Vincent, first to the small island of Balliceaux offshore and later to Ruatán Island near the coast of Honduras, where they now occupy the entire coastline from Stann Creek in British Honduras to Black River in the Republic of Honduras, and are known as the *Garif,* or *Black Carib.*

The *Carib* who remained in the West Indies also intermarried somewhat with the Negroes. They continued to reside in Dominica and St. Vincent until the end of the 19th century, when they were moved to a reservation in Dominica. At present there are some 500 survivors, less than a third of whom are full-blooded[2] (pl. 98).

SOURCES

Many of the writings of Columbus, his son, and the early explorers and historians who have been quoted above as sources for *Arawak* ethnology also contain some data on the *Carib*. The best material, however, comes

---

[2] The above account does not take into consideration the few *Carib* believed to have lived among the *Arawak* in Puerto Rico and Trinidad. Their history has already been given above in connection with the *Arawak.*

from the missionaries and other observers who had contact with the Indians between 1650 and 1700, when the Lesser Antilles were first being settled. Bouton (1640), Breton (1877, 1892), Labat (1724, 1931), La Borde (1704, 1886), Du Puis (1652), and Dutertre (1667–71; copied in Rochefort, 1665, and Davies, 1666) are the principal primary sources. These have been compiled by Ballet (1875), Harris (1904), Sheldon (1820), Cornilliac (1875), Edwards (1818–19), Featherman (1881–91), Jefferys (1760), Joyce (1916), and Ober (1895), in the last six cases in conjunction with comparable compilations of *Arawak* ethnography. Delawarde (1938), Ober (1880), and D. Taylor (1935, 1936, 1938) have provided information concerning the modern descendants of the *Carib* in the West Indies, while Conzemius (1928) and Sapper (1897 b) have described the *Black Carib* of Central America.

Although the number of *Carib* sources and compilations is smaller than for the *Arawak,* each source, being more or less ethnographic in nature, contains relatively more information, and our knowledge of *Carib* culture is therefore comparable to that of *Arawak* culture. Many of the missionaries failed to distinguish between islands, and as a result the following account will deal with the *Carib* as a whole. The period covered is that from 1650 to 1700, when the *Carib* were concentrated on Dominica, Martinique, and St. Vincent.

ETHNOGRAPHY

The *Carib* had a strong national consciousness. To distinguish themselves from the *Arawak* they used the term *Calinago* or *Calino,* which was corrupted by Columbus to *Caribales,* and later to *Carib.* From it comes our word "cannibal." The inhabitants of each island had a special name, which was formed by adding a suffix to the name of the island. Dominica, for example, was called Oüaitoucoubouli, and its inhabitants had the name *Oüaitoucoubouliri.*

Carib men and women had certain differences in language, which may have been due to the fact that many of the women had been captured from the *Arawak.* When speaking together both sexes used the men's language. The old men also had some words not found in the ordinary men's language. These were developed in the war councils.

No estimates of the original population of the *Carib* islands have been discovered. By 1700, it is said that the number of those Indians had fallen to 4,000, half of them on Dominica and the rest on St. Vincent. The *Carib* were more robust than the *Arawak.* They had well-developed, flexible bodies and broad buttocks and shoulders. Their height was medium, the skin olive-colored, and the hair and eyes black. When at ease they tended to be melancholy; when aroused they became truculent and vindictive.

SUBSISTENCE ACTIVITIES

Fishing.—The staple food of the *Carib* was the crab, which they hunted at night by torchlight. They roasted the meat, seasoning it with a sauce called taumalin,[3] a mixture of lime juice and pounded peppers with the greenish meat next to the shell of the male crab.

Sea food was an important part of the diet. The *Carib* picked up shellfish along the shore. They caught fish with small nets (at night or when the water was calm); with hook and line (the hooks being of tortoise shell); by scattering a certain kind of poisonous wood on the water; or by use of the bow and arrow. The arrows were long and three-pronged; each was attached by a string to a wooden float so that it could easily be retrieved. Harpoons (with separate points) were employed to catch the manatee and sea turtle; the land turtle was stalked. Corrals are mentioned; they may have been fish wiers.

Hunting.—On land the *Carib* hunted the agouti and the lizard with dogs, smoking the lizards out of the holes into which the dogs drove them. They also caught birds, using the bow and arrows tipped with cotton or else stupefying the birds with smoke from a poisonous wood.

Domesticated animals.—Parrots and dogs were the only domesticated animals except when, in historic times, the people kept poultry and swine, largely for trade with the Europeans.

Preparation of fish and meat.—The *Carib* took special pains in the preparation of fish and meat, broiling them sometimes for a whole day over a slow fire on a wooden grid 2 feet (0.6 m.) high. They also roasted fish and agouti meat in the ash and smoked the latter for purposes of storage, cooking the smoked meat in cassava juice when they wished to eat it. For the seasoning of fish and meat they used a sauce called coüi, which was made by boiling the juice of the manioc with crushed peppers, lime juice, and manioc flour. They made a soup from left-over scraps of fish and meat, as well as from agouti bones. These were boiled in manioc juice with peppers, manioc flour, and oysters to form a strong mixture in which the Indians dipped cassava bread. Apparently this was as close as the *Carib* came to the typical *Arawak* pepper pot.

The same sources that describe the foregoing methods of hunting, fishing, and preparing meat also mention a taboo on the manatee, the turtle, and all land animals. The sources imply that this taboo was general, a fact difficult to reconcile with the above statements.[4] It is certain, however, that the *Carib* never took salt or ate the flesh of the eel and that they avoided fat.

Farming and preparation of agricultural foods.—The Indians cultivated both the bitter and the sweet varieties of manioc, using the same

---

[3] All *Carib* terms cited here are from the men's language.

[4] This discrepancy may represent a difference between ideal and practice or it may reflect a breaking down of the system of taboos. There is some indication that the taboos were followed only during a limited period, as after fasts. (See p. 557.)

methods of planting and of preparation as the *Arawak*. The kitchen utensils, however, were more varied. The *Carib* made their graters from coral, from thorny branches, or by inserting wood or stone splinters in a plank. They removed the juice in a cylindrical basketry strainer (pl. 94), hung with a weight from a tree; sifted the flour in a basketry sieve; and baked the cake on either a stone or a clay griddle with the aid of a wooden spatula.

Corn, sweetpotatoes, yams, beans, and peppers also were cultivated, the corn being made into bread as among the *Arawak*. The sweetpotato and the yam were particularly important; they were planted as cuttings after a rain. When full grown the tubers were roasted or boiled and eaten with a sauce like that made for meat. The roots and leaves were used as a seasoning.

The *Carib* ate fruits of various kinds, including the banana (post-Conquest), the plantain, the guayba, the papaya, and the pineapple. Bananas were cooked in sugared water; both they and the other fruits were also pounded in a mortar to make a thick paste. Sugarcane, acquired from the Spaniards, was boiled in water or was chewed fresh, and honey was mixed with water to make a drink.

Eating.—Except for the morning meal taken soon after fixing their hair and bodies, the *Carib* ate irregularly. Men sat on low stools in the carbet (men's house) and were served by women on little tables (matoutou), covered with leaves. Later the women ate by themselves in the kitchen.

VILLAGES AND HOUSES

Settlements.—*Carib* villages were located in the areas least favorable for surprise attacks by the enemy, being usually on the windward side of the island and in an open space upon a rise in the land. Each village was near a stream, which provided drinking water and was used daily for bathing. The villages were moved frequently, after a death, sickness, or some other disagreeable incident. Each was small; it consisted of a carbet (men's house), various smaller houses for the women, and several storage platforms. These structures were arranged irregularly around a small plaza where the people were accustomed to sit by the light of a fire at night.

Houses.—The carbet (taboüi) was an oval building, which later became rectangular, about 60 feet (18 m.) long and 20 feet (6 m.) wide. To construct it the *Carib* set into the ground forked posts 10 feet (3 m.) high and lashed across beams to the tops of these posts. They laid on poles, extending from the ground at one end to the peak of the house at the other; bound other poles horizontally over the first set; and thatched the whole down to the ground with palm leaves. The floor was of dirt and had a hearth in the center. There were no partitions; the only openings were a door no more than 4 feet (1.2 m.) high in the middle of each side and end.

Men slept in this structure; they and the boys ate, worked, and passed the time of day there. Women, however, entered only to serve the men.

Women's houses were each about half the size of the carbet. Their construction was the same, except that each had only a single doorway and was provided with a reed partition separating the room where the women and children slept from the kitchen.

The storage platforms were built on piles and roofed, but open on the sides.

Household furniture.—Mats were used to cover the doorways of the houses. Within, hammocks were the chief articles of furniture (pl. 93). Made of a network of cotton thread, they were 6 feet (1.8 m.) long and 12 feet (3.6 m.) wide. The ends were tied by cords to two posts in the wall of the dwelling; often the cords extended along the sides of the hammock as decoration. Some hammocks were painted red or black. They had a small packet of ash at each end, which was believed to make them last longer. Small wooden tables and stools were used in many houses; some had cabinets in which to store weapons and utensils. The rafters also were a favorite storage place.

When on canoe trips the *Carib* made temporary shelters by erecting posts, to which they attached hammocks, covering them with a roof of palm leaves.

DRESS AND ADORNMENT

Clothing, hairdress, and toilet.—Like the *Arawak,* the *Carib* had no clothing except for a small cotton apron worn by women over their genitals (pl. 93). In historic times this was ornamented with beads. Every morning men washed themselves and sat in the carbet while the women combed their hair, anointing it with oil, and painted their bodies red. The women then dressed themselves in the same manner. The paint, urucú (roucou), was made by mixing oil with boiled and ground seeds from the bixa plant. It was brushed over the whole body, partially for decoration and partially as a protection against insects. On ceremonial occasions men also used black paint made from genipa; they had their wives paint it in streaks over their faces and bodies, using tiny hair brushes.

Rich black hair was considered a sign of beauty. Both men and women wore it long, cutting only the part above the eyes. They let it hang free or sometimes bunched part of it on the back of the head, tying it with a cotton cord and decorating it with tail feathers of the macaw (arara). Only slaves had their hair cut short in the *Arawak* manner. Men plucked their beards, which they considered a deformity.

Deformation and scarification.—A mother flattened both the forehead and the back of her child's head. The *Carib* pierced the ears, nasal septa, and lower lip for the insertion of fishbones, feathers, stone pendants, or pieces of wood, stone, or shell. They used the latter only temporarily, when not wearing the caracoli described below. During ceremonies men scarified their bodies, later staining the scars black. Native-born women were distinguished from captives by wearing anklets made of basketry interwoven with cotton. The anklets were assumed at puberty, and as the wearers grew they became tighter and caused the ankles to swell.

Ornaments.—Both sexes wore bracelets made of cotton or of beads of stone, crystal, bone, seed, coral, shell, or a pearllike substance obtained in shells. Men placed these bracelets around their upper arms and women around the wrists. Both men and women often wore necklaces and girdles of the same materials; it was from the girdles that women hung their aprons. Men sometimes inserted teeth and bones from the enemies they had killed into their necklaces and bracelets. On their chests both sexes hung small amulets of wood or stone carved to represent their maboya (evil spirits) and designed to frighten away other malevolent powers. Small gourd fetishes, containing bird claws and bits of jaguar skin obtained on the mainland, were also used as pendants.

The most prized possession of the men was the caracoli, a crescent-shaped alloy of gold and copper framed in wood, which the warriors obtained during raids upon the continental *Arawak* (pl. 93). Some of these caracoli were small and served as ear, nose, or mouth pendants; others were large enough to be worn on the chest. They were a sign of high rank, being passed down from generation to generation, and were worn only upon ceremonial occasions and during journeys. Certain stone necklaces, the material for which was obtained on the mainland, were also prized. They were said to have had healing virtue and were worn only during feasts. Upon ceremonial occasions men decorated their hair with feather caps and crowns and their backs with jaguar skins; some rubbed their bodies with gum and sprinkled feathers upon them.

TRANSPORTATION

The *Carib* were expert in the management of boats, of which they had four types: pirogues, large canoes, small canoes, and rafts. Both the pirogues and the canoes were dugouts, but the sides of the former were built up with planks, sewn together and pitched with bitumen. The average length of the pirogue was 40 feet (12 m.) ; some were large enough to carry 50 persons. Each one had a keel, a raised and pointed bow, a series of plank seats, and a flat-pooped stern carved with an animal's head (maboya) to frighten the enemy and often decorated with a barbe-cued human arm. The larger variety of canoe was 20 feet (6 m.) long. It, too, had a series of seats and also thwarts against which the paddlers leaned their backs. Both the stem and the stern were high and pointed; there were holes in the gunwales to which the travelers could attach their belongings. The smaller type of canoe was just large enough for one person; it had a flat stern and served mainly for fishing. The rafts consisted of a series of logs, lashed to two transverse bars.

The pirogues and canoes seem to have been better finished than the *Arawak* canoes. Their sides were smoothed, polished, and often painted to represent Indians or maboya spirits. In historic times (and perhaps earlier) the pirogues had three masts and the canoes two, each supporting a sail made from cotton or from palm-leaf matting.[5] The paddles were spade-shaped, like those of the *Arawak;* that of the steersman was one-third longer than the rest (pl. 94).

When on a raiding expedition *Carib* men traveled alone, taking only several women to prepare their food and to paint them with urucú. Otherwise men, women, and children traveled together. They carried their hammocks and kitchen utensils and landed at night to build temporary sleeping shelters.

The *Carib* were quite superstitious about traveling from island to island. While at sea they ate no crabs or lizards and drank no water, for fear of not being able to reach land. They were careful, too, not to spill fresh water into the sea, for they believed that this would cause storms and a swelling of the water. When passing a place where *Carib* had previously been drowned they threw overboard food so as to prevent the dead people, now living at the bottom of the sea, from causing them to capsize. Upon the appearance of a storm cloud they all blew into the air and waved their hands to drive the cloud away. When it did become stormy they chewed manioc bread and spit it into the sea and air to appease the spirits (omicou) who were causing the storm. If the wind were unfavorable, an old man would shoot an arrow at the prow of the canoe in order to make the canoe go straight as an arrow. The *Carib* never named or pointed at the land which they were approaching, for fear that they might not be able to get ashore.

The people traveled by foot when on land, felling a log or using small canoes to cross streams. Burdens were carried in baskets on the back; babies were suspended in little hammocks strung around the mother's neck.

MANUFACTURES

Basketry and weaving.—Next to canoes the outstanding *Carib* artifacts were baskets (pl. 94). The men made these from *Latania* leaves, which they split, scraped with mussel shells, and plaited together. Often the baskets had double walls, separated by a lining of leaves which made them watertight. Some, made large and pyramidal, were used on the back as carrying baskets. Others, which were small, rectangular, and provided with covers, served for jewel boxes. They were supplied with a cord to be attached to the gunwales of the canoes, so that the basket would not be lost

---

[5] Some sources say the pirogues had topsails as well as the usual square mainsails.

if the vessel overturned. Large rectangular baskets, turned upside down
and provided with wooden legs 4 to 5 inches (10 cm.) tall, served as
tables (matoutou). The basketry technique was used also in the manufacture of strainers, sieves, and mats, the functions of which have been
described above. In historic times the natives had brooms.

The weaving of cloth may not have been an original part of *Carib*
culture. The women had wooden spindles for making thread and used
belt looms for weaving it. They stretched the warp threads from a stick
on one side of the house to a stick on the other; then two women wove
in the weft, beating the threads down with a sword-shaped stick. The
cloth was dyed with various colors, particularly red, and was sewn with
a needle made from a palmetto spine.

Pottery and gourds.—The *Carib* baked pots and griddles of clay; the
former were indispensable for making beer. They had numerous gourd
containers, made by removing the pulp with hot water and pebbles. These
included bottles for urucú, covered bowls (coyenbouc) for carrying
trinkets, platters, cups, dippers, and spoons. Often they were engraved
or painted. Coconut shells were treated in the same manner.

Woodworking.—The men not only carved canoes of wood but also
they made bowls, which were used primarily for drinking bouts, and stools,
which either were solid or were provided with four legs.

Fire making.—The people made fire by rubbing one mahot stick
against another.

SOCIAL AND POLITICAL ORGANIZATION

Except in wartimes, each *Carib* village seems to have been an independent organization. It consisted of an extended family which had split
away from some other village and was headed by its founder. This man,
called a carbet chief or tiubutuli-hauthe, had charge of the carbet and of
the entertainment which took place therein. He probably also supervised
fishing and the cultivation of the land, which seems to have been communal. Although he was treated with deference, he had little authority.
The *Carib* men were individualists, and they looked down upon the
Europeans for taking orders.

Each island also had one or two war chiefs, called ubutu, who were
elected to hold office for life. Except that ownership of a caracoli seems
to have been one of the requirements for this chieftainship, no heredity
was involved in the office. However, a son might succeed his father if
he could prove himself worthy. He had to be an experienced warrior
with a good record, excel in swimming and diving, show that he could
carry a greater burden than his followers, and bear burning and slashing
of his flesh without flinching.

The war chief was particularly honored. He was provided with an
assistant, and wherever he went he was surrounded by a retinue. His

were the first fruits of any feast. It was his duty to conduct the war council in one of the carbets; he also had charge of some of the entertainment there.

Two or more war chiefs usually participated in each raid, one of them being chosen head chief, but only for the period of the raid. The head chief sometimes assumed command of the fleet of canoes going on the raid, or he might delegate such command to a younger warrior. The owner of each canoe was leader of the men in his craft; he was called a boat chief and bailed instead of paddling.

It will be apparent that rank was not so well defined among the *Carib* as among the *Arawak*. Descent does not seem to have been important either; no mention of it has been found in the sources.[6] Men were prominent because of their military prowess, because of caracoli obtained from their ancestors, or because they were old and full of knowledge. There was a slave class composed of captive women, but their children were free.

It is said that during historic times murders were a common occurrence at the drinking bouts. They were avenged by the relatives of the dead person. In case of theft the aggrieved person slashed the shoulder of the thief with an agouti tooth, to mark the crime. The husband punished adultery by beating his wife to death with a club.

Etiquette.—Each carbet appointed a man to act as host. He provided the visitor with tobacco and a seat. Then the other men of the carbet, dressed in their best, introduced themselves and conversed with the visitor. There might be a banquet, at which everyone drank much. Special hammocks were always provided for visitors, and a woman was assigned to paint them and dress their hair in the morning. To show great friendship, the hosts exchanged names with their guests; in case of intimacy they exchanged presents.

If the cassava provided to a guest were folded, he could have only what he ate. If it were unfolded, however, he could take with him the remnants. The people usually ate in silence and without drinking. Only one man ordinarily spoke at a time; the other men hummed if they approved.

Economic organization.—Little is known of *Carib* economics. The people used rolls of tobacco as a monetary standard and obtained beads of crystal or greenstone from South America. Land and food products seem to have been held by the village in common. On the other hand, canoes and ornaments were personal property. It is not known how they were inherited.

---

[6] It has not been possible to substantiate the statement by Gower (1927, p. 33) that descent was matrilineal.

Birth and childhood.—Sexual intercourse was forbidden during pregnancy. The birth often took place by a fire. If it caused trouble, the woman drank juice made from a certain root. Afterward she washed the child in a stream and placed it in a tiny hammock or on a couch of leaves. If the birth had taken place at night, the men of the house bathed themselves so that the child would not catch cold.

For several days after birth the mother fasted, eating only dried cassava and drinking warm water. The father, on the other hand, practiced the couvade. Immediately after the birth he complained of pains, went to a separate hut, and lay in a hammock. He remained there for at least 40 days after the birth of his first child, and for 4 or 5 days after the birth of other children. During this time he went out only at night and avoided meeting anyone for fear that they might tempt him to break his fast, thereby making the mother sick and the child cowardly. At first he took no food. After 5 days he was permitted to drink corn beer and after 10 days to eat manioc bread in increasing quantities. He ate only the insides of the bread, the crusts being hung up in the hut until the end of the 40-day period, when they served as the basis for a feast in the village carbet. Preceding the feast the father was brought into the carbet, was stood on two large flat cakes of cassava, and was scarified by two men chosen by the carbet chief. A mixture of urucú, pepper seeds, and tobacco juice was rubbed into the cuts, and the blood which fell from them was daubed on the face of the child so that he would have the courage shown by the father in undergoing scarification. The man was then fed the two cassava cakes upon which he had stood and also fish, which he had to spit out. He went back to bed for several days and had to abstain from the flesh of animals for a period of 6 months or a year, lest the child become deformed.[7]

The child received its first name 12 or 15 days after birth from a friend of the father who acted as godfather or godmother. The name was taken from that of an ancestor, from nature, or from something that had happened during birth, pregnancy, or the couvade. If the baby were strong enough to bear it, his ears, nose, and lips were pierced at the same time, but this might be deferred until 2 years had passed, when the child's hair was cut.

At first all children ate with the mother; when 4 or 5 years old the boys began to eat in the men's house. The fathers spent much time in training their sons in hunting, fishing, swimming, singing, basketry, making canoes, and particularly in shooting the bow and arrow, at which they had

---

[7] The accounts of the couvade vary considerably from source to source. The above version is taken largely from Davies (1666, pp. 336–338), with supplemental data from La Borde (1886, pp. 249–250).

to be so accurate that they could hit a bough. The girls learned from their mothers how to cook, till the fields, weave cotton, and make hammocks.

Puberty and marriage.—At the age of puberty both sexes fasted for 3 or 4 weeks and had their skins scarified with agouti teeth. This was the time when the girls assumed the aprons and cotton anklets of women. Thereafter they were not allowed to run free but had to remain close to their mothers.

The youths were taught to value courage and endurance and were periodically rubbed with the fat of slaughtered *Arawak* to make them brave. When they had reached the age of becoming warriors they were tested in these qualities. The youth having been seated on a stool in the center of the carbet, his father crushed a bird over his head, scarified his body, and rubbed the cuts with pepper sauce. Then the boy ate the heart of the bird, to give himself courage, and his father beat him. He had to endure this entire ceremony without flinching. When it was over he lay in a hammock and fasted for 3 days. Then he demonstrated his skill in wielding a club and was accepted into the company of the warriors, being given a new name. His father gave a feast in celebration.

Specialization in shamanism began in childhood, when the candidate abstained from several kinds of flesh and underwent rigorous fasts. At puberty he was apprenticed to one of the older shamans, after going through a scarification ceremony comparable to that given to warriors.

The *Carib* youth were supposed to be chaste. Except for prostitutes, contact between young men and young women was tabooed. So was marriage with mothers, sisters, and step-sisters. Cross-cousin marriage was preferred, the sororate also being practiced, but a man was allowed other wives as well. Fathers presented their daughters to the successful warriors at the feast following each raid, and the warriors could also marry the women they had taken captive during the raid. The men with the most wives were considered the most prominent.

Girls often became engaged during childhood and sometimes were brought up by their fiancé's family. The groom usually had to obtain the consent of the prospective bride's parents. There was no ceremony except for an occasional feast, the only time the wife ever ate with her husband. Residence was matrilocal, except in the case of a chief. Each wife lived in a separate hut in her own village, often on a different island. The wives were treated as servants; they dressed and fed their husbands, cleaned and thatched the houses, tilled the fields, and carried all burdens. Their husbands could abandon them without ceremony, in which case the younger children remained with the mother and the older children were divided according to sex. Teknonymy was practiced, and a man had to avoid speaking to his wife's relatives.

Death and burial.—The *Carib* sometimes killed the old and the infirm. They feared the dead and never mentioned their names. When a man died all the relatives examined his body to satisfy themselves that he had not been killed by sorcery. The body was washed, painted, oiled as in life, flexed, and wrapped in a new hammock. It was placed upon a stool in a grave dug in the carbet, near the wall in the case of an ordinary person but in the center if the man were prominent, its eyes were weighted shut, and mats were added to protect it from the soil. The grave was not filled for 10 days, during which the relatives brought food and water to the corpse twice a day and lamented over it. A fire was built around the grave to purify it and to prevent the deceased from catching cold. The deceased's possessions were either cast into this fire or were placed in the grave; sometimes the house was burned too. In prehistoric times a slave or a dog was killed and put in the grave to care for the dead person. If the deceased were a warrior, the chief delivered a funeral oration, extolling his exploits. There was also a feast over the grave, accompanied by dancing. The close relatives fasted and cut their hair in mourning; some time afterward they held a second feast over the grave. In the case of a chief the *Carib* sometimes burned the corpse and mixed its ashes into a drink.

WARFARE

The *Carib* posted sentinels near all harbors to watch for the approach of raiding parties. They held assemblies to decide upon war and to fix a rendezvous; at these meetings the old women harangued them on the cruelty of the enemy, the war chief exhorted them to revenge themselves, they became very drunk, and at the height of the festival they ate some enemy flesh, smoked and preserved from the last raid. Each warrior present was given a gourd full of pebbles, a string with knots, or a stick with notches, to tell how many days before he had to be at the rendezvous. He spent the time repairing his pirogue and his weapons, while his wives prepared food for the raid.

The principal *Carib* weapon was the bow and arrow, the former 6 feet (1.8 m.) long, the latter poisoned, occasionally feathered, and provided with a separate barbed point. The poison came from the sap of the manchineel tree; the points were of fishbone, tortoise shell, or fire-hardened wood. There were also javelins and clubs (boutou), the latter engraved and painted with geometric and anthropomorphic designs. These clubs, which varied in length according to the rank of the owner, were used after the supply of arrows had been exhausted (pl. 93).

The *Carib* attempted to catch the enemy asleep in their villages. They attacked at dawn, or at night when there was a full moon. Divided into three bands, they fell upon the village, uttering war cries and shooting fire arrows (having cotton heads).

If the enemy resisted successfully, the *Carib* retired at noon, taking with them their dead and wounded. They might re-form for another attack, but usually they returned home, carrying the corpses to be buried there. If the enemy were defeated, they pillaged the village and roasted and ate the enemy corpses on the spot, keeping only some of the bones as trophies. They bound all prisoners and carried them back to the home village.

Each warrior kept his female captives and her children as slaves, incorporating them in his family. The male captives were tortured, killed, and eaten at the feast celebrating each victory. For 5 days beforehand each prisoner was kept without food in the house of his captor, bound onto one of his hammocks. Then he was brought into the carbet, where the villagers had assembled. They thrust burning brands into his sides, cut his flesh and rubbed in pepper, and shot his body full of arrows, trying (usually without success) to make him cringe. Then one of the old men of the village dispatched him with a club. The *Carib* cut up his body, washed the flesh, and roasted it, catching the fat in gourd containers. This fat was kept by the chiefs, who used it to season the food during later feasts. Some of the flesh also was kept until later, but most was eaten then with many signs of enjoyment. The most courageous warriors received the heart, the women the arms and legs, and the other men the rest of the body.

At this time the chief recounted the exploits of the warriors, and they took the names of the enemies they had killed. A sponsor was chosen to present the new name, and he received gifts of ornaments in return. At this time, too, the fathers gave their daughters to the successful warriors to be their brides.

ESTHETIC AND RECREATIONAL ACTIVITIES

Art.—The sculpture of the *Carib* was not so well developed as that of the *Arawak*, but they did fashion images of their maboya (evil spirits) from stone and wood for use as amulets and as adornments to the sterns of pirogues. They also carved small dolls of wood for the children and engraved biomorphic and geometric designs on clubs and gourds. There are petroglyphs in *Carib* territory, but they were probably made by the *Arawak*. Painting was done on canoes, hammocks, and gourds; as in the case of engraving, the designs were either biomorphic or geometric.

Games.—The *Carib* were fond of wrestling and of boat races. When wrestling, the two contestants held each other by the upper arms while each attempted to throw his opponent to the ground.

Feasts, dances, and music.—Carib feasts were held frequently: To decide upon warfare; to celebrate victories, the birth of the first male child, or cutting the children's hair; to initiate a new warrior; to observe clearing of new fields, cutting down trees to make a new house, launching a new vessel, or recovery from a disease. They were organized by one of the chiefs, who gave notice several days in advance so that food and drink could be prepared. The feast took place in the carbet, but both men and women, dressed in their best, participated. They spent all day and most of the night in eating, drinking, singing, and dancing, usually becoming quite drunk.

Both men and women participated in the singing, not only at the feasts but also to pass the time of day. Most songs had to do with warfare; others dealt with birds, fish, and women.

Dancing seems to have been confined to the feasts (pl. 95). Men and women performed alone or together. They moved in a circle, dancing in pairs, arm in arm. The men performed violently, but the women moved only their feet. The dances were accompanied by songs, the drum, the rattle, a stringed instrument, and the flute. The drum, hollowed from a log, had a single head of skin. The rattle consisted of a gourd with a wooden handle. The stringed instrument, too, was of gourd; it had a single string. The flutes were made of bamboo or the bones of an enemy.[8]

Carib men played flutes in the morning, while their wives prepared breakfast. They used conch-shell trumpets for signaling while on raids or when hunting or fishing; at night they also had recourse to signal flares.

Intoxicants and narcotics.—They were fond of drinking and made several different kinds of beer (oüicou) from sweetpotatoes or from a mixture of sweetpotatoes and manioc. The women chewed this material, allowed it to ferment for several days, and then strained it. They also brewed beer from the coarser manioc bread which they laid aside until it became mouldy.

The *Carib* smoked tobacco, rolling it into cigars like those of the *Arawak*.[9] There is no mention of snuff, but tobacco chewing was common. The *Carib* dried the leaves over the fire, softened them with sea water, and kneaded them into rolls which served as money. Before chewing they added ashes and packed the quid between the lip and gum.

RELIGION AND SHAMANISM

The *Carib* believed in a plurality of souls, which they associated with the beating of the heart and arteries. The soul in the heart was supposed to go to an earthlike paradise in heaven, where it became part of a company of good spirits, or akamboue.[10] The souls in the rest of the body either stayed in the bones after death or went into the forests or seashores. They were regarded as evil spirits, maboya; those in the sea had a special name, omicou.

---

[8] Neither the drum nor the stringed instrument is mentioned in all the sources. They may have been historic developments.

[9] Labat (1931, p. 88) observed men smoking for pleasure. Davies (1666, p. 346), however, describes only the use of tobacco by shamans during curing ceremonies.

[10] Some believed that the paradise was on earth rather than in the heavens and that only the successful warriors went there, the rest of the people being freed to live after death in another and more barren land.

The good spirits (akamboue) were believed to be invisible, except at night when they took the form of bats. Each *Carib* had one of them as his personal deity (ichieri). From time to time, particularly during feasts, he set an offering for his deity upon a table at the end of his hut; it consisted of manioc bread and the first of his fruits; its purpose was to insure good crops and to safeguard health. There were no idols on the table, as among the *Arawak,* and no ceremony of worship. When a man died it was believed that his ichieri carried the soul of his heart to heaven.

To the evil spirits (maboya) were attributed all disagreeable and frightening occurrences, such as nightmares, sickness, shipwrecks, thunder, hurricanes, earthquakes, and eclipses of the moon (the occasion for an all-night dance). The maboya were invisible, but a bad odor sometimes revealed their presence. Each *Carib* wore a small carved image of a maboya around his neck to frighten off the other maboya.

It was the function of the shamans (boyez) to control the maboya. Each shaman had one of them as his own personal deity which he obtained at the ceremony closing his period of apprenticeship to one of the older shamans. After a fast of 5 months, the youth was brought into the carbet, before a table on which manioc bread, fruit, and oüicou had been placed. The older shaman sang a song to call his own maboya to the carbet and then blew out cigar smoke, tickling the spirit in the nose and further enticing him into the carbet. Immediately the maboya fell into the hut and was seated upon a hammock to receive the food offering. His shaman then asked him for a spirit for the apprentice. This second maboya appeared and harangued the gathering on the power which the new shaman was to have.[11]

Comparable ceremonies took place at frequent intervals to drive away other maboya who had caused evil, to bring revenge upon an enemy, to influence the course of warfare, to prophecy future events, or to cause diseases. These ceremonies were always held at night and in the dark, since the spirits abhorred light. The food offerings, and sometimes also blood, were contributed by the spectators, who sat on stools at the opposite end of the hut, but the shamans appropriated them for their own use after the ceremonies. The maboya appeared in various shapes; often it entered the body of an old woman to give an oracular answer. Sometimes it could be heard eating the food offering, or quarreling with another spirit whom it had accused of causing some evil.

Some shamans kept in their houses the hair or bones of their ancestors, which were supposed to contain maboya. The shamans put them into gourds or wrapped them in cotton; sometimes they made small cotton

---

[11] The above account is taken largely from Dutertre (1667–71, vol. 2, pp. 365–366). La Borde (1886, pp. 235–236) states on the contrary, that the apprentice went to the maboya. His body was coated with gum and with feathers so that he could fly, and he was made to take tobacco juice to induce unconsciousness.

figures through which the maboya gave oracular answers. There were, however, no household idols or priests, as among the *Arawak*.

The *Carib* often attributed sickness to the influence of sorcerers who had obtained control of maboya. They consulted a shaman to determine the identity of the sorcerer and were usually directed to a woman, from whom no reprisal was to be feared. The woman was made to pick up a shell or a fishbone and to confess that she had administered this in food to cause the disease. She was then tortured and killed.

The shaman was also brought in to effect cures. He worked in the same way as at other séances, setting up a table bearing food offerings and oüicou at one end of the hut and calling his maboya with songs and tobacco smoke. The shaman first asked his maboya whether the disease would be fatal. If so, he abandoned the ceremony and told the patient to prepare for death. If not, the shaman and his maboya approached the patient, touched the part of his body which pained him, sometimes sucking it, and drew out an object—an imaginary poison, thorns, pieces of bone, or splinters of wood and stone. These were supposed to have caused the disease. Then the shaman rubbed the sick person's body with the juice of the *Ginipa* fruit, producing a dark brown color. When the patient had recovered, he gave a feast for the shaman, at the same time providing food offerings for the latter's maboya.

The *Carib* fasted upon a number of occasions: At puberty; when becoming a chief, a father, or a warrior; after killing an enemy; and at the death of a close relative. A man might also be asked to fast when a relative was sick, in the hope that it might relieve the pain. A typical schedule of fasting has already been described above (p. 557) in connection with the birth of the first child. The people did not vomit for religious purposes, but only to rid their stomachs of an excess of food.

Women knew of certain herbs, fruits, roots, oils, and gums which they used to cure diseases. For indigestion they prepared an infusion from the bark of the chipou tree and from the *Lambys* shell; they had another drink made by pounding up the bark of certain trees and vines when the sap was thick. If the indigestion had been caused by eating crabs, they ate as an antidote the flesh of the manatee or tortoise, which caused the body to break out into pimples. Then they treated the latter with the juice of the junipa nut or with sap from the leaves of the balisier tree mixed with the ashes of burned seeds. The former was also used to heal wounds. The wives sucked the poison out of snake bites, applied an infusion to the wound, and also prepared a drink as an antidote. They had another antidote for arrow poisoning. Bathing was used to treat some wounds, sweat baths for others. Sometimes they scarified the body to draw off blood.

MYTHOLOGY

Upon questioning by the missionaries, the *Carib* stated their belief in an unnamed superior power who lived in heaven and was endowed with all goodness. They regarded the earth as an indulgent mother, who furnished them with the things necessary for life.

The sun, moon, and other heavenly bodies were supposed to be human. The sun (noun) was considered a male; as ruler of the stars he prevented their shining during the daytime. He also warmed the stars, and they were believed to become ill during eclipses of the sun when the warming was not possible. The moon (houiou) was female; at first she shone during the daytime, but the coming of the sun filled her with shame and thereafter she appeared only at night. A star named Achinoin was said to be the cause of light rain and strong winds; another star, called Couroumon, controlled the tides and caused the heavy waves which upset canoes. To a *Carib,* Savacou, who became a bird and later a star, was attributed control over the thunder and strong winds. Other stars, the rainbow, and a comet were given similar mythological backgrounds. The first waters in the world were said to be the perspiration and urine of these spirits; the waters became fresh only when the salinity was strained out of them by the ground. Later the stars caused a great flood because the *Carib* failed to worship them.

The *Carib* believed that their ancestors had emerged from the navel (or the nostrils and an incision in the thigh) of a man named Louquo, who had descended from heaven, bringing manioc roots and showing the people how to cultivate them and to prepare food. He also explained how to build houses, and according to one version he was the creator of the earth and of fish, which he made out of fragments of manioc bread. Three days after his death Louquo was said to have returned to the sky.

LORE AND LEARNING

The *Carib* recognized only four colors—white, black, yellow, and red. They counted up to 20 on their fingers and toes. As already described, they had several methods of recording the time until a rendezvous. Their chiefs, shamans, and old men kept track of the time, counting the months by the moons, the seasons by the passing of the sun over the zenith, and the years by the rise and fall of the Pleiades. They also predicted the coming of winds and rains by the ascension of certain constellations which, as described above, were believed to control the weather.

The people stated that they originally came from the mainland to conquer the *Arawak,* whom they found living in the Lesser Antilles. They were fond of recounting deeds of bravery in warfare but otherwise do not seem to have had any interest in their past history.

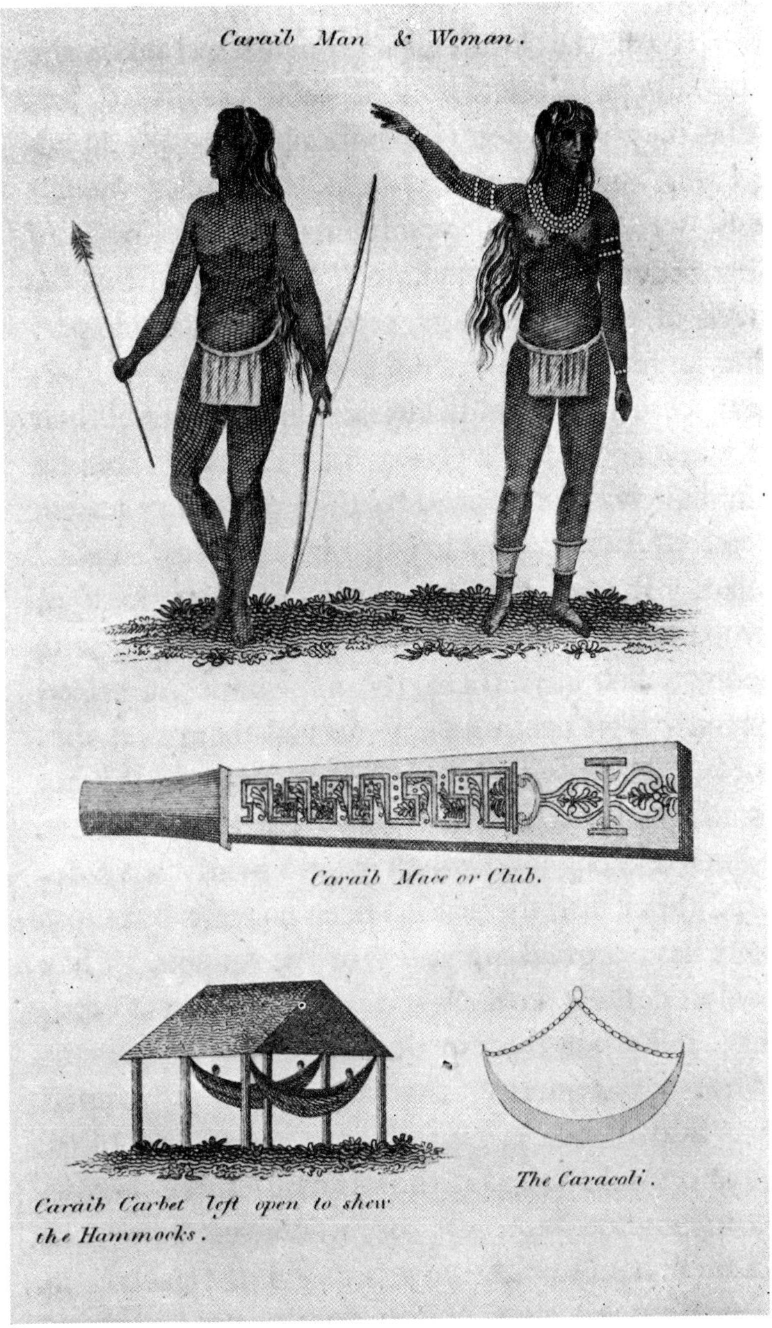

Caraib Man & Woman.

Caraib Mace or Club.

Caraib Carbet left open to shew
the Hammocks.

The Caracoli.

PLATE 93.—**Carib Indians and artifacts.** (After Sheldon, 1820, pl. 13.)

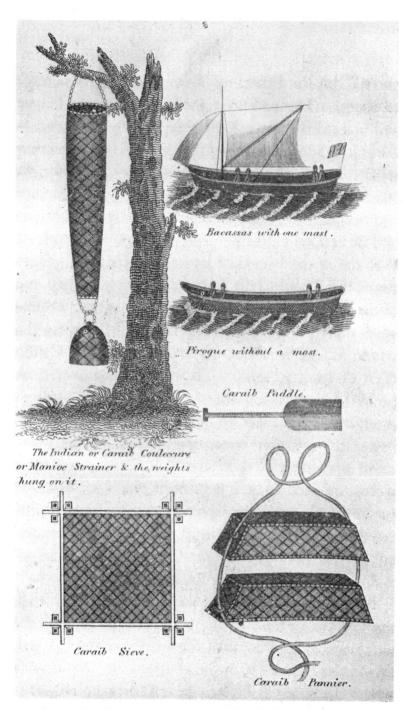

Bacassas with one mast.

Pirogue without a mast.

Caraib Paddle.

The Indian or Caraib Couleccure or Manioc Strainer & the weights hung on it.

Caraib Sieve.

Caraib Pannier.

Plate 94.—**Carib manufactures.** (After Sheldon, 1820, pl. 14.)

PLATE 95.—**Carib war dance.** (After Picard. Reproduced from Fewkes, 1907, pl. 9.)

PLATE 96.—**Cuban descendants of the Arawak.**   *Top:* Yara.   *Bottom:* El Caney.
(After Culin, 1902, pls. 62, 53, 54.)

PLATE 97.—**Cuban descendants of the Arawak.** *Top:* Playing guayo and guitar. Negro guide at left. At Yateras. *Bottom:* Spanish-Indians at Yara. (After Culin, 1902, pls. 55, 59.)

PLATE 98.—**Carib descendants.** *Top: Carib* house and basketmakers, St. Vincent. *Bottom: Carib* houses, Arima, Trinidad. (After Fewkes, 1907, pls. 8, 7.)

BIBLIOGRAPHY

Abbad y Lasierra, 1866; Anghiera, 1912 (1511) ; Arber, 1885; Bachiller y Morales, 1883; Ballet, 1875; Barlow, 1932; Bastien, 1944; Benzoni, 1857; Bernáldez, 1870 (1878) ; Beuchat, 1912; Booy, 1912, 1913 a, 1913 b; Bourne, 1907; Bouton, 1640; Brau, 1907; Breton, 1877, 1892; Brinton, 1871·; Bullbrook, 1920, 1940, 1941; Cabot, J. (See C. Columbus, 1893) ; Cabot, S. (see Arber, 1885) ; Cárdenas (see Torres de Mendoza, 1864–84) ; Casas, n.d. (1875), 1909; Castellanos, 1874; Charlevoix, 1730–31; Churchill (see F. Colón, 1811) ; Coll y Toste, 1907; Columbus (Colombo), C., 1893, 1930, 1930–33; Colón (Columbus), F., 1811; Coma (see Scillacio, 1859), Conzemius, 1928; Cornilliac, 1875; Corte Real (see C. Columbus, 1893) ; Cosculluela, 1918, 1922; Culin, 1902; Cundall, 1894; Davies, 1666; Delawarde, 1938; Dudley, 1899; Dutertre, 1654 (1667–71·) ; Eaden (see Labat, 1931) ; Eden (see Arber, 1885) ; Edwards, 1818–19; Enciso, 1519; Escalante Fontaneda, 1837–41·; Featherman, 1881–91; Fernández Duro, and others, 1885–1932; Fewkes, 1907, 1922; Fort y Roldán, 1881; Gabb, 1881·; Gage, 1928; García Valdés, 1930, 1936–37; Girard de Rialle, 1881; Gómara, 1749 (1552–53, 1852, 1901) ; Gower, 1927; Guiteras, 1865–66; Harlow, 1925; Harrington, 1921; Harris, 1904; Hatt, 1924; Heriot, 1807; Herrera Fritot, 1936, 1939; Herrera y Tordesillas, 1725–26 (1730) ; Hollis, 1941; Holmes, 1894; Hostos, 1941; Howard, 1943; Irving, 1851; Jane (see C. Columbus, 1930, 1930–33) ; Jefferys, 1760; Joyce, 1916; Kendall (see Dudley, 1899) ; Kerr (see F. Colón, 1811) ; Kidder II, 1944; Krieger, 1929, 1930, 1931; Labat, 1724 (1722, 1742), 1931; La Borde, 1704, 1886; Lovén, 1935; MacNutt (see Anghiera, 1912) ; Martyr (see Anghiera) ; Mason, J. A., 1941; Morales Cabrera, 1932; Morales Coello (see Royo Guardia et al., 1942) ; Morales Patiño (see Ortiz, Cosculluela, et al., 1943) ; Moralis (see Anghiera, 1912) ; Mulligan (see Scillacio, 1859) ; Muñoz, 1797; Münster (see Arber, 1885) ; Nau, 1894; Navarrete, 1825–37; Newton (see Gage, 1928) ; Ober, 1880, 1895; Ortiz Fernández, 1935, 1943; Ortiz, Cosculluela, Herrera Fritot, and Morales Patiño, 1943; Osgood, 1942 a, 1942 b; Osgood and Howard, 1943; Oviedo y Valdés, 1749, 1851–55 (1535), 1906; Pacheco (see Torres de Mendoza, 1864–84) ; Pané (see Bachiller y Morales, 1883; Bourne, 1907) ; Pericot García, 1936; Pichardo Moya, 1944; Puis, 1652; Rafinesque, 1836; Rainey, 1940, 1941; Raleigh, 1848; Real (see Corte Real) ; Ries, 1936; Rivet, 1923; Rochefort, 1665 (1658) ; Roth, 1887; Roumain, 1942, 1943; Rouse, 1939, 1940, 1941, 1942, 1945, 1947; Royo Guardia, 1940 a, 1940 b, Royo Guardia, Morales Coello, and Herrera Fritot, 1942; Safford, 1916, 1917; Salas, 1921; Santovenia y Echaide, 1939; Sapper, 1897 b; Schomburgk (see Raleigh, 1848) ; Scillacio, 1859; Serrano y Saenz (see Casas, 1909) ; Sheldon, 1820; Simón, 1882–92; Sloane, 1707–25; Smyth (see Benzoni, 1857) ; Sparrey, 1906; Spencer, 1873–79, vol. 6; Stahl, 1889; Stirling, 1936; Tamara, 1556; Tapia y Rivera, 1854; Taylor, D., 1935, 1936, 1938; Taylor, E.G.R. (see Barlow, 1932) ; Torre, 1890; Torre y de la Torre, 1841; Torres de Mendoza, 1864–84; Trinidad Historical Society, n.d.; Warner (see Dudley, 1899) ; Wright, 1916; Wyatt (see Dudley, 1899) ; Young (see Edwards, 1818–19) ; Zayas y Alfonso, 1931.

BIBLIOGRAPHY TO VOLUME 4

ABBREVIATIONS

Acta Amer. _____ Acta Americana. Revista de la Sociedad (Sociedade) Interamericana de Antropología y Geografía. Review of the Inter-American Society of Anthropology and Geography.

Amer. Anthrop. _____ American Anthropologist.

Amer. Antiq. _____ American Antiquity.

An. Escuela Nac. Minas _____ Anales de la Escuela Nacional de Minas. Medellín, Colombia.

An. Instr. Públ. Rep. Colombia. Anales de la Instrucción Pública en la República de Colombia. Bogotá, Colombia.

Ann. Rep. Smithsonian Inst. __ Annual Report of the Smithsonian Institution. Washington, D. C.

An. Real Acad. Cienc., Méd., Fís., Nat. Habana. Anales de la Real Academia Ciencias, Médicas, Físicas, y Naturales de la Habana. Habana, Cuba.

An. Soc. Geogr. Hist. Guatemala. Anales de la Sociedad de Geografía e Historia de Guatemala. Guatemala.

Anthrop. Pap. Amer. Mus. Nat. Hist. Anthropological Papers, American Museum of Natural History. New York, N. Y.

An. Univ. Central Venezuela__ Anales de la Universidad Central de Venezuela. Caracas, Venezuela.

Archiv. Anthrop. _____ Archiv für Anthropologie. Braunschweig (Brunswick), Germany.

Archiv. Antrop. Etnol. _____ Archivio per l'Antropologia e la Etnologia. Florence, Italy.

Bibl. Estud. Cubanos _____ Biblioteca de Estudios Cubanos. Habana, Cuba.

Bibl. Ling. Amér. Paris _____ Bibliothèque Linguistique Américaine. Paris, France.

Bol. Acad. Nac. Hist. Quito__ Boletín de la Academia Nacional de Historia. Quito, Ecuador.

Bol. Hist. _____ Boletín Historial. Cartagena and Medellín, Colombia.

Bol. Soc. Ecuatoriana Estud. Hist. Boletín de la Sociedad Ecuatoriana de Estudios Historicos. Quito, Ecuador.

Bull. Amer. Geogr. Soc. _____ Bulletin of the American Geographical Society.

Bull. Bur. Amer. Ethnol. ____ Bulletin, Bureau of American Ethnology, Smithsonian Institution. Washington, D. C.

Bull. Bur. Éthnol. République d'Haiti. Bulletin de la Bureau d'Éthnologie de la République d'Haiti. Port-au-Prince, Haiti.

Bull. Free Mus. Sci. Art. Univ. Pa. Bulletin of the Free Museum of Science and Art, University of Pennsylvania.

Bull. Soc. Géogr. Paris _____ Bulletin Société de Géographie. Paris, France.

Bur. Amer. Ethnol. Ann. Rep._ Bureau of American Ethnology, Annual Report. Smithsonian Institution, Washington, D. C.

Col. Doc. Hist. Costa Rica __ Colección de Documentos para la Historia de Costa Rica. San José, Paris, Barcelona.

Col. Doc. Inéd. Amér. y Oceanía. Colección de Documentos Inéditos, relativos al descubrimiento . . . en América y Oceanía. Madrid, Spain.

Col. Doc. Inéd. Geogr. Hist. Colombia. Colección de Documentos Inéditos sobre la Geografía y la Historia de Colombia. Bogotá, Colombia.

Col. Libr. Doc. Ref. Hist. Colección de Libros y Documentos Referentes a la
Amér.   Historia de América. Madrid, Spain.
Col. Ling., Soc. Ling. Paris __ Collection Linguistique, Société de la Linguistique de
                      Paris. Paris, France.
Comp. Ethnogr. Stud. _____ Comparative Ethnographical Studies. Gothenburg
                      (Göteborg), Sweden.
Congr. Int. Amer. _____ Congreso Internacional de Americanistas; Interna-
                      tional Congress of Americanists; etc.
Connecticut Acad. Arts, Sci. Connecticut Academy of Arts and Sciences, Memoirs.
Mem.   New Haven, Conn.
Contr. Mus. Amer. Ind., Heye Contributions of the Museum of the American In-
Foundation.   dian, Heye Foundation. New York.
Estud. Etnogr. _____ Estudios Etnográficos. Puerto Rico.
Ethnol. Abt. Königl. Mus. ___ Ethnologische Abteilung des Königlichen Museums.
                      Berlin, Germany.
Etnol. Stud. _____ Etnologiska Studier; Ethnological Studies. Göte-
                      borg, Sweden.
Expl. and Field-Work Smith- Explorations and Field-Work of the Smithsonian
sonian Inst.   Institution. Smithsonian Institution, Washing-
                      ton, D. C.
Field Mus. Nat. Hist., An- Field Museum of Natural History, Anthropological
throp. Leaflet.   Leaflets. Chicago, Illinois.
Geogr. Rev. _____ Geographical Review. New York, N. Y.
Globus _____ Globus. Illustr. Zeitschrift für Lönder-und Völker-
                      kunde. Braunschweig (Brunswick), Germany.
Hakluyt _____ Hakluyt Society.
Ind. Notes Monogr. _____ Indian Notes and Monographs, Museum of the
                      American Indian, Heye Foundation. New York,
                      N. Y.
Int. Archiv Ethnogr. _____ Internationales Archiv für Ethnographie. Leiden,
                      Holland.
Int. Journ. Amer. Ling. _____ International Journal of American Linguistics.
Journ. Amer. Folk-lore _____ Journal of American Folk-lore. New York, N. Y.
Journ. Hered. _____ Journal of Heredity, Organ of the American Genetic
                      Association.
Journ. Inst. Jamaica _____ Journal of the Institute of Jamaica. Kingston,
                      Jamaica.
Journ. Roy. Anthrop. Inst. Journal of the Royal Anthropological Institute of
Gr. Brit. and Ireland. Great Britain and Ireland. London, England.
Journ. Roy. Geogr. Soc. _____ Journal of the Royal Geographical Society. London,
                      England.
Journ. Soc. Amér. Paris ____ Journal de la Société des Américanistes de Paris.
                      Paris, France.
Journ. Wash. Acad. Sci. _____ Journal of the Washington Academy of Sciences.
                      Washington, D. C.
La Géogr. _____ La Géographie. Paris, France.
Mem. Amer. Anthrop. Assoc._ Memoirs of the American Anthropological Associ-
                      ation.
Mem. Carnegie Mus. _____ Memoirs of the Carnegie Museum. Pittsburgh, Pa.
Mem. Peabody Mus. Arch. Memoirs of the Peabody Museum of Archaeology
Ethnol. Harvard Univ. and Ethnology, Harvard University. Cambridge,
                      Mass.

Mém. Soc. Anthrop. Paris ___ Mémoires de la Société d'Anthropologie de Paris. Paris, France.

Mem. Soc. Cienc. Nat. La Salle _____ Memorias de la Sociedad de Ciencias Naturales La Salle. Caracas, Venezuela.

Mem. Soc. Cubana Hist. Nat. "Felipe Poey." Memorias de la Sociedad Cubana de Historia Natural "Felipe Poey." Habana, Cuba.

Mem. Soc. Patriótica Habana Memorias de la Sociedad Patriótica de la Habana. Habana, Cuba.

Mus. Journ. Univ. Penn. _____ Museum Journal, University of Pennsylvania. Philadelphia, Pa.

Mus. Nac. Costa Rica _____ Museo Nacional de Costa Rica. San José, Costa Rica.

Nat. Hist. _____ Natural History. The Magazine of the American Museum of Natural History. New York, N. Y.

N. Y. Acad. Sci. _____ New York Academy of Sciences. New York, N. Y.

Pap. Peabody Mus. Arch. Ethnol. Harvard Univ._____ Papers of the Peabody Museum of Archaeology and Ethnology, Harvard University. Cambridge, Mass.

Proc. Amer. Antiq. Soc. _____ Proceedings of the American Antiquarian Society. Worcester, Mass.

Proc. Amer. Phil. Soc. _____ Proceedings of the American Philosophical Society. Philadelphia, Pa.

Proc. Amer. Sci. Congr. _____ Proceedings of the American Scientific Congress.

Proc. Hist. Soc. New York __ Proceedings of the Historical Society of New York. New York, N. Y.

Proc. Nat. Acad. Sci. _____ Proceedings of the National Academy of Sciences. New York, N. Y.

Proc. Pan. Amer. Sci. Congr._ Proceedings of the Pan American Science Congress.

Proc. Roy. Geogr. Soc. _____ Proceedings of the Royal Geographical Society. London, England.

Publ. Phila. Anthrop. Soc. ___ Publications of the Philadelphia Anthropological Society. Philadelphia, Pa.

Rel. Geogr. Indias _____ Relaciones Geográficas de Indias. Madrid, Spain.

Rev. Archiv. Bibl. Nac. _____ Revista del Archivo y Biblioteca Nacionales. Tegucigalpa, Honduras.

Rev. Ethnogr. Paris _____ Revue d'Ethnographie. Paris, France.

Rev. Hist. Pasto _____ Revista de Historia. Pasto, Colombia.

Rev. Inst. Etnol. Nac. _____ Revista del Instituto Etnológico Nacional. Bogotá, Colombia.

Rev. Mus. Nac. Lima _____ Revista del Museo Nacional de Lima. Lima, Perú.

Sitz. Kais. Akad. Wiss. Wien _ Sitzungberichte der Kaiserlich Akademie der Wissenschaften. Vienna, Austria.

Smithsonian Contr. Knowl. __ Smithsonian Contributions to Knowledge, Smithsonian Institution. Washington, D. C.

Smithsonian Misc. Coll. _____ Smithsonian Miscellaneous Collections, Smithsonian Institution. Washington, D. C.

Timehri _____ Timehri. Journal of the Royal Agricultural and Commercial Society of British Guiana. Demerara, British Guiana.

Trans. Amer. Antiq. Soc. ____ Transactions of the American Antiquarian Society.

Trans. Amer. Ethnol. Soc. ___ Transactions of the American Ethnological Society.

Trans. Amer. Phil. Soc. _____ Transactions of the American Philosophical Society. Philadelphia, Pa.

Trans. Lit. Hist. Soc. Quebec_ Transactions of the Literary and Historical Society of Quebec. Quebec, Canada.

Tulane Univ. Middle Amer. Res. Ser. Tulane Univ., Middle American Research Series. New Orleans, La.

Univ. Calif. Publ. Amer. Arch. Ethnol. University of California Publications in American Archaeology and Ethnology. Berkeley, Calif.

U. S. Nat. Mus. _____ United States National Museum, Smithsonian Institution. Washington, D. C.

Yale Univ. Publ. Anthrop. ___ Yale University Publications in Anthropology. New Haven, Conn.

Ymer _____ Ymer. Stockholm, Sweden.

Zeit. d. Deutsch. Wiss. Ver. z. Kult.-u. Landeskunde Argent. Zeitschrift des Deutschen Wissinschaftlichen Vereins zur Kultur-und Landeskunde Argentiniens. Buenos Aires, Argentina.

Zeit. f. Ethnol. _____ Zeitschrift für Ethnologie. Berlin, Germany.

Zeit. f. Geopolitik _____ Zeitschrift für Geopolitik. Berlin, Germany.

Zeit. f. Vergleich. Rechtswiss_ Zeitschrift für Vergleichende Rechtswissenschaft. Berlin, Germany.

ABBAD Y LASIERRA, IÑIGO.
1866.   Historia geográfica, civil y natural de la isla de San Juan Bautista de Puerto-Rico. Nueva edición, anotada en la parte histórica y continuada en la estadistica y económica por José Julián de Acosta y Calbo. Puerto Rico.

ACOSTA, JOAQUÍN CORONEL.
1901.   Compendio histórico del descubrimiento y colonización de la Nueva Granada. 2nd ed. Bogotá.

ADAM, L. See CRÉVAUX, JULES NICOLAS.

AGUADO, PEDRO DE.
1916–17.   Historia de Santa Marta y nuevo reino de Granada. 2 vols. Madrid.

AGUILAR, M., EDITOR. See CASAS, BARTOLOMÉ DE LAS, n.d.

ALBA C., M. M.
1928.   Etnología y población histórica de Panamá. Panamá.

ALONSO DE SAN JUAN. (SUPPOSED AUTHOR.)
1873.   Relación breve y verdadera de algunas cosas de las muchas que sucedieron al padre Alonso Ponce en las provincias de la Nueva España, siendo comisario general de aquellas partes . . . Escrita por des religiosos, sus compañeros. 2 vols. Madrid. (Antonio de Ciudad Real is also believed to be the author of this work.)

ALTOLAGUIRRE Y DUVALE, ANGEL DE.
1908.   Relaciones geográficas de la gobernación de Venezuela (1767–1768). Con prólogo y notas de D. Angel de Altolaguirre y Duvale. Madrid.

AMADOR DE LOS RIOS, JOSÉ, ED. See OVIEDO Y VALDÉS, GONZALO FERNÁNDEZ DE, 1851–55.

ANDAGOYA, PASCUAL DE.
1865.   Narrative of the Proceedings of Pedrarias Dávila in the Provinces of Tierra Firme or Castilla del Oro, and of the Discovery of the South Sea and the Coasts of Peru and Nicaragua. Trans. and ed. . . . by Clements R. Markham. Hakluyt, No. 34. London.

1938. Relación de los sucesos de Pedrarias Dávila en las Provincias de Tierra Firme o Castilla del Oro. *In* Jijón y Caamaño, 1936–38, vol. 2, doc. 2, pp. 55–61. *Also in* Navarrete, Martín Fernández de, Colección de los viages descubrimientos . . . 1825–37, vol. 3, pp. 393–459.

ANDERSON, CHARLES L. G.
1914. Old Panama and Castilla del Oro . . . Boston.

ANDRADE, ANTONIO DE, and FRAY PABLO DE REBULLIDA.
[1709.] Report of Fray Antonio de Andrade and Fray Pablo de Rebullida to the Audiencia of Guatemala concerning the progress of the mission. Description and travels through Talamanca. Cartago, Jan. 10, 1709. Costa Rica-Panama Arb. Doc., 1913, Doc. 145, vol. 1, pp. 348–361. (Document published in Fernández, L., Col. Doc., Hist. Costa Rica, vol. 5, p. 450.)

ANGHIERA, PIETRO MARTIRE D' (PETER MARTYR).
1912. De orbe novo decades: The Eight Decades of Peter Martyr d'Anghera. Trans. from the Latin with notes and introd. by Francis Augustus MacNutt. 2 vols. New York. (First decade originally published in 1511.) *See also* Arber, Edward, 1885; Bourne, Edward Gaylord, 1907.

ANGULO, JOSÉ ANTONIO.
[1862.] Report, presented to the Supreme Government of the Republic ot Costa Rica, by Captain José Antonio Angulo. Status of the "Valley of Matina," "Port of Moin," "Atlantic Coast" and "Territory of Tamanaca," Year of 1862. Rep. Costa Rica, San José, May 1862. Costa Rica-Panama Arb. Doc., 1913, Doc. 529, vol. 3, pp. 136–155. fr. Nat. Archives of Costa Rica: Sec. State Dept. of Gov. Book No. 1411, Folios 1–40.

ANTOLÍNEZ, GILBERTO.
1943. Aporte etnográfico de la relación Geográfica de Nueva Segovia, 1579. Acta Amer., vol. 1, No. 4.

ANTONIO DE CIUDAD REAL. *See* ALONSO DE SAN JUAN.

ARANGO C., LUIS.
1929. Recuerdos de la Guaguería en el Quindío. Bogotá. (Another edition pub. in 1918 in Barcelona.)

ARBER, EDWARD, EDITOR.
1885. The first three English books on America [1511?]–1555 A.D., being chiefly translations, compilations, etc. by Richard Eden, from the writings, maps, etc., of Pietro Martire, of Anghiera (1455–1526) . . . Sebastian Münster, the cosmographer (1489–1552) . . . Sebastian Cabot, of Bristol (1474–1557) . . . With extracts, etc., from the works of other Spanish, Italian, and German writers of the time. Edited by Edward Arber. Birmingham.

ARENAS PAZ, BELISARIO.
1922. Guía geográfica y territorial de Colombia . . . Bogotá.

ARÉVALO, ANTONIO.
1891–94. Descripción o relación del Golfo del Darién. 1761. *In* Cuervo. Antonio B., Col. Doc. Inéd. Geogr. Hist. Colombia.

ASENSIO, ESTEBAN DE.
1921. Memorial de la fundación de la provincia de Santa Fé del Nueva Reino de Granada del Orden de San Francisco. 1550-1558. Madrid.

AVILA, GIL GONZALEZ.
  [1524.] El capitan Gil Gonzalez Davila a S. M. el Emperador Carlos V. Rey
        España, sobre su expedición a Nicaragua Santo Domingo, 6 de
        Marzo de 1524. (Doc. publ. in Peralta, 1883, pp. 3–26.)

BACHILLER Y MORALES, ANTONIO.
  1883. Cuba primitiva. Origen, lenguas, tradiciones e historia de los indios de
        las Antillos Mayores y las Lucayas. 2nd ed., corrected and augmented.
        Habana.

BALDUS, HERBERT.
  1938. Die Doppelfolge. Archiv. Anthrop., n.s., vol. 24, pp. 283–284.

BALLET, J.
  1875. Les caraïbes. Compte-rendu de la première session, Congr. Int. Amer.,
        vol. 1, pp. 394–438. Nancy.

BANCROFT, HUBERT HOWE.
  1874–76. The native races of the Pacific States of North America. 5 vols.
        New York, San Francisco. (Other ed. San Francisco, 1882.)
  1883–90. History of Central America. Vols. 6–8 of The Works of . . . . San
        Francisco.

BARAZE, PÈRE CYPRIEN.
  1819. Abrégé d'une relatión espagnole de la vie et de la mort du père Cyprien
        Baraze, de la compagnie de Jesus, et fondateur de la mission des Moxes
        dans le Pérou; imprimée à Lima par ordre de M. Urbain de Matha,
        evêque de la ville de la Paix. Lettres édifiantes et curieuses, vol. 5,
        pp. 44–70. Paris. (Earlier ed. published in Madrid, 1754.)

BARCÍA, A. GONZALES. See GÓMARA, FRANCISCO LÓPEZ DE.

BARD, SAMUEL A., PSEUD. See SQUIER, EPHRAIM GEORGE.

BARLOW, ROGER.
  1932. A brief summe of geographie. Hakluyt, 2nd Ser., No. 69, London. Ed.
        with an introd. and notes by E. G. R. Taylor.

BARNUEVO, RODRIGO.
  1942. . . . Relación apologética, así del antiguo como nuevo descubrimiento
        del río de las Amazonas . . . Quito.

BARRETT, S. A.
  1925. The Cayapa Indians of Ecuador. In Ind. Notes Monogr., No. 40,
        2 vols.

BASTIEN, RÉMY.
  1944. Archéologie de la baie de Port-au-Prince, rapport preliminaire. Bull.
        Bur. Éthnol. République d'Haiti, No. 3, pp. 33–38. Port-au-Prince.

BASURCO, SANTIAGO M.
  1894. Trois semaines chez les Indiens Cayapas. (République de l'Ecuador.)
        In Tour du Monde, t. 67, pp. 401–416. Paris.

BEALS, RALPH L.
  1932. The comparative ethnology of Northern Mexico before 1750. Ibero-
        Americana, No. 2, Univ. Calif., Berkeley.

BECKWITH, MARTHA W.
  1930. Myths and hunting stories of the Mandan and Hidatsa Sioux. Vassar
        College, Poughkeepsie, New York.

BENNETT, WENDELL C.
1936. South American Area. Amer. Antiq., vol. 1, No. 3, pp. 234–236.
1937. Excavations at La Mata, Maracay, Venezuela. *In* Anthrop. Pap. Amer. Mus. Nat. Hist., vol. 36, pt. 2, pp. 69–137. New York.
1944. Archeological regions of Colombia: A ceramic survey. Yale Univ. Publ. Anthrop., No. 30.
1946. Excavations in the Cuenca region, Ecuador. Yale Univ. Publ. Anthrop., Bull. No. 35. (Note: Nos. 35 and 36 are bound together. *See* Osgood, Cornelius, 1946.)

BENZONI, GIROLAMO.
1857. History of the New World, by Girolamo Benzoni, of Milan. Shewing his travels in American from A. D. 1541 to 1556: with some particulars of the island of Canary. Trans. and ed. by W. H. Smyth. Hakluyt, No. 21. London.

BERCKENHAGEN, HERMANN.
1894. Grammar of the Miskito language with exercises and vocabulary. Gustav Winter. Stolpen, Saxony.

BERENDT, C. HERMANN.
1876. The centres of civilization in Central America and their geographical distribution. Bull. Amer. Geogr. Soc., Sess. 1875–76, No. 3, pp. 4–15. New York.

BERGSØE, PAUL.
1937. The metallurgy and technology of gold and platinum among the pre-Columbian Indians. Tr. from Danish by F. C. Reynolds. (A, Ingeniørvidenskabelige Skrifter, A, No. 44.) Copenhagen.
1938. The gilding process and the metallurgy of copper and lead among the pre-Columbian Indians. Tr. from Danish by F. C. Reynolds. (A, Ingeniørvidenskabelige Skrifter, A, No. 46.) Copenhagen.

BERNÁLDEZ, ANDRÉS.
1870. Historia de los reyes católicos, Don Fernando y Doña Isobel, escrita por el Bachiller Andrés Bernáldez, Cura que fué de la villa de los Palacios, y Capellan de D. Diego Deza, Arzobispo de Sevilla. Soc. Bibliófilos Andaluces, 1st ser., 2 vols. Seville. (*Also in* Biblioteca de autores españoles, 1878. Madrid.)
See also Columbus, Christopher, 1930.

BEUCHAT, HENRI.
1912. Manuel d'archéologie américaine (Amérique préhistorique–Civilisations disparues).
See also Rivet, Paul, and Beuchat, Henri.

BEUCHAT, HENRI, and RIVET, PAUL.
1907. Contribution a l'étude des langues Colorado et Cayapa. Journ. Soc. Amér. Paris, n.s., vol. 4, pp. 31–70.

BLACKISTON, A. HOOTON.
1910. Recent discoveries in Honduras. Amer. Anthrop., n.s., vol. 12, pp. 536–541.

BLESSING, DON AUGUSTIN.
[1899.] An exploration of the headwaters of the River Teliri and instruction given to the Indians there by the Padre Blessing, Missionary of Talamanca. May. Costa Rica-Panama Arb. Doc., 1913, Doc. 558, vol. 3, pp. 276–280.

BOLINDER, GUSTAF.
1917. Einiges über die Motilon-Indianer der Sierra de Perijá. (Kolumbien, Südamerika.) Zeit. Ethnol. vol. 49, pp. 21-51. Berlin.
1925. Die Indianer der tropischen Schneegebirge; forschungen im nördlichsten Südamerika. Stuttgart.
1937. Över Anderna till Manastera. Stockholm.

BOMAN, ERIC.
1920 a. Adiciones al proyecto de leyenda uniforme para mapas arqueologicos de la America del Sud. Bol. Soc. Ecuatoriana Estud. Hist., No. 12, pp. 497-500. Quito.
1920 b. Vorspanische Wohnstälten Steinwerkstälten und Petroglyphen in der Sierra de Famatina. Zeit. d. Deutsch. Wiss. Ver. z. Kult.-u. Landeskunde Argent. 6th year.

BONILLA, DON JUAN DE.
[1702.] Letter of Captain Don Juan de Bonilla to the president of the Audiencia de Guatemala. Cartago, July 26. Costa Rica-Panama Arb. Doc., 1913, Doc. 141. vol. 1, pp. 333-336. (Doc. publ. in Sp. in Fernández, L., 1881-1907, Col. Doc. Hist. Costa Rica, vol. 5, p. 399.)

BONILLA, MARCELINA.
MS. Los Pueblos de la Sierra Tegucigalpa.

BOOY, THEODOOR DE.
1912. Lucayan remains on the Caicos Islands. Amer. Anthrop., n.s., vol. 14, pp. 81-105.
1913 a. Certain kitchen-middens in Jamaica. Amer. Anthrop., n.s., vol. 15, pp. 425-434.
1913 b. Lucayan artifacts from the Bahamas. Amer. Anthrop., n.s., vol. 15, pp. 1-7.
1915-16. Notes on the archeology of Margarita Island, Venezuela. In Contr. Mus. Amer. Indian, Heye Foundation, vol. 2, No. 5. New York.
1918 a. An exploration of the Sierra de Perijá, Venezuela. Geogr. Rev., vol. 6, pp. 385-410. New York.
1918 b. The people of the mist. An account of explorations in Venezuela. Mus. Jour. Univ. Penn., vol. 9, Nos. 3 and 4, pp. 183-224.

BOSCH-REITZ, G. J. A. See LA BORDE, PÈRE DE, 1886.

BOURNE, EDWARD GAYLORD.
1907. Columbus, Ramon Pane and the beginnings of American Anthropology. Proc. Amer. Antiq. Soc., n.s., vol. 17, pp. 310-348.

BOUTON, JACQUES.
1640. Relation de l'establissement des François depuis l'an 1635, en l'isle de Martinique, l'une des Antilles de l'Amérique, des moeurs des sauvages, de la situation, et des autres singularitez de l'isle. Paris.

BOVALLIUS, C.
1886. Nicaraguan antiquities. Stockholm.

BOYLE, FREDERICK.
1868. A ride across a continent: a personal narrative of wanderings through Nicaragua and Costa Rica. 2 vols. London.

BRANSFORD, JOHN FRANCIS.
1881. Archaeological researches in Nicaragua. Smithsonian Contr. Knowl., vol. 25, art. 2.

BRAU, SALVADOR.
1907. La colonización de Puerto Rico, desde el descubrimiento de la isla hasta la reversión á la corona española de los privilegios de Colón. San Juan.

BRETON, RAYMOND.
1877. Grammaire caraïbe, suivie du Catéchisme caraïbe. Nouvelle éd. Paris.
1892. Dictionaire caraibe-français, composé par le r. p. Raymond Breton, reimprimé par Jules Platzmann. Ed. facsimilé. Leipzig.

BRETTES, JOSEPH DE.
1898. Six ans d'explorations par le comte Joseph Brettes. In Le Tour du Monde, vol. 4, n.s., pp. 61–96. Feb. 1898. Paris.

BRICEÑO-IRAGORRY, MARIO.
1928. Ornamentos fúnebres de los aborígenes del occidente de Venezuela. Caracas.
1929. Procedencia y cultura de los Timotes-Cuycas. An. Univ. Central Venezuela, vol. 17, No. 2. Caracas.

BRINTON, DANIEL GARRISON.
1871. The Arawack language of Guiana in its linguistic and ethnological relations. Philadelphia, Pa.
1885. On the language and ethnologic position of the Xinca Indians of Guatemala. Proc. Amer. Phil. Soc., vol. 22, pp. 89–97.
1887. On the so-called Alagüilac language of Guatemala. Proc. Amer. Phil. Soc., vol. 24, pp. 365–377.
1895. The Matagalpan linguistic stock of Central America. Proc. Amer. Phil. Soc., vol. 34, pp. 403–415.
1901. Races and peoples; lectures on the science of ethnography. (2nd ed.) Philadelphia, Pa. (1st ed. New York, 1890.)

BRUCH, CARLOS. See OUTES, FÉLIX FAUSTINO, and BRUCH, CARLOS.

BUCHWALD, OTTO VON.
1908. Vokabular der "Colorados" von Ecuador. Zeit. Ethnol., vol. 40, pp. 70–82.
1918. Migraciones sub-americanas. Bol. Soc. Ecuatoriana Estud. Hist., Quito. vol. 1, No. 3, pp. 227–236.
1924. Notas etnográficas. Bol. Acad. Nac. Hist. Quito, vol. 8, Nos. 21–23, pp. 1–18.

BUENO, RAMÓN.
1933. Apuntes sobre la provincia misionera de Orinoco e indígenas de su territorio, con algunas otras particularidades. Los publica, con un prólogo, Mons. Nicolás E. Navarro. Caracas.

BULLBROOK, J. A.
1920. On the excavation of a shell mound at Palo Seco, Trinidad, B.W.I. MS. in Yale Peabody Museum, New Haven, Conn.
1940. The Ierian Race. In Public Lectures delivered under the auspices of Historical Society of Trinidad and Tobago during the session, 1938–39, pp. 1–46. Trinidad and Tobago.

1941.   The aboriginal remains of Trinidad and the West Indies: a commentary
on the pre-European cultures of Trinidad and the neighbouring West
Indies, in connection with the exhibition organized by the archaeological
section of the Historical Society of Trinidad and Tobago, ᒍec. 3–14,
1941. Trinidad and Tobago.

BUSCHAN, GEORG. *See* KRICKEBERG, WALTER.

BUTLER, MARY.
1940.   A pottery sequence from the Alta Verapaz, Guatemala. *In* The Maya
and their neighbors, pp. 250–267. New York.

CABELLO BALBOA, MIGUEL.
MS.   Verdadera relación de la Provincia y Tierra de las Esmeraldas. Ms. in
Archivo de Indias de Sevilla. (Excerpts from this ms. are quoted in
vol. 2 of Jijon y Caamaño, 1940–45.)

CABEZA DE VACA, ALVAR NUÑEZ. *See* NUÑEZ CABEZA DE VACA, ALVAR.

CABOT, JOHN. *See* COLUMBUS, CHRISTOPHER, 1893.

CABOT, SEBASTIAN. *See* ARBER, EDWARD, 1885.

CABRERA, VICTOR M.
1924.   Guanacaste . . . San José.

CANDELIER, H.
1893.   Rio Hacha et les Indiens Goajires. Paris.

Captain General of Guatemala.
[1742.] Notes by the Captain General of Guatemala suggesting means for the
expulsion of the Mosquitos. Nov. 23, 1742. Costa Rica-Panama
Arb. Doc., 1913, Doc. 166, vol. 1, pp. 465–472.

CÁRDENAS, FRANCISCO DE. *See* TORRES DE MENDOZA, LUIS, EDITOR.

CARDENAS PALOMINO, DON GOMEZ DE.
[1684.] Don Gomez de Cardenas Palomino having a power of attorney from
Don Francisco Nuñez de Temino, asks the Audiencia of Guatemala
to report to the king upon the subject of the Conquest of Talamanca.
Guatemala. Costa Rica-Panama Arb. Doc., 1913, Doc. 82, vol. 1,
p. 245. (Doc. publ. in Sp. in Fernández, L., 1881–1907, Col. Doc.,
Hist. Costa Rica, vol. 5, p. 330.)

CARRIÓN, HERNANDO DE, ET AL.
[1648.] Report of the Cabildo of Cartago. Cartago. Costa Rica-Panama
Arb. Doc., 1913, Doc. 83, vol. 1, pp. 249–55. (Doc. publ. in Sp.
in Fernández, L., 1881–1907, Doc. Hist. Costa Rica, vol. 5, p. 314.)

CARVAJAL, JACINTO DE.
1892.   Ralación del descubrimiento del río Apure hasta su ingreso en el Orinoco
. . . León.

CASANI, J.
1741.   Historia de la provincia de la Compañía de Jesús del nuevo Reyno de
Granada en la America. Madrid.

CASAS, BARTOLOMÉ DE LAS.
n.d.   Historia de las Indias. 3 vols., ed. by M. Aguilar. Madrid [preface 1927].
(Previous edition in 1875.)

1909. Apologética historia de las Indias. Ed. by M. Serráno y Saenz. *In* Nueva Biblioteca de Autores Españoles, vol. 13. Madrid.

CASTELLANOS, JUAN DE.
1874. Elegías de varones ilustres de Indias. *In* Biblioteca de autores españoles, vol. 4. (3rd ed.) Madrid. (Other editions, including 1847 and 1852.)

CASTELLVÍ, MARCELINU DE.
1934. Manual de investigaciones lingüísticas para uso de los investigadores del departamento de Nariño y de las regiones del Caquetá, Putumayo y Amazonas. Pasto.

CAULÍN, ANTONIO.
1779. Historia coro-graphica natural y evangelica de la Nueva Andalucía, provincias de Cumaná, Guayana, y vertientes del río Orinoco . . . Madrid. (Another edition published in Caracas in 1841.)

CEBALLOS, AGUSTÍN DE.
[1610.] Memorial to our Lord the King, giving a description and the characteristics of the province of Costa Rica. Costa Rica-Panama Arb. Doc., 1913, Doc. 77, vol. 1, pp. 212–218. (Doc. publ. in Sp. in Fernández, L., 1881–1907, Col. Doc. Hist. Costa Rica, vol. 5.)

CELEDON, RAPHAEL.
1878. Bibliotheque linguistique americaine.

CHARLEVOIX, PIERRE FRANÇOIS XAVIER DE.
1730–31. Histoire de l'Isle espagnole ou de S. Domingue. Ecrite particulierement sur des mémoires manuscrits du P. Jean-Baptiste le Pers, jesuite, missionnaire à Saint Domingue, et sur les pièces originales, qui se conservent au Dépôt de la Marine. 2 vols. Paris.

CHURCHILL, JOHN. *See* COLÓN, FERNANDO.

CIEZA DE LEÓN, PEDRO DE.
1932. La chrónica del Perú. Primera Parte. Madrid.

CIUDAD REAL, ANTONIO DE. *See* ALONSO DE SAN JUAN.

CODAZZI, AGUSTÍN.
1889. Atlas geográfico e histórico de la República de Colombia. Cartografía de Manuel M. Pas y texto del Doctor Felipe Pérez. Paris.

COHEN, MARCEL. *See* MEILLET, A., AND COHEN, MARCEL.

COLECCIÓN DE DOCUMENTOS INÉDITOS.
1898–1900. Relaciones de Yucatan. Ser. 2, vols. 11, 13. Madrid.

COLECCIÓN DE DOCUMENTOS INÉDITOS, RELATIVOS AL DESCUBRIMIENTO, CONQUISTA Y ORGANIZACIÓN DE LAS ANTIGUAS POSESIONES ESPAÑOLAS DE AMÉRICA Y OCEANÍA, 1864–84. *See* Torres de Mendoza, Luis.

COLECCIÓN DE DOCUMENTOS INÉDITOS, RELATIVOS AL DESCUBRIMIENTO, CONQUISTA Y ORGANIZACIÓN DE LAS ANTIGUAS POSESIONES ESPAÑOLAS DE ULTRAMAR, 1885–1932. *See* FERNÁNDEZ DURO, CESÁREO, ET AL.

COLECCIÓN DE DOCUMENTOS INÉDITOS SOBRE LA GEOGRAFÍA Y LA HISTORIA DE COLOMBIA, RECOPILADOS POR ANTONIO B. CUERVO. 1891–94. T. 1–4. Bogotá.

COLL Y TOSTE, CAYETANO.
1907. Prehistoria de Puerto-Rico. San Juan.

Colón, Fernando (Columbus, Ferdinand).
  1811.   History of the discovery of America, by Christopher Columbus; written
          by his son Don Ferdinand Columbus. *In* Kerr, Robert: A general
          history and collection of voyages and travels, vol. 3, pp. 1–242.
          Edinburgh. (Text taken from John Churchill.)

Columbus, Christopher (Colombo, Cristoforo).
  1893.   The journal of Christopher Columbus (during his first voyage, 1492–93),
          and documents relating to the voyages of John Cabot and Gasper
          Corte Real. Trans., with notes and introd., by Clements R. Markham.
          Hakluyt, No. 86. London.
  1930.   The voyages of Christopher Columbus, being the journals of his first
          and third, and the letters concerning his first and last voyages, to
          which is added the account of his second voyage written by Andrés
          Bernáldez; now newly trans. and ed., with an introd. and notes by
          Cecil Jane. London.

  1930–33.   Select documents illustrating the four voyages of Columbus, including
          those contained in R. H. Major's select letters of Christopher
          Columbus. Trans. and ed. with additional material, introd., and
          notes by Cecil Jane. Vol. 1, the first and second voyages. Vol. 2,
          the third and fourth voyages. Hakluyt, 2nd ser., Nos. 65 and 70.
          London.

Columbus, Ferdinand. *See* Colón, Fernando.

Coma, Guillermo. *See* Scillacio, Niccolò.

Conzemius, Eduard.
  1921.   Die Rama-Indianer von Nicaragua. Zeit. f. Ethnol., vol. 59, pp. 291–362.
          Berlin.
  1927–28.   Los Indios Payas de Honduras. Journ. Soc. Amér. Paris, n.s., t. 19,
          pp. 245–302, 1927; continued in t. 20, pp. 253–360.
  1928.   Ethnographical notes on the Black Carib (Garif). Amer. Anthrop.
          n.s., vol. 30, No. 2, pp. 183–205.
  1929.   Notes on the Miskito and Sumu languages of Eastern Nicaragua and
          Honduras. *In* Int. Journ. Amer. Ling., vol. 5, pp. 57–115.
  1930.   Une tribu inconnue du Costa-Rica: les Indiens Rama du Rio Zapote.
          L'Anthropologie, t. 40, pp. 93–108. Paris.
  1932.   Ethnographical survey of the Miskito and Sumu Indians of Honduras
          and Nicaragua. Bull. Bur. Amer. Ethnol., No. 106.

Cornilliac, J. J. J.
  1875.   Anthropologie des Antilles. Compte-rendu du Congr. Int. Amer., pre-
          mière sess., vol. 2, pp. 148–169. Nancy, France.

Coronado, Juan Vásquez.
  [1564.]   Possession taken of the province and valley of Guaymi and of the
          Bay of Zorobaró (Almirante Bay) by Juan Vázquez de Coronado,
          Governor of Costa Rica, 1563–64. Hara January 24, 1564. Costa
          Rica-Panama Arb. Doc., 1913, Doc. 51, vol. 1, pp. 131–133.

Corte Real, Gasper (or Real, Gasper Corte). *See* Columbus, Christopher, 1893.

Cortes, Hernando.
  1908.   Letters of Cortes; the five letters of relation from Fernándo Cortes to
          the Emperor Charles V. Trans. and ed., with a bibliographical introd.
          and notes compiled from original sources, by Francis A. MacNutt.
          2 vols. New York and London.

COSCULLUELA, JOSÉ ANTONIO.
1918. Cuatro años en la çiénaga de Zapata. Habana.
1922. La prehistoria de Cuba . . . Memorias de la Soc. Cubana de Hist. Nat. "Felipe Poey," vol. 5, pp. 11–50. Habana.
See Ortiz, Fernando; Herrera Fritot, René; et al., 1943.

COSTA RICA-PANAMA ARBITRATION DOCUMENTS ANNEXED TO THE ARGUMENT OF COSTA RICA BEFORE THE ARBITRATOR HON. EDWARD DOUGLASS WHITE, CHIEF JUSTICE OF THE UNITED STATES. 1913. 4 vols. Rosslyn, Va. (*See* Andrade and Rebullida, Angulo, Blessing, Bonilla, Cardenas Palomino, Carrión, Ceballos, Coronado, Criado de Castilla, Flores, Gabb, Garret y Arlovi, González y Gutiérrez, Haya Fernández, Juan and Ulloa, Laet, Landecho and San Millan, Lara, Maldonado, Margil, Matamoros, Pavon, Pinedo, Rebullida, Ribera, Rivera, Royal Cedula, Sáenz, Salinas y de la Cerda, Sandoval, San Francisco y Rios, San José, San José and Rebullida, Semano, Sójo, and Urcullu.)

CRÉVAUX, JULES NICOLAS.
1882. Vocabulaire de la Langue Guahiva. *In* Grammaires et vocabulaires roucouyenne, arrouague, piapopo et d'autres langues de la région des Guayanes, par MM. J. Crévaux, P. Sagot, and L. Adam. Bibl. Ling. Amér. Paris, vol. 8.

CRIADO DE CASTILLA, ALONSO.
[1575.] Summary description of the Kingdom of Tierra Firme, called Castilla del Oro, which is subject to the Royal Audiencia of the city of Panama, by Dr. Alonso Criado de Castilla, Senior Judge Thereof. Nombre de Dios, May 7, 1575. Costa Rica-Panama Arb. Doc., 1913, Doc. 64, vol. 1, pp. 176–186. (Doc. publ. in Sp. by Peralta, 1883, p. 527.)

CUERVO, ANTONIO B.
1891-94. Colección de documentos inéditos sobre la geografía y la historia de Colombia. 2 vols. Bogotá.
See also Arévalo, Antonio; and Sardilla, Juan Bautista.

CULIN, STEWART.
1902. The Indians of Cuba. *In* Bull. Free Mus. Sci. and Art, Univ. Pa., vol. 3, pp. 185–226. Philadelphia.

CUNDALL, FRANK.
1894. The story of the life of Columbus and the discovery of Jamaica. Journ. Inst. Jamaica, vol. 2, pp. 1–79. Kingston.

DAMPIER, WILLIAM.
1699. A new voyage around the world. 2 vols. 4th ed. London.

DAVIDSON, D. S.
1935. Knotless netting in America and Oceania. Amer. Anthrop. n.s., vol. 37, No. 1, pp. 117–134.
See also Petrullo, Vincenzo, 1937.

DAVIES, JOHN, TRANS.
1666. The history of the Caribby Islands. London. [Trans. of Rochefort, Charles de, 1665.]
See also DUTERTRE, JEAN BAPTISTE, 1667–71.

DELAWARDE, R. P. JEAN BAPTISTE.
1938. Les derniers Caraïbes. Leur vie dans une réserve de la Dominique. Journ. Soc. Amér. Paris, n.s., vol. 30, pp. 167–204. Paris.

DESCOBAR, JERÓNIMO.
1938. Relación sobre el carácter e costumbres de los indios de la Provincia de Popayán. *In* Jijón y Caamaño, 1936–38, vol. 2, pp. 149–176.

DESCRIPCIÓN DE LA CIUDAD DE NUEVA SEGOVIA. . . 2 DE ENERO DE 1579.

DIEGO Y GUTIÉRREZ, FELIPE CLEMENTE DE.
[1534.] Capitulación que se tomo con el capitan Felipe Gutierrez para el descubrimiento de Veragua. Ano de 1534. Col. Doc. Inéd. Amer. y Oceania, 1864–84, vol. 22, pp. 383–406. (Doc. also publ. in Peralta, 1883, p. 89.)

DOUGLAS, JAMES. *See* EDWARDS, BRYAN, 1823.

DUDLEY, ROBERT.
1899. The voyage of Robert Dudley, afterwards styled Earl of Warwick and Leicester and Duke of Northumberland, to the West Indies, 1594–1595, narrated by Capt. Wyatt, by himself, and by Abram Kendall, master. George F. Warner, ed. Hakluyt, 2nd ser., vol. 3, London.

DUNCAN, DAVID. *See* SPENCER, HERBERT.

DUTERTRE, JEAN BAPTISTE.
1654. Histoire generale des isles de S. Christophe, de la Guadeloupe, de la Martinique, et autres dans l'Amérique . . . Paris. (Original ed.)
1667–71. Histoire generale des Antilles habitées par les Françoise . . . 4 vols. Paris.

EADEN, JOHN. *See* LABAT, JEAN BAPTISTE, 1931.

EDEN, RICHARD. *See* ARBER, EDWARD, 1885.

EDWARDS, BRYAN.
1818–19. The history, civil and commercial, of the British West Indies. 5th ed., with a continuation to the present time by Sir William Young. (1st ed. 1793.) 5 vols. London.
1823. Poyais. An account of the British settlements on the Musquito Shore. (Drawn for the use of the Government, in 1773.) London. (Another article entitled, "Account of the attempt to form a settlement on the Mosquito shore, in 1823," by James Douglas, was published in Trans. Lit. Hist. Soc. Quebec, 1868–69, n.s., pt. 6, 1869, pp. 25–39.)

EGUILUZ, DIEGO DE.
1881–97. Entrada de Diego Aleman a los Mojos ó Mussus, 1564. *In* Rel. Geogr. Indias, vol. 4, pp. CXCVI–CC.

ENCISO, MARTÍN FERNÁNDEZ DE.
1519. Suma de geografía q̄ trata de todas las partidas y provuincias del mundo: en especial delas Indias: y trata largamēte del arte del marear: juntamēte con la espera en romāce: con el regimiēto del sol y del norte. Seville.

ERNST, A.
1870. Die Goajiro-Indianer. Zeit. f. Ethnol., vol. 2, pp. 328–336.
1872. Notizen über die Urbewohner der ehemaligen Provinz Santa Marta in Neu-Granada. Zeit. f. Ethnol., vol. 4, pp. 190–192.
1887 a. Die Sprache der Motilonen. Zeit. f. Ethnol., vol. 19, pp. 376–378.
1887 b. Motilonen-Schädel aus Venezuela. Zeit. f. Ethnol., vol. 19, pp. 296–301.
1887 c. Die ethnographische Stellung der Guajiro-Indianer. Zeit. Ethnol., vol. 19, pp. 425–444.

Escalante Fontaneda, Hernando.
1837–41. Mémoire sur la Floride, ses côtes et ses habitants, qu'aucun de ceux qui l'ont visitée n'ont su décrire. *In* Voyages, relations et mémoires originaux pour servir a l'histoire de la découverte de l'Amerique, Publiés pour la première fois en Français, par Henri Ternaux-Compans, vol. 20: Recueil de Pièces sur la Floride, pp. 9–42. Paris.

Espinosa, Gaspar de.
[1514.] Relación que ymbio el Lyscenciado Espinosa, de lo que subcedio en la entrada quel fizo por mandado del Logar-Theniente General en las provincias del mar del sur. Col. Doc. Inéd. Amér. y Oceanía, 1864–84, vol. 37, p. 575.

[1516.] Relación hecha por Gaspar de Espinosa, Alcalde Mayor de Castilla del Oro, dada a Pedrarias de Avila, Lugar teniente general de aquellas provincias, de todo lo que le sucedio en la entrada que hizo en ellas, de orden de Pedrarias. Col. Doc. Inéd. Amér. y Oceanía, 1864–84, vol. 2, pp. 467–522.

[1519.] Relación e proceso quel Licenciado Gaspar de Espinosa, Alcalde Mayor, hizo en el viaje que por mandado de muy magnifico Senor Pedrarias de Avila, Teniente general en estos Reynos de Vastilla del Oro por sus Altzas, fue desde esta Ciudad de Panama a las Provincias de Paris e Nata, e a las otras provincias comarcanas. Col. Doc. Inéd. Amér. y Oceanía, 1864–84, vol. 20, pp. 5–119.

Exquemelin, Alexandre O.
1678. De Americaensche zee-roovers. Amsterdam. (Eng. ed., "The buccaneers of America," London and N. Y., 1893.)

Fabo, Pedro.
1911. Idiomas y etnografía de la región oriental de Colombia. Barcelona.

Falkner, Thomas.
1899. Thomas Falkner's nachricht von der moluchischen sprache; separat und unverändert herausgegeben von Julius Platzmann. Leipzig.

Featherman, Americus.
1881–91. Social History of the races of mankind . . . 7 vols. London.

Febres Cordero, Luis.
1918. Colombia, del antiguo Cúcuta. Cúcuta.

Febres Cordero, Tulio.
1920. Décadas de la Historia de Mérida. Mérida.

Federmann, Nikolaus.
1557. Indianische historia. Ein schöne kurtzweilige historia Niclaus Federmanns des jüngern von Ulm erster raise. Hagenaw. (*In* Klüpfel, K., ed., N. Federmanns und H. Staden Reisen in Südamerica 1529 bis 1555. Stuttgart, 1859, pp. 1–86. Reprinted in "Bibliotek des Litteriarische Vereins in Stuttgart, 47.") [Kirchhoff cites 1840 ed.]

Fernández, Diego de la Haya. *See* Haya Fernández, Diego de la.

Fernández Duro, Cesáreo, and Others, Editors.
1885–1932. Colección de documentos inéditos relativos al descubrimiento, conquista y organización de las antiguas posesiones españolas de ultramar. 2nd ser., Real Acad. de la Historia, 25 vols. Madrid.
See also Torres de Mendoza, Luis.

FERNÁNDEZ FERRAZ, JUAN.
    1892.   Nahuatlismos de Costa Rica. San José.
        See also Fernández Guardía, Ricardo, and Fernández Ferraz, Juan.

FERNÁNDEZ GUARDÍA, RICARDO, and FERNÁNDEZ FERRAZ, JUAN, EDITORS.
    1892.   Lenguas indigenas de Centro América en el siglo XVIII según copia
        del Archivo de Indias. San José.

FERNÁNDEZ, LEÓN.
    1881-1907.   Colección de documentos para la historia de Costa-Rica; pub. por
        el Lic. Don León Fernández . . . 10 vols. San José, Paris,
        Barcelona.
        See also, Andrade, Antonio de, and Rebullida, Pablo de; Bonilla, Don
        Juan de; Cardenas Palomino, Don Gomez de; Carrión, Hernando de, et
        al; Ceballos, Augustín de; Flores, Pedro; Maldonado, Rodrigo
        Arias; Margil, Antonio; Matamoros, Juan de; and Sójo, Diego de.
    1889.   Historia de Costa Rica durante la dominación española, 1592-1821.
        Madrid.

FERNÁNDEZ PIEDRAHITA, LUCAS.
    1881.   Historia general de las conquistas del nuevo reyno de Grenada.
        Bogotá. (Madrid, 1688.)

FERRAZ, JUAN FERNÁNDEZ. *See* FERNÁNDEZ FERRAZ, JUAN.

FEWKES, JESSE WALTER.
    1907.   The aborigines of Porto Rico and neighboring islands. Bur. Amer.
        Ethnol. Ann. Rep. 25, pp. 1-220 (1903-4).
    1922.   A prehistoric island culture area of America. Bur. Amer. Ethnol.
        Ann. Rep. 34 (1912-13).

FLORES, PEDRO.
    [1611.]   Inquiry concerning the merits and services of Captain Pedro Flores
        Cartago, Dec. 29, 1611. Costa Rica-Panama Arb. Doc., vol. 2, p.
        218, Doc. 78. (Doc. publ. in Sp. in Fernández, L., 1881-1907, Col.
        Doc. Hist. Costa Rica, vol. 5, p. 165.)

FONTANEDA, HERNANDO D'ESCALANTE. *See* ESCALANTE FONTANEDA, HERNANDO D'.

FORD, JAMES A.
    1944.   Excavations in the vicinity of Cali, Colombia. Yale Univ. Publ.
        Anthrop., No. 31.

FORT Y ROLDÁN, NICOLÁS.
    1881.   Cuba indígena. Madrid.

FRANCO INOJOSA, J. M., and GONZÁLEZ, ALEJANDRO.
    1936.   Exploraciones arqueológicas en el Perú, Departamento de Puno. Rev.
        Mus. Nac. Lima. Vol. 5, No. 2, pp. 157-183. Lima.

GABB, WILLIAM MORE.
    [1874.]   Report of the Talamanca exploration, made during 1873 and 1874 by
        W. M. Gabb. This report was addressed to General Don Thomas
        Guardia, President of Costa Rica. San José. Costa Rica-Panama
        Arb. Doc., 1913, Doc. 582, vol. 4, pp. 97-142.
    1875.   On the Indian tribes and languages of Costa Rica. Proc. Amer. Phil.
        Soc., vol. 14, pp. 483-602.
    1881.   On the topography and geology of Santo Domingo. Trans. Amer. Phil.
        Soc., n.s., vol. 15, pp. 49-259.

1886. Tribus y lenguas indígenas de Costa-Rica . . . Col. Doc. Hist. Costa Rica. Barcelona. (Trans. of 1875.)

GAGE, THOMAS.
1928. The English-American, a new survey of the West Indies, 1648. Ed. with introd. by A. P. Newton. London. (1st ed. 1648, London.)

GAGINI, CARLOS.
1917. Los aborigenes de Costa Rica. San José.

GANUZA, FR. MARCELINO.
1921. Monografía de las misiones vivas de agustinos recoletos (candelarios) en Colombia . . . Bogotá.

GARCÍA, ANTONIO.
1937. Geografía económica de Caldas. Contraloría General de la República, pp. 228–236. Bogotá.

GARCÍA CARBONELL, F.
1918. Memoria sobre el descubrimiento, conquista y colonización del Chocó. Bol. Hist., Nos. 43–44, pp. 297–310.

GARCÍA VALDÉS, PEDRO.
1930. La civilización taína en Pinar del Río. Habana.
1936–37. En Vueltabajo sí hubo civilización taina. Revista Cubana, vol. 6, pp. 179–235; vol. 7, pp. 210–242; vol. 8, pp. 187–203; vol. 9, pp. 86–101, 213–29, 346–61; vol. 10, pp. 256–68. Habana.

GARRET Y ARLOVI, BENITO.
[1711.] Report of Don Fray Benito Garret. y Arlovi, Bishop of Nicaragua, concerning the Mosquitos and the way to subdue them. Nov. 30. Costa Rica-Panama Arb. Doc., 1913, Doc. 151, vol. 1, pp. 371–386.

GASPAR DA MADRE DE DEOS.
1797. Memorias para a historia da capitania de S. Vicente, hoje chamada de S. Paulo, do estado do Brazil. Lisboa.

GASSÓ, LEONARDO.
1910–14. La Misión de San José de Narganá entre los Karibes. Las Misiones Católicas, vols. 18–22. Barcelona.

GIGLIOLI, ENRICO.
1906. On rare types of hafted stone battle-axes from South America in my collection. Archiv. Antrop. Etnol., vol. 36, fasc. 3.

GILIJ (GILII), FILIPPO SALVADORE.
1780–84. Saggio di storia americana; o sia, Storia naturale, civile e sacra de' regni, e delle provincie spagnuole di Terra-Ferma nell' America Meridionale descritto dall' abate F. S. Gilij. 4 vols. Rome.

GIRARD DE RIALLE, JULIEN.
1881. Caraibes. Paris.

GÓMARA, FRANCISCO LÓPEZ DE.
1749. Historia de las Indias. Ed. by A. Gonzáles de Barcía. Historiadores primitivos de las Indias Occidentales, No. 9. Madrid. (1st ed. 1552–53, 2 parts, Saragossa; other eds. 1852 and 1901.)

GONZÁLEZ, ALEJANDRO. See FRANCO INOJOSA, J. M., and GONZÁLEZ, ALEJANDRO.

GONZÁLEZ DÁVILA, GIL. See AVILA, GIL GONZÁLEZ.

González y Gutiérrez, Diego.
[1540.] Capitulación que se tomo con Diego Gutiérrez sobre la conquista de Veragua. Ano de 1540. Col. Doc. Inéd. Amér. y Oceanía, 1864–84, vol. 23, pp. 74–98.

Gordon, George B.
1896. Prehistoric ruins of Copan, Honduros. Mem. Peabody Mus. Arch. Ethnol. Harvard Univ., vol. 1, No. 1. Cambridge.
1898. Researches in the Uloa Valley, Honduras. Mem. Peabody Mus. Arch. Ethnol., Harvard Univ., vol. 1, No. 4. Cambridge.

Goubaud Carrera, Antonio. See Stoll, Otto.

Gower, Charlotte D.
1927. The northern and southern affiliations of Antillean culture. Mem. Amer. Anthrop. Assoc., No. 35.

Grubb, K. G.
1927. The lowland Indians of Amazonia . . . London.

Guillén Chapparo, Francisco.
1889. Memoria de los pueblos de la Gobernación de Popayán y cosas y constelaciones que hay en ellos. In An. Instr. Públ. Rep. Colombia, vol. 15, pp. 144–156. Bogotá.

Guiteras, Pedro José.
1865–66. Historia de la isla de Cuba. 2 vols. N. Y.

Gumilla, Joseph.
1745. El Orinoco Ilustrado, y Defendo Historia Natural, Civil, y Geographica de este Gran Rio, y de sus Caudalosas Vertientes . . . 2nd ed. in 2 pts. Madrid. (Barcelona, 1791.)

Gutiérrez, Diego. See González y Gutiérrez, Diego.

Gutiérrez, Felipe. See Diego y Gutiérrez, Felipe Clemente de.

Habel, Simeon.
1878. The sculptures of Santa Lucia Cosumalwhuapa in Guatemala with an account of travels in Central America and on the western coast of South America. Smithsonian Contr. Knowl., No. 269, vol. 22.

Hackett, L. W.
1916. Note on the collection of Dr. L. W. Hackett in Peabody Museum, Harvard Univ., obtained from the Guaimi Indians of Panama in 1915–1916. Spec. Nos. c/7422–c/7475. Notes, file No. 200.

Harlow, Vincent T., Editor.
1925. Colonising expeditions to the West Indies and Guiana, 1623–1667. Hakluyt, 2nd ser., No. 56. London.

Harrington, Mark Raymond.
1921. Cuba before Columbus. Ind. Notes Monogr. Pt. 1, vols. 1–2, N. Y.

Harris, W. R.
1904. The Caribs of Guiana and the West Indies. Ann. Arch. Rep. (of the Ontario Provincial Mus.) : 1903, being part of Appendix to the report of the Minister of Education, Ontario, pp. 139–145. Toronto.

Harrower, David E.
1925. Rama, Mosquito, and Sumu of Nicaragua. Ind. Notes, vol. 2, No. 1, pp. 44–48.

HARTMAN, CARL V.
1901. Archaeological researches in Costa Rica. Stockholm.
1907. Archaeological researches in the Pacific Coast of Costa Rica. Mem. Carnegie Mus., vol. 3, No. 1. Pittsburgh.
See also Holmes, William H., 1908.

HATT, GUDMUND.
1924. Archaeology of the Virgin Islands. Proc. 21st Congr. Int. Amer., pt. 1, pp. 29–42, 9 pl. The Hague.

HAYA FERNÁNDEZ, DIEGO DE LA.
[1719.] Report of the Governor Don Diego de la Haya Fernández to his Majesty. Cartago, April 14. Costa Rica-Panama Arb. Doc., 1913, Doc. 156, vol. 1, pp. 404–423.

HEATH, GEORGE REINKE.
1913. Notes on Miskuto grammar and on other Indian languages of eastern Nicaragua. Amer. Anthrop., n.s., vol. 15, pp. 48–62.
1927. Grammar of the Miskito language. Printed by F. Lindenbein, Herrnhut.

HEIMANN, MAX.
1931–32. Die Cayapa-Indianer. Zeit. Ethnol., vol. 63, pp. 281–287.

HENNEPIN, LOUIS. *See* LA BORDE, PÈRE DE, 1704.

HEREDIA, DON PEDRO DE.
1915 a. Carta al Rey, fechada en la Villa de Santa Cruz de Mompox en 3 de Julio de 1541. Cartas Inéditas de Heredia. Bol. Hist., Año 1, No. 2, pp. 53–58, Junio, 1915. Cartagena.
1915 b. Encomiendas de Urabá. Bol. Hist., Año 1, No. 4, Agosto, 1915. Cartagena.
1916. Adelantado. Relación de la Conquista de Cartagena. Escrito por un soldado de Heredia. Bol. Hist., Año 2, No. 14, Junio 1916, pp. 59–63. Medellín.

HERIOT, GEORGE.
1807. Travels through the Canadas, containing a description of the picturesque scenery on some of the rivers and lakes; with an account of the productions, commerce, and inhabitants of those provinces. To which is subjoined a comparative view of the manners and customs of several of the Indian nations of North and South America. London.

HERMANO JUSTO, RAMÓN.
1943. Geografía de Colombia. Quinta ed. Bogotá.

HERNÁNDEZ DE ALBA, GREGORIO.
1936. Etnologia guajira. Bogotá.
1938. Colombia; compendio arqueológico. Bogotá.

HERRERA FRITOT, RENÉ.
1936. Culturas aborígenes de las Antillas. Habana.
1939. Informe sobre una exploración arqueológica a Punta del Este, Isla de Pinos, realizada por el Museo Antropológico Montané de la Universidad de la Habana . . . Pub. de la revista "Universidad de la Habana," Nos. 20–21. Habana.
See Ortiz, Fernando; Cosculluela, J. A.; et al., 1943; and Royo Guardia, Fernando, et al., 1942.

HERRERA Y TORDESILLAS, ANTONIO DE.
1725–26. The general history of the vast continent and islands of America, commonly call'd, the West-Indies, from the first discovery thereof: with the best accounts the people could give of their antiquities. Collected from the original relations sent to the kings of Spain . . . Trans. into English by Capt. John Stevens . . . London. (Other editions: London, 1726; 1726–43, 6 vols.; 1740, 6 vols.; 1740–43, 6 vols.; 1825–26, 6 vols.)
See Tapia y Rivera, Alejandro, 1854.
1730. Historia general de los hechos de los castellanos en las islas i tierrafirme del mar oceano. 5 vols. Madrid. (First ed., 1601; 3rd ed. Madrid, 1726, 4 vols.)

HOLLIS, ALFRED CLAUD.
1941. A brief history of Trinidad under the Spanish Crown. Trinidad and Tobago.

HOLMES, WILLIAM HENRY.
1887. The use of gold and other metals among the ancient inhabitants of Chiriqui, Isthmus of Darien. Bull. Bur. Ethnol., No. 3.
1888. Ancient art of the province of Chiriqui, Colombia. Bur. Ethnol., 6th Ann. Rep., pp. 3–187. (1884–85).
1894. Caribbean influence on the prehistoric ceramic art of the Southern States. Amer. Anthrop., n. s., vol. 7, pp. 71–9.
1908. Review of "Archaeological Researches on the Pacific Coast of Costa Rica," by C. V. Hartman. Amer. Anthrop., n.s., vol. 10, pp. 128–133.

HOLTEN, HERMANN VON.
1877. Das Land der Yurakarer und dessen Bewohner. Zeit. Ethnol., vol. 9, pp. 105–115. Berlin.

HOSTOS, ADOLFO DE.
1941. Anthropological papers. Based principally on studies of the prehistoric archaeology and ethnology of the Greater Antilles. San Juan.

HOWARD, GEORGE D.
1943. Excavations at Ronquín, Venezuela. Yale Univ. Publ. Anthrop., No. 28.
See Osgood, Cornelius, and Howard, George D.

IBI, CAMILO DE.
1919 a. Curiosos datos etnográficos y expedición del Reverendo padre Camilo de Ibi, Misionero Apostolico Capuchino, a la Sierra de Motilones. Bogotá.
1919 b. Las misiones católicas en Colombia. Bogotá.

IRIAS, DON JUAN FRANCISCO.
1853. Rio Wanks and the Mosco Indians. Trans. Amer. Ethnol. Soc., vol. 3, pt. 1, Art. 3, pp. 161–168. N. Y.

IRVING, WASHINGTON.
1851. The life and voyages of Christopher Columbus; to which are added those of his companions. The works of Washington Irving, new ed., revised, vols. 3–4, N. Y.

IZIKOWITZ, KARL GUSTAV.
1935. Musical and other sound instruments of the South American Indians . . . Göteborgs Kungl. Vetenskaps- och Vitterhets- Samhälles Handlinger, 5th följden, ser. A, Band 5, No. 1. Göteborg.

JAHN, ALFREDO.
1914. Parahuanos und Guajiros und die Pfahlbauten am See von Maracaibo. Zeit. f. Ethnol., vol. 46; pp. 267–283.
1927. Los aborígenes del occidente de Venezuela . . . Caracas.
1932. Los craneos deformados de los aborígenes de los valles de Aragua. Sociedad Venezolana de Ciencias Naturales de Caracas, Bull. 8, pp. 1–14, Caracas.

JAMES, PRESTON E.
1942. Latin America. New York.

JANE, CECIL, TRANS. AND ED. See COLUMBUS, CHRISTOPHER, 1930, 1930–33.

JEAN-BAPTISTE LE PERS, P. See CHARLEVOIX, PIERRE FRANÇOIS XAVIER DE.

JEFFERYS, THOMAS.
1760. The natural and civil history of the French dominions in North and South America giving a particular account of the climate, soil, minerals, animals, vegetables, manufactures, trade, commerce and languages, together with the religion, government, genius, character, manners and customs of the Indians and other inhabitants. Two parts, bound in 1 vol. London.

JIJÓN Y CAAMAÑO, JACINTO.
1912. Contribución al conocimiento de los aborígenes de la provincia de Imbabura. Madrid.
1919. Contribución al conocimiento de las lenguas indígenas que se hablaron en el Ecuador interandino y ocidental, con anterioridad a la conquista española. Bol. Soc. Ecuatoriana Estud. Hist., vol. 2, No. 6, pp. 340–413.
1936–38. Sebastián de Benalcázar. 5 vols. in 2. Quito.
1940–45. El Ecuador interandino y occidental antes de la conquista castellana. 4 vols. Editorial ecuatoriana. Quito. See Cabello Balboa, Miguel, MS.

JIMÉNEZ, ORTON. See POPENOE, WILSON, and JIMÉNEZ, ORTON.

JOHNSON, FREDERICK.
1940. The linguistic map of Mexico and Central America. In The Maya and Their Neighbors, pp. 88–114. N.Y.

JOYCE, THOMAS ATHOL.
1916. Central American and West Indian archaeology . . . London.

JUAN, DON JORGE, and ULLOA, DON ANTONIO DE.
[1748]. Relación historica del viaje a la America Meridional. (Historical account of a voyage to South America, etc.). Madrid. 5 vols. Costa Rica-Panama Arb. Doc., 1913, Doc. 574, vol. 4, pp. 15–18.

JUARROS, DOMINGO.
1936. Compendio de la historia de la ciudad de Guatemala. 2 vols. Guatemala. (1st ed. 1808–18.)

KANTULE, REUBEN (RUBEN) PÉREZ. See NORDENSKIÖLD, ERLAND, 1928–30, 1938.

KARSTEN, RAFAEL.
1924. The Colorado Indians of Western Ecuador. Ymer, vol. 44.
1926. The civilization of the South American Indians . . . London.

KENDALL, ABRAM. *See* DUDLEY, ROBERT, 1899.

KERR, ROBERT. *See* COLÓN, FERNANDO, 1811.

KIDDER II, ALFRED.
  1940. South American penetrations in Middle America. *In* The Maya and
        their neighhors, pp. 441–459, N. Y.
  1944. Archaeology of Northwestern Venezuela. Pap. Peabody Mus. Arch.
        Ethnol. Harvard Univ., vol. 26, No. 1.
        See also Strong, William Duncan; Kidder II, Alfred; and Paul, A. J.
        Drexel.

KIRCHHOFF, PAUL.
  1931. Die Vervandtschaftsorganization der Urwaldstämme Südamerikas. Zeit.
        Ethnol., vol. 63, pp. 85–193.
  1943. Mesoamérica. Acta Amer., vol. 1, pp. 92–107.

KOCH-GRÜNBERG, THEODOR.
  1917–1928. Vom Roroima zum Orinoco. 5 vols. Berlin (Stuttgart).

KOHLER, J.
  1887. Ueber das Recht der Goajiroindianer. Zeit. f. Vergleich. Rechtswiss.,
        vol. 7, pp. 381–84

KRICKEBERG, WALTER.
  1922. "Amerika," *in* Illustrierte Volkerkunde, herausgegeben von Georg
        Buschan, vol. 1. Stuttgart.

KRIEGER, HERBERT W.
  1926. Material culture of the people of southeastern Panama, based on speci-
        mens in the United States National Museum. U. S. Nat. Mus., Bull.
        134.
  1929. Archeological and historical investigations in Samaná, Dominican Re-
        public. U. S. Nat. Mus., Bull. 147.
  1930. The aborigines of the ancient island of Hispaniola. Ann. Rep. Smith-
        sonian Inst. for 1929, pp. 473–506.
  1931. Aboriginal Indian pottery of the Dominican Republic. U. S. Nat. Mus.,
        Bull. 156.

KROEBER, A. L.
  1939. Cultural and natural areas of native North America. Univ. Calif. Publ.
        Amer. Arch. Ethnol., vol. 38. Berkeley.
  1940. Conclusions: The present status of Americanistic problems. *In* The
        Maya and their neighbors, pp. 463–487. New York.

LABAT, JEAN BAPTISTE.
  1724. Nouveau voyage aux isles de l'Amerique, contenant l'histoire naturelle
        de ces pays, l'origine, les moeurs, la religion et le gouvernement des
        habitans anciens et modernes . . . 2 vols. The Hague. Other editions:
        Paris, 1722, 1724, and 1742.
  1931. The memoirs of Père Labat, 1693–1705, trans. and abridged by John
        Eaden . . . London.

LA BORDE, PÈRE DE (Sieur de).
  1704. Voyage qui contient un relation exacte de l'origine, moeurs, coûtumes,
        réligion, guerres et voyages des Caraïbes, sauvages des isles Antilles
        de l'Amerique, faite par le Sieur de la Borde, employé à la conversion
        des Caraïbes, et tirée du cabinet de Monsr. Blondel. A. Leide, Chez
        P. van de Aa, 1704. *In* Hennepin, Louis: Voyage ou Nouvelle
        decouverte, pp. 517–604. Amsterdam.

1886.   History of the origin, customs, religion, wars, and travels of the Caribs, savages of the Antilles in America. Trans. from French and condensed by G. J. A. Bosch-Reitz. Timehri, vol. 5, pp. 224–254. Demerara.

LADE, ROBERT.
   1744.   Voyages du capitaine Robert Lade en différentes parties de l'Afrique, de l'Asie, et de l'Amérique. 2 vols. Paris.

LAET, JUAN DE.
   [1640.]   L'histoire du Nouveau Monde ou description des Indes Occidentales, contenant dix-huit livres, par le sieur Iean de Laet, d'Anvers; enrichi de nouvelles tables geographiques et figures des animaux, plantes et fruites. A Leyde, Chez Bonaventure et Abraham Elseviers, Imprimeurs ordinaires de l'Universite. Costa Rica-Panama Arb. Doc., 1913, Doc. 571, vol. 4, pp. 4–6.

LANDECHO, DOCTOR MEXIA, and DOCTOR BARROS DE SAN MILLAN.
   [1559.]   The Audiencia of the Confies, to his Majesty the King, concerning the pacification of the Chomes Indians and Conquest of New Cartago. Santiago de Guatemala. Costa Rica-Panama Arb. Doc., 1913, Doc. 35, vol. 1, p. 96.

LARA, GERARDO.
   [1912.]   Report of Governor of Limón (on the District of Talamanca). Costa Rica-Panama Arb. Doc., 1913, Doc. 568, vol. 3, pp. 440–444.

LARDE Y LARIN, JORGE.
   1940.   Distribución geográfica de los pueblos Lencas en El Salvador. Rev. Archiv. Bibl. Nac., t. 19, No. 6, pp. 370–373. Tegucigalpa.

LAS CASAS, BARTOLOMÉ DE.   See CASAS, BARTOLOMÉ DE LAS.

LAURA DE SANTA CATALINA, MADRE.
   1936.   Cartas Misionales. 3rd ed., p. 136. Medellín.

LE BARON, J. FRANCIS.
   1912.   Description of stone ruins in eastern Nicaragua, with notes on the location of other ruins in Central America. Records of the Past, vol. 2, pt. 5, pp. 217–222. Washington.

LEHMANN, WALTER.
   1910.   Ergebnisse einer Forshungsreise in Mittelamerika und Mexico. 1907–9. Zeit. Ethnol., vol. 42, pp. 687–749.
   1915.   Über die Stellung und Verwandtschaft der Subtiaba-Sprache der Pazifischen Küste Nicaraguas und über die Sprache von Tapachula in Südchiapas. Zeit. Ethnol., vol. 47, pp. 1–34. Berlin.
   1920.   Zentral-Amerika, 2 vols. Berlin. Vol. 1, Die sprachen Zentral-Amerikas in ihren beziehungen zueinander sowie zu Süd-Amerika und Mexiko.

LEHMANN-NITSCHE, ROBERT.
   1899.   Weitere Mitteilungen über die Guayakis in Paraguay. Globus, vol. 76, pp. 78–80. Braunschweig.

LESLIE, FRANK.   See SQUIER, EPHRAIM GEORGE, 1869.

LETTRES ÉDIFIANTES ET CURIEUSES, ÉCRITES DES MISSIONS ÉTRANGÈRES.
   See BARAZE, PÈRE CYPRIEN.

LINES, JORGE A.
   1935.   Los altares de Toyopán. San José, Costa Rica.

1938 a. Sukia: tsúgür o isogro. An. Soc. Geogr. Hist. Guatemala. T. 14, No. 4, pp. 407–431. Guatemala.

1938 b. Notes on the archaeology of Costa Rica. San José, Costa Rica. (2nd ed. rev.; 1st ed. 1936.)

1939. Notes on the archeology of Costa Rica. San José, Costa Rica. (3rd ed., rev.; 1st ed. 1936.)

LINNÉ, SIGVALD.
1929. Darien in the Past. The Archaeology of Eastern Panama and North western Colombia. Göteborgs Kungl. Vetenskaps- och Vitterhets-Samhälles Handlingar, Femte följden, Ser. A, Band 1, No. 3. Göteborg.

LONGYEAR III, JOHN M.
1940. The enthnological significance of Copan pottery. In The Maya and their neighbors, pp. 268–271. New York.

1942. A southern Maya-Peten pottery correlation. Amer. Antiq., vol. 7, No. 4, pp. 389–396.

LÓPEZ DE VELASCO, JUAN.
1915. Geografía y descripción universal de las Indias. Bol. Hist., Año 1, 5 and 6. (Earlier ed. Madrid 1894.)

1916. Cronista y Cosmógrafo Mayor de Indias. Geografía y Descripción Universal de las Indias. In Bol. Hist., Año II, No. 17, pp. 193–208. Medellín.

LOTHROP, SAMUEL KIRKLAND.
1919. The discovery of gold in the graves of Chiriquí, Panama. Ind. Notes Monogr., vol. 7, No. 2.

1921. The stone statues of Nicaragua. Amer. Anthrop., n.s., vol. 23, pp. 311–319.

1926 a. Stone sculptures from the Finca Arevalo, Guatemala. Ind. Notes, vol. 3, No. 3, pp. 147–171.

1926 b. Pottery of Costa Rica and Nicaragua. Contrib. Mus. Amer. Ind., Heye Foundation, vol. 8 in 2 vols. N. Y.

1927 a. Pottery types and their sequence in El Salvador. Ind. Notes Monogr., vol. 1, No. 4, pp. 165–220.

1927 b. The Museum Central American Expedition, 1925–26. Ind. Notes, vol. 4, No. 1, pp. 12–33.

1933. Atitlán, an archaeological study of ancient remains on the borders of Lake Atitlán, Guatemala. Carnegie Inst. Washington, Pub. 444.

1937. Coclé, an archaeological study of Central Panama. Pt. 1. Historical background. Excavations at the Sitio Conte. Artifacts and ornaments. Mem. Peabody Mus. Arch. Ethnol., Harvard Univ., vol. 7.

1939. The southeastern frontier of the Maya. Amer. Anthrop., n.s., vol. 41, No. 1, pp. 42–54. Menasha.

1940. South America as seen from Middle America. In The Maya and their neighbors, pp. 417–429. New York.

1942. Coclé, an archaeological study of Central Panama. Pt. 2. Pottery of the Sitio Conte and other archaeological sites. Mem. Peabody Mus. Arch. Ethnol., Harvard Univ., vol. 8.

LOVÉN, SVEN.
1935. Origins of the Tainan Culture, West Indies. Göteborg.

LUTZ, O.
1922. Die Ureinwohner am Isthmus von Panamá. Festschrift Eduard Seler, pp. 363–378. Stuttgart.

"M. W."
1752. The Mosqueto Indian and His Golden River; being a familiar description of the Mosqueto Kingdom in America, etc. (written about 1699). A collection of voyages and travels, vol. 6, pp. 297–312. London.

MacCurdy, George Grant.
1911. A study of Chiriquian antiquities. Connecticut Acad. Arts, Sci. Mem., vol. 3. New Haven.

MacNiel, J. A.
1886. Gold and bronze relics, and Guaymi Indians. Amer. Antiq., vol. 8, p. 42.

MacNutt, Francis Augustus, Trans. and Editor. *See* Anghiera, Pietro Martire d'; *also* Cortes, Hernando.

Major, R. H. *See* Columbus, Christopher, 1930–33.

Maldonado, Don Rodrigo Arias.
[1662.] Royal Provision Granted by the Audiencia de Guatemala to Don Rodrigo Arias Maldonado, Governor of Costa Rica, Empowering him to conquer and settle Talamanca. Guatemala. Costa Rica-Panama Arb. Doc., 1913, Doc. 86, vol. 1, p. 265. (Doc. publ. in Sp. in Fernández, L. 1881–1907, Col. Doc. Hist. Costa Rica, vol. 5, p. 344.)

Marcano, G.
1889. Ethnographie précolombienne du Venezuela, Vallées d'Aragua et de Caracas. Mém. Soc. Anthrop. Paris, 2nd ser., vol. 4, pp. 1–86. Paris.

Margil, Fray Antonio.
[1703.] Letter of Fray Antonio Margil to the President of the Audiencia of Guatemala. Guatemala. Costa Rica-Panama Arb. Doc., 1913, Doc. 142, vol. 1, pp. 339–344. (Doc. publ. in Sp. in Fernández, L., 1881–1907, Col. Doc. Hist. Costa Rica, vol. 5, p. 412.)

Markham, Clements R. *See* Andagoya, Pasqual de, 1865, *also* Columbus, Christopher, 1893.

Martyr, Peter. *See* Anghiera, Pietro Martire d'.

Mason, Gregory.
1940. South of Yesterday. New York.

Mason, John Alden.
1926. Coast and crest in Colombia. Nat. Hist., vol. 26.
1940. The native languages of Middle America. *In* The Maya and their neighbors, pp. 52–87, New York.
1941. A large archaeological site at Capá, Utuado, with notes on other Porto Rican sites visited in 1914–15. Scientific Survey of Porto Rico and the Virgin Islands, N. Y. Acad. Sci., vol. 17, pt. 2.
1942. New excavations at the Sitio Conte, Coclé, Panamá. Proc. 8th Amer. Sci. Congr., Washington, D. C., 1940, vol. 2, pp. 103–107.
1945. Costa Rican stonework: The Minor C. Keith Collection. Anthrop. Pap. Amer. Mus. Nat. Hist., vol. 39, pt. 3.

MATAMOROS, JUAN DE.
[1675.] Subjection of Talamanca. Statement of Fray Juan de Matamoros in regard thereto. Cartago. Costa Rica-Panama Arb. Doc., 1913, Doc. 88, vol. 1, p. 274. (Doc. publ. in Sp. in Fernández, L., 1881–1907, Col. Doc. Hist. Costa Rica, vol. 5, p. 353.)

MEILLET, A., and COHEN, MARCEL.
1924. Les langues du monde. Paris.
See also Rivet, Paul, 1924.

MEMBREÑO, ALBERTO.
1897. Hondureñismos. 2nd ed. Tegucigalpa.

MESA JARAMILLO, JOSÉ MARÍA.
1905. Retoques históricos. Repertorio Histórico. Año 1, No. 1, Enero, 1905. Medellín.

MÜNSTER, SEBASTIAN. See ARBER, EDWARD, 1885.

MILLA Y VIDAURRE, JOSÉ.
1879–1919. Historia de la América central . . . Guatemala.

MORALES CABRERA, PABLO.
1932. Puerto Rico indígena; prehistoria y protohistoria de Puerto Rico; descripción de los usos, costumbres, lenguaje, religión, gobierno, agricultura, industrias de pueblo taino de Boriquén, según los cronistas de Indias en la época del descubrimiento de América. San Juan, Puerto Rico, "Imprenta Venezuela."

MORALES COELLO, JULIO. See ROYO GUARDIA, FERNANDO, ET AL, 1942.

MORALES PATIÑO, OSWALDO. See ORTIZ, FERNANDO; COSCULLUELA, J. A.; ET AL., 1943.

MÜLLER, FRIEDRICH. See PITTIER, HENRI FRANÇOIS, 1898.

MULLIGAN, REV. JOHN, TRANS. See SCILLACIO, NICCOLÒ, 1859.

MUÑOZ, JUAN BAUTISTA.
1797. The history of the New World. Trans. from the Spanish with notes by the translator . . . London.
See also Tapia y Rivera, Alejandro.

NAU, BARON EMILE.
1894. Histoire des caciques d'Haiti. Deuxième éd. Paris.

NAVARRETE, MARTÍN FERNÁNDEZ DE.
1825–37. Colección de los viages y descubrimientos que hicieron por mar los españoles desde nes del siglo XV . . . 5 vols. Madrid.

NAVARRO, NICHOLAS E. See BUENO, RAMÓN, 1933.

NECTARIO MARÍA, H.
1933. Descubrimientos arqueológicos en la región de Barquisimeto. Excelsior, vol. 2, No. 30. Barquisimeto, Venezuela.
1942. Contribución a los estudios etnológicos y arqueológicos de Venezuela. Mem. Soc. Cienc. Naturales La Salle, Año 2, No. 4, pp. 17–21. Caracas.

NÉLE. See NORDENSKIÖLD, ERLAND, 1928–30, 1938.

NEWTON, A. P. See GAGE, THOMAS, 1928.

NICHOLAS, FRANCIS C.
1901. The aborigines of the Province of Santa Marta, Colombia. Amer. Anthrop., n.s., vol. 3, pp. 606–649. (This is a translation of "Floresta de la Santa Iglesia Catedral de la Ciudad de Santa Marta" by Father Alvarez Don José Nicolas de la Rosa, dated 1739, plus some additional notes concerning the present condition of the Indians.)

NICOLAS DE LA ROSA, ALVAREZ DON JOSÉ. See NICHOLAS, F. C., 1901.

NOMLAND, GLADYS AYER [Mrs.].
1933. Archaeological site of Hato Viejo, Venezuela. Amer. Anthrop., n.s., vol. 35, pp. 718–741.
1935. New archaeological sites from the state of Falcón, Venezuela. Ibero-Americana, No. 11. Berkeley.

NORDENSKIÖLD, ERLAND.
1924. Des flèches à trois plumes d'empenne en Amérique du Sud. Journ. Soc. Amér. Paris, n.s., vol. 16, pp. 195–196.
1928 a. Indianerna på Panamanaset. Stockholm. Article with same title *in* Ymer, vol. 48, pp. 85–110, 1928, Stockholm.
1928 b. Les Indiens de l'isthme de Panama. La Géogr., vol. 50, Nos. 5–6, pp. 299–319. Paris.
1928–30. Picture-writings and other documents by Néle, Paramount chief of the Cuna Indians and Reuben Pérez Kantule, his secretary, published by Erland Nordenskiöld. Comp. Ethnogr. Stud., vol. 7, pts. 1, 2. Göteborg.
1929. Les rapports entre l'art, la religion et la magie chez les Indiens Cuna et Chocó. Journ. Soc. Amér. Paris, n.s., vol. 21, pp. 141–158. Paris.
1930. Modifications in Indian cultures through inventions and loans. Comp. Ethnogr. Stud., vol. 8. Göteborg.
1938. An historical and ethnological survey of the Cuna Indians, by Erland Nordenskiöld, in collaboration with the Cuna Indian, Ruben Pérez Kantule, arranged and edited from the posthumous manuscript and notes, and original Indian documents at the Gothenburg Ethnographical Museum, by Henry Wassén. Com. Ethnogr. Stud., vol. 10. Göteborg.

NUÑEZ CABEZA DE VACA, ALVAR.
1906. Relación de los naufragios y comentarios. Col. Libr. Doc. Ref. Hist. Amér. T. 5–6. Madrid.

OBER, FREDERICK ALBION.
1880. Camps in the Caribbees: the adventures of a naturalist in the Lesser Antilles. Boston.
1895. Aborigines of the West Indies. Proc. Amer. Antiq. Soc., n.s., vol. 9, pp. 270–313. Worcester, Mass.

ORAMAS, LUIS R.
1916. Materiales para el estudio de los dialectos Ayamán, Gayón, Jirajara, Ajagua. Caracas.
1917. Apuntes sobre arqueología venezolana. Proc. 2nd Pan Amer. Sci. Congr., Sec. 1, vol. 1, pp. 138–45.

Ortiz, Fernando; Cosculluela, J. A.; Herrera Fritot, René; Royo, Fernando; and Morales Patiño, Oswaldo.
1943. Las culturas precolombinas de Cuba. Actas y Documentos del Primer Documentos del Primer Congreso Histórico, 1942, pp. 192–346. Habana.

Ortiz Fernández, Fernando.
1935. Historia de la arqueología indocubana. Colección de Libros Cubanos, vol. 33, t. 2, pp. 23–457. Habana. (Revision of earlier edition published in Cuba Contemporanea, t. 30, núms. 117 y 118, 1922.)
1943. Las cuatro culturas indias de Cuba. Bibl. Estud. Cubanos, vol. 1. Habana.

Ortíz, Sergio Elías.
1944. Linguistica colombiana . . . Familia Guahibo. Rev. Hist. Pasto, Nos. 3 and 4, pp. 39–62.

Orton, Jiménez. See Popenoe, Wilson, and Orton, Jiménez.

Osgood, Cornelius.
1935. The archeological problem in Chiriquí. Amer. Anthrop. n. s., vol. 37, pp. 234–243.
1942 a. The Ciboney culture of Cayo Redondo, Cuba. In Yale Univ. Publ. Anthrop., No. 25.
1942 b. Prehistoric contact between South America and the West Indies. Proc. Nat. Acad. Sci., vol. 28, pp. 1–4. New York.
1943. Excavations at Tocorón, Venezuela. Yale Univ. Publ. Anthrop., No. 29.
1946. British Guiana archeology to 1945. Yale Univ. Publ. Anthrop., No. 36. (Note: Nos. 35 and 36 are bound together. See Bennett, Wendell C., 1946.)

Osgood, Cornelius, and Howard, George D.
1943. An archeological survey of Venezuela. Yale Univ. Publ. Anthrop., No. 27, pp. 1–153.

Ospina, Tulio.
1905. "D. Alvaro Restrepo y la Academia de Historia." Repertorio Histórico, Año 1, No. 3, pp. 145–164. Medellín.
1918. El Oidor Mon y Velarde, regenerador de Antioquia. In Repertorio Histórico, Nos. 9–11, pp. 413–414. Medellín. Dato de Relación de la visita del Oidor Herrera Campuzano en 1616.

Outes, Félix F., and Bruch, Carlos.
1910. Los aborígenes de la República Argentina. Buenos Aires.

Oviedo y Baños, José de.
1824. Historia de la conquista, y población de la provincia de Venezuela. Pt. 1. Other editions: Caracas, 1932, 1935, 1941; Madrid, 1723, 1885.

Oviedo y Valdés, Gonzalo Fernández de.
1749. Relación sumaria de la historia natural de las Indias, compuesta y dirigida al emperador Carlos V. por el capitan Gonzalo Fernández de Oviedo. In Barcia (Carballido y Zuñiga), Andrés Gonzalez de. Historiadores primitivos de los Indias Occidentales. (No. 5.) Madrid.
1851–55. Historia general y natural de las Indias, islas y tierra firme de la mar océano . . . 4 vols. José Amador de los Rios, ed. Madrid. (First part originally published in 1535.)
　　　See Tapia y Rivera, Alejandro.

1906. Extracts of Gonzalo Ferdinando de Oviedo his Summarie and Generall Historie of the Indies. *In* Hakluytus Posthumus or Purchas His Pilgrimes, containing a History of the World in Sea Voyages and Lande Travells by Englishmen and others, by Samuel Purchas, vol. 15, pp. 148–232, Hakluyt, extra ser., No. 27. Glasgow.

PABLO DEL SANTÍSIMO SACRAMENTO, PADRE. (FRAY CARMELITA DESCALZO, MISIONERO DE URABÁ.)
1936. El Idioma katío (ensayo gramatical) . . . Medellín.

PACHECO, JOAQUÍN F. *See* TORRES DE MENDOZA, LUIS, EDITOR.

PALMATARY, HELEN P.
1939. Tapajó pottery. Etnol. Stud., No. 8. Göteberg.

PANÉ, RAMÓN. *See* BACHILLER Y MORALES, ANTONIO, 1883; and BOURNE, EDWARD GAYLORD, 1907.

PAS, MANUEL M. *See* CODAZZI, AGUSTÍN.

PAUL, A. J. DREXEL. *See* STRONG, WILLIAM DUNCAN; KIDDER II, ALFRED; and PAUL, A. J. DREXEL.

PAVON, FRANCISCO.
[1578.] Act of taking possession of the Valley of Guaymi. Artieda, March 5, 1578. Costa Rica-Panama Arb. Doc., 1913, Doc. 68, vol. 1, pp. 190–191.

PECTOR, DÉSIRÉ.
1888–89. Indication approximative de vestiges laissés par les populations pré-colombiennes du Nicaragua. Deuxieme éd., Paris. (Pt. 1, pp. 1–31 not numbered as a part. Pt. 2, pp. 145–178 same title and date.)

PERALTA, MANUEL MARÍA DE.
1883. Costa-Rica, Nicaragua y Panamá en el siglo XVI; su historia y sus límites, según los documentos del Archivo de Indias de Sevilla, del de Simancas, etc. Recogidos y publicados con notas y aclaraciones históricas y geograficas. Madrid and Paris.
See also Avila, Gil González, [1524]; Criado de Castilla, Alonso, [1575]; and Diego y Gutiérrez, Felipe Clemente de [1534].
1890. Límites de Costa-Rica y Colombia. Nuevos documentos para la historia de su jurisdicción territorial con notos, comentarios y un examen de la cartografía de Costa-Rica y Veragua . . . Madrid.
See also Royal Cedula, [1521].
1892. Etnologia centro-americana. Apuntes para un libro sobre los aborígenes de Costa Rica. Madrid.
1901. Les Aborigenes de Costa-Rica. Essai de distribution géographique. Journ. Soc. Amér. Paris, vol. 3, pp. 125–139.

PEREDO, OBISPO DON DIEGO DE.
1919. [Probable autor de] Noticia Historial de la Provincia de Cartagena. Año 1772. Bol. Hist. Año IV, Nos. 47–48, abril 1919, pp. 45–80. Cartagena.

PÉREZ, FELIPE. *See* CODAZZI, AGUSTÍN.

PÉREZ KANTULE, REUBEN. *See* NORDENSKIÖLD, ERLAND, 1928–30, 1938.

PERICOT GARCÍA, LUIS.
1936. América indígena. (Vol. 1 of ser.: Historia de América y de los pueblos americanos . . . .) Barcelona.

PETER MARTYR OF ANGHIERA. *See* ANGHIERA, PIETRO MARTIRE D'.

PETRULLO, VINCENZO.
    1937.   Composition of "Torts" in Guajiro Society. *In* Publ. Phila. Anthrop.
            Soc., vol. 1, 25th Anniv. Stud. (ed. D. S. Davidson), pp. 153–160.
    1939 a. The Yaruros of the Capanaparo River, Venezuela. Anthrop. Pap.
            No. 11. Bull. Bur. Amer. Ethnol., No. 123, pp. 161–290.
    1939 b. Archeology of Arauquin. Anthrop. Paper No. 12. Bull. Bur. Amer.
            Ethnol., No. 123, pp. 291–295.

PICHARDO MOYA, FELIPE.
    1944.   Los caneyes del sur de Camagüey. Rev. Habana, vol. 3, No. 18, pp.
            523–546. Habana.

PIM, BEDFORD, and SEEMAN, BARTHOLD.
    1869.   Dottings on the roadside in Panama, Nicaragua, and Mosquito. London.

PINART, ALPHONSE LOUIS.
    1885.   Chiriquí: Bocas del Toro—Valle Miranda. Bull. Soc. Géogr. Paris,
            7e ser., vol. 6, pp. 433–452.
    1887 a. Les Indiens de l'etat de Panama. Rev. Ethnogr. Paris, vol. 6, No. 1,
            pp. 33–56.
    1887 b. Les Indiens de l'etat de Panama. Rev. Ethnogr. Paris, vol. 6, No. 2,
            pp. 117–132.
    1900.   Notes sur les tribus indiennes de familles guarano-guaymies de l'isthme
            de Panama et du Centre-Amérique. Chatres.

PINEDO, DON GASPAR DE.
    [1709.] Royal Cedula concerning the colonization of the Indians of Boruca.
            Costa Rica-Panama Arb. Doc., 1913, Doc. 146, vol. 1, pp. 363–363.

PIÑERES, EDUARDO GUTIÉRREZ DE.
    1917.   Censo de la Provincia de Cartagena. Bol. Hist. No. 29. Cartagena.

PITTIER DE FÁBREGA, HENRI FRANÇOIS. *See* PITTIER, HENRI FRANÇOIS.

PITTIER, HENRI FRANÇOIS.
    1895.   Nombres geográficos de Costa Rica. San José de Costa Rica.
    1898.   Die sprache der Bribri-Indianer in Costa Rica. Herausgegeben und mit
            einer vorrede versehen, von dr. Friedrich Müller. Wien. Sitz. Kais.
            Akad. Wissen. Wein. Philos.-histor. classe., Bd. 137, No. 6.
    1903.   Folk-lore of the Bribri and Brunka Indians in Costa Rica. Journ. Amer.
            Folk-lore, vol. 16, pp. 1–9.
    1904.   Numeral systems of the Costa Rican Indians. Amer. Anthrop., n.s., vol.
            6, pp. 447–458.
    1938 a. Apuntaciones etnológicas sobre los indios bribri. Mus. Nac. Costa
            Rica, ser. etnol., vol. 1, pt. 1. San José.
    1938 b. Capítulos escogidos de la geografía física y prehistórica de Costa Rica.
            Mus. Nac. Costa Rica, ser. geogr., vol. 1, pt. 1. San José.
    1941.   Materiales para el estudio de la lengua brunka haglada en Boruca reco-
            gidos en las años de 1892 a 1896. Mus. Nac. Costa Rica, ser. etnol., vol.
            1, pt. 2. San José.

PLATZMANN, JULES. *See* BRETON, RAYMOND, 1892; and FALKNER, THOMAS.

PONCE, ALONSO. *See* ALONSO DE SAN JUAN.

PONCE, PADRE ALONSO. *See* ALONSO DE SAN JUAN.

POPENOE, DOROTHY H.
1928. Las Ruinas de Tenampua. Tipografía Nacional. Tegucigalpa.
1934. Some excavations at Playa de los Muertos, Ulua River, Honduras. *In* Maya Research, vol. 1, pp. 61–85. New York.
1936. The Ruins of Tenampua, Honduras. Ann. Rep. Smithsonian Inst. for 1935, pp. 559–572.
See also Popenoe, Wilson, and Popenoe, Dorothy H.

POPENOE, WILSON, and ORTON, JIMÉNEZ.
1921. The pejibaye, a neglected food plant of tropical America. Journ. Hered., vol. 12, pp. 154–166.

POPENOE, WILSON, and POPENOE, DOROTHY H.
1931. The human background of Lancetilla. Unifruitco Magazine, August, 1931.

POSADO ARANGO, ANDRÉS.
1875. Essai ethnographique sur les aborigenes de l'Etat d'Antioquia en Colombie. Mém. Soc. Anthrop. Paris., 2nd ser., vol. 1, pp. 201–232.

PRINCE, J. DYNELEY.
1913 a. A text in the Indian language of Panamá-Darien. Amer. Anthrop. n. s., vol. 15, pp. 298–326.
1913 b. Grammar and glossary of the Tule language of Panamá. Amer. Anthrop. n.s., vol. 15, pp. 480–528.

PUIS, MATTHIAS DU.
1652. Relation de l'établissement d'une colonie française dans l'ile de la Guadeloupe de l'Amérique, et des moeurs des sauvages. Caen.

PURCHAS, SAMUEL.
1905–07. Hakluytus posthumus, or Purchas his Pilgrimes . . . 20 vols. (Reprint of 1625 ed). Glasgow.

QUIROGA, PEDRO DE.
[1535.] Informacion en derecho del Licenciado Quiroga sobre algunas provisiones del Real Consejo de Indias. Col. Doc. Inéd. Amér. y Oceanía, 1864–84, vol. 10, pp. 333–525.

RADIN, PAUL.
1919. The genetic relationship of the North American Indian languages. Univ. Calif. Publ. Amer. Arch. Ethnol., vol. 14, pt. 5. Berkeley.

RAFINESQUE, CONSTANTINE SAMUEL.
1836. The American nations; or, outlines of their general history, ancient and modern: including the whole history of the earth and mankind in the western hemisphere; the philosophy of American history; the annals, traditions, civilization, languages, etc., of all the American nations, tribes, empires, and states . . . Philadelphia. 2 vols. in 1. (*For* "The Haytian or Taino languages restored, with fragments of the dialects of Cuba, Jamaica, Lucayas, Boriquen, Eyeri, Cairi, Araguas. Grammar, roots, and comparative vocabularies," *see* vol. 1, pp. 215–259.)

RAINEY, FROELICH GLADSTONE.
1940. Puerto Rican archaeology. Scientific survey of Porto Rico and the Virgin Islands, N. Y. Acad. Sci., vol. 18, pt. 1.
1941. Excavations in the Ft. Liberté Region, Haiti. Yale Univ. Publ. Anthrop., No. 23.
See also Rouse, Irving, 1941.

RALEIGH, SIR WALTER.
    1848.   The discovery of the large, rich, and beautiful empire of Guiana, with a
            relation of the great and golden city of Manoa (which the Spaniards
            call El Dorado), etc., performed in the year 1595 by Sir W. Raleigh,
            knt. . . . Edited . . . by Sir Robert H. Schomburgk. Hakluyt, No. 3.
            London.

RAVENEAU DE LUSSAN.
    1689.   Journal du voyage fait a la mer du Sud, avee les flibustiers de l'Amérique
            en 1684 et années suivantes. Paris.

REAL, GASPER CORTE (or CORTE REAL, GASPAR). See COLUMBUS, CHRISTOPHER, 1893.

REBOLLO, PEDRO MARÍA.
    1919.   Tamalameque, Sompollón, El Banco y el Río Cesare. Divagaciones His-
            toriales. Bol. Hist., Año 4, Nos. 47 and 48. Cartagena.

REBULLIDA, PABLO DE.
    [1698.] Second report as to the extension of the Holy Gospel among the tribe
            of the Changuenes, of the Province of Talamanca, in the two years
            of 1697 and 1698, by the Padre Fray Pablo Rebullida, Apostolic
            Missionary. In Costa Rica-Panama Arb. Doc., 1913, Doc. 138, vol.
            1, pp. 324–327.
            See also Andrade, Antonio de, and Fray Pablo de Rebullida; San José,
            Francisco de, and Rebullida, Pablo de.

RELACIONES DE YUCATÁN. See Col. Doc. Inéd., 1898–1900.

REQUEJO SALCEDO, JUAN.
    1908.   Relación histórica y geográfica de la Provincia de Panamá (año 1640).
            Col. Libr. Doc. Ref. Hist. Amér., t. 8. Madrid. (Other ed. Madrid,
            1842.)

REQUENA, RAFAEL.
    1932.   Vestigios de la Atlántida. Caracas.

RESTREPO, VINCENTE.
    1937.   Estudio sobre las minas de oro y plata de Colombia. An. Escuela Nac.
            Minas. No. 23. Medellín. (Earlier ed. Bogotá, 1884.)

RESTREPO TIRADO, ERNESTO.
    1929.   Ensayo etnográfico y arqueológico de la provincia de los Quimbayas en el
            Nuevo Reino de Granada. Sevilla.

REYNOLDS, F. C. See BERGSØE, PAUL, 1937, 1938.

RIBERA, PERAFAN DE.
    [1571.] Relation of Perafán de Ribera, Governor of Costa Rica, to H. M.
            the King, Don Philip II, concerning the Province of Costa Rica.
            Nombre de Jesus. In Costa Rica-Panama Arb. Doc., 1913, Doc. 58,
            vol. 1, pp. 148–155.

RICHARDSON, FRANCIS B.
    1940.   Non-Maya monumental sculpture of Central America. In The Maya and
            their neighbors, pp. 395–416. New York.

RICKETSON, OLIVER G., JR.
    1940.   An outline of basic physical factors affecting Middle America. In The
            Maya and their neighbors, pp. 10–31. New York.

RIES, MAURICE.
1936. Summary report: Tulane University-Cuban Navy expedition to Cabo San Antonio, Cuba. MS. in Tulane Univ. Mid. Amer. Res. Inst., New Orleans.

RIONEGRO, FROILÁN DE.
1918. Relaciones de las misiones de los PP. Capuchinos en las antiguas provincias españolas hoy República de Venezuela, 1650–1817 . . . Documentos inéditos . . . publicados bajo la dirección y estudio de fray Froylán de Rionegro, misionero capuchino. Sevilla.
1926–. Actuaciones y documentos del gobierno central de la unidad de la raza en el descubrimiento, exploración, población, pacificación y civilización de las antiguas provincias españolas, hoy República de Venezuela, 1486–1600, siglos XV. y XVI. Coleccionadas bajo la dirección y estudio de fray Froylán de Rionegro, misionero capuchino. Editados y publicados por el gobierno venezolano. La Coruna.

RIOS, JOSÉ AMADOR DE LOS. See OVIEDO Y VALDÉS, GONZALO FERNÁNDEZ DE, 1851–55.

RIVAS, PEDRO.
1934. Monografía geográfica e histórica de la isla del Tigre y puerto de Amapala. Tegucigalpa.

RIVERA, DON PERO AFAN DE.
[1569.] Memorandum of the native villages of the Provinces of Duy, Coaza, Tariaca and Pococi, embraced in the distribution of "Encomiendas" (Allotments) made by the Governor and Captain General of the Province of Costa Rica, Don Pero Afan de Rivera, in the city of Cartago, on the 12th of January, 1569, in favor of the conquerors of the Province. In Costa Rica-Panama Arb. Doc., 1913, Doc. 636, vol. 4, pp. 406–407.

RIVERO, JUAN.
1883. Historia de las misiones de los llanos de Casanare y los rio Orinoco y Meta. Escrita el año 1736. Bogotá.

RIVET, PAUL.
1905. Les Indiens Colorados. Récit de voyage et étude ethnologique. Journ. Soc. Amér. Paris, n.s., vol. 2, pp. 117–208.
1911. La Famille linguistique Peba. Journ. Soc., Amér. Paris, n.s., vol. 8, pp. 173–206.
1912. Les Familles linguistiques du nord-ouest de l'Amerique de Sud. L'Annee linguistique, t. 4, 1908–10, pp. 117–155. Paris.
1923. L'orfévrerie précolombienne des Antilles, des Guyanes, et du Venezuela; dans ses rapports avec l'orfèvrerie et la metallurgie des autres régions américaines. Journ. Soc. Amér. Paris, n.s., vol. 15, pp. 183–213.
1924. Langues de l'Amérique du Sud et des Antilles. In Meillet, A., and Cohen, Marcel: Les Langues du Monde, Col. Ling. Soc. Ling. Paris, vol. 16, pp. 639–707.
1943. La Influencia Karib en Colombia. Rev. Inst. Etnol. Nac., vol. 1, Entrega 1, pp. 55–87. Bogotá.
See also Beuchat, Henri, and Rivet, Paul; Verneau, René, and Rivet, Paul.

RIVET, PAUL, and BEUCHAT, HENRI.
1910. Affinités de Langues du sud de la Colombie et du Nord de l'Equateur. Le Musèon, vol. 11, pp. 33–68, 141–198.

Robledo, Mariscal Jorge.
  1864.   Relación del viaje del capitán J. Robledo á las provincias de Ancerma
          y Quimbaya 1539. Col. Doc. Inéd. Amér. y Oceanía. Madrid.
  1936-38. Descripción de los Pueblos de la Provincia de Ancerma por Jorge
          Robledo. *In* Jijón y Caamaño, 1936-38, vol. 2, pp. 63-80.
          See also Sardilla, 1891-94.

Rochefort, Charles César de.
  1665.   Histoire naturelle et morale des les Antilles de l'Amérique. Rotterdam.
          (1st. ed. 1658).
          See also Davies, John, 1666.

Rodriguez, Manuel.
  1684.   El Marañon y Amazonas. Historia de los descubrimientos, entradas, y
          reduccion de naciones, trabajos malogrados de algunos conquistadores,
          y dichosos de otros, ossi temporales, como espirituales en los dilatadas
          montanas, y mayores rios de la América. Madrid.

Roth, Henry Ling.
  1887.   The aborigines of Hispaniola. Journ. Roy. Anthrop. Inst. Brit. and
          Ireland, vol. 16, pp. 247-286. London.

Roumain, Jacques.
  1942.   Contribution à l'étude de l'ethnobotanique précolombienne des Grandes
          Antilles . . . Bull. Bur. Éthnol. République d'Haiti, No. 1. Port-au-
          Prince.
  1943.   L'ontillage lithique des Ciboney d'Haiti. Bull. Bur. Éthnol. République
          d'Haiti, No. 2, pp. 22-27. Port-au-Prince.

Rouse, Irving.
  1939.   Prehistory in Haiti, a study in method. Yale Univ. Publ. Anthrop., No.
          21.
  1940.   Some evidence concerning the origins of West Indian pottery-making.
          Amer. Anthrop., n.s., vol. 42, pp. 49-80.
  1941.   Culture of the Ft. Liberté Region, Haiti. Yale Univ. Publ. Anthrop.,
          No. 24.
  1942.   Archeology of the Maniabón Hills, Cuba. Yale Univ. Publ. Anthrop.,
          No. 26.
  1945.   Excavations in Puerto Rico. MS. in the Yale Peabody Museum, New
          Haven, Conn.
  1947.   Ciboney artifacts from Ile à Vache, Haiti. Bull. Bur. Éthnol. République
          d'Haiti, March, 1947 [No. 5], pp. 16-21.

Royal Cedula.
  [1521.] Limits of the city of Panama (Castilla de Oro). Royal Cedula of
          Burgos. *In* Costa Rica-Panama Arb. Doc., 1913, Doc. 5, vol. 1, pp.
          17-20. (Doc. publ. in Peralta, 1890, p. 14.)
  [1740.] Royal Cedula to the President of the Audiencia of Guatemala, approv-
          ing the steps he took for the subjection of the Indians of Talamanca
          and giving him a commission to install a corregidor in the District
          of Boruca. *In* Costa Rica-Panama Arb. Doc., 1913, Doc. 164, vol. 1,
          pp. 460-463.

Royo Guardia, Fernando.
  1940 a. Entierros aborígenes en Cuba. Mem. Soc. Cubana Hist. Nat. "Felipe
          Poey," vol. 14, pp. 39-43. Habana.

1940 b. Notas sobre la etnología de los Tainos cubanos. Mem. Soc. Cubana Hist. Nat. "Felipe Poey," vol. 14, pp. 169–174. Habana. *See also* Ortiz, Fernando, Cosculluela, J. A., et al., 1943; and Royo Guardia, Fernando, et al.

ROYO GUARDIA, FERNANDO; MORALES COELLO, JULIO; and HERRERA FRITOT, RENÉ.
1942. Las esferas líticas como base de una nueva cultura aborigen cubana. Proc. 8th Amer. Sci. Congr., vol. 2, pp. 131–138. Washington.

ROYS, RALPH L.
1932. Antonio de Ciudad Real, Ethnographer. Amer. Anthrop., n. s., vol. 34, pp. 118–126.

RUIZ BLANCO, MATIAS.
1892. Conversión en Piritú (Colombia) de Indios Cumanagotos y Palenques, con la Práctica que se observa en la enseñanza de los naturales en lengua cumanagota, por el p. fr. Matias Ruiz Blanco de la Orden de San Francisco; seguido de Los Franciscanos en las Indias, por fr. Francisco Alvarez de Villanueva, de la misma orden. Madrid.

RUIZ DE CAMPOS, DIEGO.
1631. Relación sobre le Costa Panameña en al Mar del Sur por el Capitan Diego Ruíz de Campos, Ano de 1631. Doc. de Colombia; Sección Primera, Geografía y Viajes; t. 2, Costa Pacífica, Provincia Litorales y Campanas de los Conquistadores, pp. 13–52.

SÁENZ, DON JUAN FRANCISCO.
1675. Don Juan Francisco Sáenz, Governor of Costa Rica to His Majesty the King. Costa Rica-Panama Arb. Doc., 1913, Doc. 89, vol. 1, pp. 275–279.
1676. Don Juan Francisco Sáenz, to His Majesty the King, Invasion of the Pirates. Situation of the Province in 1676.

SAFFORD, WILLIAM EDWIN.
1916. Identity of cohoba, the narcotic snuff of ancient Haiti. Journ. Wash. Acad. Sci., vol. 7, pp. 547–562.
1917. Narcotic plants and stimulants of the ancient Americas. Ann. Rep. Smithsonian Inst. for 1916, pp. 387–424.

SAGOT, P. *See* CRÉVAUX, JULES NICOLAS, 1882.

SALAS, JULIO C.
1908. Tierre-Firme (Venezuela y Colombia) estudios sobre etnología e historia. Mérida, Venezuela, Tip. de "Paz y Trabajo."
1921. Etnografía americana. Los indios caribes, estudio sobre el origen del mito de la antropofagia. Barcelona, Talleres graficoa, "Lux." (Another edition, Madrid, 1920.)

SALCEDO, JUAN REQUEJO. *See* REQUEJO SALCEDO, JUAN.

SALINAS Y DE LA CERDA, DON JUAN FERNÁNDEZ DE.
[1651.] Letter of the Governor, Don Juan Fernández de Salinas y de la Cerda to his Majesty. Cartago. Costa Rica-Panama Arb. Doc., 1913, Doc. 84, vol. 1, pp. 255–257.

SANDOVAL, DON GREGORIO DE.
[1638.] Proposal of the Governor of Costa Rica to undertake the Conquest of Talamanca. Cartago. Costa Rica-Panama Arb. Doc., 1931, Doc. 81, vol. 1, pp. 237–245.

SAN FRANCISCO Y RIOS, BERNABE DE.

[1703.] Letter of Fray Bernabe de San Francisco y Rios to the President of the Audiencia of Guatemala. Costa Rica-Panama Arb. Doc., 1913, Doc. 142, vol. 1, pp. 336–339.

SAN JOSÉ, FRANCISCO.

[1697.] Report of Fray Francisco de San José, Apostolic Missionary to the President of the Audiencia of Guatemala, concerning the subjection of Talamanca and the houses and tribes of the Terrabas Indians. Costa Rica-Panama Arb. Doc., 1913, Doc. 137, vol. 1, pp. 314–324.

SAN JOSÉ, FRANCISCO DE, and REBULLIDA, PABLO DE.

[1699.] Memorial of the missionaries. Costa Rica-Panama Arb. Doc., 1913, Doc. 139, vol. 1, pp. 327–329.

SAN JUAN, ALONSO DE.   See ALONSO DE SAN JUAN.

SAN MILLAN, DOCTOR BARROS DE.   See LANDECHO, DOCTOR MEXIA, and DOCTOR BARROS DE SAN MILLAN.

SANTA CRUZ, ANTONIO.

1941.   Aspects of the avunculate in the Guajiro culture. Primitive Man, vol. 14, Nos. 1 and 2, pp. 1–13.

SANTOVENIA Y ECHAIDE, EMETERIO SANTIAGO.

1939.   Historia de Cuba. Vol. 1. Habana.

SAPIR, EDWARD.

1937.   Central and North American languages. Encyclopaedia Britannica, 14th ed., vol. 5, pp. 138–141.

SAPPER, KARL THEODOR.

1897 a.   Das nordliche Mittel-Amerika nebst einem Ausflug nach dem Hochland von Anahuac. Braunschweig.

1897 b.   Mittelamericanische Caraiben. Int. Archiv Ethnogr., vol. 10, pp. 53–60. Leiden.

1899.   Die Paya von Honduras. Geschildert nach einem Besuche im Jahre 1898. Globus, t. 75, No. 6, pp. 80–83.

1907.   Choles und Chorties. Congr. Int. Amer., 15th sess., 1906, vol. 2, pp. 423–465. Quebec.

1927.   Mittelamerika und Westindien. Zeit. f. Geopolitik, vol. 4. Berlin.

1931.   Die Indianer und ihre Kultur einst und jetzt. Zeit. f. Geopolitik, vol. 8, No. 5. Berlin.

SARDILLA, JUAN BAUTISTA.

1891–94.   Relación del Descubrimiento de las Provincias de Antioquia por Jorge Robledo. In Col. Doc. Inéd. Geogr. Hist. Colombia, recopilados por Antonio B. Cuervo, vol. 2, p. 392, 1891–94. Bogotá.

SARMIENTO, LUIS ALBERTO.

1941.   The Unknown age in Columbia. Nat. Hist., vol. 48, No. 1, pp. 14–18. New York.

SCHEPPIG, RICHARD.   See SPENCER, HERBERT.

SCHOMBURGK, SIR ROBERT H., EDITOR.   See RALEIGH, SIR WALTER, 1848.

SCHUCHERT, CHARLES.

1935.   Historical geology of the Antillean-Caribbean region, or the lands bordering the gulf of Mexico and the Caribbean Sea. New York.

SCHULLER, RODOLFO R.
　1928.　Las lenguas indígenas de Centro América, con especial referencia a los idiomas aborigenes de Costa Rica. San José de Costa Rica.

SCILLACIO, NICCOLÒ.
　1859.　Nicolaus Syllacius de insulis meridiani atque indici maris nuper inventis. Trans. by Rev. John Mulligan. New York. (This account seems to be almost wholly derived from the letters of Guillermo Coma.)

SEEMAN, BERTHOLD CARL.
　1853.　The aborigines of the Isthmus of Panama . . . Trans. Amer. Ethnol. Soc., vol. 3, pp. 173–182.
　　　　　See also Pim, Bedford, and Seeman, Berthold Carl.

SELER, EDUARD.
　1885.　Notizen ueber die Sprache der Colorado von Ecuador. Ethnol. Abt. Königl. Mus., vol. 1, pp. 44–56.
　1901.　Die alten ansiedelungen von Chacula im distrikte Nenton des departements Huehuetenango der republik Guatemala. Berlin.
　1902.　Die verwandten Sprachen der Cayápa und der Colorados von Ecuador. *In* Gesammelte Abhandl. z. Amer. Sprach- u. Alterthumskunde, vol. 1, pp. 18–48. Berlin.

SEMANO, JUAN DE.
　[1536.]　Royal Cedula to the Governor of Nicaragua, commanding him to undertake the discovery of the Desaguadero (San Juan River). Valladolid. Costa Rica-Panama Arb. Doc., 1913, Doc. 11, vol. 1, p. 29.

SERRANO Y SAENZ, M., EDITOR. *See* CASAS, BARTOLOMÉ DE LAS, 1909

SEVERINO DE SANTA TERESA, (Fr.).
　1924.　Creencias, ritos, usos, y costumbres de los indios Catíos de la prefectura apostólica de Urabá. Bogotá.

SHELDON, WILLIAM.
　1820.　Brief account of the Caraibs, who inhabited the Antilles. Trans. Amer. Antiq. Soc., vol. 1, pp. 365–433.

SIEVERS, W.
　1898.　Des Grafen Josef de Brettes Reisen im nördlichen Colombia. Globus, vol. 73, pp. 381–399.

SIMÓN, PEDRO.
　1882–92.　Noticias historiales de las conquistas de Tierra Firme en las Indias Occidentales. 5 vols. Bogotá. (Written in 1623 and subsequently.) (Other editions 1637 and 1819.)

SIMONS, F. A. A.
　1885.　An exploration of the Goajira Peninsula. Proc. Roy. Geogr. Soc., n.s., vol. 7, pp. 781–796.

SKINNER, ALANSON BUCK.
　1920.　Notes on the Bribri of Costa Rica. Ind. Notes Monogr., vol. 6, No. 3.

SLOANE, SIR HANS.
　1707–25.　A voyage to the islands Madera, Barbados, Nieves, S. Christopher's and Jamaica . . . with some relations concerning the neighbouring continent, and islands of America. 2 vols. London.

SMITH, ROBERT E.
  1940. Ceramics of the Peten. *In* The Maya and their neighbors, pp. 242–249. New York.

SMYTH, W. H., EDITOR AND TRANSLATOR. *See* BENZONI, GIROLAMO, 1857.

SÓJO, DIEGO DE.
  [1605.] Foundation of the city of Santiago de Talamanca. Viceita, Oct. 10, 1605. *In* Costa Rica-Panama Arb. Soc., 1913, Doc. 72, vol. 1, pp. 197–205. (Doc. publ. in Sp. in Fernández, L., 1881–1907, Col Doc., vol. 5, p. 116.)

SPARREY, FRANCIS.
  1906. The description of the Ile of Trinidad, the rich Countrie of Guiana, and the mightie River of Orenoco . . . *In* Hackluytus Posthumus or Purchas His Pilgrimes, vol. 16, pp. 301–309. Hakluyt, extra ser., No. 28. Glasgow.

SPENCER, HERBERT.
  1873–79 Descriptive sociology; or, groups of sociological facts . . . compiled and abstracted by David Duncan . . . Richard Scheppig . . . and others. No. 6, American races . . . (Div. 1, Pt. 4–A). London.

SPINDEN, HERBERT JOSEPH.
  1915. Notes on the archeology of Salvador. Amer. Anthrop., n. s., vol. 17, pp. 446–487.
  1916. New data on the archaeology of Venezuela. Proc. Nat. Acad. Sci., vol. 2, pp. 325–328.
  1925. The Chorotegan culture area. Proc. Congr. Int. Amer., Göteborg. 21st Sess., 1924, pt. 2, pp. 529–545.

SQUIER, EPHRAIM GEORGE (PSEUD., SAMUEL A. BARD).
  1852. Nicaragua; its people, scenery, monuments, and the proposed interoceanic canal. 2 vols. New York and London.
  1853 a. Observations on the archaeology and ethnology of Nicaragua. Trans. Amer. Ethnol. Soc., vol. 3, pp. 83–158.
  1853 b. Ruins of Tenampua, Honduras, Central America. Proc. Hist. Soc. New York.
  1856. Waikna; or, adventures on the Mosquito Shore. London.
  1858. The states of Central America; their geography, topography, climate, population, resources, productions, commerce, political organization, aborigines, etc. New York.
  1859. A visit to the Guajiquero Indians. Harper's Magazine, vol. 19, p. 18.
  1860 a. Collection of rare and original documents and relations concerning the discovery and conquest of America. New York.
  1860 b. Some account of the Lake of Yojoa or Taulebé, in Honduras, Central America. Journ. Roy. Geogr. Soc., vol. 30, pp. 58–63.
  1869. Tongues from tombs. *In* Frank Leslie's Illustrated Newspaper, vol. 28, Mar. 20, July 24. New York.
  1870. Honduras; descriptive, historical and statistical. London.
  1908. Honduras. Descripción histórica, geográfica y estadística de esta república de la America Central. Edición corregida y anotada por J. M. C. Tegucigalpa.

STAHL, AUGUSTIN.
  1889. Los indios borinqueños. Estud. Etnogr. Puerto Rico.

STEINEN, KARL VON DEN.
1904. Ausgrabungen am Valenciasee. Globus, vol. 86, No. 77, pp. 101–108.
STEINMAYER, R. A.
1932. A reconnaissance of certain mounds and relics in Spanish Honduras. Tulane Univ., Middle Amer. Res. Ser., Publ. 4, Pap. No. 1.
STEVENSON, W. B.
1825. A historical and descriptive narrative of twenty years' residence in South America. 3 vols. London.
STEWARD, JULIAN HAYNES.
1929. Petroglyphs of California and adjoining states. Univ. Calif. Publ. Amer. Arch. Ethnol., vol. 24, No. 2.
STEWART, T. D.
1942. Persistence of the African type of tooth pointing in Panama. Amer. Anthrop., n.s., vol. 44, pp. 328–330.
STIRLING, MATTHEW W.
1936. Florida cultural affiliations in relation to adjacent areas. In Essays in Anthropology presented to A. L. Kroeber, pp. 351–357. Berkeley.
STOLL, OTTO.
1938. Etnografía de la République de Guatemala. (Traducida del Aleman por Antonio Goubaud Carrera.) Guatemala. (Tr. from German, publ. Zurich, 1884.)
STONE, DORIS ZEMURRAY.
1934 a. A new southernmost Maya city (Los Naranjos on Lake Yojoa, Honduras). Maya Research, vol. 1, No. 2, pp. 125–128. New York.
1934 b. A mound and a house-site on Jerico farm, near Trujillo, Honduras. Maya Research, vol. 1, No. 2, pp. 129–132. New York.
1938 Masters in marble. Tulane Univ., Middle Amer. Res. Ser., Publ. 8, pt. 1.
1940 a. Demarcación de las culturas precolombinas del Norte y Centro de Honduras. Rev. Archiv. Bibl. Nac., vol. 19, Nos. 2–5.
1940 b. The Ulua Valley and Lake Yojoa. In The Maya and their neighbors, pp. 386–394. New York.
1941. Archaeology of the north coast of Honduras. Mem. Peabody Mus. Arch. Ethnol., Harvard Univ., vol. 9, No. 1.
1942. A delimitation of the area and some of the archaeology of the Sula-Jicaque Indians of Honduras. Amer. Antiq., vol. 7, No. 4, pp. 376–388.
1943. A preliminary investigation of the flood plain of the Rio Grande de Térraba, Costa Rica. Amer. Antiq., vol. 9, pp. 74–88.
STONE, DORIS, and TURNBULL, CONCHITA.
1941. A Sula-Ulúa Pottery kiln. Amer. Antiq., vol. 7, No. 1, pp. 39–47.
STOUT, D. B.
MS. San Blas Cuna acculturation: An introduction. Unpublished dissertation on file at Dept. of Anthrop., Columbia Univ.
STRIFFLER, LUIS.
1920. El río San Jorge. Cartagena.
1922. El río Sinu. Cartagena.
STROMSVICK, GUSTAV.
1935. Notes on metates from Calakmul, Campeche, and from the mercado, Chichen Itza, Yucatan. Carnegie Inst. Washington, Publ. No. 45 b, Contr. Amer. Arch., No. 16, pp. 121–127.

Strong, William Duncan.
  1925. The Uhle pottery collections from Ancón. Univ. Calif. Publ. Amer. Arch. Ethnol., vol. 21, No. 4, pp. 135–190.
  1934 a. An archaeological cruise among the Bay Islands of Honduras. Expl. and Field-Work Smithsonian Inst. in 1933, pp. 49–59.
  1934 b. Hunting ancient ruins in northeastern Honduras. Expl. and Field-Work Smithsonian Inst. in 1933, pp. 44–48.
  1935. Archaeological investigations in the Bay Islands, Spanish Honduras. Smithsonian Misc. Coll., vol. 92, No. 14.
  1937. Archeological explorations in northwestern Honduras. Expl. and Field-Work Smithsonian Inst. in 1936, pp. 75–82.
  1940. Anthropological problems in Central America. *In* The Maya and their neighbors, pp. 377–385. New York.
  1943. Cross-sections of new world prehistory . . . Smithsonian Misc. Coll., vol. 104, No. 2.

Strong, William Duncan; Kidder, Alfred, II; and Paul, A. J. Drexel, Jr.
  1938. Preliminary report on the Smithsonian Institution-Harvard University archeological expedition to Northwestern Honduras, 1936. Smithsonian Misc. Coll., vol. 97, No. 1.

Swanton, John R. *See* Thomas, Cyrus, and Swanton, John R.

Tamara, Francisco.
  1556. El libro de las costumbres de todas las gentes del mundo, y de las Indias. Antwerp.

Tapia y Rivera, Alejandro.
  1854. Biblioteca historica de Puerto-Rico, que contiene varios documentos de los siglos XV, XVI, XVII y XVIII. Puerto Rico. (This contains the sections dealing with Puerto Rico from Herrera y Tordesillas, 1725–26, Muñoz, 1797, Oviedo y Valdés, 1851–55, and others.)

Taylor, Douglas.
  1935. The Island Caribs of Dominica, B.W.I. Amer. Anthrop., n.s., vol. 37, pp. 265–272.
  1936. Additional notes on the Island Carib of Dominica, B.W.I. Amer. Anthrop., n.s., vol. 38, pp. 462–468.
  1938. The Caribs of Dominica. Anthrop. Pap., No. 3. Bull. Bur. Amer. Ethnol., No. 119, pp. 103–160.

Taylor, E. G. R. *See* Barlow, Roger.

Termer, Franz.
  1914. Ein Beitrag zum religiosen und kulturellen Lebender Guaimi-Indianer im 16 Jahrhundert. Korrespondez-blatt der Deutschen Gesellschaft für anthropologie, ethnologie und urgeschichte, vol. 45, Jahrgang 1914, pp. 52–55. Hamburg.

Ternaux-Compans, Henri. *See* Escalante Fontaneda, Hernando.

Tertre, Jean Baptiste du. *See* Dutertre, Jean Baptiste.

Thamara, Francisco. *See* Tamara, Francisco.

Thomas, Cyrus, and Swanton, John R.
  1911. Indian languages of Mexico and Central America and their geographical distribution. Bull. Bur. Amer. Ethnol., No. 44.

Thompson, J. Eric S.
  1936. Archeology of South America. Field Mus. Nat. Hist., Anthrop. Leaflet 33.

1939. Excavations at San José, British Honduras. Carnegie Inst. Washington, Publ. No. 506.
1941. Dating of certain inscriptions of non-Maya origin. Carnegie Inst. Washington, Div. Hist. Res., Theoretical Approaches to Problems, No. 1.
1943. A trial survey of the southern Maya area. Amer. Antiq., vol. 9, No. 1, pp. 106–134.

TORQUEMADA, JUAN DE.
1615. Los veynte y un libros Rituales y Monarchia Yndiána . . . (1st ed.), 3 vols. Seville.
1723. Los veinte i un libros Rituales i Monarchia Indiana . . . (2nd ed.), 3 vols. Madrid.

TORRE, CARLOS DE LA.
1890. Conferencia cientifica. An. Real Acad. Cienc., Méd. Fís., y Nat. Habana, vol. 27, pp. 325–343.

TORRE Y HUERTA, CARLOS DE LA. See TORRE, CARLOS DE LA.

TORRES DE MENDOZA, LUIS, EDITOR.
1864–84. Colección de documentos inéditos, relativos al descubrimiento, conquista y organización de las antiguas posesiones españolas de América y Oceanía, sacados de los archivos del reino, y muy especialmente del de Indias. 42 vols. Madrid. (Vols. 1–3 edited by Luis Torres de Mendoza with Joaquín F. Pacheco and Francisco de Cárdenas.)
See also Fernández Duro, Cesáreo, and others, 1885–1932.

TORRE Y DE LA TORRE, JOSÉ MARIA DE LA.
1841. Mapa de la isla de Cuba y tierras circumvecinas según las divisiones de los naturales. Mem. Soc. Patriótica Habana, vol. 13, No. 73, pp. 18–67.

TRINIDAD HISTORICAL SOCIETY.
n.d. Publications of the Trinidad Historical Society, Nos. 1–300. Trinidad. See also Bullbrook, J. A., 1940, 1941.

TURNBULL, CONCHITA. See STONE, DORIS, and TURNBULL, CONCHITA.

ULLOA, ANTONIO DE. See JUAN, DON JORGE, and ULLOA, DON ANTONIO DE.

URCULLU, MANUEL DE.
[1763.] Report of Fray Manuel de Urcullu. Mission of Talamanca in 1763. Guatemala. Costa Rica-Panama Arb. Doc., 1913, Doc. 172, vol. 1, pp. 486–491. (Doc. publ. in Sp. in Peralta, 1890, p. 130.)

URIBE ANGEL, MANUEL.
1885. Geografía general y compendio histórico del estado de Antioquia en Colombia. Paris.

VAILLANT, GEORGE CLAPP.
1927. The chronological significance of Maya ceramics. (MS. thesis submitted in partial fulfillment of the requirements of the degree of Ph.D. at Harvard Univ., Cambridge.)
1930. Notes on the Middle Cultures of Middle America. Congr. Int. Amer., Proc. Sess. 21, New York, 1928, pp. 74–81.

1934. The archaeological setting of the Playa de los Muertos culture. Maya Research, vol. 1, No. 2, pp. 87–100.

1940. Patterns in Middle American archeology. *In* The Maya and their neighbors, pp. 295–305. New York.

VÁZQUEZ, FRANCISCO.

1714–16. Chronica de la Provincia del Santissimo Nõbre de Jesus de Guatemala de el Orden de N. Seraphico Padre San Francisco en el Reyno de la Nueva España. 2 vols. Guatemala.

VERNEAU, RENÉ, and RIVET, PAUL.

1912–22. Ethnographie ancienne de l'equateur. Paris. 2 vols. (France, Ministère de l'instruction publique, mission du service géographique de l'armée pour la mesure d'un arc de méridien équatorial en Amérique du Sud sous le contrôle scientifique de l'Académie des Sciences, 1899–1906, t. 6.)

VERRILL, ALPHEUS HYATT.

1927. Excavations in Coclé province, Panamá. Ind. Notes, vol. 4, No. 1, pp. 47–60.

VILLACORTA CALDERÓN, JOSÉ ANTONIO.

1942. Historia de la capitanía general de Guatemala. Guatemala.

VON HAGEN, VICTOR WOLFGANG.

1939. The Tsátchela Indians of western Ecuador. Ind. Notes Monogr., Misc. Ser., No. 51.

1943. The Jicaque (Torrupan) Indians of Honduras. Ind. Notes Monogr., Misc. Ser., No. 53.

WAFER, LIONEL.

1903. A new voyage and description of the isthmus of America . . . reprinted from the original edition of 1699. (Edited by George Parker Winship.) Cleveland.

WARNER, GEORGE F., EDITOR. *See* DUDLEY, ROBERT.

WASSÉN, HENRY.

1933. Cuentos de los Indios Chocós recogidos por Erland Nordenskiöld durante su expedición al Istmo de Panamá en 1927 y publicados con notas y observaciones comparativas. Journ. Soc. Amér. Paris, n.s., vol. 25, pp. 103–137.

1934. Mitos y cuentos de los Indios Cunas. Journ. Soc. Amér. Paris, n.s., vol. 26, pp. 1–35.

1935. Notes on Southern Groups of Chocó Indians in Colombia. Etnol. Stud., No. 1, pp. 35–182. Göteborg.

1936. An archaeological study in the Western Colombian Cordillera. Etnol. Stud., vol. 2, pp. 30–67. Göteborg.

1937. Some Cuna Indian animal stories, with original texts. Etnol. Stud., No. 4, pp. 12–34. Göteborg.

1938. Original documents from the Cuna Indians of San Blas, Panama. Etnol. Stud., No. 6, pp. 1–178. Göteborg.

1940 a. An analogy between a South American and Oceanic myth motif and Negro influence in Darien. Etnol. Stud., No. 10, pp. 69–79. Göteborg.

1940 b. Anonymous Spanish manuscript from 1739 on the Province Darien. Etnol. Stud., No. 10, pp. 80–146. Göteborg.

See also Nordenskiöld, Erland, 1938.

WAUCHOPE, ROBERT.

1941. Effigy head vessel supports from Zacualpa, Guatemala. *In* Los Mayas Antiquos, pp. 211–232. Mexico.

WAVRIN, ROBERT, MARQUIS DE.

1937. Moeurs et coutumes des Indiens sauvages de l'Amérique du Sud . . . Paris.

WELLS, WILLIAM VINCENT.

1857. Explorations and adventures in Honduras . . . New York.

WESTON, JULIAN A.

1937. The cactus eaters. London.

WIENER, CHARLES.

1882. Les Indiens Colorados et les Sieges de pierre de Manabí. Rev. Ethnogr. Paris, vol. 1, pp. 454–458.

WILCZYNSKI, GUSTAVUS.

1888. Contribution towards a vocabulary of the Cayapas. Journ. Roy. Anthrop. Inst. Gr. Brit. and Ireland, vol. 18.

WINSHIP, GEORGE PARKER. *See* WAFER, LIONEL.

WRIGHT, IRENE ALOHA.

1916. The early history of Cuba, 1492–1586. New York.

WYATT, CAPT. *See* DUDLEY, ROBERT.

YOUNG, THOMAS.

1842. Narrative of a residence on the Mosquito Shore, during the years 1839, 1840, and 1841 . . . London.

YOUNG, SIR WILLIAM. *See* EDWARDS, BRYAN, 1818–19.

YDE, JENS.

1938. An archaeological reconnaissance of northwestern Honduras. Copenhaven. Tulane Univ., Middle Amer. Res. Ser., Publ. No. 9; and Acta Archaeologica, vol. 9, København.

ZAYAS Y ALFONSO, ALFREDO.

1931. Lexicografía antillana; diccionario de voces usadas por los aborígenes de las Antillas mayores y de algunas de las menores y consideraciones acerca de su significado y de su formación. 2nd ed., 2 vols. Habana.

☆ U. S. Government Printing Office: 1948—653334